STUDIES IN CHRISTIAN HISTORY

Bedford's Victorian Pilgrim

With the author's

best wishes,

August 2012

STUDIES IN CHRISTIAN HISTORY AND THOUGHT

A full listing of titles in this series appears at the end of this book

STUDIES IN CHRISTIAN HISTORY AND THOUGHT

Bedford's Victorian Pilgrim

William Hale White in Context

Michael Brealey

Foreword by John Hale-White

First published 2012 by Paternoster

Paternoster is an imprint of Authentic Media
52 Presley Way, Crownhill, Milton Keynes, Bucks, MK8 0ES, UK

www.authenticmedia.co.uk
Authentic Media is a division of Koorong UK, a company limited by guarantee

09 08 07 06 05 04 03   8 7 6 5 4 3 2 1

British Library Cataloguing in Publication Data
A catalogue record for this book is available from the British Library

ISBN 978–1–84227–7348

Typeset by Michael Brealey
Printed and bound in Great Britain
for Paternoster
by Lightning Source, Milton Keynes, UK

STUDIES IN CHRISTIAN HISTORY AND THOUGHT

Series Preface

This series complements the specialist series of Studies in Evangelical History and Thought and Studies in Baptist History and Thought for which Paternoster is becoming increasingly well known by offering works that cover the wider field of Christian history and thought. It encompasses accounts of Christian witness at various periods, studies of individual Christians and movements, and works which concern the relations of church and society through history, and the history of Christian thought.

The series includes monographs, revised dissertations and theses, and collections of papers by individuals and groups. As well as 'free standing' volumes, works on particular running themes are being commissioned; authors will be engaged for these from around the world and from a variety of Christian traditions.

A high academic standard combined with lively writing will commend the volumes in this series both to scholars and to a wider readership

To my Mother, and in memory of my Father,
from whom I first learned the value of books

Contents

Figures

Foreword

Michael Brealey has given us a thoroughly researched study of the context of my great-grandfather's life. Or, rather, contexts, as he has dealt separately with distinct situations in different periods of the life. I greatly admire the erudition of his research and the accumulated knowledge of this complex field it displays, as well as the manner of laying it out. In reading it I have myself learnt and understood better all sorts of things.

I remember from my childhood visits by an earlier generation of scholars, especially Catherine Maclean, Irvin Stock and Wilfred Stone. This study now analyses critically the ostensibly factual accounts of the autobiographical *Early Life* as well as the evocations in the novels. For New College and the crucial event of the expulsion, Brealey considers carefully both the figures of the College establishment and Hale White's two companions, and traces the spiritual experience opened up by the reading of Wordsworth and other influences. He gives a good account of the last years and the second marriage, and its literary and religious aspects within the family circle.

Though not a professional man of literature myself, I honour and have always felt strangely close to my great-grandfather, and hope that this book will help others to understand better his life and writings. I wish it every success.

John Hale-White
London
October 2011

Preface

This study of William Hale White (1831-1913) was prompted by a reading of nineteenth century novels categorised among the literature of faith and doubt which nonetheless exhibited a surprisingly strong attachment to faith. Hale White, better known by his literary pseudonym 'Mark Rutherford', is often included in surveys of such texts as a representative of Protestant Dissent. In his case particularly there seemed reason to believe that being typecast as a doubter obscured more about his life than it revealed, an impression reinforced by a review of the sources used in previous critical studies. The existence of four substantial biographies might have suggested there was little more to be said, until it became clear that some significant aspects of his life had not been fully explored or adequately set in context. A larger scale investigation resulted in a doctoral thesis submitted to the University of Bristol in August 2008. The work which follows is a revised and expanded version of that text.

I have been glad of the opportunity the publishers have given to introduce some new material into the original thesis, allowing a rather broader biographical treatment of White. However no attempt has been made to radically alter the overall shape of the work, which therefore in structure and form still reflects the requirements of the degree regulations under which it was first prepared. It has not been practical to follow up all the lines of further enquiry which have suggested themselves, but note has been made of some areas that might still repay investigation. It should be added that while the manuscript was essentially complete by the end of 2010 delays in the publishing schedule prevented its appearance then. It has not been possible to engage fully with works appearing after that date.

This is not an exhaustive account of William Hale White's life or writings. Literature specialists will want to say more about his fiction, and a reconstruction of his working life remains to be attempted. Until this latter task has been undertaken knowledge of his civil service career at the Admiralty remains very incomplete. Some parallels between Hale White and the novelist George MacDonald were hinted at in the original thesis, but to do full justice to these more research in primary sources would have been necessary than time permitted. Nevertheless some instances have been added, helping in a small way to better appreciate White's life by way of comparison and contrast.

I am delighted that John Hale-White, son of Dr Reginald Hale-White, M.C., has agreed to contribute a foreword to this study of his great-grandfather. This is appropriate in more than the obvious sense, for his grandfather Sir William Hale-White initiated much of the gathering of family letters and other material since deposited in archives which so greatly aid modern studies, and Mr Hale-White himself has continued this tradition by generously adding more recently to Bedford library's Mark Rutherford collection.

Acknowledgements

My first debt is to those who aided the doctoral research which forms the basis of this work.[1] The Revd Dr Ruth Gouldbourne's enthusiasm and wise counsel were a great encouragement from the start. When she moved from Bristol Baptist College her place as supervisor was taken by the Revd Dr Jeanette Sears of Trinity College, who oversaw the crucial last stages and helpfully commented on the final draft. As external supervisor Professor John Vincent of the University of Bristol guided the early planning of the thesis. On his retirement, Professor John Briggs of Regent's Park College, Oxford, kindly took over that role and gave invaluable help.

I am grateful to my examiners, Professor Clyde Binfield and Professor Nigel Scotland, for their comments and suggestions, and for encouragement to seek publication.

I owe a great deal to librarians and archivists, in particular Norman Amor and George Brandak (University of British Columbia; Norman Colbeck Collection), Susan Brown (Trinity College, Bristol), Rachel Eichhorn (Luther King House, Manchester), Susan Killoran (Harris Manchester College, Oxford; Chignell papers), Judy Powles (Spurgeon's College, London), Marion Smith (Birmingham Central Library), Barry Stephenson (Bedford Central Library; Mark Rutherford archive), Margaret Thompson (Westminster College, Cambridge; Cheshunt College archives) and the staff at Dr Williams's Library (New College and constituent colleges archives). The online launch of that library's Surman Index during the period when the thesis was being revised for publication greatly helping in tracing the ministerial careers of many whose lives in different ways illuminate White's, containing as it does much information normally impossible to locate without ready access to complete runs of the *Congregational Year Book* and similar sources. The Dr Williams's Centre for Dissenting Studies research project on the content and use of college libraries promises to be another invaluable source for writers in this field but was not completed in time to be used here.

I am grateful to the publishers, institutions, and individuals who have given permission to quote from published and unpublished sources. In particular, John Hale-White has allowed citations from the family papers deposited at Bedford and British Columbia, while Geoffrey Nowell-Smith has kindly sanctioned the use of copyright unpublished material from the Estate of his great aunt, Dorothy Vernon White, née Smith, and of his father, Simon Nowell

[1] M. A. Brealey, '"What I now set down is fact": A Study of *The Early Life of Mark Rutherford* by William Hale White (1831-1913), with Special Reference to the Development of his Faith' (unpublished doctoral thesis, University of Bristol, 2008).

Smith, as well as sharing something of his early memories of having met Dorothy.

Conversations with Dr Mark Crees have always been instructive, and members of *The Mark Rutherford Society*, especially Nick Wilde, David French, and Richard Wildman, have given much very useful information. The death of Charles Swann of the University of Keele during this research was a loss to scholarly work on Hale White. Like many before me I greatly benefited from his writings, and the readiness with which he shared his knowledge. Professor Alan Sell kindly read a draft of this text before revision and made some helpful suggestions, for which I am grateful. His forthcoming study *Christ and Controversy: The Person of Christ in Nonconformist Thought and Ecclesial Experience, 1600-2000* (Eugene, OR: Pickwick Publications, 2012) is certain to elucidate the background to some of the issues discussed here.

I very much appreciate the kindness of Professors John Briggs, Alan Sell, Clyde Binfield and Timothy Larsen in reading advance copies of the text and contributing material for the book's cover.

Other debts to individuals are indicated in the references, and to all I express my thanks.

I am much obliged to kindly proof-readers who must remain nameless lest they bear the blame for any errors which may have been introduced at a later stage, and to Wendy Baskett of the Society of Indexers for her care and patience in preparing the index.

Mindful of all those who have shared with me their knowledge of White, or offered help and support in other ways, the traditional disclaimer remains. No-one else is responsible for the presentation or interpretations offered here. These, and any mistakes, are wholly my own.

Michael Brealey
Bristol
December 2011

Abbreviations

White's works are abbreviated as follows, otherwise cited in full:

Autobiography	*The Autobiography of Mark Rutherford*
Deliverance	*Mark Rutherford's Deliverance*
Revolution	*The Revolution in Tanner's Lane*
Early Life	*The Early Life of Mark Rutherford*

References to the novels are from the undated T. Fisher Unwin Collected Works Edition (ca. 1904). Where they exist, chapter numbers are cited to assist users of other editions.

The key critical biographies are cited in the footnotes after first reference by author's name alone:

Stone	*Religion and Art of William Hale White ("Mark Rutherford")* by Wilfred Stone (Stanford, CA; London: Stanford University Press; Oxford University Press, 1954)
Maclean	*Mark Rutherford: A Biography of William Hale White* by Catherine Macdonald Maclean (London: Macdonald, 1955)
Stock	*William Hale White (Mark Rutherford): A Critical Study* by Irvin Stock (London: George Allen and Unwin, 1956)
Harland	*Mark Rutherford: The Mind and Art of William Hale White* by Catherine R. Harland (Columbus, OH: Ohio State University Press, 1988)

Archive sources frequently cited are abbreviated as below:

BPL, MR	Bedford Public Library, Mark Rutherford Collection
UBC, NCC	University of British Columbia, Norman Colbeck Collection
DWL, NCA	Dr Williams's Library, London, New College Archives
WCC, CC	Westminster College, Cambridge, Cheshunt College Archive
HAT, CHE	Hatfield House, Chelwood Papers (Lady Robert Cecil)

The index has the following abbreviations:

DVS	Dorothy Vernon Smith
MR	Mark Rutherford
WHW	William Hale White

CHAPTER 1

'A commonplace life'
Introducing William Hale White

With a modesty wholly characteristic of its author William Hale White's *Autobiography of Mark Rutherford* was offered as 'the tale of a commonplace life'.[1] While debatable even of 'Mark Rutherford', the book's pretended writer as well as its subject, this judgement certainly understates Hale White's ability and achievements. Nonetheless close identification of Rutherford with White sets the tone for almost all modern studies of White, and risks significantly misrepresenting his life. This is never more the case than when the account in the *Autobiography* and elsewhere of Rutherford's growing estrangement from his Dissenting heritage causes the writer by extension to be widely cited as an exemplary instance of Victorian religious doubt. This understanding has dominated the field, and it is time for a new look at the evidence and the wider context within which it must be interpreted.

Few contemporaries knew anything of the writer describing himself as Mark Rutherford, even after five further novels had been issued in his name. At the end of White's life many must have been equally unaware that he had published a good deal in other forms, much of it anonymous, occasional or scholarly. Those who read here and there elegant named pieces by 'W. Hale White' might have noticed some similarities in style with the novels, but had no reason to link him with 'Mark Rutherford'. The connection had been made occasionally by observant critics but only very gradually became more widely known. This changed in 1913 with the publication of his posthumous memoir

[1] *The Autobiography of Mark Rutherford* (London: T. Fisher Unwin, n.d.), p. 1, Ch. I (first published 1881; this reference from the undated – ca. 1904 - collected works edition used here). Full details of books cited are given in the bibliography. In this study White is referred to as 'White', or 'Hale White', alternatively 'Hale' (the family usage), to distinguish him from other members of the family who shared the name William. It will be made clear in context when his father William White is intended.

The Early Life of Mark Rutherford, which included White's name on the title page.[2] Consequently the modern reader almost invariably approaches the Mark Rutherford texts as revealing much about Hale White himself, and the novels have commonly been mined for the biographical information they are anticipated to yield on their writer. Their mixture of disclosure and concealment nonetheless poses an interpretative challenge, and detailed investigation is required before it is possible to judge how closely Mark Rutherford's story mirrors that of his creator. Furthermore, a tendency to read the fiction as illuminating wider trends has arguably been an obstacle to understanding the author in his proper context. A completely fresh examination of all the sources is needed to understand more fully the pilgrim progress, or regress, of Bedford's less famous son.

This historical study therefore aims to place William Hale White within the contemporary social, religious, and intellectual setting, and against the background of more recent debates about Victorian religion. It will challenge the frequent depiction of White as one who lost his faith and suggest that some key ideas about a Victorian crisis of faith are misleading. The portrayal of White as a doubter relies heavily on assumptions about his exclusion from ministerial training which a study of the evidence renders untenable, and upon a particular reading of the fiction that needs to be questioned. The priority normally given to the novels as sources must be reassessed, and less well-known texts by White brought under review to offer a wider perspective. *The Early Life of Mark Rutherford*, which the author declared to be 'fact' in explicit contrast to previous works, will be a central focus.[3] Whatever the truth of its claim, the book contained reference to important events which could not be guessed at from a reading of the novels. Therefore through this slender foolscap octavo volume of only ninety-one pages key aspects of White's life and religious experience can be explored.

Although in some ways an enigmatic figure, the broad outline of White's life is clear enough. He was born in Bedford, the second child of William and Mary Ann White, née Chignell, on 22 December 1831.[4] William senior was a member of the Dissenting congregation of the Old Meeting, while his wife came from the Lion Walk Independent church in Colchester.[5] William White was a committed Whig, active in local politics and on the hustings at election

---

[2] *The Early Life of Mark Rutherford (W. Hale White) by Himself* (London: Oxford University Press, 1913).

[3] *Early Life*, p. 5.

[4] William and Mary married in August 1829. A daughter, Susanna, had been born in July 1830 but died in November 1831, so Hale was effectively their eldest child. See the Appendix for a family tree.

[5] The Old Meeting was commonly called Bunyan Meeting after the chapel was rebuilt in White's youth (1850), recalling its most famous member. The terms are used interchangeably here.

time. A printer and bookseller by trade, he was noted for 'the purity of the English he spoke and wrote', and in this particular Hale felt indebted to his example, while also recalling the paternal advice against over-artfulness which seems an early intimation of his calling; 'if you write anything you consider particularly fine, strike it out'.[6] The young Hale White was educated locally thanks to the provision of the Harpur Trust, a significant Bedford charity, and at his mother's encouragement then trained for the Independent ministry. For this he first attended Cheshunt College (1848-50) before transferring to New College, London. Taking advantage of the opportunity accorded to Nonconformists by the recently established University of London, he proved his academic promise by gaining a BA in 1850.

In circumstances which demand careful analysis, he was expelled from New College in April 1852 with two fellow-students for holding opinions about the Bible deemed unorthodox. This traumatic reversal forced him to seek a different future, and in time resulted in withdrawal from active participation in any church. After short periods in other work, including an important spell with the radical publisher John Chapman, a civil service clerkship in the General Register Office obtained through the patronage of Samuel Whitbread, MP for Bedford, was followed by a transfer to the Admiralty where he remained until retirement from the post of Assistant Director of Contracts in March 1892. Having married in 1856, and shared a family life with six children (two of whom died young), his public face was of a respectable civil servant of increasingly comfortable means. Respectability did not extend to attendance at public worship however, and he remained alienated from institutional religion.

With a young family, the need to supplement his income turned him to journalism. His father, appointed Doorkeeper to the House of Commons in 1854 after the failure of his Bedford business, had for some years used the privileged access of this position to write sketches of Parliamentary life for the *Illustrated Times*.[7] Inspired by his example, in addition to his daily work Hale from 1861 to 1883 penned weekly columns for several regional and national newspapers in which his pronounced support for political and social reform often found voice. As was customary, these pieces appeared anonymously. From an unknown date, possibly in the late 1870s, and quite in secret from even those closest to him, he also wrote and published between 1881 and 1896 six novels under the name of Mark Rutherford. These were ostensibly brought before the reading public after Rutherford's death by a fictional editor, Reuben Shapcott. In addition, works of literary criticism and translations of Spinoza

---

[6] Quoted in the *Early Life*, p. 31. This advice on style comes originally from words reported by Dr Johnson, though neither father nor son, both admirers, mention this.

[7] A selection was published posthumously with an introduction by Hale White; *The Inner Life of the House of Commons*, ed. by Justin McCarthy, 2 vols (London: T. Fisher Unwin, 1897).

(the *Ethics* and *Tractatus de Intellectus Emendatione*) appeared between 1883 and 1910 under White's name.[8] A number of shorter pieces were published posthumously, along with the *Early Life*, representing the manuscript 'Autobiographical Notes' apparently compiled from about 1910.[9] Despite a measure of critical acclaim, sales of his writings were modest and White received little financial reward. The *Autobiography* seems to have been the best seller, but twelve years after first publication little more than a hundred copies were sold annually.[10]

White's first wife, Harriet Arthur, died in 1891 after many years of distressing invalidity due to multiple sclerosis. He retired from the Admiralty the following year, moving to Hastings, then Crowborough, and finally Groombridge, like his hero Carlyle grumbling in turn about each house and its locality. The most creative period of his literary endeavour corresponded to the years of his wife's illness, and the lonely ones after her death. He had earlier been tested by the loss of his brother Tam (1862), and two sons who lived for less than a year (1861 and 1867). Though a proud father, he was sometimes a distant figure to his children. The eldest, William Hale (1857-1949) was outwardly the most successful, having a distinguished medical career; John Harry (1861-1938), generally known as 'Jack', trained as an engineer and spent many years abroad on construction projects; Ernest Theodore (1869-1936) followed a similar technical career at home, while his twin sister Mary Theodora (1869-1957), 'Molly' to the family, remained single and always lived with her father. Something about marriage evidently made White uneasy, and he found reasons to avoid attending any of his sons' ceremonies, while nonetheless delighting in the grandchildren these unions produced.[11] A key figure in his later life, the young admirer Dorothy Vernon Smith, daughter of the Metropolitan Magistrate Horace Smith, became his second wife in April

---

[8] The work on Spinoza is considered further below. White atypically renders the title '*Ethic*'; '*Ethics*' is usual, and is used here except when referring specifically to White's text.

[9] Later deposited in the British Museum, BL Add Ms 44891. Full details of repositories and references for manuscript sources are given in the bibliography (Section b).

[10] Some of his publishers' accounts survive in the Norman Colbeck Collection of the University of British Columbia. For sales in the six months to 1 September 1893 see UBC, NCC 2-4. *Miriam's Schooling* sold only 59 copies in this period. See bibliography, Section b, for a note on the numbering of British Columbia archive references.

[11] To his eldest son he admitted the pain of seeing others happy when his wife's health had marred their life together; see letters cited by Stone, *Religion and Art of William Hale White ("Mark Rutherford")* (Stanford, CA; Oxford: Stanford University Press; Oxford University Press, 1954), p. 92.

1911, despite the great disparity of their ages (she was 34, he 79).[12] The attachment to Dorothy, one of several young women who were attractive to and attracted by White, caused severe strains between White and his now-adult children.[13] He died at Groombridge in March 1913 after a long period of poor health. Dorothy was still only thirty-six, and died aged ninety in 1967, having long outlived all her step-children.

Very shortly after his death, through the publication of the *Early Life*, the lifting of secrecy about his authorship of pseudonymous writings, and the memorial articles penned in his honour, debate began about the character and significance of this complex figure. His children generally discouraged enquirers about their father's life, in contrast to Dorothy who from the start seemed determined to bring him before a wider public. Her celebrated *Groombridge Diary* (1924) was a revealing portrait of White's last years which the children felt violated their father's privacy. It did however spur them to make their own record and therefore contributed to the survival of a substantial collection of archival material. With one or two exceptions, White was not the subject of sustained research and critical study until the 1950s, when several important monographs laid the basis for all later study.[14] A common theme was the relationship between the Mark Rutherford of the fiction (as writer and subject) and the life of William Hale White. At first it was only possible to explore his private life through the co-operation of Dorothy White and his children, who in addition to their personal memories held most of the letters and other unpublished material necessary for the task. This dependence may have affected the willingness of scholars to confront some sensitive areas, including the difficult relationship between Dorothy and her step-children. The subsequent deposit of most of the primary sources in archives has removed this possible cause of scholarly self-censorship.

Strong disagreements are evident in some of the surviving family letters, and in the contrasting memories of White by those who knew him in old age. The importance of sources relating to these later years, notably the *Early Life*, has

---

[12] Late in his career the 'very old' Horace Smith (1836-1922) sat in proceedings against Gerald Hamilton (Christopher Isherwood's 'Mr Norris'), whose allegedly pro-German sympathies led to his being held under the Defence of the Realm Act in 1914. Recalled by Hamilton, *Mr Norris and I: An Autobiographical Sketch* (London: Allan Wingate, 1956), p. 74. Dorothy's father is not to be confused – as happens – with the minor novelist and poet of the same name (1779-1849).

[13] The troublingly intense nature of some of these relationships is seen in the anonymously published account by Gladys Easdale, *Middle Age: 1885-1932* (London: Constable, 1935), pp. 216-217. See further below on Easdale, pp. 313-314.

[14] First Wilfred Stone, *Religion and Art of William Hale White ("Mark Rutherford")*, then Catherine Maclean, *Mark Rutherford: A Biography of William Hale White* (London: Macdonald, 1955), and thirdly Irvin Stock, *William Hale White (Mark Rutherford): A Critical Study* (London: George Allen and Unwin, 1956).

not always been recognised, especially where studies have concentrated on his novels, and thus mainly the years up to 1896. White's mature reflections on his experiences and beliefs have been somewhat neglected, possibly because they contain affirmations of continuing faith which are uncongenial to the prevailing 'loss' theory.

Several factors make a fresh look at White appropriate. Growth in studies of the Victorian period, along with the rediscovery of minor novelists and a new interest in all kinds of autobiographical writing, have produced a number of essays which refer to him, but the insights they promise are to some extent vitiated by common reliance on an outline taken over from the standard monographs, particularly in relation to the events leading to the expulsion from New College. A further distorting effect occurs because of the influence of the crisis of faith thesis. The early studies of White generally suggest that a viable faith of some sort marked his latter years. The nature of this *credo* might be difficult to define, but fulfilment or affirmation had replaced doubt. More recent writing, in essays, articles and theses, has been cautious about supposing any sort of theistic belief in later life, though not always by explicitly challenging the older studies. Complete loss of faith seems to be assumed, and language which suggests otherwise is interpreted as intended to keep this fact from others, perhaps especially from Dorothy, a committed believer. Earlier monographs had generally accepted her positive testimony in matters of faith, which subsequent researchers have been much less ready to receive. This may be partly due to growing belief in a Victorian religious crisis, or simply that as it became clear she had concealed the difficulties arising from their relationship other features of her account were also questioned.[15] It would be regrettable if potentially valuable evidence was too readily discarded for this reason. There have been serious weaknesses elsewhere. All studies to date have been hindered by a failure to exploit fully the records of Cheshunt and New College, reflecting a broader tendency to understate the importance of the Dissenting context. The distinctive character of this background has been recognised, but inadequately explored since studies have so often been predicated upon seeing White as a doubter in lonely exile, thereby missing significant parallels and points of contact. To the extent that he did come to live as one apart, this was not the simple or inevitable consequence of holding particular beliefs. It was a status chosen, not forced upon him.

Among the last published writings of White's life was an introduction to the 1907 reissue of Carlyle's *Life of John Sterling*. This caused him to address the

[15] She hid evidence of the conflicts between them, and those caused within the family. The sensitivity of the earliest scholars meant that this was also left unrecorded in their accounts. It was understandable that Dorothy wanted to remain silent on such a personal matter, and this does not necessarily invalidate the rest of her record, where the same motive is not present.

nature of biographical writing and the way in which Sterling's faith was to be understood. He quoted approvingly Sterling's view of another 'large-minded' writer:

> Did Montaigne believe in Christianity? A compendious question, which would be clear enough to admit of an answer, if we only knew what is meant by belief, and what by Christianity. Sad is the condition of a talker in drawing-rooms, very sad that of a writer of dissertations, who attempts to answer a question before he knows the meaning of it.[16]

This is an apposite warning. Not only is the understanding of Christian belief capable of a wide range of interpretations which are obscured in the simple opposition of 'faith' and 'doubt', but the evidence of faith in a life is not always easy to detect or define. White himself, in the same context, cited Sterling's conclusion that theology had its limits; it might have 'its use, nay, for speculative minds its necessity, but this is very different from that highest obligation upon all men, the simple as well as the sagest, to seek to realize truth in their own daily lives'.[17] True belief cannot simply be recovered from the sum of a writer's philosophical or theological statements. To this end all the circumstances of White's life which may contribute to a more accurate assessment of his religious convictions and experience will need to be explored.

Scholars have generally assumed that the youthful White held a well-defined orthodox Christian faith, which later crumbled. This begs the question as to the nature of religious belief in the young, and implies an unreasonably high standard by which any later faith might be assessed. Given White's understandable reluctance to define ultimate truths, a broader understanding of implicit Christian faith may be a more appropriate measure. This, among other reasons, is one basis on which to question the adequacy of some common theories about the nature of religious belief in nineteenth-century Britain.

Was there a Victorian Crisis of Faith ?

The phrase 'Victorian crisis of faith' has had widespread currency since a volume of essays of that name was published in 1970.[18] In its broadest sense the description refers to the challenges to religious faith which arose from social and intellectual changes during the nineteenth century, but the dominant idea is *loss* of faith. A perception that the churches were losing a battle with

---

[16] Thomas Carlyle, *The Life of John Sterling: With an Introduction by W. Hale White*, new edition (London: Oxford University Press, 1907); introduction, p. viii.

[17] *Life of John Sterling*, Introduction, p. xiv.

[18] *The Victorian Crisis of Faith*, ed. by Anthony Symondson (London: SPCK, 1970); the importance of 'loss' and 'doubt' had already been a theme in the literature for some years.

alternative world-views is commonplace, and instances of the turmoil in individual lives are cited as concrete examples of the forces at work. Vivid accounts from writers and autobiographers, the 'literature of faith and doubt', play a very significant part as proof-texts. Though studies often show some awareness of many possible stages on the continuum between faith and doubt, this is not always enough to prevent the impression being given that questioning of received orthodoxy was the start of an inevitable journey towards its total abandonment. Where this idea is present there may be a strong tendency to depict those expressing faith in alternative language, perhaps with hesitation and reserve, as attempting to hide from others (or themselves) a real lack of faith. This distorting secularising perspective needs to be guarded against. And yet doubts are now being raised about the crisis of faith meta-narrative itself, as studies increasingly recognise the richness and diversity of Victorian religious expression.

Moreover as Timothy Larsen has shown, movement between faith and doubt was not all towards the latter, and some very significant cases demonstrate a shift from doubt to definite Christian faith.[19] The examples he cites are re-conversions of those brought up in Christian homes who became aggressive secularists before a final return to faith, and are a useful warning about seeing loss of faith as typical of the age. Larsen's study also points to the crucial importance of the transition from Christian nurture in the home to intellectual and spiritual maturity. Factors which at this stage affect vulnerability to doubt are particularly relevant in Hale White's case because of his known exposure to radical sentiment after leaving New College.[20] A careless adoption of the crisis theory which gives undue prominence to now-famous individual cases may falsely suggest loss of faith as the likeliest Victorian ending, with other outcomes overlooked.

Literary examples of religious crisis need to be used with particular care, for it is impossible to say to what extent they represent similar experiences among those who have left no such record. Furthermore, some of the evidence routinely used to illustrate the personal loss of faith needs to be re-examined. In essays edited by Richard Helmstadter and Bernard Lightman on *Victorian Faith in Crisis*, themes of both 'continuity and change in nineteenth-century religious belief' were explored. But even here famous fictional doubters

[19] *Crisis of Doubt: Honest Faith in Nineteenth-Century England* (Oxford: Oxford University Press, 2006). He does not deny that some famous Victorians did abandon Christian belief.

[20] In the employ of John Chapman, a leading publisher of sceptical thought. Rosemary Ashton describes his circle in *142 Strand: A Radical Address in Victorian London* (London: Chatto & Windus, 2006). It is impossible to be sure what White picked up there, apart from an enduring interest in Spinoza. The roll-call of important thinkers he may have met cannot be linked to any particular appropriation of their ideas as documentary evidence is lacking.

continued to be cited as typifying loss while the crisis paradigm was being challenged on other fronts.[21] At least the beginnings of new and more appropriate interpretative strategies can be seen, notably in the greater sensitivity to the literary form in which 'loss of faith' accounts appear, and a recognition that individuals are often seeking new ways of believing; loss being balanced by gain.[22]

The continued popularity of the models of 'faith and doubt' and 'crisis of faith' has been attributed to 'the powerful influence of the secularisation thesis in the academic study of religion and modernity'.[23] These categories fail to recognise the ways in which nineteenth-century Christianity responded to the intellectual challenges it faced, and through which it 'emerges as a tradition in the process of radical reinterpretation'.[24] If this analysis is accepted, a change in religious views, accompanied by storm and stress as it may be, will not automatically be counted as loss because it involves a re-working of traditional beliefs. When White is compared with contemporaries who remained within the church, including prominent ministers, the similarities are often more striking than the differences. All claims to faith must be taken seriously. Those like Hale White who show a high regard for the Bible and for the person of Jesus, espouse an ethic recognisably derived from Christianity, use at least some of the terminology of creeds or doctrines, practise disciplines such as prayer, and do not formally renounce theistic belief or embrace contrary ideologies have a strong *prima facie* claim to be considered as standing within the Christian tradition, generously understood. There is no other system against which his life, experience and declared beliefs are explicable. A better understanding of faith development also allows for a spirituality which changes and expresses itself differently at various life stages. This being so, there are wider implications. If White's story has been distorted under the pressures of the crisis theory then other 'doubters' lives too may need to be reconsidered.

Questioning the value of the crisis of faith paradigm does not mean under-estimating the importance of intellectual challenges, especially those relating to

---

[21] As by Frank Turner, 'The Victorian Crisis of Faith and the Faith that was Lost', in *Victorian Faith in Crisis: Essays on Continuity and Change in Nineteenth-Century Religious Belief*, ed. by R. J. Helmstadter and B. Lightman (Stanford, CA: Stanford University Press, 1990), pp. 9-38; especially his references to Mrs Ward's *Robert Elsmere* (London: Smith Elder, 1888), and the *Autobiography of Mark Rutherford* (p. 9).

[22] On genre see again Turner, 'The Victorian Crisis of Faith and the Faith that was Lost', p. 10, and on *Robert Elsmere*, Bernard Lightman, '*Robert Elsmere* and the Agnostic Crises of Faith', also in Helmstadter and Lightman, *Victorian Faith in Crisis*, pp. 283-311 (especially pp. 290-291).

[23] So Linda Woodhead, 'Introduction', in *Reinventing Christianity: Nineteenth-Century Contexts*, ed. by L. Woodhead (Aldershot: Ashgate, 2001), pp. 1-21 (p. 1).

[24] Woodhead, 'Introduction', *Reinventing Christianity*, p. 1.

the authority of the Bible which play a large part in Victorian religious controversies. After all, the presenting cause of Hale White's college difficulties was his view of the scriptures. This prominence owes much to the growth of biblical criticism, though the discipline itself was not inherently hostile to faith. While some biblical scholarship was motivated by a desire to overthrow traditional teachings, much was produced by those committed to orthodoxy. None could control the use made of their work. At a popular level radical findings might be employed against the churches in secularist and freethinking debates, but the evaluation of new ideas raised a different set of problems in theological education. Here the issue was particularly acute in respect of the latitude available to tutors authorised by the churches they served. This forms a setting for the events to be described, for both teachers and the taught were under scrutiny. They were not necessarily judged by the same standards, for from those to whom much was committed by the church, more was expected. Doubtless many were apprehensively aware of the implications of their sacred trust.

Attacks on the historical reliability and traditional authorship of the biblical books had been a staple of sceptical writing for many years, but it was increased awareness of continental, especially German, scholarship which contributed to the febrile atmosphere in which Hale White's views came under suspicion. This background accounts for the much more serious eruption in Congregationalism over the supposed heterodoxy of Samuel Davidson, tutor at Lancashire College, in 1857. It is possible that the New College events predisposed some towards a stricter view of Davidson's case, but this link is not made in the earliest accounts. As Willis Glover points out, the reception of biblical criticism was influenced by the perceived orthodoxy of its advocates; if traditional Christian teaching was not apparently denied an exponent might employ new methods without much comment or hindrance.[25] Davidson's crime was to leave room for others to conclude that in questioning the Mosaic authorship of the Pentateuch he held too lightly the inspired nature of the sacred text in order to embrace a liberal theology.[26] In many minds traditional authorship was directly linked to the concepts of authority and inspiration. Glover sees the important changes taking place later in the century, but the 1850s showed signs of things to come.[27]

---

[25] *Evangelical Nonconformists and Higher Criticism in the Nineteenth Century* (London: Independent Press, 1954), pp. 25 and 44-48 (on Davidson). John Rogerson highlights the importance of Davidson for the transmission of German scholarship; *Old Testament Criticism in the Nineteenth Century: England and Germany* (London: SPCK, 1984), pp. 170-173, 197-208.

[26] Rogerson shows that he was in fact far from radical in his theology; *Old Testament Criticism in the Nineteenth Century*, pp. 198-199.

[27] Roger Tomes has examined the Davidson case and the general situation in the colleges, concluding that despite earlier stirrings the 1870s and 80s were more

Note continues on following page

The suspicion of unorthodoxy might thus by extension bring critical scrutiny of approaches to the biblical text which could in other circumstances go unchallenged, and it is likely that such factors lie behind the New College expulsions. White and his fellow students had some reason to argue that as young men with ideas still to form they had been treated too harshly, and there are other mid-century examples where a quite surprising liberty was permitted, as instances involving some taught by Richard Alliott at Cheshunt show.[28]

Reframing Hale White

In the belief that existing studies of White, for all their very considerable merit, fail to do justice to his life, a new look at the evidence is required. This vitally includes exploring the origin, meaning, and significance of the under-used *Early Life*. The nature of this and other writings must be explored, and the historical detail they contain on Bedford and his young life examined. This is a necessary first step towards understanding the community of faith into which he was born, and the formation in faith (or lack of formation) experienced there. Through a fresh reading of the *Early Life* the hypothesis is tested that Hale White's religious beliefs and experiences have been commonly misunderstood and misrepresented, rather finding him to be an un-dogmatic believer who questions but never repudiates Christianity.[29] A characterization of Christian faith consistent with changing understandings of conversion and other intellectual developments will be argued for in support of this contention. In the nature of the case it will be easier to question the portrayal of White as losing faith, than to define the faith he came to (or continued to) hold. He is not a systematic writer, and never fully sets out what he believes. The character of the evidence provided by his writings will be considered, challenging their common use as more or less straightforwardly historical sources. The usual dominance of the novels is questioned, and the nature of the *Early Life* as an autobiographical text analysed.

Why the *Early Life*?

The foreword and the opening page of the main narrative indicate something of

---

significant times; '"We are hardly prepared for this style of teaching yet": Samuel Davidson and Lancashire Independent College', *Journal of the United Reformed Church History Society*, 5 (1995), 398-414 and '"Learning a New Technique": The Reception of Biblical Criticism in the Nonconformist Colleges', *Journal of the United Reformed Church History Society*, 7 (2004), 288-314.

[28] For Alliott see pp. 232-235 below.

[29] Both the nature of 'faith' as a way of believing, and the *content* of faith will be explored.

White's purpose in writing the 'Autobiographical Notes' on which the published *Early Life* is based. Both make Hale seem a reluctant autobiographer. In the foreword his eldest son William took responsibility; 'a few years ago I asked my father to put down some facts of his life for those of his family who are too young to remember his early years'; this was echoed in the first sentence - 'I have been asked at 78 years old to set down what I remember of my early life'.[30] In often quoted words, Hale White's explanation went further; 'A good deal of it has been told before under a semi-transparent disguise, with much added which is entirely fictitious. What I now set down is fact'.[31] Since the title page of the *Early Life* declared it to be the life 'of Mark Rutherford (W. Hale White) by Himself', the 'stories' of Mark Rutherford and the 'history' of William Hale White were for the first time publicly declared as in some way standing together.

White's fiction is of a markedly autobiographical character, and thus has assumed great importance for exploring his life and character. But Mark Rutherford may be a decoy or substitute for the writer, an exercise in concealment not self-revelation. Putting these works to one side allows another, different, voice to be heard. White's willingness to record a distinct memoir in old age points to the incompleteness of the novels as a source for his life story. The *Early Life* may stand as a corrective, or complement, perhaps an opportunity taken to forestall the drawing of inadequate or 'unauthorised' parallels between White and Mark Rutherford. Despite the declared element of complementarity it is quite impossible to produce anything like a full life of the writer from the novels and *Early Life* taken together. For example, they contain no clue as to the importance of an Admiralty career which occupied the greater part of his working years, nor can the reader discover anything of White's children. The difficulty in giving a comprehensive biographical account of White reflects the inadequacy of the unpublished sources for the task, as well as the problem of interpreting the public writings.

One way of exploring his different works is through applying hermeneutical techniques from the study of self-writing. For example, a feature common to childhood autobiography (the *Early Life*) and fictionalised autobiography (the *Autobiography* and its sequel, *Mark Rutherford's Deliverance*) is the possibility of closure; the fictional account, as in the case of Rutherford, may include the subject's death and therefore a judgement on a whole life can be offered, while childhood too has a completion, marked by the attainment of maturity. Furthermore, the writer is distanced from his own story. These aspects may have been particularly attractive to White, and partly explain the use of both

---

[30] *Early Life*, pp. iii, 5. William made a notable contribution to medicine and was appointed KBE in 1919; he is sometimes anachronistically called Sir William in this text before that date to distinguish him more readily from his father and grandfather.

[31] *Early Life*, p. 5.

models. Critical theory on the understanding of autobiographical writing has developed greatly since the first seminal monographs on White, and offers useful new perspectives.

Though the importance of the *Early Life* has not been adequately reflected in previous studies its influence can be detected even when it is not directly cited. Its main role, whether acknowledged or not, has been as a check on the *Autobiography* and *Deliverance* as accurately reflecting White's life. It is taken as the standard against which the novels (and other sources) can be read. The additional material it provides on White's early family life, and the Bedford context, is rightly seen as especially valuable. However difficulties arise from readings that take this evidence at face value, without due consideration of genre, and which do not attempt to corroborate the historical picture from other sources. The role of faith is vital in this text, indicating its continuing significance to White, and challenging the idea that his story is simply one of loss. The work also has a unique importance as the only writing in which the critical expulsion episode is covered, but more careful analysis of this event is required, and other source material must be considered.

There is also the wider question of White's place in the tradition of autobiographical fiction which focuses on the life of faith. The story of Mark Rutherford fits broadly into this category, within which the memoirs of nonconformist ministers form a distinctive group. There is no direct evidence that Hale White was influenced by earlier accounts still in circulation, but some common features can be identified. The *Autobiography* was formally presented as that of a 'Dissenting Minister', though this designation was removed from the title-page without comment after the first edition. Inevitably there are parallels with similar 'lives', in which loneliness, spiritual struggles, hardships of various kinds, and difficulties with deacons or elders loom large. A declared hesitation in publishing such records is another staple, along with some necessary concealment of personal and place names in works nevertheless offered as truthful accounts. This was especially important when writing under one's own name, for simple changes of place or name could not prevent those who had known the writer personally from making the correct identifications. Reviewers, if not perhaps always readers, were therefore often cautious about accepting authorship as claimed, and several early reviews of the first Mark Rutherford novels in particular showed hesitation over the author's identity. The *Autobiography*, for example, one noted, '*professes* to be the autobiography of an ex-Nonconformist minister'.[32] Though Hale White withheld his name and disguised locations some people must have been able to make the connection.

William Pitt Scargill's *The Autobiography of a Dissenting Minister*,

[32] From a review by Richard Littledale in *The Academy*, 21 May 1881, p. 370 (emphasis added). His perceptive reading captured the subtlety of the book and will be referred to again below, p. 274.

published in 1834 (by Smith, Elder) and quite possibly the first book in English to describe itself as an 'autobiography', had a title similar enough to have perhaps informed White's choice, though there is nothing to show any other borrowing.[33] With the sort of statement not untypical of such works the writer declared his intention; 'I am not going to make a fiction that shall look like truth, but rather to exhibit a truth which shall look like a fiction'.[34] In an early sign of coming trends the book was published anonymously, and the common attribution to Scargill, a Unitarian minister, is very doubtful, as Michael Watts notes.[35] The writer was almost certainly an Independent minister, and there are strong criticisms of Unitarianism within the work. In places 'Scargill' is shockingly honest, as when recalling his childhood pleasure in reading of Sabbath-breaking swimmers being drowned.[36]

In a later example William Leask, supposedly encouraged by friends to tell of his *Struggles for Life*, overcame a 'reluctance to speak of myself' by 'withholding the writer's name, and slightly altering the orthography of the name of places', while stressing that the resulting text was not 'fiction ... but, strictly and literally, a consecutive narrative of facts and events of which I have been the subject, or which have come under my personal observation'.[37] The author's reflection on 'the period of his spiritual enlightenment' is worth noting for Leask's awareness of the difference between inherited beliefs and a personal faith, a vital issue for all those raised in believing families:

> I had been, up to the period under notice, like many others who are trained amidst religious influences, an intellectual Christian, but nothing more; that is to say, I believed the Bible to be the truth of God, and I believed that Jesus Christ is the true Messiah, and the only Saviour of men. But the fact is, I had never doubted these things; my state of mind therefore, instead of being the result of personal conviction and personal faith, was, more properly, acquiescence in the opinions of others; an adherence to the received doctrines, rather than a personal appropriation

---

33 James Olney makes the claim for Scargill's priority; 'Autobiography and the Cultural Moment: A Thematic, Historical, and Bibliographical Introduction', in *Autobiography: Essays Theoretical and Critical*, ed. by J. Olney (Princeton, NJ: Princeton University Press, 1980), pp. 3-27 (p. 5).

34 *The Autobiography of a Dissenting Minister*, p. 2.

35 *The Dissenters, vol. II: The Expansion of Evangelical Nonconformity* (Oxford: Clarendon Press, 1995), p. 256, note 525. At least some of the novels commonly attributed to Scargill are also very probably by another hand.

36 *The Autobiography of a Dissenting Minister*, p. 4. This story has an echo in White's life; see below, pp. 150-151, 154-155.

37 Leask (1812-1884) published *Struggles for Life: Or, the Autobiography of a Dissenting Minister* anonymously (London: W. & F.G. Cash, 1854); the quotation is from pp. 22-23. The book has also been attributed to Thomas Binney and T. T. Lynch, though the lack of plausible internal evidence makes this difficult to understand.

of the truth.[38]

He went on to describe his full participation in the spiritual disciplines and life of the church (including, as with Hale White, being a Sunday school teacher), until the day on which the sermon by a visiting preacher produced a deep conviction of sinfulness leading to conversion. He was just sixteen. The immediate blessing of his new life was soon followed by dark night of the soul before a prolonged struggle against temptation and doubt was overcome.[39] The parallels here with 'Mark Rutherford' and White himself will become clear in due course.

Another ministerial life was presented in fictional form by Florence Williamson, the pseudonym of William Kirkus (1830-1907), a Congregational minister trained at Lancashire College who was later ordained in the Church of England. The subject of *Frederick Rivers: Independent Parson* (1864) like White had no initial sense of vocation but was forced to earn a living by some respectable means; 'it was no use putting Fritz [the family name for Frederick] into a trade; he was made for a different, if not a higher, work. The choice seemed to lie between law, medicine, and the Church'.[40] There is little sense of personal faith, though Frederick assures himself - under his mother's questioning - of a call to ministry. His critical assessment of fellow students at theological college is rather similar to Mark Rutherford's, with mention of prigs and Pharisees. The chief story of the book is Frederick's long struggle with the deacons of his church as he attempts to revivify a congregation which has fallen into torpor. His preaching attracts the suspicion of heterodoxy, partly because it becomes known that he reads F. D. Maurice.[41] Each of these texts show similarities with Hale White's, but influence or dependence cannot be proved.

A further work, bearing a very similar title, was published anonymously shortly after the *Autobiography of Mark Rutherford.* In *Chapters from the Autobiography of an Independent Minister* (1882) Henry Julius Martyn, lately of Cannon Street Independent Church in Preston, detailed the trials a minister could expect at the hands of his deacons.[42] No author was given on the title page, and the protagonist was named only as 'Mr Wilkinson'. Unusually there was no explanatory preamble explaining the origins of the book, or stating that names and places had been disguised, though the text itself discreetly made that

---

[38] *Struggles for Life*, pp. 102-103.

[39] *Struggles for Life*, pp. 105-106.

[40] *Frederick Rivers* (London: Williams and Norgate, 1864), p. 51. While obviously drawing on episodes from his ministry this is not simply a disguised autobiography of the writer.

[41] *Frederick Rivers*, p. 156; he reads Schleiermacher too, p. 266.

[42] There is no indication in either book that he was aware of White's writing.

plain. An expanded edition in 1887 included additional chapters and a signed preface by Martyn in which he defended himself against some critical reviews of the earlier version. He also revealed that Williams and Norgate had completed the first printing, apart from the title page, 'upwards of ten years' before the volume was actually published.[43] No reason was given, but this situation surely relates to the power struggles at Cannon Street within the diaconate and against the minister which are fictionally reproduced. There may have been a moment of crisis which caused him to draw back after the publishers had the manuscript, or else he wished to have it immediately ready for issue at an opportune moment. In the end he waited until he broke with Independency to become an Anglican before releasing it.

The book is of particular interest because Martyn was at Cheshunt only a little later than White, probably entering in the 1856-57 academic year and leaving for his first pastorate in 1860. Details of Martyn's life, apart from those vouchsafed in the text and possibly unreliably so, are scanty, though brief local accounts record his Cannon Street days, and the shock to that congregation when he announced his intention to join the Church of England. Local journalist Anthony Hewitson observed the difficulties a congregation 'born to have their own way in sacred matters' could heap upon their minister, though Martyn he believed had 'got on pretty evenly with his flock'.[44] His pastorate was in most ways successful, but the fiction reveals more poignantly than any outsider's account the mental distress a few malcontents could inflict. Important aspects of Martyn's outward and inward life will be compared below with Hale's own.

These works and their writers have been largely forgotten, but the reputation of another minister-turned-author has endured. George MacDonald, whose life offers an interesting parallel to White's, openly declared the authorship of his novels but made significant changes when drawing on his personal ministerial experience, re-imagining himself as a clergyman of the Church of England. The travails unique to the Dissenting minister did not therefore feature and some readers believed the writer to be an Anglican, causing embarrassment to his son Greville on one occasion.[45] Since the novels were designed to set forth his wider vision of Christian faith he had never intended them to represent the Dissenting tradition. Some of the similarities and contrasts between MacDonald

---

[43] *The Autobiography of an Independent Minister, to Which is Now Added for the First Time a Second Part, Containing Six Chapters, as Also a New Preface to the First Part* (London: Williams and Norgate, 1887), p. x.

[44] *Our Churches and Chapels, Their Parsons, Priests, and Congregations; Being a Critical and Historical Account of Every Place of Worship in Preston* (Preston: Chronicle Office, 1869), p. 36 (published under the pen-name 'Atticus').

[45] Recalled in his *Reminiscences of a Specialist* (London: George Allen & Unwin, 1932), p. 38. Greville was a medical man like Hale White's eldest son, becoming a respected throat surgeon.

and White will be explored below, with special reference to early spiritual development.

White's writing was not confined to fiction and memoir, for alongside such creative literature other works, few of them now well-known, occupied him for prolonged periods. Nevertheless, presumably on the basis of his Bedford background and ministerial training, he made the claim that he was 'not educated for literature; not trained for literature', but rather belonged in 'a religious world'.[46] A survey of his output will challenge this self-deprecation, insofar as it suggests any lack of ability, by demonstrating White's breadth of literary interest and his writing skills. The claim to natural affinity with a religious world will be upheld however.

The Journalist

White's journalism is significant as a witness to the development of his style as well as for the evidence it yields of his opinions, though its range and volume means that it cannot be fully examined here. It is too easily forgotten that the larger part of Hale White's writing appeared in print before the first of the Mark Rutherford novels.[47] When the *Autobiography* was published in 1881 he had already for twenty years reported on parliamentary debates and the cultural life of the capital. His weekly contributions to several newspapers, beginning with the *Aberdeen Herald* in 1861 and continuing until 1883, were initiated by the difficulty of supporting a household on his clerk's salary.[48] He had already submitted a small number of articles for reference works and periodicals, but evidently felt the attraction of a more predicable income.[49] As he later wrote; 'needing money, I tried to get work on the newspapers. I applied to nearly a hundred and at last two replied. Those two enabled me to live for some years

[46] Reported from a conversation with Dorothy in May 1908, *The Groombridge Diary* (London: Oxford University Press, 1924), p. 33. The reference to having lived in 'a religious world' is in a letter reproduced there of 22 April 1908 (p. 15).

[47] See the study by Mark Crees, 'Before Mark Rutherford: The Translations, Journalism and Essays of William Hale White' (unpublished doctoral thesis, University of Liverpool, 1999) for a much fuller coverage of the journalism. I am grateful to Dr Crees for allowing access to photocopies of White's columns gathered during his research.

[48] White had just started at the Admiralty, on a salary of perhaps £90 p.a., and with very uncertain prospects for promotion under the prevailing rules of seniority. Maclean (p. 164) repeats family sources suggesting earnings of about two and a half guineas per weekly column, a considerable addition to his income.

[49] Among these, from about 1858, were pieces for *The Imperial Dictionary of Universal Biography* and *Chambers' Journal*; see Maclean, p. 162. Hale's fellow New College student Frederic M. White was another contributor to the *Imperial Dictionary*.

till my position improved'.[50] There is no documentary confirmation of another column coinciding at first with that in the *Aberdeen Herald* to support this recollection of starting to write for two newspapers. If there were two replies to his letters, one must have been the *Herald*; the other may have been a rejection (or fruitless proposal), for he did not begin another column until that for the *Morning Star* in 1865. His imperfect memory is suggested by the difficulty that

Dorothy Smith found in establishing the details of his newspaper connections, which White told her had begun 'around 1856'.[51]

This brief reference appears to be all the direct evidence that survives on White's approach to editors or proprietors, though the account of Mark Rutherford's similar search in the *Deliverance* is manifestly closely modelled on the writer's experience.[52] His father's success in parliamentary reporting clearly provided the inspiration (and his office of Doorkeeper access to the House), but the apparent difficulty in finding an opening suggests that William White's contacts with politicians and journalists were of no benefit. Even the briefest personal information in Hale's letters of application would probably have identified him as a Dissenter, and, in all likelihood, a political liberal, but there is nothing to indicate any friendships or family ties existing in such networks which he could call to his aid.

However the newspapers which contracted him were uniformly of a liberal or even radical stamp, and inclined towards nonconformity. There was a marked connection between nonconformity and the provincial press in the later nineteenth century, though rather typically it seems that White was not consciously part of any circle or movement within it.[53] Nevertheless his columns served these overlapping political and religious constituencies, being always marked by support for reform, especially the widening of the franchise, and sympathy for the Dissenting tradition. This meant that White was not forced (as far as one can tell) to suppress his own instincts in these writings, though he enjoyed the traditional columnist's freedom of anonymity, and could

---

[50] From a letter to Mabel Marsh, 27 September 1903, cited by Catherine Maclean, p. 162 (autograph now at Bedford Public Library).

[51] See *Groombridge Diary*, p. 94, recalling a conversation in September 1908. Of course White may sometimes have been intentionally vague under Dorothy's insistent questioning.

[52] *Deliverance*, pp. 1-3, Ch. I.; possibly White had this text in mind when writing the letter mentioned above to Mabel Marsh. It includes the detail of two replies and two columns which seems historically unsupportable.

[53] Links described by Simon Goldsworthy; 'English Nonconformity and the Pioneering of the Modern Newspaper Campaign: Including the Strange Case of W. T. Stead and the Bulgarian Horrors', *Journalism Studies*, 7 (2006), 387-402. Personal reticence and professional discretion as a civil servant must have limited White's freedom as a journalist.

not be personally held to account.[54] The success of his early writings helped him to obtain further employment in the field, and often meant a heavy work-load. The columns themselves do not betray the sense of discontent with the task which Mark Rutherford displays, though doubtless in life they were sometimes 'a great trouble' to the writer.[55] At whatever personal cost, his literary skill produced elegant and attractive copy. His contribution to the *Aberdeen Herald* carried on until early 1872 while that to the *Morning Star* lasted little more than a year, ceasing in July 1866, perhaps because of an engagement for the *Birmingham Journal* started that year and continuing until 1880 (the paper, a Tory foundation turned liberal, having by then become the *Birmingham Daily Post*). During the same period he began his 'Letters' for the *Rochdale Observer* (1867-1872).[56] In 1872, withdrawing from the *Aberdeen Herald* and the *Rochdale Observer*, he wrote for eighteen months in Edward Miall's *Nonconformist* (like the *Morning Star*, a nationally circulated title), and for many years, until March 1883, in the *Norfolk News*. There were also a number of shorter appointments and less frequent pieces appearing in other papers.

The subject matter of his columns is accurately described by their headings. They are variously titled 'Metropolitan Notes' (*Aberdeen Herald*), 'Below the Gangway' (*Morning Star*), 'Sketches in Parliament' (*Birmingham Journal* and successors; this heading also used for the *Nonconformist*, along with 'How it Strikes a Stranger'), 'Letters by a Radical' (*Rochdale Observer*), and 'Our London Letter' (*Norfolk News*). In each case political news was of the highest importance, but culture fell within the wider metropolitan remit, and during parliamentary recesses inevitably other topics were covered. Sometimes these were Hale White's reports of his holiday travels, at home or abroad, including a memorable tour of Germany.[57] Always a close observer of the natural world, and the curiosities of human behaviour, he seemed never at a loss. His eye for the absurd and sharp wit are often evident. On a slack day for other news there might be as many as six or seven paragraphs on different topics, artfully linked in a manner later echoed in the adroit changes of key and subject-matter in the *Early Life*. This allowed him to introduce his own interests, from reports on diseases caused by poor drainage to the waste of public money and despoliation

---

[54] In his fiction he shows an awareness of the problems of conscience some journalists encountered, as when M'Kay has to write 'Tory' pieces; see *Deliverance*, pp. 8-9, Ch. I.

[55] *Deliverance*, pp. 6-7, Ch. I.

[56] This was due to the recommendation of John Bright, according to Maclean (p. 173); Bright, along with Richard Cobden, was a founder of the *Morning Star*. Both men were heroes to White.

[57] With a visit – almost a pilgrimage – to Luther's rooms in Wartburg, described in the *Aberdeen Herald*, 28 September 1861 (p. 4). He has no truck with the rationalistic explaining away of the Devil's appearance to Luther and the famous ink-throwing episode; to call it a 'myth' fails to recognise its religious and psychological significance.

of the countryside.[58] Unsurprisingly, matters touching on the Admiralty and naval expenditure are often noted, though without the writer admitting his personal connection with the subject as a civil servant.[59] In political reporting he did not disguise his support for liberalism, but nonetheless praised any Member of Parliament who spoke effectively and acted honourably.

Distinctive elements of White's style were undoubtedly honed by the discipline of producing topical and lively pieces under severe time pressure and within word limits.[60] Directly addressing the reader in the first person, this kind of writing was a challenge without the authorial freedom which the novel form allowed, and, unlike in his fiction, which has a strongly retrospective element, always with the need to address current issues. It must hardly ever have been possible to craft pieces earlier than the week in which they were required to be in print. Sometimes the same basic material could be re-worked for more than one publication, but since readers also expected the interests of their locality to be respected, it was usually necessary to highlight people or subjects known to have a regional significance. The degree of overlap was therefore usually small.

Though Hale White's progress in journalism is not traceable to influential friendships, the importance of such links in the newspaper world is not to be underestimated, nor the potential disadvantage of being without them. His status as an outsider appears to be shown by the circumstances in which he ceased to write the *Norfolk News* 'London Letter', by then (1883) the only regular column from his pen. Apparently without warning or ceremony he was forced to make way for the young Henry Massingham, who as a cub reporter on the *News* had been handling his (White's) copy, a position he owed to family links with the paper's senior staff. Clement King Shorter records how Massingham, visiting the capital at the age of twenty, and intending there 'to make a living in journalism', proposed at first to supplement his private income by taking over the 'London Letter'.[61] When Shorter asked about the future of the present writer, Massingham 'replied that Mr Hale White … would cease to do so on his arrival in London'.[62] Massingham, eager in later years to laud

---

[58] As in the *Aberdeen Herald* of 18 January1862 for example (p. 4; typhoid outbreak in a hospital), and 1 February 1862 (p. 4; fortifications at Portsmouth); both dates the House not sitting. See also the *Norfolk News*, 8 February 1873, a domestic note on the most efficient kind of heating apparatus (Parliament having only just been recalled and nothing yet to report).

[59] His close knowledge of such matters was sometimes clearly displayed, as in the *Nonconformist* of 6 November 1872, on reforms to tendering processes at the Admiralty, presumably touching on his own department (pp. 1129-1130).

[60] Checks on the *Norfolk News* and *Aberdeen Herald* suggest articles of commonly around 1500 words; that is, 'a column and a half', as the *Deliverance* has it (p. 3, Ch. I).

[61] Recorded in *C.K.S. An Autobiography: A Fragment by Himself*, ed. by J. M. Bulloch (London: Privately Printed, 1927), pp. 50-51.

[62] *C.K.S.*, p. 51.

White's writings, showed little regard for him at this time, and was probably not yet aware that he had already published the *Autobiography*. If there was any resentment on White's part about this loss of work it did not prevent his later producing many articles for *The Nation* under Massingham's editorship.[63]

There is no mention of this incident in Massingham's 'Memorial Introduction' to the 1923 reprinting of the novel, but both he and Shorter have left valuable impressions of White's journalism which help to show some of its distinctive features. For Shorter 'it was full of strenuous Nonconformity', though 'it rather overdid … the gibes against the Church of England'.[64] This chimes with Massingham's verdict:

> it was hardly of that acknowledged pattern of that particular work of art. The topics were of no great variety, being, as often as not, concerned with some ceremonial freak of a High Church clergyman, treated with an irony highly agreeable to the readers of a Nonconformist newspaper, From time to time here was a little criticism of the Shakespearian drama in one of the Irving revivals, also a permitted topic in the serious circles to which the paper went.[65]

Clearly White knew what his readers liked, though there is no indication that he did not share these opinions himself. The strictures against ritualism are more than crude 'No Popery' (unless they indicate that religious prejudices remain strong even when personal ties to the tradition are weakened), since for White they arose from the ethics of belief. It was improper for Anglicans to stretch the meanings of their formularies to accommodate catholic beliefs which would have been repugnant to earlier generations. Believers should be true to 'type' and inhabit their own best traditions.[66]

Massingham's career offers an instructive parallel with White's. 'HWM' had a private income, and the family advantages which had secured him a post on the *Norfolk News* on leaving school. That apprenticeship allowed him to learn the craft and build up contacts which would open doors in the London newspaper world. He also immersed himself in politics and in adulthood became a tireless campaigner for liberal causes - he was a party man in a way foreign to Hale White, for whom in any case journalism had to be fitted around

---

[63] Edward Garnett was another significant contributor, and as a reader for T. Fisher Unwin knew Hale White's worth. See G. Jefferson, *Edward Garnett: A Life in Literature* (London: Jonathan Cape, 1982), especially pp. 54, 99-100.

[64] *C.K.S.*, p. 51

[65] 'Memorial Introduction' to the *Autobiography* (London: T. Fisher Unwin, 1923), pp. v-xxv (p. v). This rather understates the range of subjects White mentions, since Massingham based his view only on the copy he had handled for the *Norfolk News*.

[66] The ethical question also arises where personal beliefs are reinterpreted to conceal possible unbelief, which White also challenged. Here it means believing *too much*, a focus on non-essentials.

the commitments of his job and family life. Massingham admired White's writing, and felt a kinship on the basis of a shared nonconformist background (Methodist in his case); he also shared a personal reserve and beneath the public figure was curiously detached from deeper human relationships.[67] Through Mark Rutherford, Hale White expressed distaste for party spirit which may also have inhibited his own closer participation in politics:

> men must join a party, and have a cry, and they generally take up their party and their cry from the most indifferent motives. For my own part I cannot be enthusiastic about politics, except on rare occasions when the issue is a very narrow one.[68]

Rutherford's reserve was based on the complexity of issues to which no simple answer was possible (this also extends to religion), but his reasoning was presented with an unappealing pomposity:

> it disgusts me to get upon a platform and dispute with ardent Radicals or Conservatives who know nothing about even the rudiments of history, political economy, or political philosophy, without which it is as absurd to have an opinion upon what are called politics as it would be to have an opinion upon an astronomical problem without having learned Euclid.[69]

Under his own name, in a letter to *The Speaker* (a Liberal journal) White expressed great distaste for party action, on the similar grounds that no one group could have the monopoly on truth and, more bluntly, that flawed and selfish human beings all too often vitiated any good they attempted. Adopting Wordsworth's mantle he asserted that 'the world is running mad with the notion that all its evils are to be relieved by political changes, political remedies, political nostrums ... whereas the great evils, sin, bondage, misery, lie deep in the heart, and nothing but virtue and religion can remove them'.[70] This individualism brought a sharp, anonymous, response lamenting that 'Mr Hale White, alas, has no faith in humanity', which does not essentially misrepresent White's view of man and society.[71] It was why the Drury Lane experiment described in the *Deliverance* was committed to the rescue of

---

[67] Alfred Havighurst traces Massingham's career, while regretting the difficulty of illuminating the private self, in *Radical Journalist: H.W. Massingham (1860-1924)* (Cambridge: Cambridge University Press, 1974).

[68] *Autobiography*, p. 16, Ch. II.

[69] *Autobiography*, p. 16, Ch. II. White, of course, was a gifted amateur astronomer.

[70] Letter, 'Mr W. S. Lilley and the *Times*', *The Speaker*, 10 February 1906, pp. 457-458 (p. 458). From remarks made by Wordsworth to Dewey in 1833. The journal was given new life the next year under H. W. Massingham as *The Nation*.

[71] 'Mark Rutherford and Democracy', *The Speaker*, 3 March 1906, pp. 518-519 (p. 519).

individuals, one by one.[72] His Dissenting background showed the importance of community, but also a more fundamental emphasis upon personal responsibility and answers beyond the political. In a comparative study of White alongside George Gissing and H. G. Wells, Thomas Hubbard also identifies this stress upon the individual and its roots, asserting that White retained 'an essentially religious outlook', and was therefore never willing to embrace secularism.[73]

As this survey demonstrates, to single out comments on religion would give a misleading picture of White's journalism, which has a very strong political focus, naturally arising from the primary purpose of reporting from Parliament. When political battles were at their height there was frequently no other subject in a column. But it has shown a passionate concern for truth in matters of belief, and an emphasis on essentials, which does convey something important about the man. While these newspapers would hardly be the appropriate forum for declarations of doubt (and a sampling of texts reveals none), there is no reason to suppose that White was concealing his true position. Only by misrepresenting the expulsion from New College as arising from a personal loss of faith, or reading backwards from the novels, and taking *them* as expressing such a loss, could an argument even be attempted to show from the journalism also that White repudiated his natal faith. It would then be largely a most unsatisfactory argument from silence.

The evidence instead is that his unhappy college experience made him more impatient of externals, wishing to focus rather on the essentials of faith, and a bitter opponent of all that he considered hypocrisy. For example, he is astonished that a clergyman should write for the *Westminster Review* (with its 'reputation for everything but orthodoxy' which he well knew from experience) in terms which would 'appal both his flock and his bishop ... if ... made public'.[74] This might be contrasted with 'the constant collision between the living, acted Christianity of the genuine believer' and 'dead, traditional profession' which in noticing it for the public he took to be the central theme of Mrs Lynn Linton's anonymously published novel, *The True History of Joshua Davidson*.[75]

At other times his personal knowledge of the Dissenting world is clearly displayed, as for example in reference to John Campbell, 'the Editor of the

---

[72] *Deliverance*, Ch. V.

[73] In a thesis which has been curiously overlooked by students of White; 'Born in Exile: The Lower-Class Intellectual in the Fiction of William Hale White ("Mark Rutherford"), George Gissing and H. G. Wells, 1880-1911' (unpublished doctoral thesis, University of Aberdeen, 1982), p. 37. I am indebted to Dr Hubbard for making a copy of his work available to me, and for permission to cite from it.

[74] The writer must have been anonymous, or using an assumed name; *Aberdeen Herald*, 8 March 1862 (p. 4).

[75] *Norfolk News*, 21 December 1872 (p. 4). The book was brought out by Strahan in that year.

British Standard, a violent and ultra-evangelical organ' and a man 'addicted to "being on the rampage"', who had written to the Prince Consort to warn of the dangers of Popery, or when after the death of Thomas Binney he ventured that none of the published tributes had 'given a correct account of his early life' or sufficiently noted the surpassing power of his preaching.[76] Unfortunately White himself entered into error in this case, while claiming special knowledge because Binney had started his ministry at John Howard's New Meeting in Bedford, and not on the Isle of Wight as others had suggested. In Bedford (White reported) Binney's preaching attracted a great following even from among 'steady-going Church folk', until 'the usual result of such living interpretations of the Bible followed', and he was 'covertly pronounced "suspect". Some 'ism or 'ology was secretly breathed against him, and indirectly he was forced to leave Bedford'.[77] There is an element of myth-making here (depending upon the meaning to be attached to 'indirectly'), or White assumed more than he knew, for a history of the church reveals that 'it was the course of true love that caused Binney's sudden departure'; he had courted the daughter of Samuel Hillyard of Bunyan Meeting, but his suit was rejected by her parents and he left Bedford the next day.[78]

White's journalism has remained little known, largely because of its anonymous nature and relative inaccessibility. The doctoral thesis by Mark Crees is the best guide, and within the scope of this study it is only possible after this point to cite material where it provides biographical information, or has particular relevance to the argument being advanced. It is too simplistic to suggest that journalism was White's pulpit, though there is no doubt that he valued the opportunity to contribute to popular debate, and to hold the executive to account. This was not just sermonizing, but the imagery was near to him; 'it has so happened that since the House of Commons adjourned last Tuesday not a single political event has occurred which could serve as a text for the most meagre of sermons'.[79] It was, at the very least, a sort of political preaching, and a decidedly moral scrutiny of events. Recognising the power of the press, his own exercise of it was wholly responsible, against the tendencies he lamented elsewhere; 'newspapers are said, and justly said, to do more than

---

[76] *Aberdeen Herald*, 24 August 1861 (p. 4), and *Norfolk News*, 14 March 1874 (p. 5), respectively.

[77] *Norfolk News*, 14 March 1874 (p. 5). Binney went to the Isle of Wight *after* leaving Bedford.

[78] See H. G. Tibbutt, *A History of Howard Congregational Church* (Bedford: Howard Congregational Church, 1961), p. 23. There is a suggestion that the energetic Binney had already wished to move, but no evidence that this was due to conflict over doctrine.

[79] From the *Nonconformist*, 3 April 1872, pp. 350-351 (p. 350). Unusually, this piece 'By our Parliamentary Correspondent' is not headed 'How it Strikes a Stranger', but bears the title 'A British Fast'. However it stands in exactly the place usually occupied by White's column, and is in his style.

all churches and chapels in moulding men's minds, and they compete with one another for what is vile and loathsome'.[80] These years spent in journalism suggest a gifted natural writer, even if this was not how White chose to define himself.

The Novelist

This long apprenticeship notwithstanding, the novels remain White's best known texts and it is necessary to say something about the qualities which have brought this about. The first thing to strike the reader who approaches White in the context of other Victorian fiction is his elegant brevity, no doubt reflecting his newspaper experience in writing short pieces, and also the pressure on his writing time. The three-decker novel was still the norm when the one volume *Autobiography of Mark Rutherford* was published in 1881. It was followed in 1885 by *Mark Rutherford's Deliverance*. Two years later *The Revolution in Tanner's Lane* moved beyond the story of Mark Rutherford, but was still firmly located within his Dissenting world. Three further works showed a quite new emphasis on central female characters; *Miriam's Schooling* (1890), *Catharine Furze* (1893), and finally *Clara Hopgood* (1896).

White's succinctness generated some curiosities in the printing. The novels varied in length but were all comparatively short, and an attempt was made to compensate for this with a generous line spacing (in printing terms, increasing the 'leading'), and in some cases also a larger font size.[81] First impressions could therefore be misleading. An apparently substantial volume such as *Clara Hopgood* with nearly three hundred pages had three fewer lines per page - and in larger type - than the *Deliverance*, which (without the bound-in 'Notes on the Book of Job' and short essay on 'Principles') had one hundred and sixty-three pages. The extra material in the *Deliverance*, and that published with *Miriam's Schooling*, may be partially explicable by a need to add length. The printing strategy was not uniformly adopted in the first editions. *Catharine Furze*, uniquely, appeared as two volumes with wide spacings (though simultaneously published by Macmillan in New York as a single volume), whereas *Miriam's Schooling* had been so densely printed that the main story only just exceeded a hundred pages, and with the 'Other Papers' of the title the book did not double that number. The *Autobiography* and *Deliverance* were reset and issued together as a single volume in 1888, and the number of pages in each decreased, this setting being retained in later individual re-issues. The

---

[80] The verdict in his extended preface to the second edition of the translation of Spinoza's *Ethic* (London: T. Fisher Unwin, 1894), p. lxxxv, comparing them with Spinoza's emphasis on virtue.

[81] In the first editions *Autobiography* had 180 pages, *Deliverance* 210, *Revolution* 388, *Miriam's Schooling* 194, *Catharine Furze* 370 [181 + 189], and *Clara Hopgood* 298.

joint edition was extended by the addition of 'A Mysterious Portrait', which had previously appeared without attribution in the *Birmingham Daily Post* of December 1881. 'Reuben Shapcott' had poignantly described finding the extra pieces after Rutherford's death among 'a mass of odds and ends ... apparently written for publication', most of which he was sure 'had been refused'.[82] All three were retained in subsequent printings of the *Deliverance* as a single volume. Since critics have sometimes attempted to demonstrate a relationship between the short pieces bound-in and the headline texts it is important to remember that the reasons for their inclusion may have been more practical and prosaic, with a sudden need to add whatever was to hand.[83]

Possibly use of these various techniques to maximise the number of pages betrays anxiety about sales of volumes which seemed too slim in contrast to the more traditional novel form, in which the same methods had often been used to stretch material to the necessary three, or at least two, volumes.[84] Whatever the reasons, the books were noticeably of the future. The three volume form had been under attack from mid-century, but the crucial importance of the circulating libraries and the economics of publishing ensured its survival. Only when the libraries themselves supported change in the mid-1890s did single volume publication become more common and sales to individuals increased.[85] Hitherto the novel reader had typically been a borrower rather than a buyer, but White's were potentially books to own.[86]

It must be supposed that many readers were drawn to the novels because of an interest in the world they depicted, especially the *Autobiography*, *Deliverance* and *Revolution*. This was the life of Dissenting communities by one who appeared to share it as an insider. Quite apart from the subject matter,

---

[82] *Autobiography of Mark Rutherford and Mark Rutherford's Deliverance*, pp. 272-273; the same postscript had followed the main text in the original single volume issue of the *Deliverance*.

[83] 'A Mysterious Portrait' may be more significant than its companion pieces. In a work published too late to be more than briefly noticed here Max Saunders has drawn attention to the number of texts of this period in which portraiture features largely; see *Self Impression: Life-Writing, Autobiografiction, and the Forms of Modern Literature* (Oxford: Oxford University Press, 2010), especially pp. 116-119 for his suggestion that this piece 'ironizes' the autobiography which it accompanies, leaving the reader uncertain about the status of the main text (p. 118).

[84] Comparisons here are based on the first editions and the later Fisher Unwin uniform series; the Oxford University Press editions show some similar differences, but are not identical.

[85] J. A. Sutherland considers the practicalities of novel publication in *Victorian Novelists and Publishers* (London: Athlone Press, 1976), pp. 9-72.

[86] Three volume novels typically sold at 31s.6d.; the *Autobiography* was priced at 5 shillings, commonly the price of the single volume reprint which followed a successful three-decker.

White's literary style has always attracted admirers, as has his deeply moral vision. A few critics have made extravagant claims for his greatness, citing the praise of readers like André Gide and Arnold Bennett; many more have remarked on the uneven quality and weakness of plot in White's fiction.[87] Often it is his evident sincerity which attracts attention, and the high quality of his English.

Those who appreciated White's writing seem to have been relatively few in number. The initial print runs are known to have been small, normally between 500 and 750 copies, and later re-issues may have included newly bound-up copies from the first printings. While the novels remained in print for long periods, and were periodically released in new forms, as by Fisher Unwin in his six-volume 'Works of Mark Rutherford', and later by Oxford University Press, annual sales were low.[88] The surviving correspondence with publishers over the years shows that White scrutinised agreements and accounts with an attention to detail honed on Admiralty contracts and tenders. He took a close interest in the whole process, and was not slow to raise queries or challenge the interpretation of contracts.

It is impossible to disentangle fully his publishing history. The texts which caused most difficulty for writer and publisher were not the novels but the translations of Spinoza to which he dedicated many years. White seemed determined to keep these specialised and slow selling titles in print, and some of the changes in publisher seem to have been chiefly designed to achieve this end. He had been in correspondence for some time with the barrister and amateur Spinoza scholar Frederick Pollock before attempting to place his translation of the *Ethic*.[89] In 1880 Pollock offered to introduce White to his own publishers, Kegan Paul, Trench & Co. This must have come to nothing, but perhaps they recommended him to Nicholas Trübner, and so ensured that Trübner & Co. handled the *Autobiography*, which was ready for the press in 1881. The *Ethic* which followed in 1883 was well suited to Trübner's 'English and Foreign Philosophical Library', where it featured alongside similarly demanding texts. After this successful cooperation Trübner went on to publish the *Deliverance* and *Revolution*.

When Trübner, along with the firm of George Redway, was merged with Kegan Paul, Trench in 1889 the contracts were transferred to the new limited

---

[87] Stock lists the praise of literary readers from Matthew Arnold to D.H. Lawrence, pp. 3-5.

[88] The Fisher Unwin Collected Works edition (as used here) was at first issued in five volumes, without *Clara Hopgood*. This title was later added in the same uniform binding, and numbered as volume six. It is not clear if this delay related to the sexual ethic it displayed. The six volume set was reprinted many times. The Oxford University Press edition followed in 1936.

[89] Letter of 15 December 1880, Pollock to White (UBC, NCC 1-7).

company of Kegan Paul, Trench, Trübner, with *Miriam's Schooling* appearing under that imprint in June 1890. Some authors used to dealing with familiar staff in the previous firms were discomfited by these changes, and it also gradually became clear that the expense of the merger, which involved large new premises, had not been as fully anticipated as the hoped for economies.[90] The new firm ran into difficulties within a few years, and possibly it was some early indication of these (as rumours then circulating suggest), or the loss of personal contact, which prompted White to cancel his agreement with them in 1892.[91] 'For reasons with which I need not trouble you', he wrote, 'it has been arranged that the books you have hitherto published and sold for me are to be transferred to Mr Fisher Unwin of Paternoster Bldgs'.[92] As usual Spinoza posed a problem, and White had to buy out the copyright and purchase the printer's moulds for £7.10.00, along with the remaining stock.[93]

That Thomas Fisher Unwin came of a well-known and extensively connected Congregational family does not seem to have played a part in White's switch of publisher.[94] After learning the trade at Jackson, Walford and Hodder, Fisher struck out of his own, buying the failing firm of Marshall, Japp in 1882. He now courted new authors to expand the business, and was dedicated to producing single-volume novels rather than the traditional three-deckers for the circulating libraries. The advice of Edward Garnett was fundamental to his success, and it was Garnett who insisted that White be retained 'at any cost'.[95] Adept at creating the maximum value from his list, one of Fisher's common techniques was to stimulate demand by issuing books in new sets and series. Stanley Unwin makes this almost a criticism; 'he could never believe any series was finished and made constant attempts to revivify it', but the practice met with considerable success.[96] The Rutherford novels were

[90] The episode is covered in Leslie Howsam's history; *Kegan Paul: A Victorian Imprint. Publishers, Books and Cultural History* (London; Toronto, ON: Kegan Paul International; University of Toronto Press, 1998), pp. 138-154.

[91] James Nelson cites a letter of August 1892 reporting three separate rumours of Kegan Paul's imminent bankruptcy; *The Early Nineties: A View from the Bodley Head* (Cambridge, MA: Harvard University Press, 1971), p. 79 note 10 (on p. 343). Kegan Paul also sold rights and unsold stock to other publishers during this period, presumably to aid liquidity; see Nelson pp. 313-314 for a list of transfers to Elkins Matthews and John Lane at the Bodley Head for example.

[92] Letter of 29 April 1892 (UBC, NCC 1-19).

[93] Letter of 26 March 1892, Kegan, Paul, Trench, Trübner & Co. to Hale White (UBC, NCC 1-19).

[94] Something of his background and business dealings is given by Philip Unwin, *The Publishing Unwins* (London: Heinemann, 1972), especially pp. 37-49.

[95] From a reader's report quoted (without date) in Jefferson, *Edward Garnett*, p. 54.

[96] Stanley had his introduction to the trade under 'TFU', his father's step-brother, but found him a hard master. *The Truth About a Publisher: An Autobiographical Record*

Note continues on following page

produced in different impressions over the years, notably in the Cabinet Library ('The Novels of Mark Rutherford'), and as 'The Works of Mark Rutherford' (in plain black cloth, numbered on the spines). These undated uniform editions were issued periodically, and to some effect. While sales of *Pages from a Journal*, first published in December 1900, were by the end of the decade very slow, Fisher Unwin reassured White that his novels were faring better; 'it is an illustration of the influence and power of what might be called a Series or Library form of publishing books that have been successful and can be issued uniform & sold at a cheap price. The shilling editions of your books have sold very well'.[97] The smaller Spinoza translation, *Tractatus de Intellectus Emendatione*, which Duckworth took on after Fisher Unwin (who then held the rights to the *Ethic*, later also transferred to Duckworth) declined to re-issue it, was another very slow seller which probably could not have been originally tolerated without the more successful writings.[98]

In 1910 Oxford University Press joined Fisher Unwin as one of White's publishers, the rights to the novels remaining with Unwin until at least 1927. Dorothy Smith's family connection was probably a factor (her sister Marion had married Humphrey Milford), and since Fisher's business was somewhat in decline during his later years, White may already have been predisposed to consider a change.[99] The University Press found a limited market for White's books, and attempts to boost sales by co-ordinating the publication of a new edition of *Pages* (from the Fisher Unwin plates with some fresh material added) alongside *More Pages from a Journal* met with little success. At White's request in the same year they also produced a fourth edition of the *Ethic* based on Duckworth's plates, though even he doubted if the 500 copies would ever be sold.[100] The Press had no great commercial success with the novels, which it first published in 1936. Humphrey considered pulping his stock in 1943

(London: George Allen & Unwin, 1960), pp. 79-111 allowed him to set the record straight, but he could not deny Fisher's many successes. The reference above is on p. 88.

[97] Letter T. Fisher Unwin to Hale White, 7 July 1910 (UBC, NCC 4-9). Stanley Unwin remembered the shilling series, and that sales of the *Autobiography* and *Deliverance* carried the slower moving *Revolution*; *The Truth about a Publisher*, p. 91.

[98] White had to underwrite publication of both Spinoza texts, and may hardly have recovered his costs from royalties.

[99] At this date Milford was assistant to the Secretary to the Delegates of the Press; he succeeded Henry Frowde as manager of the London office and publisher to the University in 1913. Thomas Fisher Unwin did not retire until 1926, when the ailing business merged with Ernest Benn.

[100] Letter Hale White to Milford 11 February 1910 (UBC, NCC 4-13). The printers reported that 'the whole of the preliminary matter', including of course White's preface, would need to be re-set, and a good number of other plates needed 'tinkering' with before they could be re-used. The 1910 edition was reprinted (or bound up from the unsold first printing) at least twice, in 1923 and 1930.

because rarely were more than ten copies of each title called for annually and 'I cannot keep my congested warehouse groaning under six unsaleable books indefinitely'.[101] Sales of White's philosophical and literary-critical works were also typically very modest.[102]

There was a minor title change to one of the novels in these later years, though it did not endure. For reasons which are unclear the *Deliverance* was reprinted by Fisher Unwin in 1924 with the title reversed, becoming *The Deliverance of Mark Rutherford*. In this form it also appeared three years later in Jonathan Cape's Travellers' Library, along with the *Autobiography* and *Revolution*. The series contained many works which Cape printed under licence from their copyright holders, and the reason for White's inclusion surely lies in the role of Edward Garnett as Cape's principal reader during this period. He closely advised on the books thought worthy of a new lease of life under these covers and is known to have held White in high regard.[103] When Humphrey Milford announced his first issue of the novels in 1936 (Cape having been required to surrender their rights) the title was again *Mark Rutherford's Deliverance*.[104]

A varied publishing history and recurrent scholarly interest should not obscure the fact that this writer has never enjoyed a very large circulation, his readers discriminating rather than plentiful. Even with the praise of other writers and admiring modern readers White is not to be judged as belonging to the first rank of nineteenth century novelists. He nevertheless rises above almost all of the company in which he is found when narrowly considered as a novelist of faith and doubt (though this is a poor enough test). Few now read the once-famous *Stephen Remarx* by James Adderley (1893), or W. J. Dawson's *The Redemption of Edward Strahan* (1891), but at least some of White's fiction has been almost continuously in print. This is a tribute to its literary merit, and the compelling interest of the subject matter, especially the spiritual and emotional struggle of Mark Rutherford. Reviewers commonly detected some truth from life behind his story, even when they had no knowledge of the author. William Howells, writing on the *Autobiography* and *Deliverance* in *Harper's New*

---

[101] Unpublished letter to J. G. Wilson of J. & E. Bumpus, booksellers (cited from catalogue of book dealer Richard Ford of London, offering the letter for sale in March 2007).

[102] He may have earned as little as £150 from all his writings; see *Groombridge Diary*, p. 164.

[103] The fullest account of the series is by Basil Savage, 'Jonathan Cape and the Travellers' Library', *The Private Library*, n.s. 4 (1971), 165-183.

[104] At this stage Cape still had 2400 copies of the three novels in stock, from a total printing of 12,000 in 1944. Statement by the literary agents James Pinker & Son to Sir William Hale-White in a letter of 24 February 1936 arranging the copyright for Milford; UBC, NCC 17-4. Unfortunately the stocks levels of 500, 600 and 1300 are not differentiated by title.

Monthly Magazine, spoke of works which carried 'so deep a sense of truthfulness' that he hesitated to call them fiction.[105] Perhaps by design, White had created an air of mystery about his writing.

Literary Anonymity

Then as now the veiled nature of White's authorship represented a challenge to reader and critic. It was not in itself a particularly unusual stance, for Victorian authors were heirs to a long tradition of disguised publication. The device of a fictional editor, Reuben Shapcott, in addition to the pseudonymous writer Mark Rutherford added another layer of secrecy but again this was not uncommon, having already been used in Carlyle's *Sartor Resartus* for example, but the efforts White made to keep his name from the public makes his an unusual case.[106] Anonymity was rarely so successfully protected, here in part reflecting a deeply reticent personal nature. The fact of publication, albeit formally after the death of the fictional author, nevertheless shows a need for self-expression and concern for posterity.

The steps which White took to preserve his secret, including denials when challenged that appear very close to lying, suggest a serious intention to remain unidentified. His persistence in them appears to confirm this, with only a slight weakening in resolve towards the end of his life, but other writers made very similar statements for more complex reasons which highlight the difficulty in being sure about a writer's motive. In fact this is hardly recoverable with any great certainty. According to John Mullan the available evidence itself may be part of a design to intrigue:

> the elaborateness of measures taken to preserve an incognito tells us nothing of any true desire to remain unknown. The lengths to which a writer might go to keep the public, or sometimes the publisher, or occasionally the writer's own friends or family, guessing about the authorship of a work is not in itself evidence of the author's modesty, or shamefacedness, or fear. Being guessed at might be a

---

[105] 'Editor's Study', *Harper's New Monthly Magazine*, 72 (1886), 481-487 (pp. 485-486). White appreciated the review and wrote to Howells revealing his authorship, but enjoining secrecy; see Stone *Religion and Art of Mark Rutherford*, p. 124, who however omits the postscript in which White asked that his identity remain confidential (letter dated 25 February 1886 in the Houghton Library of Harvard University: MS.Am.800.20).

[106] Technically, to describe a work as pseudonymous is to assume a close resemblance between the written life and the author's own. Where a greater degree of invention is supposed the term 'heteronym' has been suggested; see the discussion in Saunders, *Self-Impression*, p. 113, and examples in Part II, *passim*. For simplicity the earlier term is used here, without pre-judging the extent of differences between 'Mark Rutherford' and William Hale White.

> writer's ambition. Provoking curiosity and conjecture - highlighting the very question of authorship - can often be the calculated effect of authorial reticence.[107]

This conclusion rests on research among authors' unpublished letters and diaries, and there are obvious similarities with White. Pseudonymity enabled public recognition to be avoided, but could be combined with openness among trusted friends, as Mullan describes in the case of Charles Dodgson. A writer who chose not to be named in a work might feel justified in refusing to acknowledge it as his.[108] Charlotte Bronte also claimed this absolute right. She revealed her authorship within a select circle, but in a close parallel to White sanctioned the use of her name to make denials. Friends could tell enquirers that they were 'authorized by Miss Bronte to say, that she repels and disowns every accusation' of having written the novels being attributed to her.[109] White's eldest son recalled that when admirers of the novels wrote to his father as the assumed author 'he got his daughter to reply, saying that her father had not among his acquaintances any one of the name of Mark Rutherford'.[110] On one occasion Hale had written to his friend Sarah Colenutt, apparently referring to the *Autobiography*, that he had 'never owned the book you name, and should be quite justified in denying its authorship'.[111] This may be a special case, for Mrs Colenutt had lent the book to Hale's cousin William Chignell, and White was anxious about his reaction; 'tell -------, *not as a message from me* but as one from yourself, that you understand I disclaim it and that he had better not say a word to me about it. I have a particular reason for not wishing to put him under any obligation to make any observation to me on that subject, and he would certainly feel such an obligation in the case of a volume acknowledged

---

[107] Mullan concentrates on nineteenth century works, though without considering Hale White; *Anonymity: A Secret History of English Literature* (London: Faber and Faber, 2007), p. 20.

[108] Even when widely identified as 'Lewis Carroll' he continued to deny the link, and friends were asked to keep silent; *Anonymity*, pp. 41-46. Mullan includes works presented as if the writer was already dead; though Shelley, De Quincey and Hazlitt all had more to hide than White (pp. 264-266).

[109] Cited in Mullan *Anonymity*, p. 91.

[110] 'Notes on William Hale White (Mark Rutherford) by his eldest son', p. 10 (BPL, MR 14-1).

[111] Cited in *Letters to Three Friends* (London: Oxford University Press, 1924), p.11, a letter of 17 March 1883. In a note Dorothy (the editor of this volume) identifies the book referred to as the *Autobiography*, but this is not given in the text. White's statement on ownership seems unlikely to be true, unless by chance he did not have a copy on his shelves at the time of writing, or used the word in the secondary sense of 'claimed as mine'.

by me as mine'.[112]

For writers interested in sales anonymity was a severe restriction to the promotion of their work, which helps to explain the number of authors who abandoned the practice after the success of their early publications.[113] This is compatible with anonymity or pseudonymity being adopted as a tactic or lure, and cast off when a text has been favourably received. Something of this lay behind the creation of T. Fisher Unwin's 'Pseudonym Library', which effectively created an uncertainty about the author's identify that in ordinary publication might never have arisen, and made it something which could then be dramatically revealed. The technique clearly worked, for 'readers and reviewers ... searched for clues in the texts for the identities of the authors'.[114] White's novels were never included in the Pseudonym Library (although this is sometimes erroneously assumed), apparently because there was no wish to advertise that 'Mark Rutherford' *was* a pseudonym.[115] That White did not soon discard his pseudonymity confirms a still deeper desire to cloak his self-disclosure, allied to natural personal reserve and an apparent indifference to commercial considerations. His newspaper column had by convention appeared without the writer's name so to publish the fiction openly would in a sense have constituted an unmasking, but in some other significant writings he did declare his role. These however were texts which were not personally revealing, and for the most part his responsibility was more editorial than creative.

The Essayist, Critic, and Scholar

---

[112] *Letters to Three Friends*, p. 11, original italics. The autograph supplies 'William' where the printed text leaves a blank (the location 'Exeter' was similarly omitted earlier in the letter; Dorothy's editorial strategy was often to remove references to place and personal names). The implication is that William (always known by this name rather than Thomas, a usage adopted here throughout) would be offended or upset by the book. Chignell could hardly have read it without guessing the authorship. See below on rediscovered letters to the Colenutts, pp. 290-293.

[113] Mullan makes this point; *Anonymity*, p. 287.

[114] Troy Bassett traces the creation and reception of the series in 'T. Fisher Unwin's Pseudonym Library: Literary Marketing and Authorial Identity', *English Literature in Transition (1880-1920)*, 47 (2004), 143-160 (p. 152). The reader, Bassett's suggests, here 'received two stories for the price of one'; the novel's plot, and the mystery of the writer's name (p. 150). His theoretical discussion of pseudonymity usefully supplements Mullan's account.

[115] Frederick Nesta has traced the history of the series; 'The Series as Commodity: Marketing T. Fisher Unwin's Pseudonym and Autonym Libraries', in *The Culture of the Publisher's Series, vol. I: Authors, Publishers and the Shaping of Taste*, ed. by John Spiers (London: Palgrave Macmillan, 2011), pp. 171-187 (p. 173). I have to thank Dr Nesta for separately confirming that Hale White's work never appeared in the Pseudonym Library.

White had published works under his own name from 1866. These show the range of his interests. His first named publication, *An Argument for an Extension of the Franchise: A Letter Addressed to George Jacob Holyoake, Esq.*, was a slim pamphlet dated March 1866. He did not return to such openly political writing in this form, but the case for reform was constantly (if anonymously) supported in his journalism. His career as a civil servant may have inhibited him from further publishing in this field. It was another ten years before he returned to print, and then in the form of an equally small piece, privately printed and circulated, on the death of his friend Elizabeth Street.[116] This tribute to the landlady with whom he lodged during some of his early years in London, celebrated her true piety nourished under the ministry of Caleb Morris. Friendships were made with the whole family; it was her half-sister Harriet Arthur who was to become White's first wife. Mrs Street was old enough to be Hale's mother, and he may have taken her as a model parent.

White's other non-fiction publications can be grouped together as philosophical or literary. The former comprise the already mentioned translations from the Latin of Spinoza's *Ethics* and *Tractatus de Intellectus Emendatione*, published in 1883 and 1895 respectively. These, especially the *Ethics*, represented a very great investment of effort, for little financial return. His interest in Spinoza presumably arose during his employment at John Chapman's, where his colleague Mary Ann Evans had started to translate the *Ethics*.[117] It is not clear why White should have worked on the same text, unless as some sort of failed cooperative venture, for which no evidence survives, or in tribute to a woman he greatly respected. The mid-nineteenth century saw a rediscovery of Spinoza's thought in England, partly because of his influence upon German thinkers who were also becoming better known. White's translation took many years, and did not immediately reach the public; 'the present translation of Spinoza's Ethic was completed more than twenty years ago, but at that time the interest in Spinoza was too slight to justify its publication'.[118] The time scale indicated in the preface to the *Ethic*, suggesting translation in the period between 1852 and 1863, shows that this work was finished before he turned his hand to other subjects.

White worked hard at his writing, snatching odd moments, and disciplining himself to write late at night and early in the morning. The novels were produced under intense pressure, alongside the demands of working life and family commitments, as well as, at first, the tyranny of deadlines for his weekly

---

[116] *A Letter Written on the Death of Mrs Elizabeth Street* (Privately printed, 1877).

[117] Completed in 1856 but not published at the time.

[118] *Ethic: Demonstrated in Geometrical Order, and Divided into Five Parts* ... by Benedict De Spinoza, translated from the Latin by William Hale White (London: Trübner & Co., 1883), p. v.

columns. The retirement years for the first time allowed tasks to be undertaken without such constraints, significantly including works of literary criticism,. This may reflect the time needed for careful textual work, as well as the attraction of tasks which were minutely consuming. Elsewhere White celebrates the release from self-absorption which such interests bring, depicted in the meeting of Mark Rutherford with the butterfly catcher in the *Autobiography*.[119] Wordsworth's verse was vital to White's spiritual development and he never lost a deep love for everything related to the poet, and likewise had an abiding interest in Coleridge. Access to manuscripts held by T. Norton Longman (on Wordsworth) and James Dykes Campbell (on Coleridge) allowed editions of each to be prepared and published, in 1897 and 1899 respectively. White's editing of these papers was marked by the keen attention to detail he brought to all his literary work, but it cannot be said that he made a significant contribution to scholarship in this area.[120] White also defended Wordsworth against accusations that in later life he quietly abandoned the more radical political and religious views of his youth. *An Examination of the Charge of Apostasy Against Wordsworth* was published in February 1898, though it seems that fewer than two hundred copies of the five hundred printed were sold.[121]

Other literary-critical works were acts of homage to figures he admired; the collection of excerpts from Dr Johnson's *Rambler* published in 1907 and in the same year the introduction to a new edition of Carlyle's biography of Sterling. White's sole full-length biography, of John Bunyan, had appeared through Hodder and Stoughton in 1905.[122] It is impossible to establish when he ceased to write fiction. A number of short stories and occasional pieces accumulated over the years were published (in some cases, republished) as *Pages from a Journal With Other Papers* (1900), *More Pages from a Journal With Other Papers* (1910), and *Last Pages from a Journal With Other Papers* (1915).[123]

These three selections were all attributed to 'Mark Rutherford', unlike the other works of criticism referred to in this section which were presented under his own name. There was probably by this date no longer any strong desire for concealment, since knowledge of White's authorship was spreading. Continued

---

[119] *Autobiography*, pp. 104-108, Ch. VIII.

[120] Stephen Gill notes White's scholarly interest in Wordsworth, but finds more space for White as an example of Wordsworth's influence. See *Wordsworth and the Victorians* (Oxford: Clarendon Press, 1998), especially pp. 51-55.

[121] Figures from Simon Nowell Smith, 'Mark Rutherford: A Short Bibliography of the First Editions', supplement to *The Bookman's Journal*, 1930, pp. 1-23 (p. 17).

[122] Commissioned by the 'Literary Lives' series editor, W. Robertson Nicoll.

[123] Hereafter cited as *Pages*, *More Pages* and *Last Pages*. T. Fisher Unwin first published *Pages*, which was later reprinted by Oxford University Press in a second edition (1910) with additional material, and all references here are to this later edition. *More Pages* and *Last Pages* were both first issued by the University Press.

use of the Rutherford name for the three collections might however usefully have attracted buyers familiar with the novels, whether or not they linked them with Hale White. The posthumous *Last Pages* volume was edited by Dorothy White, who also later gathered some of his letters for the press.[124] Publication of these late works, unlike the novels, seems to have been at least in part financially motivated, and this was certainly a factor after his second marriage. White wanted to guarantee some income for Dorothy without disadvantaging his children, especially his daughter Molly who had remained unmarried in order to look after him. The 'Autobiographical Notes' were willed to Molly so that she might receive any profit from their publication.

This is not an exhaustive list of White's lesser writings, which included dictionary articles and frequent contributions to magazines and periodicals, including on science and astronomy, a particular interest.

George MacDonald

It has already been suggested that something might be gained from a comparison between George MacDonald and Hale White. The former's publicly acknowledged success as a writer sets him apart, for after leaving the ministry, and a period of uncertainty amid financial insecurity, MacDonald earned his living almost entirely by the pen. The two had friends and acquaintances in common, and if it cannot be proved that they met, they must certainly have known of each other. As young men in London both had been grateful for the ministries and friendship of Caleb Morris, Thomas Binney and F. D. Maurice. In adulthood there was an indirect link through the painter Arthur Hughes, who collaborated with MacDonald in providing the illustrations for some of his best known books. Hughes was a frequent visitor to the family home and his nephew Edward became engaged to MacDonald's daughter Mary, though she died before they could marry. Arthur's daughter Agnes married Jack Hale-White (White's second son), and Hale had been on friendly terms with her father for some time.[125] They were near neighbours in Carshalton for a time, and several of the family sat for Hughes. An 1887 sketch of White by the artist is often reproduced.[126] These links notwithstanding, it is the parallels and contrasts between them that form an interesting series of

[124] As the *Letters to Three Friends.*

[125] As early as 1882 they holidayed together at Porlock, where Hughes was painting; *Letters to Three Friends*, p. 10.

[126] Presented to the Cecil Higgins Art Gallery in Bedford by John Hale-White through the National Art Fund in 1978. Molly was another sitter. For reproductions of these and MacDonald items see Leonard Roberts (compiler), *Arthur Hughes: His Life and Works. A Catalogue Raisonné, with a Biographical Introduction by Stephen Wildman* (Woodbridge: Antique Collectors' Club, 1997).

counterpoints, to be explored in succeeding chapters. A brief *résumé* of MacDonald's life is necessary in order to provide the background information enabling meaningful comparisons to be made between the two men.

The Scotsman was a little older than White, born in 1824 but also lived into his early eighties, dying in 1905.[127] Brought up in the farming community of Huntly, Aberdeenshire, a small market town of around 2,500 souls, he shared with White a deep appreciation of the natural world. The religious background was similar, though Scottish Calvinism was reportedly of a stricter stripe than in Bedford, at home and at church. The family worshipped at the Independent (Congregational) church in Huntly known as the Missionar Kirk from its origin in the evangelism inspired by the London Missionary Society.[128] The church was not as large as Bunyan meeting, but was nonetheless a significant presence within a smaller town. Sunday attendance in 1837 was estimated at six hundred, though far fewer - one hundred and fifty - were in membership.[129] Like William White senior in Bedford, MacDonald's father was an office holder, serving as a deacon under John Hill, minister from 1817 until his death in 1848. James Legge of China (1815-1897) was the most famous son who caught the church's wide vision. He was sent out under the auspices of the Congregationalist dominated London Missionary Society, the body also closely associated with the college run by John Jukes and William Alliott during Hale White's Bedford years which gave Bunyan Meeting a similarly global concern.

MacDonald had the advantage of an education at King's College, Aberdeen, where among others he mixed with English nonconformists who were largely excluded from higher education in England. Graduating MA in 1845, following

[127] The date of birth is unknown. The old Parish Register for Huntly (at the General Register Office for Scotland) lists George's baptism on 10 December 1824. Though invariably cited as his date of birth it was a well-known deficiency in Scottish records that before civil registration (1855) dates of birth and death were rarely given, baptism and burial standing for them. MacDonald may not have been aware of the date himself, and like many Scots of the time habitually used his baptismal date.

[128] The history of the church is given by Robert Troup, *The Missionar Kirk of Huntly* (Huntly; Edinburgh: Joseph Dunbar; John Menzies, 1901). See also W. D. McNaughton, *Early Congregational Independency in the Highlands and Islands and the North-East of Scotland* (Tiree: Trustees of Ruaig Congregational Church, 2003), pp. 384-388. I am grateful to Dr McNaughton for providing other helpful information on aspects of Scottish Congregationalism.

[129] Figures from the minister's returns to the Commissioner of Religious Instruction, given in McNaughton, *Early Congregational Independency in the Highland and Islands and the North-East of Scotland*, p. 390. The morning congregation was 'about 300', the evening 'about 500'; many attended twice and the number of individuals is uncertain. If the formula applied to comparable English figures on attendance and membership is used – a ratio of 3:1 – adherents would number around 450. As in Bedford, the congregation included those drawn from the surrounding countryside.

a period as a private tutor he three years later entered Highbury College to train for the ministry. After a shortened course, and not without some difficulty, he secured an invitation to the pastorate of an Independent church in Arundel in 1851. His testing time there illustrates the difficulty experienced by a minister through opposition from within his congregation, and usefully contextualises White/Rutherford's equally unhappy ministry. His preaching aroused suspicion, and after the failure of an initial attempt to prompt his resignation by lowering his stipend on the grounds that the church could not afford to be so generous, this was openly expressed. The discontent was said to be twofold; the holding out of some hope of post-mortem salvation for 'the heathen', and a less precisely worded unease about German theology. This is as reported by his son Greville, though without full supporting documentation. The extract he cites from the church minute book refers only to the first point:

> We do not by any means sympathize with the statement which has been made that "there is nothing in his preaching". But we do sympathize with those who are dissatisfied with the statement from the pulpit "that with the Heathen the time of trial does not (in his, the Revd. G. MacDonald's opinion) cease at their death", which certainly implies a future state of probation. And this Church considers such a view is not in accordance with the Scriptures and quite differs with the sentiments held by the Ministers of the Independent Denomination.[130]

It is probable that the issue singled out masked other hesitations which were not named, and it is unsurprising that MacDonald chose to leave.[131] After only two years there he moved to Manchester and attempted to support himself by teaching while exploring new possibilities for ministry. Already a published poet, he went on to pen novels which eventually brought financial independence and public recognition. Unlike Hale White he never hid his authorship, and became a well-known literary figure. Despite the spiritual turmoil of some earlier years he continued to preach (and publish written sermons) and attend public worship, becoming a regular communicant in the Church of England. He had assumed something of the status of a sage or mystic by the time of his death in 1905.

The ways in which MacDonald's story echoes White's are obvious even from this brief summary. At appropriate points in the following narrative some of the similarities and differences with respect to the origin and nature of his spiritual life will be highlighted.

---

[130] *George MacDonald and His Wife* (London: George Allen & Unwin, 1924), p 180.

[131] MacDonald recorded something of Arundel in his *Annals of a Quiet Neighbourhood* (serialised 1865; published in three volumes 1867), but very much altered, and presented as by an Anglican clergyman. This model was adopted in all the novels set in England which drew upon his ministerial experience, a wise precaution for one writing under his own name. He disguised his ministry, Hale White his name.

Chapter 2

Discovering an 'author of real excellence' Writing on Hale White

It was typically a desire to bring before the public a neglected 'author of real excellence' (as Wilfred Stone put it) which prompted the first studies of this writer.[1] Unlike Hale White's contemporaries many later readers now encounter him through such works before going on to read the novels. Their expectations are therefore shaped by the scholarly research and assumptions undergirding the secondary studies that serve as an introduction, especially the four major biographies. Investigating these influential texts is essential to any reassessment of White, but since there are different ways in White may be approached a number of other areas also need to be covered before any useful conclusions can be drawn. A broad review of recent critical works touching on his life and work is therefore an absolutely necessary preliminary to the task in hand.

The First Critical Biographies

Modern writing on White began with curiosity about the man and his method. As has already been suggested from John Mullan's researches on disguised authorship, it is likely that White valued the opportunity afforded by his chosen form of pseudonymous fictionalised autobiography to observe its reception by readers and critics without revealing his identity. The further arms-length device of a fictional editor very probably added to the lure while giving extra protection against discovery. Scholars continue to be intrigued by these techniques, and White's evident appeal to students of nineteenth-century English literature and culture can be readily documented. Through a series of apparently quite unconnected circumstances three seminal works were completed independently and published in successive years. The co-operation of White's widow gave these early researchers a sense of privileged access to first-hand memories of him many years after his death, and the impact of their critical biographies on later studies has been very considerable. First in importance is Wilfred Stone's *Religion and Art of William Hale White ("Mark*

---

[1] Stone, p. 3.

Rutherford"), published in 1954 but based upon a doctoral dissertation submitted in 1950. Stone acknowledged an earlier German monograph by Hans Klinke, the first full study, as well as a number of important articles and the unpublished University of Birmingham thesis by Henry Smith, but in depth and range he exceeded them all.[2]

Considering the *Autobiography* and *Deliverance* to be essentially true to White's own life, he 'fillets' the other novels for the evidence he supposes they can supply to supplement this outline. Information from other sources fleshes out the account, and there is a detailed survey of the intellectual and social milieu. That is, given the first two novels' status as 'the product[s] of a self-confessional impulse' consideration of them 'takes us immediately into a study of his [White's] biography; and a study of his biography takes us immediately into a phase of Victorian cultural history ... which was an intimate part of Hale White's own history'.[3] The close connection of literature, life, and context, while a truism, has nonetheless yielded very different conclusions in research on Hale White, depending as it often does upon varying judgements about the most significant influences, and the use made of limited and partial sources. The temptation to take White's experience of alienation from organised religion, for example, as typical of 'Victorian *Sturm und Drang*' has rarely been resisted, and Stone regards White's story - written and lived - as an attempt to fill the resulting vacuum and reconcile the tensions between past and present.[4] The dualism represented by the lives of Hale White and Mark Rutherford is a fundamental sign of unity-in-division and division-in-unity, the exploration of which underlies Stone's work; 'the basic theme of this study is, therefore, one of conflict and resolution, of dualisms slowly moving towards unity'.[5] The unity, while couched in spiritual terms, is, Stone suggests, really achieved by the 'progressive substitution' of the psychological for the theological.[6]

Some features of Stone's method and account have a particular significance for this research. His emphasis upon the historical and biographical is welcome, but he does not go far enough. While making extensive use of letters and other unpublished material held by White's children and his widow, Stone shows no awareness of the tensions between the children and their step-mother. It may be

---

[2] Hans Klinke, *William Hale White (Mark Rutherford). Versuch einer Biographie* (Frankfurt: Wilhelm Bohn, 1930). A much later European thesis by Ursula Buchmann had little impact, partly because it was completed in post-war conditions and suffered from a lack of access to sources; *William Hale White (Mark Rutherford) and the Problem of Self-Adjustment in a World of Changing Values* (Zurich: Juris-Verlag, 1950). For Henry Smith see below, p. 207.

[3] Stone, p. 3.

[4] Stone, p. 3.

[5] Stone, p. 8.

[6] Stone, p. 12.

significant that he seems to have spent least time with Molly White, and either was not shown, or chose to make no use of, letters of hers which denounced Dorothy's influence over her father.[7] Like all early studies, Stone's considers the expulsion from New College as a defining moment for White, yet his description of it is based on selected contemporary accounts, without direct use of the New College archives. Potential for a bias towards the expelled is clear. The nature of White's youthful religious views and experiences is insufficiently explored, resulting in a misleading representation of his journey of faith (or, doubt). There are assumptions about the loss of faith which must not go unchallenged, however frequently they recur in the literature.

Encountering White chiefly through his novels, the use made of these by Stone must also be questioned. Without accepting the full rigour of critical theories which effectively deny the importance of context and intent, a case can be made for a much more careful consideration of the nature of these key texts on their own terms as fiction. The relationship between art and life may be more complex than Stone allows, and later developments in the study of autobiography suggest new strategies to aid interpretation of this genre. It may be noted that the most significant additional source - *The Early Life of Mark Rutherford* - is simply accepted by Stone as a trustworthy factual account of his life.[8]

Stone's book was followed within a year by the most thoroughly biographical treatment of White, Catherine Maclean's *Mark Rutherford: A Biography of William Hale White*. Once again, the attempt to place White in context reveals a life 'almost in itself an authentic history of the Victorian era'.[9] There is nothing inherently mistaken about this approach, for one helpful way to 'place' White *is* to stress the connections with wider society. The outworking of his restless intellect produced links with the sciences (especially astronomy), architecture (through friendship with Philip Webb), politics, and the Pre-Raphaelites, even if he was on the fringes of these circles, rather characteristically hovering between being an insider or outsider. But to stress these 'typical' aspects of his life risks losing the more particular and distinctive ones.

Maclean's is a strongly chronological narrative, in which to an even greater extent than Stone the novels tend to feature as texts to be quarried for facts about their author's life. Relying on very similar sources, Maclean weaves a story of beguiling completeness. This triumph masks a significant problem of inadequate referencing. Often it is impossible to determine the authority for facts or opinions given, and it seems certain that Maclean's literary *élan* has

---

[7] The split between Dorothy and her step-children came to a head after White's death; see further below, chapter eleven.

[8] See Stone, p. 17, for example.

[9] Maclean, p. xiii.

triumphed over her scholarship.[10] While some of the rich biographical detail could have originated in family oral tradition it is impossible to avoid the conclusion that an element of creative re-imagining has taken place. Her work must therefore be used with caution. The picture she paints has a familiar outline, although giving private family life and public career more prominence than in Stone. There is less full consideration of the intellectual and social context, but Maclean, rightly, considers faith as central to understanding White's life and motivation. Though her understanding of the content and nature of this faith may be questioned, she boldly maintains the reality of White's life-long attempt to work out his own salvation. There is no suggestion here of anything pretended or deliberately ambiguous about his ultimately religious hope, albeit one imprecisely expressed.[11]

Like Stone, Maclean accepts the *Early Life* as an authentic record of White's youth and early adulthood, supplemented by her family sources. A close reading of this text will challenge the picture painted by Maclean and others of a happy childhood. Similarly, the idealised romantic view of White's second marriage - a feature of all the major studies - is thrown into doubt by sources perhaps unknown to Maclean. However, even if she did not have access to the family letters with contrary evidence, her conversations with White's children must have revealed their dismay about the relationship with Dorothy Smith. A letter to Reginald Hale-White (Hale's grandson), responding with relief to his favourable verdict on her biography, suggests that out of respect for her subject she chose to avoid this sensitive area, confiding to him that 'the last section of the book was difficult and delicate work. ... I fell back on the principle of giving only what Mark Rutherford felt'.[12] Dorothy's role as self-appointed guardian of White's reputation coupled with her control of access to key sources doubtless ensured a certain deference from researchers.

The third almost contemporaneous study of Hale White, that of Irvin Stock, relied just as heavily upon his widow.[13] He maintained friendly links with Dorothy for many years after the completion of his book.[14] Stock's chief contact with the rest of the family was not through White's eldest son, Sir William Hale-White, but through *his* son, Reginald.[15] This demonstrates both

[10] Though she did use sources which have eluded some other scholars, such as the diary of Caleb Morris (no longer traceable); see her acknowledgements, pp. vii–viii.

[11] Note Maclean's reflections on his late writings on faith, pp. 397–400.

[12] Letter dated 10 November 1955 (UBC, NCC 6-7).

[13] Stock, 1956.

[14] Copies of this correspondence have recently been deposited in the Mark Rutherford Archive at Bedford Public Library.

[15] He was not the only member of the family willing to be interviewed; Molly and Cecily also met Stock, but no-one was more ready to give their time than Dorothy. The surname was hyphenated by the generation after Hale, partly it seems to distance them from Dorothy as 'Mrs White'.

the very considerable age gap between Dorothy and Hale, and the appeal of her cooperation - unlike the grandchildren she could claim close, adult, knowledge of White.[16] Stock adopts a more thoroughly literary approach to his subject than Stone or Maclean, motivated by a high view of his writings. There is nonetheless a fairly full biographical outline, and this as usual draws on letters and other unpublished material. Stock argues for a close but not 'too simple identification of Hale White and Mark Rutherford', in places reminiscent of Stone's distinction between his subjective self-expression (in fiction) and the more objective expression (other writings, letters, and so on).[17] The striking empathy which Stock felt for his chosen author informs his writing, and is particularly clear in the unpublished journal of his extended research trip to London during 1950.[18] Stone's use of the *Early Life* conforms to what may now be termed the usual pattern, as a reliable factual record.

Religious questions are again to the fore, and White's life is depicted as the story of a 'struggle to retain or rebuild a religion, and to find love'.[19] That is, a tension between dream and reality (fact and fiction?) marks his life and writings. Giving up his Calvinist inheritance, White searches for 'that religion which lies beneath "creeds"', in an era increasingly inhospitable to faith.[20] There is much to be questioned about Stock's portrayal of White's early beliefs, especially the assumption that he was 'a devout Dissenter for his first twenty years', a statement which can hardly be supported from White's own writings.[21] Stock reinterprets his subject's adult faith too, suggesting that White has no time for a realist theology and ends in a hallowed scepticism which only faintly acknowledges the transcendent. Traditional religious language, understood as symbolic, finds its ultimate reference point in human experience and the unknown mysteries of the universe.[22]

Stock's valuable work is perceptive in its reading of the novels, but potentially misleading on historical and biographical details. This highlights the difficulty of doing equal justice to the novels and the life of their author. Despite the evident overlap in biographical detail, it is necessary to analyse the fiction according to the techniques of literary criticism rather than to approach them as lightly re-worked autobiographical texts which must somehow be reconciled with the historically verifiable facts of White's life. Given the circumstances of this writer's life and work such a tension can never be wholly

[16] Reginald was 18 on his grandfather's death, and died himself in 1967, the same year as Dorothy (obituary, *The Times*, 2 November 1967).

[17] Stock, p. 53; see also pp. 90–91.

[18] Copy now among Stock's papers (as yet uncatalogued) in Bedford Public Library.

[19] Stock, p. 94.

[20] Stock, p. 85.

[21] Stock, p. 1; the most which might be said is that White later suggested an unquestioning faith, but this is scarcely to be described as 'devout'.

[22] Stock, pp. 251-252 (a viewpoint Stock appears to share).

overcome, though the potential conflict here must always be borne in mind.

These major studies by Stone, Maclean and Stock form the backdrop to all later research, and only recently have critics advanced new understandings of White.[23] Stimulus has come from reading the novels in relation to particular themes or specific contexts. Different lenses have brought fresh interpretations, but also new possibilities for partiality and confusion. Use of a writer as illustrative of contemporary social, political, religious and economic conditions is notoriously hazardous, and circularity an ever-present risk. The sense of common interest which some scholars come to feel with White brings its own dangers of misrepresentation or misunderstanding

The Novelist, the Literary Critic and the Historian

This difficulty is evident in an important essay by David Daiches. His high view of White as a writer, and the very close identification assumed between White and 'Mark Rutherford' ('the autobiography is in all essential points wholly accurate and honest') leads him to rail against the 'narrowness, cruelty, and sometimes even the stupidity and hypocrisy bred by the English evangelical tradition' without appearing to question the accuracy of White's portrayal.[24] What is manifestly deeply felt and experienced is privileged over the mundanely historical. At the same time Daiches' admiration for White the artist leads him to recognise the originality of his form, that he:

> invented a new kind of novel, that is a kind of fable that is much richer and more complex than a fable, that is autobiography yet which transcends autobiography, that is a *Bildungsroman* without the obvious schematic development of most examples of that genre, that is a 'novel of ideas' while remaining a quietly honest narrative deeply human in its significance and genuinely moving as a human document.[25]

Daiches is a sensitive reader, even if not quite in tune with the historical context. Perhaps the concern to make White speak with 'sceptical stoicism' beyond his own time is always doomed to separate him from it.[26] However this

---

[23] For completeness the work by Stephen Merton, *Mark Rutherford (William Hale White)* (New York: Twayne Publishers, 1967) may be noted. A useful summary of critical writing on White, with contextual analysis of the novels, but really adding nothing new.

[24] *Some Late Victorian Attitudes* (London: André Deutsch, 1969), p. 92 – and citing the *Early Life* as 'proof' of the *Autobiography*'s trustworthiness. The reference in parentheses is from p. 93. Daiches clearly felt the outsider's kinship with White.

[25] *Some Late Victorian Attitudes*, p. 108.

[26] *Some Late Victorian Attitudes*, p. 17; this 'attitude' he believes is typical of the late nineteenth century, not just of White.

remains a stimulating essay, which emphasizes the significance of White in the context of Victorian faith. Daiches, recognising the challenge posed by the complexity of White's writings, closes his paper by recommending cooperation between 'the social historian, the historian of ideas and the literary critic' in exploring their full meaning.[27]

The most thorough-going attempt to combine historical research and literary criticism of White and his world is found in Valentine Cunningham's *Everywhere Spoken Against: Dissent in the Victorian Novel*.[28] Vigorously opposing literary theories which question the relevance of historical and biographical insights on the basis that the novelist creatively transforms and re-imagines the familiar world, Cunningham's campaign against ignorance and prejudice challenges reader and critic alike.[29] Fully alive to the misinterpretation possible when the literary critic disregards history, and the social historian uncritically appropriates his 'local colour' from the novel, Cunningham shows how often Dissent has been misrepresented by authors and their interpreters.[30] His original research in the records of Bunyan Meeting and Lion Walk (Colchester) adds materially to the knowledge of White and his local context. He notes that Bunyan Meeting's membership 'combined Baptists and Congregationalists', recognising that different views on baptism had at times amicably or uneasily co-existed there.[31] The Bedfordshire Union of Christians had since 1797 formally brought together in cooperative endeavour both Congregational and Baptist churches, and it was not unusual for individual chapels to hold those of both persuasions. Differences over baptism could not disguise otherwise very similar polities and culture. In an end-of-century survey of English Congregationalism Alexander Mackennal celebrated this closeness as well exemplified in the Bedfordshire Union. There were comparable understandings of membership which allowed easy transfers between the churches, and 'in most of our Churches of both denominations all offices in the Church are open to Baptists and Paedo-Baptists indiscriminately'.[32] The picture varied nationally, but much shared history and common purpose makes it possible to talk of *Two Congregational Denominations: Baptist and Paedobaptist*, as John Briggs has done.[33] This overlap notwithstanding,

---

[27] *Some Late Victorian Attitudes*, p. 123.

[28] Oxford: Oxford University Press, 1975.

[29] Cunningham returned to the question of literary theory in his *In the Reading Gaol: Postmodernity, Texts, and History* (Oxford: Blackwell, 1994).

[30] *Everywhere Spoken Against*, p. 4. He subsumes 'new' Dissent such as Methodism within his umbrella term.

[31] *Everywhere Spoken Against*, p. 39.

[32] *Sketches in the Evolution of English Congregationalism* (London: James Nisbet, 1901), p. 237.

[33] The Congregational Lecture for 2010 (London: Congregational Memorial Hall Trust, 2010).

Bunyan's size and pre-eminence set it somewhat apart from other churches, and the Meeting itself was never wholly aligned with any denomination.[34]

Cunningham criticises and corrects White's version of political Dissent, suggesting that 'his model must be as it were inverted', for Dissent did not lose influence in mid-century (as portrayed in *The Revolution in Tanner's Lane*) but actually grew in power as the century progressed.[35] Literary critics who have adopted White's viewpoint are castigated for 'reading novels as if they were history textbooks'.[36] In fact the decline (or otherwise) of nonconformity over time is a matter of dispute among historians themselves and there may be greater uncertainty here than Cunningham realises.[37] However he has usefully mapped the territory of mid-century Dissent in more detail than any other recent scholar on White.

Cunningham's work recognizes the strong regional identity dictated by the geography of Dissent. White was deeply conscious of the tradition within which he was nurtured, and perhaps only ever at home when sensing connection with his origins. The importance of community *and* place, of social change and individual response, is the theme of John Lucas's *The Literature of Change: Studies in the Nineteenth-Century Provincial Novel*.[38] There could hardly be a more appropriate subject than Hale White, studied here alongside Hardy and Gaskell. Lucas explores the way in which 'survival in and cooperation with the social process comes to much the same thing as accepting as inevitable the fact of separation: from family, friends, community. And from self'; for White, he suggests, this means placing 'his hope for survival of self in self-transcendence, in a deliverance from self through duty, political action, altruism'.[39]

The concept of the self, a key theme for Lucas, is complicated in this case by issues of identity and pseudonymity. Hale White is not simply 'Mark Rutherford', though both are the voice of 'middle-class liberalism'.[40] Lucas skilfully explores the tensions between writer and narrator, and the alienation between White and the community in which he was reared. The blurred line between writer and subject, difficult for the critic to trace, is problematic because White has not 'controlled' the distinction clearly enough himself.[41] Lucas stresses the novels as written in their time, the closing decades of the

[34] For historical reasons the church did not specify the mode of baptism, nor require proof of it as a condition of membership.

[35] *Everywhere Spoken Against*, pp. 266-268 (p. 267).

[36] *Everywhere Spoken Against*, p. 267.

[37] Cunningham thinks White's 'mistaken' view can be *partly* excused because of his estrangement from Dissent after 1852 (pp. 269-270).

[38] Brighton: The Harvester Press, (second edition) 1980.

[39] *The Literature of Change*, p. xii. But White was *not* a political activist.

[40] *The Literature of Change*, p. 66.

[41] *The Literature of Change*, p. 101.

century, and reflecting attitudes prevalent then rather than the mid-century period of their settings.[42] The danger here is that a reading of contemporary issues will be insufficiently questioning of received opinion and perhaps misrepresent White *vis-à-vis* those concerns. Lucas is not uncritical of White as a writer, though his interpretations are sometimes open to question.

White, History, and Dissent

Lucas and Cunningham give close attention to the historical context of White and his novels, and it is not surprising that historians too have been attracted to his writings. The feelings of alienation and separation which echo across all White's work arise not just from a feeling of having been displaced from the strong community of one's birth - and hence offering insights into that world - but also from much of national and social life as well. This contributes to the sense that he can be read as providing an authentic voice of history from below, as in references to the novels by E. P. Thompson, who hails 'Mark Rutherford, one of the few men who understood the full desolation of the inner history of 19th-century Nonconformity'.[43]

There were elements of Thompson's background which must have made these texts particularly evocative. The son and grandson of Wesleyan ministers deeply involved in Indian missions, his father's semi-autobiographical novels about 'John Arnison' show marked similarities with Mark Rutherford's world, which may have inspired their writer.[44] E. P. Thompson's usage involves judgements about the historical value (and interpretation) of fiction, but it is important to guard against too-ready acceptance of these sources at face value. At times there has been a failure to read them in context, or refer to other available sources of verification. Historians of nonconformity too have sometimes used White uncritically, though the more sensitive have contrasted his viewpoint with those whose experience and witness is more positive. David Thompson, for example, while appreciating White, has been careful to juxtapose his testimony with that of others and includes a warning about accepting Mark Rutherford's views too simplistically; 'it is also important to remember that many of those who described this [Dissenting] life did so in

---

[42] A case also argued by Sally Ledger, 'History, Politics and Women: A Contextual Analysis of the Writings of William Hale White ("Mark Rutherford")' (unpublished doctoral thesis, University of Oxford, 1990).

[43] See *The Making of the English Working Class* (London: Victor Gollancz, 1965), p. 350, referring to the description of services in the *Autobiography*. But he astutely notes the writer as 'evidence of values that somehow survived' (same page).

[44] *Introducing the Arnisons* (London: Macmillan, 1935), *John Arnison* (London: Macmillan, 1939). For a life, with a little on the Arnison novels, see Mary Lago; "*India's Prisoner*": *A Biography of Edward John Thompson, 1886-1946* (Columbia, MO: University of Missouri Press, 2001).

order to criticise it'.[45] More often White rates only the slightest of references in studies of nonconformity, even in important histories such as those by Watts and Munson.[46]

These instances are cited to emphasize that interest in White is not wholly the domain of literature specialists, and at the same time to note the pitfalls of reading history from fiction. As far as social history goes the critic may find richer pastures in Hale White's journalism, a field which has only recently been explored. The face of radical Dissent and middle class liberalism is there much in evidence, often expressed with humour, and an acute social commentary.[47]

White and Victorian Faith or Doubt

The importance of faith in White's life and fiction has been made clear with reference to the early critical studies, and this theme has been taken up by other scholars. Basil Willey, an early admirer of White's writings, helped to ensure him a place in the consideration of Victorian religion by including 'Mark Rutherford' in his study of 'honest doubters'.[48] Willey distinguishes Rutherford from Hale White, though perhaps inadequately, for the *Autobiography* especially is taken as essentially a true account of White's life, correlated against the *Early Life*, once more the readily accepted reliable witness. White's spiritual pilgrimage is described with some insight. He was not 'merely another sufferer from the Victorian malady of honest doubt, or loss of faith', for his had been a purely external 'faith' to start with.[49] Its loss was the beginning of growth. The expulsion from New College is treated as a turning-point, and the analysis of key influences (especially Wordsworth and Spinoza) sets White in the wider intellectual context.

On purely historical and biographical questions Willey is less sure-footed, but his work has a wider significance than questions of accuracy about White. Timothy Larsen identifies him as a prime example of the distorting effect of concentrating upon specific examples of crisis and doubt as if they are self-evidently representative of wider tendencies.[50] This is all the more misleading if

---

[45] In his anthology *Nonconformity in the Nineteenth Century* (London: Routledge & Kegan Paul, 1972), pp. 62–63.

[46] James Munson. *The Nonconformists: In Search of a Lost Culture* (London: SPCK, 1991), pp. 77-81 and Michael Watts, *The Dissenters, vol. II*, pp. 304, 603; both contain much valuable background information.

[47] This area has been opened up by Mark Crees in 'Before Mark Rutherford'.

[48] *More Nineteenth Century Studies: A Group of Honest Doubters* (London: Chatto and Windus, 1956). Willey had contact with Wilfred Stone during the latter's research in England, which may have enhanced his own sense of White's importance.

[49] *More Nineteenth Century Studies*, p. 206.

[50] *Crisis of Doubt*, pp. 6-7; Larsen cites other examples from standard works on the Victorian age.

the paradigmatic models are themselves inaccurately presented. Willey demonstrates two trends which recur constantly in the secondary literature; the tendency to accept on trust the results of earlier research, and a desire to categorise White according to some particular theme or context. The result is that the critic stops work just when further probing might challenge the established consensus. Misrepresentation is all the greater in this area if the exact circumstances and dynamics of the supposed crisis of faith are not properly understood, as will be argued has so often been the case in respect of Hale White.

Willey integrates the romance with Dorothy into White's spiritual progress, as a relationship which 'crowned [his life] with a glory well-nigh miraculous'.[51] In this he continues what becomes the unvaryingly positive appraisal of Dorothy. Willey, himself of nonconformist stock, is particularly sympathetic to religious dissent, and selected White partly to represent that important tradition, and its portrayal by an insider; formerly 'no English novelist had written thus of Dissenting life and thought from within'.[52] For this reason alone the novels are of enduring value. The resonance of this inheritance with some of these key English writers on White is marked, as is the appeal to those who have some reason to feel themselves outsiders or apart from the mainstream of national life.

A.O.J. Cockshut included Hale White among more famous 'unbelievers', in order to explore how those who leave traditional Christianity behind (as he supposes) sought new forms of believing.[53] He relies on the first two novels alone, and stresses that Rutherford is 'a fictional character', but it is impossible to be quite sure if Cockshut believes his is essentially a description of White's own spiritual history.[54] Cockshut finds difficulty in defining Rutherford's 'more puzzling' deliverance, which seems to consist in putting insoluble questions aside and finding satisfaction in the smaller things of life.[55] The significance of this work therefore is not in the analysis it provides, but the way in which it reinforces the idea that White lost or abandoned faith. Like Basil Willey, Cockshut also embraces the novelist's low estimate of provincial Dissent.

There is a danger in accepting White's pungent critique of nonconformity too uncritically, as if its vigour ensured accuracy. Where a critic identifies a shared humane liberalism with his subject the temptation to join forces against the supposedly narrow and dogmatic is strong. In fact White may misrepresent,

---

[51] *More Nineteenth Century Studies*, p. 246.
[52] *More Nineteenth Century Studies*, p. 190.
[53] *The Unbelievers: English Agnostic Thought, 1840-1890* (London: Collins, 1964), pp. 136-143.
[54] *The Unbelievers*, p. 137.
[55] *The Unbelievers*, pp. 139-142 (p. 139).

for his own reasons, the world he portrays (and especially the forces he believed were ranged against him in the 1852 expulsion episode). Even if these are fairly pictured, rather than caricatured, it may not be legitimate to consider wider nonconformity from the same perspective.

Other studies of this area are little more than general surveys and few show much concern for the psychology of faith. Standard texts like those by Margaret Maison and Robert Wolff helpfully demonstrate the range and variety of Victorian novels on this theme, but they do not deal in detail with specific questions such as the nature of religious conversion, which is so significant in understanding White.[56] Some interesting comparative features emerge, though White's literary ability and powers of analysis set him apart from the otherwise deservedly forgotten minor writers who mostly populate such studies. Even where there are similarities, these must not be pressed too far; certainly Froude's *Nemesis of Faith* (1849), shares some of the form of Rutherford's *Autobiography*, as well as demonstrating a debt to Carlyle, Goethe and Spinoza, but differences are just as evident.[57] Over time the shortcomings of writings which fail to pay due attention to the prodigious breadth and depth of Victorian religious expression have become clearer, and simplistic ideas of a crisis or loss of faith which might be almost randomly illustrated from contemporary fiction have been challenged.[58]

Nonetheless David Hempton suggests a particular association between Evangelical upbringing and later falling away.[59] In part this is linked to cultural aspects of evangelicalism, a perceived narrowness or hypocrisy, rather than beliefs. His study needs to be interpreted with care, for the evidence presented does not necessarily show individuals who were personally persuaded of a faith which they later rejected. The subtlety of Hempton's starting point that the chosen figures 'were *associated* with the evangelical tradition' is all too likely to be missed, especially given the stricter definition which follows - 'people represented here are figures of some eminence who embraced evangelicalism

---

[56] Maison, *Search Your Soul, Eustace: A Survey of the Religious Novel in the Victorian Age* (London: Sheed and Ward, 1961), and Robert Lee Wolff, *Gains and Losses: Novels of Faith and Doubt in Victorian England* (London: John Murray, 1977).

[57] White may have known this work, but it inhabits a different, Anglican and Oxford world. H. W. McCraw draws out the likeness, while admitting significant contrasts, 'Two Novelists of Despair: James Anthony Froude and William Hale White', *The Southern Quarterly*, 13 (1974), 21-51.

[58] For example Frank Turner, 'The Victorian Crisis of Faith and the Faith that was Lost', in *Victorian Faith in Crisis*, pp. 9–38. Ironically, Turner is not as careful in interpreting novels of 'faith and doubt' as he might be. Larsen's *Crisis of Doubt* must now be added as a more forthright challenge to the emphasis upon loss of faith.

[59] *Evangelical Disenchantment: Nine Portraits of Faith and Doubt* (New Haven, CT: Yale University Press, 2008). He does not claim these to be representative accounts.

for a season before repudiating it'.[60] It is important to note that these are not straightforward stories of loss of faith, instead involving 'a renegotiation of ... religious sensibilities', complicated by the continued use of traditional language with undefined new meanings.[61] A range of starting points leads to a range of outcomes, and sometimes the persistence of faith goes unrecognised because of its tentative or unsystematic nature.

Hempton's work suggests a need to distinguish more carefully the personally owned belief of individuals from their family or church context. This is particularly the case with those who relate a change of belief on attaining adulthood. It may not be meaningful to talk of loss of faith when uncritically accepted childhood teaching is later questioned, re-interpreted or even rejected. The situation is complicated by the standpoint of the subject, who may interpret a faith which failed to endure as never truly held, or describe a child-like trust in parental teaching as if it were mature faith. Hempton uses a quotation from the *Autobiography* on the 'dissolution of Jesus into mythologic vapour' to introduce his work, but does not otherwise consider Hale White's case.[62] Nevertheless his study is a reminder that an attempt must be made to understand White's experience in his own terms and context, without the undue influence of assumptions drawn from other cases. The interpretation of his fiction will always be an important part of this task. It can be informed by new literary techniques appropriate for the study of novelists like White whose art appears so closely patterned on their own lives.

White and Autobiographical Writing

The study of autobiographical or 'self-writing' has drawn many fictional accounts within its orbit, and opened up new forms of critical appreciation. It is a discipline in which competing models still struggle for supremacy, but it has potential to shed light on White.[63] It may be significant that Wordsworth, so strong an influence on the young White, was among those Victorians who ably explored self-disclosure through the written word, in his case *The Prelude* of 1850.[64] The use of pseudonymity is also of particular interest in self-writing, and several scholars have referred to White in this context. The availability of genre-specific techniques which can be applied to supposedly 'factual' writings like the *Early Life* just as readily as to fiction offers the further advantage of informed comparison between both kinds of texts.

---

[60] *Evangelical Disenchantment*, p. ix (emphasis added) and p. 11 respectively.

[61] *Evangelical Disenchantment*, p. 17.

[62] *Evangelical Disenchantment*, p.1; quoting from the *Autobiography*, p. 54, Ch. V.

[63] Laura Marcus offers a helpful survey, *Auto/biographical Discourses: Criticism, Theory, Practice* (Manchester: Manchester University Press, 1994).

[64] The poem has a complex textual history before and after this date.

Only one full-length study on White, appearing long after the initial three such works, has so far taken advantage of insights from this field. Catherine Harland's *Mark Rutherford: The Mind and Art of William Hale White* stresses the separation of writer and remembrance in the 'autobiographical act' of writing.[65] Therefore one of her main themes is White's transformation of key events in his life as they appear in the novels. The latter, she believes, are a 'truer' account of his inner life than any more obviously factual text could be, so developing a common view that 'fullest confession required the liberating mask of fiction'.[66] Comparison between the *Early Life* and the novels can test this thesis to some degree. As no further single monographs on White have been published since Harland's it is largely within the periodical literature that the self-writing theme has been developed and applied. Essays by Gamini Salgado, John Goode, and repeated contributions by Charles Swann offer new readings. At stake here are issues which are always central; how William Hale White and Mark Rutherford relate to each other, and thus where the novels are placed on the sweep of narrative writing from fact to fiction. Artistic creativity, authorial intention, and claims to truth-telling are core areas around which debate over life-writing revolves.

Analysis by type, and comparisons across a wide range of similar and sometimes contrasting texts provide new ways of placing White in context. At one extreme works like his, where the narrative appears markedly to reflect the author's own life, are nevertheless regarded as having no point of reference outside the text. Associated sometimes with deconstruction, this viewpoint finds perhaps its purest expression in Paul de Man. He argues that it is impossible to speak of an autobiographical genre as such. All texts can be regarded as in some degree autobiographical for it is the reader who is the key to understanding. The writer who attempts to record his own life is effectively the prisoner of his chosen form; 'whatever the writer *does* is in fact governed by the technical demands of self-portraiture and thus determined, in all its aspects, by the resources of his medium'.[67] Against this view the majority of scholars working on self-writing posit a definable canon of more or less self-evidently autobiographical works, though with varying degrees of precision. The effect of such divergences among theorists can be illustrated with reference

---

[65] Columbus, OH: Ohio State University Press, 1988. The phrase 'autobiographical act' originates with Elizabeth Bruss from her study *Autobiographical Acts: The Changing Situation of a Literary Genre* (Baltimore, MD: Johns Hopkins University Press, 1976).

[66] Harland, p. 5.

[67] 'Autobiography as De-Facement', in *The Rhetoric of Romanticism* (New York: Columbia University Press, 1984), pp. 67–81 (p. 69, original emphasis). The posthumous revelation of de Man's acts of collaboration in wartime Belgium forms a tragic and ironic commentary on the truthfulness of his own writing; see D. Lehman, *Signs of the Times: Deconstruction and the Fall of Paul de Man* (London: André Deutsch, 1991).

to White.

Some critics have protested against too ready an identification of Hale White and the fictional 'Mark Rutherford' on the basis that this misreads the novels. Gamini Salgado was the first to make the case; neither in content nor style can the *Autobiography of Mark Rutherford* be considered a record of William Hale White's life.[68] It is written as a novel, and can only satisfyingly be read as one. This is a sharp contrast with the earlier monographs which tended to read White's experience directly from the text. Salgado wrote without reference to the literature on self-writing (little developed at the time) but from within the discipline a powerful statement of the same basic position has come from Gerry Brookes.[69] In all this the question of 'truth-to-life' cannot be avoided, for to argue that the fiction is not autobiographical - at least in the sense of some basic outward conformity to the writer's life - involves citing events which appear to have no parallel in White's experience. One instance given by Brookes, the 'mission' in Drury Lane described in the *Deliverance*, undermines rather than supports his case. Misled by Wilfred Stone's failure to establish White's involvement in such a venture, he is left quite unaware that Mrs White's diary recorded her son's slum work, as both Maclean and Harland note.[70]

Brookes is conscious that students of autobiography typically look for something more than a simple correspondence between the life described and the writer's own (though suggesting that this is partly an attempt to maintain an autobiographical status despite the facts); 'some higher truth about the author is being told, rather than any literal one'.[71] While Brookes continues to dismiss such a reading, he acknowledges autobiographical elements, but denies that their presence needs to be detected, much less analysed and traced back to White, in order to read the novels appropriately.

As this debate shows, fictionalised autobiography is a test case for theorists and critics. The particular questions raised prompted the writer Stephen Reynolds (1881-1919) to coin the phrase 'autobiografiction' to describe his own first published book, and Charles Swann has noted the aptness of this

---

[68] 'The Rhetoric of Sincerity: *The Autobiography of Mark Rutherford* as Fiction', in *Renaissance and Modern Essays: Presented to Vivian de Sola Pinto in Celebration of his Seventieth Birthday*, ed. by G. R. Hibbard (London: Routledge and Kegan Paul, 1966), pp. 159–168.

[69] In 'Fictional Forms in William Hale White's *Autobiography of Mark Rutherford* and *Mark Rutherford's Deliverance*', *Biography: An Interdisciplinary Quarterly*, 9 (1986), 247–268.

[70] Also confirmed from conversations recorded in Florence Low's 'Walks and Talks with Mark Rutherford', *The Contemporary Review*, 187 (1955), 405–409 (p. 408). Stone knew the diaries, but misunderstood these references; see p. 277 below.

[71] 'Fictional Forms', p. 248. It is here (pp. 248-249) that he castigates Stone for suggesting some unverified (since he had misinterpreted Mrs White's diaries, unknown to Brookes) Drury Lane experiment as the basis for the fiction.

categorisation for the Mark Rutherford novels.[72] In a more recent study Max Saunders suggests just how important an example of this type White's writing is; neither he nor Swann extend their discussion to the *Early Life* however, which is clearly of a somewhat different order.[73] Reynolds had considered the experience of spiritual crisis as a vital element in autobiografiction, while Saunders argues for a broader definition, thus on his terms assuring Hale White's place in a greatly enlarged literary tradition.

Though questions about genre and its role or limitations in deciding which texts may be considered autobiographical represent a major theme in self-writing studies, scholars are often as interested in determining how writers shape their material in autobiographical writings. There is a widespread acceptance that such works are not simply mimetic, and that the literary tradition within which a writer stands very largely determines how the task is approached. Thus without accepting de Man's other premises, the controlling nature of the canon is acknowledged by many in the field.

It is not necessary to give up all hope of recovering historical information from autobiographical writing. Carl Dawson considers White among six near-contemporaries in order to trace modes of remembering and presentation which suggest the emergence of a pattern of self-understanding that illuminates writing of this type and period.[74] He believes that 'Mark Rutherford relives, with minor variations, the life of his author', and this is indeed the most common assumption of studies on White.[75] Even where the presumption is against so close an identification it is hard to see how historical research can occupy a less than central role in making such judgements. The more precisely the lines of White's life can be traced the better placed the critic is to suggest how that material may have been re-shaped and re-presented in fictional form. Dawson, like others, is still heavily dependent upon Stone and Maclean for biographical information. He also gives a high value to the *Early Life* as a source. This reliance will prove questionable in the light of the re-evaluation offered here, and the conclusion Dawson draws from the title page and declaration of authorship will be overturned. Susanna Egan has also considered White, alongside other autobiographers, in tracing the *Patterns of Experience in Autobiography*, concluding that the *Early Life* 'deals with no emotion deeper

---

[72] Swann, 'Autobiografiction: Problems with Autobiographical Fictions and Fictional Autobiographies. Mark Rutherford's *Autobiography* and *Deliverance*, and Others', *Modern Language Review*, 96 (2001), 21-37.

[73] *Self Impression*, see especially pp. 110-124. He notes how the form conveniently 'allows writers to express and efface personality at the same time' (p. 61).

[74] See *Prophets of Past Time: Seven British Autobiographers, 1880-1914* (Baltimore, MD: Johns Hopkins University Press, 1988).

[75] *Prophets of Past Time*, p. 29. His focus is on the role of memory and the remembered self for his selection of *fin de siècle* middle-aged writers.

than nostalgia', unlike the much richer *Autobiography*.[76] The third-person narration of the novel (that is, as by Rutherford, though *written* in the first person) is for her more emotionally satisfying than the later first person memoir, but all the while she underestimates the gap which exists there between truth and life.

Given the importance being suggested for the *Early Life* it is helpful that autobiographies of childhood can be analysed as a distinct sub-genre. This classification, already proposed in the seminal work of Roy Pascal, has been further explored by Richard Coe.[77] Though he does not refer to White his conclusions offer useful clues to reading the *Early Life*, and indicate common features in comparable texts. His work will be considered in more detail below alongside analysis of White's memoir. For other critics and readers content was always valued over form. Their interest lay in what White was trying to articulate rather than his mode of expression; indeed it could almost be a matter of feeling or mood more than words.

Readings from Sympathetic Admirers

Two periodical articles can be noted as representative of attempts to sum up the significance of White's life and writings - his 'message' - for different generations of readers. In this way they represent a spiritual appreciation which was not confined to any one church of tradition, rather the opposite for White is presented as the prophet without honour in his own country of Calvinist Independency. The first was prompted by White's death (and the concomitant identification of him as writer of the Mark Rutherford novels), the second by the publication of fresh source material on his life. These were typical triggers for such occasional pieces, as were the periodic reissues of the novels.

Willard Sperry, an American Congregationalist, wrote an appreciation of White in 1914.[78] He did not simply attempt to describe a life, but to identify White's distinctive ideas and lasting importance. Hale White is a witness to mid-Victorian Dissent, but his true value is as the recorder of a spiritual awakening, the discovery of true faith, for 'in renouncing Calvinism, Mark Rutherford found Christianity'.[79] The reader who knows what it is to find a personal faith will study White with interest and profit. The journey from

---

[76] Chapel Hill, NC: University of North Carolina Press, 1984 (p. 31). Egan is another writer unaware that the 'purely fictitious' ministry by Rutherford did have an equivalent in White's life (p. 26).

[77] Pascal, *Design and Truth in Autobiography* (Cambridge, MA: Harvard University Press, 1960), particularly chapter six, and R. N. Coe, *When the Grass was Taller: Autobiography and the Experience of Childhood* (New Haven, CT: Yale University Press, 1984).

[78] 'Mark Rutherford', *Harvard Theological Review*, 7 (1914), 166-192.

[79] Sperry, 'Mark Rutherford', p. 185.

negation to affirmation is traced in the *Deliverance*, and finds an echo in the later novels though human emotion. A mystical faith emerges, celebrating union with the divine.[80] Sperry's interpretation therefore elevates experience over doctrine. This tribute to White as a guide to the religious life is one example among many of the attempt by nonconformists especially to claim him as one who at a deep level remained true to his Puritan roots. Against the loss of faith model these 'the man and his message' pieces seem to claim too much - they certainly struggle to explain just what faith means for White - and yet they are able to take seriously the language about belief that many critics disregard or reinterpret too freely according to their own presuppositions.

A word of caution is necessary, for taken in isolation positive claims for faith made upon White from within the churches by men like Sperry might give a false impression. Such posthumous judgements claimed to recognise something essentially spiritual in his writing which had been unacknowledged by his contemporaries. This is not surprising, for in any attempt to measure the writer by dogmatic standards (as ministers were wont to do - the view from the pew might have been kinder) he was bound to have been found wanting, especially when, as Thomas Selby recognised, for White, like others in the field, a marked feature of his fiction was 'a recoil from many things in the theology of the decrees'.[81] Selby was uneasy about the high value given to nature, which smacked of pantheism, the perceived loosening of sexual ethics, and the deep fatalism he detected even in the later novels. By his standards, works like White's exemplified a regrettable decline from the strong belief of the Puritan tradition.[82] Only later would it be hailed as a renewal from within.

If Sperry and others were prompted to reconsider White by news of his death, some who followed were moved to write by the publication of works which shed new light upon his life. John Middleton Murry approached White with high praise for the quality of his writing and thought, as being 'radiations from a single living centre, functions ... of one unchanging soul'.[83] The occasion of his article was the publication by White's widow of a selection of his *Letters to Three Friends* (1924), which promised a more intimate picture of

---

[80] Sperry, 'Mark Rutherford', pp. 190-191. Sperry perhaps downplays White's concern with practical religion.

[81] In *The Theology of Modern Fiction* (London: Charles H. Kelly, 1896), p. 173. Selby also noted this aspect (to which as a Methodist and Arminian he must have been sympathetic) in the works of Scots novelists, including George MacDonald in particular, pp. 131-172. Oddly, Selby writes as if Reuben Shapcott is the writer's pseudonym in the Mark Rutherford books; it seems he is not aware of William Hale White at all.

[82] At least, the 'doctrinal oscillation and unsettlement of which Mark Rutherford himself is a pathetic and noteworthy example'; *Theology of Modern Fiction*, p. 175.

[83] 'The Religion of Mark Rutherford', in *To the Unknown God: Essays Towards a Religion* (London: Jonathan Cape, 1924), pp. 260-275 (p. 260). The article first appeared in *The Adelphi*, II (1924).

the writer.[84] Murry judges White's most attractive quality to be his integrity, writing always of what was most deeply felt. There is something essential which cannot be put into words however, for he found it 'impossible ... to say wherein the meaning consists'.[85] In this Murry is not so far from Sperry, and he goes on to explore the alienation of White from the institutional expressions of faith as the 'irreconcilable conflict between Christ and Christianity'.[86] Murry is not wrong to see this contrast, but fails to identify White's target clearly enough. By 'Christianity' White typically means outward forms ('Christendom' in its most negative connotation), but his attacks in these published letters are on quite specific issues, especially the failure of church leaders to speak out against the South African war, which he (like many Dissenters) fiercely opposed. Murry, a convinced pacifist, is attracted to White for this reason, but to isolate these letters from other writings is to risk misrepresenting White, who does not always judge 'Christianity' in this way.

There is a link here between White's expulsion from theological college and his consistent opposition to officially sanctioned or approved religious expression. The believer must always be absolutely free to follow his conscience. This is the lesson of White's early spiritual illumination through Wordsworth and nature, the 'habit of inner reference'.[87] White is thus true to his Independent roots, in which there was a long tradition of resisting credal tests as an infringement of personal liberty and in no way a suitable substitute for evangelical experience. Murry confesses to being unable to fully explain his subject's religious beliefs, and in this he is typical of those who are attracted by the impression of a faith which requires no external, dogmatic, support.

In their different ways Sperry and Murry bear witness to the individual responses which White and his writings often evoke, but they also represent the constant danger of interpreting him in terms of the reader's sympathies. It occurs again in Don Cupitt's introduction to the 1988 reprint of the *Autobiography* and *Deliverance*, in which rigid dogmatism is contrasted with a search for personal truth, and the conclusion is that he could find no suitable replacement for the discarded Christian meta-narrative.[88] This modernising of

---

[84] The 'friends' of the title were the architect Philip Webb, Mr & Mrs Richard Colenutt of Ryde, who he got to know in the 1850s through his cousin William Chignell, and Sophia Partridge, a retired teacher he had met when living in Ashtead sometime after 1889.

[85] Murry, 'The Religion of Mark Rutherford', p. 264.

[86] Murry, 'The Religion of Mark Rutherford', p. 270. He writes in the context of White's expulsion from college, but confuses the facts by thinking this was from Cheshunt, and that he had been intended for ministry in the Countess of Huntingdon's Connexion.

[87] *Autobiography*, p. 19, Ch. II.

[88] London: Libris, 1988. For instance, Cupitt is clearly sympathetic to White but fails accurately to identify the moderate Calvinism of his upbringing (pp. xiii-xiv). Nor is he

Note continues on following page

White can only be guarded against by attention to the historical and intellectual context.

Therefore information from both early and more recent scholarly sources must be used with due regard for the viewpoint of the writers, which needs to be identified when weighing their evidence. They may be predisposed to certain readings by their own interests, by dependence upon the research of others, or by the acceptance of dominant scholarly paradigms. Some have brought highly personal motives to their writing, for White seems to have attracted both among contemporary and later critics those feeling an empathy with his opinions, heritage, character or ideals. This can lead to imaginative insights, but also to misrepresentation as White is forced into line with a preconceived picture. The tension between individuality and being supposedly 'typical' of the historical context is always present.

Approaching White through his novels, the first introduction to his pen for almost all scholars, means that attempts to flesh out his life then start with a mental template which patterns everything about White after the narrative of his writings. An affinity with the author which readily identifies with his character and temperament, as revealed in the texts, may also inhibit any recognition of divergent views, especially from independent sources. In fact the differences between the life of Hale White and that depicted of Mark Rutherford may be more revealing than the obvious similarities and overlap. A tendency to minimise or ignore these is a feature of some studies, reinforced by the impression that his life outside writing (and especially *after* writing the novels) is of less importance. The evidence of his continuing, even reviving, religious belief late in life is commonly disregarded, as if any 'loss' in the novels was the last word on the subject. The dead Mark Rutherford thus casts a long shadow over the later years of his still-living creator.

The Contribution of Unpublished Research

There is a gap between the published criticism on White reviewed here and the latest research, which has not yet had an impact and remains largely unknown. It nevertheless forms an essential backdrop to this study and reference must be made to three unpublished theses which together provide a conspectus of current scholarship.[89] Their mix of new interpretation and new evidence, like that to be offered here, though with different emphases, challenges the conclusions of the biographies hitherto regarded as authoritative. While it is White's qualities as a writer which has attracted these doctoral studies, they

---

sufficiently alert to the nature of autobiographical texts and the impossibility of simply reading a life from them.

[89] Quotations are by permission of the authors. Reference here will concentrate on issues relevant to the task in hand, and a full description of their arguments is not attempted.

proceed with varying judgements about the relationship between form, content, and context.

Sally Ledger prioritises the late nineteenth-century context within which White writes as the key to understanding the author and his novels.[90] This provides insights which are obscured if attention is directed at the rather earlier mid-century setting of the novels themselves. He is, for Ledger, both 'distinctly original' and 'extraordinarily representative', attributes which at first sight appear to be in some tension.[91] She seems to mean that White *as a writer, in style and technique* is original and innovative, while dealing with issues which represent key areas of debate in political, religious and social life. He is therefore *inter alia* a witness to, and example of, 'the crisis of religious faith which gained momentum from about the mid-century, with the publication of Darwin's Origin of Species in 1859 and the infamous Essays and Reviews in 1860'.[92]

Ledger explores this through a study of the *Autobiography* and *Deliverance*, but does not escape the problems inherent in the crisis model. She challenges the trajectory from orthodox faith through doubt and despair to a stoical 'gospel of resignation' commonly described in the existing critical literature as being insufficiently related to the historical context. It is significant that Ledger shows least sympathy with Catherine Harland's monograph, just because it supposes a much more explicitly religious achievement for White, emphasizing a mystical belief in the 'indwelling Christ'.[93] For Ledger this is a spiritualising of White which down-plays his support for social and political reform, partly (she believes) through ignoring the importance of the journalism, with its practical emphasis. Her view is that 'White was basically not a mystic, and never completely transcended his earth-bound consciousness of immediate human needs' though (perhaps inadvertently) Ledger's wording here leaves open the supposition that White really *had* hoped to move beyond the 'immediate' of everyday life.[94] Moreover, the existence of a body of writing, especially the journalism which shows a preoccupation with contemporary social issues, does not make White an activist. He is an observer, and

[90] 'History, Politics and Women: A Contextual Analysis of the Writings of William Hale White ('Mark Rutherford'), 1990. She was one of the first to take seriously White's journalism, a subject since explored further by Mark Crees. I gratefully recall Dr Ledger's interest in this project at an earlier stage. News of her early death in January 2009 was everywhere received with great sadness.

[91] 'History, Politics and Women', p. 1.

[92] 'History, Politics and Women', p. 1 (original underlining); but there is no evidence that White was troubled by either of these texts.

[93] 'History, Politics and Women', p. 10.

[94] 'History, Politics and Women', p. 14. Christian history shows that the mystical and practical are not necessarily mutually exclusive.

commentator, but in life shied away (for example) from practical politics.[95]

Similarly, on the level of personal life Ledger asserts that White has been misunderstood by the failure to locate his novels properly in the context of their time of writing. The common depiction of troubled marriages should not be explained by supposing they arise directly from the author's experience, but in recognising that a preoccupation with gender relations was typical of the period, reflected in other 'new woman' novels.[96] She therefore underestimates the possibility of marital unhappiness in White's case, while allowing for the obvious strains caused by Harriet's ill-health, but this may be a false choice; the theme of mismatched partners is so strong and so poignantly expressed that some personal experience surely lies behind it, and clearly this does not rule out the parallel fictional exploration of the changing role of women.[97]

In describing White's religious views Ledger gives prominence to references which stress the human rather than the supernatural, and argues that these justify his being used to illustrate the Victorian crisis of faith. It is not clear if this is applicable to his view of Jesus, who is not for him just the sublime ethical teacher of Renan (whom he admires, as Ledger notes). Ledger reads the evidence all one way, and this arises from her prior acceptance of the crisis paradigm; 'the emphasis on the "human" rather than the supernatural aspects of religion', and the need to "identify the Bible with genuine human experience" [citing White's praise of Thomas Binney] 'was of course symptomatic of the crisis of faith of which "Mark Rutherford", along with so many other Victorians, was a victim'.[98]

Ledger takes the usual view of the *Early Life*, treating it as a straightforward account, though formally qualifying this by accepting White at his word when he declared; 'although I have been asked to write my own life, I have decided it cannot be done'.[99] While this does not explicitly rule out a change of mind before compiling the 'Autobiographical Notes' it does confirm the need for caution in reconstructing the life of Hale White from the his fictional writings. Most likely it expressed White's unwillingness to pen a complete factual record of his life for publication.

A thesis by Lorraine Davies completed in 1994 concentrated upon detailed study of the six Mark Rutherford novels treated as a developing series of inter-

---

[95] Ledger has to admit that on the woman question, for example, White wrote little in support, and did nothing practical, 'History, Politics and Women', pp. 71-72.

[96] 'History, Politics and Women', pp. 15-16, 192-195.

[97] Patricia Thomson believes that the difficulties described reflect White's own awareness, felt often at the time of writing, of 'the aching, *ever-present* disparity between two people which no amount of good will can bridge'; 'The Novels of Mark Rutherford', *Essays in Criticism*, 14 (1964), 256-267 (p. 257; emphasis added).

[98] 'History, Politics and Women', p. 27.

[99] In a letter to Miss Edwards, 18 October 1907; Ledger, 'History, Politics and Women', p. 90.

connected texts.[100] Innovative in form, their basic theme, repeated in different contexts, is 'the reformulation of religious consciousness within secular terms'.[101] This highlights the contrast between the early novels which feature Mark Rutherford and his Dissenting context and the last three, female-centred novels, in which characters without religious faith or upbringing seek purpose in their lives. Davies's close reading of the texts does not proceed by constant reference to external evidence from White's life, and there is correspondingly limited engagement with the historical context. The writer's mind and life are strangely separated. However she seems to accept the biographical outline of the foundational studies on White.

Her most important insight comes from a careful analysis of the complex and multi-layered references to religious conversion in the *Autobiography*, where description is accompanied by later reflection on meaning. Mark Rutherford struggles to understand his experience (or, at first his *lack* of experience?) in terms of the traditional language of Christian conversion, and is eventually forced to come to terms with uncertainty. According to Davies, this offers a breakthrough; 'it is as if the loosening up, or surrender of the "technical" language he inherited, in releasing thought from the obligation of verbal expression, makes way for the idea of unresolved being which makes doubt a means of actually admitting faith'.[102] This captures something of the openness of White's thought, but does not do justice to his passionate conviction. Nevertheless, Davies is one of the few critics to see that White is not moving from faith to doubt, as commonly supposed, but rather, potentially, from a formal adherence towards a meaningful lived commitment.[103] Davies appears to be working within the broad assumptions of the crisis of faith model, for elsewhere she writes of his early recognition of spiritual emptiness as making 'Hale White's crisis of faith untypical of his age', but detailed attention to the text has saved her from misleadingly applying it too rigidly to White.[104]

The most recent doctoral work, by Mark Crees, concentrates on White's journalism, most of which pre-date the novels, and the persistent support for social and political change it demonstrates.[105] This is a useful reminder that White lived in the aftermath of the 1832 Great Reform Act, and among the growing clamour for further widening of the franchise resulting in the Second

---

[100] 'An Awkward Rectitude: The Evolution of William Hale White's Fiction' (unpublished doctoral thesis, University of Liverpool, 1994).

[101] 'An Awkward Rectitude', abstract, p. ii.

[102] 'An Awkward Rectitude', p. 56.

[103] Just one point at which White is reminiscent of Kierkegaard (independently, for his works were not available in English during White's lifetime).

[104] See her 'Introduction' to the Everyman edition of *Clara Hopgood* (London: J. M. Dent, 1996), pp. xxv-xlvii (p. xxvi).

[105] 'Before Mark Rutherford: The Translations, Journalism and Essays of William Hale White' (1999), as cited p. 17 above.

Reform Act of 1867. Crees portrays a radical and subversive figure, while criticising the biographies which he believes have effectively obscured this truth, not least through the portrayal of a happy ending (emotional and spiritual) to his life. This is partly the result of the picture created by Dorothy White, whose writings, editing, and influence have greatly affected later understandings of her husband. Questioning her motives and role potentially allows a misleading layer of tradition to be peeled away.

The challenge Crees offers to the common portrayal of White's second marriage needs to be heard. He has particularly noted the influence of two works published by Dorothy after her husband's death in feeding this view, that is, *Letters to Three Friends* and *The Groombridge Diary*.[106] These sources need further investigation, which can be helped by the use of archive material making clear the concern White's children felt about the exploitation of their father's memory. The deep rift between Dorothy and her step-children was concealed in earlier studies.

Crees has not questioned other elements of the consensus on Hale White and seems unable to escape the 'faith-doubt' antithesis which can be so distorting when applied to White's life. It could be for this reason that he places too much store by White's knowledge of Strauss's *Life of Jesus*, implying (it seems) that since Strauss gave no place to the supernatural element in the Bible, then neither did White.[107] This is apparently contradicted by White's high view of the Bible, and resistance to 'negative criticism', for 'the New Testament without the miracles would be ruined'.[108] This phrase very probably has Strauss in mind, famous for the stripping away of the miraculous which his English translator found so painful.[109] Perhaps this evidence has been silently discounted because of its late date (1908) and the fact that it occurs in a letter addressed to Dorothy. It is nonetheless worthy of attention.

As outlined by Crees, White's 'spiritual' thought comes not from a residual Christianity but through his encounter with Spinoza, even though it is very difficult to determine what White borrowed from him. Spinoza's own thought is complex enough, and open to a wide variety of interpretations. Crees argues against any return by White to the God of his fathers, and so fails to do justice to the faith statements in his later writings, including the *Early Life*. They are interpreted as part of an emotional pull which he always resisted; 'throughout his life Hale White would be tempted to return to the comforting, familiar

---

[106] 'Before Mark Rutherford', pp. 2-3, 15-16.

[107] 'Before Mark Rutherford', p. 53.

[108] From a letter to Dorothy, quoted in the *Groombridge Diary*, p. 3. It is less clear how White understands these miracles; see further below, especially pp. 331-335.

[109] George Eliot was described by Mrs Bray in 1846 as 'Strauss-sick'; cited in *The George Eliot Letters, vol. I: 1836-1851*, ed. by G. S. Haight (London: Oxford University Press, 1954), pp. 206-207.

figure of the God he had known as a child (perhaps the largest temptation to return to this God came from his second wife) yet his vision remained resolutely secular'.[110] The implication is that White was true to his own convictions despite possible manipulation by Dorothy, but this argument ignores the signs of genuine continuity in White's religious development, and is arguably insensitive to the nature of faith itself. Nevertheless Crees has demonstrated how important it is to be aware of Dorothy's powerful effect as the self-appointed guardian of his legacy.

These theses show a substantial shift from the models of interpretation offered by the first clutch of critical biographies, demonstrating the effects of fresh readings of White, and of information newly available. But there is still a core reliance on an inadequate biographical outline, and misplaced certainty about events like the New College expulsion, giving a false impression that there is little more to say about his historical and spiritual context. The unanimous resistance to 'spiritual' reading of White is striking, mainly attributable to the triumph of the crisis view of Victorian religion. Nor has the discussion of White as a historically trustworthy witness to mid-century Dissent in general, and Bedford in particular, been searching enough. Some of this is due to continued overly simple reading of the *Early Life*.

This survey has focussed on writings in English, though the studies by Klinke and Buchmann testify to the existence of other audiences. The *Autobiography* has been translated into several languages, but this has often been due to the efforts of a few enthusiasts and may not be proof of wide interest. The publication of a French translation in 1957, still in print in another edition, suggests that country has one of the largest readerships, and French scholarship currently makes its own contribution to Hale White studies. The work of Jean-Michel Yvard is predicated upon the outline suggested in the first biographies and therefore he portrays White as a representative Dissenter who suffered a loss of faith occasioned by German thought and biblical criticism.[111] This caused the New College expulsion, while his later life is evidence of secularisation, in which a commitment to social radicalism replaces faith. The understandable reliance on previous accounts is a limiting factor however, and the value of Yvard's conclusions, for example about the denominational make up and political setting of nineteenth-century nonconformity, is also affected by an acceptance of White's writings as historically accurate. He refers to the

[110] 'Before Mark Rutherford', p. 103.

[111] His assumptions are set out most recently in 'Appartenance confessionnelle et allégeances politiques: William Hale White (<< Mark Rutherford >>) et l'évolution de la non conformité religieuse en Grande-Bretagne en XIXe siècle', *La Revue LISA/Lisa e-journal*, 9 (2011), 20-35 <http://www.lisa.revues.org/4094> [accessed 20 July 2011]. Much of Yvard's work has appeared in relatively inaccessible conference papers, hindering his impact in the field.

'multitude de <<sectes>>, Églises et <<dénominations>> en tous genres qui existaient dans la petite ville de Bedford' without realising that White mentions only a selected few of those which (as will become clear) are known to have flourished there, because too few other sources seem to have been consulted.[112]

Summary

This introduction to writing on Hale White highlights a surprising readiness to take information from White's pen on trust. This is especially true of material from the *Early Life*, with the exception that presuppositions about White's loss of faith prevent its evidence of renewed or returning faith being taken seriously. Since it appears to represent White's mature reflection on his life this text requires closer reading. Access to papers not available to an earlier generation of scholars, the unparalleled survival of the manuscript 'Autobiographical Notes', unique evidence about the publication process, and the availability of a range of little used independent corroborative sources for some of the key events combine to make such an undertaking potentially fruitful. The only way to remedy over-reliance on White's own testimony is to compare his writings with contemporary records. Because of the overlap between the novels and the *Early Life* both need to be tested, and the shaping Bedford context in particular may thereby be better understood.

---

[112] 'Appartenance confessionnelle et allégeances politiques', p. 20.

CHAPTER 3

The Rock from which he was Hewn
Bedford in Life and Writing

As 'Mark Rutherford', Hale White avowedly set out to leave a testimony for posterity about the Dissenting 'race' into which he had been born.[1] He is commonly read as a witness to his times, raising questions of accuracy which are not always addressed. It has often been supposed that the historical context can be reconstructed from the novels, cross-referenced against the *Early Life*. But his picture of mid-century Bedford cannot be squared with a reading of other sources. There is also a danger in accepting on trust his description of Bunyan Meeting, or taking it as typical of wider nonconformity. Quite apart from this aspect of the novels, their content and message will also be considered in an attempt to appreciate something of White's worth as a writer and the following he has attracted over the years. These and other texts can additionally be used to reveal how the experiences of his working life make their way into his writing, a valuable parallel check alongside the example of Bedford.

A sampling of independent sources shows that White has not represented without distortion the race or place which shaped him. The possible argument from self-writing theory that his works correspond to a felt experience more 'real' than one accurate in every historical or factual detail needs to be tested. The inevitably selective and unreliable function of memory is another factor hardly explored in writings on White, despite its relevance when considering writings separated by many years from the setting or events they describe.

The standard monographs have made very limited use of contemporary material relating to Bedfordshire, except for the few newspaper cuttings preserved among White's papers. His depiction has been accepted at face value and the accuracy of references to Bedford has not been seriously questioned. Where alternative sources such as the 1851 Religious Census are available they have not generally been employed. It is possible to demonstrate that local historians too have been so ready to incorporate White's seductively believable portrayal of Bedford in the 1830s and 40s that they have ignored the tensions

---

[1] *Autobiography*, p. 2, Ch. 1.

with other available evidence, even as they cite such sources alongside his.[2]

In White's youth Bedfordshire was a predominantly agricultural county with little industry. Cottage working was common, especially straw plaiting, hat making and lace-making by women and children. Wages were low and illiteracy high.[3] Baptists, and to a lesser extent Independents, were strongly represented, as was old Dissent generally in this region; overall the county had high figures for church attendance.[4] Bedfordshire was among the less populous English counties, with 129,000 inhabitants in 1851, but population density was above that of some larger adjoining counties with greater headcounts.[5] After Bedford the only other sizeable towns were Luton, Biggleswade, Ampthill and Dunstable.[6] At mid-century a number of towns in neighbouring counties were significantly larger than Bedford, though with a population of 12,000 (up from 7,000 in 1831) it stood comfortably above many.[7] Market gardening and other food production for London was an important part of the county's economy. Among the social elite were families like the Russells and Whitbreads, both of these having considerable influence in Bedford itself, and contributing to a strong Whig presence. As the county town Bedford was an administrative and cultural centre, hosting public buildings such as the prison, workhouse, asylum, and infirmary. The energetic support of the Whitbreads in particular meant that in some respects Bedfordshire was ahead of many larger counties in such provision. The asylum for example was only the second to be built in England after the 1808 enabling Act of Parliament.[8] Little enough of this context can be determined by reading White.

---

[2] For example Joyce Godber's *History of Bedfordshire: 1066-1888* (Bedford: Bedfordshire County Council, 1969; repr. 1984), where White's sleepy town suddenly appears amid the record of vigorous development and change, pp. 484-485.

[3] These details and other useful statistics in W. B. Stephens, *Education, Literacy and Society, 1830-70: The Geography of Diversity in Provincial England* (Manchester: Manchester University Press, 1987), pp. 162-205.

[4] Figures in K.D.M. Snell and Paul S. Ell, *Rival Jerusalems: The Geography of Victorian Religion* (Cambridge: Cambridge University Press, 2000), pp. 98-102 and 214-216.

[5] Cambridgeshire for example, 1851 population 192,864, averaged 0.29 people per acre, to Bedfordshire's 0.40; *Rival Jerusalems*, tables 7.1 and 7.3, pp. 223, 226.

[6] For towns 1835-1891 see Godber, *History of Bedfordshire*, pp. 484-498; Bedford grew steadily, while some market towns prospered and others stagnated, population statistics given on pp. 494-495.

[7] Stephens has gathered figures for eight counties west and north of London. In 1851 only five towns in these were larger than Bedford, and thirty others ranged from 3,000 to 11,000; *Education, Literacy and Society*, p. 162.

[8] Nottingham was the first, in 1811. Bernard Cashman tells the story of Bedford's asylum, and the leading role of Samuel Whitbread (the second, 1764-1815); *A Proper House: Bedford Lunatic Asylum (1812-1860)* (Bedford: North Bedfordshire Health Authority, 1992).

The apparently neutral historical material he includes provides a useful test of how White chooses to represent the times in which he grew up. Sources for comparison show his writings to be a re-creation rather than straightforward *reportage*. On this basis the need is established for a critical reassessment of the other areas on which he writes. When the historical context is more clearly understood attention can turn to the specifics of the *Early Life*.

Place - Life in Bedford

White's novels have made Cowfold (*Autobiography, Revolution, Miriam's Schooling*), Fenmarket (*Clara Hopgood*) and Eastthorpe (*Catharine Furze*) famous, and descriptions of these sleepy towns are commonly quoted in praise of his style and as evidence of the conditions of pre-industrialised English life.[9] The correspondence with Bedford, reinforced by the undisguised references of the *Early Life*, is strong. However the evocative portrayal is difficult to reconcile with contemporary sources.

The identification of Bedford with the 'small country town in one of the Midland shires' of the *Autobiography*, and 'my native town' of the *Deliverance* hardly needs to be argued given the obviously close connection between the life described of 'Mark Rutherford' and White's own.[10] Some of the features here, and of Cowfold, Fenmarket and Eastthorpe could have been drawn from other small towns round Bedfordshire, and there is no reason to suppose that a site can be identified to match every description. White's authorial freedom doubtless allows a street or building to reappear elsewhere, just as Fenmarket, though in some ways like Bedford, Cowfold, or Eastthorpe is actually located by its distance 'about ten miles north-east of Eastthorpe', and set in a different landscape.[11] It is observable however, whatever other differences there may be, that White has reduced the scale of his *locale* in every sense.

The scene of Mark's childhood, for instance, is very small. The complex, textured, life of a town like Bedford, growing from a population of less than 4,000 in 1801 to almost 12,000 in 1851 is less than fully described. The built environment of streets, businesses and institutions is so simplified, 'one long main street, with a few other streets branching from it at right angles', as to be misleading for a market town with approaching two thousand houses in

[9] In the *Autobiography* the town is given simply as 'C--------', becoming openly Cowfold in the *Revolution*. Did White have the Sussex village of Cowfold in mind, only a few miles from Ditchling, an area which he knew well?

[10] *Autobiography*, p. 2, Ch. I (see also p. 34, Ch. III), *Deliverance*, p. 31, Ch. III, 'my native town'.

[11] *Clara Hopgood*, p. 1, Ch. I; Claire Tomalin, in her 'Afterword' to the Hogarth edition (London: Hogarth Press, 1985), suggests Fenmarket represents the most negative memories of Bedford (without numbering, but third page).

addition to significant public buildings and commercial premises.[12] Cowfold's apparently busier centre in *Revolution*, 'four streets, or, more correctly, only two, which crossed one another at right angles in the middle of the town, and formed there a kind of square or open place, in which, on Saturdays, a market was held' describes the grid at the centre of Bedford, simply giving greater prominence to roads subsidiary to the High Street than does the *Autobiography*.[13] By the same token, there is little to suggest the activity that this size of population must have generated. *Robson's Commercial Directory* of 1839 lists more than ninety trades carried on by over four hundred businesses or individuals, reflecting its status as the county town.[14] The character list of the novels is highly selective, and the later reminiscences of the *Early Life* continue to give the same impression, perhaps pardonably in that case, from a child-framed perspective.

The feel of these fictional towns is very similar; dull, remote, backward places cut off from modern ways or intellectual advance. While published between 1881 and 1896 these works are typically set in the 30s and 40s, the years between White's birth and majority. Reference is sometimes to even earlier events, presumably episodes gathered from parents and older relations, for his earliest datable memory was of celebrations in June 1838 to mark Queen Victoria's coronation.[15] Examination of local sources from this period shows the pronounced tendency for Hale White to sharpen the contrast between the time of writing and the earlier period by suppressing all signs of development, emphasizing stasis rather than change. In part this may have arisen from the undoubtedly more rapid expansion of the town in the 1880s, by contrast with which White imagines a more somnolent setting for his childhood than was really the case.

It seems certain that even by eighteenth century standards White's portrayal is misleading. In a comparative study of provincial towns Peter Borsay has identified key features of a pre-nineteenth century urban renaissance which find parallels in Bedford.[16] The evidence suggests that Bedford was a little behind

---

[12] *Autobiography*, p. 3, Ch. I. Estimate of houses based on population density and census figures for 1851.

[13] *Revolution*, pp. 232-233, Ch. XVI. See Figure 1 for a town plan of 1831, giving main outline only.

[14] *Robson's Commercial Directory of the Six Counties Forming the Norfolk Circuit: viz. Beds, Bucks, Cambridgeshire, Hunts, Norfolk, and Suffolk* (London: William Robson & Co., 1839), pp. 8-11. White's father is listed, and his uncle Samuel Lovell, but the guide has less detail on churches (incidental to its purpose), with only a passing reference to the Old Meeting (p. 8).

[15] *Early Life*, p. 40; thus Robson's 1839 *Directory* coincides with White's earliest memories.

[16] *The English Urban Renaissance: Culture and Society in the Provincial Town 1660-1770* (Oxford: Clarendon Press, 1989).

some towns, but nonetheless with signs of change. For example travelling theatre companies depended here upon using any available building when others had purpose-built theatres, balls were occasional and again without dedicated Assembly Rooms, while gardens and urban walks being laid out elsewhere were not yet a feature of the town. On the other hand, already by 1683 a market house and town hall were being erected (though never completed, and later adapted for another use), horse-racing was recorded from 1730, and a parochial library existed from 1700.[17] The river was another focal point, with popular races and regattas in the nineteenth century, from earlier origins. The significance here may be the relatively slow development of distinctly cultural and genteel pursuits, suggesting a leisured class too small to support such activities. The contrast between the still more thriving nineteenth century town and Hale White's descriptions can be made evident by comparison with other local sources.

Bedford in Contemporary Sources

Two volumes published in Bedford provide appropriate information for the time under review. The first, J. H. Matthiason's *Bedford and Its Environs*, was printed and sold by Hale's father in 1831.[18] Matthiason's map of the town, engraved by Robert Havell of that distinguished family of craftsmen, is reproduced below (Figure 1). This is an outline street plan only, emphasizing key public buildings, with houses in narrow roadside blocks, giving the impression of a smaller town than his text describes. It means that neither the substantial new building to the west of the High Street during the previous decade, nor the large amount of in-filling along existing streets is visible. Here the engraver harked back to a tradition by which 'on many early town plans a map-maker may have unconsciously ignored the alleys and courtyards of the poor in deference to the principal thoroughfares, public buildings and residents of the merchant class in his conscious promotion of civic pride or vaunting commercial success'.[19] Whatever Havell's role in delineating the plan, Matthiason was not lacking in civic pride, as his lavish prose indicated.

The Reynolds map of 1841 (Figure 2 below) in fact better represents the

---

[17] Borsay has extensive comparative tables of dates and events; see appendices 1-7; *The English Urban Renaissance*, pp. 323-367.

[18] *Bedford and Its Environs; or An Historical and Topographical Sketch of the Town of Bedford and Places Adjacent, Containing Accounts of Its Public Institutions, Schools, Charities, Societies, &c. & Brief Notices of Every Thing Most Remarkable and Important Relating to the Town and Neighbourhood* (Bedford: W. White, 1831).

[19] So J. R. Harley, 'Maps, Knowledge, and Power', in *The Iconography of Landscape: Essays on the Symbolic Representation, Design and Use of Past Environments*, ed. by Denis Cosgrove and Stephen Daniels (Cambridge: Cambridge University Press, 1988), pp. 277-312 (p. 292).

town as it was in 1831, clearly showing the effects of recent development.[20] This is also evidence of changes in cartographic conventions though, for while Havell and Matthiason's plate anachronistically echoes earlier birds-eye view town maps, Reynolds' is recognisably of the modern two-dimensional type.

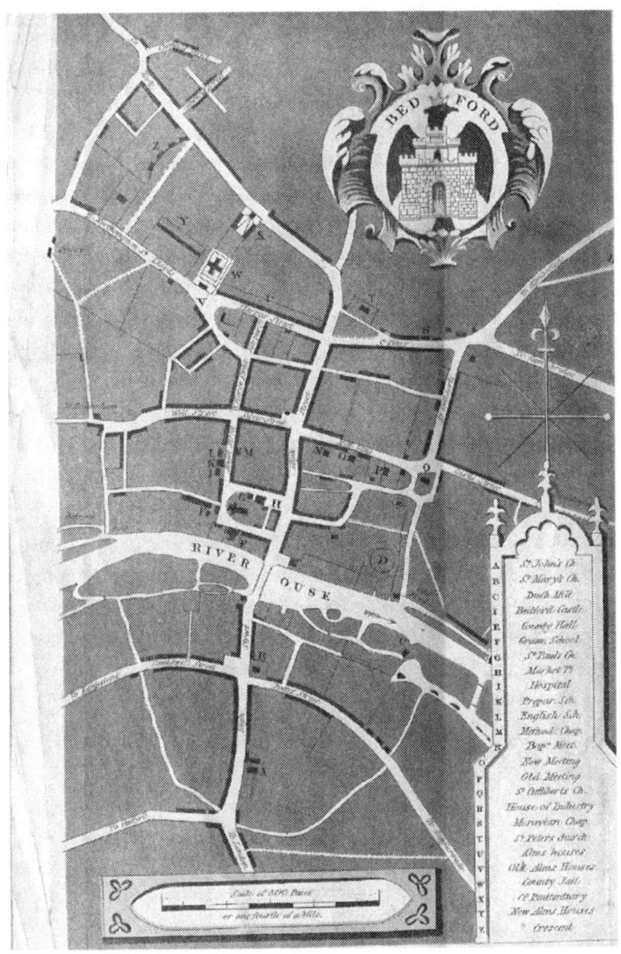

Figure 1 : Matthiason's Bedford, 1831

[20] Even at the limited scale reproduction possible here. For a description of early plans see Betty Chambers, *Printed Maps and Town Plans of Bedfordshire, 1576-1900* (Bedford: Bedfordshire Historical Record Society, 1983).

The second source is the compendium of local newspaper reports edited by J. Hamson for the *Bedfordshire Times* jubilee in 1896. The period from 1845 to the publication date of 1896 allowed 'comparisons between Bedford fifty years ago, and Bedford as it is now', with helpful descriptions of those former times.[21] Therefore from these two works, supplemented by other records, much can be gathered of the town in White's early years. Some direct links can be established between events and characters featured in the novels and other writings, but there are also divergences and omissions.

Matthiason's is the account of an enthusiastic newcomer, but his eagerness to praise does not necessarily imply inaccuracy.[22] It shows just how much could be said of the improvements to the town recently carried out, and of others anticipated. The need for paving, lighting, clearances and rebuilding had been addressed in an 'Act for the Improvement of the Town of Bedford, and for rebuilding the Bridge over the river Ouze [*sic*], in the said Town' of 1803. Commissioners were authorised to borrow money and raise rates, and although another Act was required in 1810 for increased funding, considerable changes were achieved.[23] It was the fruit of their efforts which Matthiason celebrated; the High Street 'with an excellent modern pavement which, for beauty, might certainly vie with any town in the kingdom', and a new bridge, among other evidence.[24] Progress was shown by comparison with areas not yet touched, such as the crowded roads to the east of the main thoroughfare, between Well Street and the river. He acknowledged that the town had not 'yet attained to that marked superiority ... at which it is excellently calculated to arrive'.[25] New, speculative house building as early as 1825 was also changing the townscape, evidence of prosperity, including The Crescent in Bromham Road.[26] Another witness from 1831 lauded the town as 'rapidly improving'.[27]

---

[21] *Bedford Town and Townsmen: Record of the Local History of Bedford During the Last Half Century* (Bedford: Bedfordshire Times Office, 1896), p. i.

[22] He came to the town to teach at the Modern School, but lost his position under the innovating headmaster John Moore.

[23] Details in Godber, *History of Bedfordshire*, pp. 442-443.

[24] *Bedford and Its Environs*, p. 39.

[25] *Bedford and Its Environs*, p. 7.

[26] Described by E. Moser, 'The Crescent, Bedford', in *Bedfordshire Historical Miscellany: Essays in Honour of Patricia Bell* (Bedford: Bedfordshire Historical Record Society, 1993), pp. 205-218.

[27] Samuel Lewis, *A Topographical Dictionary of England* (London: S. Lewis and Co., 1831), vol. I, p. 125.

Figure 2 : Reynold's plan of Bedford, 1841

Early-Victorian Bedford was clearly a rising town, an emphasis completely lacking in White. Other features too have been ignored. As the county town Bedford was a centre for business, justice and administration, the site of markets, fairs and horse races.[28] All this Matthiason catalogues, applauding the effect of those drawn in for such activities in making the town 'continually gay, lively, and interesting'.[29] Bustle and excitement is notably absent from White's

[28] The market square is mentioned in *Revolution*, but its activities are not described (pp. 232-233, Ch. XVI).

[29] *Bedford and Its Environs*, p. 6.

descriptions, which are therefore significantly misleading if read on their own.[30]

The review in Hamson's *Bedford Town and Townsmen* by its nature tends to emphasize change and progress, including an extensive listing of shops and small businesses which suggests that White very much understates the thriving nature of the local economy. There is insufficient detail to be sure just how many of the traders and premises mentioned by Hamson were operating in the 1830s and 40s, but for artistic reasons if no other White chose to focus on a very few. Cowfold has just five shops, along with some houses where goods could be bought.[31] At the same time, interesting links to his novels emerge from this compilation, though Hamson, while aware of 'Mark Rutherford's' Bedford connections, does not make any judgement on the veracity with which the town is portrayed, simply acknowledging 'these remarkable works, in which most of the scenes are laid in Bedford'.[32]

The only explicit detail Hamson notes is to identify a Mr Tacchi, who traded as 'a carver and gilder, and maker of the old style of barometer, examples of which are preserved in the older houses of the town', as clearly the inspiration for the heroine's father in *Miriam's Schooling.*[33] No local sources appear to identify John and Maria Furze of the Children's Hospital (orphanage), later teachers at the boys and girls elementary schools respectively, as possibly supplying the family name of Catharine Furze.[34] One instance recalled here and also mentioned in the novels is of the first shop in Bedford to have plate glass replacing the traditional bow window and domestic style façade.[35] The premises in question (no. 31), then a tailor's, was a little further up the High Street from William White's business at no. 5.

'Most beneficial to the town': Bedford's Charity

One important feature of Bedford life, noted by a contemporary as 'most

---

[30] Mention in *Revolution* of 'a travelling menagerie with a brass band' visiting Cowfold is just the occasion to remark on the otherwise total lack of entertainment (p. 263, Ch. XVIII), and Dissenting disapproval of dancing. Eastthorpe's centre has permanent pens for animal markets (*Catharine Furze*, p. 7, Ch. I). Miriam's Cowfold is busy on market days (*Miriam's Schooling*, pp. 131-132).

[31] *Revolution*, p. 233, Ch. XVI.

[32] *Bedford Town and Townsmen*, p. 48.

[33] *Bedford Town and Townsmen*, p. 48; Giacomo Tacchi is a watchmaker who also 'repaired barometers and thermometers' (*Miriam's Schooling*, p. 49).

[34] The couple worked at the Hospital from 1815-1847, and the schools from 1815-31 (John, at the boys) and 1837-60 (Maria, at the girls); see Godber, *The Harpur Trust, 1552-1973* (Bedford: The Harpur Trust, 1973), pp. 87-89 and 160-161.

[35] *Bedford Town and Townsmen*, p. 33; Hamson does not date this event. Eastthorpe's druggist, 'as a man of science and advanced ideas', introduces plate-glass windows to the town; *Catharine Furze*, p. 7, Ch. I.

beneficial to the town', was the historic Harpur Trust, a charity applying income from extensive London estates for educational purposes and eleemosynary relief.[36] Hale White benefited from the schooling provided for those born in the town by the Trust, as his father had before him.[37] Its disbursements had a great effect upon everyday life. When White writes in the *Early Life* that in his childhood 'the Bedford Charity was as yet hardly awake' this is misleading.[38] It is noticeable that the fund has no parallel in his fictional towns. It seems likely that White is again taking the 1880s as the point of comparison, for the Trust was certainly more active then and its educational provision in particular was spread even more widely, but it is nevertheless erroneous to play down its role earlier in the century.[39]

The Trust's activities were extensive. In addition to the Grammar School (attended by William White), the charity supported the English School and elementary schooling.[40] The two secondary schools for many years shared the same building, and were known as the Upper (occupying the upper floor) and Lower schools, the usage White follows in his *Early Life*, the names continuing long after they possessed separate premises. The emphasis of the Grammar School was upon possible University entrance - the curriculum included Latin and Greek - while the English School aimed to help those entering business careers (that is, particularly local children). Only under changes initiated by headmaster John Moore was Latin added in 1837, a recognition that some boys might wish to enter the new University College of London.[41]

Control of the funds was vested in Trustees, and arrangements for their selection and election were varied several times by Act of Parliament. In due course Dissenters gained the right to become trustees, William White serving in this capacity. Children of nonconformists had always enjoyed the same entitlement to free education as other residents, and upholding a similar principle William successfully combated a proposal that all teachers appointed

---

[36] The verdict of *Robson's Commercial Directory* in 1839, p. 8.

[37] Literacy in the market towns of Bedfordshire was higher than in the county generally; Stephens, *Education, Literacy and Society*, p. 8. The effect of Harpur Trust provision helps to explain this for Bedford itself. Stephens shows that this was not always true of town over countryside.

[38] See *Early Life*, p. 15. No doubt White was influenced by the even greater scope of the Trust's operations later in the century.

[39] A change in the rules in 1873 had allowed those not born in Bedford also to benefit from subsidised education. Note a Harpur-like body outside the novels, in the short story 'Mrs Fairfax' (*Pages from a Journal*, pp. 218-283).

[40] The 'English' School was so-named because classical languages were not at first taught; education beyond the 'three Rs' led to the name Commercial school. It was later known as the Modern School.

[41] See Godber, *The Harpur Trust*, p. 73. The ancient English universities were effectively closed to Dissenters in White's youth.

to the schools by the Trust be members of the Established Church.[42] The pastor of Bunyan Meeting, Samuel Hillyard (Minister 1792-1839), had also held office as a trustee. His son was a pupil at the grammar school alongside William White under the reforming John Brereton, headmaster 1811-55.[43]

Hale White's references to the Trust may have been coloured by a critical report long after he had left the town. In a review conducted by the Schools Inquiry Commissioners in 1868 the 'local, exclusive and indiscriminate lavishness' of the Trust's doles so much appreciated by ordinary townspeople was condemned as a misapplication of funds which would have been better employed for education, though this verdict is undermined by figures which show a steady increase in resources allocated to the latter.[44] Perhaps White's slighting remarks in the *Early Life* about the 'worthless' nature of the education provided, and the 'very large part' of the endowment used for relief derives from this 'exaggerated and, in the main, unjust' report.[45] They do not represent the true situation of his youth, when the Grammar and Modern Schools were being transformed and receiving a rapidly increasing share of Trust expenditure. Moreover he is simply wrong in stating that 'no part of the funds was devoted to the education of girls', for efforts had been made from early in the century to just that end.[46] The Commissioners were reflecting a wider debate about the most effective means of combating poverty, with education as the primary method gaining broad acceptance.

The Railway Era

The prosperity of Bedford was enhanced by the coming of the railway. In the *Autobiography* Hale White dates Rutherford's birth to 'just before the Liverpool and Manchester Railway was opened'.[47] While there was no line to Bedford until 1846 the town was affected as early as 1838 by the opening of

---

[42] Events described in *Early Life*, pp. 29-30. The masters of the Grammar School, appointed by New College, Oxford, *were* to be Anglicans. The change proposed was to extend this to all the Trust schools.

[43] Godber, *The Harpur Trust*, p. 66.

[44] Report quoted in F. E. Balls, 'The Endowment of Education in the Nineteenth Century: The Case of the Bedford Harpur Trust', *History of Education*, 6 (1977), 103-113 (p. 104). He includes statistics on expenditure.

[45] *Early Life*, pp. 15-16. The verdict of Balls, 'The Endowment of Education', p. 105.

[46] *Early Life*, p. 15. See Godber, *Harpur Trust*, p. 84 for an account of girls' education from 1818, an enterprise which almost foundered for lack of parents willing to send their daughters. Suspended in 1831, only in 1836 was a full-time girls school opened, a tribute to the determination of some Trustees that girls should benefit from education.

[47] *Autobiography*, p. 2, Ch. I. But it is as if he rejects the machine age, a sentiment shared with his hero Carlyle. *Revolution* has passing railway references, p. 323, Ch. XXIV, p. 387, Ch. XXVII.

that between London and Birmingham. Its construction provided some local employment in depressed times, though evidence on the scale of this is mixed.[48] If his first memories are accurately self-dated from 1838 there can never have been a time when he was not conscious of this sign of the machine age, but White has chosen to ignore it and look to a completely rural past. He acknowledges the Bedford Times coach to London as Whitbread's subsidised 'hobby', without noting that its demise in 1846 coincided with the opening of the railway.[49] The Ouse, which he celebrates, had been an important goods route for many years, but declined quickly with competition from the railways.

The Natural World: Unrest in Eden?

Enjoyment of the river and countryside surrounding Bedford features significantly in White's writing, but his is a partial view. Mark Rutherford records half-holidays from school spent exploring the river as among 'the happiest part of my life', rhapsodised also in the *Early Life*; because of the nearness to open country, 'never was there a town better suited to a boy than Bedford at that time for out-of-door amusements'.[50] These descriptions of childish delight are not simple memories, but, like similar passages in the novels, demonstrate White's special view of nature. From Wordsworth he had learned of transcending the self through the intimate connection between the creative mind and the infinite Universe.[51] In the accounts mentioned, this is expressed in feeling of ease and refreshment, the depiction fitting into the common categorisation of nature as Edenic.[52] The same connection between nature, transcendence of the self, and oneness with the divine is found in Emerson, whom White read and admired. This concept is prominent in *Catharine Furze* with the paradisiacal setting of Bellamy's farm, a stark contrast to the ugly, urban, formal newness of 'The Terrace'.[53] More immediately relevant here, in comparing White's presentation with other sources, is the extent to which he has avoided mentioning the widespread rural

[48] Too few men may have been needed, and drawn only from areas very close to the line, to have a wider impact on employment; references in W. Apfel and P. Dunkley, 'English Rural Society and the New Poor Law: Bedfordshire, 1834-47', *Social History*, 10 (1985), 37-68 (pp. 59-60 and note 83).

[49] *Early Life*, p. 15 (the facing plate of the coach on its last journey was added to White's manuscript).

[50] *Autobiography*, p. 4, Ch. I, *Early Life*, p. 49-52 (p. 49). The accounts are very close.

[51] From *The Prelude* no doubt, but also, in a life-changing encounter, the *Lyrical Ballads*.

[52] A feature specially prominent in memories of childhood.

[53] As in Ch. IV for example. Also seen in the description of Lower Hatch Farm in 'A Home-Made Religion', a veritable holy-land, where Jesus himself might be imagined at prayer in the fields; reprinted in *Pages*, pp. 320-325 (p. 322).

poverty and unrest in Bedfordshire. This can only be partly explained by his relatively comfortable town upbringing.

None who lived through those times could have been ignorant of the disturbances. Though White was too young to recall them himself, local memories would have been still very strong during his teenage years, as they were throughout the affected areas. The *Recollections* of Alderman James Coombs, sometime Mayor of Bedford and member of Bunyan Meeting, start by recalling the dark times in his native Hampshire when 'wages were low, bread was dear; and the disaffected, gathering in formidable numbers, marched from farm to farm, smashing the hated implements and levying black mail [*sic*] along their track'.[54] Although his adopted county did not see the degree of rural conflict experienced in the worst affected areas, there were 'Swing' riots and machine-breakings in several villages around Bedford. Rick-burnings, prevalent in the Eastern counties after 1830, were a particular feature of Bedfordshire into the 'hungry forties', with more than a hundred incendiary attacks over five years, peaking in 1843-44.[55] Locally high levels of seasonal rural unemployment were the inevitable consequence of the amount of land given over to corn, with full employment possible only at harvest times.[56] The extent of rural poverty is shown by the rising cost of poor relief in Bedfordshire from £36,895 in 1803 to £84,514 in 1830.[57]

Nothing of this local background could be gathered from reading White, a fact surely to be explained by a desire to present nature as a locus for transcendence, rather than strife or hardship.[58] It cannot be that White was unaware of this situation, which was still during his teens a cause of considerable social tension. Since child labour - in agriculture and especially cottage industries - was an important factor it might be expected that the youthful White should have been particularly conscious of this.[59] Poverty and child-labour was linked to poor educational provision and attainment,

---

[54] *Recollections, Personal and Political* (Bedford: Arthur Ransom, 1889), pp. 5-6. If his dating is correct, this would be from the very start of the unrest there in late 1830.

[55] Report to the Parliamentary Select Committee on Game Laws, 1846, cited in E. J. Hobsbawm and G. Rudé, *Captain Swing* (London: Lawrence and Wishart, 1969), p. 285.

[56] Apfel and Dunkley, 'English Rural Society and the New Poor Law', p. 59.

[57] Figures from Apfel and Dunkley, 'English Rural Society and the New Poor Law', p. 40, table 1. A reduction by 1847 due to the Poor Law Amendment Act did not necessarily mean an amelioration of severe poverty.

[58] Reference in *Revolution* to countrywide 'incendiarism' breaks the silence, though this is from 1816; p. 143, Ch. X; see also p. 381, Ch. XXVII however.

[59] Women were also heavily dependent upon straw-plaiting.

evidenced particularly by the reported widespread illiteracy in the county.[60]

In adulthood White's deep concern for social justice and democratic reform is clear from much of his journalism, as documented by Mark Crees, and is central to the sympathetic depiction of the plight of workers in the *Revolution*.[61] Man enmeshed in industrialisation and urbanisation is a victim, but his idealised view of nature will not allow him to recognise the alienation of the agricultural worker. The case which appears to be an exception, a set-piece of Rutherfordian commentary, does not quite disprove this reading. In *Catharine Furze* White describes the ill-repaired cottage home of Phoebe Crowhurst; scarcely habitable inside, while 'outside nothing had been done to the house for years. It was not brick built, and here and there the laths and timber were bare, and the thatch had almost gone'; of this cottage a local landowner's daughter:

> made a little sketch in water-colour ... it hung in the great drawing-room, and was considered most picturesque ... "it makes one quite enamoured of the country", exclaimed Lady Fanshawe, one of the most determined diners-out in Mayfair. "I never look at a scene like that without wishing I could give up London altogether. I am sure I could be content. It would be so charming to get rid of conventionality and be perfectly natural".[62]

White's denunciation of such blindness is total, as he condemns 'sham ecstasies over one of these pigstyes so long as it is in a gilt frame'.[63] This may be an indirect commentary on the portrayal of cottage life by some early Victorian artists who, like many writers, had often presented a rural idyll in which the poor were displayed in pleasing simplicity. Increased knowledge of rural poverty had fuelled criticism of the idealised paintings which had been in vogue and brought its own reaction. In contrast 'the paintings of the 1870s and 1880s were part of the new awareness of the extent and depths of distress [which] entered art ... fiction and ... the public consciousness'.[64] Painters had most commonly depicted cottage interiors, but the same response would apply to the scene White describes. Many in the Pre-Raphaelite group shared this concern, and its members were responsible for some significant pictures countering the unreality popularly displayed in illustrated magazines and the

---

[60] Bedfordshire's rate as measured by illiteracy at marriage between 1840 and 1850 was among the worst in England and Wales; Stephens, *Education, Literacy and Society*, Appendix D, p. 322.

[61] See Crees 'Before Mark Rutherford' chapter three for White's journalism and social comment. The London poor are a social focus of the *Deliverance*.

[62] *Catharine Furze*, p. 313, Ch. XVIII.

[63] *Catharine Furze*, p. 314, Ch. XVIII. It isn't made clear if the picture shows the ruinous reality.

[64] Julian Treuherz, introducing *Hard Times: Social Realism in Victorian Art* (London: Lund Humphries in association with Manchester City Art Galleries, 1987), p. 13.

major galleries. White, himself a thwarted artist, was probably aware of this debate and may indeed have heard something of it from Arthur Hughes, who was on the fringes of the Pre-Raphaelite circle.[65] Hale was also a regular visitor to galleries, and had the first-hand knowledge to assess what he saw.[66]

That said, he may be guilty of something similar himself. For not only, this instance apart, has he largely avoided reference to the depressed state of the Bedfordshire farm worker, but the description of his childhood nurse Jane Reed's home at Oakley has, in a lower key, something of the flavour of Lady Fanshawe. This 'little thatched cottage', of a 'very poor' family could offer 'no entertainment, no special food', but was nevertheless an:

> escape to a freer life, to a room in which we cooked our food, ate it, and altogether lived during waking hours when we were indoors. Oh, for a house with this one room, a Homeric house! How much easier and how much more natural should we be if we watched the pot or peeled the potatoes as we talked, than it is now in a drawing-room, where we do not know what chair to choose amongst a dozen scattered about aimlessly; where there is no table to hide the legs or support the arms; a room which compels an uncomfortable awkwardness, and forced conversation.[67]

This is perhaps an attitude not so very far from that condemned in the novel. The Reeds are not desperately poor, but they know their place. Even if White has accurately portrayed a family moderately well-housed and provided for, his is a romanticised, even sentimental, view. Conditions in Oakley seem to have been a little better than some other villages, but the chronic lack of employment and its seasonal nature encouraged landowners and the Poor Law authorities to promote emigration as a means of removing over-supply in the labour market. Several families from Oakley had been helped in this way around the year of White's birth.[68] Circumstances for many were as bad as the Crowhursts', but

---

[65] Christiana Payne has traced the debate with reference to some key works; 'Rural Virtues for Urban Consumption: Cottage Scenes in Early Victorian Painting', *Journal of Victorian Culture*, 3 (1998), 45-68.

[66] The *Early Life* (pp. 90-91) shows how eagerly he visited the Royal Academy and other exhibitions as a young man. The RA introduced highly popular reduced price evening opening in 1862 to benefit the urban working classes; see Payne, 'Rural Virtues for Urban Consumption', p. 67, note 18.

[67] *Early Life*, pp. 41-42; reminiscent of Mr Furze's unease in the more 'respectable' home of The Terrace. The attraction of *naturalness* is closely paralleled in the extract cited above from *Catharine Furze*.

[68] See letter (reference 4.2.1.4, dated 1840 but describing events in Oakley ca. 1831) from the Duke of Bedford's agent in Nigel Agar, *The Bedfordshire Farm Worker in the Nineteenth Century* (Bedford: Bedfordshire Historical Record Society, 1981), p. 135. Alan Cirket shows that they went to America in May 1831, funded by a special rate; 'The 1830 Riots in Bedfordshire – Background and Events', in *Worthington George*

Note continues on following page

their presence is hardly felt, and is confined to the fiction, with not a hint in the *Early Life*. Parliamentary inquiries and local newspapers reported agrarian strife in detail, and it seems that White must have been aware of much of this. In one instance local events during the 1874 agricultural workers' dispute may have supplied the idea for incidents in Rutherford's life.

Henry Havergal, vicar of Cople near Bedford, became engaged in controversy over his support for striking labourers locked-out by farmers on the Woburn estate. Copying to the *Bedfordshire Times* his letters to the Duke of Bedford on this issue, he earned the gratitude of the men, but criticism from those who regretted clerical intervention.[69] There is a certain similarity here with the (anonymous) disapproval by Deacon Snale of Rutherford's public support for improved sanitation in Cowfold, scandalised that 'a minister of religion should interfere in politics', setting 'class against class'.[70] The specific issue in the *Autobiography* is known to have been a subject of disagreement in Bedford. While with hindsight, as Godber records, 'the installation of a supply of clean piped water was perhaps the most vital measure for an expanding Victorian town', some Bedford councillors were strongly opposed to the cost being borne by ratepayers. Only after the town had been shamed by widespread publicity about regular outbreaks of typhoid fever could the reformers carry the day. Mains drainage and a piped water supply were in place by 1864 and 1866 respectively.[71] White's writing shows a keen awareness of the importance of such improvements, even when hesitant about other signs of 'progress' in rural life such as mechanisation.[72]

For while largely ignoring the railway era, he also omitted to note changes in agriculture that were a sign of the machine age. Although Eastthorpe's ironmonger selling 'all kinds of agricultural implements', with foundry attached, which features large in *Catharine Furze* is undoubtedly derived from a Bedford original, the historical significance of this enterprise for the local economy is hidden from the reader.[73] The changes to farming made possible by enclosure, and the demand for increased productivity were ideal conditions for

---

Smith and Other Studies: Presented to Joyce Godber, (Bedford, Bedford Historical Record Society, 1978), pp. 75-112 (p. 108). Inward migration to London and the growing northern industrial towns was also common.

[69] Reproduced in Agar, *The Bedfordshire Farm Worker,* pp. 189-190.

[70] *Autobiography*, p. 43, Ch. IV.

[71] Godber describes this controversy, *History of Bedfordshire*, pp. 487-488 (p. 487).

[72] One of his New College tutors, Edwin Lankester, played a key role in the fight against cholera and the campaign for improved sanitation, which may have impressed White. See Mary P. English, *Victorian Values: The Life and Times of Dr Edwin Lankester, M.D., F.R.S.* (Bristol: Biopress, 1990).

[73] *Catharine Furze*, p. 11, Ch. I.

greater use of machinery.[74] Technical innovation and production-line assembly techniques made Howard Brothers Britannia Iron Works highly successful.[75] The company became a major employer, and by the 1870s its factory was perhaps the largest of its kind in the world. But White's novels still inhabit the world of the original small shop in the High Street started by John Howard, though he handed over to his sons in 1850, who by the end of the decade had already transferred to a much larger site. Once more the town of his earliest childhood is preferred to later realities, even where obviously significant changes were already taking place.

Festivals and Amusements, Crime and Punishment

What else has White not recorded of Bedford life in the early nineteenth century? It seems that the colourful or exotic has largely been excised. Mention has already been made of the markets, fairs, and other events which drew crowds to the town. This vitality is missing, and leaves a distorted picture. Henry Hawkins, a boarder at Bedford school in 1830, recalled the colour of market-day:

> there was a good deal of merriment to divert our attention, for there were clowns and merry-andrews passing along the high road, with singlestick players, Punch and Judy shows, and other public amusers. Everyone knows [unless they read Mark Rutherford, one might add] that the smallest event in the country will cause a good deal of excitement'.[76]

He also described the sombre spectacle of public executions. The last of these in England was carried out in 1868, and though some took place in Bedford during White's youth they became markedly less common during his lifetime.[77] Changing sentencing policies and frequent commutation meant that

---

[74] It might be added that White's years at the Admiralty covered a period of unprecedented technical advance in the development of marine power, and he must have been well aware of changing times.

[75] Interesting information is found in the diaries of Charlotte Bousfield, whose husband Edward was a key employee; see *The Bousfield Diaries: A Middle-Class Family in Late Victorian Bedford*, ed. by R. Smart (Woodbridge: Boydell Press for The Bedfordshire Historical Record Society, 2007), especially Smart's introduction, pp. xiv-xviii.

[76] *The Reminiscences of Sir Henry Hawkins, Baron Brampton*, ed. by Richard Harris, popular edition (London: Edward Arnold, 1905), pp. 2-3.

[77] According to Godber, 15,000 watched a hanging in 1860; *History of Bedfordshire*, p. 497. White's journalism often comments with repugnance on public hangings, perhaps suggesting some regrettable early experience of the excitement they caused, if only at a distance. In later life, as a judge, Henry Hawkins himself pronounced death sentences.

there were only four hangings in the town between 1837 and 1878.[78] Perhaps White was shielded by his parents, unlike some who thought public hangings a wholesome warning to the young. While Lord Houghton had wondered 'who would dream of taking anybody to a public execution as a grand moral example', there were those eager to do so.[79] Matilda Betham-Edwards of Suffolk, a contemporary and later acquaintance of White, remembered meeting 'a labourer's wife and her two daughters' returning from Ipswich, the mother declaring her robust moral sensibility; 'I am anxious to do my girls all the good I can, so I have just taken them to see a man hanged'.[80] Since the events often attracted unruly crowds noted for vulgar and profane language it would be understandable if on those grounds, let alone for the horror of the hanging itself, respectable families stayed away and kept their children from the scene.

The Religious Life of Bedford

Whatever the reasons for other apparent deviations from historical accuracy White is widely taken to be a reliable witness to the religious life of his home town. The ecclesiastical inventory of Cowfold is generally accepted as a true description of Bedford - Wilfred Stone for instance refers to it without showing any doubt about its historicity - but it does not detail the range and colour of the churches actually to be found.[81] The Rector of St Peter's had occasion to complain about the 'sect[s] of which there is a melancholy variety in this town', but White is highly selective in his account.[82] The fullest detail he gives is of 'Cowfold', which in addition to the Established church has simply 'three chapels; one *the* chapel, orthodox, Independent ...; the second Wesleyan, new, stuccoed ...; the third, strict Baptist, ultra-Calvinistic'.[83] From the 1851 Religious Census for Bedford can be added five other Anglican churches, and

---

[78] Details in E. Stockdale, *A Study of Bedford Prison, 1660-1877* (Bedford: Bedfordshire Historical Record Society, 1977), p. 194. As he notes, this infrequency meant that there were several periods when the prison was without the means to carry out the sentence if passed, pp. 195, 205.

[79] Cited by Randall McGowen in following the debate leading to the cessation of public hangings; 'Civilizing Punishment: The End of the Public Execution in England', *The Journal of British Studies*, 33 (1994), 257-282 (p. 264); McGowen notes that 'in rural areas people walked for miles in order to attend' hangings, p. 268.

[80] An undated memory, most likely 1864 or 1865, from her *Reminiscences* (London: George Redway, 1898), p. 45. Betham-Edwards came to know White in Hastings during his retirement years, see below, p. 312.

[81] See Stone, p. 18.

[82] Letter of Revd Philip Hunt, 1830, in Joan Varley's account of 'A Bedfordshire Clergyman of the Reform Era and his Bishop', in *Worthington George Smith and Other Studies*, pp. 113-140 (p. 116).

[83] *Revolution*, pp. 234-235, Ch. XVI (original emphasis).

Moravians, Primitive Methodists, Howard Meeting, a second Baptist chapel, the Catholic Apostolic church, and a 'Christian Brethren' chapel, all founded before 1840 and of which he must have had some personal knowledge.[84]

The 'Christian Brethren' congregation is that of the Reverend Timothy Matthews, an Anglican in uneasy relationship with his Bishop, said in 1838 to be 'the most popular preacher in England'.[85] His biographer further acclaims him in 1841 'by far the most prominent figure in Bedford, where he dwarfed all other personalities'.[86] It is inconceivable that White should have been unaware of this messianic, street preaching, river-baptising figure. Calling people to open-air services with a trumpet, his was a highly visible ministry, frequently reported - often abused - in the press. Hale's father knew Matthews at least slightly, for the latter's Methodist-influenced system of pastoral oversight involved class tickets which were printed by William White. Matthews was also a sometime purchaser of books at the High Street shop.[87] Relegated to the fringes by his own views, Matthews was attracted to the newest teachings and thus contributed further to the religious diversity of the town. He initially welcomed his brother-in-law, Joseph Fielding, one of the most significant Mormon missionaries to Britain, who travelled extensively in the locality.[88] Latter Day Saints' historiography continues to represent Matthews himself as the would-be convert who fell away.[89] Rejection of their doctrines was a not wholly unpredictable outcome given his volatility and the fact that the most distinctive tenets of Mormonism, often at first concealed from enquirers, had been shared with him very soon after the original promising contact. Beneath the revivalist garb which appealed to Matthews was too much idiosyncratic

---

[84] Census details for Bedford reproduced by D. W. Bushby (ed.), *Bedfordshire Ecclesiastical Census, 1851* (Bedford, Bedford Historical Record Society, 1975), pp. 109-200 (pp. 128-132).

[85] Admittedly the verdict of an admirer, T. Wright, *The Life of the Rev. Timothy Richard Matthews, Friend of Edward FitzGerald* (London: C. J. Farncombe & Sons, 1934), p. 40. The name 'Christian Brethren' seems to have arisen through Matthews' admiration for the Moravian Brethren, but his was a quite independent mission (and not to be confused with Plymouth Brethren).

[86] Wright, *Life*, p. 58.

[87] A visit to order books for his son Joseph is recorded in a letter dated 9 February 1843 in Wright, *Life*, p. 78.

[88] Ronald Bartholomew tells the story of the Latter Day Saints in the county; '19th Century Missiology of the LDS Bedfordshire Conference and its Interrelationship with Other Christian Denominations', *International Journal of Mormon Studies*, 2 (2009), pp. 108-127.

[89] The fullest account (citing unpublished material from the Latter Day Saints archive in Utah) is by Malcolm Thorp, 'Early Mormon Confrontations with Sectarianism, 1837-40', in *Mormons in Early Victorian Britain*, ed. by Richard L. Jensen and M. R. Thorp (Salt Lake City, UT: University of Utah Press, 1989), pp. 49-69.

teaching derived from special revelation that even by his standards seemed at odds with the faith once delivered. The group had small causes in the county, though despite some early gains it did not flourish in Bedford itself.[90]

Perhaps White considered Matthews (and Mormons) too eccentric to merit attention, but that he gave a falsely limited picture of Bedford by silent exclusion is confirmed by his failure to mention the Moravians, who had been firmly established there since the middle of the eighteenth century. This was one of the earliest groups outside London, which by 1745 had developed into a congregation and a settlement.[91] A radical lifestyle made theirs a distinctive presence which could not be accidentally overlooked, and they made a significant contribution beyond their own circle. They co-operated with nonconformist and Anglican churches in organising the town's first Sunday schools. There were other shared activities between local churches, and doubtless family and personal links. The Dissenting congregations joined together regularly for prayer, a meeting initiated by Bunyan's Samuel Hillyard.[92] The Moravian minister was among the pall-bearers at Hillyard's funeral in 1839.[93]

Whatever the reason for White's silence, the effect is the same as that of his other omissions, to mislead the trusting reader about the nature and range of activities supported by the population of mid-Victorian Bedford. The society was not ignored by others, with J. H. Matthiason paying tribute to their 'very considerable standing in Bedford' and 'truly respectable rank', while noting that they had 'not a very extensive connection in the town: the scrupulous regard which is paid to their admissions acting probably as a considerable check to the extension of their body'; nevertheless, their chapel was 'numerously attended at the evening service when the churches are generally closed'.[94] Twenty years later, at the 1851 Census, only the Methodist churches

---

[90] The 1851 Census shows meetings at Wyboston (111), Thorncote (41), Studham (102) and Kensworth (103). Meetings known to have existed in Bedford in the 1830s had either dwindled or dispersed by 1851. Encouraged emigration to Utah could have removed the most committed.

[91] The early years are described by Edwin Welch in *The Bedford Moravian Church in the Eighteenth Century* (Bedford: Bedfordshire Historical Record Society, 1989). The settlement houses were turned over to other uses during the nineteenth century as the congregation became the focus for community life. Bedford was not, as Welch asserts, the first congregation outside London; Fulneck in Yorkshire preceded it by three years.

[92] Documented by Tibbutt, *Bunyan Meeting, Bedford: 1650-1950* (Bedford: Trustees of Bunyan Meeting [1950]), p. 46.

[93] Patricia Bell cites a local newspaper report of the event; *Belief in Bedfordshire* (Bedford: Belfry Press, 1986), p. 110.

[94] *Bedford and Its Environs*, pp. 67-69. Matthiason may be distinguishing attenders from members in the apparent contradiction between limited membership yet some well

Note continues on following page

(Wesleyan and Primitive) and Bunyan Meeting attracted more evening worshippers than the 450 who favoured the Moravians.[95]

If their organisation and strong internal bonds tended to divide the Moravians from their fellow citizens, without entirely cutting them off from the wider Dissenting community, there was another trait which set them a little apart from their closest spiritual neighbours. Scrutiny of the surviving poll-books shows that Moravians in Bedford were markedly more conservative than other nonconformists, who overwhelmingly voted for liberal candidates; 'on average ... the Moravian electors were 7.7 times more likely than the wider dissenting electorate to cast votes for a conservative candidate'.[96] It is hard to believe that a lingering discontent with their political stance would have been enough to ensure their omission. Whatever the case, while certainly different, Bedford's Moravians were far from invisible. The puzzle remains. In his novels White celebrates the exotic among the ordinary - why not in this regard? Perhaps enthusiasm in religion is to be deplored.

Bunyan Meeting

White might be expected to be a more dependable guide to his own church. The Old Meeting, attended by Hale and his parents, is at the centre of his description of Bedford life.[97] The perspective of Dissent colours everything - the acknowledgement of a long Calvinist and Puritan history, the role of Dissenters locally, and the experience of belonging within that tradition. It was in his great-grandfather's day that the family separated themselves from the established church, though not on any point of doctrine or church polity; according to legend it was disgust at the drunkenness of the Anglican minister.[98] In this sense Hale White was an accidental Dissenter, though destined to be remembered precisely for that connection. Whatever the reason for the transfer of allegiance, in Bedford it meant belonging to a faith

---

attended services. Several of Bedford's Anglican churches had afternoon services but not an evening one.

95 Census figures in D. W. Bushby; *Bedfordshire Ecclesiastical Census, 1851*, pp. 128-132.

96 From the analysis of five elections (1832, 1835, 1837, 1841, and 1847) by Richard Floyd; *Church, Chapel and Party: Religious Dissent and Political Modernization in Nineteenth-Century England* (Basingstoke: Palgrave Macmillan, 2008), note 34, p. 276. Figures from other regions show a similar trend, with variations in degree. Floyd attributes this to a natural conservatism within Moravianism.

97 It became known as the 'Old Meeting' to distinguish it from the breakaway 'New Meeting' of John Howard.

98 Reported from family sources in a study by A. J. Warner; 'Mark Rutherford, A Victorian Pilgrim: A Study of the Mind and Writings of William Hale White (1831-1913)' (unpublished thesis, University of Witwatersrand, 1949), p. 5.

community of considerable strength and influence with little sense of disadvantage.

The church is clearly described in the *Autobiography* and *Revolution* (and elsewhere), reinforcing the identification of these settings with historical Bedford. For most readers and critics it is White's record of church life and services as an insider which is of special note. Here, surely, his credentials as a witness are impeccable (with occasional recognition that his later estrangement may have coloured his account); 'when he describes Dissent he speaks with the initiate's authority; if anyone could understand nineteenth-century Dissent it should be Hale White'.[99] White does speak with authority, but with partiality too. Cunningham recognises that 'personal knowledge may sometimes generate very subjective estimates', and therefore be misleading when extended beyond the specific bounds of that experience.[100] He questions White's wider portrayal of Dissent, for it was not, as his view suggests, divorced from the social and political issues of the age, but accepts that in respect of Bedford, because of personal knowledge, he can be trusted.

In fact White has maligned the reputation of Bunyan Meeting and its minister. 'Big, gross-feeding' John Broad in the *Revolution* is a misleading caricature of John Jukes (in post 1840-1866), as at least one person with some personal knowledge declared; 'Jukes, being devoid of imagination and humour, was just the sort of man to excite Rutherford's lively pen; but, all the same, he did good work in his sturdy, solid way'.[101] This writer further declares 'the Dissenters were active', and instances the Bedford Training College run by Jukes and William Alliott (of Howard Chapel, the 'New Meeting').[102] Here between 1840 and 1866 more than a hundred students were trained for home missions and overseas, many on behalf of the London Missionary Society, a body with strong links to Congregationalism. This gave the church a pronounced missionary interest barely noted in the novels, with just the briefest of references in the *Revolution*.[103] The Society was also particularly important

---

[99] So Cunningham, *Everywhere Spoken Against*, p. 252. Ironically, if White was never baptised, or even took Communion (as will be argued below), he was an 'initiate' only in the limited sense of formal membership and attendance.

[100] *Everywhere Spoken Against*, p. 264.

[101] *Revolution*, p. 252, Ch. XVII; kinder verdict by Wright, *Life*, p. 31. Jukes has also suffered from comparison with his energetic long-serving successor John Brown (Minister 1864-1903).

[102] Wright, *Life*, p. 31. Alliott came of a family of ministers, and his brother Richard (1804-1863), an early reader of Schleiermacher, taught in Congregational colleges for many years; see Alan P. F. Sell, *Hinterland Theology: A Stimulus to Theological Construction* (Milton Keynes: Paternoster, 2008), pp. 187-224.

[103] *Revolution*, pp. 252, Ch. XVII; 'young men whom Mr Broad prepared to be missionaries', reinforcing the identification of Broad with Jukes. A slighter reference is found on p. 255, same chapter.

for the church of George MacDonald's childhood, and was responsible for sponsoring that congregation's James Legge for service in China.[104]

Although a memory of collection by missionary boxes appears in the *Early Life*, there is no mention of the training college, despite the known friendship between White and some of those who received instruction there, such as Samuel Whitmee, later of Samoa.[105] His own cousin, William Chignell, attended the college before entering the home ministry.[106] The effect of this institution on the life of Bunyan Meeting was profound, reinforced by marriages contracted between students and members of the congregation, which ensured regular visits by ex-students on furlough. The memoirs of several missionaries record their appreciation of the teaching received in Bedford, including John Smith Moffat and John Mackenzie of Southern Africa, and Griffith John of China.[107] This was not a sleepy, cut-off place, but one demonstrating an intimate connection with the furthest corners of the earth; 'essentially a missionary church. Its interests were spread nearly all over the globe'.[108] And yet White writes as if even London was a world away.

Bunyan Meeting stood out. Through the link with its most famous member it was well-known outside Bedfordshire. Within the county easily the wealthiest nonconformist church, it was also, like Tanner's Lane, 'the centre of the Dissenting activity for a whole district'.[109] For all the possible disadvantages under which Dissenters laboured there is little evidence from Bedford that these greatly affected everyday life. This was partly because of the Meeting's fame and history, but also a tribute to its very large congregations. In Bedford more people attended services there on Census Sunday in 1851 than any other single church, and the nine nonconformist churches together, for the morning service,

---

[104] MacDonald's church background is compared more fully with White's below; see pp. 161-164.

[105] *Early Life*, p. 25, the encounter between Samuel Lovell and young Keziah Fitchew. Whitmee recorded visits from White and his father; see transcripts in H. G. Tibbutt, 'From Stagsden to Samoa', *Bedfordshire Magazine*, 2 (1968), pp. 192-196 (p. 193).

[106] Later leaving Congregationalism for the freer atmosphere of a Unitarian pulpit in Exeter.

[107] For example R. U. Moffat, *John Smith Moffat, C.M.G., Missionary: A Memoir* (London: John Murray, 1921), pp. 33-34; W. D. Mackenzie, *John Mackenzie: South African Missionary and Statesman* (London: Hodder and Stoughton, 1902) pp. 21-27; R. W. Thompson, *Griffith John: The Story of Fifty Years in China*, Popular edition, (London: Religious Tract Society, 1908), pp. 22-29.

[108] The claim in *The Story of the Life of John Ashton ("Bishop of Stagsden")* (Bedford: H. Burt, 1904), p. 15. Ashton, born 1835, was son of the chapel-keeper at Bunyan Meeting in Hale White's youth.

[109] Tibbutt cites income from the 1873 Returns of Owners of Land; *Bunyan Meeting*, pp. 75-76; quote from *Revolution*, p. 251, Ch. XVII.

attracted twice as many worshippers as the six Anglican churches.[110] The Meeting was rebuilt during White's youth and in 1851 could accommodate a congregation of nearly 1,200. If the number present on Census Sunday was typical (as Jukes declared in his returns) then the church attracted around 10% of the town's population. Some worshippers travelled in from surrounding villages, but equally a number Bedford residents went out to nearby chapels which the Meeting 'supplied' and supported.

It is impossible to be certain how many individuals are represented by the Census figures. Excluding children they show 850 attending in the morning, 400 in the afternoon and 900 in the evening. Horace Mann, the Registrar General's agent responsible for the count, assumed as his working model (on no very sound statistical basis) that half an afternoon congregation were not morning attenders, and a third of the evening number had not been present earlier in the day; applying his formula to the Meeting figures gives a total of 1,350 individual worshippers. Despite the poor theoretical foundation of this method, an alternative calculation based on the ratio of attenders to members suggests a similar result. Exact membership figures are often unclear, but in 1866, at Jukes's death, the number was said to be 420.[111] Peter Yalden has collected figures showing that Congregational and Baptist churches had ratios of adherents to members from 3.07 to 4.79, and if these figures are slightly inflated by his methodology, as he believes, even at the lower ratio of 3:1 a membership of over 400 at Bunyan Meeting would suppose an attendance of around 1,200.[112] As Matthiason had noted, here old Dissent had a 'secure and extensive footing'.[113]

This church and its adherents could not be on the fringes of the life of a town where they had such a strong representation, and to the extent that White's writings suggest marginalisation they must be challenged. There is also silence about its importance beyond Bedford. At the level of families there were some significant wider connections which are missed. White's maternal grandfather's family, the Hales of Colchester (hence his middle name) were related to the Everard family (then of London) into which John Brown, minister of Bunyan 1864-1903, married in 1857. Their first child married John Neville Keynes and

[110] Figures (excluding Sunday school attendees) from D. W. Bushby, *Bedfordshire Ecclesiastical Census, 1851*. Problems over the accuracy and interpretation of data from this Census are not such as to undermine this evidence of nonconformist strength, based here for comparison simply on adult morning attendance.

[111] Tibbutt, *Bunyan Meeting*, p. 53.

[112] 'Association, Community and the Origins of Secularisation: English and Welsh Nonconformity, c.1850-1930', *Journal of Ecclesiastical History*, 55 (2004), 293-324 (p. 301). Watts, *Dissenters, vol. II*, has some further evidence, and ratios which suggest that 3:1 is a conservative estimate, pp. 671-675; his methodology (main service attendance plus one third of the others combined) gives a figure of 1,283 for Bunyan Meeting.

[113] *Bedford and Its Environs*, p. 78.

the young John Maynard Keynes played in the manse garden in Dame Alice Street.[114]

Given the special case often made for White as one uniquely well placed to chronicle the inside life of Dissent these discrepancies give pause for thought. White unfairly depicts Bunyan Meeting through his novels as a backward-looking and unchallenging congregation with few indications of spiritual depth. Signs of life and activity have been suppressed, and there are only the very slightest references to the training college.[115] It seems that the mature White regretted an over-hasty dismissal of the spirituality practised by the church and congregation of his youth. This is especially evident in the *Early Life*, but even in the *Autobiography*, there are points to celebrate; 'religious education' on the seriousness of sin was a strong incentive to 'purity of life', 'a simply incalculable gain', which no secular equivalent could have provided.[116] This education was naturally derived from parents as well as church, for the life of the family within the wider church was strongly emphasized in Dissent, and the nature of White's home life will need to be assessed.[117]

When examined below in the context of his spiritual progress the description of early inchoate faith will be seen to have been strongly coloured by the post-expulsion perspective of the writer. In essentially denying any real spiritual enlightenment during his time at Bunyan Meeting, White over-lays material which suggests just such experience. For example, he must show the falsity of the declaration of faith made for membership in February 1848, while at the same time admitting that it did then mean something to him.[118] The incident and its importance will be examined separately, along with evidence of William White senior's commitment to Bunyan Meeting.

Beyond Bedford: A Clerk's Life

It is not only in respect of Bedford that White's writing can be compared with external sources in order to weigh his representation against others. The test can be extended to his early working life in London as illustrated in the fiction and his newspaper columns. Given how little is otherwise known of White's office labours this undertaking has a value of its own in further contextualising his life.

Descriptions in the *Deliverance* of a clerk's intolerable working conditions

---

[114] Relationships traced by Neville Brown, *Dissenting Forbears: The Maternal Ancestors of J.M. Keynes* (Chichester: Phillimore, 1988), p. 3, and family tree on end-papers.
[115] As already cited above, *Revolution*, pp. 252, 255, Ch. XVI.
[116] *Autobiography*, p. 8, Ch. I.
[117] See chapter five below.
[118] *Autobiography*, pp. 9-11, Ch. I, and parallel account in *Early Life*, pp. 56-59. Date from Bunyan records, cited in Cunningham, *Everywhere Spoken Against*, p. 250, note 3.

are taken by biographers to reflect White's experience at Somerset House after his appointment to the Registrar General's Department in 1854, and later work in the same building for the Admiralty.[119] The issue was highly topical, this date coinciding with a review of the government service which recommended significant changes in recruitment and working practices, an important stage in the creation of a recognisably modern Civil Service.[120] Public debate decried the evils of patronage, sinecures and inefficiency in government offices, topics also famously addressed in the fiction of Dickens and Trollope, both writing in the 1850s from personal experience.[121]

Although adequate first-hand accounts from those at the most junior grades are lacking it is possible to reconstruct something of a clerk's life in the Civil Service. One challenge to reliably illuminating White's situation lies in his transfer from the General Register Office to the Admiralty in 1859, for despite some common factors across the service conditions were far from uniform. The influence of individual managers could also make a considerable difference to the prevailing culture. Mark Rutherford's employment is not identified by department or location, and must be assumed to represent aspects of the writer's experience in both the Admiralty and Register Office without differentiation. Office life is only portrayed at the lowest ranks, and does not therefore reflect White's promotion in the Admiralty during which his working conditions and pay steadily improved. The artistic demands in telling Rutherford's story justify this, while Hale White's move to the Admiralty which initially entailed a further period as a third-class clerk must have given him an affinity with those trapped at the bottom. Nevertheless, his depiction is a little overly negative.

The General Register Office, Somerset House

Hale White owed his place to patronage, still the commonest route to such employment.[122] Members of Parliament and office-holders were constantly begged to exercise influence on behalf of constituents, family and friends. In this instance 'Mr Whitbread obtained for me a clerkship in the Registrar-

---

[119] 'The Admiralty' is convenient shorthand for all the sections responsible for naval administration, which operated under different names and through different structures over the years; it is the term White generally uses.

[120] The famous Northcote-Trevelyan Report, completed November 1853 and published in 1854.

[121] For Dickens, see *Little Dorrit*, Ch. X (published serially 1855-57, and in one volume, 1857); for Trollope *The Three Clerks*, especially the first two chapters (published in three volumes 1858; the single volume 1859 edition omits the original chapter XII of volume two, essentially a treatise on civil service reform).

[122] And not *necessarily* always an evil; at best a sponsor would be guarantor for the character and suitable experience of the candidate.

General's office, Somerset House'.[123] (Hale's move to the Admiralty was again said to have been due to patronage, though the details are less clear.[124]) At the top no less than at the bottom personal connections counted. The Registrar General in White's time, George Graham, was appointed in 1842 by his brother the Home Secretary. The department had been created under the Registration Act of 1836, and so did not have the long traditions which shaped the practices and ethos of some other offices of state. Somerset House itself accommodated many historic departments, including the 'Weights and Measures' and 'Internal Navigation' described by Trollope, and more significantly the Navy Office and the Exchequer.

The principal rooms on the north front overlooking the Strand had been designed for the Royal Academy and the Royal Society, but the removal of the former to a wing of the just completed National Gallery allowed the evolving University of London to be housed there from 1836. When space was required for the Register Office in 1853 the university was in turn forced to find alternative premises in Marlborough House. This means that White's first clerical duties were probably at least partly undertaken in a suite of rooms he had previously visited as a student under the regulations requiring him to sign the university register held there. The Navy had had offices in Somerset House since its rebuilding largely for that purpose at the end of the eighteenth century.[125] They occupied much of the eastern side, and part of the river frontage. However competition for space between and within departments, leading to frequent changes in the apportionment of rooms, makes it impossible to establish for certain where White spent his working hours, and therefore to determine which offices might approximate to his description in the *Deliverance* of being 'shut up in a room half below the ground'.[126]

The architect responsible for the new building had planned for each

---

[123] As described in the *Early Life*, p. 88. Samuel Whitbread (the third of that name) was one of Bedford's two MPs.

[124] Robert Theobald suggested that it was the influence of 'Edwin Reed' which secured White's Admiralty post, identifying Reed as the Chief Constructor of the Navy, but there is some confusion here. The Constructor was Edward J. Reed (1830-1906), and Edwin Reed was a Shakespeare scholar known to Theobald, who seems to be conflating the two men; '"Mark Rutherford": Some Reminiscences of Mr William Hale White', *Westminster Gazette*, 17 March 1913, p. 10. The importance of Theobald himself in White's story will become clear in due course.

[125] L. M. Bates chronicles the history of the building and its uses; *Somerset House: Four Hundred Years of History* (London: Frederick Muller, 1967).

[126] *Deliverance*, p. 103, Ch. VIII. Rutherford's reference to being able to see 'a clock within a hundred yards of my window' (p. 104) seems to confirm a semi-basement room, and *may* indicate the north front, in sight of the clock of St Mary le Strand. The University of London rooms appear to have been mainly on the first floor, but this does not preclude having ancillary accommodation above or below that level.

occupying office to have 'a vertical slice of the accommodation, extending through all six storeys - cellar, basement, ground, principal, attic and garret'.[127] The lowest of these was intended for the storage of public records. The basement storey was at varying degrees below ground level according to the slope across the site between the Strand frontage and the Thames (later work on the embankment has obscured some lower features of the river facade). So it is not impossible that White toiled in approximately subterranean conditions, or visited such areas during his time at Somerset House. Mark Rutherford shared space with three other clerks, and 'all four of us kept books or copied letters from ten to seven, with an interval of three-quarters of an hour for dinner'.[128] This sort of work is entirely consistent with the primary duties of civil service clerks in their early years of employment. Algernon West, who entered the Inland Revenue in 1851, remembered the 'strictly clerical and drearily monotonous' character of the job, from which his transfer to the Admiralty in 1852 brought no relief; as 'a junior clerk ... my duties were confined to index-writing and copying letters'.[129] Only in later reforms recommended by the 1874/5 Playfair Commission were clerks divided into two classes, one 'mechanical' to serve permanently in these lowly duties, and a higher, 'intellectual', selected for early advancement to more responsible tasks.

The hours which White describes may be less typical, for the standard was from ten until four, six days a week.[130] But at both the Register Office and the Admiralty longer hours were often required of staff at busy times. This was not true for some others in the same building:

> For years past the gentlemen in the Audit Office have been envied by their less fortunate brethren of the Admiralty and the other offices in Somerset House. Punctually at four o'clock, and at two o'clock on Saturdays do they close their doors, while their harder worked companions know no such luxury, but are obliged constantly to stay after official hours, often till late into the night, till the work is done.[131]

---

[127] As described in *Somerset House: Splendour and Order* (London: Scala Publications, 1990) by John Newman (p. 7). William Chambers was the architect.

[128] *Deliverance*, p. 103, Ch. VIII.

[129] *Recollections: 1832 to 1886* (London: Thomas Nelson and Sons, 1899), p. 63 and *Contemporary Portraits: Men of My Day in Public Life* (London: Thomas Nelson and Sons, 1924), p. 37, respectively. *Contemporary Portraits* was first published by T. Fisher Unwin in 1920.

[130] The Home Office clerks, by old-established custom, attended from 11 a.m. to 5 p.m.; see A. P. Donajgrodzki, 'New Roles for Old: The Northcote-Trevelyan Report and the Clerks of the Home Office 1822-48', in *Studies in the Growth of Nineteenth-Century Government*, ed. by Gillian Sutherland (London: Routledge & Kegan Paul, 1972), pp. 82-109 (p. 103).

[131] From Hale White's 'Metropolitan Notes', *Aberdeen Herald*, 5 October 1861, p. 4.

West recollected the clerks at Somerset House as the butt of jokes for their relatively short hours and supposed idleness; like the fountains in Trafalgar Square, 'they play all day from 10 to 4', though he denied that this was true of all.[132] The difference here partly consists in the demands specific to particular offices - the Audit department presumably less likely to face extraordinary pressures than the Admiralty, affected by constant re-organizations as well as the requirements of imperial foreign policy. This period was also one of great significance for technical and operational changes to the Navy. In 1878 a joint Treasury-Admiralty inquiry implementing the Playfair Commission recommendations decided that new entrants to the lower 'mechanical' division of clerks were to work a seven hour day, from ten to five, rather than six hours as before, confirming the normal pattern of hours in White's early years at Somerset House, whatever extra might sometimes have been demanded.[133] It was the strict division of labour between higher and lower clerks, and the purging of dead wood among established higher grade staff, which gradually allowed able men like White to be promoted more rapidly than when seniority of service alone had been the almost invariable rule. There had been sporadic attempts much earlier in the century by individual reformers to institute such changes, but it was many years before the basic principles were effectively put into practice across the chief offices of state.

The General Register Office faced its own cyclical stresses. George Graham, the second post-holder, had been determined to increase efficiency in the 1840s and 50s, a task made particularly difficult because he could not appoint his own staff, the power of nomination resting with the Treasury. The unsatisfactory character and work of some of the clerks, and their poor pay, 'resulted in an unusually rapid turnover of staff, and those that remained had to work so much overtime that they often injured their health'.[134] This situation could explain a memory of very excessive hours, transferred by White into Rutherford's story.

---

[132] *Contemporary Portraits*, p. 33. He reports, doubtfully, the rhyme's attribution to Thomas Farrer of the Board of Trade. West's *Recollections* show that he had to work hard as he rose through the service. However Clement Shorter was employed at Somerset House in the 1870s, also knew the verse, and recalled that the 'easy hours gave us more time to play … than I have ever had before or since'; *C.K.S.*, p. 33.

[133] Reforms described by C. I. Hamilton in 'The Difficulties of an Admiralty Reformer in the Later Nineteenth Century: The Case of E. N. Swainson', *International Journal of Naval History*, 7 (2008) <http://www.ijnhonline.org/volume7_number1_apr08/article_hamilton_apr08.htm> [accessed 8 March 2011]. Quotations below from this source refer to the unpaginated PDF version available at this address.

[134] From Edward Higgs' summary of Graham's evidence before the 1860 Select Committee on Civil Service Appointments, in *Life, Death and Statistics: Civil Registration, Censuses and the Work of the General Register Office, 1836-1952* (Hatfield: Local Population Studies, 2004), p. 75.

Demands for extra working were connected with efforts to reduce the delay in publishing up-to-date statistics in the Annual Reports of the Registrar General, which had been particularly acute in the years immediately before White's appointment. The full report for 1848, for example, was not in print until 1852.[135] Outsiders clearly did not always link Somerset House with hard work and long hours, for in 1855 a struggling George MacDonald wished for a post there, believing that it would 'leave me time' for writing and preaching.[136]

It is highly unlikely that clerks under Graham's vigilant supervision would have had to endure the abusive treatment that Mark Rutherford describes, which might therefore be better understood as expressing in a more extreme form the humiliation Hale White felt at the constraints this employment placed upon him. Stress was certainly present. The office death of Mark Rutherford from heart failure after a particularly unpleasant encounter with his tyrannical manager may owe something to the case of a clerk "seized with mania" at his desk, who had to be admitted to an asylum. The incident was reported by the Registrar General as an instance of the harm done by frequent overwork.[137] Elsewhere White refers ironically to the 'precious quill-drivers' in that department who earned £150 a year (and who must therefore have been juniors), working 'weary hours from ten to four', suggesting that not all sections came under the pressures that required overtime.[138]

The lot of junior clerks was exacerbated by the difficulty of securing promotion and thus increased pay. Length of service was normally the key qualification for higher posts, and the route could effectively be blocked when more senior staff remained in post for many years. Eventually length of service itself was rewarded by regular salary increases, reducing resentment amongst those denied advancement. These uncertainties could have been among the factors which prompted Hale White to augment his income through journalism, and in one column he addressed the poor pay and prospects of clerks:

> Lord Derby and the *Pall Mall Gazette* have done good service in attempting to dissuade fathers and mothers from choosing the Civil Service as a profession for their children. ... Just let us see what a clerkship in an average office really

---

[135] Higgs discusses this problem, and tabulates delays; see *Life, Death and Statistics*, pp. 51-54. The time-lag became less over the years; White's 'London Letter' in the *Norfolk News* for 26 October 1872 (p. 5) noted the publication of the 1870 Annual Report within two years.

[136] In a letter to his wife, 14 July 1855, in G. E. Sadler (ed.), *An Expression of Character: The Letters of George MacDonald* (Grand Rapids, MI: William B. Eerdmans, 1994), p. 94. It is not impossible that he knew something of White's situation there, but this cannot be proved.

[137] See Higgs, *Life, Death and Statistics*, p. 75 for the original incident; compare *Deliverance*, p. 128, Ch. IX.

[138] 'Metropolitan Notes', *Aberdeen Herald*, 24 May 1862, p. 4.

> means. ... There is an office with which I used to be familiar years ago, which may be regarded as a tolerably fair specimen of the great bulk of departments at Somerset House and Whitehall. The clerks are divided into three classes. There are a certain number of juniors at salaries ranging from £90 to £220, about half that number of seniors with salaries ranging from £220 to £350, and then there are three or four superintendents who take from £400 to £500. The clerk who is now at the top of the junior list has been in the service about eighteen years. He may remain there a couple of years more, so that after twenty years' service he will receive £220 a year, advancing by an annual rise of £10 a year to £350. [139]

A little further indirect evidence on lowly workers in the Victorian office can be gleaned from characters encountered in the *Deliverance* Drury Lane project. The example of the 'young man named Clark' who copies addresses all day long 'in a house in Fleet Street, which did a large business ... in sending newspapers into the country' may be derived from personal knowledge picked up by White in connection with his time at Chapman's, or through his journalistic work.[140] Here the conditions are depicted as worse than in the public service, being overcrowded and unhealthy. Names are often significant in the fiction, and 'Clark' may stand for all clerks - it is notable that Rutherford sees his own introduction to office life as patterned after Clark's.[141] Another man aided in Drury Lane is found a position at Somerset House, but at the lowest level, as a porter carrying coals from the cellars. Suffering much under the casual mistreatment of the messengers his life was clearly significantly harder than anything White endured there, but it may be personal knowledge of such hardship which finds its way into his descriptions of Mark Rutherford's office years.[142] There is no record in White's other writings (personal or published) to suggest that he had personally borne such abuses. The common thread in these stories from Drury Lane is the misery of the sensitive soul in reduced circumstances forced to rub up against the coarseness of the less-educated, and with no alternative but to bear their harsh lot, which may traced to the writer's own experience.

This examination shows that in his fiction White has represented common

---

[139] 'Metropolitan Notes', *Aberdeen Herald*, 4 November 1871, p. 5. He excluded the Treasury and Foreign Office because their higher salaries and status made entry particularly difficult, and the Post Office and Customs, since their clerks were 'exceptionally indigent'. The Register Office had several sub-departments, and the total staff levels were higher than the figures given here. The *Pall Mall Gazette* had published articles in favour of civil service reform, also supported by Lord Derby. A piece in the *Nonconformist* of 28 August 1872 reiterated advice to parents against seeking civil service careers for their children (p. 890).

[140] *Deliverance*, pp. 77-80, Ch. V.

[141] 'his [Clark's] experience became mine'; *Deliverance*, p. 103, Ch. VIII.

[142] *Deliverance*, pp. 65-70, Ch. V.

aspects of a clerk's life in the mid-1850s, with the caveat that the bullying to which Mark Rutherford is subjected by 'the deputy-manager, who was the terror of the place' is less well attested, and that long hours were not universal.[143] As with consideration of the fictional material which relates to Bedford, the author's freedom to recast episodes from life must be respected. There is no requirement for the fiction to be historically reliable, and the reader and critic have no responsibility to take it as such. Some divergences from White's own career cannot be guessed, for example that from 1869 he no longer worked in Somerset House, but as part of the new Contract and Purchase Department, along with many other staff, had been transferred to one of the Admiralty's Whitehall buildings during the reorganisation under H. C. E. Childers.[144] The various literary accounts are clearly less than fully representative of his own experience, but the different context of Mark Rutherford's life does not lead the reader to expect such concurrence. A degree of artistic heightening for effect is not therefore essentially misleading.

At the Admiralty: Progress and Reform

These fictional references to the beginnings of his service career make the lack of comparable knowledge of his later work the more regrettable, though something of the context can be learned from the experiences of others. The major biographical studies of White are largely silent on the detail, but there must be more to be said about his time at the Admiralty. Maclean relates something of his sense of duty, the vigilance of his dockyards inspections, the care taken over his work, a particular responsibility for patents, and the trust superiors increasingly placed in his judgement, though as usual without full references.[145] These were important years for all the offices of state, as older patterns of working were gradually being supplanted by practices which rewarded ability and limited the previous advantages of patronage and promotion by seniority of service. It was still almost inevitable at the beginning of this period that a man of good family like Algernon West would prosper. Such advantages were not essential however, and like White others from humbler origins could rise to positions of considerable responsibility, a process which became easier as the century progressed.

---

[143] *Deliverance*, p. 104, Ch. VIII.

[144] As the Admiralty's *Navy List, Corrected to the 20th December, 1869* shows (London: John Murray, 1870), p. 256. Another new broom, the able and energetic Admiralty Parliamentary Secretary W. E. Baxter, outlined the changes in the House of Commons in July that year. According to Maclean, Baxter hand-picked White for the contracts post, p. 187. N. A. M. Rodger has a map showing how the Admiralty offices in Whitehall expanded into adjoining buildings to accommodate transferred staff; *The Admiralty* (Lavenham: Terence Dalton, 1979), penultimate plate between pp. 84-85.

[145] Maclean, pp. 260-264.

From slightly earlier exists the testimony of Thomas Collings, who entered the Accountant-General's department as a third-class clerk in 1833 after many years at naval stations overseas.[146] Collings, already an experienced book-keeper and storesman, did not hide his impatience with colleagues, and in their eyes was evidently something of a martinet, even seeking to intimidate his superiors if work seemed sloppy to him.[147] His duties at Somerset House were interrupted by a posting to Malta, but he returned in 1841, initially as a first-class clerk in the Storekeeper General's office, but then again to the Accountant-General's department in 1843. Among his later responsibilities there was the interviewing of new clerks, raising the possibly that it was he who inducted Hale White to the department; he must certainly have known him.[148] The *Navy List* for 1859 shows that he was then the most senior member of staff below the Accountant-General himself, for whom he deputised during the latter's extended sick leave that year.[149] Collings' intemperate memoranda about the failings of others made him too many enemies, and in 1860 he was unwillingly eased into retirement.

The strictness which could mark rising men is hinted at in some memories from Hale White's juniors, one of whom summed him up as 'a hard nut'.[150] He did not apparently arouse the deeper resentment which found particularly spectacular expression in the case of E. N. Swainson, another clerk from relatively modest circumstances, appointed in 1853.[151] A man of considerable ability, his work implementing Treasury-driven changes to working practices made him controversial and unpopular. In April 1885 he survived a bomb

---

[146] An account of his life was compiled from unpublished memoirs by his great-great granddaughter J. B. Hedderwick; *The Captain's Clerk* (London: Hutchinson, 1957). I have to thank Professor C. I. Hamilton of the University of Witwatersrand for drawing my attention to this source, and also for sharing his extensive knowledge of the Admiralty records at the National Archives. It seems certain that some of White's career could be traced there, but equally certain that this would be unlikely to shed much light on the personal life and beliefs which are at the core of this study.

[147] *The Captain's Clerk*, p. 203.

[148] *The Captain's Clerk*, p. 239. Hedderwick does not gives the dates during which Collings carried out the interviews, so it is impossible from this source to be sure. Another of the Collings family, Joseph B.E.W. Collings, later worked alongside White in the Purchase Department.

[149] *The Navy List, Corrected to the 20th June, 1859* (London: John Murray, 1859), p. 201; on his taking charge as 'Acting Accountant General', for six months, see *The Captain's Clerk*, pp. 243-244.

[150] Reported in Maclean, p. 262; summarising that 'by his subordinates he was regarded as a stern disciplinarian' (p. 261), reflecting something of his unbending nature.

[151] His story is told by C. I. Hamilton; 'The Difficulties of an Admiralty Reformer'. Starting as a third-class clerk, it took Swainson until 1870 to gain the first-class rank, showing how long this could take.

explosion in his Whitehall office, a device which had in all probability been intended to cause death or very serious injury and targeted at him personally.[152]

White's career, as far as it has been reported to date, seems uneventful by contrast, but he well illustrates the advancement possible even under the restrictions arising from entering the service at a time when 'the original sin of first appointment was all-powerful, and talent irrelevant'.[153] His progress from the lowest to the higher ranks was marked by ability, probity, and diligence, suggesting that it would be profitable to consider his career as that of an exemplary civil servant. A perception that only his work as a writer really matters (and possibly the volume of the surviving Admiralty records which would need to be investigated) may have deterred researchers from exploring this aspect of his life. It is unsurprising that men of his rank remain largely anonymous, for only now is a clear picture emerging of the level above, the Secretariat, and, however desirable, it would be a very considerable task to extend this to lower officials.[154]

'Little White Lies' - Does Accuracy Matter?

It might justifiably be claimed that the accuracy or otherwise of White's representation is irrelevant to his artistic achievement. The novels stand as an unparalleled evocation of place deeper than could be conveyed by any account of externals. It could further be argued that an expectation of verifiable correlation misunderstands the nature of these texts. Self-writing theories typically question the use of the genre as historical sources. White's method *is* perfectly valid. It is the readers and critics who take the fiction as history who allow themselves to be misled, compounded when his presentation of matters of belief is similarly accepted without question.

For in practice, regardless of the stance adopted, critics have assumed that Cowfold and its parallels faithfully represent the Bedford of the 1830s and 40s. If they have not done so explicitly, they have done so unawares by accepting the scholarly consensus of the chief critical biographies, which equate Rutherford with White and take for granted the fictional settings as in the main historically trustworthy. Using the major studies to verify the closeness of Rutherford's life and context to White's involves almost complete circularity of

---

[152] Hamilton has explored the incident in detail, and believes that other explanations – such as a random Fenian attack, or suicide bid – lack credibility; 'The Difficulties of an Admiralty Reformer', pp. 16-21 of an unpaginated PDF.

[153] As Hamilton puts it; 'The Difficulties of an Admiralty Reformer', p. 11 of an unpaginated PDF.

[154] C. I. Hamilton's *The Making of the Modern Admiralty: British Naval Policy-Making 1805-1927* (Cambridge: Cambridge University Press, 2011) is now the definitive guide to the nineteenth century Admiralty and its more senior staff.

argument. This makes it more difficult for readers of White to penetrate his multiple disguises - misled by novels *and* scholarship. Part of the reason for such a gap between representation and reality may be simple nostalgia, as Wilfred Stone suggests, heightened by London life, which initially at least White found so difficult.[155] There must have been a temptation to re-write the past in terms of his present, and portray an unattainable (and attractive) past, untroubled by the stresses and challenges of the present.

The nature of White's 'historical' record, including the possible limits of his recall as well as deliberate writing strategies, is relevant to analysis of the less easily tested areas of feeling and experience. If he is not to be trusted for the externals (presenting them to falsely align with inner feeling or a carefully re-imagined past) then the need for a more circumspect treatment of these other aspects is established.

In order to understand Hale White it is necessary to do more than explore the physical landscape and his wider social context. The novels themselves reveal the writer's engagement with and commentary on his personal setting. While not the main focus here their importance for comprehending White is not being denied. They dominate most studies of him and for that reason too need analysis. Judgements on factual questions are sometimes considered secondary when the novels take centre stage and are interpreted largely in terms of the 'message' they are presumed to contain. This plays an important part in the presentation of White as a religious doubter, and can be understood from a necessarily very brief summary of themes. To some extent this 'message' approach reads White in a time-limited fashion and does not do justice to a wider appeal to readers old and new. An attempt to go further still must then also be made, to distil - if possible - the essential features found broadly across all the novels which give them an appeal beyond any particular message. This *tour d'horizon* therefore builds on and complements the historical background already described.

Story not History? The Message of the Novels

It is becoming clear that extracting White's life from his writings is problematic. For some readers and critics this is of lesser importance than discerning the world view or ethical system which informs the novels (and other works). The tendency to identify this as a gradually evolving secularised account is associated with the loss of faith reading of White. A sketch of this supposed progress through his work will enable the outline of each novel to be introduced, inevitably omitting much detail. The positive statements of the *Early Life* can later be contrasted with an apparent regress from the life of faith in the novels.

---

[155] Stone, p. 149.

The *Autobiography* and *Deliverance* are typically bracketed out from the novels which follow because of the much more obvious alignment with the author's life, as if White wrote two volumes of autobiography before turning to works of fiction. The resemblance is closest in the *Autobiography* (1881) and it is useful to describe something of that life. The young Mark Rutherford follows a path very like White's from small town Dissent to training college, but differs in taking up a pastorate at Water Lane.[156] The spiritual experiences described are recognisably White's, from the encounter with Wordsworth to the depressing reception of his first attempts at preaching. Descriptions of the life and pettiness of the Water Lane congregation are famous, and true piety like that of the Misses Arbour was rare. Rutherford's thoughtful rarefied discourses are wasted on most of his hearers, and melancholia results. The pattern of White's thought is shaped by the need to seek the inner meaning of truths expressed in doctrinal forms. The secularist challenge of Edward Mardon brings Rutherford almost to destruction, with 'the dissolution of Jesus into mythologic vapour'.[157] A dispute with one of the Deacons, the 'contemptible' Snale, causes him to leave Water Lane, and reluctantly accept a post in the Unitarian chapel at 'D______' [Ditchling].[158] Equally unrewarding, this too is abandoned to seek work in London. Here Reuben Shapcott, the 'editor' of the novels is introduced as another ex-ministerial student. Work for the thinly-disguised John Chapman follows. The death of Mardon, and soon afterwards his daughter Mary, to whom Rutherford is attracted, closes the story.

The externals here are less important for the present purpose than the remorseless stripping away of almost all Christian faith ('emancipation' according to the chapter headings, compensated for by the experience of human love), with a poignancy which leads most readers to assume that Hale White had suffered similar loss.[159] This cannot be verified, though White is always reaching for meaning and experience over definition and dogmatising. In this way at least he is ready to question and reinterpret traditional language about belief. There is no trace of the secularist challenge to faith in the *Early Life*, nor can it be documented from other writings. It may have been imagined - feared - but not experienced.

The *Deliverance* (1885) which followed presented more of the supposed manuscript from which Shapcott brought the first book to press, with 'materials

[156] *Autobiography*, pp. 26-32, Ch. III.

[157] *Autobiography*, p. 54, Ch. V; compare *Robert Elsmere*, Ch. XXVI.

[158] See pp. 277-279 below on the Old Meeting at Ditchling, and note that many of the same intellectual currents (especially from Romanticism and the emphasis upon experience) were felt in Unitarianism as in other churches, and the formal differences are not to be exaggerated.

[159] Chapters seven and eight, the Unitarian pastorate. Emancipation may be from a false view of God (embodied in a coercive 'orthodoxy') towards a living God, rather than to unbelief.

which will enable me to represent [Rutherford] autobiographically in a somewhat different light to that in which he appears now'.[160] It will be a story of growth, though the nature of Rutherford's 'deliverance' is not entirely clear. The *locus* is now London, and Mark makes a living from journalism, while also testing his vocation further by opening the room on Drury Lane with M'Kay, a fellow writer. Practical help is there offered to the broken and oppressed. Rutherford marries Ellen, a 'simple' believer and contrast to his anxious searching. He supports Ellen and his step-daughter by enduring a degrading clerkship, resisting the brutalisation of his colleagues. His wife's death is followed shortly afterwards by his own, but not before the experience of 'actual joy' overtakes him during a Sunday excursion to the countryside. Spinoza had stressed joy as the highest spiritual experience. This may be the 'deliverance' of the title, though nothing in the text declares it to be so. Another vital lesson is that 'the very centre of the existence of the ordinary chapel-goer and church-goer needs to be shifted from self to what is outside self, and yet is truly self, and the sole truth of self'.[161] Shapcott closes the volume with his report of Rutherford's death at work from heart failure. The *Autobiography* and *Deliverance* were later (1888) published in one volume, as if representing a complete biography of Rutherford, but not before *The Revolution in Tanner's Lane* (1887) came from the press. Since Rutherford was already 'dead' by this time, the hand of Reuben Shapcott must again be seen, though apart from as 'edited by' on the title page his name does not appear and no preface or final notes are attributed to him as was previously the case.

The third novel appears to be two barely related stories set many years apart. The first is of Zachariah Coleman's participation on the edges of social unrest in 1814-16. Alienated from his wife in a cold marriage, his involvement with 'The Friends of the People' challenges conventional belief and morality. The sensual beauty of Pauline Caillaud is a reminder of White's awareness of unruly passions. The minister of Pike Street Meeting House, Thomas Bradshaw, represents radical Dissent, drawing on the figure of the Welsh preacher Caleb Morris.[162] The danger brought by his political associations causes Zachariah to flee London for Manchester, where support for the 'Blanketeers' protest brings more dangers. Imprisonment, the death of his wife, and marriage to Pauline, complete the story of a life always lived in an attempt to hold faith and action together. An apparently different story then unfolds in Cowfold, standing in many respects for the Bedford of White's youth. The ministry of John Broad at Tanner's Lane is quite unlike the prophetic one of

---

[160] *Autobiography*, p. 139, following Ch. IX.

[161] *Deliverance*, p. 87, Ch. VI; by which he appears to mean the eternal mind of a Spinoza-fashioned God.

[162] As will become clear, Morris was a significant influence on White; see for example pp. 219-222 below.

Thomas Bradshaw. George Allen's marriage to Priscilla Broad is a contrast to Zachariah's marriage, and his empty formal faith a weak echo of Zachariah's. The contrast is between radical puritanism and respectable Dissent turned in on itself. When the aged Broad is replaced by a young minister with a University of London degree the 'revolution' in puritanism has occurred, but with it the bankruptcy of modern nonconformity is complete.

White's next novel, *Miriam's Schooling* (1890), saw a complete change of focus, but not of location. Miriam Tacchi of Cowfold has an individuality which so often marks his female characters. She is self-originating, guided by no religious beliefs, and must learn to live in the present without drawing on any resources from the past (the contrast with Rutherford and Hale White is not to be missed). According to Lorraine Davies, this text exemplifies the progressive 'evolution from religious to human law' which she sees in the novels as a series.[163] Miriam 'had no religion, although she listened to a sermon once every Sunday'.[164] Her lack of a moral compass leads into destructive love for the worthless Montgomery, significantly encountered after moving to London, the secular city. Her awakening on a visit to Stonehenge suggests the mysterious power of the ancient stones and their natural setting. A return to Cowfold and marriage to Didymus Farrow does not solve her problems. The local Anglican clergyman, Armstrong, admires Didymus's practical woodworking skills, and introduces husband and wife to his special interest in astronomy (also White's). Seeing her husband's worth, and accepting the constraints of her life, is Miriam's schooling and salvation, a religion-less faith. Her story may at some points parallel the inner struggle of White's life.

Catharine Furze (1893) was a more substantial work, and again 'redemption' is the work of love, but not through marriage.[165] It is the means of Catharine's spiritual awakening and salvation, of which the Reverend Theophilus Cardew is the principal agent. And he too is saved - from a temptation towards unfaithfulness to his wife. As always, the pressures of mis-matched relationships also mark this novel. Locations are vital, especially the natural setting of Chapel Farm, but Catharine is never fully at home there, nor at the fashionable house in the Terrace upon which her mother insists. Ultimately, through Cardew's influence on her, and hers on him 'they were both saved', something which can still be described in traditional terms, 'the

---

[163] 'An Awkward Rectitude', p. 179.

[164] *Miriam's Schooling*, p. 62; nor any 'tradition, which often takes the place of religion' (same page).

[165] Vincent Newey has analysed (from a secularising perspective) the way in which salvation might here be understood; 'Mark Rutherford's Salvation and the Case of Catharine Furze', in *Mortal Pages, Literary Lives: Studies in Nineteenth-Century Autobiography*, ed. by V. Newey and Philip Shaw (Aldershot: Scolar Press, 1996), pp. 172-203.

disguises are manifold which the Immortal Son assumes in the work of our redemption'.[166] Fondness for such language is very much part of White's style.

With *Clara Hopgood* (1896), the story of two gifted sisters in Fenmarket, White gives his most intellectual novel, and one clearly drawing on his reading of Spinoza. The moral challenge represented by the portrayal of Madge Hopgood's seduction made it controversial at the time, even among readers loyal to White. For the writer it was an opportunity to reveal true rather than sham morality. Madge's later marriage to Baruch Cohen is facilitated by Clara, who then devotes her life (gains, and loses, it) to the Italian revolutionary cause.[167] Clara is forced to find work with a bookseller, where 'some heavy theology' in the shop window blocks out the sky, but when '*Calvin Joann. Opera Omnia, 9 vol. folio, Amst. 1671*' is sold 'a blessed star' is seen 'exactly in the gap the Calvin had left'; the Reformer is eclipsed by Spinoza.[168] The story emphasizes resignation and self-sacrifice, though this is not necessarily leaving Christian virtues behind. Clara's death for others echoes a deeper sacrifice; 'let us reverence also the Eternal Christ who is forever being crucified for our salvation'.[169]

In addition to the novels, several shorter writings explore similar themes, including some published within the same boards (short studies of Biblical characters prefacing *Miriam's Schooling*, and 'Michael Trevanion' concluding the volume, three short pieces with *Deliverance*, including 'Notes on the Book of Job'). Critics have advanced reasons which make these accompanying pieces appropriate to the texts with which they appear, but on the grounds already stated above it is possible that their inclusion was primarily to extend slim novellas to publishable length.[170] In which case it is possible that they were gathered together at short notice before publication, rather than crafted with the purpose of commenting on the texts alongside which they were printed.

It is not possible to do justice to the richness of these novels within the restrictions applying here (and readings are often contested), but in summary, though the later fiction increasingly explores the moral choices and world view of those without formal faith, this is not Mark Rutherford's world or Hale White's. It reflects White's fascination with the possibilities open to those who have been at best formal adherents rather than believers, and whilst set earlier in the century the social and intellectual context is that of the time of writing in

---

[166] *Catharine Furze*, p. 365, Ch. XXI.

[167] To which many nonconformists were sympathetic; see David Thompson, 'The Christian Socialist Revival in Britain: A Reappraisal', in *Revival and Religion since 1700: Essays for John Walsh*, ed. by J. Garnett and C. Matthew (London: Hambledon Press, 1993), pp. 273-295 (pp. 281-284).

[168] *Clara Hopgood*, p. 166, Ch. XVIII.

[169] *Clara Hopgood*, p. 298, Ch. XXIX.

[170] See above, pp. 25-30 on the publishing history.

the last decade of the century. White is not a child of this realm, though he skilfully presents it to the reader.

Looking at White in this way reveals something of his appeal to those who shared something of his Dissenting background or context, or found a particular resonance for other specific reasons. But an essentially descriptive approach does not go far enough to explain why he continues to find readers who have no obvious links with the culture he represents. A more analytical treatment can draw out some of the underlying themes found more or less consistently across the novels, attitudes to life which chime with the darker fears and feelings of a common humanity. These are what make White's novels accessible to modern readers, and by extension make his own life still of interest. Their key characteristic is the need for authenticity, a criterion relevant in due course to the discussion of his religious experience and beliefs.

White and the Modern Reader

Hale White's novels are concerned with the conduct of life. They address fundamental questions about behaviour in human relationships, especially between the sexes, inquire into the sources of moral authority, and weigh the claims of head and heart. Eschewing convention and the social demands of respectability White explores the beliefs which inform human actions and uncovers the tensions between theory and practice. Right choices, and the power to enact them, are at the centre of his writing, along with the sobering recognition that there are problems which cannot be solved and must be endured. The conflicting and even shameful human emotions which affect decision-making are skilfully exposed. These are features which make White's fiction continually valuable and significant.

While Spinoza had laid out a wholly abstract system, White's moral thinking is robustly embodied, initially in the life of Mark Rutherford from the *Autobiography* and *Deliverance*, and then through the characters and communities portrayed in the later books. These texts, Shapcott's editorial role reminds us, formally represent the manuscripts found after Rutherford's death, and, as the frequent authorial asides make clear, provide distillations of his experience. Selected references will provide an introduction to this aspect of White's fiction, a necessary reminder that alongside scholarly interest his writing still has relevance for thoughtful readers

White's narratives recognise that any workable ethic presupposes a shared human condition in which lessons learned can be applied beyond the single life in which they are first tested. This is also an antidote to harmful separation from society, for as Dr Turnbull warns Catharine Furze, 'nothing is more dangerous, physically and mentally, than to imagine we are not as other people', rather than 'a piece of common humanity and bound by its laws'.[171] Almost invariably such assertions address feelings to which Rutherford - by extension, White - is prone. Reuben Shapcott acknowledged that Rutherford emerges from the *Autobiography* as 'a mere egoist, selfish and self-absorbed'.[172] The originality which clearly typifies Catharine Furze is recognised, but for her own psychological well-being it must be safely channelled into 'an improved performance of what everybody ought to do' rather than 'the indulgence of singularity'.[173] The extension of the debate beyond the Dissenting community of the earlier fiction shows a determination to pursue an ethic which is potentially universal in application, and not restricted to a community of believers. This marks White's consciousness of a fragmentation in society under which previously shared values are questioned.

It was clearly easier to affirm a common humanity than to work effectively across class barriers. The Drury Lane experiment reveals the hope and limits of such a broad scope in its attempt to reach those at the lowest level of society brutalised and 'inaccessible to motives which act upon ordinary human beings'.[174] Based on work actually carried out by White, it demonstrated a courageous step beyond theorising about ethics, but also a near powerlessness to help. It highlights a focus upon the individual, for despite White's clear sympathy for social reform, in practice his ethic is a personal one and transformation must start with the individual. Character formation is more significant than political change. This is a natural corollary of the Christian moral tradition, and for this reason the novels involve the extension of fundamentally Christian values in a new form, and not their supersession.

An ethic can be commended by example or taught by illustration. Hale White first wrote in the hope that the record of his experience would be helpful. He had found consolation in 'the mere knowing that other people have been tried as we have been tried'.[175] This became the declared aim of the *Autobiography*, and the excuse for its publication by a writer uncertain of its value. Already this hints at a recurring theme in the novels, of the sensitive soul seeking reassurance in its solitude. Writing them under a pseudonym was White's paradoxical way of escaping from the isolation which resulted from his breach with the past and was compounded by the demands of his work and domestic circumstances.

That many readers did find solace is not in doubt, and specific instances have already been referred to in the writings of men as different in personality

---

[171] *Catharine Furze*, p. 334, Ch. XIX. Hale White's warning to himself also, for all too often he seemed to believe that he was made differently from other men.
[172] *Autobiography*, p. 139, postscript to the final chapter.
[173] *Catharine Furze*, p. 334, Ch. XIX.
[174] *Deliverance*, p. 65, Ch. V.
[175] *Autobiography*, p. 2, Ch. I.

as Willard Sperry, Middleton Murry, and H. W. Massingham. The key here was often a shared experience of the Dissenting world which White was held to have portrayed so faithfully. Such readers were not seeking answers to specific problems, but found reassurance in the knowledge that another had shared their perplexity. The common reader is an elusive figure who leaves little record compared with the critic or scholar, and it is correspondingly difficult to assess what the buyer or borrower of the Mark Rutherford novels found attractive or helpful. Given the range and 'openness' of these works it is likely that responses have been as diverse as the readers themselves. Nevertheless an attempt can be made to understand his appeal and identify key points at which, then as now, he challenges the reader.

Some themes are found across all his fiction, but there are significant differences between the first two novels, broadly described as spiritual autobiography, and the succeeding texts. The ruthless honesty which marks White's writing is most vividly displayed in the *Autobiography* and *Deliverance*. The reader is the privileged observer of Rutherford's mental and spiritual turmoil, which, it should be noted, is closely associated with his difficulty in leading others to a belief which he has not yet made real for himself. The crisis arises chiefly from this pressure, which accelerates to breaking point the otherwise healthy process by which inherited beliefs must be tested and personally appropriated. The stripping away of beliefs Rutherford has neither the intellectual nor spiritual resources to defend is painful for the reader to share, but creates a strong sympathetic bond with the writer, who modern readers have been trained to identify (with sometimes unhelpful consequences) as 'really' Hale White rather than Mark Rutherford. As a psychological drama Rutherford's story is accessible to all who find themselves between past certainties and the unknown future.

This is the potential for therapeutic effect which prompted publication; taking up the book becomes the equivalent of receiving a sympathetic caller; testimony to 'the healing effect which is produced by the visit of a friend who can simply say, "I have endured all that"'.[176] It is important not to mistake the nature of the spiritual struggle, which always takes place within a providential framework. Disturbed by his talks with the sceptical Mardon, and also realising that his romantic commitment to Ellen cannot be sustained, Mark is 'led past the house where the Misses Arbour lived' and 'some beneficent inspiration prompted' him to call.[177] Their meeting, which crystallises his decision to break the engagement, is typical of White's manner of setting out the conflicting views associated with right conduct, which often revolve around the poles of behaviour according to the rules of respectable society or from the dictates of conscience.

---

[176] *Autobiography*, p. 2, Ch. I.
[177] *Autobiography*, p. 59, Ch. V.

The sense of a guided life permeates the other novels, something which in *Catharine Furze* is given a universal context:

> We have discarded Providence as our forefathers believed in it; but nevertheless there is a providence without the big P ... yet surely deserving it as much as the Providence of theology, a non-theological Providence [therefore White reclaims the capital 'P'] which watches over us and leads us. It appears as instinct prompting us to do this and not to do that, to decide this way or that way when we have no consciously rational ground for decision ... it has been recognised in all ages under various forms as Demon, Fate, or presiding Genius.[178]

There is a shape to the world, and forces which cannot be denied. Everyday circumstances limit moral choices and produce encounters which challenge the idea of human autonomy. It is also compromised by emotions which are stronger than the 'prompting' Rutherford describes above. To love and be loved is always represented as the highest good, but the difficulty of misdirected or unrequited feelings is poignantly displayed in every book. The head and the heart may be in conflict. The intellect seems barely able to control such strong desires, suggesting that least in this area White himself did not find in Spinoza the means of self-control which his philosophy seemed to promise. Catharine Furze and Clara Hopgood are each able in some degree to sublimate or transfer their feelings to a nobler cause, but this is attributed to the grace of God.[179] White's readers might be reassured that a pattern can be discerned in life, and that they were not simply the victims of purpose-less forces beyond their control.

Often it is the minor characters who exemplify the highest virtue, illustrated for example from *Miriam's Schooling*. It may originate with Christian faith, as in the case of Miss Tippit, or from human experience as with Mrs Joll, who 'was utterly unintelligent as far as book learning went [but] ... was well read in departments more important perhaps than books in the conduct of human life'.[180] White in this and other ways often indirectly apologises for his own bookishness, which implied a retreat from life. These instances demonstrate a fulfilling of the duty that lies nearest (which Carlyle had lauded in *Sartor Resartus*), and the appropriate sphere of usefulness is another question to which White returns time and again. While Miriam seeks to make atonement by training as a nurse, for which she is hopelessly unsuited, the wiser Miss Tippit has already learned that 'the man who thinks he will conquer a continent has to be content with the conquest of his own kitchen-garden, fifty feet by twenty'.[181]

---

[178] *Catharine Furze*, pp. 228-229, Ch. XII.

[179] *Catharine Furze*, p. 146, Ch. VIII; *Clara Hopgood*, pp. 283-285, Ch. XXIX.

[180] *Miriam's Schooling*, pp. 106-107; for Miss Tippit see for example, p. 115 (who like Mrs Joll 'never read' a book, p. 78).

[181] *Miriam's Schooling*, p. 123.

In *Catharine Furze*, Dr Turnbull praises Jane Cardew on these grounds, for while her husband is 'luxuriating amongst the cowslips, in what he calls thinking, she is teaching the sick people patience and nursing them'.[182] The Doctor holds a utilitarian view that 'our intellect is intended to solve real difficulties which confront us, and that all intellectual exercise upon what does not concern us is worse than foolish'.[183] This theme, possibly another self-directed rebuke by the writer, occurs elsewhere, as when George Allen, inspired by a line from Dr Johnson, 'reflected that he, an ironmonger's son, was not born to save the world' but must be content with the fulfilment of nearer duties.[184] Rutherford's fictional editor Reuben Shapcott had come to a similar conclusion. In a preface to the second edition of the *Autobiography* he decried 'the danger and the folly of cultivating thoughts and reading books to which he [Mark] was not equal, and which tend to make a man lonely', an effect all too evident in the life described.[185] A few great minds are called to higher tasks, but this carries a personal cost. Notwithstanding Shapcott's opinion that 'metaphysics, and theology, including all speculations on the why and the wherefore, optimism, pessimism, freedom, necessity, causality, and so forth, are not only for the most part loss of time, but frequently ruinous', Rutherford cannot refrain from exploring these issues.[186] At the same time, intuition, naïve wisdom, and experience prove to be best guides for many of his characters, who do not concern themselves with matters too great for them, but rather work out their own salvation. Truth is not abstract or theoretical, but essentially incarnational. Cowfold 'believed that flesh and blood, and not ideas, are the school and the religion for most of us, and that we learn a language by the examples rather than by the rules'.[187]

A reflective life has its own dangers. The process of comparing 'what we are with what we might be' is 'the spring which prompts all action', but carries with it the potential for permanent discontent.[188] Comparison with others causes exactly the same problem, and is equally liberating to relinquish. Fortunately, time is a great healer, and will 'cure so completely and so gently if left to itself'.[189] Some troubles can be avoided through recognition that we have no right to happiness, perhaps a subconscious release from interpreting circumstances as representing divine punishment or blessing.[190]

White is careful to address contemporary society, and this is particularly

---

[182] *Catharine Furze*, p. 335, Ch. XIX.
[183] *Catharine Furze*, pp. 332-333, Ch. XIX.
[184] *Revolution*, p. 355, Ch. XXV.
[185] A*utobiography*, p. vii.
[186] *Autobiography*, p. ix.
[187] *Revolution*, p. 241, Ch. XVI.
[188] *Deliverance*, p. 114, Ch. VIII.
[189] *Deliverance*, p. 115, Ch. VIII.
[190] A lesson from Job; 'Notes on the Book of Job', bound with *Deliverance*, p. 156.

noticeable in the last three novels, marked as they are by female subjects, and moreover ones who are not defined by their subordinate relationship to men. These texts appeared in the era of the 'new woman', a sign of the rapidly changing context of White's writing, though as with the earlier novels the historical setting itself is retrospective. In this significant shift from the life and personal perspective of 'Mark Rutherford' the world of Dissent, and of any organised religion, recedes into the background. However the key characters are originals (Miss Leroy is like 'an Arabian bird' in the farm-yard) who exhibit a strong innate spirituality.[191] The focus on morality remains. Indeed, *Clara Hopgood* shows the most sustained engagement with this theme, though it no more speaks with one voice than the volumes which precede it. Madge goes so far as to suggest that 'it is much more important to believe earnestly that something is morally right than that it should be really right', for inner disposition is the authentic criterion for action.[192] Abstract rules and boundaries do not fit with the disorderly realities of life. Despite the obvious nod towards Spinoza in the naming of Baruch Cohen there is little to suggest that this pivotal character can master his passions by following the 'adequate' ideas which the philosopher's system described. He falls in love with Clara 'suddenly and totally .... His tendency to reflectiveness did not diminish his passion: it rather augmented it'.[193] Of course this is not a passion he intends to avoid (though he later marries Madge), but he is equally unable to strengthen himself against a subsequent unwelcome reversal. Detecting a coolness on her part, he is plunged into 'a despair entirely inconsistent - superficially - with the philosopher Baruch'; these strong emotions suggesting that despite many years of study 'he was no better able than other people to resist temptation'.[194]

There has been a constant desire to identify from Rutherford's life or words particular issues and events which may be connected to Hale White himself. This is especially difficult when it comes to ethics however as contrasting and even conflicting attitudes are represented which may plausibly represent his own. In practice, views are often expressed in order to be tested and critiqued rather than recommended. For example, Madge's seducer, Frank Palmer, meets a friend in distress who concludes 'to what is inevitable we must submit'.[195] This seems in line with a stoic acceptance White often appears to advocate, but immediately its tendency towards fatalism is questioned; 'it seemed very

---

[191] *Deliverance*, p. 40, Ch. III; Pauline Caillaud is 'a wild seagull' in contrast to the 'peaceful, clucking, brown-speckled fowls' found in the Pike Street chapel (*Revolution*, p. 86, Ch. VI.)

[192] *Clara Hopgood*, p.171, Ch. XVIII. Compare Miriam Tacchi's lie which allows the hard-pressed Cutts to escape trial for arson; *Miriam's Schooling*, pp. 61-63.

[193] *Clara Hopgood*, p. 223, Ch. XXIV.

[194] *Clara Hopgood*, pp. 231, 233, Ch. XXIV.

[195] *Clara Hopgood*, p. 240, Ch. XXV.

philosophic to him [Frank], a maxim for guidance through life. It did not strike him that it was generally either a platitude or an excuse for weakness, and that a nobler duty is to find out what is inevitable and what is not'.[196] The Puritan habit of self-examination was not lost to White.

Marriage is a central preoccupation throughout the fiction, recognition that it represents a particularly testing moral environment. Here the demands of convention, duty and desire awkwardly coalesce. Conflicts between these could be treated with startling frankness, and not just in the decision of Madge Hopgood to bear Frank Palmer's child outside wedlock that offended some contemporary readers. On several occasions spouses mentally embrace other partners during moments of intimacy, possibly reflecting Hale White's own unsettling experiences of such emotional disturbance; 'though she [Miriam] yielded, it was not Mr Farrow who held her in his arms; she purposely strove to think an imaginary Romeo's head was on her neck - his face was something like the face of Montgomery - and she kept up the illusion all that night'.[197] Yet White acutely realises that such shortcomings need not be fatal, and Miriam becomes fully reconciled to her marriage.

Unions are not idealised, and White's mis-matched couples are famous. Zechariah Coleman's first months of marriage already suggest to him a terrible mistake, a loveless match in which he is condemned to be 'dead in half of his soul' and sustained only by the faith which fills 'the other half'.[198] The soul is notionally divided here because the love which should mark marriage is to be identified with the love of God. The point is stressed in *Clara Hopgood*:

> 'No man', said Baruch once 'can love a woman unless he loves God'. 'I should say', smilingly replied the Gentile, 'that no man can love God unless he loves a woman'. 'I am right', said Baruch, 'and so are you'.[199]

Religious and secular viewpoints are complementary because all love originates in God. It therefore has a redemptive quality, and to act in accordance with love heals weaknesses large and small. Priscilla Allen dies with such final words to her husband, 'I am a poor silly girl, but I always loved you'.[200] Cardew and Catharine Furze are 'saved' by their resisted love.[201] These examples show that White's later close connection of the love of his second wife Dorothy Smith with the love of God does not mark a new departure.

This emphasis was not unique to him. In the same spirit George MacDonald on his engagement to Louisa Powell had written to her of the common divine

---

196 *Clara Hopgood*, p. 240, Ch. XXV.
197 *Miriam's Schooling*, p. 131.
198 *Revolution*, p. 18, Ch. I.
199 *Clara Hopgood*, p. 223, Ch. XXIV.
200 *Revolution*, p. 360, Ch. XXV.
201 *Catharine Furze*, p. 365, Ch. XXI.

author of their human love, and his conviction that such true love would be a sacred bond even after death; 'I want to love you for ever - so that, though there is not marrying or giving in marriage in heaven, we may see each other there as the best beloved'.[202] Already here is also seen the sense of a thin veil between human life and the spiritual life of the future evident in his later thought. The wedding incidentally highlighted a closeness to Caleb Morris which mirrors White's. MacDonald had wanted the Welshman to conduct the ceremony in March 1851 (as earlier he had hoped he would conduct the Arundel ordination, though this had proved impossible) but Louisa had not taken to Morris, and in the end John Davies had performed the ceremony at the Old Gravel Pits Meeting House in Hackney.[203] His first book, the epic poem *Within and Without* published in 1855, further celebrated the divine qualities in human love.

The similarities between marriage and the life of faith represented by White can be pressed a little further. Both rely on an inner commitment which is not to be confused with outward signs or mere habit. For example, Miss Leroy daringly suggests that marriage is the *recognition* of a bond which has already been formed, for she 'told a male person once ... that if she loved him and he loved her, and they agreed to sign one another's foreheads with a cross as a ceremony, it would be as good to her as marriage'.[204] Correspondingly for faith, the formal and ritual aspects of church life are unimportant compared with the disposition of the heart, and some of White's best Christians remain sturdily independent of outward forms (as White has his own reasons for depicting them). Miss Leroy is a constant reader of her Bible, 'had no sceptical doubts', but remained suspiciously autonomous and could not be fitted into any of Cowfold's narrow categories.[205] Mrs Butts, who, distressed by her husband's infidelity, 'laid hold ... upon heaven', is contrasted with formal religion and 'the natural man, the man of this century, uncontrolled by Christianity', who sets his own standards.[206] As elsewhere, the recurring theme of marriage suggests a focus upon the individual, though for almost every ethical strategy or opinion in the novels it is possible to find an alternative voice.

White can at times be painted as a radical who painfully recognises his own timidity and vested interest in the *status quo*. Discussion of a Chartist meeting addressed by Henry Vincent, who is regrettably 'middle-class to the backbone',

---

[202] Letter of 23 October 1848, in Sadler, *An Expression of Character*, p. 26.

[203] Ordination details given by his son Greville; *George MacDonald and His Wife*, pp. 141-142; for the marriage see p. 151.

[204] *Deliverance*, p. 32, Ch. III; wittingly or not this simply repeats the position of church and state since at least the twelfth century that *consent* makes marriage.

[205] *Deliverance*, p .35, Ch. III (no plaster saint though, being intolerant and unwilling to visit the sick).

[206] *Deliverance*, pp. 60-61, Ch. IV.

becomes the occasion for ridiculing a gradualist approach with its talk of 'the inefficiency of merely external remedies, the folly of any attempt which does not begin with the improvement of individual character'.[207] The advocates of mass action are however revealed to be out of touch with the suffering poor they purport to help, and equally tied to a dogmatic approach. In these ways the complexity of moral decision-making is repeatedly illustrated. While the past can be imaginatively ordered as 'part of a divine picture' the same can only be partially realised in the present; 'we *can* do something, if we try'.[208]

This sketch of the novels can only introduce the importance of the moral stance of White's writings, which are more intricate and nuanced than such a survey can reveal. The narrative form lends itself to the examination of issues from different perspectives, and clearly there are no simple rules to be extracted. They can best be described as representing situation ethics informed by personal responsibility and an applied, non-dogmatic, Christianity. Indeed they are inexplicable without taking the religious background into proper account, and that White intended a lively challenge to the reader is clear.

Summary

It has been too easy for the qualities and dramatic voice of the novels to overwhelm other sources on Hale White. For good reason they continue to find readers, but here they will now be put a little to one side to allow those other voices - especially the *Early Life* - to be heard. The review of previous studies has shown how unsatisfactory it is to rely on the fiction for a reconstruction of their author's life or beliefs, and some of the same difficulties of content and interpretation exist with the *Early Life*. The comparison with other sources on Victorian Bedford shows that White's writings should not be taken on trust as historically accurate. While there is no simple means by which any of his work can be persuaded to render up wholly reliable information, self-writing theory can help, along with the use of other corroborative sources. This is not to ignore the strictures of critics such as Salgado and Brookes who have argued for the artistic integrity of the novels. However like all others they in practice read with pre-existing knowledge or assumptions about White's life which play a key part in analysing the texts. Starting from the *Early Life* allows a new way of approaching White, but this requires a sensitivity to genre which has been absent from earlier uses of this memoir.

---

[207] *Clara Hopgood*, pp. 249-250, Ch. XXV.

[208] *Revolution*, p. 245, Ch. XVI (original italics).

CHAPTER 4

'All autobiographies are lies'
The Nature of the *Early Life*

'All autobiographies are lies'; so George Bernard Shaw described the inevitable result of writing about oneself. No-one could be 'bad enough to tell the truth about himself during his lifetime' or 'good enough to tell the truth to posterity'.[1] Through his novels White had the chance to address his contemporaries anonymously while still alive. The 'Autobiographical Notes' which became the *Early Life* he knew would not appear until after his death. This gave an opportunity to unburden himself in a way that he might otherwise have found impossible. It did not necessarily lead to a straightforwardly perspicuous text, and an understanding of the origins, form, and writing of the *Early Life* is essential to a proper analysis of its content.

Nature and Purpose of the 'Autobiographical Notes'

According to the foreword by his eldest son, White's 'Autobiographical Notes' were intended as a private family memoir of his father's young life. It seems that Hale had already rejected an invitation (probably from Robertson Nicoll) to 'write a full history of his own life' on the grounds that it was 'impossible' for him to do so, and as he candidly admitted, unappealing because it would bring no personal financial gain.[2] Among other issues this probably reflects unwillingness to describe his first marriage and family life. In addition to his own reserve (lacking, as he said, Rousseau's 'shamelessness') he was sensitive to the need to protect others; 'the difficulty is to be faithful without saying what may give pain'.[3] Despite the author's final caveat that this abbreviated record

---

[1] 'In the Days of my Youth', first published in T. P. O'Connor's magazine under the title 'M.A.P.' (Mainly About People), reprinted in *Sixteen Self Sketches* (London: Constable, 1949), pp. 42-47 (p. 42).

[2] In a conversation reported by Nicoll, 'Memories of Mark Rutherford' in *A Bookman's Letters* (London: Hodder and Stoughton, 1913), pp. 364-412 (p. 376); White presumed publication would be posthumous, hence the lack of financial incentive.

[3] From a letter to Miss Edwards, 18 October 1907, seemingly a source for Nicoll, above, who appears to cite it *verbatim* at points, though without reference; University of Leeds, Brotherton Library Ms 11190-07.

was 'not written for publication' eventual wider dissemination must have been foreseen. The disclaimer is better understood as Hale White's chosen method of avoiding responsibility for a decision to publish, just as he had previously hidden the authorship of the novels. The 'Notes' duly appeared, within three months of White's death, under the title *The Early Life / of / Mark Rutherford / (W. Hale White) / by Himself.*[4] The manuscript bears the marks of revision and correction by the author, as if anticipating publication.[5]

Dorothy White has left a record of the circumstances in which the manuscript was handled after her husband's death:

> When the Autobiographical Notes were handed over to Molly, she was puzzled by the last sentence, whether it left her free to publish or not. I know that her father realised that these Notes would be published; that is to say, I had asked him to leave them to Molly, and one of the reasons I gave was that they would bring in a little addition to her income. I proved my intimate knowledge of the matter by laying my hands on them, before ever the lawyer came or the Will was opened, and giving them to Molly.[6]

Given the estrangement between Hale and his children of which she was the cause, the way in which Dorothy here showed her control over this record intended for the family must have been painful for them to read. It also demonstrates the children's lack of direct access to their father - that even Molly, sharing the same house, was quite unaware of the 'Notes' until Dorothy produced the manuscript.[7] Despite their origin in a request from Sir William it suggests that her brother was equally ignorant, for surely any such knowledge would have been shared with Molly. It is a reminder that the family increasingly kept away from Groombridge.

It was partly to provide earnings after his death that in retirement White had taken the trouble to have certain writings set up in type and plates run off for ease of publication. He later asked Dorothy to make arrangements for this when the time came, and to decide what to do with any remaining manuscripts.[8] His executors were to take care of the financial aspects, and distribute the income. This work had been put in hand in about 1905, and cannot have encompassed

---

[4] Published by Humphrey Milford, Dorothy's brother-in-law, at the Oxford University Press in 1913. The description 'by himself' on the title page is very common in Victorian autobiographical writing, especially that appearing posthumously.

[5] Controversial sections, such as the New College expulsion, are among the most altered.

[6] *Groombridge Diary*, pp. 484-485.

[7] 'I knew nothing of these notes until after my father's death'; from a letter to Humphrey Milford, dated 3 May 1913 (UBC, NCC 17-5).

[8] White confirmed his wishes in a letter to Dorothy of 12 April 1908; quoted in *Groombridge Diary*, p. 12.

the 'Autobiographical Notes', then unwritten, but the need to safeguard Molly's future was clearly dominant when they were composed. Dorothy had been asked to take on responsibility for the plates before there was any thought of marriage. That event, on 8 April 1911, naturally changed her position, and in a will dated 17 April 1911 Dorothy was granted the copyright of works in print and the right to publish and dispose of manuscripts as she thought fit. Molly was not forgotten however, and there was a caveat; 'except some autobiographical notes which I bequeath to my daughter Mary Theodora White as she has always lived with me'.[9]

What Sort of Record is the *Early Life*?

The author was aware of some difficulty over the nature of his memoir, evident in a letter to Sophia Partridge dated 4 June 1910:

> I am trying to scrape together for the benefit of my children all that I can recollect of my life from my earliest childhood to my marriage. How much is *wahrheit* and how much is *dichtung*? The afternoon and evening in and on the peace-fullest of rivers, the (to me) sacred Ouse! *Wahrheit* or *dichtung*? Both.[10]

The tension, between 'poetic' and 'historical' truth illustrated by Goethe's phrase accompanies any such attempt to accurately recall childhood. White's near contemporary Eliza Lynn Linton used the same words to describe her fictionalised self-revelation *The Autobiography of Christopher Kirkland*, a work dealing extensively with her formative years.[11] The distance between the time of writing and the events described is one factor compounding the problem. In White's case the vantage point is of relatively advanced old-age, and the existence of some carefully saved contemporaneous source material (primarily on the events of 1852) could only partly offset the disadvantage of passing years and few remaining living witnesses to the times. The role of memory is therefore crucial. Perhaps for this reason crafting the record seems to have been a slow and emotionally demanding task. Dorothy noticed and recorded the intensity of the times at which he sat at his table writing 'very slowly and carefully, usually on small scraps which he afterwards thrusts between the sheets of his blotting-paper. This morning twice whilst he was

---

[9] Quoted from a copy at Bedford (BPL, MR JHW 26). The will seems to be the origin of the designation 'Autobiographical Notes', which does not appear in the manuscript; later codicils modified this will, but not affecting his literary estate. 'JHW' denotes material deposited in Bedford by John Hale-White in 1988.

[10] Given in *Letters to Three Friends*, pp. 280-281. Original italics. Evidence that despite the signs of multiple revised endings he had always intended to stop at his marriage.

[11] G. S. Layard, *Mrs Lynn Linton: Her Life, Letters, and Opinions* (London: Methuen, 1901), p. vii.

writing he gave a sob, and was evidently feeling some emotion keenly as he wrote'.[12]

The work probably occupied White intermittently for much of 1910. Some sections in the *Groombridge Diary* appear to preserve evidence about the writing process, and a little can be gleaned elsewhere.[13] A starting date early in 1910 is suggested by the opening sentence - 'I have been asked at 78 years old to set down what I remember of my early life', he having reached this age in December 1909.[14] There are clear indications that he had begun gathering material that year, making entries in his notebooks in early August which can be traced through to the 'Autobiographical Notes'.[15] Other internal evidence is found in the explicit contrast between his home town in 1831 and 'the Bedford of 1910'.[16]

The manuscript can be assumed to have been in some more-or-less complete state by the time it was mentioned in the will of April 1911, in which case the opening line in all probability marks the first writing as continuous prose. Since the manuscript is in the form of single ruled sheets, without any sign of having been fixed together, it is impossible to be sure how much revision took place after the text was initially completed. Some sheets show no changes, while others are heavily corrected. The pagination has also been altered in White's hand, and there is no way of knowing if complete sheets have been re-written or removed.[17] It is sometimes possible to make out the reason for manuscript changes, which are often stylistic; in more substantial changes the original is scored out so thoroughly as to be unreadable.[18] The material was still only loosely gathered together, 'an unbound bundle of small octavo sheets', when

---

[12] *Groombridge Diary*, p. 325; on 18 March 1910, a date which ties in with the compilation of the Autobiographical Notes.

[13] See *Groombridge Diary*, p. 335, where Dorothy reports him in May 1910 writing about his father's life.

[14] *Early Life*, p. 5; supporting the reference cited above, letter of 4 June 1910.

[15] Dorothy dates this material against her own record of conversations which can be related to sections in the Notebook; *Groombridge Diary*, p. 204. These notebooks are now at British Columbia (UBC, NCC 2-11).

[16] *Early Life*, p. 13.

[17] There are also sometimes numbers alongside his in a probably female hand, though the whole final sequencing is his. Letters quoted in the text have been copied by someone other than White, who perhaps loosely inserted the originals between his numbered sheets. This copying-in naturally affected subsequent numbering. The copyist (most probably Dorothy or Molly) may not have known the purpose of their work; evidently Molly did not.

[18] Advanced techniques for reading palimpsests might reveal interesting material where there have been more substantial alterations, but the changes cannot be made out with the naked eye.

deposited in the British Museum in October 1936.[19] The published text follows the manuscript exactly.

The apparently straightforward desire of the children to have a record of their father's life could have arisen from anxiety about his growing attachment to Dorothy. Later there were fears that she was exploiting his fame, and this tendency may have been in evidence even at this stage. The existence of his own memoir might usefully forestall her and other biographers. It is not possible to be sure of White's motives in acceding to their request, but in one respect at least the contrast with what he had already committed to print seemed clear.

He compared the nature of this record with the biographical information disclosed through fictional works; 'a good deal of it has been told before under a semi-transparent disguise, with much added which is entirely fictitious. What I now set down is fact'.[20] This is explained a little further after the description of the traumatic Stoke Newington school-teaching episode; 'At this point I had intended to stop. A good part of my life henceforward has appeared under disguise in one of my books, but I think on reconsideration it will be better to record here also what little remains to be told about myself, and to narrate it as history'.[21] An account described as 'fact' and set down as 'history' invites corroboration against other sources. The use of these in relation to the descriptions of Bedford in the fiction and this text has already demonstrated how large a gap there appears to be between their described world and reality. This needs to be further examined, with reference to the *nature* of the text. Perhaps this genre handles a 'poetic' truth which need not, or cannot, find expression in Gradgrindian 'facts'?

From Manuscript to Publication: The Title Page

Since the title page (Figure 3 below) is important in setting the reader's expectation of the text, and because information given in this way has assumed great significance for self-writing theorists, the identification there of Mark Rutherford with Hale White needs to be set in context. Critics, where they note it, have taken the page to originate with White.[22] It equates him with Rutherford, apparently signifying an intention to write of his own life. It is consonant with his declaration about facts, as opposed to fiction. But the

---

[19] Described on its accession by H. I. Bell, 'Autographs of Nathaniel Hawthorne and "Mark Rutherford"', *The British Museum Quarterly*, 11 (1936-37), 79-80 (p. 80). It was bound by the Museum in 1958.

[20] See the first paragraph of *Early Life*, p. 5.

[21] *Early Life*, p. 82. The extending of the story is one natural explanation of the re-numbering of some pages, as additional sections were inserted.

[22] See for example, Carl Dawson, *Prophets of Past Time*, p. 28.

manuscript has no title page, nor any indication of ever having had one. Even its designation 'Autobiographical Notes' comes not from the text, but simply from the reference in White's will. It seems that he avoided the choice of a title, perhaps part of the conceit that the material was not for publication, or in order not to have to put a name to the life described.

Fortunately letters of Molly White survive covering each stage of the process from manuscript to press.[23] A little over six weeks after her father's death she wrote to Humphrey Milford about publication of the Notes, Dorothy already having mentioned the subject to her brother-in-law.[24] The first of the proof pages was despatched from the Press on 5 June, and Molly in the interim obtained some suitable pictures of Bedford from Frederick Hockliffe, bookseller on the High Street and a contemporary of her father. These were to supplement the family pictures already to hand. The publisher of course wanted a title too, and in a letter of 12 June 1913 Molly rehearsed the questions this raised:

> With regard to the title for which you ask in your letter of yesterday's date, I beg to enclose a suggested title. It is difficult not to confuse this little book of notes with the original 'Autobiography of Mark Rutherford' already published. I have therefore not used the word Autobiographical. At the same time I must use the name Mark Rutherford and that must come first as many people still have no idea that W. Hale White and Mark Rutherford are one and the same person.[25]

Not for her any anxiety about the distinct *persona* of Mark Rutherford, and indeed the 'two' identities were merged to the extent that pictures of her father were described as of 'Mark Rutherford', though these captions may have originated at the press. Molly's suggested title wording was adopted, as shown below. Although critics following Philippe Lejeune have approached self-writing texts with the concept of an 'autobiographical pact' established between writer and reader through the declarations of the title page (perhaps the *only* way in which autobiography might be distinguished from fictionalised autobiography), in the circumstances of its genesis outlined here this

---

[23] Now at the University of British Columbia, and apparently not seen by previous scholars.

[24] Letter of 3 May 1913 (UBC, NCC 17-5). Valentine Cunningham, perhaps reading too much into Dorothy's connection, does not record Molly's role; 'White, William Hale', in *Oxford Dictionary of National Biography* <http://www.oxforddnb.com/view/article/36864> [accessed 19 March 2008].

[25] Letter at UBC, NCC 17-4, original under-lining. On donation of the manuscript to the British Museum in 1936 the Director wrote a letter that reads as if *he* thought the manuscript was of the *Autobiography*. He thanked Sir William for 'the autograph MS. of the Autobiography of Mark Rutherford', but this was perhaps just a careless choice of words. Letter of 10 October 1936 now at UBC, NCC 17-4.

responsibility statement cannot bear the weight expected of it by such theories.[26]

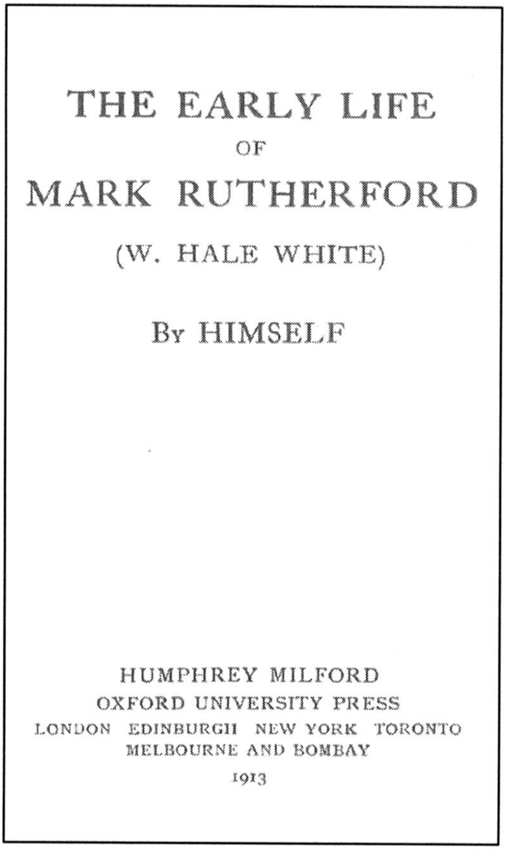

THE EARLY LIFE
OF
MARK RUTHERFORD
(W. HALE WHITE)

BY HIMSELF

HUMPHREY MILFORD
OXFORD UNIVERSITY PRESS
LONDON EDINBURGH NEW YORK TORONTO
MELBOURNE AND BOMBAY
1913

Figure 3 : *Early Life* - Title page on publication

It must be asked if Molly's choice of title was a wise one, especially in privileging Rutherford's name over White's. The name Mark Rutherford appears nowhere in the text, nor are any of 'his' novels specifically named. The running header, presumably agreed by the family, avoids the problem and is simply 'Autobiographical Notes'. The life outlined is clearly at variance with

---

[26] Lejeune, *On Autobiography* (Minneapolis, MN: University of Minnesota Press, 1989), especially pp. 3-30.

the fictional character, as, *inter alia*, the more detailed family background and fuller New College history demonstrates. At the same time it is assumed that the reader will be familiar with the world of the novels. There is no hint that White intended the 'Autobiographical Notes' to refer to any other 'self'. It seems possible that in choosing to put the work before the public in an already-familiar name Molly may have subverted the writer's purpose of leaving a final open account of his life simply in his own name.[27] For surely the putting aside of a disguise implied revealing the writer's identity.

The book did not sell particularly strongly, and must have been bought by only a small proportion of those who had enjoyed the novels. The print run was for 1,500 copies and the first account was rendered to Molly for sales to the end of March 1914.[28] It showed 818 copies supplied to home booksellers and 183 for export; assuming a proportion of these were for stock, rather than from customer orders, sales were somewhat less. The payment due to Molly was a little over £19, and nearly 500 of the print run remained with the publishers. Royalties in later years were very modest. In 1936 Molly made over the copyright to her brother William telling him that annual payments could be less than two shillings, implying sales in single figures.[29] And this was in the decade when the anniversary of White's birth had received a measure of attention, and Oxford University Press had reissued the novels. However slight the sales, distribution was still wide enough for the book to have a significant influence. This is in part due to the commonly held belief that an unguarded picture of White emerges, though this begs questions about the nature of the text.

Reading the text - Help from Self-Writing Theory?

Despite the apparently straightforward nature of the *Early Life*, represented above all by the declaration 'what I now set down is fact' (manuscript original of this shown in Figure 4 below), serious questions of interpretation arise.[30] White's literary output may be viewed as representing alternative strands within the self-writing tradition - that of fictional autobiography as well as here of the ostensibly 'true' life story.

The *Early Life* has affected readings of Hale White in two important and often un-declared respects. First, the explicit statement that the writer had previously recorded 'a good deal' of his life 'under a semi-transparent disguise'

---

[27] Dorothy knew White first and foremost as Mark Rutherford but there is no evidence of her involvement in deciding the title.

[28] UBC, NCC 17-5. There is nothing to indicate any later printings.

[29] From a letter of 15 July now at British Columbia (UBC, NCC 17-4); she also handed over the manuscript, as it would be 'safer' with William. Royalties had been agreed at 5d. for home sales, and 3d. for overseas.

[30] *Early Life*, p. 5; the text has been heavily revised at this crucial point (Figure 4).

has been taken to legitimise an understanding of the novels (most particularly the *Autobiography*) as thinly veiled autobiography in the confessional mode. This understanding is not without some significant opponents, though it represents the majority view.[31] The dissenters stress the qualification which follows the declaration quoted above; 'with much added which is entirely fictitious', or hold the two statements in tension to disallow any thoroughgoing autobiographical reading.[32] It is probable that White included this element of equivocation deliberately.

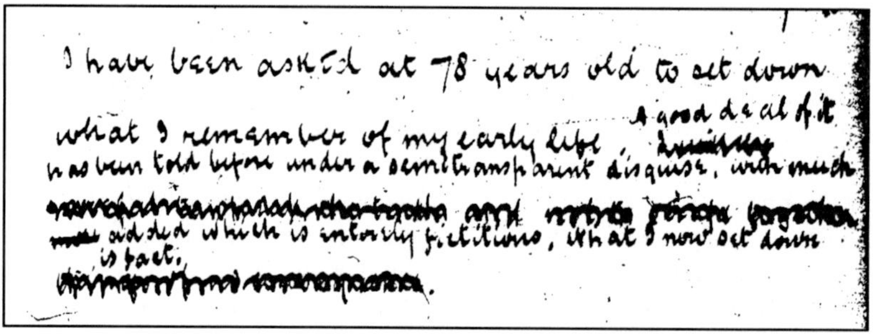

I have been asked at 78 years old to set down
what I remember of my early life. A good deal of it
has been told before under a semi-transparent disguise, with much
added which is entirely fictitious, what I now set down
is fact.

Figure 4 : 'Autobiographical Notes', p. 1 (detail)
© The British Library: Add. Ms. 44891

The second use of the *Early Life* has been as a 'control' text, one from which events in White's life can be established, and against which other (typically the fictional) accounts can be tested for their historicity. It is striking that even in discussions of the novels which draw heavily on self-writing theory and ought therefore to be alert to the difficulty of establishing the factual content of any text the *Early Life* seems able to maintain a privileged position, its truthfulness and accuracy received on trust. This is clearly shown in Carl Dawson's study, where the title page in particular is taken to be of special importance.[33] Susanna Egan compares the *Early Life* with the novels in some detail, but again without

[31] Gamini Salgado ('The Rhetoric of Sincerity') and Gerry Brookes ('Fictional Forms') are powerful champions of reading the novels as fiction; see above, pp. 52-53.
[32] So Brookes, 'Fictional Forms', p. 248; he also notes that White relates two episodes in *Early Life* directly to previous portrayals (pp. 79, 85), school teaching in Stoke Newington (*Autobiography*) and his essay on Caleb Morris (reprinted in *Last Pages*; it is not clear that Brookes knows of this essay, and he may believe this second reference is to preaching described in the *Autobiography*, where Morris is not named).
[33] *Prophets of Past Time*, p. 28; 'it is characteristic of White that he should write about his boyhood and youth under his original pseudonym'.

really doubting the simple historicity of the former.[34] If White had set out to provide an 'authorised' account of his life, he could scarcely have hoped for so grateful and accepting an audience.

The Nature of Autobiographical Writing

A mixture of memory and reinterpretation is present in all autobiographical writing, for there can be no recall *without* interpretation. This fundamental emphasis of self-writing theory may be applied to clarify differences between the novels - especially the *Autobiography* - and the *Early Life*. The *Early Life* can be additionally read as a special example of self-writing, that devoted to childhood memories, and better understood by comparison with similar accounts. Although the chief interest of self-writing theory lies in its alertness to presentations of the self implied in the selection and arrangement of the life narrative, it also has value in assessing the writer's description of the physical and social environment. This aspect is especially important for childhood autobiographies because the child's world is so notably small and bounded, and it is not irrelevant to adult examples.[35]

Roy Pascal notes that 'every autobiographer must leave out the humdrum details of everyday life', except where some special significance is thereby revealed, but the more the ordinary is excluded the greater the potential for distortion.[36] As has been demonstrated, the gap between White's fictional Bedford and the otherwise historically verifiable facts is sometimes considerable. Since critics infer so much about White from his context, and this largely on the authority of his own description (even when recycled by scholars as biography) any misrepresentation, apart from the trivial, must be a matter of concern. That his felt experience may thereby be better conveyed does not justify neglecting historical checks, which can help to identify the degree of reinterpretation, and may suggest motives for it. It is almost inevitable that a writer recalling the setting of his early years from a distance (temporally and geographically) will accentuate the contrast with the time of writing, but examination shows the wholesale omission of much which must surely have been within his recall. It cannot be wholly explained by the demands or limitation of genre.

Studies of memory confirm conclusions drawn from literary analysis of

---

[34] *Patterns of Experience*, pp. 23-33.

[35] Coe discusses these 'inventories of a small world'; *When the Grass was Taller*, p. 205. See chapter six for examples.

[36] *Design and Truth*, p. 62. 'What is the use', White mused, 'of recording the commonplace experiences of which everybody knows?'; from his letter to Miss Edwards 18 October 1907, cited above, describing why he would not write a full life (Brotherton Ms 11190-07; University of Leeds).

autobiographical texts by suggesting the constructed nature of the autobiographical record. Memories are not simply 'stored and retrieved, but are constructed anew from stored information and the immediate situation', and therefore changing circumstances, and especially changing self-understanding, affect the presentation of personal narratives.[37] This clearly supposes an important element of interpretation, and there will be a gap between the purpose memory serves for the self and 'what actually happened'. In mental and written recall, while the subject looks back, 'autobiography is the writer's *de facto* attempt to elucidate his present rather than his past'.[38]

The Literary Form of Conversion Narratives

Discussion of the literary tradition is a reminder that autobiographical writing is shaped by previous exemplars, and the understanding of the self this involves is relevant to conversion. In part this is due to the dominance of biblical models in the western literary canon. The flowering of autobiographical writing in the nineteenth century exhibits this tendency, even where the self-understanding is apparently secular, as Barry Qualls has shown.[39]

Just as in religious terms conversion means a new understanding and status, so the autobiographer seeks a new understanding or perspective on the self. This leads to narratives which frequently shape themselves by reference to typical biblical figures, pre-eminently Moses, Job, Paul, and Jesus himself. These typological associations offer writers narratives within which to tell their own stories. The Prodigal Son is a further type, one evident in White's writing, suggesting a degree of self-identification. The existence of such parallels highlights the question of truthfulness in accounts which are so obviously affected by them.[40] Since Edmund Gosse's *Father and Son* (1907) has similarities to the *Early Life*, it is instructive to note how scholars have

---

[37] For survey of current research (not always agreeing with such a constructive analysis) see David Rubin, 'Introduction', in *Remembering Our Past: Studies in Autobiographical Memory*, ed. by David C. Rubin (Cambridge: Cambridge University Press, 1999), pp. 1-15 (p. 6).

[38] Louis Renza, 'The Veto of the Imagination: A Theory of Autobiography', in *Autobiography: Essays Theoretical and Critical*, ed. by James Olney, pp. 268-295 (p. 271).

[39] *The Secular Pilgrims of Victorian Fiction: The Novel as Book of Life* (Cambridge: Cambridge University Press, 1982). He explores the influence of seventeenth century religious texts in mediating biblical models for nineteenth century writers.

[40] As Heather Henderson notes, *The Victorian Self: Autobiography and Biblical Narrative* (Ithaca, NY: Cornell University Press, 1989), p. 15.

analysed his claim of a wholly truthful account against such a context.[41] On one level this statement seems to be only a reassurance that nothing knowingly false has been included, and fallible memory excuses a merely literal truthfulness. For to convey the truth of a life is much more complex than the mere recollection of historical facts.[42] The writer's purpose - to tell a life and explore its self-significance - over-rules everything; in Gosse's case the need was to separate himself from his father. This 'story' can only be told by a mixture of external facts and the reconstruction of feeling and emotions (and more).[43] In short, a degree of artistic licence is required, or as Jean Cocteau memorably puts it, 'lies are essential if one is to tell the truth'.[44]

In this instance the biblical model acts as an anti-type. Gosse rejected the role of 'another Infant Samuel', the chosen child who was a common designation; Hale White had feared himself unable to emulate Samuel because he felt sleepy in services, unlike the boy who faithfully served in the Temple.[45] Edmund cannot model the biblical story as his parents had wished, and perversely seeks parallels with Gehazi, the cheating servant of Elisha. He rejects his father's suspicion of him as an unworthy son, which flowed from Philip Gosse's own self-identification with Job.[46] Edmund's view of truth had been shaped by the gradual erosion of respect for his omnipotent father, with whom faith in God was unwholesomely mixed for the young boy. So the biblical types can shape by reaction as well as imitation and in Gosse the progress towards salvation is by freeing himself from fatherly domination, including the tyranny of a belief system he no longer shares.

John Barbour notes this as a rare instance of 'an autobiographer [using] the conversion pattern to place the emphasis squarely on the loss of faith, using the conventions of the conversion narrative but presenting deconversion without reconversion'.[47] Some aspects of disillusionment occur in many other accounts, where the move is from falsely held beliefs to authentic ones, but Gosse

---

[41] See Ann Thwaite's biography of Philip Gosse for the context, and qualification of the claim; *Glimpses of the Wonderful: The Life of Philip Henry Gosse, 1810-1888* (London: Faber & Faber, 2002), especially pp. 189-191.

[42] As Barrett Mandel has made clear; 'Full of Life Now', in *Autobiography: Essays Theoretical and Critical*, ed. James Olney, pp. 49-72.

[43] Mandel shows how this is worked out in *Father and Son*, 'Full of Life Now', pp. 58-62.

[44] Cited by Coe, *When the Grass was Taller*, p. 5.

[45] *Father and Son*, ed. by Peter Abbs (Harmondsworth: Penguin Books, 1983), p. 153, Ch. VIII; see also p. 212, Ch. XII. White, *Early Life*, p. 46.

[46] *Father and Son*, p. 214, Ch. XII, and pp. 242-243, Epilogue (where Edmund feels an affinity with Elihu).

[47] *Versions of Deconversion: Autobiography and the Loss of Faith* (Charlottesville, VA: University Press of Virginia, 1994), p. 74.

emphasizes loss alone, which itself is liberation.[48] Like Hale White, Gosse's conscience was later troubled by the apparent insincerity of a youthful confession of faith, one which involved very similar doubts about the nature of conversion. Baptism and admission to communion had been his father's wish, despite the lack of evidence of conviction of sin and conversion which he expected of others (paralleled in White and his fellow expelled). This was because Edmund belonged to:

> another class of persons, whom early training, separation from the world, and the care of godly parents had so early familiarized with the acceptable calling of Christ that their conversion had occurred, unperceived and therefore unrecorded, at an extraordinarily early age.[49]

The dramatic public baptism which followed left Edmund 'puffed out with a sense of my own holiness'.[50] It is likely that Hale White knew this work, though he does not refer to it.

If Gosse exemplifies the subversion of biblical models in deconversion, Newman's *Apologia Pro Vita Sua* points in a quite different direction, but its biblical echoes also throw light on White.[51] The strong parallels with the story of Job highlight the importance of this figure to themes of unjust suffering. The first purpose of Newman was to defend himself against the imputation of Charles Kingsley that he disregarded the truth, the setting one of trial and defence. Kingsley takes the place of Job's accuser, and Newman defends himself against all charges by outlining the irresistible process by which he comes to Catholic faith. Job is not the only inspiration, for like Moses leading the people out of Egypt, Newman moves from the Church of England to Rome.[52] Job predominates however, joined by Saint Paul as the other great biblical figure tried for his faith. To identify with them is to give an account of reasons for a great change of belief; although in White there are hints of an identification with Jesus these do not appear here, not least because Jesus did not attempt to justify himself, as Newman is determined to do.

It is not just in this text that Newman echoes Job, for his 'sermons, letters, and journals reveal a lifelong sense of kinship with Job.'[53] It was especially in

---

48 Though Barbour notes that in rejecting his father's faith he leaves open the possibility of a different, authentic, Christianity; *Versions of Deconversion*, p. 78.

49 *Father and Son*, p. 152, Ch. VIII; a strong Calvinist doctrine of election could underpin this belief. Compare similar testimony from Frederic White, pp. 182-183 below.

50 *Father and Son*, p. 160, Ch. VIII.

51 This section draws largely on the detailed analysis of Newman by Henderson, *The Victorian Self*, pp. 19-64.

52 A theme admittedly more common in the *Lyra Apostolica*.

53 Henderson, *The Victorian Self*, p. 39.

the loss of friends because of his lonely pilgrimage that this was realised. As an autobiographer the parallels with Job are played out in his defence against unjust accusations, and in the experience of suffering for the truth. In the case of Paul, the analogy centred on the apostle's suffering as one who had 'betrayed' the religion of his birth, offering an obvious prototype of Newman's move from Anglicanism. Like Paul, he would claim a strong sense of inevitability about the rightness of this move, and assert divine blessing upon it.

Hale White uses the biblical types of Job and Paul in several places, and does not shy from what may be a deliberate echo of the trial of Jesus in his New College experience, with the three-fold questionings before the Council. The feeling for the Prodigal Son is also strong, being the subject of Cardew's sermon which so deeply affects Catharine Furze, based it must be assumed on a sermon by Caleb Morris which had thrilled Hale White.[54] In so far as White may have identified himself with the wayward son it not only suggests an alternative to the dogmatic conceptions of atonement - reconciliation is purely the result of love - but a personal sense of having ventured (intellectually, geographically, emotionally) to 'a far country' without having lost that entitlement to belonging. The Book of Job he considers at length in 'Notes on the Book of Job' published with the *Deliverance*, and these show that it is the subject of unjust suffering which preoccupies White rather than simply the character of Job. This may relate not so much to his hurt feelings and injured career after the expulsion, but the random occurrence of illness. His wife's debilitating experience of multiple sclerosis and premature death brought this home to him directly, as did the early loss of children. The link is made clear when he describes the death of a young mother and her child and declares with Job that there can be no answer to innocent suffering before the inscrutable will of God; 'this book (of Job) in a sense is terribly modern, for this is a question which is continually but resultlessly asked by us all'.[55] But it does not oblige us to keep silent - 'the example of Job protects us from the charge of blasphemy in not suppressing our doubts'.[56] This can stand on a broader canvas as White's *apologia* for exploring so fully elsewhere in his writings the moral and other objections to Christian belief.

The common emphasis in the biblical types is their ultimate vindication, so this tradition includes a strong sense of restoration which can also be found in White, and especially the *Early Life*. Even where he does not make the direct link these literary conventions may be a shaping influence.

---

[54] Reported in 'Caleb Morris', a review reprinted in *Last Pages*, pp. 244-250 (p. 245).

[55] 'Notes on the Book of Job', printed with *Deliverance*, pp. 131-157 (p. 138).

[56] 'Notes on the Book of Job', p. 138.

White's Awareness of the Writer's Limitations

White's versions of Bedford, whether from the novels or the *Early Life*, have been shown to differ from the town of his youth. This has not prevented scholars from assuming that for the most part the external conditions of White's upbringing can be read off from these texts. Since even local historians with a range of comparative material to draw on have produced an incongruously harmonised picture of early-Victorian Bedford, where White's isolated, dull and backward-looking community jostles with records of enterprise, education, progress and development, it is not surprising that literary critics too have failed to question the historical details which he seems to provide.

The fictional author's own explanation for his depiction has been largely ignored. In the *Revolution*, Rutherford declares himself not just a writer, but 'the present *historian*' when introducing the reader to Cowfold, a description repeated in the *Early Life*.[57] The self-designation surely recalls the intention of the *Autobiography* to be an authentic chronicle of his disappearing race. But he is unable 'with strictest accuracy' to 'reproduce exactly what happened' on even a single day in the town.[58] Such knowledge is compared to knowing the life of those ancient cities which represent the highest wisdom of the past - Athens, Rome, and Jerusalem; 'but, alas! the preliminary image in the mind of the writer is faint enough, and when he comes to trace it, the pencil swerves and goes off into something utterly unlike it'.[59] Following this disavowal a description is nevertheless offered, one which John Lucas suggests helps to emphasize Rutherford's distance from the world in which he was intimately involved in the earlier works. This is not wholly satisfactory as an explanation, especially since Cowfold's 'somnolent, incurious way of life' which Lucas cites in support is in this aspect quite indistinguishable from the town of the *Autobiography*.[60]

The 'swerves' of the writer's pen - and memory - must instead be attributed partly to a desire to express distance from the times and events described, but also to a deliberate literary technique. It is the 'unhistoric acts' of the inhabitants of Cowfold which matter (and supremely in the *Autobiography*, of Rutherford himself) with the physical environment simply the stage where the dramas of ordinary human lives are displayed; a stage which must be kept uncluttered. In this way, and with democratic intent, the apparently undramatic lives of his characters are revealed with a grandeur all their own:

> the history of every boy or girl of ordinary make is one of robbery, murder,

---

[57] *Revolution*, p. 238, Ch. XVI (emphasis added); *Early Life*, p. 82.
[58] *Revolution*, p. 238, Ch. XVI.
[59] *Revolution*, pp. 238-239, Ch. XVI.
[60] Lucas, *Literature of Change*, p. 81.

imprisonment, death sentence, filing of chains, scaling of prison walls, recapture, scaffold, reprieve, poison, and pistols; the difference between such a history and that in the authorised versions being merely circumstantial. The garden of Eden, the murder of Cain, the deluge, the salvation of Noah, the exodus from Egypt, David and Bathsheba, with the murder of Uriah, the Assyrian invasion, the Incarnation, the Atonement, and the Resurrection of the Dead; to say nothing of the Decline and Fall of the Roman Empire, the tragedy of Count Cenci, the execution of Mary Queen of Scots, the Inquisition in Spain, the Revolt of the Netherlands, all happened in Cowfold, as well as elsewhere, and were perhaps more interesting there because they could be studied in detail and the records were authentic.[61]

Childhood Reminiscence

Many of the features which mark the townscape of the novels are also present in the *Early Life*, along with much else that is common to Mark Rutherford. The childhood memoir was largely a new phenomenon. 'Never before this period had so many English writers been interested in recalling their early lives at length within the form of a sustained prose autobiography'.[62] One listing of British autobiographies of the nineteenth and early twentieth centuries reveals more than a hundred accounts which focus solely or chiefly upon the early years of life.[63] Richard Coe's study of this genre includes a considerable number by artists and writers, serious attempts to understand and identify the distinctive felt experiences of childhood and youth.[64] His analysis reveals a surprisingly high number of common features, many of which can be traced in the *Early Life*. Coe's chosen texts provide valuable insights, and his survey will be referred to repeatedly. An examination of working-class childhoods by John Burnett offers further points of comparison.[65]

Coe argues that the childhood memoir, for all its similarities with other autobiographical writings, has 'its own internal laws, conventions, and

---

[61] *Revolution*, pp. 243-244, Ch. XVI; 'authentic' here apparently meaning personally witnessed.

[62] So Luann Walther, 'The Invention of Childhood in Victorian Autobiography', in *Approaches to Victorian Autobiography*, ed. by George P. Landow (Athens, OH: Ohio University Press, 1979), pp. 64-83 (p. 65).

[63] William Matthews (compiler), *British Autobiographies: An Annotated Bibliography of British Autobiographies Published or Written Before 1951* (Hamden, CT: Archon Books, reprint 1968); childhood accounts indexed on p. 345.

[64] There is a strong emphasis upon the memoirs of intellectuals, which naturally affects his assessment of typical features. Note that White does *not* relate his childhood to a literary career – despite mentions of the fiction no reader can discover from this text what else he had written.

[65] *Destiny Obscure: Autobiographies of Childhood, Education and Family from the 1820s to the 1920s* (Harmondsworth: Penguin Books, 1984).

structures'.[66] The discontinuity separating the 'self-as-child' and the writer creates an obstacle between text, writer and reader rather than the common understanding which can normally be assumed when reader, writer and subject are all adults. The difference between the writer and childhood subject is such that the life described is '*qualitatively* different from adult experience, and therefore cannot be reconstituted simply by accurate narration'.[67] Necessarily, 'poetic' rather than literal truth is at the heart of this genre (and, tellingly, *The Prelude* - known to have influenced White - is noted as a very significant work of this type). Coe's formal definition of the 'childhood' includes its conscious attempt to 'reflect[s] step by step the development of the writer's self ... concluding ... with the attainment of a precise degree of maturity'.[68] This last stage, where the subject emerges as the mature self, is probably to be identified in the *Early Life* with White's transfer to the Admiralty and, more privately, with his marriage.[69] These events mark the real emergence from the shadow of the New College expulsion, and the close involvement of his parents in decisions about his future life, a measure of independence achieved.

This is congruent with the range of archetypal endings listed by Coe, but the peculiar structure of the *Early Life* allows a further identification with the smaller number of texts which have a 'double' ending.[70] Examples in his study include works with 'a clear-cut climax at the age of twelve or thirteen, followed by a long, dull, unspeakably painful period of adolescence; and then the gradual buildup to a second, definitive climax some six or seven years after the first'.[71] The duality observable in the *Early Life* is differently occasioned, for White largely avoids emotional introspection, but quite clearly displayed. It is closely linked to his method of composition. The first climax is his Wordsworthian enlightenment; 'it was a new capacity', an awakening, quickening experience which marked a fundamental reinterpretation of all that had gone before, and a reorientation for the future.[72] The second, more muted, ending is that which records the security of permanent employment, and his marriage, soberly recounted and followed by summary judgement on the Victorian age.[73] These pages constitute not simply a closure, one possible attraction of this form, but almost an anti-climax.

---

[66] Coe, *When the Grass was Taller*, p. 1.

[67] Coe, *When the Grass was Taller*, p. 1; original italics.

[68] Coe, *When the Grass was Taller*, p. 9 (italicised throughout in the original, not reproduced here).

[69] *Early Life*, p. 88.

[70] White's admission that he had 'intended to stop' after describing his engagement as a teacher, but then extended his account is not to be taken as a closure (p. 82). Endings are a more complex question than first appears.

[71] *When the Grass was Taller*, p. 77.

[72] *Early Life*, pp. 61-62.

[73] *Early Life*, pp. 88-91.

Structure and Content of the Text

The Early Life of Mark Rutherford (W. Hale White), by Himself

Frontispiece, title-page, foreword, key to illustrations
pp. 1-4 [5 pages]

Family background; brother, mother, grandmother, Colchester aunt and grandparents
pp. 5-13 1831 – 1840s [9 pages]

Bedford; town, schools / Bedford charity, Dissent, Bunyan Meeting / Calvinism / Lord's Supper / country chapels / congregation
pp. 13-21 late 1830s – early 1840s [9 pages]

White family; forbears, politics, Uncle Lovell and family, father / bookselling / Bedford charity / language / writing / House of Commons door-keeper / politics and politicians / creed
pp. 21-39 late 18th century – 1882 [19 pages]

Hale White; early memories, schooling, home life, nurse, mother, Sunday, church, Modern School, school life, amusements, town life, fishing, swimming etc
pp. 39-55 1832 – ca.1847 [17 pages]

Hale White; destined for ministry, preparation, admission to Bunyan Meeting, Cheshunt College, education at Cheshunt, discovery of Wordsworth, new insight, transfer to New College, controversy with Principal, expulsion, father's pamphlet, support from Maurice, Kingsley, consequences
pp. 55-79 1847 – 1852 [25 pages]

Hale White employment; teaching at Stoke Newington, Chapman and *Westminster Gazette*, George Eliot, Caleb Morris, leaves Chapman, Registrar General's office, transfer to Admiralty
pp. 79-88 1852 – 1858 [10 pages]

Hale White; marriage, life-style, reflections on Victorian age
pp. 88-91 1856 onwards [4 pages]

Figure 5 : Précis of the *Early Life*

A summary of the text (Figure 5 above) makes clear that the *Early Life* is not a single harmonious narrative, or one with a strict chronology. This is partly to be explained by the manner of writing, with material gathered by subject, person or place, and the sources available. For whatever reason, White chose not to order these uniformly.

The précis indicates the main areas covered in the *Early Life*, and part of the charm of the work is the movement between different subjects and experiences. Inevitably there is a good deal of common ground between almost all reminiscences of childhood - the archetypes which feature in Coe's analysis - but their arrangement and presentation can vary widely. A roughly tripartite division of White's subject-matter may be suggested. The individuals (almost exclusively family) who are remembered for their influence upon him, the sense of place - the town of Bedford and the surrounding countryside which formed and informed his boyhood - and the religious practices, experiences, and reluctant vocation which were fundamental to his early identity and later life. The text therefore invites the reader to understand White's life chiefly through the respective roles of people, place, and piety.

Analysis shows an initial emphasis upon personal relationships (pp. 5-39, with an excursus at pp. 13-21 on Bedford), followed by material on life in the town (pp. 39-55), and thirdly, an extended section on ministerial training and withdrawal from the same introduced by the formal admission to Bunyan Meeting (pp. 55-79). Brief concluding sections on employment, and reflections on the Victorian age, complete the work (pp. 79-88 and 88-91). These divisions are not precise or exclusive. Material on place inevitably overlaps with personal influences, and the role of faith and practice is a recurrent element, represented in almost every part of the book. There is a strong tendency for people and places to be described and valued according to their life-enhancing spiritual qualities. While the record of White's writing technique left by Dorothy suggests that initially composition proceeded slowly in fragmentary notes, the result in the *Early Life* indicates a tendency to build these up into blocks giving roughly eight to fifteen pages in the printed text.

The structure conveys something of the relative importance of the material included. Between the two 'endings' identified as significant markers from Coe's comparative examples (the encounter with Wordsworth, and secondly, his marriage) lies the account of the New College expulsion which forms the largest single section of material in the text. With this the writer moves beyond anything described of 'Mark Rutherford'.

White relied almost entirely upon primary sources collected at the time, chiefly newspaper reports, pamphlets, and private letters, many preserved in his cuttings scrapbook, often cited *verbatim*, with his own short linking paragraphs. This unit thus stands quite apart from all that precedes the first 'ending', and yet in one sense is the real climax of the whole work, intended to serve a definite apologetic purpose.

White was both made and broken by these events. The editorial work on the sources, and the interpretation provided in the link paragraphs, makes this clear. A series of later endings can be discerned, which heightens the sense of an uneven text. The childhood narrative of the Bedford years is basically complete in itself and hardly requires extension. It fits the model offered by Coe, and the tension identified by Luann Walther between the representation of childhood as Edenic or unhappy is relevant.[74] There is some evidence here of both views, though the former predominates, but this is clearly not all that White wants to record, even when the college years have also been added.

The signs of repeated changes of intention towards the end of this work may indicate that the writer returned more than once to a nearly completed manuscript. White uses the final ten pages to describe the steps which lay between the catastrophe of 1852 and his real attainment of adulthood, married and with secure employment. The inclusion of this material is crucial to demonstrate recovery from the set-back at New College. With a eulogy for the Victorian age to close, this seems a fitting ending. The expulsion marked one obvious if depressing end to the story of his early life, and an appropriate one, not having been described in previous writings. It was new information which in itself deserved to be recorded. A desire not to finish on such a note would be understandable however, and the immediately following failure to make anything of a teaching career would be an equally unappealing *finale*.

The short-lived Stoke Newington school-mastering experience is unutterably bleak, and marked by the onset of a depressive illness 'which has lasted all my life'.[75] It is not at all clear how re-telling this (already 'told elsewhere with some variation') makes 'my little history complete'; a perplexity increased when still more material follows.[76] It is probable that this was considered to mark the end of his failures, and thus to be separated from all that followed; the nadir but also the turning point, the escape from which brought instant relief. The corollary 'still, I had nothing to do' points at least to the chance of a completely fresh start.[77] Here again though, the sense of something lacking drove White to add further memories, for reasons which seem elusive. 'At this point', he declares, 'I had intended to stop', for much of his later life had been already described 'under disguise in one of my books, but I think on reconsideration it will be better to record here also what little remains to be told about myself'.[78] Almost everything about this statement is opaque. Perhaps the emphasis is properly upon the contrast between what was formerly 'disguised'

---

[74] See 'The Invention of Childhood in Victorian Autobiography', pp. 69-70.

[75] *Early Life*, p. 80; an experience of despair which parallels that of the sinner convicted, but still seeking salvation?

[76] *Early Life*, p. 79.

[77] *Early Life*, p. 81.

[78] *Early Life*, p. 82.

and is now related as fact, rather than upon any new revelation about himself. The idea of a full record ('what little remains') is also problematic, and can only make sense if read as referring only to the period up to his marriage (that is, what the text actually covers), rather than his whole life. That it might imply coverage of the whole of the remainder of his life in the fiction is clearly misleading.

The additional period described covers his time at Chapman's, giving an opportunity to declare his admiration for George Eliot, and regret at not having maintained that friendship. Similarly, the influence of Caleb Morris ('about him also I have written [elsewhere]') can be stressed. The power of the Welshman's sermon on the Prodigal Son is recalled, with the passionate commitment to the Bible which it demonstrated.[79] The chance to name and acknowledge these two figures may be sufficient explanation for their inclusion, with the hint that they represent the two poles, literary and religious, which exercised so great an influence upon the writer's formation and aspirations. It is probable that a reading of his manuscript up to the expulsion left White aware that the intellectual stimulus of the following years needed to be represented. This illustrates a bias towards the personal, with only the slightest mention of the writings known to have been important in his mental development.[80] The significance of the Chapman years for the effect they *failed* to have on White is not to be missed. Despite his introduction there to the most radical and sceptical literature of the time (or perhaps just because of it) he sought out the ministry of thoughtful men like Morris and Binney who taught a vividly personal faith sensitive to the challenges of the age. He did not embrace secularism or rationalism.[81] This strongly suggests the counter-productive effect of anti-religious scepticism. A letter to his father of this period repudiates all 'negativism', and indicates reaction against an 'emptiness both in books and men [greater] than I ever saw before ... [which] ... drives me back again to my old eternal friends who appear more than ever perfect, and Jesus above them all'.[82] The Bible, thanks to gifted preachers and personal association, was alive and quickening to him while radical books were found to be both dead and deadening.

One short section covers the steps from leaving Chapman's to joining the

---

[79] It also finds a place as Cardew's sermon which so affects Catharine Furze; *Catharine Furze*, pp. 216-218, Ch. XII.

[80] Goethe and Carlyle are mentioned in passing, but what of Spinoza, and many other less famous figures?

[81] Thereby a further illustration of Larsen's point that there was nothing inevitable about the path towards doubt by those disturbed in their faith. See *Crisis of Doubt*, pp. 242-243 for a summary of factors that could lead to dissatisfaction with secularism and a return to belief.

[82] Quoted in Stone, p. 52, who refers by name to some of these 'books and men', p. 51, while admitting that dependence on them is impossible to prove.

Admiralty (1854–1858). Reference to a momentous change in his private life is particularly brief; 'meanwhile I had married'. This should not be misinterpreted. John Burnett cites examples of similar reticence, concluding on the basis of his sample that 'autobiographers rarely give any extended account of their feelings for their partners, or their emotional state before marriage'.[83] To this it might be added that the relationship is typically so unlike all the others which can be described as influencing the growing self as to properly lie outside the scope of writings such as the *Early Life*. Of course marriage with its joys and sorrows had already been treated with great insight and sensitivity in the novels, whether directly from personal experience or not.

The remaining paragraphs contain reflections upon 'the Victorian age' which may be considered a coda to the main text. Its literary and artistic vigour is celebrated and by implication the current one questioned. White declares himself part of an age which has passed, but lives on through its achievements. The distance between the self as writer and the self as subject is emphasized. The life described is of another century, the author a survivor of that distant past. This ending, and the earlier additions outlined above, may simply reflect dissatisfaction with the manuscript at repeated re-readings, perhaps at intervals over several months. It is likely that composition took quite some time, and the impact of White's poor health should not be overlooked. Periods of severe illness may have led to the manuscript being prematurely put aside, and later improving health given the opportunity for further editorial work and expansion.[84]

Composition and Sources for the College Years

The sources utilised by White, from memory at the most fallible to the theoretically more reliable documentary material, produce different potential levels of veracity for the college years. The historical outline given is not quite accurate. The time at Cheshunt (two years) is disposed of briefly, ending in a blunt summary judgement, 'I learnt nothing'.[85] White would have been less eager for readers to know that his New College tutors, at least in one subject area, were inclined to agree that his academic progress had been hitherto unsatisfactory. New entrants there sat tests early in their college careers, and Hale's knowledge of the Greek Testament was judged to be 'very

[83] *Destiny Obscure*, p. 257.

[84] The British Library manuscript does not show any obvious breaks in the closing sections, but it is impossible to know what drafting changes may lie behind this final shape.

[85] *Early Life*, p. 63.

unsatisfactory'.[86] White's verdict on his fellow students was harsh, if the *Autobiography* account is to be read for Cheshunt; 'young men of no education ... their spiritual life was not very deep. In many of them it did not even exist, and their whole attention was absorbed upon their chances of getting wealthy congregations or of making desirable matches'.[87] Doubtless exaggerated, but perhaps not wholly inaccurate. James Ritchie was hardly impressed with his contemporaries at Coward College; 'the class of young men who had come to study for the ministry was not, with very rare exceptions, of a high order, either in a religious or intellectual point of view'.[88] And he did not exempt himself from this criticism.

White describes himself as 'hardly nineteen' (in fact the age at which he left Cheshunt in 1850) and expresses surprise that he did not question the strict Calvinism taught there, so much so that an apology must be offered; 'the only approach to explanation I can give is that all this [i.e. doctrine] belonged to a world totally disconnected from my own, and that I never thought of making real to myself anything which this supernatural world contained'.[89] This statement acknowledges that he had once believed such doctrines, but that from the perspective of his renewal through nature the 'supernatural' has been relegated to meaninglessness, for all nature is recognised as imbued with the divine.

As at other points in the text, this is an example of the way in which different strands can be identified, when youthful experience and adult reflection upon it are placed side by side. The sequence so far - admission at Cheshunt, orthodox but un-questioned belief, renewal through Wordsworth - covers the years to '1851 or 1852' and the move to London.[90] This vagueness may arise from a lack of evidence among his sources, and a belief that such detail is unimportant, for very soon specific dates in the controversy are noted, obviously derived from his primary sources.

The climactic events at New College are described with the help of *verbatim* reports, including quotations from Principal Harris and others. These are taken from contemporary newspaper reports, and his father's counterblast to the college, *To Think or Not to Think?*.[91] A little new detail is added which may faithfully preserve Hale's own memory, as in recalling the Principal's manner

---

86 Minutes of Senate, 1851, a record of Examiners' Reports, minute 118 (DW, NCA 159).

87 *Autobiography*, p. 17, Ch. II.

88 *Christopher Crayon's Recollections: The Life and Times of the Late James Ewing Ritchie, as Told by Himself* (London: James Clarke, 1898), p. 98. His memoir gives few dates, but this must be ca. 1840.

89 *Early Life*, pp. 60-61.

90 *Early Life*, p. 63.

91 Sub-titled *Remarks upon the Late Expulsions from New College* (London: Robert Theobald, 1852).

and expression.[92] White does not here name the other students, Frederic White and Robert Theobald (whose stories will be told more fully below), and their views and writings are not quoted. There was clearly a need for White to omit much from the extensive material he had to hand. The resulting picture allows conclusions to be drawn about the principles guiding his selection.

First, precedence has been given to direct quotation wherever possible, with the probable aim that the college authorities would be seen to be condemned out of their own mouths for intolerant persecution. Secondly, and perhaps in support of the aim above, statements from the three are not mentioned. It is impossible to discern their views from this report. Thirdly however, the part of their defence which relied upon natural justice is included. That is, the repeated request (echoed in a personal appeal by their parents) for clarification of the charges against them, for sight of the creed against which they were judged, and that 'our moral character should be placed above suspicion'.[93] Fourthly, White refuses to enter again into discussion on the question of biblical inspiration, for the practical reason that argument is unprofitable, but again with the effect of enhancing the stature of the defendants.

The cumulative effect of this editorial work is to emphasize the unequal nature of the struggle, and cast the authorities as harsh and arbitrarily judgemental. A certain simplicity is preserved by a focus upon the chief participants; the appeals for support to Caleb Morris and John Jukes are omitted (perhaps because they were fruitless). A desire to pay homage to his father may have prompted the brief extracts from *To Think or Not to Think?*, giving White the opportunity to endorse the considered response to questions on the inspiration and authority of scripture which it contains. It is impossible to explain *how* the sacred writings are inspired, and their truth and authority can only be experienced 'out of a living sense of them', not debated.[94]

The reflections which follow the descriptive material are of vital importance in assessing the religious beliefs held in old age. Although detail is lacking, the emphasis is firmly upon a continued belief 'under new forms', and a solid appreciation of the Puritan spirit. It is, he seems to say, better to follow a religion which makes strenuous demands upon the believer ('earnestness'), than to adopt the more optimistic view of human nature found in 'modern religion' with its 'flowery' path.[95] Since belief and behaviour must be intimately related the practical effects of doctrines in daily life are always to be considered. These preoccupations occur frequently in the *Groombridge Diary*, and their appearance here justifies regarding Dorothy's record as in this respect an accurate reflection of life-long concerns. Taking this evidence of continuing

---

[92] *Early Life*, p. 64.

[93] *Early Life*, p. 66.

[94] *Early Life*, p. 71; a quotation from *To Think or Not to Think*?

[95] *Early Life*, p. 78.

belief seriously offers a corrective to the idea that White's religious journey is one of loss. A more sophisticated conceptualisation of the origin and testing of his faith, referenced to the *Early Life* and other sources, is needed to achieve this. It is evident that the drama of the expulsion as told in the *Early Life* has seized imaginations in a way in which the under-stated pointers to later recovery have not.

The Importance of Religious References in the *Early Life*

It is impossible, and illegitimate, to set aside other evidence completely, but an attempt will be made to read the *Early Life* afresh for indications of White's religious beliefs and development. This task cannot be limited to the text itself. A thorough investigation of the events it describes is also necessary, the task of the succeeding chapters. At the same time the memoir must not be too artificially separated from the *Autobiography*, because the closeness in language suggests that White had the novel before him (or at least, clearly in mind) as he composed the manuscript.

Conclusions already reached about the *Early Life* from the application of self-writing theory need to be borne in mind. The work is not a simply a factual account of White's youth, but a carefully controlled narrative which can be read on several levels, reflecting the writer's attempt at a mature self-understanding. Simply in terms of the space given to different topics it is clear that two issues dominate; White's relationship with his father and with the faith tradition in which he was raised. It seems wholly justified therefore to take seriously what he has to say about matters of belief in this text. Only here can the reader learn from him about the New College expulsion, although many do so second-hand through the critical biographies. They then read or re-read the fiction with a quite different set of expectations from those of the first readers of Mark Rutherford. The danger of turning the novels into 'autobiography after the fact' needs to be guarded against.[96] One vital question is whether he most fully revealed himself through the fiction, or if other evidence, such as from the *Early Life*, is more reliable.

If the novels appear to show an increasingly 'secular' outlook (though such an analysis might be challenged) this memoir contains some of the strongest language pointing to continuing faith. Other late writings contain mature reflections on faith which are relevant. Privileging the supposed world-view of the later novels against other interpretations is one explanation for the dominance of the loss of faith view. Some critics find reasons to disregard or

---

[96] The warning of Paul Eakin, *Touching the World: Reference in Autobiography* (Princeton, NJ: Princeton University Press, 1992), see particularly pp. 27-28, supportive of Lejeune's contention that the *writer* needs to establish an 'autobiographical pact' with the reader, who must not be left to make extra-textual estimates of authorial intention.

play down late mentions of religious belief or commitment as due to the influence on White of Dorothy Smith, a dedicated Anglican. It is possible, according to this argument, that he suppressed his questioning out of deference to her faith (or more sinisterly, that *she* concealed evidence of them or otherwise distorted his opinions). Contemporary sources which express dismay over Dorothy's influence, and her portrayal of White, need examination to see if this charge can be substantiated. If it is assumed that White composed the *Early Life* without direct reference to Dorothy, as the meagre evidence available suggests, then this possible distortion may not be present, at least directly. On this basis, what the careful reader might learn of White's faith from this text can only be determined by analysis with due reference to the context and an understanding of how religious faith develops (or fails to develop).

Summary

In the *Early Life* Hale White is preoccupied with identity and belonging, issues closely related to conversion. The perspective of old age, and increasing signs of mortality, reinforced the need to acknowledge his roots while simultaneously exploring his separation from them. The pressures experienced in early family life cannot be hidden, and the sense of the prodigal is strong. His reconstruction of these years focuses upon poetic rather than factual truthfulness. It is not a strictly biographical or historical record, consisting instead of the remembered experiences, impressions, and 'emotion recollected in tranquillity'.[97] This does not diminish their value in representing religious experience, where any connection to external historical circumstances may be less important. The evidence presented here challenges the common view that in this text White revealed himself without artifice. The text obscures a good deal which may be determined more reliably from other sources, and is far from a plainly factual account. It does however reveal the overarching importance of certain key events from the years covered. In this, as has been demonstrated, it stands firmly within the 'childhood' genre isolated by Richard Coe, and exhibits a range of classic features.

White's children were not in a position to test the accuracy of these reminiscences, but their actions revealed a true grasp of the importance of the 'Autobiographical Notes'. The speed with which they were published, and later the decision (in 1936) to deposit the manuscript in the British Museum, showed an awareness of the need to safeguard this record. Conflicting views of Hale White entered the public domain in 1913 immediately after his death, through

---

[97] As Wordsworth describes it in his preface to the second edition of *Lyrical Ballads* (1800); *The Poetical Works of William Wordsworth*, ed. by E. De Selincourt, 5 vols (Oxford: Clarendon Press, 1940-49), II (1944), p. 400.

obituaries and newspaper reports.[98] At least some of these may have been considered a distortion of the father they knew, and the need for a corrective to appear in print as quickly as possible would then have been compelling.[99] Already elements emerge of the posthumous struggle between the children, his widow, and other friends to be regarded as true guardians of White's memory.

The elements of disclosure and reticence intertwined within the *Early Life* itself do not make it easy to arrive at a true picture of White. However with a clearer understanding of the nature and limitations of texts of this genre, and greater knowledge of the historical context, attention can turn more specifically to the content and its evidential value. The earlier years covered by the text, so important to White's formation, will be reviewed first, before turning to the crucial events which flowed from the decision to pursue a ministerial career.

---

[98] Detailed in chapter eleven below.

[99] This might have been intended to forestall the publication of still further accounts, or perhaps, more prosaically, for commercial reasons publication seemed best while public interest was likely to be at its greatest.

CHAPTER 5

People, Place and Piety
Themes in the *Early Life*

Like many childhood autobiographies the *Early Life* is generally descriptive and lacking in dialogue (the reported speech in the New College episode is an obvious and independently sourced exception), a consequence of the way in which such memories are recalled and presented.[1] The text is fragmentary compared with the sophisticated fictionalised or stream of consciousness examples in which a fuller and more continuous narrative has been crafted. This reflects both the status of the work as, modestly, 'Autobiographical *Notes*' rather than a full life, and the linking together of remembered people and places (Coe's 'archetypes'). This form shows White's distinctive style to advantage; the elegant summaries and link sentences as he moves from subject to subject - 'To return to Bedford', 'To me he [Uncle Lovell] was kindness itself', 'I now come to my Father', 'My mother was by no means democratic', 'To him [William Chignell] I owe much'.[2] Instances might be multiplied, for every word is used to maximum effect.

Much remains unclear, and there are very significant gaps. Some of the lacunae and uncertainties are due to technique, others possibly to tricks of memory and the inevitable lack of corroborative sources for the earliest years, while a few must reflect polemical intent. The consistent misrepresentation of family involvement at Bunyan Meeting is not obvious to the casual reader. There are surprising silences. While something is revealed of the young Hale's taste in books no indication is given of Bible reading or, extraordinarily, of familiarity with the works of Bunyan.[3] It is inconceivable that the Bible and Bunyan were not both read and heard; these are the most commonly cited books in nineteenth century autobiography. Their ubiquity may simply have been assumed, but one who wrote elsewhere of the Bible as 'the most precious of books' might have been expected to mention something of his early

---

[1] Coe, *When the Grass was Taller*, p. 117.

[2] *Early Life*, pp. 13, 22-23, 27, 42 and 55 respectively. Subsequent page references to the *Early Life* are given within parentheses in the text, except where clarity dictates otherwise.

[3] Note that the *Norfolk News* of 7 September 1878 appears to preserve some record of White's early reading, including of the Bible (briefly summarised by Maclean, p. 32).

encounters with it in this text.[4] Possibly his long and constant study of the scriptures dimmed the memory of first impressions, which he simply could not accurately recall.

Throughout the *Early Life* people are largely described by their connection to Hale White. The emphasis is firmly upon his paternal ancestors, who 'had lived in Bedfordshire beyond memory', rather than his mother's relations, much more fleetingly introduced, and quickly passed over (p.21). This may simply reflect the connection with place, but possibly also a degree of alienation from the maternal line. There is no evidence that White was close to his mother, even if regular visits with her to Chignell relations in Colchester are described (pp.9-11). His cousin William Chignell was an influence, though most of what is known about his role in White's life must be gleaned from elsewhere. Family predominates, and there is little sense of the wider chapel community which was a significant aspect of nonconformist life. It may be assumed to have been so here, but excluded from comment by the narrow focus upon closer ties. Embarrassment over the memory of a rather negative portrayal of fellow members in the *Autobiography* may be showing itself in a circumspect and more generous silence. It is known from other sources that friendships were made through the faith community, as with the Whitmees of Stagsden.[5] William White's regular trips to preach at Bunyan-supported causes nearby, often accompanied by Hale, are not declared in the *Early Life*, understating his commitment to the church.[6]

The only relationship beyond immediate family shown to have real importance here is that with the servant 'Nurse Jane' (Reed), who seems to have joined the household to help care for Samuel and the recently born Anne (pp.40-43).[7] Her early influence was considerable - she regularly took Hale and his sister to her parents' home for holidays - and the friendship extended well into his adult life (pp.40-41).[8] The naturalness of life with her is contrasted with the formality and expectations which restricted life at home, such that visits with her were 'a delight as keen as any which could be given' (p.41). This welcome freer life is noticeably a common feature of time spent away from home, even with close family members like the Lovells. Such opportunities seems to have been keenly anticipated, naturally enough in the excitement of seaside holidays (the only activity with his mother positively reported), but

---

[4] Said of Mark Rutherford; see *Autobiography*, p. 15, Ch. II.

[5] See recollections of S.J. Whitmee in *The British Weekly* of 3 April 1913 (cited in Maclean, p. 40).

[6] Maclean reports these preaching visits, though without references, pp. 38-39.

[7] White gives his age at the time as about ten, making Samuel less than two; Anne (formally Mary Anne) was born in April 1841.

[8] There is no mention here of Samuel and the narrative reads at this point as if White and his sister were the only children.

surely indicating some domestic unhappiness when so often mentioned. With his Uncle Lovell, part of the pleasure of his company was the chance to be 'out all day' (p.23). The mature White's appreciation of simplicity and disregard for convention seem to have their roots in these childhood years.

It is noticeable that descriptions of houses, gardens, and interiors always highlight the attractions - the freedoms, indulgences and pleasures - of places outside the family home. The *Autobiography* has almost nothing on the home life of Mark Rutherford, which suggests a wish to avoid treating such an intimate subject and scrupulousness in not writing of those still living and potentially able to read it on publication. Quite apart from other relations, his father was still alive in 1881 (having been widowed in 1867), and there must have been some risk that a retired nonconformist bookseller would become aware of a new work describing a town and life which could easily be identified with Bedford.[9]

White and his Father: An Awkward Relationship?

The joyful note of pleasures enjoyed is stilled as the subject turns closer to home; 'I now come to my father' (p.27). The relative paucity of references to his mother has been noted. Her concern for status and respectability evidently grated upon White (this surely informs the portrait of Mrs Furze), and the possibility of tension and disharmony within his parents' marriage on this and other matters cannot be discounted. William White was a man scarred by his own upbringing, suffering the death of his mother and the cruelty of a stepmother, in an uneasy household where his step-mother's natural child was favoured above him.[10] He had an 'explosive' temper; a figure to be respected, feared even, but not perhaps to be loved (p.38). A good deal of critical comment has discussed the possibility of Hale's marriage as the basis for descriptions of mismatched relationships in the novels; it is probable that his youth also provided at least some other experience of the tensions between temperamentally unsuited partners.[11] William White is the dominant figure in White's account, for in terms of text he has more space in the memoir than any other individual. This is not necessarily the whole truth of the father-son relationship, but there is nothing here to support the view proposed by Catherine Maclean, that 'Hale's dearest friend throughout his boyhood was his

---

[9] In 1881 William was living in Carshalton near Hale, and within a circle of family and new friends; he died in February1882. Possibly Hale thought he could ensure that his father saw no reviews or advertisements for the *Autobiography*.

[10] She supposedly encouraged severe beatings at school; see *Early Life*, pp. 27-28.

[11] As, for example, Irvin Stock suggests, p. 35. Might William's later financial difficulties have partly resulted from his wife's aspirations to a more refined lifestyle, a prototype of Mrs Furze?

father'.[12] White may have spoken more warmly of his father than he wrote, and naturally spent a good deal of time in his company when growing up, but generally the record shows a sense of respectful distance rather than intimacy.

Richard Coe has drawn attention to several key depictions of fathers in childhood memoirs. Alongside the father as violent 'brute' are found the figures of 'the dead father, the absent father, the failed father'.[13] These themes, linked by their 'subtly varied degrees of inadequacy', initially seem ill-suited to define Hale's view of his father. The one real failure in that life, the bankruptcy of his business, was not due to weakness or neglect, but was the result of a principled stand over Bedford education which alienated many of his customers; moreover the recovery from a burden of debt demonstrated the iron will and principles of the man, vindicating his integrity.[14] Rather, any taint of inadequacy stems from the greater success of his son, for a common feature in such narratives is that 'the father has been outdistanced by the son', a truth which may have been uncomfortably clear to White and to his father even during the latter's lifetime.[15] Though the literary success was apparently hidden from his father, the Admiralty position was a considerable achievement. In parts the text here reads more as an *apologia* for William White's life than as a recollection of his son's. A sense of unease may be identified alongside the deferential tone of an obedient son.

The place given to the elder White's political views and parliamentary involvement is not unexpected, for they were a well-known part of his life in Bedford and a matter of public record. But the representation of his links with Bunyan Meeting, where public and private merge, is inadequate and misleading. There seems to be a desire to play down his involvement, with no reference to his role as a deacon and trustee, his preaching, or Sunday school

---

[12] Maclean, p. 35.

[13] Coe, *When the Grass was Taller*, p. 142.

[14] William White senior has in one place been identified with a bookseller at 24 Pall Mall, recipient of a letter from Thomas Carlyle of 22 March 1852 which refers to involvement in the scandalous sale of forged Byron and Shelley manuscripts; *The Collected Letters of Thomas and Jane Welsh Carlyle*, ed. by C. de L. Ryals, K.J. Fielding, and others (Durham, NC: Duke University Press, 1999), XXVII, pp. 73-75. However Hale's father was still in Bedford at this date, and checks made by two current editors of the Carlyle letters project, Aileen Christianson and Jane Roberts (University of Edinburgh), and by David Southern (Managing Editor at Duke University Press) reveal notes filed with the holograph in the Duke archives proving William White of Pall Mall to be a long-standing London resident unconnected with Bedford. The misattribution has now been corrected in the Carlyle Letters Online (<:http://www.carlyleletters.dukejournals.org/>) [accessed 20 September 2010].

[15] *When the Grass was Taller*, p. 146.

teaching and superintendency.[16] There is no way to test what White says about his father's changing religious views - the embrace of 'moderate Calvinism' - but the facts do not show that he distanced himself from the chapel, for he only ceased to be a trustee on leaving Bedford.[17] He had held that position from 1836, and was chairman when he resigned in April 1853, shortly before the already planned move to London.[18] This makes inexplicable Hale's contention that his father 'left' the Meeting 'in 1850'.[19]

The Trustees had expressed concern for some time about members who absented themselves from Communion services, and several reviews of membership were carried out after the 1850 rebuilding of the chapel. Those unable to meet this obligation of membership were to be removed from the roll, and in May 1854 letters were sent to more than forty members in this position.[20] Like William White many of the other recipients were no longer resident in Bedford, and did not apply to renew their membership. There is no evidence here of estrangement. Perhaps behind his son's account lies some embarrassment that William White had been put in an uncomfortable position because of the events at New College, or possibly it marks an attempt by Hale to demonstrate that his loosening of ties with formal religion had its real origin in his father's similar disengagement. The records of Lion Walk offer a parallel which suggests a wider problem of out-of-date membership lists, and therefore no reason to suppose any special animus against William White for the pruning at Bedford. At the Colchester church, in 1853 'steps were ... taken to deal with a considerable list of non-resident members, and each was notified that unless transfer was taken to another Church within twelve months ...their names would be erased'.[21]

The considerable space devoted to his father highlights the comparative silence about life within the family circle, specifically of siblings. This is not

---

[16] His ties with the chapel were shaped by a close friendship with the minister, Samuel Hillyard; see Tibbutt, *Bunyan Meeting*, p. 56. The *Autobiography* suggests White senior's larger role (p. 8, Ch. I).

[17] Maclean (p. 97 note 2) describes him as a trustee until his death, but this seems to refer to continued inclusion on an official list by some oversight.

[18] *Trustees of Bedford Old Meeting Minute Book*, entry for 26 April 1853 (Bedfordshire Record Office, BY 9/2).

[19] Writing to Sophie Partridge in a letter of 20 December 1906, from *Letters to Three Friends*, p. 249. He seems to have ceased leading the Sunday school in around 1850 however. Conceivably financial embarrassment as his business weakened caused unease at Bunyan and prompted a desire for withdrawal.

[20] Details from the *Trustees Minute Book*, entries for 1853 and 1854 (BY 9/2).

[21] In E. A. Blaxill, *History of Lion Walk Congregational Church, Colchester, 1642-197* (Colchester: Benham & Company, Printers, 1938), p. 34. The problem caused by non-resident members is not specified, but the context was the poor financial state of the church.

unusual in the genre, for a distinctive element in such accounts is the quest for understanding about one's development. The self is perceived as unique, and 'almost without exception, the man or woman who, later in life, returns in imagination to revisit and re-create a past childhood was, in that childhood, a solitary, an alienated, an exceptional child. Not necessarily lonely, but, in all essential ways, conscious of being alone'.[22] There is a little more family information in the *Early Life* than might be gleaned from the *Autobiography*, but it hardly diminishes the sense of isolation. His sisters are mere shadows without delineation or personality. Tam might also have featured as slightly, had not his wildness, artistic ability and early death called for comment (pp.5-9). His tragedy had a lasting effect. Hale's thwarted desire to follow his brother as an artist brings into sharp relief the expulsion from the 'higher' path chosen for him; suggesting also that this failure might not have been wholly undesired. While memory naturally centres on the self, and an accurate recollection of all the details of early years cannot be expected, this in itself cannot fully explain the phenomena here described. White is one set apart, and the influence of the Prodigal Son motif is probably to be discerned; the vivid recollection of a sermon on this parable by Caleb Morris is a notable inclusion at the end of the *Early Life*. (pp.86-87). Separation and inclusion are in tension, reflecting the profound insider/outsider duality so often displayed in Hale White's writings.

Although White's father lived in retirement near his son at Carshalton, this does not remove the suspicion that some unease marked their relationship.[23] When considering where to settle in his own retirement White ruled out Bedford, for despite having 'many friends in the place of my birth', his 'father's shade' seemed to haunt the place; the subsequent 'dislike' of the town suggests very mixed memories of the man.[24] It is with some relief that White leaves the narration of his father's life and returns to his own story - though straight away he is dependent upon others for the first datable event after his birth, the danger posed by a mob attacking his parents' home during the violently contested election of 1832 (p.39). He was just a year old. The place in which he grew up was as important as the family and community into which he was born, and this he next describes.

People and Place

White's fictional writings on Bedford cannot always be reconciled with evidence from other sources, and in the supposedly factual *Early Life* due

---

[22] Coe, *When the Grass was Taller*, p. 51.

[23] White had earlier often used his parents' house in Denbigh Place as a London base, and they in turn spent many weekends in Surrey; see Maclean, p. 169.

[24] From a letter to Mrs Colenutt in November 1891, given in *Letters to Three Friends*, p. 52.

allowance must still be made for the attempted recall of a child's perspective. This releases the writer from full responsibility for accuracy in historical detail, though this must be balanced by the reader's awareness of such limitation.

The immediate physical surroundings of childhood have great significance, given the smallness of the world which children inhabit. The home is vitally important, and the general *locale* hardly less so. For the city-dweller a few streets may make up the whole of the known world. White was more fortunate, enjoying the town of Bedford and its surrounding countryside. In later life, on return visits, he felt as if he had never really belonged anywhere else, despite the evidence presented that some memories were painful.[25] The sense of exile is often present in his writings. Place determines many of the influences on the growing child, especially in this case the heritage of Dissent and Bunyan Meeting. For White, it is the simple country pleasures which stand out from his early years, in the depiction of childhood as Edenic. Powerful impressions of life arise in the homes of family and friends, followed by the immediate surroundings of the town, with access as a growing child to a wider geographical area encompassing the countryside up to natural boundaries (of roads, rivers and the sea) to the known and experienced world.

People - Close Relations and Friends

In this record the influences of people and place overlap. First to be described is the home of his maternal grandmother in Colchester; fine detail and the memory of sense experiences are common in recollections of this type. The smell of the privet hedge, the note of the old-fashioned harpsichord and - absolutely typical of White's character sketches - the piety of his grandparents (pp.9-10). Equally typically, in relating his grandparents' spiritual exercises it is his grandmother who is particularly marked for her devotion. This feature is repeated in the description of his aunt, the wife of Uncle Thomas Chignell and mother of William. Her disturbingly individualistic spirituality, coupled with personal kindnesses, endeared her to the young Hale; 'the survival in my memory of her cakes, gingerbread, and kisses; has done me more good, moral good … than sermons or punishment' (p.12).[26] The importance of authentic and generous relationship over right belief portrayed time and again in the novels, frequently in female characters, surely has its origin in these early experiences.

The houses of Bedford relations were evidently open to him a good deal, and visits are lovingly recalled. The closest family were the Lovells, his father's sister and brother-in-law. Uncle Lovell 'was kindness itself', and the young

---

[25] After a visit made in August 1893 he wrote to his son about having 'a right to be there'; quoted in Stone, p. 154.

[26] These memories, with an emphasis upon the kindness appreciated by children, add weight to the possibility that at home this was not the case.

Hale enjoyed sharing in his business trips around the area (pp.22-26). With an emphasis upon outdoor attractions his home and business are not described in detail, but at this house, after the age of ten, Hale would often join his parents for supper. This privilege may have been an important rite of passage in growing up, but no home receives higher praise than that of Jane Reed's parents. Here was real pleasure in unfeigned simplicity, an 'easier' and 'much more natural' life (p.41). The joy of living in one room is keenly contrasted with the over-furnished interior where discomfort is the rule, and there can be little doubt that the family home is in mind here. Likewise, Jane's 'unbounded generosity, and ... unreasoning spontaneity' has, by implication, an authenticity lacking at home (p.43). The liberality of the friend in Potter Street 'in some way related to my father' is celebrated in much the same way for the access granted to his garden fruit (pp.44-45). It is scarcely possible here to separate the attractions of houses or gardens from the attractiveness of their inhabitants, for people and place are so closely linked. The warmth and richness of these recollections make the contrasting silence on home life more revealing. Against all expectations, the White home and household life are barely touched upon. There are no descriptions of the daily routines, of family meals, or shared activities within or outside the home. The nearest exception to this is the detail given of Sunday observance, and much less is included than in the *Autobiography*.

The possibility that tensions within the family made life uncomfortable is reinforced by this paucity of references. This most immediate of childhood worlds is often described in detail in texts of this type - the rooms, furniture, furnishings, domestic habits, and so on.[27] There is hardly a trace of that here. A few details are given, and others may be inferred. The High Street address, the house's lack of drainage, back yard well, and the breaking of windows by a mob in 1832 are very briefly mentioned (pp.5,13,39). Without being made explicit, it seems that the High Street premises consisted of his father's shop and printing business with living accommodation above.[28] There are just three aspects of home life which are remembered as enjoyable, and none involve his parents. They emphasize the solitary aspects of White's childhood; reading *Chambers' Journal* in the warm kitchen during the breakfast break after early school, reading the *Tales of Ulysses* in his father's shop, and exploring the pages of the 'Battle Book' military atlas in the dining-room with his sister (pp.48-49). The interiors are not described at all, and while no unhappiness is recorded it is surely significant that activities elsewhere are so favourably reported, and going to Oakley with 'Nurse Jane' is significantly characterised

[27] See examples in Burnett, *Destiny Obscure*, pp. 223-228.

[28] Compare *Catharine Furze*; 'up to the year 1840, the tradesmen of Eastthorpe had lived at their shops', p. 22, Ch. II. The Whites were certainly living over the High Street shop after that date, and throughout Hale's childhood.

as an 'escape' (p.41). Clearly the real pleasures of White's early years were found outside the home, and perhaps supremely, by his own description, in the countryside rather than the town.

Place - Town and Country

'Never was there a town better suited to a boy than Bedford', he writes - not for itself, but because 'the fields were then close at hand' (pp.49-50). In describing the town, the stress is very much upon its sleepy and unchanging nature. It has often been noted of the novels that the date of setting predates the time of publication by perhaps thirty or forty years, but this does not go quite far enough. There, as here, the descriptions of a stagnant and remote backwater are not true to the facts for the years of White's conscious memories, which by his own admission at the very earliest date only from the coronation celebrations of June 1838, aged six and a half (p.40).[29] The contrast between his description and one exactly contemporary account has been noted. While J. H. Matthiason had every reason to stress change and renewal, his picture of Bedford accords with that from other sources.[30] There were many signs of change and development which White omits, continuing a stance already adopted in the novels. White's High Street is marked by the lack of sanitation, while Matthiason extols the shops there 'vieing in taste and show even with those of the metropolis itself'; his Bedford is a town full of 'life and bustle', on market days 'one of the most crowded little capitals that can easily be imagined'.[31]

The reluctance to embrace development, and nostalgia for the unchanging past, are persistent aspects of White's writing. In the *Early Life* the pull of the past is further represented by stories pre-dating his own life, and presumably learnt in the family circle and at his grandparents' fireside - for example, of the famous Bedford flood of 1828 (p.14).

Though spending more years at school than many of his Bedford contemporaries, White records this time perfunctorily. He was probably unhappy at the Modern School, and almost certainly failed to achieve his potential, though whether this was due to poor teaching or lack of application cannot be determined. His feelings are unconvincingly concealed by feigned indifference, while the appeal of life outside school is accurately conveyed; 'the recollections of school are not interesting to me in any way, but it is altogether otherwise with playtime and holidays' (p.48). Nevertheless, the little included

---

[29] Earliest memories are commonly linked to significant national or local events, as Burnett demonstrates, *Destiny Obscure*, pp. 24–26.

[30] Joyce Godber's history fails to demonstrate this when she draws upon White without recognising the resulting inaccuracies; see *History of Bedfordshire*, pp. 484-485.

[31] *Bedford and Its Environs*, p. 43; the writer notes older and unimproved areas also. His is not a falsely positive account.

on education adds something to the sense of place. The memory of his arrival one morning at the first school - advertised for "young ladies" - in a shop boy's wheelbarrow evidently pleased him (p.40), but the Modern School was largely put from his mind.[32] The reason for this may lie in the knowledge that it lacked the prestige of the Grammar School, and in not preparing pupils for university entrance emphasized the barriers facing the children of Dissenters. While recording his father's unhappiness at the Grammar School, it may be imagined that Hale felt cheated of the wider opportunities which education there might have afforded him, possibly fuelling a sense of alienation from his father.

Emphasis upon pleasures is not simply a device intended to distract from less happy memories. The attractions of outdoor life to the young boy are recalled with deep feeling, even if the descriptions of the Bedfordshire countryside are more vividly re-created from the far side of his Romantic enlightenment. Love of nature is a constant theme in the fiction, as in later short stories and other occasional writings, but here the aspects of freedom and unhindered (usually physical) pleasure are to the fore. Once more there is an implicit contrast with the constraints of home life. The natural world is unspoilt, inviting, and wonderfully open. Richard Coe has traced the importance in many childhoods of the boundaries of the immediate world, and also of the routes which lead beyond it. This is not specially evident in the *Early Life*, but can be seen in the fiction, where the sea and open sky in one direction and the Great North Road in the other feature as boundaries or thresholds.[33]

The countryside offers rare glimpses of White at ease among those of his own age, the un-named friends with whom he explores the fields and rivers. The solitary, even timid figure suggested by much of the *Early Life* becomes the hunter, swimmer, skater and explorer. Several 'we' passages describe joint expeditions, while 'in the winter, fishing and boating gave way to skating' (p.54).[34] One incident is of unusual significance. Having already described his learning to swim at school, he now recalls the terror of panicking while swimming in the sea, as the fear of drowning needlessly came upon him; 'there was no real danger of failure of strength, but my heart began to beat furiously, the shore became dim, and I gave myself up for lost' (p.53). Learning in a moment to conquer this dread, he safely made the shore. His mature conclusion that 'it was not nature or passion which carried me through, but a conviction wrought by the reason' (p.54) ascribes triumph to the will; it can be argued that

---

[32] In the *Autobiography* the good intentions of the headmaster are mentioned, but the teaching itself nevertheless condemned as ineffective, p. 3, Ch. I.

[33] *When the Grass was Taller*, pp. 205-206, and note the importance of the Great North Road in *Revolution*, p. 230, Ch. XVI.

[34] Did Hale explore with his troubled younger brother Tam (Samuel)? There is no hint of this. Compare some very close parallel passages in the *Autobiography*, as on p. 4, Ch. I.

the role of the mind shows something of the influence of Spinoza. The fear of drowning is represented in the fiction - as in the story 'Michael Trevanion' bound with *Miriam's Schooling* - and there may be a subconscious link between this unwelcome absorption into a watery absolute and examples of union with nature equally unsought, but welcome and liberating (another possibly Spinozan emphasis); for example as portrayed at the close of *Mark Rutherford's Deliverance*. Thus nature is not always benign or restorative, and this complex area has a part to play in White's religious development. Early exposure to Sabbatarian tracts featuring the drowning of children daring to swim on Sundays probably feeds into this at some level.[35]

Believing and Belonging: Faith, Nurture and Spiritual Development

White was very aware of the heritage into which he entered as the child of Dissenting parents in a town whose most famous son was John Bunyan. His biography of the great puritan affirmed the continuing importance of Bunyan's legacy; 'the effect of religion in those for whom it is alive is the same as it was for him. It increases the value of the whole man; it deepens love, it exalts the stature, and adds force to every faculty'.[36] White's memory of Bunyan Meeting however is generally taken to be negative, as Sunday is described in unhappy contrast with the rest of the week, though the evidence in the *Early Life* is more ambiguous than this verdict suggests.

Bunyan Meeting is portrayed as living off its past and ill-adapted for the present or future. There is no suggestion of a narrow or restricting upbringing however, but 'belonging' without a personally challenging belief seems all too possible, for the whole social world and self-understanding is based upon the chapel and its congregation. Yet piety is represented by family beyond the chapel. The relations introduced are probably among those who have inspired characters in the fiction, especially the females noted for godliness and individuality. His grandmother, 'a most pious women', and especially his Colchester aunt who 'read *George Herbert* in the porch' of a nearby church in the early morning, clearly made a deep impression upon him (pp.10-11). The recognition of true faith in private practice is noteworthy - it is not tied to communal worship and church membership, though this was obviously a key part of White's upbringing. Significantly, there is no mention of the religious practices of the White household. The intention may be (in support of his own separation from public worship) to show that such externals are always less important for the true believer. It is notable that the holy exemplars are female,

---

[35] See *Early Life*, p. 46. It is not clear if White intends the reader to understand that he bathed on Sundays and thus had special reason to fear drowning (baptism too might be deemed a 'unitive' experience though he does not explore this).

[36] *John Bunyan* (London: Hodder and Stoughton, 1905), p. 233.

for this is in contrast to the free-thinking nature of the late fictional heroines. What they have in common is also important; both groups think for themselves and have scant regard for convention.

Bunyan Meeting is further presented as ossified and rudderless. Though well attended, its spiritual capital had been severely eroded; 'the reason why it held together was the simple loyalty which prevents a soldier or a sailor from mutinying, although the commanding officer may deserve no respect' (p.16). The historical accuracy of this judgement may be questioned, for it seems to reflect a certain animosity between the Whites and John Jukes, minister from 1840 to 1866. His predecessor, Samuel Hillyard, had enjoyed a long and fruitful ministry, and, significantly, had been a friend and mentor to the young William White.[37] This close sympathy was not repeated under Jukes, who also faced criticism for not better supporting Hale and his parents during the turbulent New College experience. Tibbutt's history of the church however indicates that in many areas his was a successful ministry which saw increased membership, the rebuilding of the chapel, and a commitment to overseas mission.[38] The Bedford Training College itself was a very significant enterprise, under-reported by White. His is an unfairly jaundiced account. Such a negative picture prepares the reader for White's disillusionment, while almost placing the blame upon the church for failing to nurture faith, exonerating him from responsibility.

The dominant theology appears as a form of modified Calvinism, specifically that 'moderate Calvinism' which played down predestinarian doctrine, and tended towards universalism.[39] Traditional Calvinism was not formally repudiated, but in practice 'some of the congregation were a little Arminian, and St. James could not be totally neglected' (p.17). If White's story is one of disenchantment with rigid doctrine and abstract theologising, this was reflective of the wider Dissenting community too, for the emphasis was commonly on the personal and experiential. This subjective turn was fuelled by the spiritual experience of nature, as influentially displayed for example in Carlyle's writings. The resulting 'depreciation of the sacraments, discipline and church order' helps to explain why such features appeared to be so unimportant

[37] Hillyard had been a particular supporter of William after his father's early death when the boy was only eight years old; see Maclean, p. 35. The Reverend James Harden of Tanner's Lane owes something in character to the principled Hillyard; *Revolution*, pp. 252-253, Ch. XVII.

[38] Tibbutt, *Bunyan Meeting*, pp. 53-66.

[39] Associated in Independency with Edward Williams; studied by W. T. Owen, *Edward Williams, D.D., 1750-1813: His Life, Thought and Influence* (Cardiff: University of Wales Press, 1963).

for White.[40] White's lack of interest in theology proper, and questions of church life and order therefore do not in themselves necessarily differentiate him very greatly from many who retained a formal allegiance to the church and attended public worship.

There is much about church life that cannot be gleaned from the *Early Life*, but it gives an account of the services, including the Lord's Supper. This 'strangest' of services (p.18) emphasized division not unity, as the unregenerate who had to sit in the gallery watched friends and neighbours partake; 'the mistress might be seated aloft while her husband and her conceited maid-of-all-work, Tabitha, enjoyed full gospel privileges below' (p.19).[41] A silence on baptism is hard to explain unless White himself had not been baptised. The mode of baptism had caused controversy during Hillyard's pastorate, eventually leading to the secession of a Baptist minority.[42] This divisive issue in the life of the church is not referred to in White's writings, and it seems possible that baptisms (however administered) were in his day conducted outside public worship, though in earlier times this had not been the case.[43]

White's vivid recollections of services have become famous and are often quoted. The oppressively stale atmosphere of the evening services in which he struggled to keep awake and women fainted refers to the building demolished in 1849, which was known for its poor ventilation; 'the windows of the meeting-house streamed inside with condensed breath, and the air we took into our lungs was poisonous' (p.45). There is no sense of inspiration or real engagement with the services, or recall of Sunday school instruction, though his father was Superintendent. The absence of any reference to the specifics of faith instruction and worship is remarkable.

The material on Bunyan Meeting is not all presented together, but appears in discrete sections interspersed with other subject matter, as if the writer cannot approach directly this part of his history. The introductory section on the loyal but inert membership is followed by the description of the Lord's Supper (pp.18-19) and then a sketch of the 'elders of the church' (p.20). One such, a family friend, 'was perfectly straightforward, God-fearing also, and therefore wise', but for all that frowned on innovations such as 'pōtry (poetry) in the

---

[40] So Ian Sellers, *Nineteenth-Century Nonconformity* (London: Edward Arnold, 1977), p. 23; he writes of the 1890s, but this is the outcome of trends discernible much earlier in the century.

[41] A typically fine piece of social commentary and acute observation; with nothing to imply that White ever took communion, despite admission to membership.

[42] Hillyard's predecessor, Joshua Symonds, had come to a Baptist position during his Pastorate; he continued as minister, under some restrictions, but then a paedobaptist group left to form Howard Meeting, Tibbutt, *Bunyan Meeting*, pp. 35-36.

[43] Tibbutt, *Bunyan Meeting*, p. 43, describes cases of public sprinkling and immersion in 1815, perhaps both of adults however. Note just one description of baptism in the fiction, at Zoar Strict Baptist chapel in *Revolution*, pp. 237-238, Ch. XVI.

pulpit' (pp.20-21). This is nevertheless a positive assessment compared with the *Autobiography* ('the horrible hypocrisy' of the long prayer, 'totally unlike the model recommended to us in the New Testament', for example) tempered by the perspective of old age.[44] There is comparison with 'the superficial young person of the present day' (pp.19-20). Thus at the end of his life White can be seen revising an earlier, harsher judgement on these men, whose true value he had been slow to recognise. The importance of what is immediately apprehended and proved in everyday experience has been affirmed, the same lesson learned in life by the author himself.

The writer's father is not to be taken as typifying the religious outlook of the average church member, though even so there is a frustrating lack of detail. White highlights the period in his father's life between 1849 and 1851 as one of significant change, an estrangement from chapel and the stricter doctrines of Calvinism (pp.37-38). It cannot be unimportant that this coincides exactly with Hale's time at Cheshunt College. The cause is given as the reading of Carlyle's *Heroes and Hero Worship* and *Sartor Resartus*. In language reminiscent of that used to describe the effect of his own discovery of Wordsworth, he notes 'there is nothing in these two books directly hostile either to church or dissent, but they laid hold of him as no books had ever held, and the expansion they wrought in him could not possibly tolerate the limitations of orthodoxy' (p.38).[45] The implication, not quite spelled out, is that William White became distanced from Bunyan Meeting, though the evidence does not show any formal breach. The relevant factor in Carlyle's thought is probably the stress in *Sartor* upon the difference between the external language of belief (including the doctrinal expression) and the underlying truth it represents; the changeable 'clothes' in which reality is dressed. Hale next turns more directly to his own experiences.

Early Religious Impressions: The Fear of Hell

At first this is to recall a powerful early fear that he might not be 'one of God's children, like Samuel' because he was insufficiently attentive in services, and prone to childish temptations (p.46). A stress upon election might naturally produce such anxiety in young and old alike, depending upon the doctrine of assurance taught. Here a genuine memory appears to be unaltered by later reflection. Identified temptations include Sabbath-breaking to swim in the Ouse; such activities were prohibited in the starkest terms by popular tracts for

---

[44] *Autobiography*, p. 6, Ch. I; presumably White has the Lord's Prayer in mind. Under John Jukes the prayer at the Old Meeting might last more than half-an-hour, the congregation standing (Tibbutt, *Bunyan Meeting*, p. 59).

[45] Compare with Hale and Wordsworth, p. 62, and some parallel passages in the *Autobiography*, pp. 18-21, Ch. II.

children. White mentions one 'by a certain divine named Todd' (p.46), which included the sort of warnings that others encountered in the more famous *Token for Children* by James Janeway.[46] Fear of hell (and of sudden death) was a common feature of such works, though there is an incongruity that moderate Calvinism sought to modify it with a softening of teaching on eternal punishment; evidently this message had not yet penetrated children's literature or Bunyan Sunday School. White's fears, and exposure to tracts such as Todd's, may have arisen in the context of Sunday school instruction, an important subject for understanding expectations upon the young at Bunyan Meeting and relevant to the confession later made to enter into membership. He recalled another point of Todd's, an argument ridiculing a universe without a designer, in which 'the geese had hoofs, and "clamped about like horses". Such was the awful consequence of creation by a No-God or nothing' (p.47). In fact this came not from the same book as the Sabbath warning but from Todd's equally widely disseminated *Truth Made Simple*, though White's account of it is otherwise tolerably accurate.[47]

These references notwithstanding, the character of his religious nurture is hampered by a lack of detailed evidence since White is unhelpfully vague about any formal religious instruction. This is regrettable, for the teaching offered to children reveals prevailing assumptions about their spiritual status and potential. Despite this some useful indicators of the growing significance of such teaching can be adduced from studies of the British and American Sunday school movements, which show changes in understanding about their role and purpose. Charles Cashdollar notes how often the religious press released works in both British and American editions, leading to a constant exchange of ideas and teaching material between the two countries throughout this period.[48]

Hale White and Nineteenth-Century Sunday Schools

The earliest Sunday schools were typically concerned with the teaching of reading and only later did their primary purpose become one of spiritual education and nurture. The first provision in Bedford, in 1787, was of the

---

[46] The American Congregationalist John Todd (1800-1873) was the author of improving books widely used on both sides of the Atlantic, including *Lectures to Children, Familiarly Illustrating Important Truth: First Series* (London: George Routledge and Sons, n.d.), which includes the Sabbath story to which White alludes (pp. 135-140); Michael Watts notes the importance of early teaching about hell in conversion accounts, including references to Janeway; see *The Dissenters, vol. II*, p. 78.

[47] *Truth Made Simple: Being a System of Theology for Children on the Attributes of God*; first published in England by Ball, Arnold and Co., 1839, quoted here from an undated later edition, p. 44 ('Sequel to Lecture 1').

[48] *A Spiritual Home: Life in British and American Reformed Congregations, 1830-1915* (University Park, PA: Pennsylvania State University Press, 2000), p. 9.

'Town Meeting' type, in which individuals representing their different churches co-operated to provide teaching 'under one management and their expenses paid out of one fund' but delivered separately on multiple sites.[49] Five Anglican parishes and four nonconformist churches, including Bunyan Meeting, participated in the venture. Since in many centres nonconformists were excluded from such arrangements, this situation reflects the strength of Dissent in Bedford and its vital role in the religious affairs of the town.[50]

Commonly in the growing Sunday school movement reading (and sometimes writing, though this was controversial for some) was taught from the Bible and catechism. Elementary skills were learned though appropriate religious texts which reinforced a moral purpose. Again this can be traced in Bedford, where the paid teachers were each responsible for about forty children, and attached to a particular church. This level of staffing reflected the aim of imparting religious knowledge and rudimentary education, for it gave neither time nor opportunity for attention to personal spiritual development. It does not therefore seem that conversion was directly intended, rather the promotion of a civilizing ethic. Boys and girls were instructed separately under a teacher of the same sex, in Bunyan's case often in the teacher's house, before joining the congregation for the morning service.[51] At Bunyan, the scholars also gathered during the afternoon for a further lesson, probably organised by voluntary helpers and more focussed upon Christian education. Teaching might have been related to the content of the morning service which the children had attended, a practice already recommended elsewhere.[52] The tensions inherent in cross-denominational working caused problems in many areas, and in Bedford the joint organisation of Sunday schools broke down by 1812.

The pattern for Bunyan's children in White's youth is described in the *Autobiography*; 'after family prayers and breakfast the business of the day began with the Sunday-school at nine o'clock. We were taught our Catechism and Bible there till a quarter past ten. We were then marched across the road into the chapel .... There were three services every Sunday'.[53] J. Guinness Rogers, a near contemporary, in his recollections confirms this as entirely

---

[49] Tibbutt, *Bunyan Meeting*, p. 67. Philip Cliff describes the differing early methods; *The Rise and Development of the Sunday School Movement in England, 1780-1980* (Redhill: National Christian Education Council, 1986), especially pp. 6-7, 32-33.

[50] See Cliff, *Rise and Development*, pp. 41-43, for common tensions between Anglicans and nonconformists.

[51] Tibbutt, *Bunyan Meeting*, pp. 68-69.

[52] Described with approval in an early outline of Sunday schools in the *Evangelical Magazine*, 1798, cited by Stephen Orchard, 'From Catechism Class to Sunday School', in *The Sunday School Movement: Studies in the Growth and Decline of Sunday Schools*, ed. by Stephen Orchard and John H. Y. Briggs (Milton Keynes: Paternoster, 2007), pp. 1-16 (p. 12).

[53] *Autobiography*, pp. 5-6, Ch. I.

typical of the nonconformist Sunday.[54] At Lion Walk in Colchester the model again was nearly identical.[55] Tibbutt's history of Bunyan Meeting clarifies the activities of a normal Sunday, and adds some details not recorded by White.[56] The main service took place after morning Sunday school, attended by the children, who returned to the chapel after lunch for a short afternoon service timed to suit members living outside the town, followed by a further teaching period. The scholars sat in the gallery for the services, but did not attend in the evening as a group. It is not known how typical White was in accompanying his parents for the last service of the day. Thomas Green, a grocer and chapel trustee, was Superintendent of the Sunday school in Hale's earliest years, until William White took over in 1840. William served for ten years, and with his 'natural ability and force of character greatly improved the school'.[57] Detailed records have not survived, but in 1847 there were more than two hundred pupils and twenty-three teachers, indicating that teaching could be provided in small groups, which would favour spiritual encouragement. This is significant, for it demonstrates the changing nature of instruction, and the underlying intention.

As Superintendent, White senior saw the need for better provision for the children, which surely reflects new ideas, and at his instigation they ceased to attend the morning service, instead meeting for worship on their own after the morning teaching session. This was also the case at Lion Walk from at least 1849 and was clearly part of a trend.[58] The ideal relationship between churches and their Sunday schools had long been debated, often fuelled by ministerial fears about too great an independence of schools as well as by practical and pedagogical concerns.[59] Hale remembered his father as having 'revolutionized the system of the children's Sunday School by releasing the children from attendance at the long and (to them) unintelligible morning service in church, and giving them a suitable service of their own'.[60] As the pattern described for

---

[54] See *J. Guinness Rogers: An Autobiography* (London: James Clarke, 1903), p. 28; he also bears witness to the moderate Calvinism which marked that era (p. 25).

[55] Described from a slightly earlier date, ca.1829, in Blaxill, *History of Lion Walk Congregational Church*, p. 55.

[56] *Bunyan Meeting*, pp. 56, 67-70.

[57] Tibbutt, *Bunyan Meeting*, p. 70.

[58] Blaxill, *History of Lion Walk Congregational Church*, p. 35.

[59] 'The Sunday School is not a distinct and independent organization apart from the church. ... Hers is the arm that toils ... hers the lap into which the fruit is poured out', argued a *British Banner* writer in a supplement celebrating the jubilee of the Sunday School Union; 21 July 1852, p. 489 ('Claims of the Sunday-School').

[60] Reported from a conversation with Dorothy in 1910, *Groombridge Diary*, p. 315. Tibbutt uses this reference without attribution and possibly indirectly through Catherine Maclean (who shared information with him before her book was published), adding nothing new, *Bunyan Meeting*, p. 56.

Bunyan has shown, children had already been treated as a group, and seated in the gallery during morning worship. Separate services was a natural development, but elsewhere they were not without criticism from those who feared a weakening of parental responsibility for the spiritual nurture of their children; 'a false or an exaggerated individualism which would send us to the house of prayer as isolated units, each one for himself'.[61] Nevertheless, Bunyan was among many other churches which established their own age-appropriate children's services, a common practice by the 1860s.[62] The new system suggested a close pastoral concern for the children and their spiritual welfare.[63] Though note that it is represented as a sign of change for the worst when at Tanner's Lane 'the afternoon service was dropped and turned into a service for the Sunday-school children'.[64]

It is curious that Hale does not mention anything about life in the school, especially since he taught in it himself in his teenage years. Dorothy records a conversation with him on this in February 1910, the year in which the 'Autobiographical Notes' were begun; 'he says that he remembers teaching a class of little boys in Sunday School when he was 13 or 14 years old'.[65] The intention must be to play down any positive influence from Bunyan Meeting, and this suggests again the need for caution in accepting without question what else he says about his time there.

It is not clear if conversions were a direct aim of teaching in the Bunyan Sunday School. If Hale was a teacher before having been admitted as a church member, and therefore (it appears) without having testified to any conversion, this implies little emphasis upon conversion. However if he undertook this responsibility following his admission (which would fit with his age as described in reminiscence to Dorothy), because only after that confession could he be approved to do so, then at least formally conversions might have been the goal. It might also have been deemed a suitable occupation during his time of preparation before enrolling at Cheshunt.

---

61 The Baptist, S. G. Green, cited in J. H. Y. Briggs, 'The Baptist Contribution to the Sunday School Movement in the Nineteenth Century', in *The Sunday School Movement*, pp. 42-63 (p. 56). Green was writing in 1884, but reflecting on an issue very much alive earlier in the century.

62 Among Baptist churches at any rate; Briggs, 'The Baptist Contribution to the Sunday School Movement in the Nineteenth Century', p. 56.

63 William White's positive role here does nothing to support the indications his son gives of alienation from the Meeting by the end of the decade.

64 *Revolution*, p. 387, Ch. XXVII; see also the interesting reflections on college-trained clergy with London degrees, and advanced views on the atonement.

65 *Groombridge Diary* p. 315, a reference again to the material taken over by Tibbutt, *Bunyan Meeting*, p. 56.

Children and Spiritual Development

A key issue in the evolving work of Sunday schools was the spiritual status of children from believing families and the means suitable for their faith development. White's reflections on conversion highlight the difficulties faced by churches in which admission to membership depended upon a confession of faith derived from the traditional evangelical model.[66] His case, paralleled by others, shows by mid-century a tacit admission that children's experience did not naturally conform to this archetype. Where an application for church membership involved testifying to conversion, confession could mean explaining the *absence* of any dramatic change. A theological and psychological reappraisal was needed to explain and justify this adaptation. A Baptist writer, Samuel Green, argued that improved religious education in Sunday schools would reduce the number of children able to assign a specific date to their conversion, as progressive illumination replaced crisis conversions. Events aimed at inducing conversion could be unhelpful, and warnings of hell fire were deprecated. Children were to be made aware of God's encompassing love.[67] The anxiety induced by emotional approaches was to be regretted, and Green showed pastoral insight into the dangers posed by the resulting self-absorption.[68] At least in retrospect, White too was well aware of this risk.[69] These questions were understandably of concern in many churches, nationally and beyond, as pastors and teachers sought to engage more effectively with the young.

Some transatlantic Parallels

In American Sunday schools important conclusions were being drawn about children's spiritual development, and these gained widespread currency in other parts of the English-speaking world. Anne Boylan has shown how similar transatlantic practice was to that in Britain during the early decades of the nineteenth century. Teaching was based on learning to read the Bible, with the aim of spreading 'religious knowledge, and the behaviour associated with it',

---

[66] On the origins and development of a stereotypical narrative see Bruce Hindmarsh, *The Evangelical Conversion Narrative: Spiritual Autobiography in Early Modern England* (Oxford: Oxford University Press, 2007), especially the first two chapters.

[67] Green's views as summarised by Briggs, 'The Baptist Contribution to the Sunday School Movement in the Nineteenth Century', pp. 50-51.

[68] See Briggs again, 'The Baptist Contribution', pp. 54-55. Green also notes a concern that children would repeat what adults wanted to hear – as White clearly did.

[69] This schema 'concentrated my thoughts upon myself, and made me of great importance', *Early Life*, p. 59. The same objection could also be argued from a traditional Calvinist perspective; man becomes exalted, as if God's grace depends upon human decision rather than divine election.

and teachers did not expect to build up a close relationship with their pupils.[70] This mirrors the first phase of the movement in Britain, and the situation described in Bedford. Significant changes were to come, associated with the growth of free day schooling, leading to a much greater emphasis in Sunday schools upon religious instruction as a first step towards conversion. Sunday schools were becoming primarily composed of children from church families, and were thus the spiritual nurseries of the faith community. Class sizes and teacher rotation were adjusted to allow a much closer personal oversight of pupils, perhaps approximating to the sort of relationships which may have developed in the afternoon teaching at Bunyan Meeting.

Adolescence was seen as an appropriate age for the conversion towards which earlier teaching had been preparatory.[71] Not yet hardened to sin, and emotionally susceptible, teenage children were particularly suitable subjects for conversion. The difficulty of achieving this goal was one factor in a reappraisal of childhood religion which questioned the assumption that adult experiences could be simply replicated in the young. Separating children's experience from that of adults was a step towards a new understanding of their psychological make-up. Under the influence of a moderation of the doctrine of total depravity (especially regarding very young children who had never consciously sinned) and the romantic idealisation of childhood, a new conceptualisation of Sunday school teaching emerged.[72] Horace Bushnell's writings on Christian nurture typify these changes, as teaching aimed at conversion gradually gave way to an emphasis upon God's loving acceptance of the children of Christian parents, who would grow up within the church in a state of grace. Famously summarised in his view that 'the child is to grow up a Christian, and never know himself as being otherwise', naturally Bushnell opposed any approach to children which encouraged pressured emotional responses.[73] The idea of conversion was never entirely supplanted however, and where it was seen as a process rather than a crisis it could co-exist with more developmental views.[74] Bushnell was sensitive to the mental harm which could result from inappropriate demands on children, and wished them to come to faith in their own time.

It was not just at the level of teaching and institutions that changing views of

---

[70] *Sunday School: The Formation of an American Institution, 1790-1880* (New Haven, CT: Yale University Press, 1988), p. 133.

[71] Boylan, *Sunday School*, pp. 141-142. Studies of conversion routinely show the importance of these years.

[72] As Boylan details for America, *Sunday School*, pp. 143-149.

[73] Quotation from his classic work cited by Margaret Bendroth with some valuable context; 'Horace Bushnell's *Christian Nurture*', in *The Child in Christian Thought*, ed. by Marcia J. Bunge (Grand Rapids, MI: William. B. Eerdmans, 2001), pp. 350-364 (p. 350). Bushnell's books were widely sold in Britain.

[74] Boylan explores the tension between conversion and nurture, *Sunday School*, p. 149.

children's spiritual status made themselves felt. The same story might be told over a longer time-scale through the hymns in popular use. Alan Sell suggestively traces a change from regarding fallen humanity in general as 'worms' to a more optimistic view of human nature in which children especially were depicted as 'sunbeams'.[75] The gradual modification of high Calvinism on moral and doctrinal grounds is the essential background to these changes, but the need for individual conversion (however understood) is not diminished. Indeed Sell argues that the early Victorian period marks the beginning of the end for the older covenantal theologies of church membership in this tradition, supplanted by the emphasis upon personal conversion.[76]

In White's case the need to publicly testify to conversion was a significant factor in his later difficulties. The focus here has been upon the years leading up to Hale White's move to Cheshunt, though of course the *Early Life* text continues well beyond this point. The vital college years, and the application for membership at Bunyan which entering Cheshunt necessarily entailed, require separate treatment. This will include a detailed study of his admission to Bunyan Meeting, illuminated by some parallel instances of adolescent conversion. At several points George MacDonald's experience will be compared and contrasted with White's. The Scot's home background and church involvement must be outlined to make these points of comparison meaningful, although some details are impossible to recover.

George MacDonald: Context and Spiritual Development

In MacDonald's youth the Scottish churches were being disturbed by challenges to Calvinist orthodoxy, and especially to the doctrine of the atonement. As in England, a moderate Calvinism arose which rejected extreme interpretations of limited atonement, a change taking place alongside a wave of spiritual renewal encouraged by the influence of Charles Finney's *Lectures on Revival*.[77] The holding of meetings extending over several days which were a feature of the American revivalism took root, as they did in England, and preaching was often directed to securing conversions among existing

---

[75] 'From Worms to Sunbeams: The Dilution of Calvinism in English Congregationalism', *Journal of the United Reformed Church History Society*, 7 (2004), 253-274. This article also offers a useful introduction to the rise of English moderate Calvinism.

[76] 'From Worms to Sunbeams', p. 266.

[77] Escott writes of 'a remarkable revival of religion' among Scottish Congregational churches from 1839, though this is native-born in his examples, rather than attributed to American influence; *A History of Scottish Congregationalism* (Glasgow: Congregational Union of Scotland, 1960), p. 106. Richard Carwardine highlights the important American connection; *Transatlantic Revivalism: Popular Evangelicalism in Britain and America, 1790-1865* (Westport, CT: Greenwood Press, 1978), pp. 95-97.

adherents.[78] Finney's ideas were embraced by James Morison, who ministered in Banffshire, not far from Huntly, contributing to the turbulence which split Scottish Congregationalism in the early 1840s.[79] Conflicting ideas from this ferment may have been known to MacDonald in Aberdeen and earlier, for they surfaced from time to time at Huntly, but there is no reliable early evidence about the young man's beliefs.[80] Probably his son reads back into these days some advanced views, for instance of a wider hope which is evident in his fiction, without sufficient justification.[81] MacDonald's later confession that his faith was not personally alive until sometime in the 1840s implies a negative judgement of the Missionar Kirk's John Hill, and his own distinctive theological emphases can be seen as having developed in reaction against the example of an undue strictness which resisted engagement with new ideas. This is in tune with Robert Troup's description of his predecessor:

> Mr Hill ... was a Calvinist. He began his work as such, and so he continued, conservative, all but unchanged, from the first day of his ministry to the last. He had no sympathy with those who in his later years were earnestly proclaiming the universal love of the Father, the universal influence of the Holy Spirit, nor probably with those moderate Calvinists who preached the universal atonement of Christ.[82]

As Troup's comments suggest, the nature and extent of the work of Christ was not the only troublesome issue relating to salvation under discussion, for John Kirk of Hamilton (1813-1886) further undermined the Calvinist understanding of election by advancing a new view of the role of the Holy Spirit in conversion. Moderate Calvinists open to a wider scope for the atonement preserved the doctrine of election by positing a special work of the Spirit in the lives of those who received the Gospel message, enabling them to respond positively. Kirk argued instead that the Spirit was universally active in pressing

---

[78] Documented by William McNaughton, *Early Congregational Independency in the Highlands and Islands and the North-East of Scotland*, pp. xxiv-xxvi.

[79] David Robb has explored this background to MacDonald's Aberdeen years in 'George MacDonald at Blackfriars Chapel', *North Wind* [Journal of the George MacDonald Society], 5 (1986), 3-20 (pp. 5-7).

[80] Robert Troup records that the minister, John Hill, 'spoke strongly' against 'Morrisonianism' (the name sometimes attracted a second 'r'); The *Missionar Kirk*, p. 114.

[81] Following Robb therefore in hesitating to accept Greville's account (in *George MacDonald and His Wife*, p. 85) without corroboration, based as it is on interpreting much later fiction as faithfully portraying his father's experience.

[82] Troup goes on to mention MacDonald, and may have shaped this account to match the latter's beliefs; *The Missionar Kirk*, p. 133.

the claims of Christ upon all people, though only some found salvation.[83] There was room for Kirk's critics to suggest that he exalted human agency over Divine sovereignty, and these on-going disputes parallel the divisions caused in English Calvinism during the same period by challenges from within and without.[84] During his visit to Scotland Finney himself had some difficulty in understanding Kirk's teaching, which evidently left him uneasy.[85]

MacDonald's Aberdeen years were a stepping-stone towards independence. He worshipped at the city's Blackfriars Chapel during a time commonly held to have been one disquieting for his religious beliefs. However a tendency to read events from the fiction into his life, and a relatively uncritical reliance on Greville MacDonald's memoir in particular, has led to the significance of his Aberdeen experience being inadequately portrayed. David Robb demonstrates the importance of Blackfriars to MacDonald, and especially the role of the charismatic young minister John Kennedy who made it particularly popular with students.[86] In this he stands almost as a Scots equivalent of the London preachers like Caleb Morris and Thomas Binney, though he was a theological conservative and did not sympathise with those who welcomed James Morison's overturning of stricter Calvinist tenets. Kennedy's rejection of doctrinal modification led to a division in the church, and action against those who did not fully support him. MacDonald, in another parallel with Hale White, helped to teach children, but he and several others who had laboured in the Sunday school were among those relieved of their posts.[87] It may be for this reason that MacDonald never became a church member at Blackfriars, a status he had not entered into at Huntly either. This suggests that it was not seen as a

---

[83] As Escott summarises a complex controversy, see *Scottish Congregationalism*, pp. 107-108; for parallels in James Morison, who moved towards Kirk's position over time, pp. 116-124.

[84] The importance of John Kirk and James Morison in this period of revival and controversy is assessed by Carwardine, *Transatlantic Revivalism*, pp. 94-101. The Evangelical Union of Scotland was formed in 1843 by those who followed Morison out of other churches.

[85] Finney left a record of his dealings with Kirk. The first edition of the *Memoirs of the Rev. Charles G. Finney, the American Evangelist, Written by Himself* (London: Hodder & Stoughton, 1876), often deviates from his manuscript. Garth M. Rosell and Richard A.G. Dupuis reinstate much useful information in *The Memoirs of Charles G. Finney: The Complete Restored Text* (Grand Rapids, MI: Academie Books/Zondervan, 1989); for Kirk see pp. 590-593.

[86] Kennedy reported an average attendance of 500, most of whom were not wealthy, and a membership of 145; information for the Commissioners of Religious Instruction, 1837, given in McNaughton, *Early Congregational Independency in the Highlands and Islands and the North-East of Scotland*, pp. 425-426.

[87] Events described by Robb, 'George MacDonald at Blackfriars Chapel', pp. 11-12; by some slip he has *George* Kennedy mistakenly for John Kennedy.

rite of passage appropriate to teenagers but required a distinct cause, possibly an invitation from the minister, and was not necessarily at the instigation of the would-be candidate.

When a student, as probably at home, MacDonald was familiar with a Sabbatarianism in some aspects more severe than White describes.[88] Kennedy promoted careful observance of the Lord's Day, and presumably carried many of his church members with him. George and his brother Charles found lodgings with one of the Blackfriars' deacons, Peter Taylor, who each Sunday required the window blinds to be kept lowered throughout the day.[89] The church was also marked by a lively social concern however, so this was not an arid or inward-looking orthodoxy. Causes from reform of the Corn Laws to the abolition of slavery were vigorously supported.[90] Here and elsewhere MacDonald may have been introduced to English nonconformists, who were well represented at Scottish universities, and consequently in Scotland's churches. A little before this date George Dawson, later of Birmingham and an acquaintance of Hale White's, worshipped at Blackfriars while at Marischal College during the 1837-1838 session, though his views came to differ very markedly from anything he encountered there.[91]

Summary

While the *Early Life* provides relatively little information about White's home life as a child it is nevertheless possible from this and other sources to reconstruct something of that background, and especially the spiritual influences upon him in these formative years. The expectations of chapel, and probably of family too, lay heavy upon him, particularly as they showed an inadequate understanding of the psychological and spiritual needs of the young. Sunday schools were gradually changing, but the long-term effects of insensitive teaching and unrealistic expectations could be considerable. Although White's own account is shaped by later events there are points of contact with the memories of others, to be explored below, which suggest that his story was far from unusual. However further evidence from Macdonald's

---

88 William Raeper describes childhood restrictions on Sunday walks for example, *George MacDonald* (Tring: Lion Publishing, 1987), p. 26.

89 Robb, 'George MacDonald at Blackfriars Chapel', p. 8. Taylor's housekeeper and her husband honoured her employer's memory, and a generous legacy, by naming their son born in 1848 Peter Taylor Forsyth. The boy was destined to become one of Congregationalism's finest theologians, and perhaps the most famous New College alumnus.

90 Robb lists some of these causes, 'George MacDonald at Blackfriars Chapel', p. 8.

91 He then moved to Glasgow, where he studied alongside J. D. Morell, later a possible influence on Hale White. Dawson's Church of the Saviour was regarded with suspicion in some circles, see p. 221 below.

life will show that it is not possible to predict particular outcomes from early experiences of church which came to be negatively assessed in maturity.

With this understanding of the content and wider context of the *Early Life* in place attention can turn to the events leading up to the crisis at New College. In this there will again be scope to consider records left by others of their moves towards church membership, and of ministerial training. White was far from being alone in reporting a disturbed or unsatisfactory college life. If anything, his difficulties have been less well understood for being falsely isolated.

CHAPTER 6

'The great blunder of my life'
An Uneasy Vocation

White describes the vocation chosen for him by his parents as 'the great event and the great blunder of my life, the mistake which well-nigh ruined it altogether' (p.55). The final third of the *Early Life* is devoted almost entirely to the consequences, encompassing the two episodes which so profoundly affected him, the formal admission to Bunyan Meeting and the expulsion from New College. The decision to train for ministry is attributed to his mother being 'a little weak in her preference for people who did not stand behind counters', as her husband had cause to do in his business (pp.55-56).[1] This is the period which also includes Hale's Wordsworthian enlightenment however, and is not therefore a wholly negative time. That experience has close parallels in the *Autobiography*, but the expulsion is publicly acknowledged only in this text.

Becoming a Church Member

The need to declare his faith and be admitted to membership at Bunyan Meeting arose directly from the decision to train for the ministry. Cheshunt College sought references showing that applicants were members in good standing of their originating churches, and Hale was accordingly interviewed by two of Bunyan's deacons in early 1848. It is likely that membership would not have been taken up quite so early without this specific need.

Remembering that all surviving sources are informed by a post-expulsion perspective, care is needed to interpret how White describes these events. Memories are not repeated un-glossed, and the distance between the time of writing and the years described typically shows itself in a measure of reinterpretation, including the author's commentary which attempts to bridge the temporal gap. The language from the start of this sequence suggests the passive subject in the grip of decisions taken beyond him. If an echo is heard of Jesus setting his face towards Jerusalem and the start of a passion narrative this

---

[1] Mark Rutherford is sent to college 'after much deliberation' with no further details given; *Autobiography*, p. 12, Ch. II. Mrs Broad was determined that her son would train for ministry; *Revolution*, p. 258, Ch. XVII (and not be employed in trade, an attitude which might recall Mrs White).

probably reflects something of White's later understanding of this time of trial. It may also mark an inability or unwillingness to take responsibility for his part in the unfolding story. In any event, despite his reservations, the 'decision was against me' and his mother's preference for the 'sacred calling' meant that he 'was handed over' to a tutor to be prepared for Cheshunt (p.56).

In recording this time White struggles to understand conversion, a spiritual transformation he felt he had not experienced (pp.56-58). This lies at the root of his life-long reluctance to speak publicly of faith, and to join churches or participate in services where a confession of faith was required. The act itself had an exceptionally high status at the Old Meeting. Following the dictum of Bunyan himself that no particular form of baptism should be demanded for membership, confession of faith alone sufficed, and there was no obligatory initiatory rite of incorporation into the church (admission to the Lord's Supper *followed* and sealed membership). In all probability White himself was not baptised, and certainly there is no record of such an event. He did not wish any of his children to be baptised, and when the teenage Willie wrote home from Framlingham College asking why, his father replied with an attempt to disprove any dominical command on the subject ('the words "and be baptized" are of very doubtful origin'), and affirm that the 'religion of Christ' rested upon 'perfect truthfulness, perfect tenderness, perfect purity, perfect kindness and perfect reverence for the great God who made us', not 'ceremonies and churchgoings'.[2] However if belonging to the church rested on confession alone, feelings of insecurity and disaffection might be engendered precisely in proportion to any perceived failing to live up to that early avowal. Donald Davie suggests that some of White's difficulties arose from supposing 'the crux of the religious life to be the mental act of belief, not the physical act of worship', including participation in the sacraments.[3]

George MacDonald, by contrast, was definitely both baptised and a communicant. His baptism on 10 December 1824 was recorded in the Huntly Parish register as witnessed by his two uncles, indicating a rite performed outside the Church of Scotland, presumably by their own minister, John Hill. In contrast, some other attenders of the Missionar Kirk, including James Legge a few years before (1815), are shown in the register as having been baptised 'before the congregation', that is, within the established church. This was also

---

[2] Letter of 1874, quoted in Maclean, pp. 193-195. White was clearly troubled by Willie's letter, which also asked why he did not attend church; because, he replied, 'I do not know anyone who can teach me anything at church which I want to know' (as cited, p. 194). He did occasionally attend services, for example in Exeter under William Chignell, before their mysterious estrangement.

[3] *A Gathered Church: The Literature of the English Dissenting Interest, 1700-1930* (London: Routledge & Kegan Paul, 1978) p. 98; Davie sees more real faith in White than many discern.

the case for MacDonald's friend Robert Spence in 1822.[4] There could have been residual family ties which brought some nonconformists back to the church for this rite, while for others there was no alternative since at the Missionar Kirk baptism was not offered to infants unless their parents were in membership. George's certainly were, for his father was a deacon. This was the policy during John Hill's tenure, a practice relaxed when Robert Troup became minister. Troup's 'startling innovation' of extending baptism to the children of non-members (that is, to those of attenders) was not implemented without a struggle.[5] The question was a particularly sensitive one because as at Bunyan Meeting there were some who favoured adult baptism, an issue which caused controversy over the years.[6]

Since church membership in Congregationalism was synonymous on both sides of the border with admission to communion, White's silence on any such participation is surprising. MacDonald considered his membership at Trevor Chapel in London as starting from his first communion. In English congregationalism communion services were usually held monthly while in Scotland six-monthly celebration was the norm. The Missionar Kirk of MacDonald's youth met around the table each month, but this frequency had been introduced by John Hill only after great resistance which had nearly persuaded him against accepting the pastorate.[7] The solemnity which for MacDonald surrounded the event, especially at first, must owe something to this Scottish background.

Membership required White's declaration 'that a certain change called conversion had taken place in the soul' (p.57).[8] His confession, sincerely meant at the time, later struck him as false and hypocritical, 'very near lying' (p.59). The authorial aside, 'I can see myself now' (p.59) is not simply a figure of speech, but an example of recollective memory in which the viewpoint is that of an external observer. This type of childhood memory (distinguished from 'field memory', in which the original perspective as subject is retained) is a

---

[4] I am grateful to Dr William McNaughton for help in understanding these elements of nonconformist baptismal practice in nineteenth century Scotland.

[5] Recalled in the anonymous memoir of Troup, preface to *The Missionar Kirk*, p. xix.

[6] The matter is noted among others which sometimes caused distress in John Hill's time; Troup, *The Missionar Kirk*, pp. 114-115, perhaps hinting at deeper and more widespread discontents.

[7] Hill would have preferred weekly communion, but had to settle for monthly; *The Missionar Kirk of Huntly*, pp. 104-106. It was such an important issue for him that he felt the necessity of having it agreed in advance of taking up the appointment.

[8] 'William Scargill' records admission to membership by an examination of 'religious attainments', with conversion not specifically mentioned; *The Autobiography of a Dissenting Minister*, pp. 46-48.

feature of older memories.[9] The element of hindsight is particularly obvious here, though it operates at some level in much of the material relating to faith. It is interesting that no attempt is made retrospectively to justify the belief which he clearly did then hold ('I was satisfied I understood'), or to refer to any genuine element of religious experience (p.59). This may be in order to heighten the contrast with the 'new capacity' brought about by reading Wordsworth and appreciation of the revelatory power of nature (p.61). With this came a gradual 'modification' of traditional belief that provided a means by which the 'artificial God of the churches' might be challenged and eventually supplanted (p.62).

White accepts responsibility for the statements made at Bunyan Meeting, even though these were presumably arrived at after careful coaching by his parents or the examining deacons. There is no realistic portrayal of the spiritual understanding of a child. At Bunyan Meeting lip-service was paid to the notion of a genuine spiritual change, but the assumption seemed to be that the children of adult members would be admitted without reporting any dramatic experience. The temptation to present one's 'experience' according to expectation was clearly strong, as White recalled; 'it is very often inaccurately picturesque, and is framed after the model of the journey to Damascus' (p.57). He exaggerates, for his own confession of a singularly uneventful nature was completely acceptable to the Church Meeting, who it seems were used to receiving in this way the children of 'godly parents' (p.58).[10] The description of Thomas Broad's letter of admission to Tanner's Lane may well reflect what had become common practice at Bunyan Meeting; Thomas wrote as 'the child of pious parents, and of many prayers, [who] had never been exposed to those assaults of the enemy of souls which beset ordinary young men, and consequently had not undergone a sudden conversion'.[11] The norm became the exception, as shown in White's belief that this 'miracle' by which a man became 'something altogether different to what he was previously' was only 'in rare cases ... occasionally a reality'.[12]

White's fellow student Robert Theobald is another witness to the changing nature of conversion, arguing that '*sudden conversion* is rare and exceptional,

---

[9] See William F. Brewer, 'What is Recollective Memory', in *Remembering Our Past: Studies in Autobiographical Memory*, ed. by David C. Rubin, pp. 19-66 (p. 37).

[10] As in the case of John Ashton, whose testimony to 'the comforts of a pious home' in 1861 explained his lack of a sudden conversion; *The Story of the Life of John Ashton*, p. 17.

[11] *Revolution in Tanner's Lane*, p. 260, Ch. XVII; Cunningham supposes that this recalls White's own admission, but it just as likely alludes to a common pattern; see *Everywhere Spoken Against*, p. 263. Thomas is portrayed as a pious hypocrite, representing what White despises most.

[12] *Autobiography*, pp. 9-10, Ch. I.

[though] I would not be understood to deny that it does occur'.[13] The much younger Edmund Gosse, it will be recalled, had required no crisis experience (or so his father argued) to justify his baptism and church membership.[14]

White's report does not suggest that radical conversion was normative, for otherwise he would surely have been encouraged to that end instead of presenting himself to explain why it was not the case. He records the procedure as having both private and public faces:

> two deacons are appointed to examine the candidate privately, and their report is submitted to a church-meeting. If it is satisfactory, he is summoned before the whole church, and has to make a confession of his faith, and give an account of his spiritual history (p.57).[15]

It was the confession before the whole church which later haunted him, though this act was possibly easier in familiar settled churches where intermarried families of long standing made up the core of the membership. Before this date there are already signs that such public testing was not always insisted upon, with private interview or application by letter becoming more common.[16] Different concepts of propriety and respectability may have played their part, and certainly some large urban churches had moved to make the process less demanding. In a case at Binney's King's Weigh House, for instance, as early as 1830 one candidate had only to present evidence of her conduct and Christian experience to representative deacons and the minister privately, while at a subsequent church meeting they spoke for her, and after a vote on admission the minister welcomed the new member with a handshake. When the church next gathered to celebrate communion names of the newly enrolled were simply read out.[17] Over time the responsibility of the minister grew, and applications became a more private matter for discussion between the candidate and the minister, on whose recommendation the church meeting then voted for

---

[13] *Passages from the Autobiography of a Shakespeare Student* (London: Robert Banks & Son, 1912), p. 17; a view arising from his own difficulties on conversion (emphasis added).

[14] See above, p. 125.

[15] A reminder that the conversion narrative is closely related to the 'requirement that candidates for admission to the [gathered] church had to offer not only a profession of orthodox belief but also evidence of personal saving faith'; so Hindmarsh, *Evangelical Conversion Narrative*, p. 46.

[16] In 1821 a Congregational journal regretted the decline in public examination; cited in Sell, *Commemorations: Studies in Christian Thought and History* (Calgary, AB; Cardiff: University of Calgary Press; University of Wales Press, 1993), p. 347.

[17] Described in Cashdollar, *Spiritual Home*, p. 101. William Scargill, writing in the 1830s of earlier times, describes candidates being interviewed by both minister *and* deacons; *Autobiography of a Dissenting Minister*, pp. 46-50.

admission. Perhaps this explains the process followed when George MacDonald joining Trevor Chapel.

His action never generated the trauma which White later associated with his application to Bunyan Meeting. MacDonald was anxious about taking the step, but this was in all likelihood engendered by the admission to communion which it signified, and the immediate unease soon passed. He was more mature than White, took a greater personal responsibility for the decision, and the event in any case was less intimidating. The chief encouragement, suggesting that the minister often took the initiative, had come from John Morison, as George explained to his father:

> Dr. Morison sent me a letter by a messenger who waited for an answer, saying that he wished to propose me a member that evening, but did not like to do so without a line from me to say *yes*. I consented but with fear & trembling as I told him I have had a good deal of distress since, but am better now - much. I think I am a Christian although one of the weakest. I do not think Christ will allow me to go to his table unworthily although I should not have come forward so soon had not the Dr. urged me. I am sure he never saw Mr Still's recommendation, but he seems satisfied with me himself. I shall have to see one of the deacons next week[18]

There is no reason to suppose that this was an unusually abbreviated handling of membership. MacDonald needed this status in order to enter a training college, but that further move was not taken for three years, even if it had been in mind for some time. More probably, Morison, well aware of the possible consequences of withdrawal from church life to anyone uncertain in faith, was keen to bring MacDonald to a commitment which might otherwise have been avoided. In due course those dangers were to become evident in Hale White's life. That Morison was a long-standing family friend would help explain his willingness for things to proceed so swiftly. MacDonald's report, albeit it very compressed, reads as if Morison was the chief determinant. 'Mr Still' in this source is perhaps a transcription error from the original for John Hill, who as MacDonald's home minister could well have been approached for a reference, but even without it Morison, 'satisfied with me himself', makes the recommendation to the church meeting. So acting, the deacon's visit seems a formality, further suggesting a process of invitation by the minister rather than application by the candidate, unless Morison's act was simply to put MacDonald's name forward for consideration without any recommendation, the real decision only to follow from the deacon's report. This would be an

---

[18] Letter dated 8 November 1845; text in Sadler, *An Expression of Character*, p. 11 (original italics). John Morison, also the influential editor of the *Evangelical Magazine*, was not related to the James Morison involved in the Scottish controversies over conversion.

awkward reading of the letter however. The apparent lack of rigour might have been easier to understand if MacDonald was transferring membership from another church, but in Aberdeen he had not joined Blackfriars, and only became a member at Huntly after doing so at Trevor.[19]

Outside London change was sometimes slower coming, but in 1861 the church at Lion Walk in Colchester 'decided to discontinue the practice which had been in vogue from earliest times of appointing a deputation of members to interview personally each candidate for church fellowship and report on their suitability and their experience in the faith'.[20] Charles Cashdollar shows that the move to make requirements less stringent can be widely documented in Britain and America.[21] The example from the King's Weigh House suggests something about the role of the Dissenting ministry in becoming a professional class with specific competencies, and the retreat of religious expression into the private sphere. It may be imagined that very often personal character rather than Christian 'experience' now became the crucial test for membership.

That these instances were not simply local adaptations without wider significance is confirmed by passages in Henry Martyn's *Chapters from the Autobiography of an Independent Minister*. It was clearly a topical issue, for the Cheshunt students (who incidentally are here presented more positively than by White) discussed the 'best method of introducing members to our churches' in their weekly debating class.[22] The opening paper suggested the weaknesses of the traditional pattern. Asking the applicant to share their Christian experience expected too much of the inarticulate and ill-educated, creating 'a temptation to unreality'. The personal visit by two church members did not help because many candidates found it difficult to talk of their deepest feelings. Furthermore, there is an appropriate reticence in such personal matters which ought not to be breached. This marks a definite retreat from the vital religion of earlier days. Other speakers recounted their experience of the process, of questions on 'the new birth' which they found too intrusive, or doctrinal cross-examination on matters which seemed remote and irrelevant. One represented what must have been a common occurrence; the visit by members who had known the family for many years and looked forward to each new generation entering into membership, the process becoming a mere formality. A strongly opposing view was voiced however, arguing for strictness

---

[19] As his application to Highbury reveals; he dates his membership at Trevor from first communion in December 1845, at Huntly only from April 1848, where he had returned before leaving again for London. The form is copied in Sadler, *An Expression of Character*, pp. 22-25.

[20] Blaxill, *History of Lion Walk Congregational Church*, p. 42.

[21] *Spiritual Home*, pp. 102-103.

[22] *Some Chapters from the Autobiography*, pp. 18-21. The quotations in the remainder of this paragraph may all be found on these pages.

in order that only the 'thoroughly converted' should be admitted. This was rejected by the original speaker, on the grounds that it 'took away from the candidates a sense of personal responsibility'. This weakness it shared with traditional practice, under which the recommendation for membership became 'a kind of certificate of character' and too little was subsequently expected of the new member.[23] This again reflects the move away from the demands of more radical days. Congregational thinkers were aware of the difficult balance to be struck between encouraging the hesitant believer without weakening the admission requirements until the process became meaningless, at worst a legalistic justification by works supplanting that of grace.[24]

In retrospect White felt that the traditional scheme of conversion evoked in the process encouraged unhealthy self-obsession. Ironically the Calvinist system as he encountered it, despite its theoretical emphasis upon divine sovereignty, turned on a moment of human decision; 'it concentrated my thoughts upon myself, and made me of great importance' (p.59). For all the stress upon Christ's atoning death as the ground of conversion, White betrays little sense of sin or fear of punishment. Although there are signs of both in the recollection of early moralistic teaching (temptations to bathe on the Sabbath, to sleep in services), they do not feature in his adult life. It has been suggested that his depression and melancholia represent the psychological equivalent of sin, but the chief reason for this divergence from evangelical patterning is probably to be found in the sense of complete acceptance and security experienced through 'Nature' (and not previously by nurture) after his Wordsworthian 'conversion'.[25] When he returns in other writings to the idea of conversion he is loath to relegate all such experience to the past; as with Eastthorpe's 'Orkid Jim', and people known in life, such a change is still possible.[26] In the *Autobiography* he writes of true conversion as rare in his childhood, but 'now altogether untrue', and 'altogether unmeaning'.[27] It has a possible modern equivalent however, in the redeeming power of human love. The main reason for White's unease with the concept of conversion lies in the

---

[23] Since the student who espoused the rigorist view turns out to be untrustworthy, it is probable that Martyn himself rejected such a view. His own ministerial experience of difficult members would have suggested the inadequacy of a once-for-all test of Christian experience and good standing.

[24] Alan Sell describes Robert Vaughan and Robert Mackintosh wrestling with this question, *Commemorations*, pp. 346-347.

[25] See Basil Willey on sin, in his introduction to the Victorian Library edition of the *Autobiography and Deliverance* (Leicester: Leicester University Press, 1969), pp. 7-20 (p. 9). But White's long-term depressive illness is a parallel to the prolonged periods of self-despair which those convicted of sin sometimes endured.

[26] See *Catharine Furze*, pp. 356-358, Ch. XX.

[27] *Autobiography*, p. 10, Ch. I; surely some hyperbole here - not his last word on the subject.

feeling that hypocrisy is thereby encouraged; a trivialised notion of change undermined by a smug religiosity. This is shown especially in the *Autobiography*, where sin is confessed with an air of unreality, 'brother Holderness ... never prayed without telling all of us there was no health in him', yet it was difficult to believe that he was confessing actual sins.[28] It was with good reason that White hesitated about the 'real' meaning of conversion.

Confusion Over Conversion: Old Words and New Meanings

All attempts to understand White's religious life include assumptions about the origin, nature and growth of faith, though these areas are often inadequately addressed. For White the knowledge that conversion had been, and still could be for some, sudden and dramatic played a part in the negative assessment of his own experience.[29] Yet his understanding of belief might be more profound than some have granted and show a truly existential grasp of the religious commitment. In trying to relate his experience to traditional language, his dilemma is often (as Lorraine Davies says of the *Autobiography*) 'an attempt to find the right words to describe his condition, having started with the wrong words'.[30] According to this reading his problems stem from putting words before feeling or intuition. When this effort can be relinquished, 'releasing thought from the obligation of verbal expression makes way for the idea of unresolved being which makes doubt a means of actually admitting faith'.[31] It is curious that Davies does not go on to make more of White as a believer after this promising analysis, possibly through over-reliance on the novels alone, and these read as progressively more secular. She does show clearly that Rutherford (and for her this means White) is searching for the faith which is 'a matter of personal apprehension rather than dogma, of imagination rather than knowledge, of individual conviction rather than institutional authority' - and what Puritan could disagree?[32] There is no sign that the young White found traditional language an obstacle, but the *Early Life* shows that during the college years he began to test it for inner meaning.

Religious language is not freely chosen, and as noted White suggests there was pressure at Bunyan Meeting to dramatise one's experience in imitation of the Damascus road archetype. This debased the very concept, and on later reflection lent an air of artificiality to the explanation of how the experience ought to be understood and received. The key features were the conviction of

---

[28] *Autobiography*, p. 11, Ch. I.

[29] Though note that his reading of Wordsworth brought about a sudden and unsought change.

[30] Davies, 'An Awkward Rectitude', p. 51.

[31] 'An Awkward Rectitude', p. 56.

[32] 'An Awkward Rectitude', p. 63.

sin and the awakened dread of divine punishment, from which the atoning death of Christ rescues the subject; 'I was guilty of original sin, and also of sins actually committed. For these two classes of sin I deserved eternal punishment. Christ became my substitute, and His death was payment for my transgression' (p.58). This is not to be conceived in the abstract, but spiritually applied in a uniquely personal way - 'appropriated' (p.58). Against this background the Wordsworthian 'conversion' is more properly described as an enlightenment or revelation, rather than a moral turning from sin as in Christian conversion.

The most serious problem with the traditional model of conversion illustrated by White and many of his contemporaries lay in the expectation that an essentially adult experience could be similarly worked out in the children of Christian parents. Naturally enough many such candidates, whatever the effect of tracts designed to frighten them into an act of commitment, had little real consciousness of sin and struggled with the idea of a sudden spectacular change (the more so, if as White suggested the nearest adult role models failed to demonstrate such a pattern). The result was a sense of 'unmeaning' about this critically important spiritual process, the knowledge that something apparently vital to understanding conversion from the inside was missing.[33] White was never satisfied that he had understood all that the Dissenting tradition meant by conversion, and his language about it is tentative and uncertain; it is simply too 'difficult to explain', though he turns the idea over and over in his attempt to do so (p.58). There is no necessary link between these uncertainties and later unsettlement. Men who went on to forge successful ministries had experienced similar misgivings; for example both John Pye Smith and Joseph Parker had been deeply troubled that their conviction of sin was not profound enough to meet the expected standard of testimony for admission to church membership.[34]

Understandings of the atonement were linked with ideas of conversion, both matters of dispute in England and Scotland. These controversies could have a lasting impact. The sometimes fiercely argued differences disturbed George MacDonald, especially during his time in Aberdeen, and along with the split in the church they caused may explain why he did not become a member there. His experience at Blackfriars, following that of Huntly, left him with a strongly expressed distaste for abstract theological speculation and the harsher aspects of his church background: 'to have to believe in the God of the Calvinist would drive me to madness or atheism; to believe in the God of our Lord Jesus Christ, is to feel that, if such a God there be, all is well, he may do with me as he

[33] White attempted to express this in the *Autobiography*, p. 10, Ch. I.

[34] Cited in Sell, *Enlightenment, Ecumenism, Evangel: Theological Themes and Thinkers 1550-2000* (Milton Keynes: Paternoster, 2005), pp. 346-347. Pye Smith's experience is from a somewhat earlier date than White's, but Parker (born 1830) was an almost exact contemporary.

pleases, I am blest'.[35] On the subject of the atonement both MacDonald and White show impatience with theories and explanations. They do not dispute that a work of reconciliation has taken place (language of sacrifice and redemption is used), but taking a lead from the Gospels rather than the New Testament epistles stress the revelation of God as a loving father. This becomes the key motif in MacDonald's writing. White favours the related concept of the Prodigal Son, and his report of sermons on this theme always suggest the artificiality of the theologies grafted on to the 'simple' story of the Gospels, which does not require such explanation.

Nurture and Conversion

The malign effects of a gap between expectation and experience, especially in respect of children, were addressed by Bushnell in his previously cited *Christian Nurture*.[36] Christian parents, he argued, needed to be re-educated against 'unwittingly ... taking up notions of conversion that are mechanical, and proper only to the adult age', while 'asserting the universal necessity of a new spiritual birth; not perceiving under what varieties of form that change may be wrought. ... A child [they believe] can be born of God only in the same way as an adult can be'.[37] This approach condemned children to a 'nurture ... of despair' unable to emulate the adult experience of conversion held out to them as the only escape from sin and its penalties.[38] Clearly this situation could all too easily prompt the sort of premature or insincere confession of faith which Hale White afterwards felt he had made at Bunyan Meeting. In place of simply applying the evangelical model to children Bushnell urged their full acceptance into the community of faith from an early age (he assumed infant baptism marked this inclusion, something problematic in White's case because of the unusual baptismal context of Bunyan Meeting), and insisted that within the family they should be brought up as Christians.[39] His whole emphasis, as Margaret Bendroth notes, is against the notion of 'a single emotional experience as the mark of true conversion', though this was the heritage of churches affected by the Evangelical Revival, as well as the hallmark of transatlantic revivalism.[40] Writing in 1896, Thomas Selby argued that the regret expressed in the *Autobiography* at a decline in sudden conversions was

---

[35] A statement from 1886, see R. Hein, 'George MacDonald: A Portrait from His Letters', *Seven: An Anglo-American Literary Review*, 7 (1986), 5-19 (p. 9).

[36] First published in his native America in 1847, and widely distributed in Britain soon afterwards.

[37] *Christian Nurture*, third edition (London: Alexander Strahan, 1866), p. 45.

[38] *Christian Nurture*, p. 46.

[39] *Christian Nurture*, p. 4.

[40] 'Horace Bushnell's *Christian Nurture*', p. 352.

unnecessary, for Rutherford had not appreciated 'the new emphasis put upon the doctrine of prevenient grace, and the just and reasonable expectation of finding signs of spiritual life in children who have been nurtured in Christian homes, without abrupt transition' as its laudable cause.[41]

It was a key difference between MacDonald and Hale White that the former successfully made the transition from childhood instruction in faith to adult profession without unreasonably condemning his early lack of reflection, despite a not dissimilar awareness that he then had no living faith. Scottish Congregationalism was born in the desire to witness to vital religion, and this must surely have extended to children. The history of the Missionar Kirk is unhelpfully vague in this respect. Robert Troup records that under the ministry of John Hill 'time after time the children of pious parents, trained in Christian nurture, confessed the name of the Redeemer who they had learned to trust and love'.[42] This does not suggest crisis conversion, rather the familiar acceptance of the 'children of many prayers', though without more detail certainty is impossible. MacDonald's own reflection on the past came in his application to Highbury, where he was required to describe his Christian experience. He acknowledged his birth into a Christian family and community, but without claiming that this had brought him to faith; 'I have been familiar with the doctrines of the gospel from childhood. I always knew and felt that I ought to be a Christian'.[43] This said, and reflecting the importance of 'ought to be', he robustly declared that 'the truths of Christianity had no *life* in my soul' until 'about five years ago'.[44] The language of becoming a Christian, implying a process rather an event, had an affinity for him, as shown in the 1845 letter to his father already quoted.[45]

Though gradual, his awakening originated in a specific period in his student life tentatively dated from the reference above to the summer of 1843, a time when MacDonald's movements are unclear, for it seems that he did not keep full college terms that session. The assumption that he was exposed to sceptical books while temporarily working in a castle library lacks evidence and the church context in Aberdeen is much more likely to explain his grappling with theological questions.[46] In all likelihood MacDonald used circumspect language

---

[41] *Theology of Modern Fiction*, p. 175.

[42] *The Missionar Kirk*, p. 113. Significantly or not, in his summary of Hill's fruitful ministry Troup lists these children between conversions of the ungodly and adult members added to the church.

[43] The whole form is reproduced in Sadler, *An Expression of Character*, pp. 22-25 (p. 22).

[44] Sadler, *An Expression of Character*, p. 22 (original emphasis).

[45] See p. 172 above.

[46] It was Greville MacDonald who popularised the supposed library experience, but Rolland Hein points out just how flimsy the evidence is; *George MacDonald: Victorian*

Note continues on following page

on the Highbury form because he did not wish to refer openly to the problems at Blackfriars, and this has left room for unfounded speculation about other reasons. McDonald writes as if he had been rescued from growing infidelity, his mind eventually concentrated by the thought of becoming a church member (presumably at Blackfriars, and not pursued because of internal strife there), but it was a slow process of learning and re-learning. 'All I had been taught in my youth I required to learn over again'; throwing himself on God's mercy he gradually 'began to see some of the beauty of religion, some of the grandeur of the Truth'.[47] If the date of these events is reliably given as the second half of 1843, the reminiscences of Robert Troup (a contemporary at Aberdeen) confirm a distinct spiritual unease noticed by those around MacDonald. 'His elder friends were anxious about his spiritual state', Troup recorded, attributing this to a reaction against Calvinist harshness, especially regarding everlasting punishment.[48]

His case illustrates some of the challenges to finding faith faced by those born as insiders. And if children found it difficult to enter into their inheritance the position of those more mature could not be taken for granted. As ideas changed about the appropriate nurture of children within the faith community, concerns were expressed that adults in many congregations were in a parlous spiritual state due to misunderstandings about the true nature of conversion. Since these issues were aired by some close to White it is helpful to be aware of these arguments, as well as the evidence they provide about changing theological positions. The subject also fuelled debate about what kind of ministers the churches needed - academically qualified or evangelistically zealous - and hence the nature of the college system.[49]

Revivalism and Conversion

A common factor in concern about children being falsely pressured into confessions of faith and the lack of an effective challenge to adults was the question of the subject's ability to respond. The rise of moderate Calvinism in both America and Britain played its part, as modification of the doctrines of total depravity, limited atonement, and absolute predestination lessened the sense of the complete passivity of the individual in conversion.[50] In America,

---

Mythmaker (Nashville, TN: Star Song Publishing, 1993), p. 410 (note 7). Hereafter cited as *Victorian Mythmaker.*

[47] Application form, Sadler, *An Expression of Character*, p. 22.

[48] Unpublished notes quoted in Raeper, *George MacDonald*, p. 50. It is always possible that, like others, Troup was reading too much back into these early days.

[49] The debates are explored by Dale Johnson in *The Changing Shape of English Nonconformity, 1825-1925* (New York: Oxford University Press, 1999), though mostly after mid-century.

[50] On this see for example Carwardine, *Transatlantic Revivalism*, pp. 60-65.

and less so in Britain, this enabled some Calvinists to embrace revivalist techniques aimed at more vigorously securing conversions. Caleb Morris was among the leading Congregationalists who welcomed to Britain American ministers promoting revival. Edward Kirk of Albany, New York, held services with Angell James at Carr's Lane church, Birmingham and then in 1838 at James Sherman's Surrey Chapel, London, specifically 'for the revival of religion'; these special protracted meetings, with their rooms set aside for ministry to those affected by the message, were controversial and successful.[51] Morris himself was a platform speaker during the week at Surrey Chapel.

Another supporter of revival was John Campbell of Whitefield's Tabernacle, Moorfields, where Charles Finney preached in 1850, and again the following year.[52] Finney's *Lectures of Revival*, published in Britain in 1837, had been important in preparing the theological ground for the new conversionist preaching. In this way Morris and Campbell, though different in many ways, were united in promoting a religion which was truly alive. The currency of revivalist thinking among Calvinists in the late 1830s and 40s may reflect concern that the churches of old Dissent were failing to see the kind of growth evident in newer nonconformist churches and thus sheds light on the importance of trends affecting conversion during White's youth. It was becoming clear that both within (including adult attenders, but also the children of church families) and externally (the challenge of converting un-reached adults) there was much to be achieved.

It seemed that revival was urgently needed among the professedly religious, for Finney's record of his time in England demonstrates a concern that many within the churches were strangers to vital religion; even at Angell James's church, a friend reported to the American visitor, there were 'not less than fifteen hundred impenitent sinners'.[53] The situation was apparently as serious among John Campbell's congregation. Campbell had been taken aback by the number of his congregation who answered Finney's call to decisive commitment, initially quite unable to accept that there were so many

---

[51] Carwardine, *Transatlantic Revivalism*, pp. 73-77, and, at length, *The Church Awakened: Report of Special Meetings for the Revival of Religion, Held in Surrey Chapel, London, November 5th, 1838, and following days* (London: Thomas Ward, 1838). Sherman had a link with Bedford; he preached at the stone-laying of the new Bunyan Meeting in 1849, and a member of his church, Joseph Insull, trained at Cheshunt, was inducted as assistant to John Jukes in 1854; from Tibbutt, *Bunyan Meeting*, pp. 62, 63-64.

[52] Carwardine, *Transatlantic Revivalism*, pp. 140-142; later Campbell was less enthusiastic, pp. 176-177.

[53] C. G. Finney, *Memoirs of the Rev. Charles G. Finney*, p. 391. Rosell and Dupuis supply the name of the 'friend' who told of the spiritual stagnation at Carr's Lane as Charles H. Roe, a Baptist minister; see *The Memoirs of Charles G. Finney: The Complete Restored Text*, p. 486.

unconverted among them. Finney reported the conversation; 'I told him there were hundreds of inquirers in the congregation. But at this he laughed, and said it was impossible'.[54] The evangelist had been quite explicit that his call was to those 'who are not Christians, but who are anxious for the salvation of their souls'; a very large number responded, to Campbell's 'great astonishment'.[55] Charitably accepting Campbell's claim that many present were not his regular attenders, Finney explained his success in terms of London being 'cursed with hyper-calvinistic preaching'; its emphasis upon 'waiting God's time' for conversion had only to be challenged by an urgent, expectant, appeal to achieve decisive results.[56] Finney had long held that dogmatic Calvinism produced a spirit of 'cannotism' which had to be broken.[57] 'People have sometimes called me crazy', he complained, 'because I addressed sinners as if I expected them *then* and *there* to become Christians. But if I believe the Gospel, what else should I expect?'.[58]

Campbell was naturally deeply affected by these events, which seem likely to have reinforced his belief that the college system could not produce ministers capable of such effective preaching. He was already concerned that the quest for educational attainment might have deleterious consequences. By the end of that decade he was quite sure that 'the affiliation of our Theological Institutions with the University of London, and the introduction of Examinations for Honours and Degrees ... [had] ... introduced an evil element, supplying the strongest temptations to personal vanity and sinister ambition'.[59] He thus stands as a representative figure for those unconvinced that the educated ministers then being produced were meeting current needs. He had some grounds for doubting the system. In 1850 Finney shared with him the details of a letter from a disillusioned Independent minister whose 'piety never recovered the tone it

---

[54] *Memoirs*, p. 403.

[55] *Memoirs*, p. 405.

[56] *Memoirs*, p. 406; Campbell's later disagreements with Finney (see *Memoirs*, p. 451) may have been the result not just of his quarrelsome nature, but resentment over the revelation of such spiritual weakness in his own church. There could also have been theological reasons, just as Angell James came to believe that Finney and others were over-emphasizing human agency in revival.

[57] Finney's criticism is studied by C. E. Hambrick-Stowe in *Charles G. Finney and the Spirit of American Evangelicalism* (Grand Rapids, MI: William B. Eerdmans, 1996), especially pp. 153-155.

[58] This passage was omitted from the first published text but is in the restored edition; *The Memoirs of Charles G. Finney*, ed. by Rosell and Dupuis, p. 510. Italics here represent underlinings in the manuscript.

[59] *Academic Reform*, a letter 'To the Presidents, Professors, Managers, and Supporters of Theological Colleges', November 1859, printed in *John Angell James: A Review of His History, Character, Eloquence, and Literary Labours*, etc. (London: John Snow, 1860), pp. xvii-xxxii (p. xix).

lost in [his] passage through college', and later turned to Unitarianism, thence to deism, but who had regained his orthodox faith after hearing him preach at Carr's Lane. Campbell had read the letter 'with manifestly deep emotion'.[60] Finney's manuscript names the man as James Cranbrook, who however was afterwards again suspected of unorthodoxy.[61]

Against this background it is not surprising to find other examples similar to White's. His co-expelled came from just as secure church backgrounds, and they too demonstrate uncertainty about what conversion might mean.

The Expelled Students and Conversion - A Common Thread

Robert Theobald, expelled alongside White in 1852, has left striking testimony to the feelings provoked by pressure for conversion among the young. Brought up at Carr's Lane church under John Angell James, he was given the latter's famous tract addressed to the 'Anxious Inquirer'. It did him no good:

> Mr James's book was the cause of inexpressible mental agony to me. I tried to follow its directions, to be as penitent and lachrymose as I ought to be .... But it was all in vain; I could never assure myself that I was a new creature, and at last I gave it up in despair, hoping that some flash of divine influence might reach me, as it did St. Paul on his way to Damascus.[62]

The 'helpful' aid should be re-titled, he suggested, 'The Anxious Enquirer After Personal Safety Driven to Despair'; he also shows the same concern as Hale White that the focus upon personal salvation unhealthily exalted the self.[63] Later he came to see conversion as a process rather than a sudden event. His mother (who had distinguished clerical relations), like White's, had urged a ministerial career upon him, suggesting a motive for him to escape from this when the opportunity presented itself in 1852.[64] The third expelled student, Frederic White, has left no record of disquiet about conversion, but there is confirmation that, like Hale White, he was unable to point to any moment at which the great change had come upon him.[65] Frederic's application to Homerton (where he started his studies before transferring to New College) required evidence of his Christian experience, but he could not date any

---

[60] Finney, *Memoirs*, pp. 396-399. Desertion to Unitarianism was a trend which must have worried Congregationalists.

[61] *The Memoirs of Charles G. Finney*, ed. by Rosell and Dupuis, p. 495, and note 81.

[62] *Passages from the Autobiography*, p. 17; his age is not given, but the narrative suggests adolescence.

[63] *Passages from the Autobiography*, pp. 16-17.

[64] It had been his mother's deathbed wish (though he had shared it); *Passages from the Autobiography*, p. 15.

[65] See below however for later evidence of his awareness of the problem; pp. 328-329.

conversion, attributing his lack of a crisis change to 'the assiduous instructions of a pious Father'.[66] The three were not untypical in this respect, and some points of tension might have been expected between such men as theological students and their tutors who represented a generation in which witness to a definite moment of conversion had been the norm; conflict which did not come to the surface unless students challenged traditional ideas, whatever their experience of conversion.

Wider Trends on Conversion in Nonconformity

Other research has yielded firm evidence that White and those cited above were correct in believing that the evangelical conversion experience was less common in their youth than formerly. It was becoming accepted that many from Christian homes would not exhibit the same conviction of sin and subsequent release as those outside the fold. Figures derived from records of ministerial candidates by Kenneth Brown show that from mid-century the ability to precisely date conversion declined very markedly.[67] In so far as trends over a longer term can be identified, taken from a study of nonconformist obituaries with a strong bias towards Calvinism and Independency, there seems to have been a tendency to emphasize the element of human effort and response in conversion.[68] A prolonged period spent under conviction of sin became rarer as the sinner was urged to seek immediately the proffered salvation. The experience of that salvation could be confidently known too, for uncertainty about assurance or 'elect' status was actively preached against. The spiritually awakening subject could take a dynamic role in achieving salvation. This appeared to elevate human choice over divine agency, and may have been a factor in the decline of the classic puritan conversion during the nineteenth century. White saw the result of this, accurately describing a change which can be documented from other sources without having been equipped to discern the causes. With a growing stress upon immanence, the divine near at hand, or within, as against transcendence, it is easy to see how the conviction of sin could become less important.[69] Whatever the type of conversion envisaged, the evidence suggests adolescence as overwhelmingly the time at which it might be

---

[66] Letter in New College archives, DWL 218/24, June 13 1848.

[67] *A Social History of the Nonconformist Ministry in England and Wales, 1800-1930* (Oxford: Clarendon Press, 1988), pp. 49-50, and table 1.11, facing p. 50. Brown attributes this to growing materialism and a move towards social activism.

[68] See David Bebbington, 'Evangelical Conversion, c. 1740-1850', *Scottish Bulletin of Evangelical Theology*, 18 (2000), 102-127 (especially pp. 119-127).

[69] The 'transcendentalism' of Emerson and Carlyle which influenced White, despite its name, stressed the divine within.

expected to take place, which fits exactly with Hale White's situation.[70]

The importance of early religious impressions formed within home and church has long been recognised. It was only from mid-century that the psychological aspects of child development also began to be taken into account.[71] The modern study of faith development can now inform historical research, though it is not easy to hear the child's voice.[72]

Faith Development

Insights from this field have not been applied to those held to have suffered from a crisis of faith during the Victorian period. It has therefore been difficult to make properly informed judgements about believers who showed enduring faith (with or without periods of 'storm and stress') and those who suffered alienation or loss. James Fowler has suggested a six-stage theory of faith development, drawing on earlier work by Piaget and Kohlberg, which will be used here as a guide to what might be expected among children and young people exposed to religious instruction and nurture.[73] If applied too rigidly the theory may distort interpretation, and it does not engage with a more recent highlighting of the socially constructed nature of experience, but in this case there is still much which seems worth considering. Briefly summarised from Fowler's densely descriptive terms, the believer may be expected to move from an undifferentiated infantile faith through steps labelled intuitive-projective (fantasy-filled and imitative of nearest adult exemplars), mythic-literal (first appropriation of beliefs, in literal form), synthetic-conventional (synthesizing norms and values encountered beyond the immediate family), individuative-reflective (a move towards responsible individual commitment), and conjunctive (second *naiveté*, integrating symbols and conceptual meaning) towards the rarely-attained mature 'universalizing faith'. The 'stages' show a

---

[70] Fully 82% of Bebbington's examples in the article cited above are of those under 25, a figure also borne out by Watts' study.

[71] This is to simplify. The study of education had paid attention to the psychology of the child since Locke, greatly extended (after Rousseau) in the eighteenth century; see Friedrich Schweitzer, 'Developmental Views of the Religion of the Child: Historical Antecedents', in *Stages of Faith and Religious Development: Implications for Church, Education and Society*, ed. by J. W. Fowler, K. E. Nipkow and F. Schweitzer (London: SCM Press, 1992), pp. 67-81.

[72] Marcia Bunge identifies the problem of studying an adult perspective instead of the authentic child's view; see her 'Introduction', in *The Child in Christian Thought*, ed. by Marcia J. Bunge (Grand Rapids, MI: William B. Eerdmans, 2001), pp. 1-28 (p. 9, note 20).

[73] *Stages of Faith: The Psychology of Human Development and the Quest for Meaning* (New York: Harper & Row, 1981). His empirical research was not limited to Christian belief. This is 'faith' development in the broadest sense.

gradual build-up of faith, and roughly correlate different ages with increasingly sophisticated understanding of religious concepts. [74] Although sudden changes such as conversion experiences are allowed for, the emphasis is upon a dynamic understanding of developing faith. Conversion can occur at any stage, and at the transitions between them.[75]

Fowler also stresses the vital importance of the community setting within which conversion may take place, and 'the ongoing sponsorship of the new convert', meaning 'the way a person or community provides affirmation, encouragement, guidance and models for a person's ongoing growth and development'.[76] Against this measure Bunyan Meeting may seem to have failed to fulfil its proper part after the application for membership. Affirmation was missing, for White had only done what was routinely expected, encouragement was wanting for the same reason, teaching (at least as recorded) was too concerned with not offending the hearers, and role models were singularly lacking, if White's description of lukewarm or hypocritical members is at all accurate. By contrast, charismatic figures like Caleb Morris and Thomas Binney did fulfil these necessary functions, appealing to many like-minded young men.[77]

The usefulness of Fowler's theory can be judged by comparing his summaries against what can be determined of White's religious life. Despite the difficulty of assessing such evidence some aspects seem strikingly applicable. There is no meaningful information for infancy, or for the first, intuitive-projective stage, which typically covers the years between three and seven, but the second stage, of mythic-literal faith, can be documented. It commonly occupies the years from eight to twelve, and here the literal replaces the earlier imaginative understanding. The meaning of beliefs is carried in the narrative of the faith community, and is not yet the subject of reflective analysis. As this starts to occur, transition to stage three becomes possible - synthetic-conventional faith. This is one which can very appropriately be used to 'read' White.

According to Fowler it is:

> a "conformist" stage in the sense that it is acutely tuned to the expectations and judgements of significant others and as yet does not have a sure enough grasp on its own identity and autonomous judgement to construct and maintain an independent perspective. While beliefs and values are deeply felt, they typically are tacitly held - the person "dwells" in them and in the meaning world they

[74] Fowler's work has found wide acceptance; for its continued importance see S. Lownsdale, 'Faith Development Across the Life Span: Fowler's Integrative Work', *Journal of Psychology and Theology*, 25 (1997), 49-63.

[75] *Stages of Faith*, pp. 281-286.

[76] *Stages of Faith*, pp. 286-287.

[77] The importance of such informal 'ecclesial' groups for White must be stressed.

> mediate. But there has not been occasion to step outside them to reflect on or examine them explicitly or systematically. At Stage 3 a person has an 'ideology' ... but he or she has not objectified it ... and in a sense is unaware of having it.[78]

Fowler also notes the fragility of this state, where progress to a deeper, reflective, faith cannot be assured. A crisis may be precipitated by exposure to other beliefs, and especially by 'the experience of "leaving home" - emotionally or physically, or both'.[79] This analysis is obviously apt for Hale White, both in explaining the degree to which he at first accepted without question the beliefs of his faith community, and the challenge posed by new experiences, whether in reading Carlyle and Wordsworth, or through other aspects of the college years. Beyond this stage lies the need during the 'individuative-reflective' phase to develop an identity which is not wholly dependent upon one's background and early personal relationships, and to nurture beliefs which are sustained without such recourse. This explains the importance of guides like the independently-minded Caleb Morris, as well as the inability ever again fully to relate to his dissenting roots. But if the controversy at New College had not forced matters to crisis point it is perfectly possible that White would have made spiritual progress without this degree of alienation. The prize is a 'conjunctive faith'. Again much in Fowler's description of its typical features fits White's situation well:

> Here there must also be a new reclaiming and reworking of one's past. ... Importantly, this involves a critical recognition of one's social unconscious - the myths, ideal images and prejudices built deeply into the self-system by virtue of one's nurture with a particular social class, religious tradition, ethnic group or the like. ... Stage 5 knows the sacrament of defeat and the reality of irrevocable commitments and acts. ... Alive to paradox and the truth in apparent contradictions, this stage strives to unify opposites in mind and experience'.[80]

Telling his story will demonstrate just how much of White's life was marked by these sorts of tensions.

An understanding of faith-development shows that the content of faith is often not very clearly delineated, and it is not surprising that in this area White is elusive. For this reason the evidence of private religious practice - prayer and Bible reading especially - is a significant indicator of his indebtedness to the Christian tradition. Fowler emphasizes that development is usually gradual, and

---

[78] *Stages of Faith*, pp. 172-173 (italicised throughout in the original, not reproduced here).

[79] *Stages of Faith*, p. 173 (italicised in the original, not reproduced here).

[80] *Stages of Faith*, pp. 197-198 (italicised in the original, not reproduced here). Some of these features point to the significance of the new self-image generated for White by his second marriage and Groombridge years.

except in the case of conversion (which disrupts the normal stages), change in the content of faith is not the key element.[81] For White it can be shown that pivotal events resist analysis in terms of doctrines affirmed. The encounter with Wordsworth is such an occurrence, of great significance but not immediately reducible to any change in particular beliefs.[82] Rather it enhanced that to which he had previously assented. Fowler's analysis suggests how it is quite possible for White to have appeared as a 'natural' believer, and yet suffer a severe dislocation of faith and community in the turmoil of the college years. Wordsworth represents White's first significant spiritual experience, though acting as a catalyst rather than bringing fresh knowledge.

Wordsworth's Balm for the Soul

The crucial encounter with Wordsworth through a reading of the *Lyrical Ballads* is recorded in both the *Autobiography* and the *Early Life*.[83] In the former, reference is immediately made to Pauline conversion; it producing a change which 'could only be compared with that which is said to have been wrought on Paul himself by the Divine apparition'.[84] The effect is described as the death of 'systems' and a new focus upon personal experience - 'substituting a new and living spirit for the old deity, once alive, but gradually hardened into an idol'.[85] This is renewal which does not inevitably overturn previous belief but seeks its living heart. It was not in itself a mystical experience however, and nor is any content indicated. This makes it comparable to the 'borderline' examples which lie between the more common extrovertive and introvertive types identified (following Rudolf Otto) in W. T. Stace's classic study.[86] It is to be distinguished from the sort of nature mysticism which experiences union with the external world. Already in this version, composed some thirty years afterwards, White cannot disguise an element of dissatisfaction, a puzzling over just how Wordsworth's verses made such a difference, and a recognition that 'preciser problems' still to come would still require their own 'preciser answers'.[87] Yet it was a sign that conversion, in some shape, was still possible.

By the time of the *Early Life*, after a much greater interval, this emphasis has disappeared, and only the positive remains. Very probably White had the

---

[81] Described in *Stages of Faith*, pp. 285-286.
[82] Hence it hardly fits Fowler's definition of conversion as marked by content change.
[83] *Autobiography*, pp. 18-19, Ch. II; *Early Life*, pp. 61-62.
[84] *Autobiography*, p. 18, Ch. II.
[85] *Autobiography*, p. 19, Ch. II.
[86] *Mysticism and Philosophy* (London: Macmillan, 1961) pp. 81-84; extrovertive states focus upon the visible world and oneness with it, while introvertive experience is internal and without sense perceptions, seeking union with the Infinite. Aspects of Stace's analysis may be questionable; see further below, pp. 304-305.
[87] *Autobiography*, p. 19, Ch. II.

Autobiography to hand - or at least in mind - as he retraced these years. The encounter is still described as one entirely unsought and unexpected, the awakening of 'a new capacity' (p.61) for the enjoyment of nature but also now a 'modification ... of religious belief' (p.62). The contrast is essentially between the 'living God' encountered in nature and 'the artificial God of the churches' (p.62). The newly enlivened cannot for long endure the formal religion of churches and creeds, since 'the revolution wrought by him [Wordsworth] goes far deeper, and is far more permanent than any which is the work of Biblical critics, and it was Wordsworth and not German research which caused my expulsion from New College' (pp.62-63). Spiritual awakening is the severest challenge to institutional religion, not intellectual advance. The insistence that no particular change of doctrine or belief *necessarily* results from this experience - the essence of faith remains whatever reservations there might be about particular expressions of it - can be compared with examples of others who found solace in Wordsworth.[88]

The poet evoked responses at different levels, including an 'effect [which] can only be described paradoxically as a loss of faith and at the same time a spiritual awakening. The loss is a loss of faith in the value of the dogma and creeds of organised religion, and the awakening is a new awareness of the indefinable but insistent intimations of significance ... [which may be called] ... transcendental'.[89] This is very much how White interprets the significant moments for himself, but with such an 'open' experience the result might be a renewal of existing religion as much as its abandonment. Something of this mysterious quality is evident from his description of the impact of the key lines 'Knowing that Nature never did betray/The heart that loved her'; 'what they meant was not clear to me, but they were a signal of the approach of something which turned out to be of the greatest importance, and altered my history. It was a new capacity' (p.61).[90] The suggestively capitalised 'Nature', a feminine quality, does not (at least here, and not explicitly) mean a form of pantheism.

White speaks of a 'living God, different from the artificial God of the churches', but there is no suggestion in the *Early Life* of a new divinity *replacing* the Christian God. Rather, there is a sense that the 'real', living God, could not be adequately described in language at all - and could too easily be imprisoned by attempts to do so. Instead the Romantic emphasis upon feeling

---

[88] See examples in M. Paffard, *Inglorious Wordsworths: A Study of Some Transcendental Experiences in Childhood and Adolescence* (London: Hodder and Stoughton, 1973); on White pp. 53-55.

[89] *Inglorious Wordsworths*, p. 53.

[90] The phrase is from Wordsworth's *Lines written a few miles above Tintern Abbey* (fourth stanza).

and the intuitive comes to the fore.[91] Such themes were already part of the cultural milieu, penetrating Dissent as well as the wider community. A review of other similar experiences suggests that the prior disposition of the subject is the main determining factor in the form of response to the initial stimulus.[92] If this is the case, White's early attachment to the natural world (the only reported *locus* of childhood pleasure in this text or elsewhere) may at least partly explain its impact in his life, coupled with a lack of any real sense of spiritual inclusion at Bunyan or Cheshunt (possibly linked to sacramental *exclusion*). He writes with sufficient honesty and self-awareness to acknowledge that at the time his new spiritual awareness did not seem incompatible with fulfilling his vocation ('I had no thought of heresy') though in retrospect it seemed inevitably to be so; 'the seed was there, and was alive just as much as the seed-corn is alive all the time it lies in the earth apparently dead' (p.63). This 'conversion' involved an intensification of original belief, not its abandonment.[93]

In a later reflection posthumously published White suggests a measure of reinterpretation over time; 'When first I read Wordsworth I saw God in Nature. A I grew older I felt difficulty in saying so much. Nevertheless, the "something added" has always remained and will remain as long as I live'.[94] Effectively he realises what the other examples cited have already suggested, that the effect of this enlightenment is related to existing beliefs. Only two options are given for the 'something' which exposure to Wordsworth's verse adds 'to the wonder and the glory of the world'; 'for a few it is the Godhead; for almost all of us it is a something which demands reverence'.[95] Such a shift would be in accordance with an increasing hesitation about claiming too much and need not necessarily be interpreted as a weakening of belief. It could equally have arisen from a keener appreciation of the problems caused by an over-identification of 'God' and 'Nature', an attempt to avoid lapsing into pantheism. He is careful to separate religious belief from an intoxicated love of the natural world; 'a man

---

[91] The emphasis in Schleiermacher on feeling as the basis of religion could also have been a factor. J. D. Morell's *Philosophy of Religion* (London: Longman, Brown, Green, and Longmans, 1849), known to White, was very sympathetic to Schleiermacher. German idealism infused Romanticism by various routes. See quotes from Schleiermacher, and on Spinoza, in A. P. F. Sell, *Philosophical Idealism and Christian Belief* (Cardiff: University of Wales Press, 1995), pp. 12-14.

[92] Examples throughout Paffard's *The Unattended Moment: Excerpts from Autobiographies with Hints and Guesses* (London: SCM Press, 1976), and his earlier *Inglorious Wordsworths*.

[93] That is, a type of 'Christian deconversion', in which inauthentic - nominal or inherited - belief becomes real, as described (following Lewis Rambo) by John Barbour, *Versions of Deconversion*, pp. 10-33.

[94] From the essay 'Revolution' in *Last Pages*, pp. 88-94 (p. 94).

[95] *Last Pages*, p. 94. He doesn't quite say that he moved from the first to the second position, but this is surely implied.

who devotes himself to Wordsworth *and* is religious *and* a lover of nature will find himself looking at the world in certain way'.[96]

There are other interesting literary parallels. Richard Coe notes how frequently questions of faith appear in childhood autobiography; 'religious belief, or the lack of it, forms an integral part of those particular preoccupations which inspire and inform the Childhood genre'.[97] Often this is connected with a loss of conventional belief, sometimes anguished, sometimes liberating. Coe's examples do not have quite the combination of renewal *and* discovery which marks Hale White's story, but in one illuminating respect a similarity does exist. His concentration upon poets and writers draws out the importance for them of being 'suffused by some form of otherness - some degree of transcendental awareness of another dimension of experience, whether in art, in nature, in language, or in the very mystery of being in the world', a sense often accompanying a traditional belief system, and threatened by any withdrawal from that.[98] Even after a 'loss' of conventional faith however, what remains may often be characterised as 'an instinctively realized transcendentality', and a common trajectory takes the subject 'from a sense of magic in the very young child, to an awareness of beauty, thence to a sense of the mystery of the beautiful, and finally to a kind of pantheism, frequently with existential overtones'.[99] This wider experience of wonder, especially in nature, is clearly fundamental for White (and feeds into the Edenic view of the Bedford years), though indications of more orthodox belief remain. Pursuing this theme, Coe cites Bernard Berenson's memory of a childhood experience of oneness with nature; 'I climbed up a tree-stump and felt suddenly immersed in *It*-ness. ... *It* and I were one'.[100] This instance, given as proof that the decline of formal religious belief in no way reduces the sense of the mysterious, is very close to some of White's experiences (especially, that fusion with nature recalled in the short piece *An Epoch*), though it differs from the Wordsworth episode which is not explicitly unitive.[101] The significant references to natural beauty in the *Early Life* and other late writings suggest that White consciously sought such numinous encounters.

---

[96] *Last Pages*, p. 93 (emphasis added).

[97] Coe, *When the Grass was Taller*, p. 43. It is worthy of note that in his examples of spiritual reflection Burnett finds more examples of male adolescent conversions than female; see *Destiny Obscure*, p. 39.

[98] Coe, *When the Grass was Taller*, p. 43.

[99] Coe, *When the Grass was Taller*, pp. 113-114.

[100] From Berenson's *Sketch for a Self-Portrait*, cited in *When the Grass was Taller*, p. 116, and demonstrating remarkable recall of an event in early childhood (original italics).

[101] Printed in *More Pages*, pp. 181-183. Presuming this piece to be autobiographical, an experience from the age of more than sixty. See further below on this important text and its interpretation, pp. 303-306.

This spiritual renewal leads him to downplay the significance of his formal tuition at college - 'I learnt nothing' - probably an unduly harsh verdict, but in line with a tendency to blame others for shortcomings, and echoing the 'understood nothing' verdict on attendance at Bunyan Meeting (pp.63, 45 respectively). This also clears the way for the unique material in the *Early Life* on the New College expulsion. In length as well as content this section stands out from the rest of the memoir, and it is also marked by the obvious and significant reliance on primary sources. This dependence is unusual in White, and potentially allows his interpretation and use of contemporary records to be objectively assessed. Though widely recognised as of fundamental importance, this episode has been inadequately contextualised, and some evidence which may throw light on it has not been explored. While the reasons for the expulsion remain partly obscure, they by no means necessarily point to a loss of faith by the three students involved.[102] What White goes on to explain in the *Early Life* has made this clear to all those prepared to take his account seriously.

Clearly Wordsworth did not mean the same for all his readers, or produce such a change in them. George MacDonald for one felt that Coleridge offered something more; 'we find in him what we miss in Wordsworth, an inclined plane from the revelation in nature to the culminating revelation in the Son of Man'.[103] Coleridge's poetry led to a deepening experience of God, marked especially by *joy*. This quality, so important for White, who may draw something of his meaning from Spinoza's usage, recurs in MacDonald's private and published writings, but is never fully defined by him. Rolland Hein suggests that it was borrowed from Coleridge's poem *Dejection: an Ode*, where it appears as the gift of God to the faithful, but MacDonald does not make the link himself.[104] Rather he describes it as relief from 'sin, difficulties, anxiety, & forgetfulness'.[105] Its essence seems to be a loving trust in God's goodness, effectively the opposite of fearing a wrathful God. It means to participate in the very life of God, rather than to speculate upon his nature, an echo of Hale White's regular protests against 'over-definition'.[106] Christ is not for 'definiteness', but 'for life, for the joy of deliverance, for the glory of real creation, for the partakings of the divine nature' due to those who believe in

---

[102] Though it *may* have triggered that effect in Theobald and Frederic White; evidence is scant.

[103] From *England's Antiphon*, quoted in Raeper, *George MacDonald*, p. 111.

[104] *Victorian Mythmaker*, p. 31. (See especially stanza V of the Ode; Coleridge fears the loss of joy.)

[105] In a letter home, 11 April 1847, reproduced in Sadler, *An Expression of Character*, p. 17.

[106] See for example pp. 281-282 below.

him.[107]

MacDonald did not intend to slight Wordsworth, whom he praised for his 'Christian pantheism', a holding together of transcendence with the religious experience of nature which truly reveals God, without allowing nature to replace the divine.[108] Coleridge seems to have had the same effect upon MacDonald as the Scot claimed he had first had upon Wordsworth, in opening the eyes of his imagination, releasing that creative power in man which mimics his Creator.[109] It may have been as early as this date that MacDonald had read some of the poems of Novalis whose mystical emphasis was already congenial to him, and also included something close to a panentheistic understanding of the world.[110] In his Arundel pastorate this familiarity with German authors was used against him to raise the spectre of heterodoxy.

Summary

Careful reading of the *Early Life*'s description of his years at Bunyan Meeting and entrance to Cheshunt College, supplemented from other sources, suggests that White had accepted the traditional doctrines of Calvinist Dissent without serious thought or question. Though harshly judged in retrospect, his confession before the church was not false. The later layers of reflection on how he had been able to hold and unhesitatingly confess such beliefs reinforce the unreflective nature of his first assent. Though reproaching himself for it, the nature of this belief up to early adolescence fits with the psychological development appropriate to his years, as predicted by Fowler's theory of faith development. Recognising the limitations of such 'assent' means that the young White can be described as an unthinking believer, rather than falsely expecting him to display an adult understanding. This sort of faith, as Fowler also demonstrates, is fragile, and Hale White's life shows only too clearly how development to maturity can be disrupted by critical events. Serious obstacles soon lay across White's path, though the reasons for the unfolding tragedy are difficult to establish with certainty.

---

[107] As MacDonald put it in a letter of 1886, quoted in Hein, 'George MacDonald: A Portrait from His Letters', pp. 8-9.

[108] Stephen Prickett praises MacDonald's rare insight into Wordsworth; see *Romanticism and Religion: The Tradition of Coleridge and Wordsworth in the Victorian Church* (Cambridge: Cambridge University Press, 1976), p. 86-87. 'Pantheism' as used by MacDonald has a broad sense; the more precise term panentheism (which seems his meaning) was little known in English writing before the mid-twentieth century.

[109] Described by Raeper, *George MacDonald*, p. 111, citing again *England's Antiphon*.

[110] Here is an indirect link with Spinoza – it was Novalis [Georg Friedrich von Hardenberg] who had called him a 'God-intoxicated man'.

CHAPTER 7

'Our condemnation'
The Cheshunt and New College Years

The abrupt end to Hale White's training at New College has always been recognised as a pivotal event. The description of 'our condemnation' in the *Early Life* is the standard account, repeated in the secondary literature with only slight acknowledgement that subjective bias may have affected White's report.[1]

A failure to investigate thoroughly the primary sources combined with an over-readiness to read the *Early Life* as a simply factual record has led to other evidence going unnoticed or being ignored. The temptation has been to incorporate White's one-sided and partial account into a harmonised story of the journey from faith to doubt. When referring to White's description allowance must be made for the results of long reflection on bitterly experienced events, as well as the shaping effect of the literary genre within which he expresses them. While three students were involved it is only White who leaves such a full record of his feelings, though this does not prove that he was the crucial figure at the time. There is no known account of the life of Frederic White (*obit* 1895), but Robert Theobald (*obit* 1914) penned an autobiographical sketch, already cited above, which has not been noticed in previous studies.[2]

Although White introduces the crucial years in the most casual way - 'my expulsion from New College, of which a page or two further on' (p.63) - this narrative forms the largest continuous section in the *Early Life*. From the qualifying admission at Bunyan Meeting to the immediate consequences of his dismissal occupies fully twenty-five pages, over a quarter of the whole work. This was clearly a rooted sorrow which time had barely healed.

Unusually for White, the sources of his account are easily traced. As for almost all other writing on the subject, the primary text is the letter sent jointly by the three expelled to the weekly *Nonconformist* newspaper.[3] The accused

---

[1] *Early Life*, p. 69 (collectively describing the fate of the three). Wilfred Stone, among others, suspects the view of Principal John Harris is not quite fair, pp. 36-37.

[2] *Passages from the Autobiography of a Shakespeare Student*. Theobald later trained as a Doctor, while Frederic White took up a career in journalism, eventually working for the newly established Press Association.

[3] *The Nonconformist*, 31 March 1852, p. 240.

writing in their own defence are thus the most cited witnesses. The college published (or allowed to be published) a semi-official version of the circumstances, in addition to a brief notice in the Annual Report, but with much less detail. Versions by William White senior and Robert Theobald are also to be noted, though both draw heavily on the *Nonconformist* letter.[4]

Background to the College Years

The classroom discussion on 3 February 1852 which marked the start of this episode was not White's first contact with Principal John Harris. They had been in the same relation at Cheshunt College before both transferred to New College. There was no indication then of difficulties to come. White's recall of the Principal's cold reception of one of his early trial sermons at Cheshunt is doubtless made more pointed by being written from a post-expulsion perspective.[5]

Admission to church membership had been only the first step towards training. Another need was for 'some months of preparation'.[6] Such extra coaching was common and necessary, since there was recurrent concern from colleges about the weakness of candidates.[7] For some students ambition or ability was the spur to extra preparation, seeking special instruction because they intended to register for a degree when at college, and had to meet specific entry requirements. The provision of '*Preparatory Training for Young Brethren*' was officially encouraged and supported, '*so that they may enter the colleges qualified for their studies and advantages; and so that the Committees* [of the colleges] *may uniformly require a specified advance in learning, as an essential qualification for entrance*'.[8] Frederic White is an example, spending six months at William Legge's Fakenham Academy before going up to

---

[4] *To Think or Not to Think?* and (Theobald) *Statement of Facts Connected With the Expulsion of Three Students from New College London* (London: Robert Theobald, 1852).

[5] *Autobiography*, pp. 22-23, Ch. II; not repeated in the *Early Life*.

[6] *Autobiography*, p. 12, Ch. II, gives an idea of the time-scale, not mentioned in the *Early Life*.

[7] Kenneth Brown has written on this and other aspects of early Congregational training; 'The Congregational Ministry in the First Half of the Nineteenth Century: A Preliminary Survey', *Journal of the United Reformed Church History Society*, 3 (1983), 2-15.

[8] *Minutes of the Proceedings of a Conference of Delegates from the Committees of Various Theological Colleges Connected with the Independent Churches of England and Wales, Held in the Congregational Library, Blomfield Street, London, on Tuesday the 7th, and Wednesday the 8th of January, 1845* (London: Blackburn & Pardon, Printers, 1845), pp. 18-21 (p. 18; original italics).

Homerton.[9] Aaron Buzacott and Joseph Stuchbery, who transferred from Cheshunt to New College with Hale White, had also been under Legge. The diary of another Fakenham student shows that for some tuition was of the most practical kind, such as the preparation and delivery of trial sermons.[10] Pupils lived closely with their teacher, followed him in his ministerial duties, and shared much of the family life of his household. Unless Hale White's experience was very different it is surprising that he does not say more about it, though in his case (as one hoping to work for a degree) the emphasis might have been more upon academic work. He gives no indication where this learning took place, writing simply 'I was handed over to a private tutor to prepare for the Countess of Huntingdon's College at Cheshunt' (p.56).[11]

There was a college in Bedford itself, run jointly by John Jukes and William Alliott of Howard Meeting from Jukes' arrival in 1840 until 1869.[12] Students were equipped for the home ministry, while from 1849 to 1866 there was the significant addition of men training for overseas service with the London Missionary Society (which also placed men at Fakenham). Hale White's name does not appear in any surviving lists of students, but it is possible that short-term students were not always registered, or that his tuition was entirely private and he remained living at home.[13] The *Early Life* reference suggests individual teaching, and the University of London Calendar, which recorded the institutions at which its candidates had been prepared for matriculation, has 'Private Tuition' against his name.[14] Why did White not disclose the place of

---

[9] Letters relating to his Homerton application are in the New College Archives, DWL 218/18-25. T. G. Crippen briefly describes the establishment and lists many students, though his work shows that F. M. White was sometimes mistaken for another White, who ministered in Wiltshire; 'The Fakenham Theological Seminary', *Transactions of the Congregational Historical Society*, 8 (1920), 50-53. The Surman Index at Dr Williams's Library betrays the same confusion, cross-referencing Frederic with Joseph Metcalfe White, at Tisbury from 1854 until his death in 1888. J. M. White is shown at the town during these dates in the decennial national censuses, and Frederic has no connection there.

[10] William Astbury was at Fakenham a little later than Frederic White; see S. Orchard, 'Fakenham Academy in 1845', *Journal of the United Reformed Church History Society*, 2 (1978), 9-17.

[11] The college is not named in the *Autobiography*, but from the description is clearly Cheshunt.

[12] Jukes had conducted an academy during his previous ministry in Yeovil.

[13] Information on the seminary in H. G. Tibbutt, 'The Bedford Congregational Academy', *Transactions of the Congregational Historical Society*, 20 (1966), 114-118, and L. T. Towers, 'The Bedford Missionary Training College, and its Connection with the London Missionary Society', *Transactions of the Congregational Historical Society*, 15 (1945), 33-40.

[14] *The London University Calendar, 1849* (London: Richard and John Edward Taylor, 1848), p. 103. White matriculated in July 1848 (the same year as R. W. Dale, from

Note continues on following page

preparation? He surely could not have forgotten, and though the *Autobiography* often omits or disguises the identity of friends and colleagues, this is less the case in the *Early Life*.[15]

If it *was* in Bedford, the most likely explanation for his silence must lie in the later rift between Jukes and the White family. Both father and son felt that their minister could have done more to defend Hale during the New College difficulties, a feeling expressed in an angry exchange of letters. William White was told of remarks made privately in company by Jukes which appeared to impugn his son's integrity, and on complaining Jukes responded that he also 'had been too often and too cruelly misrepresented' with respect to the expulsion.[16] Although Hale White denied that Jukes appeared in *The Revolution in Tanner's Lane* as John Broad, there is no doubt that the depiction owed much to his painful memories of that time. The issue clearly rankled, for when Jukes' successor John Brown in 1882 suggested that William White had left the church piqued at the lack of support offered to the family, Hale was quick to respond by stating that his father had become disillusioned by the Meeting, while stressing that he remained a life-long member of the church universal.[17] In a poisoned atmosphere it is understandable that neither Jukes nor White made later reference to any pupil-teacher relation.[18] The minister's son was also at theological college and there was perhaps a fear that the family might be tainted by too close an association with Hale White.[19]

This is conjecture, but the need for an academic grounding highlights the importance of degrees for groups largely excluded from Oxford and Cambridge. Cheshunt was among those colleges forging links with the new University of London, where the option to register as external students was a particular attraction.[20] Much later, as always in reference to his formal education, White was dismissive of the institution - 'I never was at a University - the London University is not one - and was never properly taught Latin or

---

Spring Hill). Nonconformist and Catholic institutions are numerously represented in this listing.

[15] Maclean supports Bedford - 'he now studied at home instead of at school' – but, typically, without referencing this assertion (p. 52).

[16] Letter to White dated 8 April 1853 (BPL collection, MR 1/33).

[17] The story is told by George Jackson from White's own book of cuttings, which contained the relevant extracts printed in the *Bedfordshire Mercury*; 'Mark Rutherford's Scrap-Books', *London Quarterly Review*, 131 (1919), 191-204 (pp. 193-194.

[18] In due course Jukes had problems nearer to home, with his younger brother Edward being involved in a small way in the controversy over T. T. Lynch's *Rivulet* volume.

[19] John Griffith Jukes entered Lancashire College in 1847, leaving in 1852.

[20] The Cheshunt College annual *Report* for 1849 shows another student entering alongside White had also matriculated. For the importance of London, especially as a provider of external degrees, see James Munson, *The Nonconformists*, pp. 92-94.

Greek'.[21] The importance of the university to Dissenters is demonstrated by the numbers graduating; by 1851 *alumni* of Congregational colleges amounted to 130 of the 546 awarded degrees in Law and the Arts since the foundation.[22]

This total might have been higher but for the number of Scottish students attending the colleges after having completed degrees in their home universities, for whom there was usually no incentive to take the London qualification. George MacDonald was in this category, which also allowed exemption from some years of the typical college course, usefully reducing costs to the student. (Robert Theobald, unusually, attended University College for a year before going on to take a Glasgow MA and returning to study at New College.[23]) MacDonald was in a quite different position to White in applying to college of his own volition, and there is interest in his choice of Highbury. No explanation is given for White's parents selecting Cheshunt. They may have followed their minister's advice, or its rural situation and relative nearness may have commended it.

The reason for MacDonald choosing Highbury is also unclear. Other Scottish students had links with the college, including some MacDonald knew from home, but the letter referred to above shows it had not been his first preference; 'I should like to go to Homerton, to Dr Pye Smith, certainly not to Highbury'.[24] Kenneth Brown notes 'a considerable influx of university-trained Scots into the ranks of [English] Congregationalism in the 1840s, following the disruptions in the Scottish Church in those years', so MacDonald could be almost certain to train alongside fellow countrymen.[25] MacDonald gives no grounds for his apparent early inclination towards Homerton, nor any argument against Highbury. William Raeper portrays one of the Highbury professors, John Godwin, as 'fearsome', and suggests that the college discouraged

---

[21] In a letter to Sophia Partridge, 17 November 1896 (*Letters to Three Friends*, p. 157). Such criticism was common from opponents of the new non-residential degree factory; see T. L. Humberstone, *University Reform in London* (London: George Allen & Unwin, 1926), pp. 47-48. White may only have meant to highlight that his teaching was not delivered through the university (which at this date did not provide any), but at Cheshunt.

[22] Figures from A. J. Grieve, 'A Hundred Years of Ministerial Training', *Transactions of the Congregational Historical Society*, 11 (1932), 258-264 (p. 261).

[23] A year at University College had been recommended by examiners for Dr Williams's Trust, which sponsored his Glasgow studies; *Passages from the Autobiography*, p. 43.

[24] Raeper lists some of the Scottish students, but while referring to this letter of 11 April 1847 shows no awareness of the caveat about Highbury; *George MacDonald*, p. 62. MacDonald declared at Highbury that he had not applied to any other college; see Sadler, *An Expression of Character*, p. 25.

[25] *Social History of the Nonconformist Ministry in England and Wales*, p.84; overall, at least 10% of students admitted before 1851 to Highbury, and its predecessor at Hoxton, were from Scotland (p. 47).

independent thought by its 'worthy rather than inspiring' teaching 'conducted along narrow, doctrinal lines', but MacDonald did become close to Godwin, and Raeper may be reading too much back into the context from other reasons for his unsettlement.[26] MacDonald's friend Robert Troup, afterwards minister at Huntly and a year before him at Highbury, regarded Godwin as the best teacher on the staff, leaving no hint of difficult relations with students.[27] Godwin transferred to New College at its opening, and it will be seen that his role in the expulsion suggests a certain sympathy for the students concerned.

There may have been a straightforward motive for MacDonald's initial leaning towards Homerton. Pye Smith was celebrated for his scientific learning and MacDonald could well have known and admired his writings. The sciences had formed an important element in his Aberdeen studies, and were a continuing interest.[28] For some unknown reason Homerton was not to be, but positive suggestions offered in respect of Highbury fall short. His Huntly minister, John Hill, and John Kennedy of Blackfriars Chapel, are both said by Raeper to have trained here, thus explaining his application, but the association seems to be mistaken.[29] Whatever the cause, in joining Highbury MacDonald was welcomed into one of the most prestigious colleges, which could afford to choose its students carefully.[30] He was following closely in the step of another Huntly student, James Legge, also a graduate of King's College, Aberdeen. MacDonald was among the last to train at Highbury, which ceased to exist on the merger with Coward and Homerton to form New College in 1850.

Cheshunt College

In the *Autobiography* Mark Rutherford completes all his training at the (un-named) Cheshunt College; 'I had now reached the end of my fourth year at college, and it was time for me to leave', whereas the *Early Life*, closer to life,

---

[26] *George MacDonald*, pp. 63-64. In contrast, Rolland Hein speaks of a great warmth between Godwin and his student, though this may be reading back from later friendly relations; *Victorian Mythmaker*, pp. 45-46.

[27] Reminiscences imparted to his friends and included in the memoir prefacing his posthumously published history of *The Missionar Kirk*, p. xiii.

[28] According to Raeper, MacDonald offered his own lectures in chemistry to fellow Highbury students; *George MacDonald*, p. 73. It was perhaps partly due to his scientific training that MacDonald was not disturbed by Darwin's theories.

[29] *George MacDonald*, p. 62. William McNaughton lists them as alumni of the Glasgow Theological Academy in *The Scottish Congregational Ministry, 1794-1993* (Glasgow: Congregational Union of Scotland, 1993), pp. 65, 76-77, respectively.

[30] Kenneth Brown has compiled figures showing that between 1825 and 1850 Highbury (one of the larger colleges) accepted 181 students and declined places to 51; *Social History of the Nonconformist Ministry in England and Wales*, p. 68.

notes the start at Cheshunt and subsequent transfer to New College.[31] These narratives are naturally completely focussed upon White, but much of the significance of the events they describe is missed if they are not located within a wider context. Changes in the educational possibilities open to mid-century Dissent (and in expectations), and the growing self-assurance of the Free Churches are vital factors. The repeal of the Test and Corporation Acts in 1828 and the establishment of the Congregational Union in 1831 are part of this upsurge in confidence.[32]

Cheshunt had never simply trained ministers for the Countess of Huntingdon's Connexion, as the *Early Life* makes clear, though occasionally this is overlooked in studies of White.[33] Students from the London Missionary Society were an increasing presence in the 1830s (including some prepared at Bedford), representing a link with Independency. The appointment of Harris as Resident Tutor (Principal) in 1839 was a further significant identification with Congregationalism.[34] This 'elderly gentleman who had an American degree of doctor of divinity' has been misrepresented by White.[35] He was forty-eight on arrival at Cheshunt, and his degree recognised an appreciative readership for his works in America.[36] His sermons and essays were widely read, and his works on geology and human origins were serious attempts to relate scientific discoveries to the Christian understanding of creation.[37] Moreover he was posthumously celebrated (in words which must not be misunderstood) 'as a theologian [who] sought to infuse a more genial and humane spirit into the dry

---

[31] *Autobiography*, p. 26, Ch. III; compare *Early Life*, pp. 56-63.

[32] For this mood see C. Binfield, *So Down to Prayers: Studies in English Nonconformity, 1780-1920* (London: J. M. Dent, 1977), p. 12. Those who trained for ministry but did not continue in it now had wider opportunities.

[33] *Early Life*, p. 56. David Daiches seems to confuse Independent (Congregational) churches with those loyal to the Countess, to suggest that the College *excluded* all but Connexional students; *Some Late Victorian Attitudes*, p. 95.

[34] See Stephen Orchard, *Cheshunt College: A Record of the College Founded by Selina, Dowager Countess of Huntingdon, etc* (Cheshunt: Governors of Cheshunt College, ca. 1968), p. 11.

[35] *Autobiography*, p. 12, Ch. II. Harris was never 'elderly', dying aged 54 in December 1856.

[36] English higher degrees were not granted to non-Anglicans, and American (or Scottish) degrees were common among nonconformist leaders. See Timothy Larsen, 'Honorary Doctorates and the Nonconformist Ministry in Nineteenth-Century England', in *Modern Christianity and Cultural Aspirations*, ed. by David Bebbington and Timothy Larsen (London: Sheffield Academic Press, 2003), pp. 139-156.

[37] Posthumous re-publication of his works in America was justified because of the 'immense sales' which had testified in his lifetime to 'their intrinsic worth and great popularity', according to a notice from Gould and Lincoln of New York, fronting their edition of 1858.

dogmas of theology, and to urge Christians to reduce their belief to practice'.[38]

John Harris as a Scholar

Writers on Hale White have also presented an inadequate picture of John Harris. Some of his scholarly work has been too readily overlooked because of the recondite subject, and the ease with which it can be simplistically identified with biblical conservatism. Two major texts, *The Pre-Adamite Earth* (1846) and the later companion volume *Man Primeval* (1849), displayed a wide knowledge of the most up to date biblical and scientific writing.[39] The history of speculation about the life of a pre-Edenic world is a complex one with many associations.[40] David Livingstone demonstrates how theories about the existence of humanoid figures before Adam arose as a challenge to biblical orthodoxy but were later recast by writers who sought to harmonize the findings of science with the received teaching of scripture, Harris among them.[41] Some aspects of the theory also had a sinister appeal for those who at different times and for different reasons argued that Adam was the father of the white race only, and therefore regarded other racial groups as sub-human.[42] This was impossible on Harris's account, in which all mankind traced their ancestry to Adam and Eve. There was a pre-Adamite world, but no pre-Adamic creatures.

His work was not driven by the question of human origins, but rather by the challenge geological discoveries posed to the traditional biblical chronology, and his response shows him to be far from a biblical literalist. While hostile to evolutionary thinking, he exploited the suggestions in the Genesis text that allowed for a lengthy period between the initial act of creation and the

---

[38] The verdict of G. C. Boase in the original *DNB* entry; *Dictionary of National Biography*, ed. by Leslie Stephen and Sidney Lee, vol. XXV (London: Smith, Elder, 1891), p. 15. The word 'reduce' was unfortunately chosen; the sense surely requires something like 'relate'. Not re-appearing in the entry as revised by A.B. Baker, 'Harris, John', in *Oxford Dictionary of National Biography* <http://www.oxforddnb.com/view/article/12402> [accessed 8 July 2008].

[39] *The Pre-Adamite Earth: Contributions to Theological Science* (London: Ward and Co., 1846); *Man Primeval: Or, the Constitution and Primitive Condition of the Human Being. A Contribution to Theological Science* (London: Ward and Co., 1849).

[40] In *Adam's Ancestors: Race, Religion, and the Politics of Human Origins* (Baltimore, MD: Johns Hopkins University Press, 2008).

[41] For the history of this view see Livingstone, *Adam's Ancestor's*, chapter seven.

[42] Livingstone, *Adam's Ancestors*, pp. 84-85. Livingstone also records the positive verdict of several reviewers, but clearly not all readers were convinced; the copy of *The Pre-Adamite Earth* used here has 'absolutely unscriptural' and 'stuff and nonsense' boldly scrawled across the margins, in a possibly contemporary hand (pp. 27 and 30-31 respectively, both sections on the role of the divine pre-existent Logos in creation).

appearance of man. In the divine plan, the earth was then being dramatically prepared for its first inhabitant; 'for him, volcanic fires had fused and crystallised the granite, and piled it up into lofty table-lands .... For him, the earth had often vibrated with electrical shocks, and become interlaced with rich metallic veins'.[43]

There were similarities and differences with the contribution to the debate of John Pye Smith.[44] A friend of Harris, and colleague in the work of ministerial training (tutor, then Principal, of Homerton College from 1800 until the merger to form New College in 1850, when he retired), Pye Smith was a keen student of the geological sciences. Like Harris, he intended to demonstrate the congruity of scientific findings with the biblical revelation. Pressing for a reverent yet scholarly approach, he rejected undue literalism in biblical study and also argued that Genesis did not rule out a long geological epoch before the creation of Adam. Moreover he suggested that the Mosaic account was not necessarily universalistic, but described only a portion of the earth, seeming to accept a polygenic account of human origins, a possible but not necessary conclusion of such geographical restriction.[45] Harris and Pye Smith demonstrate a deep engagement with contemporary thought, including an extensive knowledge of German theologians and scientists, which warns against portraying either as backward-looking obscurantists.[46]

Harris devoted much of his life to education, and argued strongly for the necessity of an academically able ministry, notably in an address at the opening of Lancashire Independent College. For the sake of increasingly well-educated congregations, and to understand intellectual trends affecting those outside the churches, godliness needed to be matched with learning. Christian experience and character remained the indispensable foundation however: 'on this account we call for evidence of the personal piety of every one seeking admission to our collegiate institutions; we take the opinion of his pastor, and of others likely to form a correct judgement of his character, and we subject the whole to the test of a patient and anxious examination'.[47] Some popular feeling in the churches

---

[43] And much more in the same vein; *Man Primeval*, p. 1.

[44] Smith's teaching is set out by Richard Helmstadter; 'Condescending Harmony: John Pye Smith's Mosaic Geology', in *Science and Dissent in England, 1688-1945*, ed. by Paul Wood (Aldershot: Ashgate, 2004), pp. 167-195.

[45] Helmstadter, 'Condescending Harmony', pp.184-187. Though Smith believed this view was plausibly scriptural, Helmstadter suggests that geological findings were the chief determinant. Harris too argued that a local setting was possible, turning on the same interpretation of the Hebrew for 'earth'; *Man Primeval*, pp.16-17.

[46] By contrast, in the *Autobiography* the President 'knew nothing of German literature' (p. 14, Ch. II).

[47] 'The Importance of an Educated Ministry: A Discourse Delivered on the Occasion of the Opening of the Lancashire Independent College, Manchester, at the Preparatory Service, on the 25th of April, 1843'; reprinted in *Sermons and Addresses Delivered on*

Note continues on following page

viewed academic study with suspicion, believing that the best preachers were not necessarily the most highly educated.[48] This tendency Harris emphatically rejected. It was necessary to learn the Biblical languages and become familiar with the techniques of biblical criticism.[49] There is no suggestion in this clearly written and cogently argued piece that learning is dangerous or to be discouraged.

Yet elsewhere are clues to Harris's cast of mind which might explain the clash leading to the New College expulsions. His scientific writings were essentially works of synthesis which reflected 'astonishing power in collecting and moulding materials, giving them a perfect harmony, and making them his own', without his being 'a mere compiler' or 'wholesale plagiarist'.[50] To this assessment made at his funeral by George Smith must be added the high praise of Harris's Christian character and behaviour which makes it difficult to suppose that his treatment of the three students in 1852 could have been motivated by personal hostility or petty-mindedness.[51] Another tribute was presented by Thomas Binney. He had known Harris since both were young men offering for the ministry. He had admired his colleague's first published work, *The Great Teacher*, and noted his well-deserved reputation as a preacher.[52] References to the theological writings are a little more guarded, and Binney seems to distance himself from endorsing the way in which Harris worked:

> to collect and arrange the facts of science and the conclusions of philosophy, and to make them subservient to a sacred purpose, showing, with some originality of application, doubtless, how every thing natural and providential concurred in one grand design, harmonized with it, or threw light upon it.[53]

This has the feel of dutiful recognition of a self-imposed task important to

---

Special Occasions, by John Harris, D.D., Second Series, ed. by Philip Smith (London: James Nisbet & Co., 1857), pp. 230-256 (p. 232). See also similar expressions in Sermon XI in the same collection, 'The Christian Ministry', pp. 203-229.

[48] James Ritchie trained at Coward College, which had an academic reputation, but he found this meant students could be regarded with distrust; *Christopher Crayon's Recollections*, pp. 100-101.

[49] 'The Importance of an Educated Ministry', p. 241.

[50] From a tribute by George Smith, 1856; printed in *Christians at the Grave: Paul at the Cross: and Christ on the Mount. The Funeral Services Occasioned by the Death of the Late Rev. John Harris, D.D., Principal of New College*, ed. by Thomas Binney (London: Ward & Co.; Jackson & Walford, 1857), p. 11.

[51] Though lasting grief after the early death of his wife during childbirth in 1842 might have reduced his sensitivity to others.

[52] *Funeral Services*, pp. 73-75; high praise from such a noted preacher as Binney himself.

[53] *Funeral Services*, p. 78; this section is followed by un-attributed quotations from colleagues to the same effect.

Harris but less well received by others. Again it is accompanied by the warmest acknowledgment of Harris's personal qualities as minister and teacher. There are no references in the funeral addresses to the 1852 difficulties, but it is obvious that an emphasis upon submitting all knowledge to the judgement of scripture and received Christian teaching would have made it hard for Harris to respond positively to any radical restatement of doctrine. He must however be cleared of any suspicion of personal malice or a refusal to engage with the intellectual trends of his time.

White does not refer to the scientific side of Harris's work, and also presumably did not know that a witness he greatly respected had declared her admiration for aspects of the Doctor's ministry. George Eliot heard him preach, read his *Great Teacher* and praised his 'stirring eloquence'.[54] White's picture of Harris has triumphed so that even those who allow for some misrepresentation conclude that in the later crisis 'Harris was unquestionably defending a reactionary position with a shaky argument'.[55]

White at Cheshunt College

White's summary of these years is brief, bleak, and misleading; 'I learnt nothing at Cheshunt, and did not make a single friend' (p.63). It needs testing. His submission was first discussed by the Trustees' Meeting on 15 May 1848; 'an application for admission was made through the Rev. J. Jukes's Church, Bedford, and was referred to Dr Harris'.[56] This reference to Harris is unusual, as the College Secretary normally processed applications. It does not appear to demonstrate a special link between Bedford and Cheshunt, for students from the Jukes' academy went to a wide range of colleges, as did members of Bunyan Meeting who trained for the ministry. In a pamphlet history of the Meeting of 1849 Jukes noted five ex-Sunday school teachers who had recently offered for ministry, including his own son, Hale White and William Chignell (White's cousin), but all had applied to different colleges.[57] This leaves the possibility that Jukes had been responsible for preparing White, and Harris

---

[54] J. W. Cross, *George Eliot's Life as Related in her Letters and Journals*, new edition (Edinburgh: William Blackwood & Sons, 1885), p. 52, and letter (quoted above) of October 1840 in *The George Eliot Letters, vol. I*, ed. by G. S. Haight, p. 72. *The Great Teacher* had been published in 1835.

[55] Stone, p. 37. This episode clearly did not stand out to all, for the expulsion is not mentioned in the *Oxford DNB* entry on Harris.

[56] Trustees' Minute Book, 1837-50, Westminster College, Cambridge, Cheshunt Archives C1/7,

p. 250; White's name does not yet appear, but associated papers allow the identification to be made.

[57] *A Brief History of Bunyan's Church, etc* (London, Bedford: Partridge & Oakey, Rowland Hill, 1849), pp. 45-46.

wished to verify with him White's academic suitability for the course, perhaps in connection with matriculation at London University.

There is nothing in the Cheshunt archives to suggest anything unusual about the time there. After the normal probationary period White was admitted as a full member of the college in November 1848. As well as classroom teaching there was practical training in homiletics, with students supplying about thirty chapels in the surrounding area each Sunday on preaching assignments. The College Preaching Book for April 1844 to May 1851 details the engagements undertaken by Hale White and his fellow students in the college chapel and these local churches; the entries for White are entirely typical, showing regular appointments in the first and second terms of the 1848-49 and 1849-50 sessions, with the summer term free.[58] Henry J. Martyn also recorded something of the student experience in local churches during his time, showing the very mixed reception their sermons might receive.[59]

It is disappointing that White leaves almost no account of the teaching at Cheshunt, possibly deliberately to reinforce the impression that he did not learn anything. He refers to one theological text, but without sufficient detail to identify it with any certainty. He was recommended to study 'a book on the Atonement, by somebody named Williams', who 'justified the election of a minority to heaven and a majority to hell on the ground that God owed us nothing, and being our Maker, might do with us what He pleased' (p.60). This uncompromising text does not seem likely to be by the otherwise most-likely candidate, the moderate Calvinist Edward Williams who played down the concept of double predestination and limited atonement, unless White has seriously misrepresented his teaching. It could possibly be a confused memory of something by Thomas William Jenkyn, theological tutor at Coward College from 1840, who had written *On the Extent of the Atonement, in its Relation to God and the Universe* (1833) but gained a poor reputation as a teacher.[60] His work was probably in the Cheshunt library, but it did not expound limited atonement, and while upholding divine sovereignty rejected any motivation for the atonement not based upon God's love. Whatever the truth, by accident or design White succeeds in making it impossible even in this one area to assess the sort of instruction he received.

---

[58] Preaching Book April 1844 - May 1851 (WCC, CC C8/1). Thomas Broad's college preaching seems to be based on White's experience, including a sermon which ought to have been 'a little simpler'; *Revolution*, pp. 282-284, Ch. XX.

[59] *Chapters From the Autobiography*, pp. 15-16.

[60] The book went through several editions. Rosell and Dupuis suggest that Jenkyn's writings on the Holy Spirit helped make Finney's understanding of active conversion acceptable; *The Memoirs of Charles G. Finney*, p. 493, note 72. John Thompson records students' less favourable impressions of their tutor in *A History of the Coward Trust: The First Two Hundred Years, 1738-1988* (Cambridge: United Reformed Church History Society, 1998), pp. 63-64.

From the *Autobiography* it is known that White was deeply affected by the Principal's criticism of one of his sermons, that he had 'talked over [the] heads' of his congregation.[61] The subject was the atonement, but his attempt to uncover a deep universal meaning in the virtuous suffering for the wicked, not leaving aside all traditional language, but describing it as 'an exemplification, rather than a contradiction, of Nature herself, as we know her in our own experience' was perhaps simply incomprehensible.[62] Rutherford's reaction to criticism betrays White's sensitive nature, and the years of reflection following the later experience of rejection at New College; 'his words fell on me like the hand of a corpse ... the man who of all men who ought to have welcomed me, had not a word of warmth or encouragement for me (contradicting his earlier words, 'he said that my sermon was marked by considerable ability'), nothing but the coldest indifference, and even repulse'.[63] His sense of hurt is strikingly paralleled in the experience of modern students, who have been found to react just as strongly to academic praise or criticism, and long to retain such memories.[64]

White's mystical, almost uncontrolled spontaneity, results from the discovery of Wordsworth; 'the effect which was produced upon my preaching ... by this change was immediate'.[65] Although he is specific that this new awareness did not inevitably threaten traditional belief - which he appears to have hardly questioned by this date - he realised that this alternative, subjective, source of authority at one level made simple assent to orthodoxy impossible. The metaphorical nature of such language had been made clear. The suspicion that traditional terminology was used with a meaning not wholly in line with received belief lies behind the controversy yet to come. Nevertheless, if further proof were needed that nothing in White's time at Cheshunt can be definitely linked to the forthcoming storm it can be found in the decision to transfer to New College.

New College

White left Cheshunt at the end of the 1849-50 academic year, though he gives

---

[61] *Autobiography*, p. 23, Ch. II. Not mentioned in the *Early Life* however.

[62] *Autobiography*, p. 22, Ch. II. Compare Larsen's example of Joseph Barker's very similar (but secularist) defence of a universal principle of vicarious suffering, *Crisis of Doubt*, p. 163.

[63] *Autobiography*, pp. 22-23, Ch. II. The implication that Harris is spiritually dead, a 'corpse', must be deliberate.

[64] Evidenced in the study by D. B. Pillemer, M.L. Picariello, A.B. Law and J. S. Reichman, 'Memories of College: The Importance of Specific Educational Episodes', in *Remembering Our Past: Studies in Autobiographical Memory*, ed. by David Rubin, pp. 318-337.

[65] *Autobiography*, pp. 20-21, Ch. II.

no reason for doing so. He had completed the London University BA, which may have been a factor. Changes were being canvassed to the provision of ministerial training, and the uncertainties surrounding these could have prompted the move. There was a widespread recognition (with some vociferous opposing voices) that better educated ministers were required for a new generation, and that the existing colleges were not suited to meet the times. In Congregational circles particularly there were regular debates about the need for change; the subject was discussed at every Annual Assembly of the Union from 1840 to 1845.[66] Specific proposals for the amalgamation of Coward, Highbury, Cheshunt and Homerton were put forward in 1848.[67] The colleges were small and expensively duplicated their efforts. In the event Cheshunt, governed under the Trust established by the Countess of Huntingdon, faced insurmountable difficulties in agreeing to a merger, but the others went ahead to form a new college in St John's Wood. The college was to break fresh ground in being non-residential (like the Scottish universities and the University of London), and was also to encourage lay students alongside ministerial candidates. There was a formal affiliation to the innovative 'secular' university, and students could sit for the BA.

John Harris was appointed Principal of the new venture, his Cheshunt Senior Tutor Philip Smith leaving with him. White's application to the college survives. His letter of 6 May 1850 expressed a specific wish to follow his 'respected and beloved teachers' Harris and Smith.[68] This appears to rule out the possibility of antagonism between pupil and Principal dating from the Cheshunt years, unless White was dissembling. He was offered a place, the New College Council having agreed (10 June 1850, minute 73) to accept Cheshunt students who had the permission of their tutors and the Trustees to apply. This meant that Harris as Cheshunt Resident Tutor signed the authorisation for White, before as Principal of the new institution welcoming him to New College, suggesting that he had no reservation about the move (or, no power to stop it).[69] The Congregational Fund Board, which had previously given financial support to Homerton continued this for New College in the forms of grants to support ten students; White's letter of application asked that he might be considered for such aid, perhaps one reason for transferring.[70] His father's business was in decline at this time, and no doubt this made it difficult

---

[66] Details in A. D. Gilbert, *Religion and Society in Industrial England: Church, Chapel and Social Change, 1740-1914* (London: Longmans, 1976), p. 156.

[67] The invitation to consider amalgamation came from William Smith of Highbury, cited in M. J. Mercer, 'New College, London: Its Origins and Opening', *Journal of the United Reformed Church History Society*, 6 (1999), 327-336 (p. 329).

[68] DWL, New College Archives 336/4/1.

[69] Permission in DWL, NCA 366/4/2.

[70] The record does not show if he was successful.

for William senior to be sure that he could continue funding Hale's education.[71]

Other Cheshunt students applied to move at the same time as White, and the obvious reading of the *Early Life* is that they were his fellow-accused. 'I was transferred, with two other students, to New College ... [and when the Principal held his examination on the inspiration of the Bible] ... the two students before mentioned were members of this class, and asked some questions about the formation of the canon and the authenticity of the separate books' (pp.63-64).[72] White's letter accepting a place at New College, on 20 August 1850, had requested that the Cheshunt students might lodge together. The other three (not two, as the *Early Life* suggested) are there named as Aaron Buzacott, Joseph Stuchbery and Eliezer Griffiths, all of whom went on to serve as Independent ministers.[73] The identity and origins of the expelled students must be sought elsewhere.

The Three Expelled

The applications files for New College reveal details of the controversial students, and suggest possible links between them. When all three were believed to have studied together at Cheshunt experiences there might be presumed to have formed a common bond, but separate roots make their shared stand more difficult to explain.

Robert Masters Theobald was the oldest of the group, the best educated, and with impeccable dissenting credentials.[74] Born in 1829, he had already received an MA in classics and philosophy from Glasgow University, funded by a Dr

---

[71] This may have been the reason for a visit to Cheshunt by William White (un-dated, but ca. mid-1850) in which he asked Harris about Hale's progress and prospects. Noted in William's *To Think or Not to Think?* (p. 14), it could just as easily have been an ordinary visit to see Hale and a chance meeting with Harris. It was however at a time when a decision may have been taken to apply to New College.

[72] H. A. Smith questioned this identification, misled by White's declaration (*Early Life*, p. 63) that he made no friends at Cheshunt; 'The Life and Thought of William Hale White' (unpublished doctoral thesis, University of Birmingham, 1938), p. 99.

[73] The four students are listed together in the Cheshunt College Report for 1850 as permitted to transfer to New College. They could have been in the same class as White, but were not directly involved in any controversy. On leaving New College Buzacott spent a year of rural ministry in Suffolk before serving at Fetter Lane for twelve months from 1854, bravely accepting a cause burdened by debt and still dispirited after the withdrawal of an ailing Caleb Morris in 1849. He was followed by another New College man, Samuel March, who after many trials left in 1859 and was ordained as an Anglican. Details in Arthur Pye-Smith, *Memorials of Fetter Lane Congregational Church, London* (London: Warren Hall and Lovitt, 1900), p. 29.

[74] Biographical information derived from *Passages from the Autobiography*, confirming information preserved in his application (DWL, NCA 366/13; 366/14).

Williams's bursary. Theobald's grandfather was the Reverend Stephen Morell of Little Baddow, who supplied his reference for New College. His uncle, J. D. Morell, through his philosophical writings and personal example was a significant influence and may be a point of contact with the other expelled.[75] Less is known about Frederic Meriton White, whose sister Jessie achieved fame through marriage to the Italian revolutionary Alberto Mario. The family worshipped at the Independent church at Gosport during the pastorate of J. D. Morell, before a move to Portsmouth's Highbury Chapel. There William Chignell became minister in 1849. While Theobald entered New College as an outside student, Frederic White, at Homerton since 1847, was enrolled on the terms available to members of the constituent colleges. The course of study at New College lasted for five years, but students were to be credited for the time spent in the uniting bodies, by special agreement Cheshunt too being treated in this way. For this reason the three were all to be found in the 'second theological class', representing the official fourth year of the programme of study. It is just possible that Mark Rutherford's reference in the *Autobiography* to students from other colleges with whom he formed important friendships while at Cheshunt alludes to Frederic and Robert, but no clues to identity are included.[76]

Correcting the Chronology

The imprecision with which White records his age and dates in the *Early Life* has suggested a false chronology. He applied during the summer of 1850, with his letter of acceptance dated 20 August that year. This is in contrast to the *Early Life*, 'in 1851 or 1852 I was transferred ... to New College' (p.63). The passive tense here may reflect a financial imperative under which his father required him to remove from Cheshunt, but the style adopted again suggests White as the unwilling subject. A difficulty in dating arises from a mistake easily made about the establishment of the college itself. The lecture on 'The Inspiration of the Scriptures' seen as the immediate cause of the crisis was, the title page declared, 'delivered at the opening of the College, October 1, 1851'.[77]

---

[75] Another uncle was the Reverend Stephen Morell (the younger) who died in 1824, before Theobald was born, after a most unhappy pastorate in Exeter.

[76] *Autobiography*, p.20, Ch. II. Theobald reported that he 'knew [White] first when he was a student at Cheshunt College', but without giving any context; '"Mark Rutherford": Some Reminiscences of Mr William Hale White', *Westminster Gazette*, 17 March 1913, p. 10. Probably only slight prior acquaintance is to be understood.

[77] *New College, London: The Introductory Lectures Delivered at the Opening of the College. October, 1851* (London: Jackson and Walford, 1851), pp. 3-65. In the *Autobiography*, 'the President had a course of lectures, delivered year after year to successive generations of students' on inspiration (p. 13, Ch. II). Harris may have dusted down existing notes for his inaugural lecture, but White is probably being unfair.

This statement has been used to date the college's first academic session. In fact the college began its life a full twelve months earlier, and October 1851 marked the delayed completion of the building.[78] This means that White and his fellow students had already been enrolled at the college under Harris and the other professors for more than a year before incompatible views became clear, though the amount of contact might have been slight, as a reduced programme of study was in place at first.

The Controversy

The disagreement between Harris and the accused students is variously said to involve the authority of the Bible, the nature of its inspiration, and the meaning of canonicity. In the *Report* for 1852 the official college notice of the expulsion fixed on rejection of the 'Supreme Authority of the Sacred Scriptures', and 'the *Divine Authority* of the Bible' to describe the students' position.[79] Uncertainty over the issue is matched by the difficulty of discerning from the surviving record just what was said and argued. Moreover the expulsion was not simply about different views of the Bible, but fundamentally opposed ideas about the purpose of theological education, and the authority of teachers and of the church.

The basic, undisputed, facts are given in Figure 6 below. The chief sources are the letter of the three to the *Nonconformist*, the *Statement of Facts* by Robert Theobald, and William White's *To Think or Not to Think*? Other accounts, including White's in the *Early Life*, largely depend upon these records. The New College Minute Book is a vital additional source.[80]

A discussion on 3 February 1852 sparked the clash. Harris examined the class on the doctrine of biblical inspiration as set forth in his inaugural lecture of October 1851. Such question and answer sessions were quite normal, students having been able to speak 'with that freedom which had become recognized and habitual in the class', but on this occasion (according to William White), they were 'stopped by the Principal in ... peremptory style'.[81] To this Hale White, in the *Early Life*, adds '*immediately* stopped' (p.64).[82] There is already a suspicion here that William White (then copied by Hale White) has presented his material to suggest intolerance, and ultimately

---

[78] Its early days are described by M. J. Mercer, 'New College, London', p. 333.

[79] *Report of New College, London, 1852*, pp. 9-10 (original italics and capitalization).

[80] The record is heavily corrected in some sections covering the crisis, something rare elsewhere and a possible sign of dispute among Council members over decisions or actions taken.

[81] As given in Theobald's *Statement of Facts*, p. 6, then White's *To Think or Not to Think?*, p. 11.

[82] Emphasis added. Possibly changed from his father's account to avoid slavish copying, but to Harris's detriment.

unfairness towards the students. Theobald's *Statement of Facts* does not support them, for he states that 'the conversation held on the 3rd of February lasted for about three quarters of an hour'.[83] Though brought to a close by the Principal's unwillingness to pursue matters which he declared not 'an open question' for ministerial students, the sense of abruptness is not present. It is surprisingly difficult, for such an apparently well-documented event, to discover just what was said in this conversation, and quite impossible to find who took part. It would be very valuable to have evidence from others in the class, but this seems lacking, perhaps a sign that the episode was soon forgotten by those less centrally involved.[84] From William White it might be inferred that only the three accused had asked questions, from Hale White that only his two fellow expelled did so, but from Theobald that '*other members of the class besides our three selves*' took part.[85] Extraordinarily, there is no record of any questions which may have been posed by Hale White himself, and his own account makes him silent. Although his name is the one now chiefly remembered from the incident this is an indication that he was probably not the central character at the time.

The Events of February - April 1852

Tuesday, 3 February : Class discussion and dispute over Harris's lectures on inspiration.

Tuesday, 10 February : Senate meeting to discuss the incident.

Friday, 13 February : Meeting of the College Council, and interview with each of the 'accused'.

Saturday, 14 February : Council's resolution that the men are not suitable 'for the Christian ministry' sent to the three.

---

83 *Statement of Facts*, p. 6.

84 In a least one case a fellow student recalled overlapping with Hale White at New College, but it seems without leaving a record of his memory. James Donaldson (1831-1915) did not enter the ministry but became a noted patristic scholar while pursuing a career in Scottish higher education. Obituarists (for example in *The Athenaeum*, 13 March 1915, p. 238) noted his New College years and mentioned White, presumably derived from something said or written by Donaldson. It is conceivable that his unpublished papers at the University of St Andrews contain relevant material but unfortunately these were unavailable at the time of writing due to reorganisation of the library's Special Collections.

85 *Statement of Facts*, p. 9, emphasis added.

Wednesday, 18 February : Meeting of the Council to decide what action to take against the three; Thomas White and William White petition the Council.

Monday, 23 February : Council meeting attended by Mr Theobald (copies of two letters of Robert Theobald promised to the Council).

Letter of Council same day to the three requesting them to meet with 'a Committee of three or four ministers' on Wednesday, 25 February for a 'friendly conference' on the issues.

Wednesday, 25 February: Meeting of the Committee appointed above.

Monday, 1 March : Letter of the three to the Council; they will not resign or leave the college of their own will. Three demands made of the Council (moral character to be affirmed, charges to be specified, copy of college basis of faith to be supplied).

Wednesday, 3 March : Council meeting (receiving letter above and report from the Committee meeting on 25 February); students are found wanting, but offered the chance to 'withdraw ... for a period of three months' to reconsider their views.

Monday, 15 March : Letter of the three to the Council refusing to withdraw, reiterating request for specific charges against them.

Wednesday, 17 March : Council noted letter above, confirms that the accused must therefore leave 'either by their own secession or by the authority of the Council'. Read to the three, who had waited for such a summons. They repeated their dismay at such a demand, and repeated their three requests of 1 March.

Undated letter of the Council to the three declining to meet their requests.

7 April : Letter of the Council removing the three from all connection with New College.

Figure 6 : Chronology of the New College crisis, 1852. Drawing on Theobald's *Statement of Facts* and the New College Minute Books

There is a tension between the openness suggested by the practice of classroom discussion and the resulting charge against the students. That such debate was common in the college system is suggested by Henry Martyn's account of

Cheshunt in the 1850s under the principalship of Richard Alliott. The reported dialogues are remarkable for the tolerance of widely divergent opinions, and show the apparent gulf which could exist between teachers and the taught without precipitating action against those most outspoken.[86] At least some degree of latitude is known elsewhere from a later date, so whatever the repercussions of the New College crisis it did not inhibit all freedom allowed to students. On his appointment at Spring Hill in 1869 D. W. Simon adopted an enlightened teaching method in which 'lectures were subservient to question and answer' in order to encourage students to develop their own views, though this was not without its drawbacks.[87] At New College the learning environment seems by comparison to have been more constrained.

The students, as William White recorded it, 'wished to consider the formation of the Canon, the authenticity of the separate books, and such like subjects', while Harris had responded 'I must inform you that this is not an open question within these walls. There is a great body of truth received as orthodoxy by the great majority of Christians, the explanation of which is one thing, but the foundation must not be questioned'.[88] The letter to the *Nonconformist* has the fullest indication of the substance discussed:

> they related chiefly to the propriety of treating the Bible as one book, before examining the critical evidence of the connexion between the several parts, and to the question, Whether the authors were miraculously impelled to write every part of these compositions as we now have them? Another question referred to the formation of the canon, and to the degree in which we are dependent on the compilers for the selection of the writings included therein.[89]

From reports of the subsequent interviews between the College Council and the three it is possible to identify more closely where the differences between the two sides were thought to lie. However the testimony is only of questions asked by the Council, and not the students' replies. Presumably the three, who went in separately, were asked the same or very similar questions and conferred later to record them with some degree of accuracy. As written up by William White, they were said to include, *inter alia*, the way in which 'the sacred writers' were influenced, whether statements in the Bible were to be believed as true in their own right or because of their inclusion there, how the inspiration of the Bible differs from others books deemed inspiring, and whether they believed their own views coincided with those 'held by the supporters of this

---

[86] Examples are considered below, see pp. 232-235.

[87] Powicke comments on this in *David Worthington Simon* (London: Hodder and Stoughton, 1912), p. 216. For Simon as a teacher see pp. 282-283 below.

[88] *To Think or Not to Think?*, p. 11.

[89] *The Nonconformist*, 31 March 1852, p. 240.

Institution' and as 'expressed by the Principal in his introductory lecture'.[90]

The last point echoed the distinction earlier drawn by Harris about the propriety of questioning foundational beliefs. It was a clash of views about inspiration - was it 'from above', a doctrine to be received on the authority of the church, or 'from below', something which could only be subjectively experienced by the believer? Clearly this kind of divergence could apply to any number of doctrinal formulations. It is not hard to see how Theobald's questions in class must have disturbed Harris; 'I stated my conviction, that man's religious life must rest upon realities, the truth of which must find its confirmation in the experiences of his own nature and the whole course of Divine Providence in the world, and that nothing which cannot find some natural response in the purified life of man can exert any moral power over him, or be of any spiritual value to him'.[91] This of course is very close to the concept of 'inner reference' which White derived from Wordsworth and the Romantic tradition.

Ironically, both parties were trying to avoid a purely mechanical view of inspiration, but their different starting positions made common ground hard to find. Harris' lecture acknowledged inspiration as 'the topic of the day'; 'tradition now assumes to supplement the Bible ... Tractarianism appears with another revelation. ... Reason, not satisfied with interpreting the book, assumes to be its judge; and, with the appearance of Rationalism, revelation disappears. Emotion, inward experience [seen as] truth itself, gives birth to a pious mysticism, which modifies revelation at pleasure'.[92]

A true view of the biblical writers' inspiration, he went on to argue, recognised it as quite distinct from an enhanced 'natural' genius, or the result of especially clear-sighted piety. Though he disavowed any concept of dictation (warning of the dangers inherent in words like '*plenary*' and '*mechanical*'), inspiration did result in a divinely authoritative text, the purpose of which is 'to publish truths which it had not entered into the mind of man to conceive'.[93] The role of human reason is to receive these truths with due respect to their origin. That he declared this a truly scriptural doctrine of inspiration was hardly likely to mollify critics like William White who did not share his premises. Although writers on White have routinely depicted Harris as woodenly dogmatic this reflects their instinctive sympathy for Hale White, and support for his supposed progressive opinions, rather than the facts. Harris was no fundamentalist, and his lectures on inspiration have recently been cited as an example of

---

[90] *To Think or Not to Think?*, p. 4.

[91] *Statement of Facts*, p. 6.

[92] 'The Inspiration of the Scriptures', p. 4; see p. 30 on the defects of 'mechanical' views.

[93] 'The Inspiration of the Scriptures', pp. 30, 62 (original emphasis).

imaginative thinking aimed at avoiding the pitfalls of holding to infallibility.[94]

The ideas expressed in the class discussion, and later in interviews with the Council, could not be reconciled with this high view of scripture. Theobald was anxious (at least after the event) to stress the undeveloped and tentative nature of the beliefs he articulated, but acknowledged that the debate had turned too much on what he did *not* believe about inspiration. In his *Statement of Facts* he denied that the three had ever likened biblical inspiration to that of Homer's poetry, or compared Jesus with Shakespeare, but admitted that for him the inspiration of the biblical authors was not of a different *kind* (as Harris would have insisted) to that available to the modern believer.[95] There was a reluctance to use traditional terminology, but Theobald realised this left the three exposed; 'if we dare not assent to certain forms in which important truths are stated, because we think that the truths themselves are misrepresented by the terms used to express them, there is a danger of our being regarded as entire disbelievers in all the truths which these forms are supposed and intended to convey'.[96] This well expressed the quandary in which the accused found themselves, while their assertion of the need and right of private judgement was quite unacceptable to the college authorities. However issues of process and fairness formed as great a bone of contention as the doctrinal matter supposedly at the centre of the case.

Although William White stressed the imbalance between the power of the authorities and the weakness of the students' position, the three resolutely refused all opportunities for compromise. The well-meaning intervention of Professor Godwin, like each offer of time to reconsider, came to nothing.[97] (Godwin had taught George MacDonald at Highbury, and evidently took a strong pastoral interest in his students. He gave friendly advice to the Scot thereafter, and following the death of his first wife married MacDonald's sister-in-law.[98]) The students, though effectively powerless, tried to occupy the moral

---

[94] In the volume *Protestant Nonconformist Texts, vol. 3: The Nineteenth Century* (Aldershot: Ashgate, 2006), ed. by David Bebbington, with Kenneth Dix and Alan Ruston, p. 82; also included in this collection is an extract from the *Autobiography* (pp. 120-121), without any recognition of a link between Harris and Hale White on this issue (moreover it is wrongly stated that White 'served as a minister at Bedford', and some of the other details are seriously misleading or inaccurate).

[95] *Statement of Facts*, pp. 9-12.

[96] *Statement of Facts*, p. 4.

[97] Godwin was censured in 1858 for a Congregational Union lecture expressing an exemplarist view of the death of Christ. He stopped teaching his New Testament courses, but remained lecturer in philosophy (Tudur Jones, *Congregationalism in England, 1662-1962* (London: Independent Press, 1962), pp. 261-262). See below for his later contact with Theobald.

[98] Godwin's contacts with MacDonald are explored by William Raeper; *George MacDonald*, see especially chapters six and ten.

high ground with three counter-demands upon the college; to remove the suspicion that their suspension implied moral error, to know exactly which of their opinions were condemned, and to have a copy of the college creed against which their views were judged.

The college stalled, and finally refused to comply. It is likely that the Council could not frame any charge with sufficient precision to prove that the students were in error; William White taunted that the staff themselves were not of a common, orthodox, mind on the Bible. It seems that there was no declaration of faith by which the students could be judged, and to which they had pledged allegiance. Theobald at one point admits as much ('Students, upon entering the College, are not asked to subscribe to any documentary creed.'), and if the students believed this to be the case a repeated demand for the basis of faith, to embarrass the college, would be understandable.[99] The surviving 'New College Register of Student Declarations' does not specify to what assent was made, and separately printed rules relate to behaviour, not belief.[100] Congregationalism, reflecting its fundamental principles, had little place for formal subscription, and while discussions on a basis of faith took place when the founding colleges united it is possible that no such text was agreed.[101] Students might have concluded that a greater freedom of thought was permissible where no specific statement of belief had to be formally endorsed on entry. At Cheshunt students had been required by the Trust deeds to give assent to a statement drawn from the Anglican Thirty-Nine Articles and the Westminster Confession; Harris was in a new situation at New College where there was not such a clear test.[102] His authority, as well as that of the scriptures, was under question.

Since neither side were willing to compromise, the students were ordered to leave the college by a letter of 7 April 1852. It is difficult to see any victors in this situation, but undoubtedly the room for manoeuvre diminished as attitudes hardened. William White implied that the authorities were simply dishonest, because the professors, including Harris, had scholarly dealings with advanced critics, some from Germany, while at the same time restricting the students' intellectual freedom. Though the Congregationalist *Biblical Review*, of which Harris was an editor, brought to public attention a range of modern theological opinions, it is impossible to show that such reporting constituted advocacy of

---

[99] *Statement of Facts*, p. 38.

[100] DWL, NCA 154/1. White signs at no. 23, January 1851; Theobald at no. 47 and F. M. White at no. 35.

[101] See DWL, NCA 159: Minutes of Senate, No. I, 17 January 1851, referring to the Preliminary Statement of the United Committee, Section VI, cap. 7, c, p. 19.

[102] Though Henry Martyn's reports of students' views at Cheshunt suggest they felt little constrained by subscription; see pp. 232-235 below.

their views, or hypocrisy if rejecting them from students.[103] The prospectus in the first volume reassured potential readers that 'scriptural Congregationalism' would be upheld, but there was a hint of openness to a higher principle in the support pledged for 'every pious attempt to look at old truth from new points of view', particularly for 'the benefit of the students of our theological colleges, of the rising ministry, and of the religiously-educated and intelligent among the young of all classes'.[104] While calling for a critical and scientific approach to biblical study, it was not quite clear (perhaps deliberately) what this meant in practice, leaving scope for criticism and resentment from progressive and conservative elements alike. Congregationalism had its own fierce guardians of orthodoxy. John Campbell, the energetic editor of a number of newspapers including the *British Banner*, closely scrutinised the colleges, as they must have been very well aware. Michael Ledger-Thomas describes how Campbell's aggressive campaigns in the 1850s contributed to 'a full-fledged panic about the infestation of Congregational colleges and pulpits by "Germanism"', which included erroneous views on sin and atonement, and belief that the Bible was 'no more inspired than any other literature'.[105] This accords completely with Mark Rutherford; 'it was a time in which the world outside [the college] was seething with the ferment which had been cast into it by Germany and by those in England whom Germany had influenced'.[106]

In fact in this instance the *Banner*'s reaction to events was remarkably low key, and deliberately so, for the paper held that 'where evil exists, unless publicity be essential to its rectification' no good purpose could result from 'holding it up to the gaze of an idle world'.[107] At the same time the importance of the issue, and the rightness of the Council's action was affirmed; 'we have perfect confidence in all who have to do with the College ... these are not times for half-measures on the subject of Inspiration'.[108] The criticism of Dr Harris by the students was rejected. The expulsion of the three might therefore have served as a welcome sign that the college was orthodox and the staff aware of the need for vigilance. This is at least hinted at in reports of a *soirée* at New

---

[103] *To Think or Not to Think?*, pp. 16-20. For the role of the *Review* in the reception of German thought in England see J. Rogerson, *Old Testament Criticism in the Nineteenth Century*, pp. 178-179.

[104] 'Prospectus', *The Biblical Review, and Congregational Magazine*, 1 (1847), 1.

[105] In '"Glimpses of the Great Conflict": English Congregationalists and the European Crisis of Faith, circa 1840-1875', *Journal of British Studies*, 46 (2007), 826-860 (p. 839).

[106] *Autobiography*, p.17, Ch. II.

[107] *British Banner*, 24 March 1852, p. 193, 'New College, London'; the tone is Campbell's, whether or not he actually penned this piece.

[108] *British Banner*, 24 March 1852, p. 193, 'New College, London'. The paper was treading the difficult line of rooting out error without giving ammunition to enemies of the churches in general or Congregationalism in particular.

College arranged to coincide with that summer's Congregational Union meeting, and hosted by Harris. John Angell James spoke to express 'the most tender sympathy of the Churches under the painful circumstances in which it [the College Council] had recently been placed (cheers) - and he fully believed that the event which had occurred would tend, not only not to diminish, but to increase general confidence in the Institution'.[109] John Campbell also addressed the guests, not referring to the expulsion, but perhaps having it in mind when he stressed the need for strengthened oversight of students, especially through the pastoral care exercised by the churches at which they worshipped while in London.

This context makes credible the reading suggested here, in which the expelled by their intransigence became convenient scapegoats to establish the New College's credentials in a battle which neither side had desired. William White suggestion that there had been muttering about the professors' own heterodox views is not repeated in other sources.[110] The wider exposure could hardly been seen as favourable to the college however, and it was a high risk to proceed in this way. John Harris held office as Chairman of the Congregational Union for 1852, so it seems likely that there would have been a desire to avoid adverse press comment at that time, unless to the contrary his position inclined him to act with severity against any threat to the college's reputation or orthodoxy. Limited coverage in the *British Banner* suggests the publicity was not as important or harmful as later critics believe, though the authorities might nevertheless have been wiser to temper their reaction. Some years earlier Thomas Binney had foreseen that it would be impossible to stem new ideas, especially from Germany, and had recommended the need to 'deal gently with the younger men' who were exposed to them.[111] It was unfortunate for the students concerned that such a potentially sympathetic member of the New College Council had been prevented by illness from taking any part in the process. As the *British Banner* solicitously reported in March 1852, Binney had been 'for some weeks laid aside', at worst 'confined to his room', and even when convalescing unable to read or write because of a muscular problem affecting his sight; only in June was his recovery signalled.[112] The outcome of the crisis might otherwise have been different.

The incident was a gift to the critics of dogmatic religion. Ebenezer Syme's pungent attack in William Maccall's *The People* on the 'parson-manufactory

---

[109] *British Banner*, 19 May 1852, p. 330, 'Soirée at New College'.

[110] *To Think or Not to Think?*, p. 16; the Professors had already served in other colleges without apparent problems.

[111] Cited by Ledger-Thomas from Binney's opening address to the Congregational Union meeting, 1848; '"Glimpses of the Great Conflict"', p. 835.

[112] *British Banner* 10 March 1852, p. 162 ('Rev. Thomas Binney') and 9 June 1852, p. 377 ('The Rev. Thomas Binney').

for the Independents at St. John's Wood', 'a quasi-prelatical institution, built with Babylonish bricks designed to give Dissent a "*status*" in the eyes of world', revelled in the college's discomfort; using Theobald's *Statement of Facts* and the *Nonconformist* letter from the expelled, Syme castigated the authorities that they dared not allow students to follow the truth, but he had to be content with generalities, admitting that 'what the precise sentiments of the students are, it is difficult to make out'.[113]

Reports of expulsions or difficulties between staff and students in theological colleges were not uncommon, and this incident may not have attracted an unusual level of attention. For some, however, its importance lay in confirming that the colleges generally were failing to produce the ministers appropriate to the churches' needs. There had been debates on this issue at Congregational gatherings throughout the 1840s. R. W. Dale's *The Old Evangelicalism and the New* looked back to those years as ones of conflict in which younger men frequently found themselves under suspicion for their opinions, especially about the Bible.[114] The colleges defended their work, but a significant number of older ministers remained suspicious about the emphasis upon academic qualification for ministry. To them each failing proved the need for spiritually-minded men over the intellectually gifted. Some of these concerns can be traced in the anonymous articles Dale refers to in the *Congregational Magazine*. When 'An Aged Minister' wrote that the 'Unhealthy State of the Churches' was due to more recently trained ministers, who though highly educated were pastorally weak and unable to preach 'pointed and prominent doctrine', 'A Young Minister' robustly countered all the charges.[115] Against this background the New College incident is more important as part of a tendency than for the individual cases involved.

Some Underlying Factors

It has proved impossible to explain why the class discussion in February 1852 grew into such a severe crisis. It may be that the three intentionally stated views which they knew would be provocative, though they seem to have had little direct contact with Harris before that date. Despite this, Harris claimed to have formed a high view of Hale as one he had known 'so long, and having felt no ordinary interest in' because of his youth and 'promise', seeming to rule out

---

[113] 'The Bible and the Truth: The New College Heresy', *The People: A Journal of Social, Education, and Religious Progress*, 8 May 1852, pp. 149-151 (original italics). He separately noted Harris's lectures on inspiration (pp. 147-149).

[114] London: Hodder and Stoughton 1889; pp. 22-28. It is just possible that Dale has the 1852 dispute in mind, though the dates do not tie up; he probably writes from memory.

[115] *Congregational Magazine* for February 1844, pp. 124-128 (p. 127) and March 1844, pp. 199-202.

any longstanding differences.[116] But William White mentions a letter from his son in January 1852 which indicated some looming difficulty, though he does not include any details.[117] A letter from Harris to William early in the crisis must relate to this, for he describes having had a discussion in January with Hale which alarmed him, though having discovered (from Hale presumably) that father and son shared the same 'unorthodox' theological opinions, he had not brought the matter to White senior's attention.[118] It does not seem to have turned on questions directly at issue in the expulsion however, for Hale recalled it as 'one private conversation, of about an hour's length, a month before, though not specially about Inspiration or Scripture authority'.[119] Robert Theobald had 'never had any private conversation with [Harris] ... on any theological topic', while Frederic White had only one brief meeting.[120]

The treatment of the expulsion in the secondary literature shows the result of taking the *Early Life* as an accurate record, and the power of the 'loss of faith' paradigm - there is nothing too surprising about this spectacular fall from grace, because (arguing backwards from his supposed final position) White was always on a trajectory from faith to doubt. The reality is more complex, especially when it is recognised that the expulsion did not involve students who transferred with him from Cheshunt - as the *Early Life* suggests - but others from quite separate backgrounds, who then acted together at significant personal cost. Some connections which might explain this can be identified.

Caleb Morris (1800-1865)

Although only enough evidence for tentative conclusions can be found, this is suggested by the three belonging to several overlapping circles. It would be unsurprising to find some points of contact as members of Independent churches and families with histories in Dissent, but two individuals in particular had ties of blood or affection to all three men. The Welsh preacher Caleb Morris is well-known as an influence on White and his cousin William Chignell. The corrected date for the opening of New College gives further indirect evidence of White's friendship with Morris. The delay in the opening of the college's own building meant that initially a full programme of study did not operate. In particular, students of the University of London were excused

---

[116] Letter to William White, 16 February 1852 (BPL, MR 1/6).

[117] Cited in *To Think or Not to Think?*, p. 14. The letter presumably referred to the conversation which Hale White mentions having had with Harris in that month.

[118] Letter of 21 February 1852 (BPL, MR I/10).

[119] Recorded in Theobald's *Statement of Facts*, p. 5.

[120] *Statement of Facts*, p. 5. If a reference from the college was necessary to obtain a pastorate this would explain the Principal interviewing students, and their resentment if such an assessment was anticipated to be damaging to future prospects. This was perhaps where the college authorities' real power lay.

classes until after their BA examination.[121] White had already taken his degree by this date, but it seems that such men may well have been treated in the same way as those still to complete. This is very likely the period recalled in reminiscences with Dorothy, when he 'was about one-and-twenty, and apparently for the time being at loose ends' and had much conversation with Morris.[122] It was probably through Chignell that Hale was first introduced to Morris in 1849, but the Welshman had his own links with Cheshunt during Hale's time there, as an external examiner.[123] He took on similar responsibilities at other Independent colleges (but declined to act in this capacity for New College on health grounds). While obviously considered orthodox enough to fulfil these functions some mystical elements to his faith and preaching, though deeply attractive to many young followers, were disquieting to others. Looking beyond the doctrinal expressions of belief, Morris preached a living encounter with Christ; as Hale White saw, 'with him Christianity was not assent to certain propositions, nor external obedience to its precepts. It was an indwelling of the Christ of the Gospels, shaping thought, speech, and life'.[124] Some suspected his orthodoxy, showing to his friends how easily 'large-hearted, sympathetic men are liable to be misinterpreted'.[125]

This may explain why the New College authorities were so obviously disturbed by the attendance of students at the meetings held in Morris's home in Mecklenberg Square after the end of his Fetter Lane public ministry.[126] This was *prima facie* a breach of the college rule that each student must attend a *church* in London, and 'inform the Principal with what church he has become connected'.[127] Effectively this meant attendance only at approved places of worship, and the perceived need for this rule was another consequence of the change from residential training establishments where students worshipped in the college chapel except when out preaching on 'supply'.[128] Anxiety about the influences to which students might be exposed was widespread, but at least in

[121] DWL, NCA 159: Senate Minute Book, vol. I, 4 October 1850, Minute 9 (the very first Senate meeting); White is among those named. The Cheshunt Report for 1850 already lists him as BA.

[122] *Groombridge Diary*, p. 28.

[123] Listed in the Cheshunt College Annual Report 1850, p. 6.

[124] In his review of a memorial volume of Morris; republished in *Last Pages*, pp. 244-250 (p. 247).

[125] D. Tyssil Evans, *The Life and Ministry of the Rev. Caleb Morris* (London: Alexander and Shepheard, 1902), p. 354.

[126] George MacDonald possibly among them; see Raeper, *George MacDonald*, pp. 83, 92, 144, 237-238 for the Scotsman's links with Morris.

[127] DWL, NCA *New College, London: Rules* (London: Printed for Private Circulation, n.d.), Rule X.

[128] In the case of preparatory establishments such as Fakenham students normally joined the congregation of the tutor's cause.

some places healthier attitudes came to prevail. When Principal of Spring Hill College in Birmingham from 1869-1884, David Simon argued successfully against students being forbidden to attend George Dawson's Church of the Saviour.[129] His instinctive trust in them made him confident that they would be able to learn from Dawson's preaching without swallowing his deficient theology. While there is little sign at an official level of a similar rapport between staff and students at New College, it is clear from the intervention of Professor Godwin that in different circumstances greater leniency might have been displayed.

The Senate had discussed the question of 'students attending on the private ministry of the Rev. Caleb Morris' on 16 January 1852.[130] The Principal was mandated to write to each student involved. At the next meeting (30 January) Godwin reported that *he* had spoken to the students, and was assured that a church was shortly to be formally established, though on the grounds of confidentiality he declined to pass on details of his conversations. Individual students are not named in this record but it seems likely that at least Hale White and Theobald were among them, and the nearness in date to the start of the controversy cannot be coincidental. Against a background of some sort of reprimand it is easier to see how even a small further disagreement could cause open conflict. Freedom of assembly, thought and expression were all at issue. The non-residential nature of New College was changing the relationship between tutors and students.

Morris can be tied directly to White, but less closely to the other expelled. Frederic White's family worshipped at Highbury Chapel, Portsmouth, where William Chignell was minister between about 1849 and 1854. This was the time at which Chignell was much influenced by Morris. Something of this must have been passed on in Chignell's preaching, and Morris himself was so famous a preacher that many training for the ministry in London - as Frederic White then was - gladly heard him. It cannot be proved that Robert Theobald was among his hearers, but his uncle J. D. Morell was 'a constant visitor' to Morris's home, making Robert's attendance perfectly possible.[131] Morell himself is another plausible link between the three.[132]

John Daniel Morell (1816-1891)

Morell had some personal contact with the expelled, though the evidence is sketchy. He entered Homerton College in 1833 to train for the ministry. On a

---

[129] See Frederick Powicke, *David Worthington Simon*, pp. 87-88.

[130] DWL, NCA 159, Senate Minute Book, p. 86, Minute 230.

[131] Tyssil Evans, *Life and Ministry*, p. 282 (from the diaries of Morris, present whereabouts unknown).

[132] See further below on Morris's theology, p. 330.

Dr Williams's scholarship he continued his education at Glasgow University (MA 1841), followed by theological and philosophical studies in Germany. He served his first and only pastorate at Gosport, after which he became a Schools Inspector, combining this with philosophical and other writing.

The Morells and Theobalds were related by marriage. John Daniel Morell was uncle to Robert Masters Theobald, who was the son of his sister Jemima and brother-in-law Robert Theobald.[133] John Daniel's father, Stephen, minister at Little Baddow, had supported Theobald's New College application, answering the standard questions about the candidate for the college authorities.[134] With these family links it can be taken as certain that Theobald would have spent time with Morell and been aware of his religious development.

The connection with Hale White is less direct. Morell was a close friend of Caleb Morris, and regular visitor to his home in Mecklenburg Square; it is almost inconceivable that he did not at some stage meet Hale White there too.[135] Hale recorded how greatly in this period he had been influenced by Morris; 'from 1850 up to the time when he went away from London ... he was my friend and guide'.[136] William White cites Morell's *Philosophy of Religion* in support of his case that staff at New College - at least those involved with *The Biblical Review* - were supporters of a critical approach to the Bible for which they persecuted their students.[137] Hale too must surely have also known the work.

Morell became the minister of Gosport Independent Chapel in August 1842 on returning from study in Germany. The parents of F. M. White were members there.[138] The young Frederic was greatly influenced by Morell, and very probably maintained contact when the latter left Gosport (and formal

---

[133]Genealogical data from R. M. Theobald, *Memorials of John Daniel Morell, M.A., LL.D, Her Majesty's Inspector of Schools* (London: W. Stewart, 1891). See also A. R. Buckland and C. A. Creffield, 'Morell, John Daniel', *Oxford Dictionary of National Biography* < http://www.oxforddnb.com/view/article/19200> [accessed 19 March 2008].

[134] Dr Williams's Library, NCA 366/13 (letter dated 15 June 1850) and 366/14 (completed questions). Stephen Morell identified himself as Theobald's grandfather.

[135] See D. Tyssil Evans, *Life and Ministry of the Rev. Caleb Morris*, p. 282; a reference to Morris's later years (ca. 1865), but emphasizing familiarity pre-dating the publication of *The Philosophy of Religion* in 1849, which he suggests shows the influence of Morris.

[136] From the article 'Caleb Morris' in *British Weekly*, XXXI (6 March 1902), p. 532, reprinted in *Last Pages*, pp. 244-250 (p. 244).

[137] *To Think or Not to Think?*, p. 16.

[138] Information from the papers of Frederic White's sister Jessie in the Archivio Jessie White Mario, Museo Centrale del Risorgimento, Rome, as reported by Elizabeth A. Daniels, *Jessie White Mario: Risorgimento Revolutionary* (Athens, OH: Ohio University Press, 1972), chapter one.

ministry) for London in 1845, the Whites moving to Portsmouth at the same time. Jessie White reported that her brother had been very much a 'pupil' of Morell and that she too was deeply indebted to him.[139] Frederic, like Morell before him (student 1833-1838) trained at Homerton under John Pye Smith.

This outline demonstrates individual links of kinship, friendship, and common interest between John Morell and the three expelled; they hint at some shared beliefs and ideas which might illuminate the events at New College in 1852, though in places the evidence is more suggestive than definite. The case is naturally difficult to prove. It is clear that all three were open to new ideas, significantly through interest in European thought; German criticism, theology, philosophy, literature, or indeed Italian politics. Theobald, like Morell, had studied in Europe, and the other expelled had their own connections with movements and ideas from the Continent.

Whatever the personal links, Morell's writings may have had more influence upon the three. His *Philosophy of Religion*, published opportunely in 1849, could have been known to all three men. Frederic White and Robert Theobald are likely to have been aware of it because of their links to the writer (by friendship, and through family, respectively), while William White cites it in his *To Think or Not to Think?* pamphlet, making Hale White's knowledge of it almost certain. While it cannot be proved that the three adopted the ideas it expressed on biblical inspiration there are similarities of approach which are worth noting. Morell was a key figure among those who introduced the ideas of Schleiermacher to an English audience, and the concept of inspiration he outlines draws on similar ideas of intuition and feeling.[140]

The *Philosophy of Religion* explores the philosophical ideas implicit in religious thought (for example through rival epistemologies), and gives a detailed examination of the nature and content of belief itself, all indebted to Schleiermacher. Morell stressed the experiential nature of faith, and its primacy over 'dogmatical systems'; already in the preface a pugnacious note was struck by an attack on the hypocrisy of those who show 'an *outward* respect for theological sentiments when they have been inwardly abjured', including 'many of the public teachers of religion'.[141] The potential for conflict in training colleges from students who had read these words is obvious.

His concept of revelation made any idea of verbal inspiration impossible.

---

[139] Daniels, *Jessie White Mario*, pp. 18-21.

[140] On Morell's role see I. Ellis, 'Schleiermacher in Britain', *Scottish Journal of Theology*, 33 (1980), 417-452 (especially pp. 438-440). While Schleiermacher's views on inspiration were available in English only in 1850, through William Farrer's translation of his *Brief Outline of the Study of Theology* (Edinburgh: T. & T. Clark, 1850), Morell's knowledge of German probably meant he was already familiar with the content.

[141] *Philosophy of Religion*, p. xxx (original emphasis).

Since knowledge of God is immediate and intuitive, rather than logically perceived, all true revelation is directly received in the mind; it follows that the record of this revelation, as in the biblical writings, is secondary. The biblical writers were inspired, not the text.[142] Inspiration and revelation are intimately connected; revelation needs 'an intelligible *object* presented, and a given power of recipiency in the subject' - this latter is inspiration.[143]

The other essential feature of Morell's understanding is his insistence that inspiration comes by the use of 'a faculty, already enjoyed, elevated *supernaturally*' to a higher degree.[144] This qualification 'supernaturally' is presumably intended to answer the critic who suggests that the biblical writers are being considered simply as 'inspiring' after the manner of celebrated poets and authors. Morell does indicate however a '*resemblance*' between the sacred authors and secular writers.[145] The distinction hovers uneasily between one of difference and kind. In commending his views Morell emphasized their dynamic as opposed to mechanical nature, and noted that many problems associated with previous notions of inspiration were thereby avoided. For example, minor disagreements between biblical writers were valuable as evidence that theirs are honest accounts which have not been harmonized, the discrepancies also proving that inspiration was not an absolute state of the writers. Given the moral qualms expressed about various Old Testament passages his explicitly progressive view of revelation and inspiration allowed Morell frankly to describe the Old Testament as morally inferior to the full Christian revelation.[146] Touching on another topical question, Morell was untroubled by inconsistencies between the finding of modern geology and the creation accounts, for the stories were not inspired to be scientifically accurate.[147]

The Expelled and Inspiration - Theobald's Account

It is not easy to ascertain the beliefs about inspiration and biblical authority held by White and his fellow-accused, despite these supposedly being at the heart of the case brought against them. Theobald's *Statement of Facts* is the only source to discuss the issue at length. He denied that the three spoke of the Bible as inspired after the same manner as Homeric poems, or compared Jesus

---

[142] *Philosophy of Religion*, pp. 129, 146.

[143] *Philosophy of Religion*, p. 150 (original emphasis).

[144] *Philosophy of Religion*, p. 151 (original emphasis).

[145] *Philosophy of Religion*, pp. 184-185 (original emphasis).

[146] *Philosophy of Religion*, p. 170. He does not enter into detailed discussion of this moral aspect however, as indeed is hardly required when sections of the Bible can be thus classed as sub-Christian.

[147] Morell is writing before Darwin, so wider evolutionary questions are not addressed.

with Shakespeare; positively, he held that modern Christians may be inspired in a similar fashion to the biblical writers.[148] The authority of the Bible is only such as Christians find to be inherent and all theories of inspiration are necessarily inadequate.[149] Returning to the example of Shakespeare, he denies that such writings can be directly compared with the scriptures; the 'inspiration' is of a different kind, and the subject matter quite unlike.[150] Perhaps the most significant statement is his suggestion that the Bible 'is not *in itself* a revelation, but it contains the *record* of a Revelation'; this is clearly very much in accord with Morell, though not necessarily proof of dependence upon him.[151] It was a view opposed by Harris. Finally, in calling for support for his views from the pages of the *Biblical Review* it can be presumed that Theobald intends to damn his persecutors as hypocrites.[152]

William White's pamphlet contains only a little information about the inspiration debate, and it is not clear to what extent father and son agreed on the doctrinal details. In following the questions asked of the students by the council, William shows that the example of Shakespeare was introduced on this occasion.[153] However, he pays particular attention to the lecture by Principal Harris on the subject, the ostensible cause of the whole controversy. He finds it quite unsatisfactory, and at variance with the known views of respected contemporary nonconformist scholars, including those writing for the *Biblical Review*.[154] Harris's concept that the sacred writers were supernaturally prepared to receive divine revelation, and inspired in their recording of such revelation, is ridiculed for the emphasis which then effectively falls upon the full inspiration of the biblical text itself, with discrepancies and apparent contradictions to be awkwardly explained away.[155]

The students' views on inspiration were probably not unusual among their contemporaries in turning from anything which smacked of the mechanical. How the Bible is received by the hearer or reader was the key test. George MacDonald discussed the doctrine of biblical authority in a letter of 1866 to an

---

[148] *Statement of Facts*, pp. 2, 10.

[149] *Statement of Facts*, pp. 11, 13.

[150] *Statement of Facts*, p. 21. Shakespeare was of special interest to Theobald, who later joined the debate over the authorship of his works in the often-reprinted *Shakespeare Studies in Baconian Light* (London: Sampson Low, Marston, 1901) and elsewhere.

[151] *Statement of Facts*, p. 32, original emphasis.

[152] *Statement of Facts*, p. 35; *The Biblical Review, and Congregational Magazine*, 4 (1847), 38-49 (pp. 41-43), a review article of recent publications showing 'The Present State of the Greek Testament Text' (unsigned, as were all the journal's contributions).

[153] *To Think or Not to Think?*, p. 5, see also p. 7.

[154] In fact the contributors were not named, but the editors, John Harris, William Smith, Joseph Sortain, George Smith, and Philip Smith, may well have penned many pieces themselves.

[155] *To Think or Not to Think?*, p. 9.

unknown correspondent concerned that he had abandoned something of his ancestral faith. He stressed the essential continuity of his belief with that of 'the old Scottish manse' but this meant understanding the truths underlying the old 'forms'.[156] This recalls Carlyle's concept of fundamental beliefs that need to be re-clothed in every age. The Bible is 'the most precious thing in the world' because of its witness to Jesus as Son and Saviour.[157] It cannot for that reason be reduced to a text:

> the common theory of the inspiration of the words, instead of the breathing of God's truth into the hearts and souls of those who wrote it, and who then did their best with it, is degrading and evil, and they who hold it are in danger of worshipping the letter instead of living in the Spirit, of being idolaters of the Bible instead of disciples of Jesus.[158]

'Jesus alone is the Word of God' he concludes, observing that if the Bible was God's 'very word' (which it 'nowhere claims'), 'it would have been a good deal better written'.[159] Such a combination of reverence, sophistication, and bluntness is nowhere found in White or his fellow accused, though at this date MacDonald was much older than they at their trial and could speak more freely as answerable only to his conscience. He elsewhere compared the inspiration of the Bible with Shakespeare, showing how commonly this was done, but the reference in a novel scarcely elevated Shakespeare to the level of the Bible by saying that in each case the 'word of God' must be received 'after its kind'.[160]

On the evidence from Theobald and William White it cannot be stated with certainty that Morell's views lie behind those of the expelled. There are some close similarities, but not enough to prove direct borrowing from Morell. Most of the opinions and beliefs referred to were within the common currency of debates on inspiration. The sense that open discussion was possible on these questions might just explain the willingness of Hale White to transfer from Cheshunt to New College, with the assumption that new ways of thinking too would be tolerated. When this proved not to be the case the hints from Morell that theological tutors were privately accepting theological views as admissible which they publicly disavowed and deplored in students would very likely inflame the situation.

Like White, Theobald returned to consider the expulsion in old age, and left some interesting detail in his autobiography, including memories of influential

---

[156] Letter printed in Sadler, *An Expression of Character*, pp. 153-154 (p. 153).

[157] Sadler, *An Expression of Character*, p. 153.

[158] Sadler, *An Expression of Character*, pp. 153-154.

[159] Sadler, *An Expression of Character*, p. 154.

[160] From a minor novel, *The Marquis of Lossie* (1877), cited in Kerry Dearborn, *Baptized Imagination: The Theology of George MacDonald* (Aldershot: Ashgate Publishing, 2006), p. 172.

supports of the three. He shows that sympathy with their plight must not be confused with support for their views, or a willingness to become directly involved in their struggle.

Theobald's Later Memoir

The importance of the New College episode beyond those immediately affected has been overstated by a false estimation of sympathetic letters from Charles Kingsley and F. D. Maurice which Hale White cites in the *Early Life*.[161] These were responses elicited after receiving from William White copies of his pamphlet *To Think or Not to Think?*; equally significant figures may have been addressed, but declined to commit themselves on the issue.

Maurice had his own opportunity to play a part in the dispute. Theobald attended Maurice's services in Lincoln's Inn and had become friendly with him: 'he was very kind to me when my position at New College was endangered by my heresies. Invited me to breakfast at his house, talked over the differences between me and the authorities, and suggested modes of accommodation without the sacrifice of truth or sincerity'.[162] This link explains Maurice's reference 'I know one of the expelled students' in his letter to William White, but it is clear that there was a reluctance even among well-wishers to become personally involved in the affairs of another church.[163]

Theobald's autobiography is disappointingly vague about his interrupted studies at New College, but it is nonetheless a valuable and previously unused counterpoint to the *Early Life*.[164] It is confessedly a record 'of all the remarkable people' he had known, a collection of eighty-one hardly linked vignettes and characterisations unaccompanied by any real narrative.[165] He names his fellow-accused, noting, *inter alia*, that a marriage between himself and Jessie White (sister of Frederic) had once been predicted, and shows the friendly relationship they all enjoyed during college days. He visited both their homes, but does not mention any connection after 1852.[166]

He treats Harris more gently than White does, though considering him unimpressive; both his and Godwin's lectures were 'self-originated'.[167] Another Professor, Maurice Nenner, not named in the controversy, retained Theobald's friendship and respect, though his later suggestion that Theobald 'must admit,

---

[161] *Early Life*, pp. 72-77.

[162] Robert Theobald, *Passages from the Autobiography*, p. 52.

[163] Letter given in *Early Life*, pp. 72-73.

[164] *Passages from the Autobiography*, p. 5.

[165] *Passages from the Autobiography*, p. 5; quotation from a letter encouraging Theobald to write; as in so many autobiographies, including the *Early Life*, a note of modest hesitation.

[166] *Passages from the Autobiography*, p. 6.

[167] *Passages from the Autobiography*, p. 8 (seemingly a term of approbation, meaning too little based on scholarship?).

on reviewing my College experiences, that I had been very unwise, not sufficiently conciliatory, and that my fate was not entirely underserved', did not command the latter's agreement. 'After sixty years', he wrote, 'I am still impenitent'.[168] But his writing is not an occasion to re-visit the controversy (though he suggests that if Thomas Binney had not been absent through illness the episode would not have ended as it did, which suggests a clash of personalities that a mediator might have averted), and he does not seem to have suffered the degree of psychological trauma evident in White.[169] In part this may be attributed to his having found satisfaction in work, family, and many personal interests later in life.

This hypothetical reconstruction of the background cannot present the full picture, but the shortcomings of the traditional account of White's role at this time force attempts at revaluation which necessarily draw upon slender evidence.

A *Cause Célèbre*?

The wider significance of the New College crisis must not be overstated because of its great importance for White. In a detailed study of nonconformist ministerial training it is possible for Dale Johnson to mention the episode only in a footnote.[170] Many writers on White have been willing to portray Harris in the worst light by contrast with their subject's more reasonable views, as well as assuming that an event so central for him must have been more than a little local difficulty. Lorraine Davies hails it as 'a *cause célèbre*', but it is misleading to isolate the expulsion of the three in this way.[171]

While the incident was widely reported, especially in the religious press, it was rarely discussed at any length. The tracts published on the controversy ensured that it could not be ignored, and it must be assumed that Robert Theobald arranged for his *Statement of Facts* to be sent out to editors. It is among the sources most commonly cited. There was often a natural sympathy with the three, but this did not necessarily imply approval of their conduct or opinions. Brewin Grant, himself an Independent minister, is an instance. Theobald's pamphlet came into his hands at a convenient moment, and could be included in his monthly periodical *The Bible and the People*. He agreed that inspiration was a topic of the day, sympathised with the 'first movements of a

[168] *Passages from the Autobiography*, p. 8.

[169] *Passages from the Autobiography*, p. 27; Hale White knew and admired Binney too, and regretted that he did not come to his aid (had the Whites missed the newspaper reports on Binney, and doubted the severity of his illness?).

[170] In *The Changing Shape of English Nonconformity*, p. 65, note 14. White himself describes the event as 'without much significance', *Early Life*, p. 72.

[171] In a prefatory 'Note on the Author and Editor' before her 'Introduction' to the Everyman edition of *Clara Hopgood*, p. vii.

youthful spirit, in its efforts to harmonize or philosophize upon received opinions', but regretted that the students left:

> prominent doubts so undefined, and ... felt themselves bound by a conscientiousness ... in itself praiseworthy but misapplied in its exercise, to peril or change their position for opinions that are not formed, or rather for doubts which are shadowy and undefined.[172]

He found Theobald's comparison between biblical and literary inspiration, such as that of Shakespeare, uncompelling, and charged him with misrepresenting the views of the New College tutors expressed in the *Biblical Review*. The council could not be blamed for taking the action that they did.

Outsiders often found it easier to lampoon those in authority, at New College or elsewhere. Matthew Arnold's reading of the *Nonconformist* had impressed upon him that 'disputes' were almost a way of life among the free churches.[173] Hale White was hardly exaggerating when he declared that 'the Dissenters in England are always in trouble about their Colleges'.[174] Figures compiled by Kenneth Brown show that a not inconsiderable number of students failed to complete their courses.[175] A loss of more than 10% might be expected, and this from institutions which were never very large. Some departures resulted from transfers to other colleges or early calls to ministry (a persistent problem which the authorities could do little to prevent) but a significant number were of those required to leave for moral failings, or due to changes in religious opinions. Brown suggests that Congregational colleges were the 'most susceptible to the intellectual storms that swept over theological thought in the second half of the century' because of a traditional reluctance to require subscription to doctrinal statements.[176] Certainly the figure for losses at New College in this period is higher than for any other institution he lists, partly due to losing the three in 1852. Some disputes were exacerbated by an underlying dissatisfaction over apparently trivial issues which caused disciplinary friction between staff and students, as at the Newport Pagnell Academy in 1847. In this instance one observer wryly suggested that a larger conflict which centred upon

---

172 'The Expelled Students, and Their Doctrine of Inspiration', *The Bible and the People*, 2 (1852), 252-260 (pp. 252, 255). This is an unusually restrained piece for Grant, who rarely shied away from controversy.

173 The famous essay on 'Sweetness and Light' in *Culture and Anarchy*, (London: Smith, Elder, 1869, repr. ed. by Stefan Collini, Cambridge: Cambridge University Press, 1993), p. 70.

174 *Aberdeen Herald* article, 15 January 1863 (quoted in Stone, p. 40).

175 *Social History of the Nonconformist Ministry*, see Table 2.2 for comparative Methodist, Baptist and Congregational figures, p. 70.

176 *Social History of the Nonconformist Ministry*, p. 78; figures for Congregational colleges in Table 2.3, p. 72.

a student's wish to speak at a meeting of the British Anti-State Church Association despite failing to secure his Tutor's permission might have been avoided had the men not been denied mustard at breakfast, an indication that lofty principles might often be mixed up with a more general discontent.[177]

Men of later high reputation had not always escaped controversy in their youth. In 1820 Thomas Binney temporarily withdrew from his training at Wymondley College in support of two fellow students he believed to have been unfairly excluded by the new Resident Tutor (John Atkinson) who had been appointed with instructions to restore discipline.[178] Alternatively, trouble in the student years was sometimes a sign of things to come. Brewin Grant, at Highbury from 1839 to 1843, was briefly suspended when a fractious dispute between students and the Resident Tutor became a matter of personal honour and trial of strength.[179] Resisting authority became a habit, and (notwithstanding the mildness of his comments on the New College situation) he spent many subsequent years engaged in the conflicts with officialdom which he clearly relished.

One difference between New College and some of the other older academies was its closer relationship with the Congregational Union and the Independent churches who received into their pastorates the men it prepared. Harris and the college were clearly identified with the denomination they served and the students they sent out to ministry. There was close scrutiny, and a greater sense of accountability regarding the training for which they were responsible. This added a set of pressures which could have exacerbated internal tensions. Over time all the colleges also had to come to terms with student expectations of greater respect for their views. A simple appeal to authority was likely to miscarry. Unrealistic hopes of a deferential attitude toward tutors were the cause of many problems and may have often been the real reason for breakdowns in relations between staff and students, even where other presenting causes can be recognized.

A crisis at Cheshunt College under William Stowell, John Harris's successor

---

[177] The Academy's problems attracted widespread publicity; see F.W. Bull, 'The Newport Pagnell Academy', *Transactions of the Congregational Historical Society*, 4 (1910), 305-322 (p. 314), and also Marilyn Lewis, 'The Newport Pagnell Academy, 1728-1850', *Journal of the United Reformed Church History Society*, 5 (1994), 273-282, with information on the generational tensions between staff and students in a time of growing professionalism. The student at the heart of the controversy, Henry Batchelor, later ministered at Fetter Lane from 1851-1853, a post the church had found difficult to fill after the retirement of Caleb Morris through ill-health in 1849.

[178] Reported by J. H. Thompson; *A History of the Coward Trust*, p. 50.

[179] The authorities suspected that a student had broken the rules by returning one evening later than the permitted time, and wanted each man to give an assurance that they had not done so; described in *The Dissenting World: An Autobiography*, 2nd edn (London: W. Macintosh, 1869), pp. 21-25. Grant does not date this incident.

as President, illustrates the point. His forced resignation in 1856 has been described as the result of a student rebellion against an unduly strict regime, but the truth is more complex.[180] Stowell had been in post during Henry Martyn's first year at Cheshunt, and though un-named the circumstances of his going were alluded to in *Chapters from the Autobiography of an Independent Minister*. They were addressed more directly by Stowell's son, who edited *A Memoir of the Life and Labours of the Rev. William Hendry Stowell, D.D.*, in which he sought to defend his father's honour.[181]

Martyn respected the prematurely aged man and criticised the motives of the College Committee in engineering his resignation as cowardly and misjudged, a base attempt to blame Stowell for a decline in student numbers actually due to their disunity.[182] He mentions no student ill-feeling. The anonymous reviewer in *The British Quarterly Review* 'corrected' his account; 'the case of the college tutor referred to ... was exactly the reverse of that here put. ... The committee had nothing whatever to do with the trouble; it came upon them as a surprise. They did their utmost to harmonize matters. ... It is impossible that a single student in the house could be ignorant of this'.[183] All this Martyn rebutted in his 1887 preface, referring to the extensive correspondence he had had with the journal's editor, Henry Allon (who was quite possibly the reviewer), but there was no meeting of minds. This instance demonstrates how elusive the truth might be in such disputes. Notably Martyn did not answer criticism by asserting that his was a fictional account not intended to be accurate.

Unlike Martyn, Stowell's son had access to documentary sources for the Cheshunt years. He first put the dispute in context. 'The disturbance was quite an ordinary one; just such an affair as occurs almost periodically in all colleges,

---

180 Problems were not even hinted at by C. W. Sutton, 'Stowell, William Hendry', in *Dictionary of National Biography*, ed. by Sidney Lee (London: Smith, Elder, 1898), vol. 55, pp. 7-8, but are highlighted by K. D. Reynolds, 'Stowell, William Hendry', in *Oxford Dictionary of National Biography* <http://www.oxforddnb .com /view /article/26615> [accessed 20 August 2010], apparently adopting the verdict of Kenneth Brown, *Social History of the Nonconformist Ministry*, p. 106. But Brown, using the Cheshunt Governors' Minutes, has only one side of the story.

181 References here are to the second edition (London: Judd and Glass, 1860), which omitted sermons given in an appendix in the first edition of 1859, and on representations from early readers removed some of the more critical remarks against those supposed to have treated Stowell badly. Material on the Cheshunt years was unchanged in essentials however.

182 *Chapters from the Autobiography*, pp. 24-26. He is described as 'an old man' (p. 25) though he cannot have been more than 56.

183 Review, *Chapters from the Autobiography of an Independent Student, The British Quarterly Review*, 150 (1882), 476. The *British Quarterly Review* was almost a Congregationalist house journal, and Allon a prominent Congregationalist minister (moreover a Cheshunt man, and friend of Stowell).

and indeed in all families, in all corporate bodies, and even in larger associations of human beings. The question to be tried was the limit of authority ....'.[184] What made it an exceptional case, on this account, was the way in which Stowell was undermined and betrayed by members of the college committee. Some felt that discipline had been neglected, and encouraged Stowell to act against infringements of the rules. Stowell preferred to build up personal relations with the students in order to exert an improving influence, but pressure for formal measures continued until it was decided that a new set of rules should be drawn up, based on those operating at other colleges. The President was then 'especially empowered to enforce the adopted rules', by the committee, but this 'was resented as a violation of personal and social liberty by the students'.[185] Since, as his son has it, Stowell honourably refused to distance himself from the new system by blaming the committee for insisting upon it, he bore the brunt of dissatisfaction from both sides. A sub-committee set up to find a way out of the impasse accused the students of a 'temper and manner ... disrespectful, and destructive of all proper and reasonable subordination in a College'; the President while cleared of any failings of 'moral character', was nonetheless censured for 'both in lecturing and general deportment [showing] a want of that dignity and wisdom of speech and bearing which are imperative in the President of a College'.[186] Broken in health and spirit by years of struggle Stowell tendered his resignation in March 1856.

This case shows the subtle and various pressures at work in the colleges, and the difficulty in acting against students. While open to Congregationalism the place of Cheshunt within the Countess of Huntingdon's Connexion may have introduced particular tensions, especially among any of the college committee who might have resented increasing Congregationalist influence (for by 1868 'its students almost uniformly [became] Congregational ministers').[187] Stowell's case illuminates the question of authority, but makes the New College situation no more explicable. Equally the example of that expulsion does not seem to have restrained the Cheshunt committee in their actions through Stowell. The doctrinal aspect at New College might be thought to differentiate it from more straightforward disciplinary situations, but later events at Cheshunt show a surprising tolerance over matters of belief.

A considerable breadth of opinion was allowed if Henry Martyn's account

---

[184] *Memoir of ... William Hendry Stowell*, p. 288.

[185] *Memoir of ... William Hendry Stowell*, p. 290.

[186] Quotations from the official report, given in *Memoir of ... William Hendry Stowell*, pp. 291-292.

[187] This was the estimate of Henry Allon at the college's centenary. Other prominent Congregationalists joined in the anniversary events, although controversially the Dean of Canterbury had been invited to give the address. See *Centenary Celebration of Cheshunt College: 25th June 1868* (London: Hodder and Stoughton, 1868), p. 33.

of instruction under the new President, Richard Alliott (without name in the text), is to be believed. Alliott was a more considerable figure than Martyn gives credit for, and this shows the need for caution in using his memoir.[188] Alliott had served with distinction at Western College before moving to Cheshunt, a post which attracted him partly because of the liturgical worship and other distinctive features of the Countess's Connexion.[189] He stayed only three years before moving to Spring Hill, Birmingham, leaving behind him a reputation as a fine lecturer.[190] Despite this, and a range of scholarly interests including psychology and German theology (he was an early English reader of Schleiermacher), Martyn portrays him as upholding an outdated orthodoxy. This was one-sided rather than completely false, for Alan Sell shows how Alliott combined a respect for the traditional evangelical doctrines with the subjective emphasis of Romanticism and a concern for vital religion.[191] Martyn asserts that the 'new President was elected because he was a safe man', who 'had only published one work', which understates Alliott's reputation and output, for in addition to his major work on *Psychology and Theology* (1855) he had published sermons and lectures, some lengthy and significant in themselves.[192] In fact his college duties surely left little time for other scholarly endeavours, and Martyn admits that he was a dedicated and conscientious teacher.

More relevant here is what is reported about the learning process itself, which included the sort of classroom discussions which had some years earlier caused such conflict at New College. These opportunities seem to have been a common adjunct to formal lectures. D.W. Simon for instance had raised sometimes 'startling and as it seemed perilous opinions' during his own education at Lancashire College in the 1850s, and as a teacher himself moved further away from the traditional style of formal lectures to embrace a 'Socratic' method in which teacher and taught 'think and learn together whilst they are wrestling with each other'.[193]

Martyn describes Alliott's theological lectures as dogmatic and sincere ('he not only endorsed, but honestly believed in all the old traditional theology'), but 'some of the men ...were not very remarkable for their orthodoxy, and this

---

[188] Sell devotes a chapter to him; *Hinterland Theology*, pp. 187-224.

[189] From a posthumous tribute to Alliott, quoted in Sell, *Hinterland Theology*, p. 199.

[190] Student tributes noted by Sell, *Hinterland Theology*, p. 202.

[191] As illustrated and summarised in *Hinterland Theology*, pp. 210-224. Here Sell also discusses Alliott's reading of J. D. Morell, and his views on biblical inspiration.

[192] *Chapters From the Autobiography*, p. 31. Clearly this is a compressed and selective record; for instance it does not mention the ten month interregnum between principals.

[193] From his own summary of his method, in Powicke, *David Worthington Simon*, p. 260; it was a fellow Lancashire College student who recalled Simon's questioning mind, p. 19. His extensive experience of German higher education had probably made him a more reflective teacher.

occasionally gave rise to exciting conversation, either in the middle or at the close of a lecture'.[194] He cites instances which represent Alliott as an unthinking literalist, possibly exaggerated for effect. The dialogues he reports therefore need to be interpreted with caution, but are nonetheless full of interest. In the first example, a lecture on the Fall was interrupted by the question 'if he [Alliott] really believed the narrative was literal', countered by 'What else can it be, Sir?'.[195] The student suggested a different explanation, the doctrine 'symbolising the terrible change which sooner or later comes over every mortal born into it'. At each point Alliott answered with some argument for the traditional view, but the exchange reveals that his exegesis had not posited a literal serpent, and ruled out it having spoken. The discussion seems fruitless, and if a real report this must include only selected extracts for Alliott in particular is allowed to say very little. From this first case the difference seems to be that the tutor wished to keep more closely to the text, even if the details are explained in a sophisticated fashion, while the student was more ready to reject an outmoded world view in favour of his own.

The second problem arose in a lecture on the resurrection of the dead, when one of the class preferred the Swedenborgian view, 'namely, that death is the resurrection'. Alliott responded by asking when the last trumpet would then be heard, which while represented as naïve in fact stands for the whole Christian eschatological schema, including the last judgement. The student dismissed texts which speak of the tombs being opened and the dead raised as 'very vivid representation, but clearly figurative and pictorial'. Alliott anchored the resurrection of the dead in that of Christ, ending the discussion but without any assent bring recorded from the questioning student. The third topic, of contemporary significance, was on everlasting punishment. A student simply dismissed traditional teaching; 'I cannot bring myself to believe it'. Alliott replied that 'thousands of people have believed it', including 'people with all kinds of minds'. An appeal that 'our Lord declared it' made no impact, for the questioner implicitly doubted the relevant texts, and in any case preferred to believe that Jesus' words were wrongly recorded.

Even with some allowance for dramatic heightening of contrast in reporting these discussions the apparent lack of concern shown by students ready to dismiss important doctrines is surprising. White's hesitation over the nature of biblical inspiration seems insignificant in comparison. Martyn himself struggled to explain how students who had subscribed to the college's articles of faith could then suggest such deviations, but supposed that each assumed that they 'represented his faith when he signed them, and for anything he knew

---

[194] *Chapters From the Autobiography*, p. 33. The students must in some cases have been deliberately provocative.

[195] This and the following quotations in these paragraphs are from *Chapters From the Autobiography*, pp. 34-36.

to the contrary would do when his curriculum was concluded'.[196] His supposition, possibly shared by Alliott despite his unease, was that as long as some fundamental beliefs were firmly held a degree of fluidity about others was acceptable, at least for a season. What these fundamentals might be is little developed, and limited to 'acceptance of the Bible as God's great and authoritative communication to our world, and of Jesus Christ as His only begotten Son', with silence on doctrines such as the Trinity, and notably on the Holy Spirit.[197] Naturally to others the delineation of core and secondary beliefs, and the relationship between them, might be very differently understood.

While Alliott responded to every objection to his views he is not shown to desire that the students' intellectual liberty should be curtailed. He 'looked very grave' but 'believed that in time students would come to his way of thinking'.[198] This tolerance is surprising in the light of the bad publicity which the New College controversy had generated and the knowledge (as Martyn put it) that 'there was enough of this kind of heresy amongst us to have caused quite a consternation in the churches, and to have supplied old Dr. Campbell with fifty letters on the "deplorable state of our colleges"'.[199] Whatever the precise truth behind Martyn's account it reveals an officially tolerated diversity of theological opinions five years after White's expulsion which makes it impossible to regard White and the other expelled students as exceptional in their views. This is in addition to later evidence from the 1877 Leicester Conference (which included students from this generation) showing many ministers whose beliefs were instinctively more liberal than White's and yet who remained firmly within the church.[200] In neither context do White's known beliefs mark him out as unacceptably unorthodox, suggesting that his separation from the church was a personal choice because of unhappy experiences, rather than an exclusion imposed by the unacceptability of those beliefs. For this reason all attempts to prove that White was *necessarily* forced out of the community of faith distort the facts and can never convince.

An Open Verdict

The review here of the New College years fails through lack of evidence to explain precisely what happened and why, though it reveals a more complicated series of events than summarised by White. Of Frederic White

---

[196] *Chapters From the Autobiography*, p. 38.

[197] *Chapters From the Autobiography*, p. 38. Another instance suggesting that White's reserve in doctrinal expression was not unusual.

[198] *Chapters From the Autobiography*, p. 37.

[199] *Chapters From the Autobiography*, p. 37; note the inclusion of Cheshunt among 'our colleges'.

[200] See p. 281 below for details of the Leicester gathering.

little can be known with certainty, while the evidence suggests a larger role for Robert Theobald. His report of the events is detailed and shows a keen engagement with the issues; it is likely that he was the most articulate and determined. It is far less certain that Hale White had clearly formed ideas on biblical inspiration, but his Romantic enlightenment made a subjective approach to the Bible congenial. Much has been made by some critics of his later interest in Spinoza, who has his own considerable importance in changing views of the Bible, but it cannot be shown that White read Spinoza before the expulsion.

That a clash of generations and sympathies was involved is hard to doubt. Under a system of ministerial training in which 'the teaching methods and principles ... were certainly not designed to encourage much independent thought and enquiry' the potential for conflict, especially where students already had university education and degrees, was clear.[201] If rote learning and the repetition in examination of material previously delivered in class was often the norm (evidence of some more flexible practices notwithstanding) it was unlikely to satisfy the rising generation. There remains the possibility that Hale White welcomed the crisis as a way of abandoning the ministerial career on a point of principle. When White's initial deep reluctance about this 'vocation' chosen for him is remembered it is not difficult to see the attraction of avoiding it. If he had by this time also come to view his confession before Bunyan Meeting as false, this was an opportunity to right a wrong by standing fast for the truth as he perceived it.

To consider these questions is already to seek the motives behind White's account of these years in the *Autobiography* and *Early Life*, to try and separate *dichtung* and *wahrheit*. Was White as well aware as Wordsworth of the 'two consciousnesses', of the remembered, remembering self, and the distorting results of 'aftermeditation'? [202] Even where this is recognised, the expulsion narrative of the *Early Life* is a special case, because it is not freely written, but based so fully on identifiable primary sources. It requires literary as well as historical investigation.

Autobiography and the Literary Tradition

The treatment of the college years shows significant divergence between the *Autobiography* and the *Early Life*. Mark Rutherford completes his training and enters the ministry, though his message is not received, and eventually he

---

[201] Brown, *Social History of the Nonconformist Ministry*, p. 76.

[202] From *The Prelude*; on this see M. H. Abrams *Natural Supernaturalism: Tradition and Revolution in Romantic Literature* (New York: W.W. Norton, 1971), p. 75. Abrams seems to mistake the date of the *Autobiography* and thus disallows the influence of *The Prelude* on White, p. 137.

retires disheartened. There is some parallel with Hale White, since despite the expulsion he did continue to preach for some time, including an extended appointment at Ditchling Meeting. In reconstructing a biography of White the two accounts are typically harmonised to present a picture which is believed to be historically accurate. The analysis above has shown that even the *Early Life* version is unreliable in detail, despite the use of contemporary records. This reflects the partial nature of the sources White drew upon, and possibly some failing of memory in matters where he could not refer to documentary evidence. On one level this may not matter. Self-writing criticism insists that autobiographical writing is not an attempt to portray a factual history, but to make sense of a life as a continuous narrative. The felt experience is a combination of events and interpretation revealing what is really important for the writer. For some the fictionalised autobiography is a medium which allows the deepest self to be revealed; or as Oscar Wilde put it 'man is least himself when he talks in his own person. Give him a mask, and he will tell you the truth'.[203] This does not mean that by contrast the *Early Life* is, as White's description of it suggests, an undisguised factual account.[204] The evidence presented shows that not to be the case, a reminder that 'if readers hope for impartiality they must look elsewhere than in autobiography'.[205]

White's expulsion narrative is shaped by genre and subjectivity. One result has been to make the writer appear to be the chief player, a typical feature of the *Bildungsroman*, despite the signs that make this implausible (no record of questions in the class discussion, or of his words before the Council, nor any attempt like Theobald to explain his views in detail). This is more curious still, if, as it appears, one motive for this memoir was to record his previously undisclosed part in these events. It suggests a further necessity, to mark the end of any rebellion against faith. Frederic White and Robert Theobald may have had a greater estrangement from church and faith, and for them the expulsion seems to have closed a chapter without leaving a sense of life-long grievance. It is certainly not evident in Theobald's reminiscences. White's instinct to throw over all belief did not last long ('the beliefs of childhood and youth cannot be thus dismissed. I know that in after years I found that in a way they revived under new forms'), but it took the whole of his life to sufficiently come to terms with this rude disruption, and be able to tell the story.[206] The trajectory in the later novels *may* seem one of increasing secularisation, but this is not

---

203 From 'The Artist as Critic', reprinted in *The Artist as Critic: Critical Writings of Oscar Wilde*, ed. by Richard Ellmann (London: W. H. Allen, 1970), p. 389. In a similar vein Harland writes of the 'liberating mask of fiction', p. 5.

204 'What I now set down is fact', *Early Life*, p. 5.

205 B. J. Mandel, referring to Gosse's *Father and Son*; 'Full of Life Now', in *Autobiography: Essays Theoretical and Critical*, pp. 49-72 (p. 60).

206 *Early Life*, p. 78.

reflected in the *Early Life*, where faith returns, at least in *some* form.

Biblical Myths, 'Secular' Pilgrims, and Literary Form

The suggestion of a falling away from faith followed by restoration picks up biblical motifs which were a significant influence on the form of much Victorian fiction. The themes of exile and return, fall and salvation, Edenic beginnings and a lost Paradise, pilgrimage and conversion, are fundamental. 'Conversion' may include any moment of crisis and change, even what might in terms of faith be termed a 'de-conversion'.[207] The expulsion, and all it represents, is clearly such a moment for White, a change with the potential to shape the rest of his life. Though it does not appear in the *Autobiography*, the same degree of alienation is represented over time by Rutherford's withdrawal from ministry in the face of his listeners' incomprehension and indifference, such that these literary figures can be applied. Having a personal story to tell is vital to the autobiographical project, and another correspondence with scriptural archetypes lies in it being told for the instruction of others. As White writes; 'it is not impossible that some few whose experience has been like mine may, by my example, be freed from that sense of solitude which they find so depressing'.[208]

The 'personal myth' which lies at the core of Western autobiography typically incorporates 'the biblical narratives of conversion and salvation', while also being related to key biblical characters in whose lives these narratives are definitively enacted.[209] The earlier autobiographical tradition avoided identification with Jesus, as verging on the blasphemous, but there is some indication that White did see a parallel.[210] His version of the expulsion, especially the questioning before the Council has echoes of the trial of Jesus, noticeable in his silence as one who opened not his mouth (not true to life, for surely he *must* have made some defence); also in the implicit assumption that the college did not have rightful jurisdiction, and that the charges themselves were unjust. These overtones of the Passion show that White's account has something of the martyrology about it - the sufferer for the cause of truth, unjustly accused but afterwards vindicated (in this case perhaps by the divinely appointed meeting with Dorothy Smith and the sense of renewal that brought).

---

[207] Considered by John Barbour, *Versions of Deconversion*, especially chapters two and three.

[208] *Autobiography*, p. 2, Ch. I.

[209] For a full discussion see H. Henderson, *The Victorian Self*, pp. 4-9.

[210] Paul Delany describes the earlier tradition in *British Autobiography in the Seventeenth Century* (London: Routledge & Kegan Paul, 1969); see p. 29 on Jesus. Compare *Autobiography*, p. 47, Ch. IV, for White's implied identification with Jesus, and, with some reserve, p. 91, Ch. VI.

Biblical themes could persist even where explicit Christian faith had been questioned or abandoned, the concepts re-interpreted in terms of human experience, a factor making construal of such literary texts particularly difficult. The dominant concern for the self rather than the soul (as in the Puritan tradition) is a particular feature of nineteenth-century autobiography. If, as Heather Henderson suggests, the loss of a divine authority and the hope of a real resurrection led to 'a widespread attempt to resurrect the self in autobiography' then the writer becomes the author and father of his own self.[211] This may be reflected in the portrayal of the human father, which in White's case is more complex and less favourable than has normally been supposed. The influence of Carlyle on the century, especially through *Sartor Resartus*, has been shown by Qualls and others to be very considerable, and while Carlyle judged that the Romantics had largely failed in their attempt to give 'human-centred meanings' to religious language, his own writing contributed to that process.[212] R. W. Dale had noted the enormous influence of Carlyle and the nervousness of many in the church about the unsettling nature of his writings, especially in the 1850s; 'he was more to us for a while than all our tutors; more to us than all the theologians and fathers of the church'.[213] Carlyle was certainly significant for Hale White and William White, as the *Early Life* records (p.38). It seems then that White represents two important strands in self-writing; the fictional autobiography with re-interpreted Christian themes, and the factual memoir in which fall and spiritual redemption are prominent. This may explain some of the difficulty critics have in deciding if White exemplifies the loss of faith or its psychological re-interpretation with traditional religious language retained.

Summary

The New College episode has not previously been adequately situated within its true context. The nature of ministerial training and the rising expectations of students and the Dissenting community created their own problems. The expulsion of the three can be seen as one example among others of these pressures. It was not a particularly unusual event, and its later fame is tied closely to White's gifts as a writer. The views expressed by the three seem hardly radical compared with other examples cited and the apparent cause may not be as significant as the underlying factors and personal antagonisms which also appear to have played a part. To rely on White's presentation alone is in

---

[211] Henderson, *The Victorian Self*, p. 14.

[212] See Qualls, *The Secular Pilgrims of Victorian Fiction*, p. 3 and chapter 1 *passim*.

[213] From his tribute on Carlyle's death in 1881, quoted in Mark Hopkins, *Nonconformity's Romantic Generation: Evangelical and Liberal Theologies in Victorian England* (Carlisle: Paternoster Press, 2004), p. 51.

any case misleading for circumstances and characters have been imaginatively reconstructed as memory and history coalesce. The creative influences of the autobiographical literary tradition can explain some of these changes, but gaps in any reconstruction of the historical events remain. Certainly the truth is more evasive than depicted.

Nevertheless it is clear that the expulsion in no way indicates that White suffered a loss of faith, rather it arose, among other factors, from a refusal to express belief solely within existing ('orthodox') categories, resulting from a search for the inner meaning of traditional doctrines. A personal spirituality was being constructed and explored, with the self - not the college, church or tradition - the arbiter of authenticity. The contours of beliefs underpinning such a spirituality are inevitably difficult to trace since there was no need to systematically articulate or record them. Fragmentary sources and occasional writings must be explored, as well as the reflections of those who knew White well enough to discuss religious matters with him.

In most previous treatments of this question White's engagement with Spinoza has assumed great importance. His earliest reading of the philosopher apparently dates from shortly after the expulsion, and this is taken to indicate that White was searching for (or happened upon) something to fill the void caused by a loss of faith. Since it has further been assumed that philosophical monism is both formally and practically incompatible with Christian theism, any borrowing from Spinoza is seen as inevitably displacing previous belief. White's study of Spinoza was lengthy and intensive, the single most important intellectual work of the adult years. This complex material requires full and careful investigation, with special attention to late writings that suggest need for a reconsideration of just how much White finally owed to Spinoza. Once this has been undertaken attention can shift to a review of other material, itself made more significant when Spinoza is put in his rightful place.

CHAPTER 8

The Consolation of Philosophy? Hale White Reading Spinoza

The literature on White shows that the nature of his debt to Spinoza has proved difficult to assess and easy to exaggerate. White dealt selectively with the philosopher's output, making only limited reference to writings beyond the *Ethics*, and even his purpose in first taking up that work for translation is unclear. If he was attracted by the philosopher's doctrine of God, this brings its own questions. Given Hale's high view of nature as mediating a spiritual encounter, and the strongly immanentist character of Spinoza's system, attention has focussed on the charge of pantheism, though this is among the hardest areas of Spinoza's thought to interpret. His treatment of the Bible, an important element in the pre-history of modern biblical scholarship, also came within White's purview, but was peripheral to his main interest in the *Ethics*. Engagement with this philosophy at some level lasted for the greater part of White's life, from an assumed introduction in the 1850s until preparation of the fourth edition of the *Ethic* for the press in 1910.[1] The changing shape of successive prefaces to the *Ethic* translation needs to be considered, though it will be suggested that these texts reveal less about White's mature estimation of Spinoza than several shorter occasional pieces. Exploring the issues raised is an unavoidably complex task which must cover a good deal of ground and is further complicated by uncertainties in chronology.

Spinoza is nowhere mentioned in the *Early Life*, despite its covering the time at John Chapman's (October 1852 to February 1854) in which White probably first encountered his philosophy, perhaps even in conversations with George Eliot, herself then contemplating a translation of the *Ethics*.[2] It is

---

[1] Here, as elsewhere, '*Ethic*' refers specifically to White's translation by his preferred usage; otherwise the normal '*Ethics*' is used.

[2] In conjunction with G. H. Lewes, and started in November 1854. Though completed in 1856, the translation did not appear in her lifetime because of a disagreement with Henry Bohn, who Lewes believed had promised publication, but Bohn disputed the details (Eliot had already translated the *Tractatus Theologico-Politicus*, in 1849, but it too went unpublished). Dorothy Atkins has the first full assessment of Eliot's use of Spinoza; *George Eliot and Spinoza* (Salzburg: Institut für Englische Sprache und Literatur, Universität Salzburg, 1978). The Eliot text was finally published in 1981,

Note continues on following page

unlikely that her project was far advanced at this stage, for White's own efforts would then be inexplicable. His silence here may signal that in retrospect White did not wish to stress indebtedness to Spinoza. Naturally his ideas might be present where his name was not. There was indirect influence through the importance of Spinoza to the growth of German idealism and English Romanticism, as well as to the theologies of Schleiermacher and Strauss among others, which in varying degrees contributed to White's intellectual development.[3] The memoir does report an incident possibly glossed with later Spinozan overtones, and testifying to a practical purpose. White describes his mental struggle during a swim which could have ended in tragedy if he had not been able 'to bring my will to bear directly on my terror' of drowning, when it threatened to overwhelm him.[4] This event could have been brought to mind by his renewed study of Spinoza for the paper probably being worked on at the same time as the 'Autobiographical Notes', and published posthumously as 'Revolution'.[5] Even with the slightness of any proof of Spinoza's apparent impact in the *Early Life* the adult years which White devoted to studying his philosophy and the large place given to him by previous critics makes a full examination of the subject essential.

Although elsewhere White suggests the artificiality and fragility of systematic theology, as taught at Cheshunt through a manual in which 'the author then mechanically built up the Calvinistic creed, step by step, like a house of cards', in the *Ethics* he encountered a philosophy of the most exacting and remorseless logic.[6] In part this must have appealed to his scientific impulse, and implied a system which did not rely on a prior faith commitment.[7] But White's was not an abstract philosophical interest, and his reason for taking up Spinoza must always be kept in mind. The essential question was '*Wherein can*

---

edited by Thomas Deegan. There is no sign of textual dependence between the White and Eliot translations. Articles in Chapman's *Westminster Review*, including some by Lewes, also periodically dealt with Spinoza.

[3] Schleiermacher's use of Spinoza also laid him open to charges of pantheism, but Julia Lamm argues that he can be acquitted; *The Living God: Schleiermacher's Theological Appropriation of Spinoza* (University Park, PA: Pennsylvania State University Press, 1996), her case summarised on pp. 1-11.

[4] *Early Life*, p. 53; water seems to have a special significance for White. A parallel instance, presumably based on this one, is in 'Michael Trevanion' (bound with *Miriam's Schooling*), p. 160. In Spinoza the will represents mastery of the passions (for White, in this case, fear).

[5] *Last Pages*, pp. 88-94.

[6] *Autobiography*, p. 14, Ch. II.

[7] Though later critics have suggested this is just what Spinoza's understanding of God demands; for example G. Lloyd, *Spinoza and the Ethics* (London: Routledge, 1996), pp. 31-34. By contrast, Steven Nadler believes Spinoza is not even a theist; see *Spinoza's Ethics: An Introduction* (Cambridge: Cambridge University Press, 2006), p. 118.

you help me?'.[8] The reading was an ethical task for an ethical end, with other significant matters treated along the way, though without straying too far from the central purpose.

Prefaces to the *Ethic* and Other Writings on Spinoza

White's work on the *Ethic* had occupied him for many years, and despite sluggish sales he was determined to keep the text in print.[9] He made relatively slight changes to the translation itself, with the assistance of Amelia Hutchison Stirling, but between the first (1883) and second (1894) editions greatly extended his introductory preface. There were more than sixty extra pages, a total now of nearly a hundred. The same lengthy preface was retained in the third edition, but was further revised in the fourth of 1910. Charles Swann has explored the significance of changes to the prefaces, concluding from a comparison of the second and fourth editions that for the 1910 printing White systematically deleted personal opinions to project 'neutral scholarly exegesis'.[10] On this analysis the passages excised from the second edition show what was personally most important for White. The value of this interpretative strategy must be treated with some caution. Dorothy noted a similar process in comparing her husband's manuscript note-books with material prepared for printing; 'I find ... again and again, that the personal element has been entirely eradicated and the whole paragraph reconstructed on an impersonal basis', albeit that this reference is to occasional jottings rather than longer pieces written on a particular topic or to address a specific issue.[11]

The extent of the changes was not obvious to a casual reader. The brief 'Preface of the Fourth Edition' spoke of 'some additions to the biographical part' and revision of the remainder, and was followed by the three-line 'Preface to the Third Edition' before the 'Preface' proper, where a footnote informed the reader that 'this preface is based on the preface to the second edition'.[12] White had made the alterations some years previously, but then judged that 'a new edition would not pay', and the manuscript was put aside, only to be resurrected

---

[8] Preface to the first edition, p. ix, original italics.

[9] Correspondence with his publishers survives at British Columbia (UBC, NCC 4-12 and 4-13).

[10] 'William Hale White's (Mark Rutherford) Revisions to the Second Edition Preface of His Translation of Spinoza's *Ethic*', *ANQ: American Notes and Queries*, 13 (2000), 16-28 (p. 18). This edition was put out by Oxford University Press after Duckworth, the publishers of his previous edition, declined to reprint because of poor demand (papers on this at British Columbia: UBC, NCC 4-13).

[11] 'Editor's Preface', *Last Pages*, pp. v-vi, and examples cited pp. 251-252.

[12] See pp. v, vi, vii, respectively (London: Oxford University Press, 1910).

when Oxford University Press expressed willingness to print a fourth edition.[13]

Many changes between prefaces were minor, and even the reason for substantive ones is often unclear. A pejorative second edition comment about the 'immense mass of very uninspired nonsense' from which the admirable Old Testament prophetical writings were 'a selection' was removed.[14] The wording does not make it completely plain if 'nonsense' refers to other parts of the biblical books, which would be a surprisingly harsh judgement, or to extra-canonical literature, with which it seems unlikely that White would have been familiar. Given his known reverence towards the Bible the first explanation is improbable but perhaps this very lack of clarity and the consequent possibility of offence caused the reference to be struck out. More significantly, a statement suggesting Spinoza's very high view of scripture (that he had wanted 'to strengthen its authority') was omitted. This cannot be taken as simply promoting Spinoza *over* the Bible because a second edition affirmation of his philosophy was also cut:

> the decay of popular religion may bring about a relaxation of the bonds which have hitherto in Christendom held us in their grasp, binding the intellect and passions of man into character and man into society, there must be no harking back into what is past and dead, over even any sentimental lingering over it, Whatever the end may be, there is only one road open before us, and that is the sunlit road of Spinoza's *lumen naturale*.[15]

This is a complex passage, in which the uneasy anticipation of what *may* happen has been countered by a willingness to look forwards not backward, but the change is hardly willed or gladly embraced. Removing the section suggests a lessening commitment to this philosophy, and lack of confidence in an unguided inner light.

There is typically a controversial or combative tone to the deleted sections. For example, a robust defence of Spinoza's rational approach to the scriptures was severely toned down, a statement on the study of nature as the only 'source of salvation' omitted, and a paragraph asserting the importance of human concepts of justice and mercy in testing the revelation of God removed.[16] Often what Swann calls 'moralizing' passages are omitted, though he does not note how often the changed text reflects the spiritual elements in Spinoza. A possible alternative explanation for the tendency shown by these variations is that on mature reflection White wished to distance himself from an early enthusiasm for the philosopher. He wanted to leave a record of scholarship, and

---

[13] Quotation from White's draft of a letter to Duckworth's dated 7 April 1907 (UBC, NCC 4-12).

[14] Preface to the second edition, p. lx.

[15] Preface to the second edition, p. lxi.

[16] All quoted by Swann, 'William Hale White's Revisions', pp. 18, 19, 21, respectively.

not a testament to his personal commitment, which had waned. An appreciation of its high ideals remained, but with less certainty how they might be successfully applied. It may be that his work on Spinoza over many years was as much a tribute to the high opinion of the philosopher held by his own heroes like Goethe and George Eliot as to any sense that (some general principles apart) he was a practical guide for everyday life. The essentials of Spinoza were anyway easily available mediated by thinkers like Schleiermacher with his emphasis upon human capacity for an immediate consciousness of God, including through the natural world. Deeper engagement with such thinkers might have been more fruitful for White, but the expulsion seemed to breed in him a distrust of Christian theology which effectively hampered this sort of intellectual development.

The revisions Swann highlights after the second edition should not overshadow significant alterations between the first and second. Much had been added and the original material adapted to suit. An outline of Spinoza's life was included, and there was more about his writings and their reception. A new section described the *Tractatus Theologico-Politicus*, which had not been mentioned by name in the 1883 preface, and this required comment on the view of scripture it contained. Hale always rejected the notion of Spinoza as harmful or negative. It is wrong to laud his work 'as a prophecy of German erudition of a century later', for his 'object was most distinctly not rationalistic criticism, but to put the Bible upon a pedestal and to strengthen its authority'.[17] This sentence was deleted in the fourth edition preface, possibly reflecting uncertainty about the accuracy of this particular summary of the *Theologico-Politicus*, rather than to retract the essential point, for equally strong statements about Spinoza's respect for scripture were retained. Commenting on the anti-rationalistic view of scripture taken in the *Theologico-Politicus* (as in 'God used some kind of real voice' to speak to Moses), he wonders 'is Spinoza really speaking here in his own proper person' or rather representing a traditional view for the sake of argument?[18]

In the preface to the first edition White had mentioned this aspect of Spinoza's work in order to rebut a common interpretation:

> [Spinoza] is usually supposed to be destructive. In reality he belongs in a remarkable degree to the constructive class. It is quite true that he is the founder of modern Biblical criticism, but he criticised merely in order to remove obstacles. Were he simply negative, his influence would have disappeared long ago. It is the builder and believer whom we worship. ... although the Spinoza who is current amongst those who have never read him is a sceptic or atheist, it is impossible for any person who will even look at him not to be aware that here is no waste no-man's land with nothing on it but a deposit of broken potsherds and miscellaneous

[17] From the preface to the second edition, p. lxii.

[18] From the preface to the second edition, p. xlv.

> rubbish, but at least architecture. A closer acquaintance will prove that we have before us a temple'.[19]

This emphasis needs to be borne in mind against the impression sometimes given that White's engagement with Spinoza meant a rejection of previous beliefs. The issue was developed a little further in the second edition preface. The matter was complicated because while Spinoza ruled out a literal interpretation of miracles on the grounds that nothing recorded in the scriptures must be contrary to the laws of nature, he exempted 'prophecy' (under which category he included divine and angelic messages - revelation as received) since no such test from nature could be applied. The reason that sits in judgement on miracles is insufficient to bring knowledge of God, for which revelation alone suffices.[20] White was manifestly uneasy about this distinction, and unsure what 'revelation' here entails, but stopped short of accusing Spinoza of inconsistency or bad faith, admitting therefore that on this point 'what his belief really was it is difficult to discover'.[21] It is likely that White was trying to clarify his own thinking on the subject, which never involved simply dismissing such events, but realised that their significance lay in the meaning attached to them. What this reading of Spinoza might imply for White's view of miracles is discussed below, with a more detailed examination of Spinoza's own position.[22]

Whatever inconsistency White may have suspected in Spinoza's treatment of the Bible, he agreed with the need to attend to meaning and not externals. Some traditionally important teaching about the Bible could be put aside without affecting its core message. For instance, as he made clear elsewhere, questions about the authorship of biblical books seemed simply irrelevant. 'The discovery that the book of Leviticus was not written by Moses and that there were two Isaiahs has made no difference to me'.[23] Biblical criticism of this sort might become a distraction, he felt, preventing deeper engagement. Like criticism in other spheres it could easily be sterile and even harmful, to the

---

[19] Preface to first edition (London: Trübner, 1883), pp. viii-ix. The wording is surely significant; a temple is the dwelling place of God, and the Old Testament context is most likely in mind. The passage did not survive as such in the fourth edition preface, but the sentiments were there, especially in stressing that the *Tractatus Theologico-Politicus* was *not* 'simply destructive' (p. xlv).

[20] Preface to the second edition, pp. li-liii. This is referenced to his discussion of the *Theologico-Politicus*, so had not been relevant in the first edition, where that treatise was not considered.

[21] Preface to the second edition, p. lvii.

[22] See pp. 333-335.

[23] In the article 'Revolution', reproduced from an unrevised manuscript in *Last Pages*, pp. 88-94 (p. 88). That traditional authorship (alone) carries little weight was implicit in the views put forward by the three students during the expulsion crisis.

extent that it would 'divert us from what is positive, indisputable, life-giving'.[24]

Since the changes discussed do not point in only one direction it might be a mistake to read them as revealing 'a coherent strategy', as Charles Swann suggests, rather than a practical need to shorten the preface, allowing some refinement alongside compression.[25] The printers at the University Press had found the plates for the preface of the third edition to be unusable, requiring them to be expensively re-set for this edition, giving the opportunity for a revision.[26] Hale White had advised Duckworth in April 1907 that he had reworked the preface, but evidence of recent sales had convinced him that it was not worth attempting a reprint and the Oxford edition was a completely unexpected opportunity.[27] It is possible that Duckworth had earlier warned that the plates would need replacing, prompting a re-write, but it is more likely that White's new prefaces show his interest in keeping abreast of recent scholarship on Spinoza, as well as his own changing opinion. There was another practical incentive, for a new preface represented almost the only significant advertising point for each successive edition, and this when R.H.M Elwes's translation, so unfortunately published in the same year as White's, was becoming more firmly established in the market. There was an ever-present need to recoup the costs of keeping the translation in print, and sales mattered. He could not be quite indifferent to commercial success, as he seemed to be with the novels.

Spinoza and Nature: Was White a Pantheist?

It would be a significant departure if in reading Spinoza White intended to embrace pantheism. His spiritual view of nature has led some to assume this, though White nowhere employs the concept. His summary of the relationship between God and nature in Spinoza theoretically rules it out. In writing that 'all Nature is in Him', the notion that they are simply coextensive is rejected, and panentheism implicitly affirmed.[28] Moreover, giving too high a place to Spinoza is to overlook Wordsworth as the chief influence in forming White's mystical view of nature. Ideas of a divine-imbued natural world, especially strong in German thought, were also available to him through writers like

---

[24] From an undated (but post-1908) notebook entry included in the 'Notes' of *Last Pages*, p. 317.

[25] 'William Hale White's (Mark Rutherford) Revisions to the Second Edition Preface of His Translation of Spinoza's *Ethic*', p. 17. The fourth edition preface was nearly ten pages shorter than the third.

[26] Letter of H. Milford, 9 February 1910; UBC, NCC 4-13.

[27] Details from White's minute of letter to Duckworth's 7 April 1907 (UBC, NCC 4-12).

[28] In the article 'Spinoza' from ca. 1883 printed in *Pages*, pp. 32-58 (p. 39). Panentheism underlies some significant modern theologies, as described by John W. Cooper, *Panentheism: The Other God of the Philosophers. From Plato to the Present* (Nottingham: Apollos, 2007), notably chapter nine and following.

Carlyle who were familiar with continental writing. The 'natural supernaturalism' described in *Sartor Resartus* was certainly known to White, and this understanding of the natural world as expressing the divine accords with his view that 'miracles' are not to be seen as violations of the laws of nature.[29]

It is doubtful if Spinoza himself is to be accurately described as a pantheist. The concept of God outlined in the *Ethics* as a unique substance existing in an infinity of attributes need not be understood in this way. Despite being 'one of the most difficult and contentious areas of Spinoza's thought', Richard Mason believes that 'nature' stands for 'those most general principles of order described by the fundamental laws of nature' and Spinoza can be cleared of the charge of identifying God with '*corporeal* nature'.[30] He does not link creator and creation in a simple monism. While the *Ethics* defines reality as one absolute substance, this is qualified as existing in two modes or aspects (Book I, Proposition XXIX, '*natura naturans*' and '*natura naturata*').[31] Those who (like Hobbes, and many modern commentators) read this as "God *is* Nature" reduce 'God' to an empty symbol and can accuse Spinoza of being an atheist, but this is unjustified, reasoning as it does that the words can be used interchangeably. The idea of unity in difference is also present. Carlos Fraenkel's examination of Spinoza's philosophical context also suggests a strong continuity with Jewish and Aristotelian roots (that is, reconciling his monism with monotheism) which makes the 'atheist' claim implausible.[32] White does not enter this debate, but his notes on the text show that he recognised the issue. These phrases signify 'by the same verb the oneness of God and the world, and yet at the same time ... mark by a difference of inflexion that there was not absolute identity'.[33]

This is not necessarily incompatible with Christian belief, for it can be argued that the Christian doctrine of creation requires an ontological link between creator and creation, despite the dualistic separation found in classical theism. Similarly, the conviction that God's creative activity continually sustains the world lends weight to the suggestion that theist metaphysics

---

[29] M. H. Abrams explores this theme in *Natural Supernaturalism;* see especially the first chapter for his analysis of the underlying concepts of Romanticism, characterised by T. E. Hulme as 'spilt religion' (p. 68). White understood Spinoza to rule out 'miracle[s] in the ordinary sense of the word', preface to the second edition of the *Ethic*, pp. l-li.

[30] Analysing the *Ethics* and the *Tractatus Theologico-Politicus* in *The God of Spinoza: A Philosophical Study* (Cambridge: Cambridge University Press, 1999), pp. 29, 31, original italics.

[31] The famous '*Deus sive Natura*' ('God or Nature') comes later, in Spinoza's preface to Book IV.

[32] C. Fraenkel, 'Maimonides' God and Spinoza's *Deus sive Natura*', *Journal of the History of Philosophy*, 44 (2006), 169-215.

[33] *Ethic*, p. 30, note (all editions).

depends upon an undeclared ontological connection.[34] Even if White has imbibed a measure of philosophical monism from Spinoza, this can co-exist alongside more 'orthodox' beliefs. Coleridge for instance wrote of a time when his 'head was with Spinoza, though [his] whole heart remained with Paul and John'.[35] Understanding the concept of 'pantheism' in this philosophy had long been troublesome. Julia Lamm traces some of the different interpretations in order to explicate how Spinoza could be labelled both atheist and 'God-intoxicated'. There was no necessary link between indebtedness to his thought and an absolute identification of God and the world, indeed this conclusion was often resisted. In the context of the continental *Pantheismusstreit* controversy, and disputes over the meaning of key terms, Lamm concludes that:

> the [German] Romantics did not simply identify God and nature, nor did they deny the transcendence of God; rather, they developed a theory of what may be called a dynamic coincidence of opposites that helped them reunite what had been separated, while yet maintaining the distinction.[36]

Clearly some were holding in tension concepts which others though irreconcilable, a warning against too readily assuming what Spinoza's readers took from him. In White's context the label pantheist is certainly misleading and unhelpful, suggesting a great divergence from his inherited faith that cannot be proved.

This claim mars Roger Ebbatson's account of White's place in 'the nature tradition' of English literature.[37] Too much is made of the importance of nature, and too little of the continuities with the Christian tradition. He does however usefully note the influence of Carlyle on White in his understanding of 'divinized' nature, as well as Emerson's transcendentalism, with which White

---

[34] This case has been presented by Robert Oakes; 'Does Traditional Theism Entail Pantheism?', in *The Concept of God*, ed. by Thomas V. Morris (Oxford: Oxford University Press, 1987), pp. 57-71, citing Aquinas as in agreement. On modern process theology and pantheism, see his 'Classical Theism and Pantheism: A Victory for Process Theism?', *Religious Studies*, 13 (1977), 167-173.

[35] *Biographia Literaria* ed. by J. Shawcross (Oxford: Clarendon Press, 1907), vol. I, p. 134. This may not be an unfair summary of White's position, at least for some periods. Coleridge was quite sure that the *Ethics* was compatible with Christian faith, p. 99.

[36] Julia Lamm, 'Romanticism and Pantheism', in *The Blackwell Companion to Nineteenth-Century Theology*, ed. by David Fergusson (Chichester: Wiley-Blackwell, 2010), pp. 165-186 (p. 166). This she names 'Neo-Spinozism'; for pantheism see especially pp. 181-182, and on an often-accompanying mysticism among the Romantics, pp. 178-180.

[37] *Lawrence and the Nature Tradition: A Theme in English Fiction, 1859-1914* (Brighton: Harvester Press, 1980), pp. 165-208.

probably became familiar in the Chapman years.[38] Inevitably in a literary study the novels dominate, but engagement with the *Early Life*, a more comprehensive biographical treatment, and clearer understanding of Spinoza's (limited) role would have offered a different perspective, in which the persistence of faith demands explanation. White's life thus viewed is not the journey 'from puritan to pantheist', which Ebbatson insists his fiction discloses.[39]

White's might not be a 'correct' interpretation of Spinoza, as he frankly admitted; 'the present writer does not pretend to understand the whole of Spinoza, and, so far as he can make out, nobody has fully understood him'.[40] His interest is largely confined to matters of practical application, constantly asking how Spinoza can *help* us. It is noticeable that the *Ethics*, despite its forbidding geometric conceptualisation, evoked deep feelings in many readers, as it laid out the nature of God and the world, the truly free human life, and the way to an intuitive knowledge of God through a perfect intellectual love. In and through this state the human mind can find union with the eternal mind.[41] The key features for White (according to one of his accounts) were an understanding that thought and matter - or, mind and body - are not to be set over against each other but considered as the same individual or 'substance' viewed under different attributes; that the properly informed mind allows actions free from imperfect passions; and the mind itself is in some sense immortal through its participation in the universal, eternal mind.[42]

This summary from a late piece of writing largely repeats the emphasis of an article written at about the time his translation of the *Ethic* was first published, in 1883. Spinoza offers an escape from the purely materialist outlook, for 'the sorrow of life is the rigidity of the material universe in which we are placed'.[43] Against the fear that 'we are nothing but common and cheap products of the earth to which in a few moments or years we return' is a recognition that both matter and mind relate us to the one 'substance' that is God, offering a route to joy by '*thinking*'.[44] Deliverance through the intellect (better, emotion guided and shaped by the will) is immensely attractive to White, no doubt because of an antipathy towards false emotion arising from the early pressure to relate experiences he did not really own.

It is hard to know what to make of White's tribute to Spinoza's teaching

---

[38] *Lawrence and the Nature Tradition*, pp. 171-175.

[39] *Lawrence and the Nature Tradition*, p. 206.

[40] *Ethic*, preface to the second edition, p. lxii.

[41] For a helpful analysis of the text see Lloyd, *Spinoza and the Ethics*; a guide which by silence shows that White's scholarship on Spinoza has had no lasting effect in the field.

[42] The outline given in the article 'Revolution', *Last Pages*, pp. 80-94.

[43] 'Spinoza', in *Pages*, pp. 32-58 (p. 33).

[44] 'Spinoza', in *Pages*, pp. 33-34, original emphasis.

about overcoming the passions by the mind, for there are signs that his views changed over time. Moreover interpreting the relevant texts is not straightforward. In addition to information from the prefaces, and the indirect evidence of possibly Spinozan themes in the novels, there are three significant essays which relate to White's reading of the *Ethics*. All appeared in print after the fiction, though their dates of composition cannot be definitely established. Two contrasting pieces, 'Spinoza' and a 'Supplementary Note on the Devil', were included in *Pages from a Journal* (first edition December 1900, second 1910), the third, 'Revolution', was published from a manuscript after White's death, initially in *The Nation* (August 1913), and subsequently in *Last Pages from a Journal* (1915). It is at least arguable that some of these articles indicate a weakening loyalty towards Spinoza's philosophy which parallels the emergence of a less committed tone in the last preface to the *Ethic*. Charles Swann's suggestion that White made those changes to present a more dispassionate scholarly assessment has already been weighed against Dorothy's evidence of similar alterations in other manuscripts as they were prepared for publication.[45] Judgements about a possible shift in White's attitude towards Spinoza cannot be made on these stylistic grounds alone.

If it can be shown that he had growing doubts about Spinoza's helpfulness, and that the texts supporting this view at least partly (like the fourth edition preface) post-date the novels, their own apparent witness to White's borrowings from this philosophy will need to be reassessed. They must not be considered to be the last word about the personal stance of the writer, whose intellectual and spiritual development continued after their publication. Dating has a further significance. Given the suspicion voiced by critics about Dorothy's influence over Hale - that she might have pressured him into statements of faith which he did not really mean, or that in seeking acceptance he freely conformed his beliefs to hers - writings which predate their relationship and appear to show a move from Spinoza towards a more distinctly Christian viewpoint are for that reason especially important. Such pieces potentially include some of the essays referred to here, and the fourth preface itself, which evidence from his letters has shown was completed by April 1907 (before he and Dorothy first met, in October that year), although not published until 1910.

The 'Spinoza' essay opens with the statement that 'twenty years have passed since I began the study of Spinoza'.[46] This would refer most obviously to White's work on the *Ethic*, which from internal dating he cannot have started much before the mid-1850s.[47] The close similarity with the opening sentence of the *Ethic* first edition preface ('the present translation ... was completed more than twenty years ago') makes it conceivable that they date from the same

[45] See p. 243 above.
[46] 'Spinoza', in *Pages*, p. 32.
[47] Preface to the first edition, p. v.

period. The essay might originally have been written to accompany the translation, where the reference to twenty years would have been completely appropriate. The sentence could have been accidentally retained when the essay lost its original purpose, this going un-noticed when finally prepared for printing many years later. Since White was normally a meticulous editor this hypothesis is not entirely satisfactory, and it might better be argued that the 'study' to which White refers was the reading of scholarly works undertaken in preparing the successive prefaces, starting when the long-completed translation itself was in sight of being published, say from the early 1880s. This agrees with the essay being written ca. 1900, or possibly a little earlier, since *Pages* was compiled from existing rather than specially composed papers. This explanation begs fewer questions and on grounds of simplicity is to be preferred. Certainty is impossible.

The content gives little clue to the time or circumstances in which it originated. Its relative brevity (twenty-seven pages) marks it out from all the prefaces except the first (of thirty-four pages, including extensive quotations from Spinoza), while the detached tone is nearest to the 'voice' of the fourth. There is a single closing sentence of personal commendation; 'I have found his works productive beyond those of almost any man I know of that *acquiescentia mentis* which enables us to live'.[48] The essay is less densely technical than any of the prefaces, despite the twenty years of study remarked upon, and reads more like an introduction for those with little knowledge of philosophy, perhaps an account once intended for a serious but not specialist periodical. It does not enable an informed judgement about White's personal application of Spinozan principles.

The deeply felt nature of the corrective 'Supplementary Note on the Devil' which immediately follows in *Pages from a Journal* is a distinct contrast. Wilfred Stone considered it 'almost ludicrously irrelevant', as if a hangover from a primitive past, but this verdict overlooks the possibility that White seriously intended to withdraw something of his former assent from Spinoza, and re-emphasize elements of the traditional Christian world view.[49] There is some sophistication in the language used. White stops short of claiming a physical existence for the Devil, though this figure is not just the 'invention of priests for priestly purposes' or 'merely a hypothesis to account for facts', but somehow necessary; for 'unless we act as though there were an enemy to be resisted and chained' the reality of our struggle between good and evil will be

[48] 'Spinoza', p. 58; 'of almost any man' is intriguing and tantalisingly vague. Could any other hero, such as Carlyle or Goethe compare? What about Bunyan or St Paul?
[49] Stone, p. 115.

compromised.[50] Here might be another clue to White's understanding of some of the traditional Christian language he uses; it represents truths which cannot be adequately expressed in any other way, though the words apply metaphorically or analogically, and do not form propositional statements. He does not intend to mislead by silently re-interpreting the meanings of these words. White prided himself on plain meanings and truthfulness, and found attempts to hide changing opinions behind different possible meanings of words abhorrent.

This language of an 'enemy to be resisted' reminds Bedford-born White of Bunyan's *Holy War*, in which 'the chosen regiments of Diabolus are the Doubters', who are armed with 'deadlier weapons than the theologic doubters of to-day'.[51] These traditional assaults upon the pilgrim soul bring fear of 'damnation', of being 'past-hope', and lead to 'despair'. White here locates himself firmly in the tradition of Puritan spiritual self-examination, and there is nothing to suggest that he is not in earnest. The 'theologic doubters of to-day' who by comparison are not troubling, presumably cover the questions raised by biblical criticism (such as on the authorship and dates of texts) and the challenges to traditional doctrines, neither of which relate to the essence of spiritual experience, and therefore do not touch the soul. There is little here to speak of how much White might once have valued Spinoza. For this purpose the third of these occasional pieces on the philosopher, almost certainly the last to be written, is more useful. 'Revolution' cannot be exactly dated, but it was included with other papers published after White's death that Dorothy claimed had been 'written during the last years of my husband's life'.[52] Its reference to a passage in Spinoza being 'first read fifty years ago', indicates a likely origin between 1905 and 1910.[53] Hale White listed concepts from the *Ethic* which had remained important to him; the unity of body and mind, the intimation of immortality arising from the participation of every mind in the eternal mind, and two ideas concerning the passions, though he could not quite express how these had helped. The article therefore represents a memory of the one-time significance of the latter rather than an argued case for their continuing value. It carries no real sense of their present worth. Given that the appeal of the *Ethic* allegedly lay in its utility the difficulty of finding direct testimony to this is surprising.

---

[50] 'Supplementary Note', pp. 58-59. Compare his 'Belief, Unbelief, and Superstition' for a challenge to the modern idea that 'belief in a personal devil is ... a sign of imbecility', in *Pages*, pp. 83-86 (p. 83).

[51] 'Supplementary Note', pp. 58-59.

[52] 'Editor's Preface', *Last Pages*, p. iii. It had already been published a few months after White's death in *The Nation*, 9 August 1913, pp. 708-709.

[53] 'Revolution', p. 89; dating assumes he first read Spinoza no earlier than the 1850s, and before 1860.

On the passions, he cites Proposition III from the third part of the *Ethic*; '*the actions of the mind arise from adequate ideas alone, but the passions depend upon those alone which are inadequate*', and Proposition XL from the fifth, '*the more perfection a thing possesses, the more it acts and the less it suffers, and conversely the more it acts the more perfect it is*'.[54] These remain abstractions without further explanation, but some have argued that the novels might supply this deficit. They portray a number of occasions, quite possibly drawn from life, which demonstrate self-control due to mastery of the will, and others which reflect on an inability to control it, while in several places the importance of self-awareness is emphasized.[55] However these instances may not always represent or require a Spinozan interpretation. On the contrary, some may demonstrate the difficulty of subduing the passions by adopting this philosophical outlook. A closer examination of Spinoza's teaching on this point is necessary to gauge White's appropriation.

Spinoza offers his readers a vision of the good life in which by the exercise of reason man may gain control over the passions or 'affections'. These are part of the *conatus*, the striving for existence which is the essence of all things. The key definition and its implication is that recorded by White above. A passion is an inadequate idea, since to act truly, from reason alone, is to be un-swayed by external influences which if followed may be damaging. The three key passions of desire, sadness, and joy, under different forms or combinations give rise to all other human emotions. As embodied creatures human beings are subject to external forces from which they can never be wholly free, and these cause troubling emotions. An active life springing from internal causes is higher than a 'passive' one (that is, led by the passions) in which external causes dominate. Pursuit of money and status are undesirable passions, as are all forms of sensual indulgence, and the notion that a correct understanding might release one from the morally damaging consequences of being directed by them is straightforward enough. It is congruent with many ethical traditions, including Christian teaching, and clearly suited to the long-term development of moral character.[56] Spinoza goes further than these parallels, since for him all passions are regrettable, with perfect control of the self the highest good.[57] Such a vision represents a never attainable ideal. This gives rise to the importance of

---

[54] *Last Pages*, pp. 88-94 (p. 90, original italics).

[55] See below, pp. 255-256 for an instance from the *Autobiography* used to support a Spinozan reading of White.

[56] Spinoza's testified to his experience in this regard in the *Tractatus de Intellectus Emendatione* which White also translated.

[57] Susan James has examined this aspect of the *Ethics*; see 'Freedom, Slavery, and the Passions' in *The Cambridge Companion to Spinoza's Ethics*, ed. by Olli Koistinen (Cambridge: Cambridge University Press, 2009), pp. 223-241 (especially pp. 223-225). Spinoza here follows Plato rather than Aristotle, for whom some emotions (such a righteous anger) were virtuous.

fulfilment beyond death in union with the eternal Mind (Part 5, Proposition XXIII), a parallel to the Christian *summum bonum*.

Spinoza has no sense of sin as transgressing divine commands, and his view of human nature is markedly optimistic, as in Proposition XIX in the fourth part of the *Ethic*; 'according to the laws of his own nature each person necessarily desires that which he considers to be good, and avoids that which he considers to be evil'. This view, alien to Judaism and Christianity alike, inevitably follows from Spinoza's premise that 'the essence of man consists of certain modification of the attributes of God'.[58] It cannot in any obvious way be accommodated within traditional Christian doctrines about the created order or the fall of man. These differences did not initially seem to trouble Hale White, who found refreshing an anthropology which rejected punishment, and welcomed thinking of moral development in terms of 'limitations' to be overcome, not sins to be expiated.[59]

But what of the practical implications? Spinoza's supposition that the individual will always make every effort for self-fulfilment (*conatus*), shunning evil and cleaving to the good, is a generous assumption. It is not always easy to see how his teaching could be readily applied in demanding circumstances, seeming to be better suited to a life of semi-monastic withdrawal. It is not clear for instance how a sudden regrettable emotional outburst might be guarded against. This example is relevant because it has been suggested that one such case, Mark Rutherford's loss of temper when confronting the deacon who had anonymously criticised his ministry, shows evidence of White's debt to Spinoza. The episode in question had been preceded by several months of growing personal unhappiness, in addition to discontent in the church, leading to a dramatic loss of control. During the conversation with Snale, 'the blood rushed to my brain. I was as little able to control myself as if I had been shot suddenly down a precipice', and he blurts out; 'Mr Snale, you are a contemptible scoundrel and a liar', words which he immediately realises will force his resignation.[60] It is Rutherford's reflection on this critical moment which could be thought to have an echo of Spinoza; 'When I got home I bitterly regretted what had happened. I never regret anything more than the loss of self-mastery'.[61]

This might just as plausibly be understood as an entirely natural human

---

[58] This premise is explained in Proposition X of the second part of the *Ethic*; the 'corollary' is quoted here.

[59] See for example, from the second preface, pp. lxxviii, lxxix ('hell ... is forthwith abolished'), and lxxxiv.

[60] *Autobiography*, p. 82, Ch. VI. 'Contemptible' had originally been Edward Mardon's description of Snale, p. 46, Ch. IV. Mark Crees illustrates his discussion of White's debt to Spinoza from this passage; 'Before Mark Rutherford', pp. 77-79.

[61] *Autobiography*, p. 82, Ch. VI.

reaction, and further one fully in accordance with the Christian ethic, in which self-control is a notable spiritual good. It is fully explicable without reference to Spinoza. Moreover the pattern of White's explanation almost demands an interpretation in terms of the Christian tradition. In analysing his 'betrayal' - already this word distances him from full responsibility - he describes it as resulting from an apparently overwhelming and irresistible force:

> I had been betrayed, and yet I could not for the life of me see how the betrayal could have been prevented. It was upon me so suddenly, that before a moment had been given me for reflection, the words were out of my mouth. I was distinctly conscious that the *I* had not said those words. They had been spoken by some other power working in me which was beyond my reach. Nor could I foresee how to prevent such a fall for the future. [62]

This could be read as describing the divided self, or even the influence of the Devil. The passage is strongly reminiscent of verses in the Epistle to the Romans with which White would have been very familiar, and to which he refers more than once. The apostle's dilemma is graphically summed up; 'for the good that I would, I do not: but the evil which I would not, that I do' (Romans, 7. 19, Authorised Version).[63]

A psychological interpretation of White's remarks cannot be ruled out (the reference to another *I* might encourage it, though there was not yet in this period an idea of conflict between the *id* and the *ego*) but since he recorded his belief that Spinoza's views on evil - and by extension, sin - were inadequate it would not be at all unexpected if he felt the remedy also to be lacking. Rutherford, implicitly, needs to be delivered from 'the body of this death' as the apostle puts it, and not just philosophically enlightened.[64] Unlike Spinoza's created order, which *cannot* be separated from the Divine, of which it is an extension, this 'body' is at enmity with God. White elsewhere recognises that a philosophical analysis can be accepted as true without finding 'that as it stands it is applicable to practical problems'.[65] Spinoza's teaching seems incapable of modifying this sort of hot-headed behaviour, and Rutherford can only warn the

---

[62] *Autobiography*, p. 83, Ch. VI (original italics). There is a later reference to the 'I' in the 'Notes' gathered in *Last Pages*, p. 297; 'It is impossible to exclude the 'I' in our most unselfish acts'.

[63] A strong contrast to Spinoza's belief that the human will always rationally seek the good. The Authorised Version was the Bible of White's youth; in later life he favoured the Revised Version. They render the verse almost identically.

[64] Romans 7. 24. Note the importance in *Catharine Furze* of Cardew's sermon on this passage from Romans; pp. 118-120, Ch. VII (which hinges on the different understandings of 'the body of this death', the subject of a marginal note in the Authorised Version, and later the Revised).

[65] See 'Supplementary Note on the Devil', in *Pages*, pp. 58-61 (p. 58).

reader to 'watch the first risings of the storm, and to say "Beware; be watchful", at the least indication of a tempest'.[66] The advice was likely to be of limited value given his recognition that such situations arise suddenly and with overwhelming force. There is more here to suggest the inadequacy of Spinozan self-discipline than its endorsement, and claiming this as an example of Spinoza's influence goes beyond anything which can be substantiated from the evidence. Such uncertainty inevitably arises when the teaching of Spinoza, at least as White apprehended it, is applied within a moral schema still largely indebted to the Calvinist tradition of his birth. This incident seems to undermine his assertion in the 'Spinoza' article that the philosopher sets us free 'by *thinking*'.[67]

The dating of these two pieces significantly affects the overall assessment of White's use of Spinoza. The earlier the 'Spinoza' essay the more striking the change of emphasis in the 'Supplementary Note on the Devil', if that can be reliably tied to a late date. It is unlikely that they are contemporaneous compositions, for if he had already conceived this practical objection to Spinoza it would surely have been included within the main essay.[68] It appears that he did not wish to re-write the original piece but felt a need to frankly state the method's shortcomings. Just as Calvinism had erected an impressive system which had earlier failed him save, so too with philosophy. The earliest possible dating for 'Spinoza' of the late 1850s or the 1860s, though rejected as less plausible on other grounds than the 1880s, would make it easier to suggest reasons for such a change of emphasis.

The most likely cause would lie in the personal experience of passions which he had found it impossible to subdue. The tensions arising from the loss of intimacy occasioned by his wife's progressive disability, which was a severe affliction within a few years of their marriage, would be an obvious source of unease. This probably also contributed to his bouts of depression. On his own testimony the writing of the fiction, which spanned the years of her illness and into his widowhood, was a form of psychological release, a view reinforced by his statement that if he had met Dorothy earlier there would have been no novels. This he declared in a letter to her of 17 June 1909, doubtless with some exaggeration; 'I wish I had never written stories. They are somewhat of a degradation. If I had been given you as a wife when I was thirty I would never have let the public hear a syllable from me'.[69]

---

[66] *Autobiography*, p. 83, Ch. VI.

[67] 'Spinoza', in *Pages*, pp. 32-58 (p. 34, original emphasis). Again, this piece was also in the first edition.

[68] It seems impossible to argue that the 'Supplementary Note' could have been written *before* 'Spinoza'.

[69] Reproduced in the *Groombridge Diary*, p. 176. A remark possibly owing something to Jane Welsh Carlyle having said of her first suitor 'There would have been no tongues

Note continues on following page

Even assuming a much shorter interval between the two writings, it is possible that after the almost constant work on Spinoza made necessary by the revision of successive editions of the *Ethic* a latent dissatisfaction suddenly crystallised in his mind. The 'Revolution' essay would reflect that, and (if late enough in date) probably shows something of Dorothy's influence. The renewed sense of purpose, love, and affirmation which this relationship brought could have made White question how practically useful Spinoza's doctrines had been (perhaps only 'working' because he had neutralised his emotional life). Even this small indicator of a changing attitude is significant, since it is hardly to be expected that he would have completely repudiated the system over which he had laboured for so much of his adult life.

As White realised, the *Ethic* is not concerned only with right conduct in a narrow sense. While the Snale incident raises issues of personal behaviour which any moral code must address, there are other episodes in White's writing where echoes of Spinoza's teaching may be detectable without any obvious ethical implication. This highlights Spinoza's broader understanding of human passions, which goes beyond a need to control potentially harmful impulses, and covers all excited mental states. It includes other causes of psychological disturbance, not merely thoughts or actions traditionally judged as virtuous or reprehensible. The emphasis on self-understanding and analysis is surely something which attracted White, even if the insights gained do not seem to have been as helpful in social relationships as this naturally solitary figure might have hoped. In the following examples testing comes to the isolated individual against whom the forces of nature are ranged.

Several instances of near-drowning are reported in which survival is achieved by a triumph of the will. The childhood case in which he had been 'overtaken by a mad conviction' that he would drown which he overcame by a supreme effort of will has already been mentioned.[70] This is formally congruent with Spinoza's system, though the remedy is employed in a moment of crisis which does not seem to allow for the sort of calm reflection which the philosophy advocates. The fictional examples (as in the story of Michael Trevanion) are very probably inspired by this experience Hale White reports from long before his exposure to Spinoza, and cannot prove the value of his philosophy. There does seem to be a Spinozan gloss on the re-telling of the story however, and it is not necessarily false for White to make this link, if he sensed an early awareness of the power of the mind. In other words, he was predisposed towards Spinoza's teaching because it chimed with something

---

had [Edward] Irving married me'; quoted in J. A. Froude's *Thomas Carlyle: A History of the First Forty Years of His Life, 1795-1835*, 2 vols (London: Longmans, Green, 1882), I, p. 162. White had read the book on publication with 'burning fervour'; see a letter to Richard Colenutt of 30 April 1882, in *Letters to Three Friends*, p. 7.

[70] *Early Life*, p. 53.

from his own earlier experience.

One case remains which may plausibly be inspired by Spinoza, though with a twist in the interpretation. Again, significantly, it does not originate in moral perplexity. The short story 'Faith', which first appeared in *The Nation* in 1910, tells of a clock-maker and amateur astronomer cut off by the rising tide while crossing an estuary.[71] The mental test reminiscent of Spinoza comes in an absolute reliance on his time-piece (of his own making) and knowledge of the tides. As the water rises his composure is threatened, and 'he was assaulted with horrible fears' that his watch might have gained, for he had not checked it recently. This disbelief comes from 'the Devil', but it is the appearance of the stars which calms his fevered imagination, and allows him to fight back until 'his faith was restored.'[72] In renewed trust he waits for high-tide to safely pass, as he calculates it must, without overwhelming him. He survives to tell the story, calling it 'a trial of his faith', and White distinguishes simple belief in the watch's accuracy - which on its own is 'impotent' - from the actions issuing from that belief. Really *inaction* in this case, paradoxically, in the patient waiting for the tide to turn. Such faith cannot be defined, but 'it comes by the grace of God'. The story becomes a parable, 'he that hath ears to hear, let him hear'; this man's watches are to be trusted, above any other watch or clock, 'even if it be church or cathedral'.[73] There is a great deal compressed in this short piece. While mental self-control and the importance of action seems to recall Spinoza, and the stars (as elsewhere in White's writings) evoke Kant's ordered universe, the moral of the story is surely Christian; salvation comes ultimately from outside the self by the grace of God. Only when this is personally appropriated - not reliant on a 'church or cathedral' - can it become effective.

Taken together, the writings considered here show that it is a mistake to assume that teaching from Spinoza replaces a previous belief-system. This is to state the case too simply, for critics have always recognised that Christian elements co-exist with Spinozan and other concepts, but the nearly universal tendency has been to see Spinoza's philosophy eclipsing former beliefs, which survive piecemeal only because White lacked the will or courage to throw them off. Here the Christian language and allusions have been taken with due

---

[71] Reprinted in *Pages*, pp. 326-332. This was among the pieces hurriedly gathered for an enlarged second edition of this work to mark the debut of Oxford University Press as White's publisher with the new *More Pages* (and the fourth edition of the *Ethic*). There is a somewhat similar story of a couple saved from drowning by the turn of the tide in an autobiographical novel by Sarah Grand, of which White, an acquaintance of the writer, might well have been aware; *The Beth Book: Being a Study of the Life of Elizabeth Caldwell Maclure, a Woman of Genius* (London: W. Heinemann, 1897; repr. London: Virago Press, 1980), pp. 238-243, Ch. XXVI.

[72] *Pages*, pp. 329-330.

[73] *Pages*, pp. 331-332.

seriousness. In fact the ethical examples show Spinozan 'salvation' to be inadequate. A parallel might be found in the account of the Drury Lane theology of the *Deliverance*, where the 'unity of our nature' assumed in an un-named 'philosophy' is contrasted with the absolute 'distinction between right and wrong' in Christianity; summed up in the mission of the latter 'not to propound a theory of man [but] to redeem the world'.[74] Despite White's belief that 'the goal of all ethics' ought to be the 'annihilation' of the self, Spinoza failed to deliver this result, for the body of death cannot be ruled by the will.[75] Instead White interprets, and as necessary corrects, Spinoza within the framework of his inherited faith, though this compromises both systems to a degree.

Spinoza and the Novels

This analysis suggests that White revised his view of Spinoza late in life, admitting that despite the intellectual attraction of the philosophical system it was not practically helpful. This puts attempts to read the novels through a Spinozan lens in a different light. The extent of Spinozan themes is debatable in any case, with critics who emphasize White's supposed loss of faith most likely to discover them. The question arises if there are sufficiently clear references in the novels to demonstrate a substantial dependence on Spinoza unprompted by a need to show the result of White's reading of the philosopher. Whatever echoes might be detected, there is also a danger to be avoided since the fiction cannot tell the whole story of their author's life. Too close an identification of White's personal pilgrimage with the stories of the novels causes distortion if it leans towards the unspoken assumption that his belief-system was static after the publication of *Clara Hopgood*, though he lived for a further seventeen years. Especially when these texts are treated as an unfolding series it makes little sense effectively to deny any continuing personal development after their writing.

John Goode has made the most determined attempt to demonstrate the impact of Spinoza on 'Mark Rutherford'.[76] Moreover he argues that *Catharine Furze* may be read not just as influenced by Spinoza but as an anti-Spinozan text, for example in its emphasis on imagination over thought.[77] While earlier critics hesitated to propose such complex and subtle influences, the recognised *locus classicus* is *Clara Hopgood*, the most intellectual of White's novels. The book was written at the time when the translation of the *Ethic* was being

[74] *Deliverance*, p. 90, Ch. VI.

[75] 'Ixion', *The Secular Review*, 11 September 1880, pp. 164-165 (p. 165).

[76] His 'Mark Rutherford and Spinoza' is the most extensive discussion of the fiction in this respect; *English Literature in Transition*, 34 (1991), 424-453 (p. 424).

[77] 'Mark Rutherford and Spinoza', pp. 428-429.

prepared for a second edition. The characterisation of Clara and Madge Hopgood allows an exploration of the triumph of reason over impulse or intuition, and the control of the passions. The figure of Baruch Cohen points to Spinoza (who is not mentioned by name).[78] These references do not make Mark Rutherford a Spinozan however, and there can be a forced air to readings of the novels which find resonances of Spinoza at every turn. Significantly, *Clara Hopgood* ends with a reflection on the 'Eternal Christ', through whom and in whom the work of salvation is still worked out, as in the sacrificial lives and deaths of ordinary people like Clara.

Baruch himself is imperfectly Spinozan. Though portrayed as unable to control his romantic feelings, this is not lamented, pointing to the wider significance of desire in White's writings seen in the reiterated concern for those trapped in loveless marriages. More surprisingly for one who upholds the absolute distinction between right and wrong, elsewhere love can be praised even when yielding to its impulses leads to a disregard for the moral law. This Hale had taken to be the message of Henry Arthur Jones's controversial play *Judah*, which he saw in its first season at the Shaftesbury Theatre in 1890. The minister-hero, Judah Llewellyn, perjures himself to protect the young woman he loves from exposure as a fraudulent faith-healer. White wrote to Jones acclaiming the drama for showing 'the attraction of love against the ten commandments' while regretting the sham morality of the day; 'the curse of curses nowadays is not that we don't keep the Law, although we don't do much in that line, but that we don't know what Love means and touch another with the tips of gloved fingers'.[79] To know all passion untimely spent indicates not calm, but a dehumanising loss more regrettable than the failure of Spinozan self-control.

The evidence of the novels is therefore rather mixed, as themes and ideas from the *Ethics* appear alongside profoundly Christian concepts. John Goode exploits the separate authorial voice to represent this in terms of a 'basic tension between the programme of Rutherford's novels and White's involvement in Spinoza'.[80] He further admits that 'Spinoza is not there in the texts only as a set of influences, but also as a possibility against which the text is sometimes constructed'.[81] Certainly White was always struggling for life and light. The tendency by scholars to highlight apparent borrowings from Spinoza

---

[78] See the analysis by Linda Hughes, 'Madge and Clara Hopgood: William Hale White's Spinozan Sisters', *Victorian Studies*, 18 (1974), 57-75.

[79] In a letter of 15 August 1890, given in Doris A. Jones, *The Life and Letters of Henry Arthur Jones* (London: Victor Gollancz, 1930), p. 111. Lying for a higher purpose finds a place in *Miriam's Schooling* and the included story of Michael Trevanion, but these were published in June 1890, before White had seen this play.

[80] 'Mark Rutherford and Spinoza', p. 427.

[81] 'Mark Rutherford and Spinoza', pp. 428-429.

and regard Christian themes as somehow regressive owes much to wider assumptions about White's own spiritual journey, and is not the only defensible reading of these texts.

This is not to deny signs of Spinozan themes in the early novels, most significantly in the 'actual joy' which Mark Rutherford experiences just before his death, but to resist over-interpreting them. For the importance of nature there is no need to look further than Wordsworth, and it has been demonstrated that the encounter with him was not *necessarily* destructive of faith. It must also be remembered that Spinoza's thought is thoroughly impregnated with his Jewish roots, so some 'Spinozan' features in White are also traceable to an Old Testament background. Joy is a biblical concept, and George MacDonald too valued it for just that reason, largely in ignorance of Spinoza.

White left other indications that Spinoza did not wholly satisfy, or at least that he could not derive the anticipated benefit from his system. Among the 'Notes' printed in *Last Pages* is the admission that 'in reading Spinoza again [presumably in work for the fourth edition, somewhere between 1905 and 1910] I have often felt on the verge of some great discovery which was not fully completed'.[82] A baffling obscurity remained. The clue to the real answer lay elsewhere, as the same set of 'Notes' explains; 'it is of little use to reason against our failings. They must be overcome by aspiration; by religion'.[83] In an earlier article he had already concluded that the definite everyday 'lessons of experience' were always to be preferred to enticing 'speculative propositions'.[84]

Monism's Accommodation with Christian Faith?

The conclusion must be that White never fully adopted Spinoza's system because it could not accommodate fundamental aspects of his inherited and lately reviving Puritan world view. Caution is needed before assuming too great a dependence on Spinoza since features identified in the philosopher's writings and traced in Hale White's thought may have common roots and do not always prove a direct connection. Nor must any possible influence be read wholly in a direction opposed to Christian belief, as the test case of the monism represented by Spinoza demonstrates. On three key points at which theists suggest monism is incompatible with orthodoxy - its impersonal understanding of the Absolute, the difficulty in explaining evil within a literally divine world, and denial of personal immortality - White shows his own reservations. Theism itself can to some extent accommodate concepts more often associated with monism, as consideration below of White's mystical experiences will reveal.[85]

---

[82] *Last Pages*, p. 305.

[83] *Last Pages*, p. 310.

[84] In the person of 'Tom'; see 'Some Letters', in *Pages*, p. 333-344 (p. 339).

[85] See pp. 303-306.

While he can hardly be said to have a 'doctrine' of God, the sense of a personal and relational understanding is present in White, especially in writing of the love of God (albeit experienced through humankind - Dorothy's love as the love of God for example).[86] Here there is no sense of an impersonal Monad. The understanding of divine fatherhood implied in White's reference to the Prodigal Son, though less clearly articulated than George MacDonald's, again bespeaks personality. Even the qualities of good and evil require something personal for expression. To preserve his belief in these fundamental categories White had found it necessary to add the 'Supplementary Note on the Devil' to his article on Spinoza. The statement that if Satan is the opposite of God he is 'the Nothing' may as 'a philosophical doctrine be true', but it does not accord with personal knowledge of temptation and resisting evil.[87] The brute facts of experience cannot be denied. On the issue of post-mortem survival he may not differ so greatly from Spinoza, for this is perhaps the clearest point at which White questions traditional Christian belief. It is by no means plain if Spinoza intended to suggest the survival of individual minds after death, or if all would be subsumed within the divine mind, an uncertainty shared by White.[88] '*The human mind*', he read in the *Ethic*, '*cannot be absolutely destroyed with the body, but something of it remains which is eternal*'. 'This proposition', he noted, '... contain[s] everything which I have ever found to be a reality touching the so-called immortality of the soul'.[89] Some of White's unease about the traditional Christian understanding arises from the sense that it is tainted by the idea of reward and punishment.[90] For Spinoza the moral life is furthered by the pure, disinterested, intellectual love of God, and joy results in measure accordingly. The knowledge of God is immortality. These reservations imply that White was not moulded by his reading of Spinoza, but rather was able to take over what was most useful for his own situation.

Even with the difficulty of understanding this last issue, it would be a mistake to assume that White sought through Spinoza to replace rather than supplement or creatively re-interpret Christian belief. Instead a philosophical rationale was found which could offer support to beliefs often having some essential continuity with orthodoxy. For White did not put down his Bible to read Spinoza, and continued to live as a believer. During his early encounter

---

[86] In his '1910 MS' (UBC, NCC 2-10); see also the poem 'Belief' in *More Pages*, pp. 184-185. It should be noted that Spinoza's monism admitted the 'love' of God, though it was severely intellectual.

[87] 'Supplementary Note on the Devil' in *Pages*, pp. 58-61 (p. 58).

[88] See the discussion in Lloyd, *Spinoza and the Ethics*, pp. 116-120.

[89] Quoted in 'Revolution', *Last Pages*, pp. 88-94 (pp. 90-91, original italics). Commenting on *Ethics*, Proposition XXIII, Part 5.

[90] A reward for good behaviour was the more serious moral problem, since human experience *expects* punishment for misdeeds; 'an instinct that wrongdoing demands a penalty', see 'Notes' in *Last Pages*, p. 285.

with the *Ethics* at Chapman's he was an active preacher in Unitarian chapels, with the real possibility that he might still have fulfilled a ministerial vocation; he supplied the pulpit at Ditchling Old Meeting for the 1856-57 year, a more regular commitment than has normally been noted.[91] If White's reading of Spinoza informed his preaching, there would have been nothing strange about any Unitarian appreciation, for James Martineau was among those who helped to popularise his thought, recognising the attraction of 'language [that] seemed to ring with the very tones familiar and dear to the devout', without accepting everything he wrote.[92] There was much of the Old Testament prophet about Spinoza.

Summary

This analysis shows the need to be cautious about claiming Spinoza as a major influence on White. Despite his lengthy study of the philosopher, and especially the *Ethics*, there are significant points at which the Christian world-view inhibited a closer embrace. The moral usefulness of his system among the trials of life must be doubted, and the problem of evil stubbornly resists Spinoza's relative optimism.[93] If the engagement with Spinoza is of limited value in assessing White's mature beliefs, there remain other useful public and private writings to consider. Where the novels have been prioritised as sources for White's life it has been especially difficult to give due weight to evidence of continuity in belief because of their arguable move away from faith, and, especially, the challenges to Christian belief portrayed in the life of Mark Rutherford. This needs correction and a fresh perspective, first by returning to the immediate post-expulsion period and then moving on to consider the remainder of White's life. The wider picture must also be brought into view through comparisons with others.

---

[91] Dated from the list of ministers reproduced in G. E. Evans, *Vestiges of Protestant Dissent* (Liverpool: F. & E. Gibbons, 1897), pp. 72-73; this was simply to preach, and not it seems to work pastorally. Dorothy had learned the length of his engagement there; *Groombridge Diary*, p. 463, note 1.

[92] See *A Study of Spinoza* (London: Macmillan, 1882), p. 327; Martineau believed that Spinoza argued against personal immortality, p. 301.

[93] J-M. Yvard is currently researching White's use of Spinoza, but regrettably his work has not been published in time to be referred to here. His conclusions may suggest a need to revise the present account, or themselves require adjustment in the light of the reconstruction offered above.

CHAPTER 9

'I was adrift'
The Aftermath

Any attempt to describe White's spiritual life after 1852, when he confessed himself 'adrift', faces formidable obstacles.[1] There is no continuous narrative through which the story may be told, and constructing one from the sources which are available risks misrepresenting the whole. The novels depart too obviously from life to be relied upon in this respect, though it is essential to engage with the material in them which has been taken to prove a dramatic loss of faith. An account which honestly reflects the evidence will inevitably appear disjointed, but the signs of a lasting interest in faith and commitment to belief are everywhere. Although references are scattered in writings of all kinds, many of which cannot be dated accurately, their widespread occurrence makes it plain that engagement with faith never ceased to be part of his intellectual or ethical life. In order to avoid falsely separating White from his context other contemporary witnesses will again be invoked in order that some common features can be identified. By implication the loss of faith apparently experienced by Mark Rutherford would correspond in White's life to a date in the 1850s and this, together with the issue's importance for establishing a vantage point from which to survey his other writings, makes it necessary to start by considering the key passages from the fiction.

Belief and Unbelief: Contrary Evidence from Mark Rutherford?

It has been suggested here that once false ideas of White's earliest spiritual experience have been put aside there are many texts which indicate spiritual life, and that he grappled honestly with questions of belief in search of authentic faith. Sections of the *Autobiography* have an apparently different emphasis, and seem to show the disintegration of belief. The psycho-spiritual drama presented there has greatly influenced accounts of White's faith, given the strong tendency to conform his pilgrimage to Rutherford's. It must be remembered however that the novel form naturally lends itself to and even requires an intensification of experience for dramatic effect. Events which in life cover a lengthy time-span may be concentrated into a much shorter period,

---

[1] *Early Life*, p. 79; 'After the expulsion I was adrift'.

reshaped, and otherwise adapted in order to suit the writer's artistic purposes.

The relevant material here, found in the dialogues with Edward Gibbon Mardon (chapters four and six), is largely responsible for the loss of faith interpretation of White. Rutherford is surprisingly ill-equipped to withstand these challenges; 'negative criticism, in which Mardon greatly excelled, was all new to me, and I had no reply to make'.[2] This fictional representation of White's mental struggle can be compared with the internal self-questioning by which Mrs Ward's Robert Elsmere later examined his cherished beliefs.[3] For White there may be an echo of secularist attacks on Christian belief, which find a place in the freethinking debates of the *Deliverance*.[4]

The similarities between Elsmere and Rutherford can be taken further. R. M. Schieder has shown that there is a 'surprisingly consistent' pattern in the conversion theme (of which these crises are a part) across a wide range of such fiction.[5] He identifies distinct stages; the chief character, a minister or ministerial student, begins with a formally accepted orthodox faith. This is found under examination to be intellectually or spiritually wanting, and after a struggle against the inevitable, is lost. An experience of desolation follows, relieved when a guide out of distress is found. With this help a new set of beliefs is forged, by which some form of service is enabled. Variations in details are smoothed out in this analysis, but most interesting here is the emphasis upon gain as well as loss, and the period of desolation. However a concentration on 'doubters' is too restrictive, and misses the possibility of a more positive assessment, for there is a significant overlap with characteristics of the classic dark night of the soul which indicate spiritual growth, not failure.[6]

This is a bold claim for Hale White, but it makes better sense of his early faith, and the persistence in maturity. Isolating Rutherford's breakdown has always made it difficult to understand what went before, and what follows, especially if simply transferred to White's life. For this reason critics have been unable to do justice to White's spiritual development, and show embarrassment over signs of later faith.

---

[2] *Autobiography*, p. 52, Ch. IV; the questioning may represent the 'preciser problems' of which he had earlier written (p. 19, Ch. II). Mardon explains his middle name, changed from 'Gibson', stands for the great historian, and scourge of 'believing' history.

[3] *Robert Elsmere*, Chs. XXV and XXVI (for example); it is also carried out in open dialogue with the sceptical Squire Wendover.

[4] *Deliverance*, pp. 13-16, Ch. I; based on White's attendance at such events, which he also described in his newspaper columns.

[5] 'Loss and Gain? : The Theme of Conversion in Late Victorian Fiction', *Victorian Studies*, 9 (1965), 29-44 (p. 33).

[6] See the classic introduction by Evelyn Underhill, *Mysticism: A Study in the Nature and Development of Man's Spiritual Consciousness*, 14th edn (London: Methuen, 1942), chapter nine. The illumination which in her outline precedes the dark night would in White's case approximate to his Wordsworthian 'conversion'.

Mardon is the mouthpiece for questions with which White would have already been familiar at the time of writing through his knowledge of secularist arguments, as illustrated in his newspaper columns from years before the *Autobiography* was published. The challenges are blunt rather than subtle and arise during conversations over several months. Rutherford's lonely meditations in between the personal encounters further serve to crystallise the issues at stake. The timescale indicates a period of gradual unsettlement with some moments of particular tension rather than a sudden crisis, though Mardon has 'a sledgehammer way of expressing himself' which forces Rutherford to face questions he might have preferred to avoid.[7] They revolve around the historicity of the Gospel narratives in particular, including doubting that the historical person of Jesus existed, and the doctrine of God, as attributes like omnipotence are declared meaningless. The variations between the Gospels are used to question their value, and to suggest that they are myth not history. While Strauss is not mentioned by name it is safe to assume that his theories lie behind the discussion.[8] Beyond the verbal exchanges, the simple truthfulness and hospitality of Mardon and his daughter form an uncomfortable contrast to the conduct of some in his own congregation, notably Deacon Snale.

Subsequent meetings with Mardon raised questions about the idea of immortality, and Rutherford is impressed by the manner in which the sick man faces death with quiet composure despite admitting no future hope. The subject was already one of concern to Rutherford, and is known to have preoccupied Hale White. Rutherford's ministry changes as he reflects on the doubts sown in his mind. 'I could no longer preach any of the dogmas which had always been preached in the chapel', and while avoiding the supernatural he aims instead to bring the scriptural characters to life.[9] In another visit Rutherford is challenged to name any belief which separates him from the atheist Mardon; simple belief in God is offered, but Rutherford admits he can never gain in logic over his opponent. Nevertheless the sense of purposefulness in the universe, of mind meeting mind, means that when he parts from Mardon 'the old superstition' arises 'unsubdued'.[10]

Mardon's position is not impregnable, and there is a hint that he has himself

---

[7] *Autobiography*, p. 52, Ch. IV.

[8] Timothy Larsen shows the importance of Strauss in debates about the truth of Christianity, though concluding that his works were actually read by very few; *Honest Doubt*, p. 247. In a separate study he offers a useful reminder that Strauss did not set out to overturn Christianity but to refine it; 'Biblical Criticism and the Crisis of Belief: D.F. Strauss's *Leben Jesu* in Britain', in *Contested Christianity: The Political and Social Contexts of Victorian Theology* (Waco, TX: Baylor University Press, 2004), pp. 43-58 (p. 44).

[9] *Autobiography*, p. 78, Ch. VI. White had greatly appreciated Thomas Binney's similar ability to illuminate biblical history, see p. 373 below.

[10] *Autobiography*, p. 89, Ch. VI.

been alive to more than logic. His wife had enjoyed singing parts from Handel's *Messiah*, suggesting that at least a reverence for the human character of Jesus had once permeated the home. Women were often identified more strongly with religious belief than men, and her early death perhaps raising in acute form the problem of innocent suffering might be supposed to have been at least partly responsible for Mardon's determined atheism.[11] A profound emotional attachment to the human Jesus still marked many who had turned away from formal religion.[12] None of the arguments advanced by Mardon would have been in the least surprising to Hale White by the date of the *Autobiography*. It is impossible to say how many were troubling him in the notional 1850s setting indicated by the novel, but even a slight awareness of anti-Christian debates would certainly have included several of the same lines of argument. It remains most likely that these chapters represent the distillation and re-presentation of ideas which White personally encountered and struggled to come to terms with over a longer period, but this does not prove a similar breakdown. The challenges are quite consistent with Underhill's analysis of the dark night, especially her emphasis that the crisis reflects the temperament of the sufferer; intellectual turmoil (as here) predominating in those who live by the mind.[13]

Although just how much of Rutherford's crisis is White's cannot be established, two key aspects are analogous to the dark night experience; the mental distress (including depression and physical disorders), and the sense of separation from the divine.[14] White's life-long tendency towards melancholy is dated from the period immediately after the expulsion. It is represented by the brief Stoke Newington school-teaching episode, which produces a 'most dreadful sense of loneliness', 'a kind of terror', and 'nameless dread'.[15] This is more severe than the circumstances described can account for, and could well represent a delayed reaction to the expulsion.[16] The *Early Life* report is less dramatic ('then there fell upon me what was the beginning of a trouble which has lasted all my life', p.80), in part reflecting the longer perspective, but a reminder that in fiction experience is naturally amplified. The 'powerlessness to

---

[11] Reference is made to the lines taken from Isaiah and identified with Jesus as the man of sorrows, *Autobiography*, pp. 90-91, Ch. VI.

[12] This factor was instrumental in the re-conversions of some secularists featured in Larsen's *Honest Doubt*, as summarised, p. 243.

[13] *Mysticism*, pp. 388-389 (surely here too some parallel with Henry Martyn, whose breakdown is described below).

[14] Mark Rutherford had already identified with the despised Jesus, as Mary Mardon sings from Handel's *Messiah* (*Autobiography*, pp. 90-91, Ch. VI); did he also feel for the abandonment on the cross?

[15] *Autobiography*, p. 113, Ch. VIII.

[16] Even allowing for the generally damaging effect on spirituality which White attributes to city life.

believe' which Rutherford reports is a feature of the hidden-ness of God in the dark night as beliefs previously taken for granted are tested, and it is more fully realised that religious language is provisional; 'God was obviously not a person in the clouds'.[17] As a result of his earlier Wordsworthian enlightenment Mark Rutherford had already understood that religious language was not identical with the truths it attempted to convey (and so should have been better armed on meeting Mardon), and in this narrative for dramatic purposes White may have separated events which are more nearly related than he suggests.

On this reading Hale White experienced a dark night (though he may not have identified it as such), precipitated by his expulsion from New College, which has been so heightened and re-drawn in the fiction as to mislead critics into taking it as a simple story of loss, essentially transferable from Rutherford to the author.[18] White's earlier and later spiritual experiences are then harmonised with this understanding, misleading in both instances. This radical interpretation of White conflicts with previous studies but is offered for consideration as better fitting the facts as now established. It explains the quite different emphases of the fiction and other sources; the former an intense and intensified experience, the latter calmer reflection. It removes the puzzle that nowhere outside the *Autobiography* is there any clear reference to the catastrophic loss of faith which is habitually ascribed to White himself on the basis of this text.

Henry Martyn's autobiography offers an apparently similar case, though one explicitly accompanied by the full recovery of faith. It highlights the particular difficulties faced by those whose faith was professional as well as personal. Ministry to the unappreciative and opposition from church members must inevitably challenge faith, while the inherent loneliness of the work all too easily leads to introspection and personal crisis. The breakdown which Martyn describes is not identical to Rutherford's, but it shares some key features. He starts by excluding ill-health, overwork or depression as contributory factors, and posits that unknown 'causes must have been operating for some time'.[19]

---

[17] *Autobiography*, pp. 78, 84, Ch. VI (compare pp. 90-91, already cited above, for feeling 'despised' like Jesus). White is generally thought of as a pessimist, quite apart from the more serious depression he periodically suffered, but E. Vincent Tempest argues that this is better understood as a resolute facing up to difficulties, and belief that salvation of some sort awaits the troubled soul; 'Optimism in "Mark Rutherford"', *Westminster Review*, 180 (1913), 174-184.

[18] His unsuccessful ministry (if the fiction contains truth from life here) is another possible trigger, as his beliefs are reviewed in the light of their lack of acceptance and the incomprehension of his hearers. Hence the depiction of Rutherford as peculiarly ill-fitted for this vocation, for example by Peter Allen, 'Mark Rutherford: The Anatomy of a Failure', in *The View from the Pulpit: Victorian Ministers and Society*, ed. by P. T. Phillips (Ontario: Macmillan of Canada, 1978), pp. 143-159.

[19] *Chapters From the Autobiography*, p. 89.

Despite these denials, surely prompted by a desire to stress the outward success of his ministry, in all probability the elements mentioned did play a part. The same defensive concern may affect the rest of his presentation. He is carefully specific about the nature of his crisis; 'when I say that I lost my faith in what had once been the rock on which I stood, I fully express myself. I never utterly disbelieved, and ignored the fundamental facts of our religion, but I could not believe with heart and soul, nay, could not believe in any sense'.[20] 'Believe' is used in two different senses here, which must not be confused. Martyn means that he could not trust or have faith, that any belief was wholly inert. He did not think God 'a myth', but 'feared that this was so' and suffered 'an agony which I cannot describe'.[21] The introduction of 'myth' naturally again suggests the influence of D. F. Strauss.

Martyn found prayer empty and unfruitful, the Bible lifeless, any sense of God's presence eluded him, and the concept of life after death became meaningless. Even the superstitious beliefs of ordinary people seemed suddenly attractive at an emotional level.[22] In searching for renewal of faith he considers and finds wanting the beliefs of other religions and traditional proofs of Christianity such as miracles. That so many topical issues occur in his description suggests a narrative shaped by artistic demands as much as personal experience, undermining rather than enhancing the feeling that a real situation is being documented. Seeing no alternative to resignation he announces this intention to his deacons, but is persuaded instead to take an extended break from ministry. One deacon claims to have been in a similar disturbed state for many years, though this is styled in more traditional terms as a lack of assurance of salvation. A sympathetic observer counsels Martyn that he cannot expect to be immune from stresses caused by the time of transition in which he lives, one 'more tormented with honest doubt than any age which has gone before it'.[23]

Martyn's cure is rest and time 'spent in reading the books which represented the sceptical spirit of Germany, France, and England'; their strange effect was to expose the difficulties that their own theories presented by 'the boundlessness of their assumptions, and the feebleness of their explanations when dealing with the miracles, and especially with the life of Jesus'.[24] Once faced, their power was destroyed. This finding could reinforce a reading of Mark Rutherford's crisis as the fictional exorcism of doubts which had

---

[20] *Chapters From the Autobiography*, p. 91.

[21] *Chapters From the Autobiography*, p. 91.

[22] *Chapters From the Autobiography*, pp. 93-95. This includes reports of visits from dead loved ones, a belief which overlaps with spiritualism, for which see below, pp. 316-323.

[23] *Chapters From the Autobiography*, p. 102.

[24] *Chapters From the Autobiography*, pp. 103-104; Strauss is mentioned by name.

presented themselves to Hale White, and which could not otherwise be named or overcome. In another parallel, Martyn's account shows the same dissatisfaction with what Rutherford calls the 'shallow prating' of an atheist who imagined that a world could exist in which none of the moral problems of suffering or inequality so testing for theism could arise.[25] Gradually Martyn returns to the simple truths of the gospel, with natural theology finding its rightful place not as leading to the truth but following from it. His second *naïveté* is marked by an intensely personal belief in Christ which sits lightly on doctrine ('my theory of the Atonement went utterly') but gives great *joy*.[26]

Whatever the degree to which a personal crisis has been overlaid with additional material to suit the author's purpose the description of loss is as powerful as anything described of Mark Rutherford. The strong reclamation of faith shows that at least for this writer loss was not the end of the story. As perhaps it was not in life for Hale White. The essential feature to note analogous with White (and echoed in MacDonald) is the necessity for inherited beliefs of merely formal adherence to be painfully challenged as the prelude to spiritual growth. This process largely neutralises the harmful scepticism of the day. White elsewhere suggests a slightly different connection between scepticism and faith, but with the same stress upon the importance of apprehension; 'false dogmatism is not extinguished by simple scepticism. Its effectual enemy is belief'.[27] In fact he recognized that some beliefs are not the result of conscious mental processes or 'assent'; 'we want some word to express a condition ... in which something is undoubtedly *taken on* or assumed to be our own without any mental *act* whatsoever'.[28] In this he seems to be reaching after something like the illative sense of which Newman spoke, and the accompanying grammar of assent, but an inability to go further is a factor hindering his spiritual development.[29]

George MacDonald offers a further comparison and contrast. Like White he came to look upon his childhood faith as lifeless, but gave no indication that this arose from or produced a sudden crisis. The events which brought him to this conclusion are something of a mystery, especially when the traditional reference to time spent among sceptical books has been dismissed as without credible foundation. The conflicts in Scottish Congregationalism must have had some effect, especially while a student at Blackfriars church in Aberdeen where these convulsions were felt, but the result that he needed to relearn the truths of religion was wholly beneficial. The very concept of learning and growth was healthy, and increasing assurance in the idea of God as a loving father

---

[25] *Autobiography*, p. 85, Ch. VI.

[26] *Chapters From the Autobiography*, pp. 107-108 (emphasis added).

[27] In an undated note given in *Last Pages*, p. 276.

[28] Again from notes in *Last Pages*, p. 268 (original italics).

[29] On which see also below, p. 307.

transformed his life and thinking. White suffered from the lack of such a unifying principle for his own belief, and even when he began to grow again in confidence never fully attained the Scotsman's own deep sense of assurance.

The distinction between sign and thing signified had already been probed by Rutherford. He had realised that 'nearly every doctrine in the college creed had once had a natural origin in the necessities of human nature, and might therefore be interpreted as to become a necessity again'.[30] This needs explanation, for it might be construed as suggesting that belief is entirely a human construct, but this is to misunderstand White's meaning. For him, only what is verified in human experience can be trusted (as in his 'inner reference') and no outward truth can have the same authority. Beliefs traced to the experience of others can be appropriated, and this may include the realisation of their universal nature, an aspect Rutherford explores with regard to the atonement.[31] That which must be received on authority, in creeds and official teaching, cannot have the same status. The originating impulses are themselves responses to creaturely status within the world, and illustrations of the basic credo 'I *do* believe in God'.[32]

Sermons by Theophilus Cardew in *Catharine Furze* demonstrate the application of this principle. These paradigmatic examples, indebted to sermons preached by Caleb Morris, take occasions from the Gospels and aim to 'make [the] scene real' to the hearers in order that they may enter vividly into the story. The appeal is personal, direct, and emotional. Rutherford regrets that 'the conclusion was a piece of the most commonplace orthodoxy, lugged in, Heaven knows how, and delivered monotonously, in strong contrast to the former part of the discourse'.[33] A second sermon, on the Prodigal Son, rising to even greater heights, is also marred by the closing addition 'on Christ's mediatorial work [which] had no particular connection with the former part of his discourse. It was spoken in a different tone, and it satisfied the congregation that they had really heard nothing heterodox'.[34] This is not necessarily a denial of the place of doctrine, but recognition of the vital experience that has always

[30] *Autobiography*, p. 21, Ch. II.

[31] As illustrated below, pp. 296-297.

[32] *Autobiography*, p. 87, Ch. VI, original emphasis; he resists Mardon's challenge that this is meaningless - there is an intellect which finds expression in the world, and is detected within man.

[33] *Catharine Furze*, pp. 109, 113, Ch. VI. Cardew's text is Luke 18. 18, the rich young ruler. Thomas Binney was praised by his biographer for lively preaching from the Bible not marred by 'the pernicious addition of Church theories as to the mode of its production', though apparently without any wider avoidance of traditional doctrine; see E. Paxton Hood, *Thomas Binney: His Mind Life and Opinions, etc.* (London: James Clarke, 1874), p. 290.

[34] *Catharine Furze*, p. 218, Ch. XII. White reports Morris preaching on this; 'Caleb Morris', in *Last Pages*, pp. 244-250 (p. 245).

preceded it. To repeat the doctrine alone is idolatrous, but to discard it risks also losing the reality it seeks to represent.

As already argued, there is no need to suppose that in describing Rutherford's crisis White is simply restating his own. At the very least the dramatic tension has been increased and fears magnified. The context of ministry explains the emphasis upon how little is certainly believed ('I was alarmed to find ... that the older I got the less I appeared to believe'), since it serves the purpose of explaining Rutherford's eventual withdrawal from ministry, and by extension White's too.[35] As the later fiction continues to show, through characters like Miss Tippit (*Miriam's Schooling*), a few personally held beliefs are sufficient for ordinary Christian life. In the Rutherford-Mardon dialogues doubts are strongly expressed such that Rutherford is forced to suggest that it hardly matters if Jesus really existed, for the 'Christ-idea' alone is essential for belief.[36] It is not surprising that he is unable to defend such a (possibly Hegelian) view against Mardon's sharp intelligence, and it is not clear that White ever entertained such a thought. Some of the concepts here may represent not uncertainties which he shared but those he wished to show untenable. It is likely that in his darkest moments White was exposed to serious doubts, but if the many later faith references are to be accepted as valid, they did not overcome him or persist. When Mark Rutherford reflects on conversion however, surely a resonance of White's abiding fear is heard; that one could all too easily 'remain pretty much the same kind of being that he was before'.[37] In the *Deliverance* the narrative turns on the absurdity of unthinking faith and simple negativism; 'to waste a Sunday morning in ridiculing such stories as that of Jonah was surely as imbecile as to waste it in proving their verbal veracity'.[38] He has no interest in that which cannot feed the soul.

The novels also contain positive information on the application of faith which has been down-played and misunderstood. The Drury Lane episode in the *Deliverance* therefore needs to be re-examined, but first it is useful to consider the *Early Life* material which describes faith returning after the New College expulsion, since this indicates that the Drury Lane venture need not be considered to arise from a failure of faith but its revival. Naturally this cross-over between life and fiction is only possible because the Drury Lane ministry is based upon an historical episode. Other writings, some never intended for publication, also show that White continued to engage with questions of faith which can best be understood by reference to the faith community of his birth. The mismatch between the *Autobiography* and White's personal experience

---

[35] *Autobiography*. p. 84, Ch. VI.

[36] *Autobiography*, p. 51, Ch. IV. George Eliot's translation of *Leben Jesu* had been published by Chapman in 1846 (though her name did not anywhere appear).

[37] *Autobiography*, p. 47, Ch. IV.

[38] *Deliverance*, p. 16, Ch. I.

contributes to a difficulty in establishing the proper sequence of events. For instance, insofar as Rutherford's ministerial career draws on the writer's Ditchling appointment, a post-expulsion consciousness has been inserted into a narrative that knows no such disruption. In contrast, the *Early Life* makes the expulsion pivotal, but gives no hint of Ditchling. In the face of these alternative trajectories here the *Early Life* material is considered next, since as far as can be determined it is nearer to the facts of White's life.

Post-Expulsion Belief

White used the opportunity provided by the *Early Life* to take the long view of his earthly pilgrimage. Some thoughtful paragraphs on the significance of the New College expulsion challenge any simplistic view that he had lost his faith, despite the acknowledgment that the breach left him 'adrift' (p.79). Reference to his marriage in 1856 marks the intended close of this short life, and it was not absolutely necessary to include anything more on faith. Yet he was obviously unwilling to leave the reader with the impression of one permanently alienated from his spiritual roots:

> It would be a mistake to suppose that the creed in which I had been brought up was or could be for ever cast away like an old garment. The beliefs of childhood and faith cannot be thus dismissed. I know that in after years I found that in a way they revived under new forms .... At first, after the abandonment of orthodoxy, I naturally thought nothing in the old religion worth retaining, but this temper did not last long (pp.77-78).

While modern readings of the novels which focus on a spiritual crisis make any renewal of faith seem incongruous careful readers had recognised that White was a spiritual being often impatient of religion, but never of faith itself. Reviewing his first novel Richard Littledale had noticed what eluded too many others:

> the distinguishing peculiarity of the book, marking it off from many not dissimilar narratives ... is that the doubter is represented as never sure of his very doubts themselves, nor at all convinced that he is in the right path in his negations any more than he had been in his affirmations.... [he is] the sceptic haunted by an uneasy suspicion that the right may lie with his former beliefs, and yet quite unable, intellectually and morally, to project himself backwards into them even for a moment's hypothetical re-examination'.[39]

---

[39] Review of the *Autobiography*, *The Academy*, 21 May 1881, p. 370. In 1885 he found the *Deliverance* much less satisfactory, feeling it failed to provide the resolution promised by the title (*The Academy*, 21 February 1885, p. 131). The *Revolution* he praised highly (*The Academy*, 7 May 1887, p. 322). Littledale, an Anglican priest of

Note continues on following page

It was the closing of this gap between what was past but evocatively real and the demands of the present day which occupied White for much of his life.

The *Early Life* section on returning belief can be teased out a little; 'it would be a mistake to suppose that the creed in which I had been brought up *was or could be* for ever cast away like an old garment' (pp.77-78, emphasis added). The clothing imagery may be a nod towards *Sartor Resartus*, and the tenses used are revealing. At first reading 'was' suggests that beliefs remained unaltered, but this is qualified when he writes 'I know that in after years ... they revived under new forms', with its implication of initial rejection. This is soon clarified; 'at first, after the abandonment of orthodoxy, I naturally thought nothing in the old religion worth retaining, but this temper did not last long' (p.78). The 'abandonment of orthodoxy' might be read as taking leave of the church (even, being 'abandoned' *by it*), or of the doctrines considered orthodox. These doctrines had already been discovered to be the imperfect though necessary forms describing essential truths, so it cannot be said with any certainty that White suggests giving up the beliefs themselves, rather than relinquishing a commitment to state them only under the acceptable traditional formulae.

Though it has been impossible to ascertain the exact issues at stake during the New College controversy or to identify fully the roles of each of the three accused there is no *prima facie* reason why White's beliefs should have been fundamentally altered by the experience. A rejection of institutional religion can be explained as the natural reaction to a process seen to be lacking in natural justice, but insofar as his sense of a personally liberating spiritual awakening lay behind the crisis, a *reinforcement* of those subjective beliefs might rather be predicted.[40]

Evidence from the *Autobiography* suggests that at Cheshunt White accommodated his *Lyrical Ballads* renewal within the traditional language of Christian doctrine, in line with his earlier acknowledgement that reading Wordsworth did not make alienation inevitable.[41] The expulsion may be presumed to have removed both the need and the desire to continue to do so. His inner beliefs did not change, but the language in which he had clothed them could now be put aside; in that sense only can 'loss' be spoken of. How they were 'revived under new forms' is not described, but it is significant that in his

---

Tractarian sympathies who died in 1890, was a prolific writer and reviewer with a record of outstanding academic achievement.

[40] Lewis Rambo describes an 'intensification' type of conversion, which fits post-Wordsworth White well, but without the renewed commitment to the faith community with which Rambo aligns it, the expulsion in any case preventing that; *Understanding Religious Conversion* (New Haven, CT: Yale University Press, 1993), p. 13.

[41] If it is acceptable here to apply information from the fiction (pp. 19-21, Ch. II); compare *Early Life*, pp. 61-63.

other writings White often continued to use the language of orthodoxy.[42]

It was not just because of a strong sense of tradition and loyalty to dissenting forbears that he did not find 'the modern Christianity of church or chapel' congenial (p.78). He had little time for attempts to reinterpret faith which made it less demanding - the 'flowery' route to popularity (p.78). His own struggles with (possibly sexual) temptation as a young man reinforced his view that only an absolute 'distinction between right and wrong' was powerful enough for the realities of human life (p.78).[43] Though he explicitly disowned any Christian teaching which crudely linked behaviour to rewards and punishment it appears that old-fashioned religion alone supplied the necessary moral stimulus. There seems little doubt, despite his own interest in social and economic reform, that he feared the distinctive nonconformist witness was compromised by increasing social respectability and political engagement. For this reason too there is nostalgia for 'the Calvinistic Independency of the sixteenth and seventeenth centuries' (p.78) which did not seek approval from outsiders.

In the sense of connection with, and loyalty to, the Dissenting past lies a key distinction between White and the characters created in his later fiction. Their attempts to find meaning within a secular world-view are made without the historic resources and values available to Mark Rutherford and his creator. It is a mistake to assume that their travails are White's, for his deliverance can only come from a meaningful engagement with the past as well as the present. This is clear from the *Early Life*, and equally in the short piece on 'Faith, Unbelief, and Superstition' printed in *Pages from a Journal*:

> a child-like faith in the old creed is no longer possible, but it is equally impossible to surrender it. I refer now not to those who select from it what they think to be in accordance with their reason, and throw overboard the remainder with no remorse, but rather to those who cannot endure to touch with sacrilegious hands the ancient histories and doctrines which have been the depositaries of so much that is eternal, and who dread lest with the destruction of a story something precious should also be destroyed.[44]

He acknowledges with regret that old beliefs have passed from view, fearing 'truths have been lost, or at least have been submerged', but expects 'some day they may be recovered, and in some other form may again become our

---

[42] See references below from letters of the 1890s – the same period as his most 'secular' fiction. This does not preclude a measure of reinterpretation.

[43] Note the link between Wollaston's advanced beliefs and his sexual ethics (writ large in John Chapman's life, from which White recoiled); *Autobiography*, p. 123, Ch. IX. In *Clara Hopgood*, Frank Palmer, seducer of Madge Hopgood, is described as broad church.

[44] *Pages*, pp. 83-86 (p. 86). Unfortunately this piece cannot be dated.

religion'.[45] He does *not* say that these beliefs, in their essential nature, are lost to him. On this reading White may be seen as the faithful believer in a faithless age, rather than a doubter.

The *Early Life* material can be put in context by a consideration of the information on faith available from other sources. White's pilgrimage is demonstrated in repeated serious engagement with matters of faith, a persistent seeking of understanding, and dissatisfaction with easy answers. The years from birth to early adulthood, 1831-1852, have been described above. This time saw the acceptance (in 'unthinking', age-appropriate manner), renewal (through Wordsworth's influence) and testing (during the college years) of the Christian beliefs inherited from family and the faith tradition. The clash at New College did not completely quench faith, but severely disrupted the sense of belonging necessary to its development.

The period of maturity, from 1853-1891, shows a further gradual withdrawal from even informal groupings like those around Morris (who left London for Wales in 1856), Binney, and Maurice. The exercise of pulpit ministry, marked above all by the commitment at Ditchling, also ended after about 1857. These changes need not necessarily be attributed to altered beliefs, but probably reflect the growing pressure of other responsibilities. He had married in 1856, and a first child was born the following year. In addition to his clerkship in the Registrar General's Office at Somerset House he took on the post of Registrar for Births and Deaths in the Marylebone district. Maclean links this with ceasing to preach at Ditchling, and it is possible that Hale had to be available in town for the weekends in connection with local registration.[46] If his congregations were as unresponsive as those in the fiction this discouragement must also be taken into account. Advancement to the Admiralty in early 1859 meant extra work pressures. His translation of Spinoza extended into the 1860s, a decade which also saw significant journalistic commitments. To some extent this secular 'pulpit' effectively replaced preaching. Somehow he still found time for other writing too, with further novels and many shorter pierces being produced. These were practical reasons which limited other involvement, in due course exacerbated by his wife's illness and the additional burden then placed upon him. Nonetheless the late 1850s saw him exercising a preaching ministry and participating in a very incarnational theology.

Indications from the novels that he did not simply give up all attempts at

---

[45] *Pages*, p. 86.

[46] Maclean, p. 149; Ditchling had been a fixed appointment in any case, but perhaps White did not seek a renewal. Stone notes from Mrs White's diaries Hale preaching as late as 1860, but misinterprets these (partly because he discounts the existence of an historical equivalent to the Drury Lane room) as references to Caleb Morris's chapel, whereas they are to White's own Portland Street scheme (pp. 45-46). It is probable that White preached nowhere else in these years.

publicly fulfilling a Christian calling come in their descriptions of ministry at Ditchling and of the Drury Lane project. These have been considered in previous studies but in respect of both misconceptions have arisen that have been too often repeated. For Ditchling it is the impression commonly given that the Unitarianism loosely represented there stands as a half-way-house while faith ebbs away which needs to be questioned. In the case of Drury Lane parallels with real and fictional religiously inspired work amongst the urban poor have been taken to show that practical service was commonly undertaken following the disintegration of orthodox belief, exemplified by those abandoning a formal vocation. When the events are properly contextualised neither set of assumptions can be upheld and different conclusions may be drawn.

Ditchling and Unitarianism

The Meeting at Ditchling operated under a trust deed which laid down no doctrinal test for members.[47] Associated with the General Baptists in mid-century, the 1851 Religious Census return was made in the name of the 'Unitarian General Baptist Chapel, Ditchling', but the extent to which the congregation represented principled doctrinal Unitarianism as opposed to accepting a breadth of opinions is impossible to determine.[48] Many chapels would for one reason or another have been closed to White after his expulsion, so the Ditchling appointment cannot be said to represent a deliberate theological choice on his part as against a readiness to serve where an opening occurred. He occupied the pulpit regularly during 1855-56, with at least occasional preaching into 1857.[49]

George MacDonald gives further evidence of the potential appeal of Unitarian hospitality to those who had no obvious intention to embrace Unitarian theology *tout court*.[50] In his case the freedom which the absence of a religious test gave allowed, he felt, a more authentic view of Jesus. Like White in maturity he preached among Unitarians, having once considered a greater commitment, but been inhibited by his *fiancée's* serious reservations.[51] Too

---

[47] 'An Open Trust: Note on the Ditchling Trust Deed', unattributed article in *Transactions of the Unitarian Historical Society*, 1 (1916-18), 23-24.

[48] Returns edited by J. A. Vickers, *The Religious Census of Sussex, 1851* (Lewes: Sussex Record Society, 1989), p. 76, showing 140 free seats and 60 others; compare *Autobiography*, p. 93, Ch. VII, 'a plain-looking building designed to hold about two hundred people'.

[49] Rutherford was 'with my Unitarian congregation for about a twelvemonth', *Autobiography*, p. 104, Ch. VIII.

[50] There was in any case no common standard which might constitute such a theology.

[51] Already expressed before they were married, after he had written in 1849 of his sympathy for Unitarianism. She felt the work of Christ depended upon his full deity,

Note continues on following page

much should not be read into this. At the date in question (1849) his openness towards Unitarianism surely reflected anxiety that no invitation to a charge had yet been forthcoming from within Congregationalism. His time at college was coming to an end and both marriage and future ministry depended upon securing a post. A sense of greater liberty might however be a powerful draw for others moving *from* the Independent ministry, as Hale White's cousin William Chignell did on taking the pulpit of George's Meeting in Exeter. He wanted a church where there would be no 'little framework of theological points; and, if you cannot fit your mind to it; if the bed is not long enough to stretch yourself upon it', resignation was the only option.[52] Differences should not be exaggerated, for some contemporary themes found expression across the traditions. A stress upon the fatherhood of God for example, so important to MacDonald, was naturally fundamental to Unitarianism. This point of connection could also play a part in enabling movement *away* from Unitarianism, as in F. D. Maurice's journey to ordination in the Church of England.[53]

Men like Chignell were making a statement about legitimate freedom of expression in the ministry rather than advertising a change in their views. MacDonald was sure that in any case doctrinal conformity did not ensure faithful belief. It was a wish to redress the balance against accounts of Christ causing him to appear barely human by falsely promoting his deity which made the Scot unable simply to reject all Unitarianism as unorthodox:

> The first thing is to know Jesus as a man, and any theory about him that makes less of him as a man - with the foolish notion of exalting his divinity - I refuse at once. Far rather would I be such a Unitarian as Dr Channing than such a Christian as by far the greater number of those, that talk about his Divinity, are. The former truly believes in Christ - believes in him far more than the so-called orthodox.[54]

One implication might be that each generation must discover the divine nature of Jesus for themselves (the truths 'have to be fresh expounded every age' he goes on to say), rather than accept an inherited 'orthodoxy'.

Unitarian churches and ministers themselves covered a broad spectrum of belief, and it must not be assumed that there was a universal sympathy with everything regarded as religiously liberal. Even from the days of the Salters'

---

guaranteed by Trinitarian belief. Letter reproduced in part in Hein, *Victorian Mythmaker*, p. 54.

[52] From Chignell's welcome address at Exeter, reported in the *Devon Weekly Times* of 25 April 1862; cutting preserved in MS. Chignell 2, Harris Manchester College.

[53] As shown by David Young in *F. D. Maurice and Unitarianism* (Oxford: Clarendon Press, 1992); see especially chapter seven, 'God the Father'.

[54] From the letter of 20 May 1853 already cited, in Sadler, *An Expression of Character*, p. 60. Channing stressed the loving nature of God.

Hall controversy (1719) there were those who declared themselves Trinitarian while declining to subscribe to credal statements affirming this, on the basis that to do so undermined the sufficiency of scripture.[55] By the nineteenth century 'Unitarian' views on the person of Christ ranged from near orthodoxy to semi-Arian belief in his subordinate divinity or simply to acclaiming him as the perfected example of humanity. They did not speak with one voice, and could be found defending traditional 'orthodox' positions. Timothy Larsen shows how significantly Unitarians were represented among the early opponents of D. F. Strauss in England, even before Eliot's famous translation had been published.[56] It is evidently hazardous to argue from an association with Unitarianism to a necessary liberalism in any particular areas of Christian belief or practice.

Avowed Christians of whatever stripe might believe less or more than any formally declared doctrines. The background to nineteenth-century religious allegiance is clearly complex, with different traditions overlapping at their boundaries as well as wide variations within each. It is not intended to claim here that White became (or remained) an orthodox Christian believer, a task for which the sources are in any case inadequate, but to trace some essential continuities with the tradition into which he was born, and demonstrate that he represents a sincere attempt to present faith without a dogmatic overlay. This is White the seeker and Reformer. There are beliefs on which he is almost entirely silent - the Trinity is one instance - but this is of uncertain significance, especially given the documented history of resistance to extra-scriptural credal language within Congregationalism (and elsewhere).[57] In later life he rejected the possibility of a comprehensive dogmatics. 'Theology and metaphysics as *systems* must be failures', since this 'demands a position from which complete, systematic survey is possible', whereas the best that can be hoped for is to map 'a number of points here and there which might not appear to have any connexion with one another'.[58] He had no need to cover all areas of doctrine (avoiding some while in ministry, and later having no occasion to refer to them), and some supposedly more orthodox figures might be found to mention no broader a range. Another reason for him to be suspicious of systematic

---

[55] Described by Alan Sell in *Dissenting Thought and the Life of the Churches: Studies in an English Tradition* (San Francisco, CA: Mellen Research University Press, 1990), pp. 75, 137-138.

[56] See 'Biblical Criticism and the Crisis of Belief: D.F. Strauss's *Leben Jesu* in Britain', in *Contested Christianity*, pp. 43-58 (p. 44). Ironically that translator had her own connection in Unitarian circles.

[57] Perhaps a reaction against accounts which claimed to uncover the internal relationships within the Godhead, a kind of speculation always anathema to him. Compare F. J. Powicke's criticism of David Simon on these grounds and preference for F. D. Maurice, noted in Sell, *Hinterland Theology*, p. 281.

[58] A fragment in 'Notes', *Last Pages*, pp. 269-270 (original italics).

theology was the credibility it gave to the false idea that how *much* one believes is important, rather than the 'depth to which it is felt'.[59] Both these references are to material reprinted by Dorothy from Hale's manuscript notebook, which often shows a concern for matters of faith and belief, the record of long engagement with such issues. This is evidence itself that White remained a believer who did not give up the 'faith ... [which] is not to be preserved without a struggle'.[60] His status as an exile has led to conclusions about the nature of his belief which really arise from his lack of formal participation.

On these doctrinal questions it is particularly misleading to treat White in isolation from the wider background. The intellectual trends to which he was exposed made themselves felt within the churches, sometimes welcomed, often not. They were well represented within Independency. The Leicester Conference on Religious Communion of 1877 organised to coincide with the Congregational Union autumn meeting that year had the explicit purpose of defending the principle of a spiritual communion which tolerated a very wide breadth of theological views. The participation of some who appeared close to Unitarianism and others verging on pantheism caused an extensive controversy, though many supported its aims, if not the extreme position of some leading exponents of the ideal.[61]

David Simon of Spring Hill expressed his concern at the time. He returned to the subject in 1891, speaking of his worry that insufficiently rigorous philosophical training and shallow theology had weakened the church, leaving only 'the two foci of the Fatherhood of God and the Living personality of Christ'.[62] This description fits men like MacDonald, but there were plenty of other like-minded believers nearer to home. A retreat to the subjective and an emphasis upon personal experience rather than doctrine was common. White's views would not have been abnormal alongside the range of beliefs found by others to be compatible with church membership. Nor was his approach to faith unusual in being severely practical - its applicability to everyday life - rather than theoretical or metaphysical. He could have been thinking of himself when he wrote how 'very indefinite' was much of the religion represented in Wordsworth's verse; but 'because this religion is indefinite it is not therefore the less supporting'.[63] Over-definition is always to be resisted; 'it is a common

---

[59] Actually a critique of *all* dogma; 'Notes, *Last Pages*, p. 318. Depth of feeling as a test would of course have alarmed the more keenly orthodox of his contemporaries. There may be an echo of Schleiermacher here.

[60] From the same source, 'Notes', *Last Pages*, p. 302.

[61] The most reliable account of the meeting and its aftermath is given by Mark Hopkins in *Nonconformity's Romantic Generation*, chapter four.

[62] In an address to the International Congregational Council, cited in Sell with more detail, *Hinterland Theology*, pp. 270-273 (p. 271).

[63] 'Extracts from a Diary on the Quantocks', in *More Pages*, pp. 186-204 (pp. 196-197).

mistake to demand a definition of that which can have none'.[64] This is recognition that 'a perfectly consistent, unassailable creed, in which conclusion follows from premiss [*sic*] in unimpeachable order, is impossible'.[65]

Simon, born in 1830, was an almost exact contemporary of White, and his address to the 1891 International Congregational Council can be taken as a useful summary of theological trends in Congregationalism from mid-century. The background was marked by withdrawal from the strict Calvinism of an earlier era and a growing hostility to systematic theology, making it clear beyond question that there was nothing unusual about White's views in the 1850s, and that (no matter how ill-defined) in the following years they were also within the spectrum of opinion expressed by church members and ministers. Simon himself was a formidable thinker who had studied for several years in Germany and brought new rigor to theological education. The son of a minister, he endured considerable stresses during his spiritual development, not only when a student but also into his early teaching career.[66] This made him an exceptionally understanding guide to his own students, who he trained to think for themselves. This gave him and them something of a reputation for unorthodoxy, but those who knew him well did not doubt his fundamental soundness. Guinness Rogers considered him 'thoroughly evangelical', a man who 'has gone through serious sifting himself and has come right', and he was equally highly thought of by R. W. Dale.[67]

Though impatient of dogmatism he did not set out to overturn orthodox beliefs, instead critically examining the relationships between doctrines. For example, while agreeing that the scriptures were inspired he held that this belief could only flow from faith and not be a basis *for* faith.[68] This inversion means that apologetics cannot proceed from such claims to authority. One assumes that he would have agreed with George MacDonald that miracles have meaning only from the perspective of faith and cannot persuade unbelievers.[69] He saw

[64] 'Notes', in *More Pages*, p. 222.

[65] *Revolution*, p. 85, Ch. VI; an aside on Pauline Caillaud's 'lamentable inconsistencies' in belief. White's interest in Spinoza seems by this definition to be the pursuit of an impossible order.

[66] His private diary from his student years at Lancashire College reveals struggles against sin and the search for stronger faith, while his daughter testified that even the early days as Principal of Spring Hill were similarly marked, though he later found 'firm ground'. Both recorded by his ex-student Frederick Powicke in *David Worthington Simon*, pp. 21-31 and p. 309 (describing the 'firm ground').

[67] Writing to reassure the committee of Edinburgh Congregational Theological Hall when Simon was being considered for the Principalship there in 1883; cited by Powicke, *David Worthington Simon*, p. 140.

[68] Sell conveniently sets out his position; *Hinterland Theology*, pp. 261-262.

[69] Dale Johnson describes how Simon revolutionised teaching at Spring Hill by this new approach to natural theology; 'The End of the "Evidences": A Study in Nonconformist

Note continues on following page

the need to differentiate between 'the facts to be believed ... and the interpretation which may be put upon them', an analysis congruent with White's Carlylean distinction between underlying ideas and the 'clothes' in which they are presented.[70] It was partly for this reason that he was taken to be theologically liberal as a younger man but conservative in maturity, and here too there is an instructive parallel with White. Simon had found his way to some core beliefs (especially relating to redemption and the incarnation) which then controlled his interpretation of the other historic Christian doctrines. In his teaching he encouraged others to wrestle with the implication of their own faith, rather than imparting to them what he believed. This could be perceived as dangerously liberal, and the risk was that students taught on his principles who never attained the sort of 'firm ground' on which their teacher stood might lose touch with anything distinctively Christian. Hence his anxiety at the Leicester Conference and subsequently that neglect of serious theological study coupled with an emphasis upon experience and the subjective might undermine the gospel itself. This then gave him the status of a conservative figure, as he ruefully noted; once 'best maligned ... for heterodoxy: now I am becoming the best maligned for orthodoxy'.[71]

Simon's value for understanding White's context derives from his unpartisan status. He spoke of a 'widespread distaste' in the church for serious theology, especially in the pulpit, where ministers 'earn cheap applause by denouncing dogma and contrasting it with life'.[72] In this atmosphere even gifted ministerial students adopted the prevailing tone. Not all doctrinal questions were ignored, and he identified biblical inspiration, the atonement, and future punishment as still of enduring interest. He dated the movement away from systematic theology to the 1850s and the decay of the Puritan heritage. The moderate Calvinism which emerged had itself by the time of writing been subject to 'a process of disintegration, in the course of which some doctrines have been dropped, others modified, others transmuted'.[73] He gives examples of the confusion which has arisen; on biblical inspiration everything is 'at sixes and sevens'; on the doctrine of God qualities such as infinity and transcendence are subordinate to those which bring God near to man, especially Divine Fatherhood, and in Christology the humanity of Jesus in emphasized over a

---

Theological Transition', *Journal of the United Reformed Church History Society*, 2 (1979), 62-72; see further on Simon in Mark Johnson's *The Dissolution of Dissent, 1850-1918* (New York: Garland Publishing, 1987), pp. 137-143, also making clear how dangerously exposed he (and his students) became to charges of unorthodoxy.

[70] This is Powicke's assessment of Simon; *David Worthington Simon*, p. 221.

[71] His summary in a letter of 1897 after a controversial lecture on the decline in Congregational theology; Powicke, *David Worthington Simon*, p. 222.

[72] Report of *The International Congregational Council: London 1891. Authorised Record of Proceedings* (London: James Clarke, 1891), p. 77 (col. 2).

[73] *International Congregational Council*, p. 78 (cols. 1 and 2).

previous stress on divinity. The Holy Spirit is largely ignored and 'the personal Trinity seems to have been practically dropped'.[74] In short the 'heresies' of yesteryear have become acceptable:

> those of us who remember the "Rivulet" and "Divine Fatherhood" controversies; ... the outcry about German theology and the New Lights, or Morisonians; the professorial difficulties in the New and Lancashire Colleges; and the student expulsions in London and Glasgow; not to mention the Leicester Conference; ... will scarcely hesitate to apply the word revolution to the change that has come about.[75]

It would be misrepresenting Simon to fail to say that he welcomed many of these changes, not as surpassing earlier beliefs, but insofar as they represented 'the beginning of the end, among ourselves, of a struggle with one of the most grievous perversions of Christianity ... the transformation of the Gospel into a body of truths supernaturally revealed; with its correlate notion, that salvation hangs on the holding for true of certain saving doctrines'.[76] This vindicates Independency's suspicion of man-made creeds and also justifies opposition to ideas or structures which support and enforce them, denounced as 'the ecclesiasticism, sacramentarianism, and priestism which more than anything else hinder the progress of the kingdom of God'.[77] There should be no tests or coercion in religion, for what matters is personal faith in Christ. All true theology follows from this, as understanding is sought for the faith which already exists.

Against this background White was hardly remarkable in his beliefs or attitudes, and indeed might be portrayed as on the advanced wing in the 1850s and yet in later years out of sympathy with liberalism as a creed. He was affected by the intellectual climate but not simply the creature of it, owing a good deal to his own experience. In these circumstances labelling him as liberal or conservative would be inappropriate. He had no interest in making belief easy or palatable, so his later unfavourable comparison of contemporary faith with Puritanism is hardly a surprise.[78] Nonetheless the New College event was

---

[74] *International Congregational Council*, pp. 78 (col. 2) and 79 (col. 1).

[75] *International Congregational Council*, p. 79 (cols. 1 and 2). Simon had studied under Samuel Davison at Lancashire College and regretted his being forced out for endorsing higher criticism; the Glasgow Congregational College had in 1844 expelled students believed to be unsound on the question of conversion.

[76] *International Congregational Council*, p. 79, col. 2. It is clear that Simon would have made a stimulating dialogue partner for Hale White.

[77] *International Congregational Council*, p. 80 (col. 1).

[78] 'I sympathized more with the Calvinistic Independency of the sixteenth and seventeenth centuries than with the modern Christianity of church or chapel', *Early Life*,

Note continues on following page

a severe shock from which it took time to recover and his is not a story of steady progress. That it was one of growth rather than decay is indicated by his assessment in the *Early Life*, as it had previously been demonstrated though his preaching ministry, and by the practical service he undertook and went on to describe in the *Deliverance*.

Faith in Action - Drury Lane

Even many friends were unaware of this aspect of White's applied belief. It has often been assumed that the experiment in practical Christian action among the poor portrayed in his second novel has no equivalent in life, and there is some confusion on this point in the secondary literature.[79] In fact White had been active in the opening of a room for such a purpose, though the project was of relatively short duration, spanning perhaps two years, 1859-1860. Space was found in the building shared by his brother-in-law John Arthur's business, in Little Portland Street.[80] This area of London had notorious problems of overcrowding, poor housing and sanitation. White's descriptions of 'a most foul stench' and 'a blast of corruption, made up of gases bred by filth, air breathed and rebreathed a hundred times, charged with odours of unnameable personal uncleanness and disease' which issued from the lived-in cellars combines his sense of horror with the Victorian miasmic theory of infection.[81]

The work included spiritual encouragement and practical support, and the parallel with other fictional examples is important. Such missions are associated in several novels with ministers who because of a failure in belief leave a clerical vocation, instead proving themselves through the Christ-like practical service of their fellow men. Robert Elsmere is the most famous of such examples, Stephen Remarx another.[82] It found slightly different expression in Eliza Linton's *The True History of Joshua Davidson* (1872), which White had read. This might suggest that White's social involvement is indirect proof of his loss of orthodox faith. However this goes beyond the

---

p. 78. Here 'Christianity' surely includes the negative connotations of an apostate or Erastian 'Christendom'.

[79] *Deliverance*, Ch. II. See the survey in chapter two above for different understandings of Drury Lane.

[80] Information from Maclean, p. 155. Presumably John Arthur supported the mission in some way.

[81] *Deliverance*, pp. 24-25, Ch. II. The dead made their contribution; among other reformers, Dr George Walker campaigned against overcrowded burial grounds which caused injurious emanations around Drury Lane, and in many other part of the metropolis, initially in his *Gatherings from Grave-yards: Particularly those of London, etc.* (London: Longman, 1839).

[82] J. G. Adderley, *Stephen Remarx: The Story of a Venture in Ethics* (London: Edward Arnold, 1893).

evidence and overlooks contrary examples. The late-Victorian settlements founded in London by the universities and major public schools for work among the distressed poor were associated with strongly religious motivation (mainly Anglican in these instances), demonstrating that practical action did not necessarily arise from weakening faith.[83] The study by Ian Shaw of activism by definitely orthodox Calvinist nonconformists further shows it is not safe to infer that social concern was the handmaiden of doubt.[84] Blackfriars church in Aberdeen offers a Scottish example from George MacDonald's experience in which doctrinal strictness and a commitment to good causes were combined.

Other evidence adduced confirms that in White's case too the connection is not doubt and activism, but a long-term concern for a faith which made a practical difference in all areas of life. The Drury Lane concept is one of personal service aimed at the liberation of those in need. In this way he explored his Christian vocation, as one put beyond the church by his own expulsion, to those for whom 'I do not think that church or chapel would have done ... much good'.[85] The religious discourse of institutional Christianity was set too far from their experience of life, and they required practical help in the face of overwhelming problems. It met a need in White too; 'I felt as if somehow, after many errors, I had once more gained a road, a religion in fact'.[86] The experiment had the benefit of turning the helpers away from a narrow concern with their own 'salvation' (however conceived), always presented by White as a temptation to be avoided.

References outside the novels are found in the diary kept by White's mother, though this is a disappointingly brief record, with no description of the work the room supported.[87] With her husband she 'went to Portland St, heard dear Hale' on 13 and 27 February 1859, 13 March 1859, 16 October 1859, but then not again until 1 April 1860, against which entry Sir William notes that the diary records his mother was often unwell, preventing more regular attendance. Some diaries are missing (or never kept) but the timings indicated agree overall with the 'two years or thereabouts' for which the fictional mission endures.[88] A fuller account of the meetings would have been invaluable, but even these brief

---

[83] The movement is documented in Nigel Scotland's *Squires in the Slums: Settlements and Missions in Late-Victorian London* (London: I.B. Tauris, 2007); note however that Mary Ward's University Hall *was* the expression of a distinctly liberal theology (pp. 175-195).

[84] See *High Calvinists in Action: Calvinism and the City; Manchester and London, c.1810*-1860 (Oxford: Oxford University Press, 2002).

[85] *Deliverance*, p. 82, Ch. VI.

[86] *Deliverance*, p. 84, Ch. VI.

[87] They are engagement diaries rather than journals, with very little space for each day. Originals at the University of British Columbia (7-1 to 7-4), with typescript extracts by Sir William Hale-White at Bedford.

[88] *Deliverance*, p. 64, Ch. V.

mentions, and the very fact of his parents' visits, suggest a recognisable church-like meeting. In the *Deliverance* the essence of M'Kay's purpose was 'to teach Christ in the proper sense of the word'; to become like Him, indwelt as was St Paul.[89] The parallel with St Paul suggests that Christ is taken as more than an example of supreme humanity. In a Christ-like spirit M'Kay would not only give talks, but hoped 'to gain admittance for himself and his friends into the houses of the poor and do some practical good'.[90]

The justification for this hard and often unrewarding work, the 'Drury Lane theology', is explained by Mark Rutherford, and may accurately represent the Portland Street ethos. First, to provide a sanctuary with 'peace and room for reflection', encouraged by reading or listening to the simple talks given, and secondly by such instruction to 'create in our hearers contentment with their lot, and even some joy in it'.[91] The essential message was a somewhat attenuated or reinterpreted Christianity, emphasizing the 'not new but old … religion … of the Reconciliation … of man with God', 'differing from the current creed in so far as I did not lay stress upon sin as the cause of estrangement, but yet agreeing with it in making it my duty of duties to suppress revolt, and to submit calmly and sometimes cheerfully to the Creator'.[92] This was religion pared down to what lay within the reach of the desperate hearers, offered in the knowledge that for them teaching on 'the fallacies of Arianism', or 'the personality of the Holy Ghost' would not have spoken to their need.[93] This is completely in accord with White's conviction that any religion which does not help in daily life is simply worthless. Traditional language is reinvigorated but not wholly overwritten, for the aim is always to bring out the essential meaning. The fictional experiment was short-lived, as it appears was the Portland Street mission, which ended sometime in 1860. While the fiction would suggest disenchantment as the cause, the year corresponds with White's transfer to the Admiralty (which soon brought extra responsibilities and the need to travel to dockyards), and increasing family responsibilities. It cannot be shown to be due to any change in religious convictions, and in many shorter writings he continued to address questions of belief.

Several further areas, treated separately to avoid imposing a false coherence, provide information about White's beliefs during the adult years generally, but assessing their significance (partly due to uncertainty over dating) is not always easy. In some cases meanings are elusive but it may at least be possible to guard against misinterpretations tempting to the unwary.

---

[89] *Deliverance*, p. 28, Ch. II.
[90] *Deliverance*, p. 29, Ch. II.
[91] *Deliverance*, p. 83, Ch. VI.
[92] *Deliverance*, p. 84, Ch. VI. White is writing of curbing personal 'revolt', while surely betraying his anxiety about the risk of wider social upheaval.
[93] *Deliverance*, p. 82, Ch. VI.

The Religion of the Letters

One window into Hale's life was provided by Dorothy's publication of selections of his *Letters to Three Friends* covering the years 1872 to 1913. In private correspondence his language is very traditional, especially with those who shared a similar background. 'Dissimilarity of previous history is a bar to close intercourse. ... although many of us may more or less widely have separated ourselves from the Christianity *of the day*, Christianity in a way is in our very blood and all our thoughts are coloured by it'.[94] It is always possible to sense the sacredness which for him surrounded talk of the Bible and key elements of belief. This could be experienced, even if it could not be defined. These writings point to an instinctive and never abandoned faith. The often negative self-consciousness of White's fiction, reflected also in the *Early Life*, is balanced by the informality and variety of the letters, which can be supplemented by reference to some still unpublished.[95]

Of the family letters which survive, few have significant references to faith, though the exceptions are telling, especially an early example to his father. This was sent in May 1853, when Hale was working for John Chapman's radical *Westminster Review*. Already cited above, it bears repeating for what it says about his high view of the Bible and dislike of negative criticism:

> Granted that all that the Strausses, Foxtons, and Newmans have made out is correct - that there is no miracle, that Palestine's laws of nature were really England's, and so on, yet I turn round on them and say "You cannot deceive my eyes". Here are words in these gospels in black and white, and such words I maintain were never spoken before. [96]

He goes on to mention 'the writer's *soul* ... there', and the direct impact upon the reader of the spiritual experiences described. The Jesus of the gospels, he seems to be saying, cannot be destroyed by the theories of Strauss or Francis Newman, for the reader encounters a distinctly human figure, released from dogmatic interpretation ('no clothed, disguised man'), and immediately available ('blood beating and the touch of warm flesh').[97] The 'granted' is perhaps to be taken as a sign of reservation, an agreement for the sake of

---

[94] Writing to Miss Partridge about his (Greek) acquaintance Mrs Dannreuther 26 October 1893, *Letters to Three Friends*, p. 146; emphasis added – an indirect claim to uphold 'true' Christianity?

[95] White often asked correspondents to destroy his letters, and many must be assumed to have been lost in this way.

[96] Original italics. Quoted in Stone, p. 52 (does Stone assume White is writing of entering the experience of the human writers, rather than encountering Jesus?).

[97] Stress on the humanity of Christ naturally does not preclude the idea of a unique openness to the Divine, or a growing revelation of his divinity.

argument rather than acceptance those premises, which even if true cannot touch the personal heart of faith.

Robertson Nicoll recalled that 'of Christ he [White] never speaks save with the sincerest reverence and love'.[98] This veneration was not marked by the use of a specific vocabulary. Ian Sellers finds beliefs about Jesus expressed in designations such as 'the Christ Hero, Captain of Souls, Elder Brother, Comrade, Guide' which were increasingly used in mid-1850s Dissent, but White does not seem to share this popular trend.[99] Titles mattered less than substance, and part of the attraction of Caleb Morris's inspiring preaching was his ability to present a very human Christ without denying traditional beliefs or appearing reductionist. Mystical union with this figure was the highest attainment of the Christian life. In so far as White had imbibed philosophical views from Spinoza and others which tended towards panentheism he would in any case have found it difficult to articulate a Christology which focussed on ontological difference. He shows no interest in metaphysical speculation.

Much later letters show the continuing importance of the Bible, which he read almost daily. In 1898 he reports using Kautsch's translation of the Old Testament (notes in German on the Hebrew text) to aid his study, by which an earlier knowledge of the text was renewed and his soul 'quickened'.[100] He at one time followed a 'triennial passage through the Bible'.[101] More than once he writes of 'having been brought up on the Bible', and therefore of what is 'in my blood and can never by any chemistry be extracted'.[102] This means that later readings are made more precious by the power of 'association', a word which recurs in White's letters.[103] The thrust of these occasional references tends to be the same; the importance of the Bible, the value of an experiential religion which must not be confused with dogma or external rules, and again and again the recognition that for him ultimate truth must be related to his Christian heritage. Others may despair at the follies and failures of 'Christianity' (often a negative term), but 'I cannot' turn from it.[104] His criticism of 'Christianity' has

---

[98] 'Memories of Mark Rutherford', p. 407.

[99] *Nineteenth-Century Nonconformity*, p. 22. George MacDonald however regularly refers to Jesus as 'Elder Brother'.

[100] Letter to Sophia Partridge of 4 April 1898, in *Letters to Three Friends*, p. 176.

[101] Letter to Sophia Partridge of 8 October 1899, in *Letters to Three Friends*, p. 189. He favours the newly published Revised Version (1881-85), and appreciated the marginal notes on disputed points of translation, rather a hobby-horse ('I do not remember that I ever once heard a mistranslation corrected', *Autobiography*, p. 6, Ch. I).

[102] Letter to Sophia Partridge of 31 December 1901, in *Letters to Three Friends*, p. 222 (see also, similarly, to Mrs Colenutt, 1897, p. 86).

[103] Not just in the context of faith; see the report of a visit to the Whitechapel art exhibition in 1905 to view again pictures from his youth, in *Letters to Three Friends*, pp. 244-245.

[104] Letter to Mabel Marsh of 16 July 1901, in *Letters to Three Friends*, p. 212.

misled some into believing that he thereby intended an overthrow of Christian doctrine and practice, rather than its reformation. A major complaint was the churches' failure to speak against the South African war; such 'Christianity' in its embrace of 'the official, symbolic, ecclesiastical Christ' had lost sight of 'the real Galilean of Matthew, Mark, Luke, and John'.[105] There is perhaps an echo of Renan here, whose *Life of Jesus* he had read with interest. Religion is for life, and is not 'an intellectual subtlety'.[106]

There are occasionally more philosophical reflections however, as when (in accordance with what he may have learned indirectly from Schleiermacher, among others) he rejects an antithesis between the natural and supernatural, for one can be found within the other; 'thou in me and I in thee'.[107] White often gives the impression that his true beliefs changed little over time, at any rate after his discovery of Wordsworth, and he declared that in essence his faith was little removed from that of the outwardly more orthodox Dorothy Smith; 'I am much, much closer to it than many people, *not* you, would suppose, and have been all my life', he told Miss Partridge.[108] Of course there were reasons to stress a deep unity between them, but Dorothy's faith did exhibit a mystical spirituality. Christianity and morality are inextricably linked, and White places great stress upon the distinction between right and wrong (eroded in 'modern' thought), for 'Christ dies to save us from the consequences of our ill doing', a surprisingly 'orthodox' view.[109] In this same letter, written just twelve months after publication of the *Autobiography*, there is not a trace of the anguish Mark Rutherford experiences in his encounters with Edward Mardon; Carlyle is praised as 'to the very core a Christian' and 'the inestimable worth of Christianity' celebrated for its moral worth and witness to essential 'divine truths', including 'monotheism'.[110] If White had been describing a personal crisis of catastrophic loss in his first novel it is not apparent here.

Newly Discovered Autograph Letters to the Colenutts

Evidence from this source is not confined to the texts as selected and presented by Dorothy in *Letters to Three Friends.* She edited the holographs, as periodic ellipses show, but without any explicit notice or explanation. A cache of 173 letters to Richard and Sarah Colenutt, including all those (106) represented in

[105] Letter to Mabel Marsh of 26 October 1901, in *Letters to Three Friends*, p. 217.

[106] Letter to Sophia Partridge of 2 December 1902, in *Letters to Three Friends*, p. 231.

[107] Letter to Sophia Partridge of 13 November 1905 (quoting the words of Jesus, Gospel of John 17. 21), in *Letters to Three Friends*, p. 247. See below on White's implied monism here, pp. 303-306.

[108] In a letter of 19 July 1908, explaining the nature of his friendship with Dorothy, in *Letters to Three Friends*, p. 265 (original emphasis).

[109] Letter of 30 April 1882 to Mr Colenutt; *Letters to Three Friends*, p. 7.

[110] *Letters to Three Friends*, pp. 7-8. White always admires hard-fought-for belief.

the book, has recently come to light, revealing the nature and extent of Dorothy's excisions.[111] They also disclose something more of White's private life, and hint at matters they fail to illuminate.

Many cuts were simply the removal of personal references. In some cases this was presumably to spare White's children, particularly Ernest and Willie, who Dorothy knew would be antagonised by her publication of such private material. So Hale's reference to Ernest's first, broken, engagement was omitted, along with the later description of the woman he did marry as 'not one of our set', and wonder at 'why he [Ernest] married her'.[112] However a rather similar but not necessarily derogatory description of Willie's wife as belonging 'to a different world to ours' *was* published.[113] This 'otherness' presumably signals their non-Dissenting backgrounds. Molly, because she continued to live with her father after her brothers left home, naturally featured more often in the original letters. Her periodic illnesses, sometimes amounting to physical and mental prostration, go largely unmentioned in the book selection. Given her father's melancholia, and constant fault-finding with houses and his surrounding, it is not surprising that at times she too became miserable, but Dorothy chose to edit out such episodes. In other cases of names in the autographs but withheld on publication Dorothy may have believed them to be of no interest beyond the family and a small regular circle of friends, or have been unable to identify those mentioned herself.

It could have been her Anglican loyalty which prompted the suppression of passages criticising that church. Similarly, some references to White's continuing sympathy with the tradition of his birth may have been cut for their implied rejection of other churches, despite occasionally more positive comments on the Church of England and even Catholicism.[114] Evidently there

---

[111] They are now in the hands of the Mark Rutherford Society. I am indebted to the Secretary, Nick Wilde, for allowing use of his transcriptions. It is hoped to publish the letters and deposit the originals with the Bedfordshire and Luton Archives and Record Service. The texts can be viewed online at the Mark Rutherford Resource website; <http://www.concentric.net/~djfrench/index.htm> [accessed 10 March 2011]. Numbering given here is to this collection, and not of the abbreviated series in *Letters to Three Friends*.

[112] Letters of August 1898 (no. 103) and 23 October 1904 (no. 143) respectively (edited in *Letters to Three Friends*, pp. 87-88 and 126).

[113] See *Letters to Three Friends*, p. 32, a letter of 28 November 1886. Or did Dorothy *mean* to wound Willie and Edith, who seem to have been the most opposed to her relationship with Hale?

[114] There were negative references to Dissent too however, as in a letter from Hastings (no. 75) of 18 December 1892, describing meeting a Dissenting minister on a visit to Colchester, a 'big, weighty animal'. Clericalism in any form antagonised White; 'I am no friend to priests of any sect', unpublished part of letter of 13 July 1907, no. 165 in sequence (remainder in *Letters to Three Friends*, pp. 139-140).

was no significant dilution of Hale's identification with nonconformity. An intense sense of belonging persisted, and he was troubled by a tendency for the offspring of Dissenters to transfer their allegiance to Anglicanism. Though recognising that children must be allowed to make their own choices he could not disguise his regret. In a wholly unpublished letter of 1907 mentioning Molly's Anglican baptism and confirmation he made his most positive statement of a long-remembered believing participation. 'Children grow up; they will and must take their own course; they do not care for your books, they do not believe in your creed; they go off to church and desert *the worship which was your support and delight*'.[115]

He had not anticipated facing this situation personally. A much earlier letter on the subject (also unpublished) contains just the sort of comment which is so easily misconstrued when approaching White with the preconception that he was a doubter or denier. In congratulating himself (prematurely as it turned out) that his children would not 'revert' (explicitly using this term as 'a Darwinian phrase') he says they all remain, with him it is implied, 'in the church of the d____d'.[116] A casual reading might suppose that White means to place himself and them beyond salvation, when this is surely a scorning of the implicit or explicit *extra ecclesiam nulla salus* claims of Canterbury and Rome. He mocked the Anglican clergy he met in Groombridge as 'a sillier set of creatures' than could be imagined, who regarded their own church as 'the sole catholic communion', and all outside it as 'mere contemptible schismatics'.[117] There was a continued principled objection to priestcraft and any role for the church as gatekeeper to salvation. On the same theme, it was hardly to be expected that Dorothy would print the letter in which White reported offending Maud Chignell by assuming she shared a contempt for the 'respectability' of Anglicanism only to discover that Maud herself had been confirmed.[118]

Mentions of William Chignell are of particular interest for showing a long-standing estrangement between the cousins, but unfortunately without revealing the reason for this. Each heard some news of the other through third parties, but the breach between them remained unhealed. Earlier concern on Hale's part that something in the *Autobiography* would offend William remains a possible cause, but precisely what it might have been is far from clear. Some of Chignell's letters and paper survive, but they shed no light on this subject.[119]

---

[115] Letter of 27 November 1907, no. 167 in the unpublished sequence (emphasis added).

[116] For which read 'damned'; letter of 16 January 1890, wholly unpublished, no. 56 in full sequence.

[117] Letter of 20 February 1904, section omitted from *Letters to Three Friends* text (pp. 122-123), no. 137 in the unpublished sequence.

[118] This was the sort of unattractive tribalism to which White was all too prone. Letter to Mrs Colenutt, no. 56 of the unpublished collection, dated 16 January 1890.

[119] Thomas William Chignell Papers, MSS. Chignell at Harris Manchester College.

There is a slight clue that suggests Hale may have precipitated the split. The unpublished letter in which he described his ill-chosen remarks in front of Maud Chignell closed with a paragraph about his wife's worsening health. He had evidently shared with his cousin something of his distress about her illness which was 'simply ferocious in its slow wasting cruelty', but was nonplussed by the response; 'William wrote to me the other day to tell me that there was no darkness in the world, otherwise God would not be God'.[120] Whatever White's reply it is not difficult to imagine a cooling in the relationship if he felt that William refused to face up to the theological issues raised by human suffering and had contented himself with what was received as a platitude.

These letters demonstrate his life-long concern for faith, and illustrate how context shapes the portrayal of White. To the Colenutts and Sophia Partridge, long-standing friends belonging to the same Dissenting tradition, he writes often of religion, but to Philip Webb, of different upbringing, he does not.[121] If only the letters to Webb had survived they would have suggested a picture quite other than all do together. The Webb correspondence touches on many subjects but architectural themes predominate. This is hardly surprising, for their friendship developed after White sought Webb's professional advice on design and construction, the answer to years of frustration living in, to him, poorly designed and maintained rented accommodation. A correspondence with Ruskin in the pages of the *Daily Telegraph* over the quality of modern housing first introduced White to Webb. This had an incidental significance for Webb's career. The subsequent commission resulted in Park Hill, Carshalton, White's home from 1868 to 1889.[122] This was 'the first of Webb's smaller houses other than the studio-houses to be designed for a client's own use', and Sheila Kirk cites it as a prime example of Webb's willingness to take the user's views fully into account at the design stage.[123] This was White the technically knowledgeable (or at least, opinionated) practical man.

Although most of the letters cited in *Letters to Three Friends* are from later life it is significant that they cover years during which his supposedly more secular novels were being published. Faith continued to be worked out in dialogue with his own tradition, even while his fictional heroines ranged more freely. The letters show a continuity of belief, however hard it is to define.

---

[120] Unpublished letter of 16 January 1890, no. 56 in the sequence. Earlier letters make clear that William had been an irregular correspondent, so there may not have been closeness for some years.

[121] Except to describe Dorothy's religion, see the letter of 22 September 1909, *Letters to Three Friends*, pp. 359-361.

[122] As described by Sheila Kirk, *Philip Webb: Pioneer of Arts and Crafts Architecture* (Chichester: Wiley-Academy, 2005), pp. 212-213 (Park Hill pictured, p. 212).

[123] Kirk, *Philip Webb*, pp. 212-213. Given White's very strong opinions on the subject, agreeing the design must have been a demanding process, perhaps explaining why Webb's pupil C.G. Vinall undertook most of the work (p. 213, note 18; text on p. 317).

They support White's statement in the *Early Life* that faith could not be 'cast away like an old garment' (pp.77-78), but they do not contain as much personal information about his later years as Dorothy White's *Groombridge Diary*. This text will be considered below along with reactions to its appearance.[124] In that context, as elsewhere, there must be sensitivity to the psychology of faith, which needs to be understood as more than mental assent to formal propositions. Where this is not recognised false judgements on White, and on the nature of religious belief, will result.

The Nature of Believing Faith

The evidence reviewed from the *Early Life* and elsewhere shows that White grew up in an atmosphere of apparently unquestioning orthodoxy. He accepted the Calvinist teaching of Bunyan Meeting, and assented to it as far as was possible for one of his years and psychological development. The combination of leaving home and the spiritual enlightenment from reading Wordsworth created the potential for growth (to the next 'stage' in Fowler's terms). The expulsion, which was not simply related to matters of belief, interrupted that process, and dramatically undermined his sense of belonging. The importance of inclusion and approval is hard to exaggerate, and weakening of commitment, for whatever reason, took its toll. James Ritchie praised the piety and simplicity of 'those old Noncons' of East Anglia among whom he was raised, but feared that in promoting early decisions they 'failed to understand childhood and youth'. Their 'children of many prayers' (plainly a stock phrase) too easily fell away because, *inter alia*, 'if you did not see your way to become a church member and a professor of religion you were cut off, or felt inwardly that you were cut off'.[125] One was of the church or of the world, and evidently neither early membership nor profession guaranteed later adherence. Although partially offset by the support of other guides such as Caleb Morris, White was left isolated and prey to self-absorption. He testifies to the continued traditional spiritual disciplines of prayer and Bible reading however, and did not lose a sense of connection with his Dissenting past. Though never a believer who relied upon doctrine or metaphysics, he can fairly claimed to have sought real faith, while resisting exact formulations of it. His unease about credal statements or tests does not mark him out from contemporaries also affected by Romanticism and other tendencies towards subjective affirmation, as documented from the life of David Simon.

The difficulty in defining his faith therefore arises from its very nature, as constituted to a large degree of feeling and experience.[126] Religion, he wrote

---

[124] See chapter eleven.

[125] *Christopher Crayon's Recollections*, p. 58. A memory of the 1820s and 30s.

[126] Part of Schleiermacher's heritage, indirectly transmitted.

was not 'a thing to be taught', but was 'inspired by looks, by tenderness, and by a certain attitude towards great objects'.[127] It was 'not a tangle of metaphysical subtleties nor a nostrum for preserving eternally the salt that keeps our carcases [*sic*] from putrefaction'.[128] Where such an elusive, allusive, non-metaphysical faith is held it is naturally hard precisely to explain. It was intensely personal, but without drawing attention to the self (a weakness he had identified in traditional Calvinism), informed by the type of numinous unity with God implied in his encounter with nature. He seems in some respects to approach the rare sixth stage which Fowler designates 'universalizing faith'.[129] This includes vivid spiritual awareness, and a move away from preoccupation with the self. An experience White reports in old age seems to contain something of this quality; 'I was looking at a great, spreading, bursting oak. ... It seemed to be no longer a tree away from me and apart from me. The enclosing barriers of consciousness were removed and the text came into my mind, *Thou in me and I in thee*. The distinction of self and not-self was an illusion.'[130] The natural world is not the *locus* of an abstract encounter (as pantheism might imply) but a personal one - literally an 'I-Thou' revelation, rather than 'I-It'. White would have been open to such a possibility from his earlier reading of Emerson, for whom the idea of man losing and finding himself in oneness with nature *and* God was a powerful motif. [131]

Only by privileging selected passages from White's fictional writings (and then on one possible reading) can his real and continued engagement with faith be denied. The *Early Life* alone is a powerful corrective, which can be corroborated from other material. His case illustrates the difficulty faced by the use of traditional Christian language where there is a suspicion that it is being reinterpreted. In several places he addresses just this question, through Mark Rutherford's experience, and in the ethics of subscription by which Anglican clergy were required to signal doctrinal assent on admission to orders (and affirm key doctrines in creeds during services). Independent churches did not historically require detailed consent, indeed resisted such tests, and this

---

[127] From a letter to Sophia Partridge, 10 April 1901, in *Letters to Three Friends*, p. 209; compare *Early Life*, p. 12 on the 'cakes, gingerbread, and kisses' of White's Colchester aunt.

[128] To Sophia Partridge again, 16 July 1901, *Letters to Three Friends*, p. 212.

[129] *Stages of Faith*, pp. 199-213; there are also possible links with the 'second *naiveté*' of the preceding stage, see pp. 197-198. The content of faith seems less important here.

[130] From the undated piece, ca. 1890s, 'An Epoch', printed in *More Pages*, original italics, pp. 181-183 (p. 182), apparently citing John 17. 21 (compare reference in letter to Miss Partridge, *Letters to Three Friends*, p. 247). See below for an analysis of this experience, pp. 303-306.

[131] Roger Ebbatson stresses the importance of Emerson, along with Carlyle, Goethe, Spinoza and others; *Lawrence and the Nature Tradition*, especially pp. 165-175, though exaggerating the influence of Spinoza.

doubtless shaped White's views.

In the *Autobiography* the dilemma is posed in respect of preaching, as Mark fills with new meaning doctrines which he knows his hearers interpret differently; 'it was not true, when I, understanding what I understood by it, taught it to men who professed to believe in the Westminster Confession'.[132] This must be interpreted in context, for White illustrates the preacher's dilemma with reference to the story of Balaam; like him Rutherford is in fact speaking the word of the Lord, not 'smooth things for Balak'.[133] He criticised those who may mislead by mental reservation or subtlety, in 1897 privately condemning Benjamin Jowett for his willingness to sign the Thirty-Nine Articles after his orthodoxy had been questioned.[134] White, by contrast, had refused to compromise at New College, and suffered for it. But at the same time he is aware that there is no simple 'this is that' correspondence between such language and what it seeks to represent. White is stranded between a Calvinist tradition which had pushed the inscrutable God and His eternal decrees beyond the knowable and the subjective emphasis imbibed though Romanticism and liberal Protestantism which stressed experience. In a changing intellectual context, and affected by shifting views of conversion and nurture, White was, like Mark Rutherford, a 'victim of the century' as well as victor in the long battle for faith.[135]

The Content of Believing Faith

White's reaching after meaning is based on a unified theory of truth which helps to hold together these examples collected from a disparate range of writings. Alongside the insistence that beliefs must be personally appropriated is the idea of the universal meaning to which traditional doctrinal language points. His writings on the atonement, like the sermon on this theme reported in the *Autobiography*, show this concern. In his preaching, alongside the phrases conventionally employed, Mark Rutherford locates the atonement in the 'scheme of the world', by which the innocent constantly suffer for the wicked, such that the atonement is 'the exemplification, rather than a contradiction, of

---

[132] *Autobiography*, p. 41, Ch. IV; note the force of the word *professed.*

[133] *Autobiography*, p. 42, Ch. IV; a reminder that Rutherford (and White) seeks to be faithful to the message he must deliver. The implied prophetic task marks out Rutherford – and White – elsewhere as called to denounce false religion, showing how the insider may have a special role speaking from outside the religious establishment.

[134] Letter to Sophia Partridge, September 1897, *Letters to Three Friends*, pp. 159-164, also a similar reference from October 1907, pp. 257-258. White never had much time for Oxford men. Peter Hinchliff presents Jowett's dilemma sympathetically in *Benjamin Jowett and the Christian Religion* (Oxford: Clarendon Press, 1987), pp. 43-44, 63-64.

[135] His description of Mark Rutherford in a letter to George Holyoake of 20 January 1882 (BPL, MR 6/13).

Nature herself, as we know her in our own experience'.[136] In doing so it chimes with the lessons on human experience. Calvinism itself is vindicated by its correspondence with the facts of life, for it could not have endured if this had not proved to be the case.[137] If the *Autobiography* can be taken here to accurately reflect White's mature view (that is, of the 1880s and not the 1850s the setting suggests), it is helpful in determining how his thinking developed. The believer must penetrate the symbolism of traditional language to reach the experience which gave it birth, in contradistinction to the prevailing college view, in which the 'essence of our orthodoxy [which] was not this or that dogma, but the acceptance of dogmas as communication from without, and not as born from within'.[138] This is recognisably an issue in the debate about biblical inspiration.

A casual reading, especially if conditioned by prior acceptance of White as losing faith, is likely to conclude that this 'religious' faith is a human invention, and that the universality argued for undermines any concept of Christian truth. But all truths must find expression in forms accessible to those who would be guided by them; hence White's concern that 'the ancient histories and doctrines which have been the depositaries of so much that is eternal' should not be forsaken.[139] For those born within the Christian faith tradition, the associated symbols are to be the primary means for their understanding of fundamental truths. All such statements are provisional, of things seen in a glass darkly, and time-conditioned approximations of eternal truths. His references to miracles show that recognition of the universal nature of truth is implied in acceptance of the laws of nature. In this he acknowledged the propriety of approaching the biblical text with the same critical judgement as other ancient texts, though to treat the Bible in this way did not necessarily mean that it would fail to mediate a uniquely authoritative disclosure. He demonstrates a writer's sensitivity to the text, and any demand, then or now, for a simple affirmation or denial misunderstands him.

White's exposure to sceptical thought from the Chapman years must have made him aware of what was at stake if traditional beliefs were overturned. It is instructive to compare his views against the chief reasons which Timothy Larsen has identified for once-convinced secularists to return to previously held Christian belief.[140] Most of these find at least an echo in Hale White. Larsen

---

[136] *Autobiography*, p. 22, Ch. II.

[137] So *Revolution*, p. 11, Ch. I.

[138] *Autobiography*, p. 21, Ch. II.

[139] From 'Faith, Unbelief, and Superstition', in *Pages*, pp. 83-86 (p. 86).

[140] *Crisis of Doubt*, pp. 242-244; these are reconstructed from converts' stories, and secularist thinkers would have a defence against some of the charges. It should be noted that Larsen's examples are drawn from nonconformist backgrounds, and may not represent the 'doubts' of university-educated Anglicans for example.

shows that there was a common reaction against the negative and destructive emphasis of much anti-Christian polemic, accompanied by the belief that secularism provided an inadequate basis for morality. This is already seen in White's descriptions of his time under Chapman's roof. Stress upon the power of human reason was at variance with acknowledgement of the intuitive and subjective, and a purely materialist view of the universe failed to convince (Larsen notes the importance of spiritualism). Once more, there are similarities with White, for whom despite his appreciation of science, the natural world supplies 'a sense of the infinite, extinguishing all mean cares'.[141] The use of the Bible in freethinking debates could be woodenly literalistic, failing to do justice (for example) to preaching which dramatically brought the text to life. The figure of Jesus claimed renewed allegiance, as biblical criticism failed to prevent moving encounters with the Gospel texts. This Jesus could be a radical figure too, inspiring Christian socialists and activists of other stripes - it could not be claimed that Christian commitment always meant social conservatism. In these further examples White would again concur. Finally, an intellectual defence of Christianity continued to be made by able thinkers and the secularists did not always win the argument, recalling here that White had little time for the debates between closed-minded dogmatists on both sides.

In this he was not alone. They were widely felt by thoughtful Christians to be counter-productive, and in the 1870s the newly formed Christian Evidence Society set its face against such encounters. This type of meeting rarely allowed arguments to be fully set out, while the faith was too easily ridiculed and misrepresented by its opponents. When the popularist Congregationalist-turned-Anglican anti-secularist speaker Brewin Grant offered to support the Society his help was curtly declined, since 'they [the Society] so entirely disapprove of the spirit and manner in which Mr Grant conducts his debates with Secularists'.[142] The place of miracles in White's thinking, and more broadly, will be considered further below.[143]

Of course matters of belief were not abstract, but shaped, nurtured, or challenged through personal contacts, and this context is equally valuable for understanding Hale White. Although many references have suggested White's solitariness, the letters cited earlier demonstrate the importance of friendships which he assiduously maintained. These were often relationships sustained at a distance, but informal groups were of practical importance in the years immediately after the expulsion for linking White personally with other

---

[141] *Autobiography*, p. 95, Ch. VII; Rutherford on viewing the night sky, taking this as true for White.

[142] Quoted by Dale Johnson, 'Popular Apologetics in Late Victorian England: The Work of the Christian Evidence Society', *Journal of Religious History*, 11 (1981), 558-577 (p. 561). Admittedly Grant was an unusually divisive and provocative figure.

[143] See pp. 331-337.

believers, some of them similarly dissatisfied with normal church life. These were typically clustered around figures who gained the respect of the young, and especially of ministerial students.

White Amongst Friends

The *Early Life* has some pointers to the spiritual and intellectual influences on White, though it is difficult to prove their extent or nature. Personal links were arguably more important than texts. The role of Caleb Morris is widely recognised, as White made clear his indebtedness ('he *made* me'[144]), and paid fulsome tribute in the *Early Life*. He credited Morris with a vital role in keeping faith alive, when official church bodies had done so much to crush it. It was probably while composing the manuscript of this record that he told Dorothy but for Morris he might have 'settled down as a mere partisan in the Church, or else broken away from creeds altogether'.[145] There were others for whom Morris may have had a similar significance. David Thomas records that his hearers were 'students, ministers, teachers, philosophers, men of science, and men of letters', who prized Morris's '*originality*', in which his personal apprehension of truth was to the fore.[146] His 'conversational' rather than aridly 'rhetorical' style engaged his audiences, though his teaching that the scriptures *contained* the word of God left him open to criticism from the orthodox.[147] Since he did not cultivate close friendships with denominational colleagues he was isolated when attacked, and had few to defend him in those circles. It is easy to see why the New College authorities had been concerned about their students' links with him.

Although the habit of 'inner reference' in matters of belief brought about by the Wordsworthian enlightenment suggests a sturdy independence the influence of Morris and others shows that White still needed a teacher and guide for spiritual growth, as well as the encouragement of a circle of friends; effectively a substitute 'church'. It was perhaps the gathering around Morris of such a self-selecting group which made officialdom wary of him. The special sense of belonging engendered made it impossibly difficult for White afterwards to tolerate ordinary church life. Christianity here was personal and vital, lived and experienced, not a system of belief or a set of structures. In following Morris,

---

144 As he told Dorothy in 1908; *Groombridge Diary*, p. 27 (original italics).

145 *Groombridge Diary*, p. 28; the reference to creeds suggests a claim to continued orthodoxy.

146 'Caleb Morris' [Memoir], in *Pulpit Memorials: Photographs and Specimen Sermons of Twenty Congregational Ministers, With Brief Memoirs by Several Friends*, ed. by E.J. Evans and W.F. Hurndall (London: James Clarke, 1878) pp. 381-398 (p. 384; original emphasis).

147 As described by Thomas, 'Caleb Morris; in *Pulpit Memorials*, pp. 385-396 (p. 388).

White was part of a group of like-minded young men, including William Chignell and his fellow expelled.

There was probably a degree of overlap between the membership of this circle and several others in which he moved. Thomas Binney is a well-documented example of the lively and directly personal style of preaching which proved so attractive to a new generation, and Carlyle is a lay parallel. Something of Binney lies behind the portrait of Pike Street's Thomas Bradshaw in *Revolution*, and White often sat under him. The passionate, committed and demanding nature of his sermons marked him as 'a pioneer in the modern mode of preaching, which is practical and colloquial, rather than theoretical and rhetorical'.[148] White felt tributes after Binney's death failed to capture the essence of his appeal; an ability 'to identify the Bible with genuine human experience. Abraham, Paul, and the other Biblical heroes ... were made to stand in our place, and their experience became our own. That was the meaning of his almost miraculous influence.'[149] According to another witness 'Binney was a king among men', and 'all that was intelligent in Dissenting London, among the young men especially, heard him gladly'.[150] Listeners were challenged and inspired to action. The young George Williams, effectively founder of the YMCA, was greatly influenced by Binney and the life of the King's Weigh House church, as well as appreciating the ministry of Caleb Morris, expressing himself 'much pleased' with the Welshman's preaching.[151]

There were others, where evidence is very scanty. Robertson Nicoll mentions that White 'became acquainted with Alexander M'Laren' during his first pastorate in Southampton through visits to Chignell in Portsmouth.[152] Maclaren, a Baptist of Congregational background then noted for his unconventional ways and 'advanced' views (later more widely known as a biblical expositor), re-invigorated Portland Chapel by his preaching, and 'young men were attracted to him'.[153] A friend described his direct pulpit style,

---

[148] Horton Davies, *Worship and Theology in England: From Newman to Martineau, 1850-1900* (London: Oxford University Press, 1962), p. 227.

[149] From his column in *The Norfolk News*, 14 March 1874 (also quoted by Maclean, p. 192). A typical resistance against any 'religious' message with no relation to ordinary life.

[150] From James Ritchie (born 1820), another would-be minister turned journalist, *Christopher Crayon's Recollections*, p. 189.

[151] A context described in rich detail by Clyde Binfield, *George Williams and the Y.M.C.A.: A Study in Victorian Social Attitudes* (London: Heinemann, 1973), especially pp. 23-36 and p. 45 (for Morris).

[152] 'Memories of Mark Rutherford', p. 371; this information came from White, confirmed by Robert Theobald. 'M'Laren' was often rendered 'Maclaren' (as here) or 'McLaren'.

[153] See John Carlile *Alexander Maclaren, D.D.: The Man and His Message. A Character Sketch* (London: S.W. Partridge, 1901), p. 49. Carlile is the only one of Maclaren's

Note continues on following page

and sermons that 'were a mixture of the Ten Commandments, the Beatitudes, and Thomas Carlyle'; it is easy to see how attractive a figure he must have been.[154] White himself refers to this time only fleetingly, in a letter to Mrs Colenutt recalling William Chignell's friendship with Maclaren (and implying his own meeting with the young preacher).[155] By the nature of such informal groupings evidence of them is elusive, and they are untraceable except for the haphazard survival of sources. It is known for example that Robert Theobald and Hale White attended the chapel of Lincoln's Inn to hear F. D. Maurice, White much later remembering 'what he did for the young men of that time', but details are lacking.[156] There is no doubt about Maurice's influence among Congregationalists, to the extent that at Spring Hill College in Birmingham in the 1870s there was a 'Mauriceian cult', while the principal himself attested that as a student Maurice's works had first convinced him that 'living real human lives' lay behind the biblical text.[157] Theobald's memoir speak of Maurice's kindness to him during the New College crisis, evidence of his personal charisma; 'to know him was to love and revere him'.[158]

White was noted in adult life for his reserve, but there is no doubt that the camaraderie of these groups was an important element in their appeal, arising from a shared sense of the opening up of Dissent to new ideas and opportunities. External constraints were being eased, there was a new confidence about the nonconformists' role in public life (buoyed by the results of the 1851 census), and less inclination to turn inwards against a hostile world. Doubtless many of the young men who took the opportunity to hear such figures were, like White, ministerial students. In the *Autobiography* he bears witness to the importance of meeting those from other colleges; 'especially one who had undergone experiences similar to my own'.[159] This is the language of the convert, in which shared experience makes for soul-friendship. The outworking of his faith, as in the Drury Lane theology, shows that it was not just something shared within congenial groups.

---

biographers to give very much attention to his early years, and then in little enough detail. Concern for experiential reality also marked his later ministry.

[154] Recorded in *The Life of Alexander Maclaren: Preacher and Expositor* by David Williamson (London: James Clarke; Baptist Union Publication Department, 1910), p. 29. Maclaren later regretted his early reputation for unorthodoxy (which may not have been deserved).

[155] A note of 26 April 1899, not published in *Letters to Three Friends*. Numbered 106 in the recently discovered collection of Colenutt letters.

[156] From a conversation noted in the *Groombridge Diary*, p. 3.

[157] D. W. Simon cited in Sell, *Hinterland Theology*, p. 257; on Spring Hill, from the reminiscence of F. J. Powicke, see p. 266. Note a parallel with the preaching of Thomas Binney, which also vividly brought home the humanity of the biblical characters.

[158] *Passages from the Autobiography*, p. 52.

[159] *Autobiography*, p. 20, Ch. II.

Shorter Writings

Not all the occasional pieces that witness to White's continued engagement with questions of belief can be dated. This serves as a reminder that no time-line can be drawn up, but some instances show that while publishing novels which seem to engage less with a religious world-view his was still a faith seeking understanding.

Several articles appear to question faith, but in context show a constructively critical approach rather than rejection. Wrongly understood these have contributed to the depiction of White as hostile to Christian belief. The most significant of such writings appeared in the *Secular Review*, alongside articles attacking traditional belief and those praising the teachings of Jesus in order to condemn the failings of the churches supposedly founded in his name. The article 'Ixion' (which was publicly attributed to 'W. Hale White') suggested that doctrinal systems may approximate to idolatry.[160] Here was an argument that traditional descriptions of God's attributes, such as omnipotence and omniscience, were strictly meaningless, and an abstraction. Nor were they to be found in the creeds. This is not a dismissal of orthodoxy but a plea for reserve in defining God.[161] The prophetic White is arguing against the creation of a God limited by our understanding and fettered by our desire; 'a God who would reverse the rules of this great universe to gratify the whinings of foolish children'.[162] The refined concept of God commended might seem to owe more to Spinoza than the Christian tradition ('Special Providence' replaced by being 'citizens of a vast and equal Republic, whose laws are never turned aside for their convenience', a God of Love replaced by a love 'which pours sunlight over the whole globe, and returns affection for affection through human hearts'), but this reflects White's deep-seated antipathy towards self-centred religion and any concept of rewards and punishment in the spiritual life.[163] Philosophy, ethics, and radically interpreted Christian beliefs are intertwined.

Other short extracts have a gnomic quality, as when he writes on Socrates and the shortcoming of logic. 'Perhaps we may find that something less than logic and more than a dream may be of use to us'; and when logic is put aside, the end of life can be recognised as the return of the mind to the 'One' of which

[160] 'Ixion', *The Secular Review*, 11 September 1880, pp. 164-165. It is not clear why White chose the title 'Ixion', or what aspect of the mythical figure's history might have arisen in his readers' minds.

[161] Definition entails 'clipping the Infinite and reducing it to a finite'; 'Notes' in *More Pages*, p. 238.

[162] As previous reference, 'Ixion', p. 165.

[163] Again 'Ixion', p. 165.

en-souled human beings are 'the manifold expression'.[164] This is a reminder that White could not easily believe in a life after death; 'personal immortality ... seems to me unthinkable'.[165] It was perhaps not an outright denial so much as an admission of defeat in trying to conceptualise such an idea.

Nature Mysticism and Monism

Reference to the 'One', like White's reading of Spinoza, again seems to imply a monism formally incompatible with theism.[166] The issue occurs most plainly in the only mystical encounter which White directly records, the 'thou in me and I in thee' moment cited above in which 'the enclosing barriers of consciousness' between him and an oak tree faded and 'the distinction of self and not-self' was felt to be 'an illusion'.[167] This is described as having taken place when he was 'well over sixty', and in 'a favourite wood', probably indicating his years at Groombridge, where woodland arose directly behind the house. The incident is prefaced by an explanation of the life-long importance of nature, and his 'belief', 'if this the right word, that the same thought, spirit, life, God, which was in everything I beheld, was also in me', which on its own appears simply pantheist.[168] However another layer of interpretation follows the exhilarating feeling of aliveness and unity with his surroundings, or rather, almost instantly accompanies it - 'the text came into my mind, *Thou in me and I in thee*'.[169] The effect is a conviction that 'there is no death', implying a non-personal survival through union with the divine, though no certainty is possible from such an abbreviated reference.[170] With these apparently conflicting elements care is needed in not over-interpreting his recall, but this occurrence has not received the attention it deserves.

Such extrovertive mystical experiences of oneness with nature (implying that external objects are illusory) occur across many cultures and traditions.[171] The shared features in their reporting lead many to suppose a universal basis, with differences arising from the interpretative categories through which they

---

[164] From 'Faith', an undated piece printed in *Pages*, pp. 70–73 (p. 72).

[165] As he told Florence Low; 'Walks and Talks with Mark Rutherford', p. 409.

[166] Notwithstanding the conclusion above that White does not unreservedly embrace monism, and that there may be shades of 'Christian' monism, with a blurring of boundaries; see pp. 262-263.

[167] Described in 'An Epoch' in *More Pages*, pp. 181-183 (p. 182).

[168] 'An Epoch', p. 181.

[169] 'An Epoch', p. 182 (original emphasis).

[170] 'An Epoch', p. 183.

[171] R.C. Zaehner cites examples in his *Mysticism Sacred and Profane: An Inquiry into Some Varieties of Praeternatural Experience* (Oxford: Oxford University Press, 1957), pp. 30-49, and further notes belief that 'death was an almost laughable impossibility' as a very common conclusion (p. 41).

are filtered, but the debate is far from settled and some elements are poorly explained by this model. Those who assume a common core may argue that in the Christian tradition a theistic gloss is added to events which are basically monistic; that is, of impersonal 'oneness' with the divine.[172] White's reference to the words of Jesus from John's Gospel shows his immediate recourse to Christian language, and this is apparently an intrinsic part of the experience rather than a later addition. It is obviously personal and theistic - 'thou', 'thee', 'me' - though the exact relationship intended is not absolutely clear. It suggests that at this time, no less than after reading Wordsworth in his youth, White's response to numinous experience was mediated through and controlled by the inherited faith tradition in which he continued to dwell. There was some tension in the constituent elements, but this is far from unique to his encounter. Grace Jantzen argues that medieval Christian mysticism exhibited a monist spiritual tendency which was not fundamentally incompatible with orthodox belief and that language deemed monist is often more subtle.[173] In doing so she stretches the boundaries of traditional orthodoxy considerably, but it represents an attempt to integrate theology and experience which illuminates White. His spirituality is hardly on a par with the great mystics, but he too may be holding together philosophical concepts and inherited beliefs which cannot be fully reconciled, though his expressions of faith are not to be taken less seriously for that reason.

Jantzen further argues that the concept of mystical union found in some of the most significant Christian writers actually 'requires monism as its underlying metaphysic, a unity of substance or essence between God and the soul, in which all things are one, and the distinction between subject and object is lost in unity'.[174] In this 'introvertive' mysticism the sense of self-identity is swallowed-up in the Absolute, as distinct from the more obviously dualistic variant in which a personal encounter with the Divine is reported, and self-identity reinforced.

Explication of extrovertive experiences poses a philosophical as well as theological challenge. Paul Marshall has explored a range of mystical states arising from contact with nature, some of which are very similar to White's.[175] Moreover his analysis corrects and extends the work of significant earlier

---

[172] Alister McGrath argues that the universality of transcendent experiences, far from threatening faith, can form the basis of a rehabilitated Christian natural theology; see *The Open Secret: A New Vision for Natural Theology* (Oxford: Blackwell Publishing, 2008), especially p. 40.

[173] ' "Where Two are to Become One": Mysticism and Monism', in *The Philosophy of Christianity*, ed. by Godfrey Vesey (Cambridge: Cambridge University Press, 1989), pp. 147-166.

[174] ' "Where Two are to Become One"', p. 149.

[175] P. Marshall, *Mystical Encounters with the Natural World: Experiences and Explanations* (Oxford: Oxford University Press, 2005).

writers like Stace and Zaehner, who he shows to have been strongly motivated by presuppositions which were largely concealed from their readers. Stace was influenced by the belief that a 'pure consciousness' lay behind all mystical experiences, which he therefore took to be essentially content-less (and interpreted accordingly), while Zaehner ranked nature mysticism as distinctly inferior to theistic mystical encounters.[176] Zaehner's resulting separation into two categories was driven by this imperative, rather than derived from the evidence. Marshall's much closer attention to reported cases allows him to do better justice to such experiences, while showing the difficulties in assuming that they demonstrate a common origin regardless of social, cultural or religious context, and equally that they cannot be adequately described in terms of the subject's cultural predisposition. A rigid distinction between a virgin experience and subsequent interpretation must be resisted. An assumption that all mystical experiences are at root the same across religions and cultures too readily reduces them to core features at the cost of ignoring or smoothing out variations, while novelty and features which challenge existing belief are a problem for theorists who insist that cultural conditioning is crucial. Also, the 'radical contextualists' (as Marshall labels them) tend to reduce the significance of the mystical experience itself *vis-à-vis* the place given to the interpretation which is derived from existing beliefs.[177]

More pertinent in this case is Marshall's discussion of some predisposing factors, and the place of monism.[178] Leaving aside drug-induced states, and those arising from specific religious practices, some frequently accompanying features can be identified which may act as triggers. These include a natural setting, fine weather, and being alone - all as in White's reported case. The emotional mood may be important too, which can paradoxically include both inner peace and mental disturbance. Spiritual preparation also has an association, and it would be interesting to know in this instance if White's Bible passage on the day in question, or otherwise near in time, had included the verses from John's Gospel which came to mind (though one might have expected him to have mentioned such a link). Depending upon the date, it is also conceivable that his reading of Dean Inge might have caused an openness to new experiences. Inge was a prominent exponent of the emphasis upon transcendence *and* immanence which Marshall notes as particularly linked to his liberal Christian tradition.[179] There were more general factors too, and the background of Romanticism, with its new emphasis upon retreat into nature, and of thinkers like Schleiermacher who stressed the importance of feeling in religion must have played their part. In White's case the example of Richard

---

[176] *Mystical Encounters*, pp. 49-59.
[177] *Mystical Encounters*, summarising their position, pp. 181-193.
[178] *Mystical Encounters*, particularly relevant here pp. 82-93.
[179] *Mystical Encounters*, pp. 129-137.

Jefferies might be significant; White very much admired his nature writing, and would presumably have been aware of his reported mystical encounters. His own enjoyment of the natural world, and the rich descriptions of it in a number of short articles, may well have been inspired by his reading of Jefferies.[180]

Monism can provide the philosophical context for understanding extrovertive experiences, with variant forms being important for different writers on the subject. A Platonic idealism underlay Inge's thinking, but a dual-aspect monism derived from Spinoza was another attractive option because of the shared ontological status given to mind and matter. Although Marshall ultimately finds such a system unsatisfactory on several grounds it may have played some role in White's understanding of his experience, and even in his predisposition. It certainly shows how in practice an 'absolute' monism could be closer to a theistic position than might be assumed.[181]

Returning to the question of certainty which introduced this 'monist' note in White's reflections on the end of life, the elusiveness suggested by 'something less than logic and more than a dream' is not by him deplored, for 'none of the formal arguments for the existence of God really convince. The proof lies in hints and dreams which are not expressible by human language'.[182] Faith means wrestling with doubt, and the struggle is often represented. 'True belief is rare and difficult' but worth striving for, since 'there is no security that the fictitious beliefs which have been obtained by no genuine mental process, that is to say, are not vitally held, may not be discarded for those which are exactly contrary'.[183] A sentiment repeated in a later notebook entry, the first part of which has already been cited above:

> Faith, the belief which saves, is not to be preserved without a struggle. It is not a conclusion which comes automatically from evidence presented. A hundred times a day suggestions are made within us to abandon this or that result we have achieved with much effort, and we are not then to balance but to hold fast with claws.[184]

This provisional, open-ended, but deeply felt faith does not lend itself to subscription or conventional doctrinal statements, and reflects a freedom in

---

180 'Every scrap of his is precious', White wrote to Mrs Colenutt on Jefferies' early death in 1887; *Letters to Three Friends*, p. 36.

181 For these and other mind-body relationships which affect interpretation, see Marshall, *Mystical Encounters*, pp. 240-260. A version of idealism is his preferred model, pp. 260-268, though it has been challenged as philosophically inadequate by Anthony Perovich, 'Taking Nature Mysticism Seriously: Marshall and the Metaphysics of the Self', *Religious Studies*, 47 (2011), 165-183.

182 From 'Faith', in *Pages* (p. 72) and 'Notes', in *Last Pages*, p. 274.

183 From 'Faith, Unbelief, and Superstition', in *Pages*, pp. 83-86 (p. 83).

184 'Notes', in *Last Pages*, p. 302.

belief not open to a preacher or teacher, or one in any way accountable to others for the content of belief. It seems a long way from the relentless logic of Spinoza's system. Possibly White had realised its shortcoming in generating or sustaining faith, or he was able to hold intellectual and experiential aspects faith together under tension. These late but undated pieces reinforce the supposition that Spinoza was becoming less important to him. Logic was being put aside for a less definable faith. He was working out his own salvation, and had by now realised his inability to teach others; 'I have never had a system in any subject, religion, poetry, philosophy, morals, manners, health. This makes me useless as a guide to anyone in a difficulty'.[185] This gathering of occasional pieces, indefinite as the resulting outline inevitably is, shows the constant importance of faith to White. If it is claiming too much to describe him without explanation as a Christian believer, to deny him the name is to say too little.

Faith Seeking Understanding

There remains another clue to the real nature of White's mature faith. He was conscious of something lacking in his ability to apprehend or explain faith. It is as if he was always straining after that which could not quite be attained, and which engagement with Spinoza and other thinkers was unable to supply. Newman had described an 'illative sense', a knowledge arising from actions of the mind which is held with a measure of certainty not based on conscious mental analysis.[186] He discerned something of it in the peasant's knowledge of the weather, and this is very similar to Hale White's appreciation of Bedford's farmers. Although the figures of his youth were 'ignorant' in much compared with even 'the most superficial young person of the present day', the farmer 'understood a good deal about the men around him, about his own fields, about the face of the sky, and he had found it out all by himself, a fact of more importance than we suppose'.[187] It occurs elsewhere. Miss Tippit in *Miriam's Schooling* did not have a faith 'secure against Strauss', but she is a true believer, whose 'few principles by which she regulated this present life' are worth more than any intellectual mastery of faith.[188] Again, from *Revolution*,

---

[185] From the late, undated (but ca. 1907-1912) "White" Notebook, UBC, NCC 3-1 (p. 21 of an unpaginated manuscript). Having no 'system' in 'philosophy' reads like further evidence of a distancing from Spinoza.

[186] Newman coined this 'grand word for a common thing', but it rises beyond simple intuition; see the description by Sheridan Gilley in *Newman and His Age* (London: Darton, Longman and Todd, 1990), pp. 360-362 (p. 360). Stone also notes this parallel with Newman, p. 77.

[187] *Early Life*, pp. 19-20. M. Betham-Edwards reports the woeful ignorance of Suffolk farmers in the same period, without any compensating insight; *Reminiscences*, pp. 42-44.

[188] *Miriam's Schooling*, p. 78. A typically saint-like minor figure in the fiction.

the lessons of everyday life have great value:

> The young scholar fresh from his study is impatient with what he considers the unprofitable gossip about the people round the corner; but when he gets older he sees that often it is much better than his books, and that distinctions are expressed by a washerwoman, if the objects to be distinguished eat and drink and sleep, which he would find it difficult to make with his symbols.[189]

At the same time he was aware of the difficulty of establishing an intellectually satisfactory account of belief. Indeed, despite the time spent on the study of Spinoza in earlier years it is noticeable that he did not attempt any real engagement with contemporary theological writing. But he grappled with serious intellectual issues, as his faith sought understanding. Books recommended by friends continued to stimulate him. After reading Francis Warre Cornish's clerical novel *Sunningwell* (1899) as the century turned, he reflected on the relationship between doctrine and belief.

While not identifying himself with the hero's position, he felt something of the same temper. The issue for the Reverend Philip More, increasingly tested as the novel progresses, was the latitude of interpretation consistent with prescribed adherence to traditionally expressed beliefs. Just how a doctrine is related to the truth it attempts to represent is precisely the question which holds White's attention. He had had many years to ponder this, as the work of Strauss and others on the nature of 'myth' had focussed attention on the inner meaning of many biblical stories. While personally unable to belong again to 'any Christian sect', White endorses More for 'his refusal to deny formulas which have been the means of conveying so much truth to him', and affirms, 'I would even go further and say that the doctrine in those formulas in some shape or other is fact and indispensable fact. Christian supernaturalism is almost always the objectifying if one may coin such a word of some spiritual reality'.[190] As an illustration White offers the Catholic doctrine of the Mass, a way of making real an abstraction, and declaring the continued 'living presence' of Christ. This is, he acknowledges, too big a subject to develop in a letter, but with the idea of 'objectifying' conceptualisation he strangely foreshadows the debate initiated later in the century by Rudolf Bultmann in his programme of 'demythologisation'.[191] This theologian's declared aim was to preserve the essence of the biblical message, and White too saw how an 'object' could

---

[189] *Revolution*, p. 241, Ch. XVI.

[190] From a letter to Rose Paul (who had lent him the novel), 18 February 1900 (UBC, NCC 2-7).

[191] For a classic discussion of Bultmann's project see the important contemporary assessment by John Macquarrie, *The Scope of Demythologizing: Bultmann and His Critics* (London: SCM Press, 1960).

replace true faith in God; 'we are more content the more definite the object becomes, no matter whether or not it is in any intimate relationship with us, and we do not see that the moment God can be named he ceases to be God'.[192]

This sophisticated understanding is noted by James Fowler as an element of 'individuative-reflective' faith (his fourth stage), with the warning that religious symbols so understood can become 'broken', with potential loss of meaning.[193] The compensating growth in real understanding may not be experienced by all individuals. It is easy to think of White as one sometimes stranded between the emotional resonance of traditional language and a more complex awareness of the symbolic nature of such wording. This explains why he is equally reluctant to drop doctrinal terms or to explicate them, making it is so difficult to state with exactness what he believed. On the evidence presented here, whatever the extent to which he was an 'honest doubter' White demonstrates the persistence of the 'more faith ... than in half the creeds' of Tennyson's dictum, and writes no more than the truth when claiming a faith which 'revived under new forms'.[194]

Summary

Although the material has come from scattered references and different settings, a measure of consistency can be detected. The faith of the past is respected, but engaged in a radical dialogue. Nothing can be accepted on trust or simply inherited, but must be worked out anew in each life, and indeed in each generation. Criticism is of misunderstandings or misrepresentations of faith, especially those which fail to identify the spiritual impulses from which dogmatic statements first arose. A mystical element shows that doctrines are for life, not speculation. Direct experience is always the highest good.

Further important information about late faith (covering the dates from April 1908 until his death in March 1913) is found in the *Groombridge Diary*, a source which might be regarded with suspicion because of Dorothy's influence. William Kent, writing in *The Literary Guide*, appreciated publication of Hale's *Letters to Three Friends*, but dismissed the *Diary* as part of her 'futile attempts to make the old man more orthodox'.[195] It is most appropriately considered as part of the wider reappraisal of White's life and writings which followed the

[192] From 'An Epoch', in *More Pages*, pp. 181-183 (p. 182).

[193] *Stages of Faith*, p. 180; that is, both loss and gain can follow from recognising symbols *as* symbols.

[194] *Early Life*, p. 78.

[195] 'Mark Rutherford', *The Literary Guide*, March 1932, p. 58. Kent (born 1884) was an admirer of White, and saw parallels in his own nonconformist upbringing - *inter alia* as 'the infant Samuel' - drawn out in *The Testament of a Victorian Youth: An Autobiography* (London: Heath Cranton, 1938). It meant reading White very much as a doubter however, and interpreting his experience against the writer's.

publication of the *Early Life*. Before that task is undertaken some other material to flesh out his later years can be assessed. It is partly the concern raised about Dorothy's portrayal of White's old age that makes it necessary to broaden the view. The sketches of White's life in retirement among other things show him becoming more at ease in circles which were far removed from those of his birth. This is also a useful foil to the more intellectual reporting on belief, rooting him in everyday life and concerns. It can serve as a preface to considering the later careers of his fellow accused. Frederic White and Robert Theobald were both once significant in Hale White's life but are now hardly known. In their own way they demonstrate a number of important signs of the times, though their lives took quite different directions. In particular there will be an opportunity to consider the place of other spiritualities which arose to challenge, complement, or even replace commitment to orthodox Christianity. In this way a number of contemporary figures - including again George MacDonald - can be linked to the three men, enriching the context and identifying common themes.

Chapter 10

'Rudely and roughly altered'
The Later Lives of the Expelled

The careers of the three expelled were, as Robert Theobald wrote of his own, 'rudely and roughly altered' by the events of 1852.[1] Something of White's new course in life has already been recorded, but there is more to be told of the other expelled students. His later years were marked by new interests and friendships, demonstrating a widening social world, if not necessarily any lessening of felt attachment to the world of Dissent with which he still exhibits a strong affinity. He had moved from Park Hill to a house in Ashtead in 1889, where his wife died on 1 June 1891. Shortly afterwards he applied to retire from the Admiralty, and on receiving permission to do so removed with Molly to Hastings in April 1892. After a further move in 1899 to Crowborough he finally settled at Groombridge in 1903.

The Writer in Retirement

His life naturally changed when he left the Admiralty, and more so when bereavement, despite its attendant sorrows, freed him from the burden of caring for his sick wife. The following years provided the first opportunity to give sustained attention to interests which had been put aside among the demands of working life and his earlier writing, though towards the end they were clouded by his own ill-health. Hence the immersion in literary-critical works, and penning of short pieces, some later gathered together and re-published in the *Pages*, *More Pages* and *Last Pages* volumes. There were also two novels published in retirement, though the first (*Catharine Furze*, 1893) may have been already in hand. These tasks, and the contacts allowed in new spheres, superficially represent a distancing from the Dissenting past. Acquaintance in circles well beyond those of his own background, while broadening in some ways, probably also served to feed his sense of separateness and difference. As already demonstrated, his private writings continued to reveal a strong sense of belonging in that tradition, from letters exchanged with old friends to entries in his manuscript notebook. There is interest in the further light this time sheds on the human figure of White, with indications of his mental and emotional state.

[1] *Passages from the Autobiography*, p. 5.

Despite his claim not to belong in a literary world, growing openness about his work ensured an *entrée* to just such a sphere, and it is possible in the memoirs of others to catch sight of White in the company of writers. Hastings especially was noted for the number of artistic figures who settled in the town. White had known the area well before choosing to rent a house there in 1892, and Mark Rutherford spends an idyllically happy day in the area at the end of the *Deliverance.*[2] He was on visiting terms with a number of authors, and his books were becoming known and admired, if not universally. The popular novelist Matilda Betham-Edwards recalled meeting White around the town, naturally without admitting to him that she 'could hardly indeed wade through' his 'melancholy' works.[3] There remained a reluctance to mix more freely in such society, and it seems that he made excuses to avoid Henry James, despite their having friends in common in Mrs Dannreuther (regarded locally as 'the most cultured woman in Europe') and Betham-Edwards, suggesting that White was more at ease in the company of women than with men.[4] He may also have been intimidated by someone of James' reputation, though the latter had a high opinion of him.

When White established himself in Groombridge he met Sarah Grand, the well-known 'New Woman' novelist who moved to nearby Langton in 1900. She recalled his memories of George Eliot, and thought him quite in love with her.[5] This might imply that he preferred to talk about the past and safe topics rather than discuss his writings, despite an overlapping interest in fictionally exploring the lives of newly confident women. However given the occasional nature of Grand's remarks this inference must remain uncertain. Sarah was friendly with Betham-Edwards, who was possibly the means of her being introduced to Hale White. Not all in his new orbit were local. From Groombridge he corresponded with Erica Storr, who had asked him to comment on her writing; during this period she married A. D. Lindsay (of Balliol), again showing that White was forging connections much more widely.[6]

His identity less rigorously disguised, at Groombridge the reclusive author

---

[2] *Deliverance*, pp. 117-120, Ch. IX.

[3] See her *Mid-Victorian Memories* (London: John Murray, 1919), pp. 141-142.

[4] Mrs Dannreuther's high reputation reported by Gerald Brodribb, *Hastings and Men of Letters* (Hastings: Old Hastings Preservation Society, 1971), p. 32. Greek by birth, her German husband was a professional musician and critic.

[5] Grand (assumed name of Frances Elizabeth Bellenden McFall, née Clarke) recalled these meetings in conversation with her young admirer Gladys Singers-Bigger. See Gillian Kersley, *Darling Madame: Sarah Grand and Devoted Friend* (London: Virago Press, 1983), p. 238. Grand appears to believe that Hale and Eliot might have been lovers but this surely impossible suggestion could be the result of careless reporting of Grand by the unstable Gladys.

[6] Letters preserved in the Special Collections of the University of Sussex, SxMs6.

was becoming more accessible to his readers, at least until Dorothy's arrival, when they could feel less welcome. Some pursued him there, while for others the encounter seems to have been entirely fortuitous. A sense of shared background could transform such a chance meeting, as in the case of Gladys Ellen Easdale, the daughter of Walter Frederick Adeney (1848-1920), a Congregational minister who trained at New College and having taught at both Cheshunt and New College went on to become Principal of Lancashire Independent College in 1903.[7] Ellen (as he always called her) met the writer in 1904 or 1905 when staying with her uncle Edwin Adeney in Tunbridge Wells, who happened to be Hale White's doctor. Having been introduced to his books by her parents who were 'great admirers of his work', she immediately treated their author with great respect.[8] Her tendency to hero-worship was deeply appealing to White and they were soon on the friendliest of terms, indeed she spoke of an instantaneous bond, which on her side at least endured.

This is very similar to the sense of immediate attraction later reported by Dorothy Smith, and included a feeling of triumph in the meeting, even if it had not been a carefully engineered one as in Dorothy's case. The friendship between Ellen and White, sustained by visits and many letters, could not withstand Dorothy's need to take control of White. Ellen later boasted of having kept 'heaps of his letters' despite the writer's normal request that they be destroyed after reading.[9] Her claim did not impress Virginia Woolf, who apparently had not before heard of 'an old prophet called Hale White who lived at Groombridge'.[10]

It may be that on this occasion Easdale and White discussed something of their common experience as children in Dissenting families, for she left a manuscript record of her life described as having been written 'at the request of

---

[7] Easdale (sometimes given as Easedale) became rather eccentric, and this badly affected her gifted daughter Joan (later known as Sophie). For more on the family see *Who Was Sophie?: My Grandmother, Poet and Stranger* by Celia Robertson (London: Virago Press, 2008). Some of Joan's poems were published by the Hogarth Press, and Virginia Woolf was on friendly terms with mother and daughter, as Stephen Barkway describes in 'An "Incredible Goose" and a "Country Flapper": Virginia Woolf and the Easdales', *Virginia Woolf Bulletin*, 28 (2008), 5-35.

[8] *Middle Age*, p. 142. She remembered herself as aged 'about twenty', suggesting the year 1905, but a manuscript autobiography possibly inspired by this meeting is dated as prompted by him in 'about 1904'.

[9] Virginia Woolf reporting Easdale's words in a letter to Lady Robert Cecil, 18 August 1932, cited in Barkway, 'An "Incredible Goose"', p. 12. In *Middle Age* Ellen reports destroying 'many of the most precious letters I received', but keeping twenty-one with the writer's (reluctant?) consent (pp. 142-143). The holographs do not appear to have survived, but typescript copies are deposited in the University of Reading Special Collections, RUL MS 4991/4 (and some were cited in *Middle Age*).

[10] From a letter of September 1931 in Barkway, 'An "Incredible Goose"', p. 11.

Mark Rutherford' in 1904.[11] Much of this presumably made its way into her published autobiography *Middle Age: 1885-1932*, which from a mid-life perspective included an account of her childhood. Easdale's tendency to exaggerate her links with those whom she admired (witness her later contact with Virginia Woolf) means it is necessary to treat with caution her claim that he encouraged her in this task, but it is nonetheless entirely possible that their conversation turned on autobiographies.

These meetings date from the period before Dorothy had managed to secure her own *entrée* to Groombridge, in 1907. As she became closer to White, and especially after their marriage, older friends and acquaintances felt excluded or kept their distance for other reasons. When Henry James wrote in August 1911 to Betham-Edwards hoping that neither of them would 'emulate the surprising Hale White' in something 'disappointing of him - a false note in his fine figure', the date suggests reference to his second marriage.[12] White's correspondence with Ellen Easdale petered out as the relationship with Dorothy deepened, suggesting that to some extent she supplanted these friends of older standing. Ellen clearly felt utterly rejected when the 'good man' whose close friendship she felt had caused her own husband to leave her went on to marry 'a woman I detested'.[13]

White's retirement pursuits were not all literary or solitary. It was in Hastings that he, the most improbable of joiners, took up golf.[14] This may well have been with the direct or indirect encouragement of another resident, Harry Furniss, the artist and illustrator, who was a keen sportsman and advocate of the game.[15] Possibly he had been White's landlord. He later lived in 'The Mount', which White had rented, and also owned the nearby East Cliffe property, which White too had taken for a time (Furniss afterwards using it as his studio). In 1914 he was refusing to allow a memorial tablet to be affixed to The Mount,

---

[11] Manuscript now in the University of Reading Special Collections, RUL MS 4991/29.

[12] Letter of 16 August 1911, given in Betham-Edward's *Mid-Victorian Memories*, p. 109. Hale and Dorothy were married in April 1911, though the news only gradually spread beyond their immediate families. Matilda adds a note to say she cannot recall to what James refers, which is puzzling – but perhaps by then she too had little to do with the Whites and wasn't yet aware of the marriage (mentioning also that she did not see White again after this date). Nothing else from this period suggests itself as explaining James' dismay.

[13] From a conversation between Easdale and Virginia Woolf in August 1932, repeated in a letter from Woolf to Lady Robert Cecil, quoted in Barkway, 'An "Incredible Goose"', p. 12. Did Woolf realise that Lady Robert and Hale White had been friends?

[14] Described in a letter of May 1893, *Letters to Three Friends*, p. 61; later Molly also took up the game (see p. 83).

[15] A talk by Furniss in 1894 was said to have been instrumental in popularising the game in Hastings, in which case White must have been among the earliest of local players; see Brodribb, *Hastings and Men of Letters*, p. 32.

joining forces with Sir William Hale-White against Robertson Nicoll and the local group who were eager to celebrate Hastings' famous connections.[16] White was amused by the social niceties of the club rules, which excluded those in 'trade', thus admitting the local dentist but not his pharmacist brother. Something from this episode may have found its way into the description in *Clara Hopgood* of the Brighton boarding school attended by Madge, where a similar discrimination was made against tradesmen's children, but space was found for the daughter of a druggist, the father of a lucratively large brood.[17]

Despite this evidence of White mixing with others, there were also less positive signs. Over time there was a continued withdrawal into the self, and White could choose the people and situations with which he engaged. This sometimes unhealthy introspection was challenged by the association with Dorothy, which (whatever its strains, and effect on other relationships) allowed a nature 'here and there ... very much curled up' to be 'straightened out'.[18] This was an indication of what might have been if his life had not been overshadowed by the sadness of his first wife's illness and early death.

Comparisons and Contrasts

Although there is no evidence that friends from students days remained in touch, there is value in considering the lives of his fellow accused in the aftermath of their shared disgrace. They illuminate trends in Victorian thought and spirituality, while allowing some unexpected Bedford connections to be made. There are wider links to other figures, including George MacDonald, through whom it is possible to explore the contemporary debate about the place of miracles in Christian belief, by which White's understanding can be probed, as well as his possible appropriation of Spinoza on this question.

The Later Lives of Robert Theobald and Frederic White

White's story cannot be considered separately from those of his contemporaries without the risk of serious distortion. This is as much the case for later life as for the college years. Having traced something of the effects of the climactic events of 1852 in Hale White's life it is equally worthwhile to track the consequences for his fellow accused students. Many have been misled about the origins of Robert and Frederic by assuming from a reading of the *Early Life* that they had attended Cheshunt with Hale White. The evidence presented here has established their separate paths before joining New College

[16] A letter from Furniss to Sir William dated 14 May 1914 is preserved at Bedford (BPL, MR 25/8), alongside others on this subject.

[17] *Clara Hopgood*, pp. 18-22, Ch. II.

[18] As Dorothy described it, *Groombridge Diary*, p. 394.

(notwithstanding Theobald's claim that he had at least met White before they both joined New College), indicating that the expelled seem to have shared at most only a fairly loose previous connection. The difficulty in demonstrating any lasting relationship thereafter further suggests that their friendship was a product of the times, which it did not long outlast. Possibly strains developed as it became clear all would be forced to give up their vocations, while the need for each to establish new careers sent them in different directions. There was no initial sign of disharmony however, for they shared an extended holiday in Portsmouth immediately after leaving London.[19] No further proof of contact between them appears to have survived. Nevertheless what can be discovered of their lives - though it is little enough for Frederic White - offers a potentially valuable comparison with Hale White's post-expulsion experience.

Spiritualism and the Theobald Family

Information can more readily be gathered on Robert Theobald, with the most interesting material only hinted at in his autobiography. For alongside mention of an already known medical career, and the pursuit of Shakespeare studies, one section notes his familiarity with spiritualism, albeit too briefly to give any real idea of the nature of his involvement in the movement. Hale White had expressed a less than favourable view, and ridiculed the inconsequential nature of so many spirit messages. He regarded 'spiritualism ... as a science, or as a revelation [as] beneath contempt' and in a typically witty dismissal of one manifestation gave short shrift to the claim that communication by telegraphy made clairvoyance somehow more believable; 'when clairvoyants are put into every post-office, and everybody can consult them and test their accuracy for a shilling, we shall then believe them'.[20] At a later date, in private correspondence, he seems to have been more open to persuasion, hoping that scholars might 'laboriously and faithfully collect from the sciences all well-established facts, and there are not a few, which might be a basis for spiritualism and for hope'.[21] Since publication of his earlier comments the

---

[19] As he later remembered it, 'for six months to Portsmouth'; see *Groombridge Diary*, p. 71. Maclean, pp. 98-100, fills in some details, but typically without references by which these might be verified. This was possibly the start of his long friendship with the Colenutts of Ryde, initially through his cousin William Chignell, then minister of Highbury Chapel in Portsmouth.

[20] 'How It Strikes a Stranger', *The Nonconformist*, 15 January 1873, pp. 69-70. He may not have known that the rise of spiritualism in America mysteriously coincided with the invention of the electric telegraph. His remarks came after attendance at a series of public debates between Charles Bradlaugh and James Burns held at the former's Hall of Science.

[21] From a letter to Miss Partridge, 19 March 1894, discussing a speech on science and theology by Lord Salisbury, President that year of the British Association for the

Note continues on following page

Society for Physical Research had been founded (1882), and its reports had shown that some phenomena could not easily be explained away, probably affecting White's opinion.[22] More pertinently perhaps, both his parents had died between these years. Another late note left the matter open, insisting that 'the existence of a world of spirits may not be provable, but it certainly cannot be proved untrue'.[23] He suggested that while the category of things un-provable could be reduced as knowledge advanced, those who held beliefs presently incapable of being disproved were entitled to have their views respected.

Many people welcomed manifestations which seemed to affirm the vivid reality of a spiritual realm.[24] Reports of psychic phenomena were too widespread to be ignored, and in private if not always more openly serious thinkers showed sympathy with the movement. Some names are surprising. David Simon's daughter claims that while at Spring Hill her father 'held the strong conviction that he was in close contact with the spirit world, and he wrote many things which he said were not his own'.[25] These he later destroyed, but he refused to rule out the possibility of spirit communication. He was not deterred by his daughter's argument that the spirits ought to 'have something better to say than the foolish things so often attributed to them', which he met with the matter-of-fact response that since such talk was common enough to many in life it might equally be so after death.[26]

Robert Theobald was certainly glad to explore the new field, aided by family friendships with some of the most important leaders. His brother Morell Theobald (1829-1908) is a significant example of the 'Christian' spiritualism described by Alexandra Owen, which flourished among an educated metropolitan elite, in contrast to the northern, often lower class, spiritualism

---

Advancement of Science. See *Letters to Three Friends*, p. 151. Dorothy (as editor) ends this sentence with an ellipsis, but the manuscript in the Colbeck Collection shows nothing has been omitted, though 'hope' is marked with '**xxx**' in the margin (UBC, NCC 1-22), apparently the writer's emphasis.

[22] Spiritualism's 'proofs' which could be observed raised some questions more starkly than did reliance on the historical accounts of biblical miracles to support faith claims, as Peter Lamont describes; 'Spiritualism and a Mid-Victorian Crisis of Evidence', *The Historical Journal*, 47 (2004), 897-920.

[23] A fragment in 'Notes', *Last Pages*, pp. 304-305, probably to be dated shortly before 1908.

[24] Janet Oppenheim stresses this appeal in an age of uncertainty; see *The Other World: Spiritualism and Psychical Research in England, 1850-1914* (Cambridge: Cambridge University Press, 1985), pp. 1-2. Evidence of a future life was especially welcome, p. 63.

[25] A memory she shared with Frederick Powicke, *David Worthington Simon*, p. 310.

[26] Powicke, *David Worthington Simon*, p. 132.

which was often hostile to organised religion.[27] In this first group, participation was not accompanied by a rejection of Christianity, and, as with Morell Theobald, could sit alongside church attendance.[28] For him spiritualism confirmed the essential truths of Christianity, and was a bulwark against encroaching materialism. *Spirit Workers in the Home Circle* was his dramatic record of these experiences, and in this family at least *séances* started with prayer, the scriptures were frequently read, and Christian hymns sung.[29] The 'spirit' of spiritualism was closely identified with the Holy Spirit, and mediumistic and other gifts held to be manifestations akin to those described in the New Testament.[30] His specifically Dissenting allegiance is shown in a small way by a subscription to Edward Miall's weekly *Nonconformist*, and more interestingly there were personal links to the publisher.[31]

Morell's brother William married Edward Miall's daughter, while both Theobalds shared a partnership with Edward's son Arthur in the accountancy firm of Theobald Brothers & Miall. (Edward Miall had a pre-existing connection with the Morell side of the family, having trained at Wymondley under Thomas Morell, and gone on to marry his tutor's niece.) It was a hostage to fortune that Morell Theobald, anticipating the critical spirit of some readers, stressed his character as a 'respectable householder' with 'a tolerably reputable position in my own very responsible city business, where a bias towards fraud would find innumerable opportunities and irresistible seductions', for the firm was soon exposed to most unpleasant publicity.[32] The collapse of Jabez Balfour's Liberator Building Society and its web of linked companies in 1893

---

[27] In *The Darkened Room: Women, Power and Spiritualism in Late Victorian England* (London: Virago Press, 1989; repr. Chicago, IL: University of Chicago Press, 2004) she explores both strands, and devotes a chapter to Morell Theobald. The distinctions must not be pressed too far. Spiritualist journals, for example, often appealed to the widest possible audience, even if ostensibly editorially aligned with one particular viewpoint.

[28] The Morell Theobalds remained firm nonconformists, proud of the Morell ministerial lineage, and Morell refers to his church attendance, though the place is not named in his writings. Perhaps he wished to save that congregation's embarrassment. Minnie Theobald declares that one local church did denounce her uncle but gives no name or date; *Three Levels of Consciousness: An Autobiography* (London: John M. Watkins, 1960), p. 6; problems after the publicising of his spiritualist experiences would be quite understandable, or indeed after his business calamity, described below.

[29] *Spirit Workers in the Home Circle: An Autobiographic Narrative of Psychic Phenomena in Family Daily Life Extending Over a Period of Twenty Years* (London: T. Fisher Unwin, 1887).

[30] Apparently endorsed by the spirits themselves; on one occasion the 'ever-active spirit friends directed us to read the 12th chapter of I Cor., on spiritual gifts'; *Spirit Workers in the Home Circle*, p. 45.

[31] *Spirit Workers in the Home Circle*, p. 168.

[32] *Spirit Workers in the Home Circle*, p. 269.

caused widespread scandal and much hardship. Balfour, a Liberal MP, was publicly identified with Congregationalism, and had particularly targeted nonconformists as savers and investors. Edward Miall had lent his name to the society as one of the two Arbitrators, and the choice of his son's firm as auditor may not have been coincidental.[33] In 1895 Morell was found guilty of falsifying the accounts of Balfour's Lands Allotment Company and sentenced to four months hard labour.[34] The reputation of the firm had already suffered, for William Theobald had been heavily criticised earlier in the same year for his inadequate auditing of the London & General Bank which Balfour also controlled.[35] It is not entirely clear that Balfour's fraud was premeditated, but he was caught out when the complex 'asset-juggling' which kept his companies afloat started to unravel.[36] He always protested his innocence and even the journalist J. A. Spender (who had helped bring him to book) doubted his real culpability and was shocked at the fourteen year sentence handed down by Sir Henry Hawkins.[37] It is unlikely that Morell would have publicised his

[33] J. A. Spender did much to expose Balfour's misdeeds in articles which appeared in the *Westminster Gazette* and were later published as a pamphlet; *The Story of the Liberator Crash: With Some Account of the Career and Character of Jabez Spencer Balfour.* (London: Westminster Gazette, 1893); see pp. 14-15 for details of Balfour's careful courting of nonconformists. The pamphlet did not name its author, but this was declared in Spender's *Life, Journalism and Politics*, vol. I (London: Cassell, 1927), pp. 59-60. David McKie provides a lively modern account in *Jabez: The Rise and Fall of a Victorian Rogue* (London: Atlantic Books, 2004). Jabez was not related to the Conservative Balfours.

[34] The cases is discussed by R. A. Chandler, J. R. Edwards and M. Anderson, 'Disciplinary Action Against Members of the Founding Bodies of the ICAEW', *Accounting, Auditing and Accountability Journal*, 21 (2008), 827-849 (for Theobald see pp. 840-841). Morell, denying dishonesty, admitted incompetence.

[35] Described by R. A. Chandler and Nadine Fry, 'Audit Failure, Litigation, and Insurance in Early Twentieth Century Britain', *Accounting History*, 10 (2005), 13-38 (p. 20). The case was a complicated one; Morell's work on the Lands Allotment Society accounts was related to the Liberator Society and its bankers, the London & General.

[36] George Robb outlines how an inadequate regulatory framework allowed assets to be transferred between holding companies at artificially inflated prices to produce paper profits, all under the noses of quiescent directors and auditors who failed to notice the dangers; *White-Collar Crime in Modern England: Financial Fraud and Business Morality, 1845-1929* (Cambridge: Cambridge University Press, 2002), pp. 125-142 (p. 141).

[37] Spender declared that Balfour 'was by no means a common thief; his companies were originally sound ones with good and genuine schemes; and his transactions, though fraudulent, were for the most part desperate flounderings in the hope of covering up temporary embarrassments due to trade conditions'; *Life, Journalism and Politics*, vol. I, p. 60. Balfour's severe sentencer was the Henry Hawkins who had been schooled in Bedford, his memories of the town noted p. 81 above.

spiritualistic encounters after having being involved in these calamitous events.

The evidence given of spirit activity in the Theobald household makes for extraordinary reading, as much for the remarkable nature of the incidents described as for the credulity with which Morell reported them. The role of his daughter and the young maid Mary, who together or separately witnessed so many of the later occurrences, would suggest to more sceptical readers a material cause. But at its heart Morell's experience of spiritualism was rooted in the belief that among the spirits revealing themselves were those of his children who had died in infancy; against this consolation outsiders' criticism could make little headway. He also reported that his grandfather Stephen Morell - Robert Theobald's referee for entrance to New College - had 'told me of his seeing and holding conversations with the spirit of his son, Stephen, in the old manse at Little Baddow'; Stephen junior had died in 1824, his health permanently affected by the difficult circumstances of his first pastorate in Exeter.[38] This type of event is not uncommonly reported as an unrepeated experience of the recently bereaved however, and is thus of a somewhat different character than mediumistic spiritualism.[39]

George MacDonald provides another perspective, as one introduced to spiritualism while a student, later mixing with those who participated in *séances*, yet for himself firmly rejecting the practice. William Gregory, professor of medicine and chemistry at King's College, Aberdeen, under whom he studied, was a notable researcher in the field of mesmerism, phrenology, and spiritualism. This did not spring from any desire to defend faith, or prove the existence of a supernatural world, for the 'animal magnetism' of which he wrote was simply an instance of 'obscure natural phenomena', though curiously he did allow that spiritualism demonstrated the 'immortality of the soul'.[40] Gregory's wife Lisett took a less detached view than her husband and was a significant figure in spiritualist circles, especially during her London widowhood. Gregory represents an important strand of scientific interest in these subjects on the fringes of the physical sciences, though his later popularisation of the concept of an invisible 'odylic' force opened a gulf

---

[38] *Spirit Workers in the Home Circle*, p. 17 (erroneously numbered p. 3 in some or all printings). Significantly, the reported experience predates the flowering of modern spiritualism, which originated in America in 1848.

[39] George Macdonald's family provides a parallel instance; his father reported seeing his dead son John just after his funeral, an incident from 1858 described by Greville MacDonald; *George MacDonald and His Wife*, pp. 292-293.

[40] Quoted from his chief published study on the subject, *Letters to a Candid Inquirer on Animal Magnetism* (London: Taylor, Walton, and Maberly, 1851), by David Robb, 'George MacDonald and Animal Magnetism', *Seven: An Anglo-American Literary Review*, 8 (1987), 9-24 (p. 11).

between him and many fellow academics.[41] Chemistry long remained an interest of MacDonald's. Indeed, after graduating in 1845 he seems to have briefly considered a scientific future, writing in April to ask Gregory, recently elected to a chair at Edinburgh, if he might have need of an assistant.[42] This came to nothing, and the chance to pursue such a career foundered on lack of money, but a closeness to Gregory is implied.

Gregory's esoteric researches, though dismissed by many of his colleagues, probably informed MacDonald's knowledge of contemporary spiritualism despite his later criticism of it as sub-Christian.[43] The strong ethical impulse in Christianity was just one feature which he found wanting in spiritualism, though at this early stage it is conceivable that he welcomed 'scientific' support for belief in an unseen world. Sympathy with anti-materialism was matched however by distaste for the idea that the spiritual world could be coerced or controlled, let alone unease about the problem of fraud and misrepresentation. In the novel *Castle Warlock* (1882) he strongly condemned spiritualism; it was 'to creep through the sewers', to approach the Divine, its adherents 'thieves, impostors, liars, plagiaries, and canaille of all sorts'.[44] Perhaps the novel allowed him to express a disapproval which he could not otherwise name, for his friends the Cowper-Temples (later Lord and Lady Mount-Temple) were among those fascinated by spiritualism who did not regard it as incompatible with Christian faith. Georgina Cowper-Temple was apparently more eclectic in her approach to spiritualism than her husband, but both attended *séances*, taking along friends like John Ruskin, though he became uneasy about these events.[45] MacDonald seems to have kept himself apart, but regularly attended the ecumenical religious conferences organised at their home, Broadlands, and

---

[41]An odylic force was proposed by Karl Reichenbach, whose work Gregory translated into English. For a summary of Gregory's career see W. H. Brock, 'Gregory, William', in *Oxford Dictionary of National Biography* <http://www.oxforddnb.com/view/article/11475> [accessed 9 July 2010].

[42] See Raeper, *William MacDonald*, p. 55.

[43] David Robb suggests parallels between themes in Gregory's writings and those in *David Elginbrod*; 'George MacDonald and Animal Magnetism', pp. 17-19. He also notes (p. 22) a reference to Gregory in *Castle Warlock*, strengthening his case.

[44] Quoted in K. Dearborn, *Baptized Imagination*, p. 90.

[45] Carlyle warned Ruskin against taking part; Raeper, *George MacDonald*, pp. 219-220. Van Akin Burd tells the story of Ruskin's involvement, typifying the search for evidence of an afterlife and for the supernaturally miraculous, in *Ruskin, Lady Mount-Temple and the Spiritualists* (London: Brentham Press, 1982); Ruskin attended his first *séance* in the home of Mrs William Gregory (p. 12). Like other prominent spiritualists, Mrs Cowper-Temple became a member of the Society for Psychical Research. Robert Theobald was another visitor, who notes that she was also sympathetic towards homeopathy, *Passages from the Autobiography*, p. 70.

was sometimes a speaker.[46] Differences over spiritualism, if he articulated them, did not harm his friendship with the Cowper-Temples, which was lifelong.[47] Their range of interests in the spiritual sphere was truly extraordinary, from William's early admiration for Caleb Morris to Georgina's involvement in a sitting with the now-widowed Lisett Gregory at which the manifestations were 'horrible if imposture - almost still more horrible if reality'.[48]

It is not clear how often Robert Theobald joined in *séances* held by Morell and others, or to what extent he shared his brother's belief that spiritualism was compatible with church membership, though it is implied in his support for the Reverend T. T. Lynch, who he was glad to say 'was not deterred from a belief in spiritualism by the vulgar contempt with which it is regarded by small pressmen and scientific authorities'.[49] He strongly asserted the reality of spiritualist manifestations.[50] Unlike Morell, it is uncertain that Robert retained any church-going habit, but he did pursue a more esoteric course, leading to membership of the occult Order of the Golden Dawn.[51] This secretive society founded in 1888 drew much of its ritual and order from Freemasonry and Rosicrucianism (believing that Francis Bacon wrote many works traditionally ascribed to Shakespeare, Robert may have been attracted by Bacon's supposed Rosicrucian involvement), but the oath of secrecy sworn by members hinders investigation of its membership and activities. Though never large in numbers, the Order, dedicated to the practice of ritual magic, was 'the most significant and influential occult organization of its era'.[52] There was an overlap with those

---

[46] The meetings started in 1874, and MacDonald first attended in 1876; Raeper, *George MacDonald*, pp. 337-338.

[47] Hale White greeted William Cowper -Temple's social commitment with appreciative comments in a newspaper column of 1875, cited in Stone, p. 137.

[48] Quoted from her diary for February 1874 in James Gregory, *Reformers, Patrons and Philanthropists: The Cowper-Temples and High Politics in Victorian Britain* (London: Tauris Academic Studies, 2010), p. 211; on Caleb Morris p. 199. See his chapter eleven for the fullest modern account of the Cowper-Temples' religious interests and activities.

[49] *Passages from the Autobiography*, pp. 42. Theobald also there reports that Lynch had spoken out in support of the expelled students (p. 40). Lynch had been born (1818) in Great Dunmow suggesting possible friendly links with Morells and Theobalds locally. Robert worshipped at his Grafton Street church for a time after leaving New College (*Passages*, p. 45).

[50] *Passages from the Autobiography*, pp. 58-62.

[51] A full history of the Order is given by Ellic Howe, *The Magicians of the Golden Dawn: A Documentary History of a Magical Order, 1887-1923* (London: Routledge & Kegan Paul, 1972). Alexandra Owen has considered the Golden Dawn's setting within emerging modernity; *The Place of Enchantment: British Occultism and the Culture of the Modern* (Chicago IL: University of Chicago Press, 2004).

[52] Alison Butler's assessment, in the first scholarly attempt to situate the order properly within the wider magical context; *Victorian Occultism and the Making of Modern Magic: Invoking Tradition* (Basingstoke: Palgrave Macmillan, 2011), p. 2. By 1896

Note continues on following page

involved in spiritualism and theosophy, despite the groups being opposed in many of their teachings, and the number of literary and medical figures involved is notable.[53] Theobald's membership indirectly proves that his involvement in spiritualism was limited to that of an observer, for the Golden Dawn did not admit practising spiritualists. The completely passive role of mediums was deemed inappropriate for a movement based on willed learning and practical engagement.[54]

It is known that Theobald progressed through the grades of the Golden Dawn until he was invited to join the elite Second Order (*Ordo Rosae Rubeae et Aureae Crucis*), passing the necessary examination in May 1892 alongside W.B. Yeats.[55] Unlike Yeats however, there is no evidence about his attendance at Temple ceremonies, though since members pledged themselves to do so he must have participated in them. The Order had something of the character of an exclusive club, and only later achieved a sinister reputation, through the membership of Aleister Crowley (who joined in 1898, but the London temple declined to admit him to the Second Order, for which he had to travel to Paris in 1900), after which the group splintered. Some Golden Dawn members saw no incompatibility between their participation in the Order and a professed Christian faith, but it is impossible to be sure how Robert stands in this matter.[56] None of this is mentioned in his autobiography, as no doubt he felt constrained by his membership oath, for which reason it is also impossible to discover information on his involvement through accounts left by fellow members.

All this is far beyond anything demonstrable in White's life or beliefs, perhaps a sign that he took more seriously the deeply biblical and Puritan aspects of the tradition in which (however inadequately) he was nurtured. Like MacDonald, there could well have been repugnance at the claims of spiritualism, including its sense of privileged access and private revelation through gifted individuals. While not uninterested in the possible evidence of the spirit world, he was nonetheless held back by moral qualms. It is impossible to imagine his going the extra step and being tempted to join occult activities. The idea of magical control of the spirits would have been anathema to him, even if everything else about his nature did not recoil from such practices. For

---

there were around 300 members of the main order (in five temples), but fewer than 100 were admitted to the Second Order (*Victorian Occultism*, p. 34).

[53] Owen registers the appeal to Doctors and professionals (*Place of Enchantment*, p. 61), and Howe suggests that Edward Berridge, a fellow homeopath, may have invited Theobald to join the Order (*Magicians of the Golden Dawn*, p. 51).

[54] Illustrative anti-spiritualist quotations are given by Butler, *Victorian Occultism*, p. 83.

[55] Extract from the Second Order's diaries in Howe, *The Magicians of the Golden Dawn*, p. 92.

[56] One or two Anglican clergymen were prominent in the Order, and other members used definitely Christian language.

Robert Theobald spiritualism was not the only reaction against emerging materialism. In his medical career too he was particularly open to alternative treatments which were regarded as a challenge to the dominant view of the scientific establishment.

Theobald and Homeopathy

It is only through the investigation of other sources that this aspect of his life can be uncovered, confirming that there are substantial gaps in his autobiography. These are not simply a consequence of its presentation as selective reminiscences, for subjects are introduced only to be covered so sketchily as to mislead the reader. Possibly they no longer seemed important to him, but his involvement with homeopathy is of interest because this was often found alongside belief in spiritualism. Both can be seen as reactions against increasingly mechanistic and scientific world views. The Golden Dawn itself had a significant number of homeopaths among its members.[57]

Espousal of unconventional remedies caused Theobald to be struck off the Medical Register. The autobiography shows that he had been conscious of risking official disapproval in administering homeopathic treatments to patients on his rounds during his training at University College Hospital. He claimed however that when these 'medical heresies' became known he then faced only 'ridicule and dark looks' and 'no other inconveniences'.[58] His difficulties - not recorded by him - came later, as he continued to use and recommend homeopathic cures against a background of increasingly hostile medical opinion.[59] It led to his removal from the list of the Royal College of Surgeons in May 1894, and then to his being summoned before the General Medical Council.[60] It was charged that he been responsible for the publication of:

> a book named *Electro-Homeopathic Medicine*, in which was contained a description and recommendation of the so-called electro-homeopathic cures and medicines of one Count Mattei, and in which it was suggested to persons suffering from disease by him (Theobald) as a registered medical practitioner, to adopt such so called cures and medicines as therein stated to be practised and used by him.[61]

---

[57] Noted by Phillip Nicholls, *Homeopathy and the Medical Profession* (Beckenham: Croom Helm, 1988), p. 262.

[58] *Passages from the Autobiography*, p. 45.

[59] In *Homeopathy and the Medical Profession* Nicholls charts in detail the rise of homeopathy and the reaction of the medical establishment.

[60] His cousin Minnie Theobald included in her autobiography this information suppressed by Robert, which cannot have been kept secret since the General Medical Council's meetings were publicly reported; *Three Levels of Consciousness*, p. 6.

[61] As given in the *British Medical Journal* report of the winter session of the General Council, 8 December 1894, pp. 1329-1335 (p. 1334). The *British Medical Journal*

Note continues on following page

Theobald admitted having had an interest in homeopathy since 1856, and to using Mattei's remedies. In the 1860s he held positions with both the Blackheath Home for Gentlewomen and the Blackheath Homeopathic Dispensary, as well as practising independently.[62] He can hardly have been unaware even at this time of the opposition of many in the profession towards homeopathy, which was frequently denounced as quackery. As early as 1861 the British Medical Association threatened 'excommunication' (scientific *orthodoxy* was clearly the issue) for doctors who had anything to do with homeopathy.[63] Attitudes hardened and pressure grew for action against those who continued to recommend alternative treatments. As the charge made clear, the translation of Mattei laid Theobald open to particular criticism because he had personally endorsed the method and reported its practical application. Summing up the homoeopathist sense of grievance, his language in the preface must have seemed provocative:

> the ruling medical faculty has surrendered itself to the viceroyalty of chemists and microscopists - a microbe must be found for every disease and a chemic symbol for every remedy; and so the whole realm of infinitesimal and occult forces is entirely withdrawn from its observation.[64]

The efficacy of Count Mattei's treatment, which used plant extracts taken as pills ('globules') or in liquid form (the six 'electrals'), was at this very time being fiercely disputed in exchanges between its defenders and many senior doctors.[65] Nor was Mattei's work always understood or accepted within the

---

(house journal of the British Medical Association) was prominent in attacks upon Mattei and his followers.

[62] Listed in the *Homeopathic Medical Directory of Great Britain and Ireland* for 1869 (London: Henry Turner, 1869). He also practiced at St Saviour's Hospital, Osnaburgh Street, which favoured Mattei's treatments; *Passages*, p. 70.

[63] Cited from the *British Medical Journal* of 1861 by Mark Weatherall, 'Making Medicine Scientific: Empiricism, Rationality, and Quackery in mid-Victorian Britain', *Social History of Medicine*, 9 (1996), 175-194 (p. 186). Ironically for Theobald, defender of Francis Bacon as the real author of Shakespeare's plays, alternative medicines were being found wanting against the standards of Baconian induction.

[64] *Electro-Homeopathic Medicine: A New Medical System, Being a Popular and Domestic Guide Founded on Experience*, 2nd edn (London: David Stott, 1891), p. xv. 'Occult' of course indicates unseen forces in the widest sense, and includes the link with spiritualism.

[65] The system is described by Joseph Baylen in 'The Mattei Cancer Cure: A Victorian Nostrum', *Proceedings of the American Philosophical Society*, 113 (1969), 149-176. Nonconformists were well represented in homeopathic circles; one of Mattei's most active English supporters was the some-time Twickenham Congregational minister

Note continues on following page

broader homeopathic community. Most controversial to conventional science was the claim by his disciples that cancer patients were to be cured, or at least their lives prolonged. (Theobald was closely questioned before the Medical Council about his having treated a cancer sufferer.[66]) The debate was a very public one, since the journalist W. T. Stead was strongly sympathetic to homeopathy, and used the columns of his *Review of Reviews* to promote it while criticising the medical establishment's antagonism. Among the testimonies he cited was one from Samuel Whitmee, the Bedfordshire boyhood friend of Hale White, then a missionary in Samoa. Whitmee had used Mattei's electro-homeopathy on his wife and family, the native population, and on Robert Louis Stevenson, reporting very favourable results.[67] Stead was among those who combined support for homeopathy with a great interest in spiritualism, also played out in the *Review of Reviews*. Naturally it was less controversial to be a lay enthusiast for homeopathy than to combine it with professional medical practice, and many prominent figures were supporters, George MacDonald among them.[68]

Bedford affords an example of local tensions within the medical profession over homeopathic remedies, with another link to Bunyan Meeting. The doctor at the centre of the dispute there, James Coombs, was an alderman of the town and twice mayor as well as a trustee of the Old Meeting for many years.[69] Although the controversy arose from his sympathy towards homeopathy he seems to have quite as often employed 'orthodox' methods, and there is no evidence in the sources that he embraced the wider metaphysics sometimes associated with homeopathy. His initial medical education took place at the private Aldersgate School of Medicine from 1834 to 1837, but it was much later at St Bartholomew's Hospital (1857-1859) that he undertook the further practical training which allowed him to become a member of the Royal College of Surgeons.[70] This was probably linked to the passing of the Medical Act of

---

Aurelius Gliddon (1857-1929), who seems to have taken responsibility for book depots and medicine sales, perhaps leaving the ministry to do so.

[66] The question presumably prompted by reference in his preface to having successfully treated a tumour of the eye; *Electro-Homeopathic Medicine*, p. xviii.

[67] Stead's report is found in the article 'Matteism, its Successes and its Failures', *Review of Reviews*, November 1894, p. 475. Whitmee published a pamphlet on his *Personal Experience in the Use of Count Mattei's Remedies* (London: T. Cheverton, 1895).

[68] He had personal friendships with several practitioners, and benefitted from treatment himself. F. H. Broome includes homeopathic belief as among 'The Scientific Basis of George MacDonald's Dream-Frame', in *The Gold Thread: Essays on George MacDonald*, ed. by William Raeper (Edinburgh: Edinburgh University Press, 1990), pp. 87-108 (especially pp. 97-98).

[69] See his brief *Recollections*, cited above, p. 77, in which however homeopathy does not feature.

[70] Information from a letter of Coombs to *The Lancet*, 14 February 1863, p. 192.

1858 which introduced compulsory registration for doctors involving scrutiny of their credentials, and Coombs may have hoped that his time at Barts would have been sufficient proof of fitness to practise. However his application to join the register also revealed a degree gained from the Homeopathic College of Cleveland, Ohio. After taking legal advice on their powers from the Attorney-General, the General Medical Council refused to recognise such homeopathic qualifications.[71]

The ensuing controversy kept his name in the medical press, and Coombs found himself shunned by doctors in Bedford who had previously happily worked with him but were now determined to have 'no dallyings with the trickeries and fopperies and quackeries which hang about the skirts of the profession'.[72] This was the background to the formation of the Bedford Medico-Ethical Society, from which Coombs was excluded, even after he had agreed to forsake homeopathic remedies, for he would not also give up the title 'M.D.'.[73] He did not apparently cease to practice medicine in some form, continuing to be listed as 'surgeon' in local directories through the 1880s. He obtained a further medical degree from the University of Erlangen in 1863 or 1864, though the reason for this is obscure. The founder of modern homeopathy, Samuel Hahnemann, had been a graduate of the college (1779), but at least in the nineteenth century the Faculty of Medicine there did not have an emphasis on alternative treatments. Cases like James Coombs's form part of the historical background to Theobald's arraignment, when scientific medicine was confidently in the ascendant.

Theobald and his counsel were unable to persuade the Medical Council that his actions did not amount to 'infamous conduct' within the terms of the Medical Act of 1858, and his name was removed from the Register. An appeal for reinstatement the following year was refused, but he was finally re-admitted in 1899. This episode further demonstrates that Theobald's memoir, no less than White's, is partial, misleading, and incomplete. It also serves as useful reminder of how much underlies the surface of the published records, and of the multiple social networks, not all of them visible, to which individuals might belong.

There are insufficient sources to be more certain of Robert Theobald's intellectual and spiritual development, but the case of Morell Theobald is a reminder of the elasticity of Christian language, and signifies personal

---

[71] As widely reported, especially, with indignation, in the homeopathic press. See for example an unattributed notice on 'Consultations with Homeopaths', *British Journal of Homeopathy*, 21 (1863), 332-333.

[72] Quoted in a report for the *British Medical Journal*, 'The Week', 18 July 1863, p. 64.

[73] The moves against Coombs were reported in the name of the Society; 'Meeting of the Medical Practitioners of Bedford and its Neighbourhood', *The Lancet*, 11 July 1863, p. 51.

independence in determining acceptable spiritual practices, including spiritualism despite the long-standing church condemnation of necromancy. It would be difficult to argue that William Hale White believed fewer of the core Christian beliefs than Morell, but he has been unreasonably refused the name Christian largely on the grounds of his non-attendance at worship while Morell's claim to the name, and outward respectability, might not be questioned. Despite that, a church broad enough to include Morell could well have seemed unattractive to one of Hale White's more Puritan sympathies.

Frederic White

About Frederic White very little can be said with certainty. In part this reflects a working life spent as a journalist with the Press Association, where his writing would appear anonymously, credited to the Association. A rare signed piece from 1863, written in a personal capacity, shows however that he continued to wrestle with questions of faith. His 'Life and Logic: or, The Life of Jesus in Relation to Modern Speculations' appeared in *Pitman's Popular Lecturer and Reader*.[74] This study of Jesus in the Gospels was predicated on the belief that doctrines and creeds represent second-order speculations which too easily obscure the highest religious impressions. He protested:

> It is not enough that a man have, as far as may be, the Spirit of CHRIST; not enough that his chief struggle be to get every day more of the Truth as it is in JESUS, and to live it. He is not held to be religious, hardly held to be honest, while professing this, unless he professes also to believe a string of propositions about Persons and Essences, Trinities and Unities, Incarnations and Immaculate Conceptions.[75]

So far, this is reminiscent of some of the students' attitudes during the New College episode. The re-telling of the Gospel story unfolds with a psychological portrayal of Jesus as teacher and preacher.[76] Given Frederic's presuppositions, his use of the canonical text was inevitably highly selective, leaving the very human story of a revolutionary figure whose essential message was of the Kingdom of God and the Fatherhood of God. The modern church is implicitly condemned through an extended description of Jesus' struggle against the first century Judaism - identified as 'the Established Church of his

---

[74] *Pitman's Popular Lecturer and Reader*, 5 (1863), 129-148. He has other occasional pieces in this journal however, suggesting that he may have been a hack writer for Pitman, perhaps with limited choice as to subject. He was then living in Aylesbury.

[75] 'Life and Logic', p. 131.

[76] The rich detail and imaginative reconstruction is at times suggestive of Renan, though the latter's *Vie de Jésus* was only just about to the published, and was not available in English until nearly the end of 1863.

day' - which turned him over to the Roman authorities and certain death.[77] Traditional language of sin and salvation is noticeably absent, and he explains why:

> Of the conventional phrases in which preachers speak of him [Jesus] I have nothing to say, except that, they convey no meaning whatever to me; they sound like Old Bailey jargon gone mad. I grant, however, that a phraseology that has gained such currency, must be related, somehow or other, to the truth ....[78]

This closely echoes the claim in 1852 that the students were looking for the essential truth behind traditional formularies, and he went on to address the problem of those who fail to feel the expected sense of sin, in a way which again evokes memories of the shared experience of the three expelled, who as the children of godly parents had found it impossible to make sense of such language:

> but is it not, to say the least, defective? Does it not dwell almost exclusively in one phase of this manifold life of ours, that terrible fact which we call sin? A Saviour of sinners, truly; but evil is not the chief part of our life, let us hope.[79]

Jesus 'brings not medicine only; he leads the soul upwards into its pure native air', for while the dramatically converted -'a Paul or a Magdalene' - felt the 'weight of evil' from which they had been delivered, this did not apply to all:

> a pure, loving woman, whose life has never been stained by passion, seldom been chargeable with any defect, though she knows her own shortcomings better than any save God, does *not* find this fact of sin the over-mastering, ever-recurring experience of her life.[80]

This Dissenter had travelled a long way from the robust doctrines of the Westminster Catechism, and yet, notwithstanding the obvious differences in comparing children with adults, this is not so far from the testimony of all three New College students that their 'conversions' were without the expected conviction of sinfulness. But it is impossible to believe that Hale White then, or at this date, could have shared Frederic's view, for his certainty that Calvinism expressed an essential truth about the human condition cannot be reconciled

---

[77] 'Life and Logic', pp. 142-144.

[78] 'Life and Logic', p. 145.

[79] 'Life and Logic', p. 145.

[80] 'Life and Logic', same page, original emphasis. It is just possible that Frederic chose a woman, traditionally pure, to illustrate his case because the perceived greater susceptibility to sexual temptation would have made a male exemplar less convincing.

with his namesake's apparent optimism.

As the Victorian fascination with 'Lives of Jesus' demonstrates, Frederic was not unusual in his emphasis on the Jesus of the Gospels. Despite the challenges to traditional Christian belief felt to be posed by scholars like Strauss, privileging the Christ of the Gospels over the doctrines about him did not necessarily mean a reductionist approach. Caleb Morris is a significant example, and one who was certainly in a position to have influenced Frederic. Without being able to prove the link, it is nonetheless useful to look again at Morris's thought. Here, as elsewhere, the Welshman had attracted suspicion, and his friends had some difficulty in acquitting him. For Morris was willing to allow errors and discrepancies in the Gospel accounts while being confident that they reliably presented the essential truths about the life, teachings and character of Jesus. Saving faith exists in a living relationship with Christ and must not be confused with 'faith in His history - that is *faith in His biographers*'.[81] Other New Testament writings were to be used with equal discrimination. Morris believed that the Gospels offered 'facts, events, history ... the Epistles, principles, doctrines, philosophy'.[82] Tyssil Evans stresses that Morris did not therefore wish to purge the supernatural, deny the doctrines of incarnation and resurrection, or reduce the teaching of Jesus to 'a few colourless aphorisms'; rather, drawing from 'the Bible, the Church, Christ, and the soul as revelations of God', he remained secure in faith and more orthodox that he might have sounded.[83]

No doubt Evans worried that his subject had carelessly left himself open to some of these charges. In making the experience of Jesus' first followers central to faith - the modern believer, no less than they, comes to faith in a personal encounter - traditional doctrines were effectively regarded as secondary reflections. The teaching role of the church was thus reduced, a threat to the modern institution easily seen as subversive, especially given the following of young men attracted to Morris. While it cannot be shown that the New College expelled had made such views their own in any systematic way, there is certainly a similarity with points developed in Frederic White's article above.

It is unfortunate that so little else has been discovered about Frederic, and nothing at all to show if he attended any place of worship. His essential reverence for the person of Jesus is not in doubt however, and it is likely that he regarded himself as a Christian in, for him, the truest sense, a follower of the teaching and example Jesus. When he died at Richmond in 1895 his simple

---

[81] D. T. Evans, *Life and Ministry of the Rev. Caleb Morris*, p. 362 (original italics).

[82] *Life and Ministry of the Rev. Caleb Morris*, p. 362. Morris looked for the substance of the Gospels in the first experience of the followers of Jesus, asking what he must have been like to inspire records such as these.

[83] *Life and Ministry of the Rev. Caleb Morris*, pp. 364-365.

tombstone recorded his BA degree, profession ('Journalist'), and concluded with a scriptural text, 'Blessed are the pure in heart'. This suggests at the very least a residual claim to faith, albeit one probably to be defined on his terms.

There remains another area of contemporary debate in which Hale White may be situated, one linked to the interpretation of the Bible and, like spiritualism, to the place of the apparently supernatural in the modern world. Argument and discussion over the meaning and significance of biblical miracles in relationship to Christian faith were widespread. Although there are no clear parallels in the surviving writings of Frederic White or Robert Theobald, interesting comparisons can be made with the thinking of George MacDonald.

Miracles: A Test Case for Belief?

The use (or, misuse) of miracles as proving the truth of the Bible or the divinity of Jesus was a standard feature in the anti-Christian debates popular with free-thinking and secularist advocates, as sometimes reported by Hale White.[84] Exchanges were not always edifying, and some believers hesitated to take their stand on such grounds. A rugged controversialist like the Congregationalist Brewin Grant when confronted over Balaam's ass (a common topic) thought he had sufficiently defended himself by comparing his opponent unfavourably with the animal, which had at least spoken sense.[85] In this context apologists who had come to doubt the value of such exchanges banded together to form the Christian Evidence Society, urging a more carefully targeted approach to those who might be affected by the rising tide of scepticism. The prominent Congregationalist John Stoughton was an early supporter, contributing to the cause a public lecture on 'The Nature and Value of the Miraculous Testimony to Christianity' in which he recommended a more broadly based apologetic starting from the historical facts concerning the life of Jesus attested in the Gospels.[86] However the question of miracles did not cease to be important for both believers and unbelievers.

Hale White does not address the issue as thoroughly as MacDonald, also to

---

[84] And described by Timothy Larsen with reference to Bradlaugh; 'Biblical Criticism and the Secularist Mentality: Charles Bradlaugh and the Case Against Miracles', in *Contested Christianity*, pp. 97-112.

[85] *The Dissenting World*, p. 78. Does White make Rutherford read the story of Balaam devotionally in order to show its positive value (albeit a depressing message in the circumstances) by silent contrast with such fruitless debates (*Autobiography*, p. 42, Ch. IV)?

[86] Published in *Modern Scepticism: A Course of Lectures Delivered at the Request of the Christian Evidence Society* (London: Hodder and Stoughton, 1871), pp. 179-227. For the wider picture see Dale Johnson, 'Popular Apologetics in Late Victorian England: The Work of the Christian Evidence Society', as cited above.

be considered here, but the nuances of his references are important, and may show something more of his reading of Spinoza. There are three elements to White's position, and since they emerge chronologically it is possible they result from a developing understanding. At an early stage, 'as the New College Council had tested my orthodoxy, so Chapman tested my heresy' by probing him on this point.[87] The *Autobiography* account makes the question specifically about 'the miracles in the Bible', and in response Rutherford sums up a miracle as 'a very intense statement of a divine truth'.[88] In other words the meaning and purpose of the miracle stories matters and should not be obscured by dogmatic opposition to their possibility, even though they had not 'actually happened as they are recorded'.[89] In the *Early Life* John Chapman's question is answered differently, with reference to Livy's account of Curtius and the saving of Rome, but has a similar import; the story was spiritually rather than factually true. 'I did believe in the spiritual truth set forth in the legend', though no 'actual Curtius leaped into the gulf in the Forum and saved Rome'.[90] This passed muster with Chapman, despite a feeling that the young man's scepticism was not quite rigorous enough. These examples show White declining to give the Bible a privileged status exempting it from critical scrutiny. The historical criticism then being increasingly applied to other ancient works could be legitimately extended to religious texts, for the rules of evidence and of nature are universal. The significance given to understanding the narrative context saves his approach from being simply sceptical or negatively rationalistic. It is equally possible to miss the point by stressing only the outward event detached from its truth-telling purpose, leaving as Mark Rutherford puts it, 'the artificial, the merely miraculous, the event which had no inner meaning'.[91] It seems that miracles can be signs, but not proofs, with a possible implication from the example of Curtius that some have an aetiological origin.

This means, secondly, that it is mistaken and destructive to imagine that such narratives should be purged of these key elements. This is probably the force of the statement that the New Testament would be 'ruined' by so doing, referring most likely to the thorough-going work carried out by D. F. Strauss.[92]

---

[87] *Early Life*, p. 82.

[88] *Autobiography*, p. 119, Ch. IX.

[89] *Autobiography*, p. 119, Ch. IX.

[90] *Early Life*, pp. 82-83.

[91] *Autobiography*, p. 21, Ch. II.

[92] As he wrote in a February 1908 letter to Dorothy; see *Groombridge Diary*, p. 3. Strauss ruled out miracles understood as supernatural intervention, but conceded a category of remarkable events in the ministry of Jesus not created by tradition, rather resting on a historical tradition, and the result of some remarkable power. Peter Hodgson shows how Strauss subtly altered his views (or their expression) between different editions of the *Leben Jesu*; 'Editor's Introduction', David Friedrich Strauss, *The Life of Jesus Critically Examined* (London: SCM Press, 1973), pp. xv-l (pp. xlii-xliii).

His English translator famously found her task made more painful as the most sacred stories in the Gospels were dissected in this way. The lack of respect this showed to the text and the religious impulses which produced it was also anathema to White. Sometimes it seems that White faces both ways. He had little sympathy with Bishop Colenso's mathematical analysis of the Pentateuchal stories, but it was impossible to close one's mind to the difficulties such researches posed. It was not enough to simply defend the Bible uncritically, as he criticised others for doing.[93] What mattered most to White (as so often in the rise of biblical criticism) was the intention of the critic. He was impatient of the merely negative, but could be undisturbed by the radical if it showed a proper feeling for the text. The value of the Bible to him was never determined by what he believed to be minor details but rested on deeper fundamentals.

Thirdly, it was a far from simple task to establish just what the 'laws of nature' really were, and hence what science might allow or deny. White's most extensive consideration of the subject is not really his own, but came through explaining Spinoza's position in the *Tractatus Theologico-Politicus*.[94] The issue did not directly arise in the *Ethics*, but the presumption there that nature is an extension of the divine renders the idea of the supernatural in any crude sense impossible. White's remarks on the subject in the second edition *Ethic* preface remained unchanged in all essentials through to the 1910 fourth edition, suggesting that his views too remained very similar over those years. While it cannot be certainly established that White shares in all respects the position he describes, at the very least some broad sympathy can be assumed. He does not take the opportunity afforded to distance himself from Spinoza here, nor does he draw attention to any shortcomings. Nevertheless it has to be admitted that if he aimed increasingly at neutral commentary such a critique might have been ruled out, so nothing absolutely beyond question can be drawn from this lack of engagement in itself.

White follows the common reading of Spinoza in asserting that 'he denies the possibility of miracle *à priori*'.[95] It appeared to be his clear meaning:

> we conclude absolutely that everything which is reported in Scripture to have actually taken place, necessarily happened, as everything happens, in accordance with the laws of Nature: and if anything be found which it can be conclusively demonstrated is in opposition to the laws of Nature, or cannot follow from them, we must consider it as settled that it has been added to the sacred books by

---

[93] He set out his view in a letter of 1864 to *The Exeter and Plymouth Gazette* after a controversial talk by his cousin William Chignell had been attacked locally; quoted in Stone, p. 53.

[94] In the second edition preface White's discussion covers pp. l-liii.

[95] Second edition preface, p. li.

sacrilegious men.[96]

The significant qualification introduced by the need to 'conclusively' demonstrate the impossibility of events reported effectively puts Spinoza's position itself almost beyond proof. It is noteworthy that he also dismisses the possibility that miracles as breaches of the natural law could have any positive theological value. White concurs that they would rather 'cause us to doubt's God's existence, and not to believe in it', because no satisfactory conclusions can be drawn from events beyond our understanding.[97] (Elsewhere he stresses that 'faith, the belief which saves .... is not a conclusion which comes automatically from evidence presented'.[98])

The situation is further complicated by the possibility that Spinoza's rejection of miracles was not quite as absolute as it seemed, and that it is in any case subject to a declared exemption for occurrences which might ordinarily be classed as miraculous.[99] For Spinoza's apparently straightforward test that reported 'miracles' could not be contrary to the laws of nature still allowed him to grant room for events such as angelic messages and hearing the voice of God that could not be disproved by science. Appropriate criteria had to be applied in each case:

> I have adopted a method in dealing with miracles different from that which I adopted in dealing with prophecy. For of prophecy I have affirmed nothing, excepting that which I could conclude from principles revealed in the sacred books; but with regard to miracles, I have deduced the main part of what I have asserted solely from principles within the realm of natural reason: this I have done advisedly because, inasmuch as prophecy surpasses human comprehension [it] is a theological question.[100]

Perhaps Spinoza's openness here was meant to disguise the fact that the two questions could not be so easily separated or subject to different tests. As later commentators have noted, Spinoza's was inconsistent in his treatment and the distinction between miracles and prophecy was unstable.[101]

---

[96] The *Tractatus Theologico-Politicus*, as cited in the second edition *Ethic* preface, p. lii (most of White's quotations are taken from Book VI of the *Theologico-Politicus*).

[97] White's summary of Spinoza on this point, second edition preface, p. li.

[98] From 'Notes' in *Last Pages*, p. 302.

[99] Against a strong scholarly consensus, Graeme Hunter argues that Spinoza allows for 'miracles' as events which are beyond human understanding while objecting to anything which breaches natural laws; see 'Spinoza on Miracles', *International Journal for Philosophy of Religion*, 56 (2004), 41-51.

[100] *Theologico-Politicus*, as quoted in the second edition *Ethic* preface, p. lii.

[101] See the discussion by Alan Donagan, 'Spinoza's Theology' in *The Cambridge Companion to Spinoza*, ed. by D. Garrett (Cambridge: Cambridge University Press, 1996), pp. 343-382 (especially pp. 360-364).

All this was difficult for White to interpret, who indeed satisfies himself mainly with direct quotation from the *Theologico-Politicus*, but it was nevertheless in tune with his own understanding that the sacred was not susceptible to proof or disproof by tests operated outside their competencies. Science had its limitations, and White did not intend to make it the ultimate arbiter in matters of faith. Even where the critic and believer apparently shared an acceptance of scientific principles the real question was how widely they might be applied. Although White does not set out his thinking in full he seems sympathetic to the view developed more comprehensively by MacDonald. Miracles prove nothing to the outsider, and disproving them is equally pointless. Their meaning is what matters, and this is only accessible by faith.

In *The Miracles of Our Lord* (1870) MacDonald affirmed his belief in the Gospel miracles while carefully delineating their nature and function. He was largely concerned with the meaning of miracles for the believer, though without completely ignoring wider questions. They should not appear as a difficulty when viewed in the correct light; 'I do not wonder at most of those to whom the miracles are a stumbling block', he wrote, but 'I do a little wonder at those who believe in Christ and yet find them a stumbling-block'.[102] The solution lies in recognising them as works to reveal the Father through the Son. The nature of their relationship to the laws of nature was perhaps too easily dealt with by presuming the existence of higher laws:

> So long as they [people] regard only the surface of them, they will, most likely, see in them only a violation of the laws of nature: when they behold the heart of them, they will recognize there at least a possible fulfilment of her deepest laws.

And again,

> We know so little of law that we cannot certainly say what would be an infringement of this or that law. That which at first sight appears as such, may be but the operating of a higher law which rightly dominates the other.[103]

In a similar attempt to avoid the 'how' question John Stoughton had pointed out that the New Testament did not itself describe miracles as breaches of natural law.[104] MacDonald stopped short of an unquestioning fideism by a warning to 'beware lest what we call faith be but the mere assent of a mind which has cared and thought so little about the objects of its so-called faith, that it has never seen the difficulties they involve'.[105] Miracles were important not

---

[102] *The Miracles of Our Lord* (London: Strahan, 1870), p. 226.

[103] *Miracles of Our Lord*, pp. 5, 227, respectively.

[104] 'The Nature and Value of the Miraculous Testimony to Christianity', pp. 182-183. The vital question was rather what miracles might *mean*.

[105] *Miracles of Our Lord*, p. 228.

as breach of the natural order, but as demonstrating the significance of Christ. They are 'one of the modes in which his unseen life found expression', a life which participates in that of the Father:

> This, I think, is the true nature of the miracles, an epitome of God's processes in nature beheld in immediate connection with their source - a source as yet lost to the eyes and too often to the hearts of men in the far-receding gradations of continuous law. That men might see the will of God at work, Jesus did the works of his Father thus.[106]

MacDonald clearly engages with these issues more deeply and imaginatively than Hale White, in particular through the sophistication with which he relates the natural world to the extraordinary events in the Gospels. The miracles are not just signs (visible words in fact; 'actions, which, with him, were only another form of word'), but rather a concession to the human weakness which fails to discern God at work in his world.[107] For those with eyes to see, the hand of God is evident everywhere; 'I will say that his [Jesus'] miracles in bread and in wine were far less grand and less beautiful than the works of the Father they represented, in making the corn to grow in the valleys, and the grapes to drink the sunlight on the hill-sides of the world, with all their infinitudes of tender gradation and delicate mystery of birth'.[108]

The nature miracles might be thought to raise particular problems, but MacDonald takes the story of the stilling of the storm to illustrate that 'nature herself must be shown subject to the Father and to him whom the Father had sent', making it clear that he cannot be accused of pantheism, even if his language elsewhere might be so construed.[109] Implicit in this treatment of nature is a Romantic rejection of any mechanical understanding of natural laws in favour of a natural supernaturalism.

There seems to be a parallel here between the role of faith and the power of human imagination; both depend upon an ability to 'see' something not immediately obvious. In this sense MacDonald's use of fantasy in his writings (now often more highly regarded than his novels, reversing the general opinion of contemporaries) serves a similar purpose to a miracle in lifting the veil between outward appearance and possibly contrary underlying reality. Roderick McGillis shows how such an understanding of both miracles and fantasy as examples of liminality might be further explored.[110]

---

[106] *Miracles of Our Lord*, pp. 1, 3, respectively.

[107] *Miracles of Our Lord*, p. 1.

[108] *Miracles of Our Lord*, p. 4.

[109] *Miracles of our Lord*, p. 232; it is precisely from the 'fear' or 'worship' of nature that some need to be delivered, trusting in the Creator instead.

[110] 'Fantasy as Miracle: George MacDonald's *The Miracles of Our Lord*', in *George MacDonald: Literary Heritage and Heirs*, ed. by R. McGillis (Wayne, PA: Zossima Press, 2008), pp. 201- 215.

For MacDonald reports of miracles in the Bible could not induce faith (they *require* faith to understand them at second-hand as signs), so neither should sceptical attacks on them destroy faith. Nonetheless relentless challenges to all supernatural aspects of Christianity could be very destructive, as Mark Rutherford testified to his great cost. His creator's private writings however show that whatever the difficulties he did not intend to give up a commitment to true faith.

Summary

This necessarily wide-ranging review has helped to situate Hale White more firmly within the context of nineteenth-century religious thinking and debate. It has also shown something of the alternatives and challenges to mainstream Christian belief and practice. Much of this information could not have been derived from White's published writing. A good deal on Frederic White and Robert Theobald is even less accessible. Sources for their lives were largely unknown to previous scholars, or ignored, all too often because of a narrow focus on White, who was taken as having sufficiently described his life and religious progress through the Mark Rutherford novels. The inadequacy of such an approach has become clear. Personal knowledge might seem to have offered contemporaries better insights, but White was not an easy man to know thoroughly. Yet it was largely on White's writings, some unpublished letters, and the imperfect memory of family and friends, that debate about his meaning and legacy was based after his death. Even some who claimed to know him well were challenged to reconsider that belief by the differing memories and understandings of others. This wider circle of readers and interpreters is considered next, where the role of his closest relations in promoting or protecting White also comes to the fore.

CHAPTER 11

'A book that must not be neglected' The Reception of the *Early Life*

The publication of the *Early Life* ushered in a new era of comment on White by family, friends, readers and critics. It was welcomed as 'a book that must not be neglected by any interested in one of the remarkable minds of the past era'.[1] In life he had shared only sparingly his authorship of the Mark Rutherford novels. The new text marked the end of that secrecy, though apart from the title-page rather obliquely. A connection was implicitly made with the *Autobiography* and *Deliverance* by reference to what had been 'told before under a semi-transparent disguise', and in the clear biographical overlap, but even this was without giving the titles.[2] Many authors' autobiographies include reflection on their growth as writers, and their literary output features prominently, but this is not so here.[3] Nevertheless, the appearance of the *Early Life* released information which seemingly allowed readers to judge how nearly his life paralleled that of 'Mark Rutherford'.

The memoir was widely and uncritically accepted as true, in accordance with the writer's declaration, no doubt because so few readers knew anything of White's personal circumstances or beliefs. Yet this final account still left much unsaid and White the man remained mysterious.

Publication of the Book

The *Early Life*'s publication coincided with a re-issue of the novels in Hodder and Stoughton's Sevenpenny Library, and notices sometimes covered the fiction and this new text from the author. Even where this was not the case, it was clearly the light that each shed on the other which was of interest to most reviewers, and, they must have surmised, to many of those who had read the Mark Rutherford novels without knowing anything of their writer.

---

[1] From an anonymous piece; 'Shorter Notices', *Times Literary Supplement*, 8 August 1913, p. 330.

[2] *Early Life*, p. 5.

[3] Coe gives examples, *When the Grass was Taller*, see especially chapter four. Chronologically, the *Early Life* stops short of his first novel, but the omission of any mention of his later writing is nonetheless surprising.

For the *Morning Post*, Ralph Jefferson greeted the book as lending 'a new interest to the work of that remarkable and neglected author'.[4] In a characteristic note he suggested that 'by the new volume of memories the "Autobiography" and the "Deliverance" are proved - if proof were necessary - to be almost without disguise the spiritual autobiography of their author'. An anonymous reviewer in the *Spectator* did not refer to the novels in detail, but highlighted that 'a great part of the book is devoted to an account of the author's religious experiences', concluding that 'those who are admirers of "Mark Rutherford's" work will read these pages of self-revelation with interest'.[5] As a self-appointed enthusiast for White, Robertson Nicoll naturally found space in the *British Weekly* to take note of the memoir, and boast of his knowledge of the writer.[6] It is noticeable that as a nonconformist Nicoll makes strong claims for White as one who 'though he had been badly treated by the Dissenters ... remained a fervent Dissenter'. This belonging is not described in detail, but consists in personal Bible study, admiration for the 'older Dissenters' over the new, and cultural affinity, rather than any public adherence. The importance of religion in the *Early Life* is noted, but Nicoll did not find it 'easy to define Mark Rutherford's ultimate theological position'.[7]

A piece in the *Journal of Education* for October 1913 deftly summarised one contemporary view of White's importance:

> In life Mark Rutherford had his devoted admirers; but they were mostly personal friends. He shunned popularity, preferred to be known only by his assumed name, dissociated himself from any school of religious thought or social reform, and stood apart from any literary coterie. It was only after his death that he came by his own - that the literary critics of the press discovered that a master of style and one of the most original thinkers of the age had passed away. The story of his inner life has been fully and faithfully told in his romances; nor was it difficult for the intelligent reader to separate the essential facts from the fictitious setting.[8]

The confidence of this last sentence was perhaps misplaced. The most important influences on White, the reviewer judged, were Wordsworth and Carlyle. Strangely there is no reference to events uniquely described in the *Early Life*, such as the expulsion. This was an unusual omission, and the *Times*

---

[4] From an undated cutting, believed to be 17 March 1913. This and many similar clippings preserved in Bedford or British Columbia have been cropped, removing page and publication details. The fullest known reference is always given here.

[5] *Spectator*, 9 August 1913.

[6] *British Weekly*, 7 August 1913, writing as 'Claudius Clear'.

[7] *British Weekly*, 7 August 1913; this was among the material reprinted *verbatim* in his 'Memories of Mark Rutherford'.

[8] *Journal of Education*, October 1913 (from a cutting at British Columbia lacking page numbers).

Literary Supplement was more typical in paying attention to these new features. The college episode is 'of lively interest to students of Victorian religious thought', while the whole volume offered 'welcome opportunities of seeing a little more closely into Mark Rutherford's mind'.[9]

The chief features of notices of the *Early Life*, illustrated in this modest but representative sample, are a revived interest in his novels, fuelled by their timely release in a new edition, a conviction that the memoir proved the first two books to be largely an autobiographical record of White's life, and better appreciation of the religious context of White's life and writing. On this last point there was less clarity about the extent to which he still inhabited the beliefs of his earlier life. However there is no suggestion that the insistence upon continuing faith which marks the *Early Life* required interpretation of the novels to be revised, showing that stress upon loss of faith was not a feature of early readings.[10] This makes persuasive Timothy Larsen's thesis that the crisis of faith interpretative model for Victorian novels is largely a later and often unhelpful development.[11] At the same time it must be admitted, as the reference from Nicoll shows, that critics found it hard to determine the exact contours of White's faith, and this was due not to inattention, but the innate difficulty of the subject and the paucity of evidence. It was not surprising that they dealt with the subject by allusion or studied vagueness, when this was so often White's method too. Obituarists also had to tackle these questions, in the wider context of White's life and without the benefit of having read the not yet published *Early Life*.

Death notices were generally based on very limited sources, as Ralph Jefferson noted; 'the Press provided a tolerably adequate exhibition of the generally prevailing ignorance of the fact that he had ever existed, or that there was any particular reason for reading [his] books'.[12] As these tributes appeared before the *Early Life*, there is value in the picture they give of his faith and religious experience while lacking this source. On a reading of the novels alone, a modest contribution from other writings and a sparse biographical outline, they tended to acknowledge his Dissenting roots and remain silent on his personal *credo*. The little that was securely known about Hale's life helps to explain the prominence given to his father in so many instances, on whom more information was available as a result of his political involvement in Bedford, and later position in the Commons (readily found from *his* obituaries, which may sometimes have been on file).[13]

---

[9] Issue for 8 August 1913, p. 330.

[10] Or that early critics overlooked and undervalued the signs of later faith, as later ones have done?

[11] In *Crisis of Doubt*, especially pp. 1-17.

[12] From the 1913 *Morning Post* cutting referred to above.

[13] Presumably including his detailed obituary in *The Bedfordshire Times*.

The Times' notice of the death of 'Mark Rutherford' was weak on analysis and contented itself with a brief *résumé* of his career and writings.[14] By contrast, in its weekly edition the coverage was more detailed and better informed. His father again received attention, but there is clearer appreciation of Dissent and its importance for his son. The major themes of Hale's writing were summed up; 'Dissent, past and present, and particularly ... Calvinism ... mean, trivial, and malignant women, and the tortures they inflict on their husbands; ... the tyranny of conscience; ... country life in the "hungry forties", and of the misery of diffidence and self mistrust'.[15]

That White recorded the life 'neither of the few great nor of the crowded mass, but of the obscure, lower-middle class people who built our country chapels and carried on the Puritan tradition through the eighteenth and nineteenth centuries' was a cause of celebration to *The Nation's* 'Wayfarer' columnist.[16] The same paper's 'Life and Letters' feature also included a tribute to White's literary skills, but concentrated upon the novels, with no detailed information about the man, despite White being a regular contributor to the paper. In contrast, the *Athenaeum*, which had also printed his articles, showed knowledge of the expulsion before publication of the *Early Life,* perhaps derived from White himself, though it had always been known to readers of contemporary pamphlets on the case (such as William White's *To Think or Not to Think?*, and Robert Theobald's *Statement of Facts*), as well as having being repeated the week before in Theobald's *Westminster Review* memories of White.[17]

The divide was between those aware of White's college past, and others who simply knew the life of 'Mark Rutherford'; only where a link was recognised between the two could the failed student be identified with the published writer. Though the expulsion was not quite the famous event which some have depicted, it had never been very difficult to discover the names of those involved. White's authorship was the real secret of his life. Notwithstanding the greater knowledge of White's past that the *Athenaeum's* obituary displayed, the chief stress was upon his literary style and achievement, recognising a portrayal of 'the world as a pilgrim's way, or as a disciplinary college where the only master is the desire of the soul for justice and love', a contrast to the scepticism or hedonism apparent elsewhere. That White could be appreciated only by the discerning, and that he conformed to no model of what was acceptable or expected is a recurring theme in critical comment. The *Morning Post* too was

---

[14] *The Times*, 17 March 1913.

[15] *The Times Weekly Edition*, 21 March 1913 (one might demur that he faithfully portrayed the "hungry forties").

[16] *The Nation*, 22 March 1913.

[17] *The Athenaeum*, 22 March 1913, p. 335; here the expulsion is dated to 1851 however, not 1852 as (correctly) in Theobald.

keener to appreciate his style than to analyse his character.[18] His nonconformist sympathy is stressed, along with his acute social conscience, and feeling for the victims of injustice, pain, and poverty. Understandably newspapers of a nonconformist stamp were generally more ready than others to emphasize White's links with Dissent and sympathy for that tradition.

It is not just formal obituaries, but the contribution of friends, specially from his early life, which might be expected to illuminate the impression made by White. Robert Theobald's memories shared in the *Westminster Gazette* naturally centred around their time together as students at New College, with little to say about his literary achievement. His unfortunately influential verdict that White 'was certainly very unorthodox' while at New College, and 'as great a heretic' as his cousin William Chignell, is certainly misleading, full of hindsight, and possibly really reflects the distance Theobald himself may have travelled from traditional belief.[19] It means little more than that White was careless in using words and phrases that could be misconstrued. He was 'unorthodox' in not working to fit in, but it is impossible to show that he had essentially departed from orthodox Christian belief at this time. Theobald may have wished to make clear that he was not alone in having separated himself from the church (if that was the case), and was reading this too far back into White's life.

There were still people alive who remembered Hale White from the Bedford years. Samuel Whitmee, one-time missionary in Samoa, was a childhood friend who wrote of the high esteem in which the family were held locally. His testimony is too slight to be really valuable, but it does contain an interesting reminiscence from his mother, who knew the Whites well. She was 'very indignant' at the expulsion, not doubting Hale's spiritual vitality - 'I feel sure Hale White is a disciple of Christ and a pupil in the School of Christ' she had declared, and even if in error he would 'come right'.[20] Those who had only known him late in life were unable to assess the autobiographical value of the *Early Life*, but others with a personal connection were more concerned about the trustworthiness of subsequent accounts such as the *Groombridge Diary*, and publicly or privately expressed their misgivings.

---

[18] *Morning Post*, 17 March 1913.

[19] '"Mark Rutherford": Some Reminiscences of Mr William Hale White', *Westminster Gazette*, 17 March 1913, p. 10. Theobald erroneously described White's father as the editor of a Bedford newspaper, another reason for caution about accepting his accuracy, though he had less reason to know that background.

[20] S.J. Whitmee, letter to the *British Weekly*, 3 April 1913; partly cited in Maclean, p. 98. The suggestion that his problems were caused by growing faith, not loss, is noteworthy.

Family, Friends and Critics

After his death many wished to claim that *they* had best understood White. Close friends were sensitive to any mis-portrayal, including on matters of belief. Churches which he had shunned were eager to reclaim him. In 1933 he was even listed among the *Great Christians* of his generation, as a 'singular genius' of Victorian nonconformity, though the writer had to acknowledge that White was one who 'traces the footprints of the veiled God'.[21] In this way the thoroughly religious nature of White was admitted, as well as his diffidence about public utterance on matters of faith. Articles in the nonconformist press paid similar tributes, indicating the role that White played at the boundaries of belief. For the present purpose the tributes of those with a personal knowledge are more relevant. These were united in stressing his deeply spiritual temperament, though they typically declined to explain it further. His family were often as reticent as he was in exploring such private beliefs (any confidence that they knew him best surely eroded when they discovered the novels, of which some had been quite unaware until late in his life), and he seems to have been most open with friends. White enjoyed and sought out the company of women, and these are the chief witnesses.

Three in particular defended him from what they deemed false interpretation. Lady Robert Cecil (*née* Lady Eleanor Lambton) and the sisters Florence and Frances Low came to know White during his retirement. Lady Robert met him in 1909, after having written in praise of his biography of Bunyan and been invited to Groombridge.[22] The Lows also became friendly with Molly, and it is possible that at times they speak for her. This may be significant in the context of responses to Dorothy's *Groombridge Diary*, for Frances can be identified as the anonymous author of the manuscript 'Refutations' of this work.[23] She had introduced herself to White by noting that her brother Walter, editor of the *St James's Gazette*, had been an early and appreciative (anonymous) reviewer of the *Autobiography*.[24] In this way Frances became a welcome visitor, as in later years was Florence also, and knew him when quite at ease. In contrast, he 'seemed rather perturbed' after a meeting at which 'a reverend gentleman had bothered him most persistently by asking; "What, sir, are we to deduce about your religion from your writings?"'. White had escaped only after baffling the enquirer by quoting Cicero; 'there will not

---

[21] Ed. by R. S. Forman (London: Ivor Nicholson and Watson, 1933), pp. 607-615 (pp. 608, 614); the entry on White was by Ernest Jeffs.

[22] According to Kenneth Rose, *The Later Cecils* (New York: Harper & Row, 1975), p. 149. Probably one of the three women was the unnamed 'later admirer' who contributed to the 1913 *Westminster Review* memorial article alongside Theobald.

[23] Evidence for this attribution is given below, p. 351 (notes).

[24] Told in 'Mark Rutherford of the Books: As I Knew Him', *Great Thoughts From Master Minds*, 96 (1931), 122-124.

be one law at Rome and another at Athens ... but the same law everlasting and unchangeable will bind all nations at all times', and God will be the ruler of all.[25] This draws attention to the provisional nature of all theological knowledge under the inscrutable wisdom of God, and shows the reason for White's freedom in matters of belief. It was just at this most private level that White's friends resented the intrusions he was forced to bear, while aware that his reserve prevented them from knowing quite what he believed. It was easier for them to deny what others asserted, possibly from having heard White's own reactions to some of the speculation about him.

Lady Robert took a more public role in defending him from false assumptions. She especially disliked the way in which William Robertson Nicoll seemed to lay claim to White and take responsibility for making him better known. Nicoll had already antagonised White by identifying him in the *British Weekly* as the writer of the Mark Rutherford novels.[26] The force of a scribbled note by Lady Robert to Molly, 'I simply hate Robertson Nicoll', must owe something to White's own antipathy, as well as the critic's later writing, possibly in mind when she complained of those who wrote with 'a touch of faintly patronizing superiority'.[27] Nicoll's 'Memories of Mark Rutherford', published in *A Bookman's Letters* just after the White's death, could be read as supposing a closeness which had never existed.[28] They contained little which could not be gleaned from already published sources, but with a proprietorial air which suggested White was Nicoll's *protégé*. Nevertheless his attempt in one section to trace 'the spiritual history of Mark Rutherford' was worthwhile, but its conservatism - 'he held fast by essential Christianity' - may have seemed too bold an attempt to claim White for the church.[29] Even so Nicoll is arguably closer to the truth here (especially on the significance of Caleb Morris) than friends who knew White only partially and imagined they were protecting him from dogmatic capture. They could recognise his spiritual depth however. Lady Robert (an Anglican) spoke of being humbled by his faith; 'I always felt that my religion was a very thin trickle compared to his', as she wrote to Molly.[30] A feeling repeated when she welcomed a reprint of the novels in 1923; 'His name is associated with unorthodoxy, but to our own time his faith is more

[25] Reported in 'Mark Rutherford of the Books', pp. 122-123

[26] In the 'Claudius Clear' column of his *British Weekly* for 9 July 1896, p. 185, also noting White's place of retirement.

[27] In an unpublished letter of 10 March 1932 (UBC, NCC 6-15); for her criticism of other writers see 'Mark Rutherford' in *The Nation and Athenaeum* for 27 October 1923, pp. 151-152 (p. 151).

[28] Though he did admit never having known him 'intimately' (p. 373).

[29] 'Memories of Mark Rutherford', pp. 405-412 (p. 407). Like the rest of the text of the 'Memories', this section had first appeared in Nicoll's *British Weekly*.

[30] Letter of 31 October 1934 (UBC, NCC 6-16).

remarkable than his scepticism'.[31] Like many who knew White, she distrusted attempts by others to convey this in statements of belief.

Her appreciation of White's engagement with faith can be followed in their surviving correspondence. Books and ideas were discussed, and she became a *confidante* about the developing relationship with Dorothy Smith. With her encouragement he grappled with the writings of Dean William Inge. After reading the latter's *Personal Idealism* he rehearsed his difficulties over defining belief. Phrases like 'a partial depotentiation of the Divine Energy' were of no help, but 'I look at the stars or into the heart of a rose, and in a moment [they] compel the confession that in nothing do I believe so earnestly as in Him'. In the same letter he also has something interesting to say on sin (remembering that he found Spinoza wanting on the nature of evil). The Western tradition, he believed, explained sin in relation to a whole system holding that because of 'definite rebellion against a definite King, definite punishment follows, or could follow if it were not for definite payment'; the artificiality ('dead abstraction') of this makes it 'a word which has no effect on me'. [32] This is understandable in terms of his much earlier objections to over-rigid views of atonement, and reward or punishment. White does not suggest that the underlying idea is untrue, but that it is misrepresented by 'its crude, sharp definition'.[33]

This is entirely typical of his desire to seek the ultimate meaning of religious language, and explains the appeal of reading Inge; 'usually theological books do not touch me, but there is much in Inge, disguised, it is true, in a dialect not my own, which expresses my own thoughts and hopes'.[34] Another reference to the Dean makes the point of essential agreement clear. Reading his *Faith and Falsehood in Religion*, despite the problems of understanding the writer (White always defensively claims such difficulty), Inge he holds is right to say that 'a logical account of this Being, which satisfies the understanding is of necessity false', for 'I know nothing more important than to dissolve and make fluid that which was rigid and fixed but which went by the name of religion. Given freedom and susceptibility and a man may, not only every day enlarge his idea of God, but add substance and reality to it'.[35] Once more the stress is upon a real and lively faith, and it is not surprising that in her writings on White Lady Robert sought to defend the reality of his belief. Elsewhere White stresses the

---

[31] 'Mark Rutherford', *The Nation and Athenaeum*, 27 October 1923, pp. 151-152 (p. 151).

[32] Letter to Lady Robert Cecil, 24 July 1911 (HAT, CHE 35/65-66). I gratefully acknowledge the permission of the Marquess of Salisbury to reproduce extracts from these letters, and the assistance of Robin Harcourt Williams, Librarian and Archivist at Hatfield House.

[33] Same letter, 24 July 1911, original underlining (HAT, CHE 35/66).

[34] Letter to Lady Robert, 19 February 1912 (HAT, CHE 35/81).

[35] Letter to Lady Robert, 6 March 1912 (HAT, CHE 35/83-84).

need to 'properly recognize the important fact that relative truth is of more consequence to us than any abstract truth', another appeal against over-intellectual theorising.[36]

It was natural for these who knew White personally to regret the sometimes ill-informed comments of others. The dating implied in Frances Low's statement that she had known him *before* 'he was "discovered" by the various gentlemen who later on appropriated him' apparently rules out a reference to Robertson Nicoll, but probably includes some who 'discovered' him through that critic's endless puffing of the writer.[37] Her implication is that inferences drawn from the novels were misleading, and that personal knowledge was vital to understanding their author. Friends wrote articles which typically made this claim, as in the piece cited from Low, titled 'Mark Rutherford of the Books: As I Knew Him'. They were a snub to those who wrote without ever having been close to White. Something of the same feeling that White had been 'taken over' was aroused again as his relationship with Dorothy developed, extending to her published accounts after his death. Dorothy's representation of White was complicated by the fact that he explicitly linked her love with the love of God, and wrote of it as a 'spiritual regeneration answering to what is known as conversion in the language of religion'.[38]

The *Groombridge Diary*

The *Early Life* was to some extent eclipsed by the works published by Dorothy in 1924 which offered views of the private figure. The already discussed *Letters to Three Friends* was accompanied by the more intimate *Groombridge Diary*, covering the period from April 1908 until his death. Unlike the *Early Life,* the *Diary* was explicitly a portrait of Hale White as a thinker and writer. It is not without justification that Mark Crees describes Dorothy as almost adopting the role of a literary stalker.[39] The most negative reactions to her part in bringing these books to press were private ones, and public notice of the texts was less than might have been expected. A reviewer in *The Times Literary Supplement* praised the 'perfect taste' in which Dorothy described her relationship with

---

[36] In the article 'the Bible' in *Last Pages*, pp. 108-130 (p. 129), mostly a catena of biblical passages with brief expositions. By 'relative' White surely means 'in relation to us', rather than in opposition to absolute truth.

[37] See 'Mark Rutherford of the Books', p. 122.

[38] From the '1910 MS' in which he recorded his feelings about Dorothy, preserved in part by her (UBC, NCC 2-10, p. 2). In the *Autobiography* Rutherford had written of a deep desire to be loved, to find a soul-mate (pp. 109-110, Ch. VIII). Consider also the poem 'Belief' in *More Pages* (pp. 184-185) for another expression of this, in curiously un-White like style.

[39] See his unpublished thesis, 'Before Mark Rutherford', especially pp. 12-15.

Hale, but the family were much less impressed.[40] White's sister Annie had earlier articulated her concern to her nephew Jack; 'I think Dorothy ought to be carefully watched for unless your Father told her he wanted nothing of the kind I think she will write some sort of memoir or life!'.[41]

Dorothy must have realised their unease, explaining the enigmatic last sentence of her preface, 'I earnestly trust that only those will read it who really wish to do so'.[42] The *Groombridge Diary* was literally extracts from the record she kept at the time, interspersed with information from letters and other private sources. The manuscript survives, enabling changes for publication to be traced, though there seems no consistent reason for material withheld, except that signs of Hale's emotional distress are routinely toned down. In the preface Dorothy claimed that it had not been her intention to publish it in her lifetime (an echo of the *Early Life*), but it is no longer clear what 'the reasons for allowing it to appear now seem sufficiently strong' might mean.[43] It may be that, aware of the unremitting hostility of her step-children, she decided it was time to place on record her story of the relationship with their father.

'Hale's Book' on which the published *Diary* was based was kept as a private journal; by agreement he kept an equivalent 'Dorothy Book'.[44] This too survives, but is a much shorter document than Dorothy's. It consists almost entirely of copies of her letters and prayers, with a few observations. There is very little of Hale in it, and nothing like the emotional disclosure of the *Groombridge Diary*.[45] (By contrast, the '1910 MS' which in places recorded more frankly his psychological state, was so revealing that Dorothy removed several pages, presumably those which suggested his unease about their relationship.) It does however contain one letter of remarkable intimacy from Dorothy revealing her vow of perpetual virginity; 'you can never possess me, but no-one else ever shall, and I want you to comfort me with this thought. It is my only comfort to feel that you are to be mine for always, all through my life, however long'.[46]

---

[40] *Times Literary Supplement*, 15 May 1924, p. 299. The *TLS* archive names Harold H. Child as the reviewer.

[41] Letter dated 18 April 1913 to White's son Jack (BPL, MR, copy in uncatalogued Stock deposit).

[42] *Groombridge Diary*, p. vii.

[43] *Groombridge Diary*, p. vii.

[44] This agreement she outlined in the manuscript of the *Diary*, but it did not appear in print. The books were named for each other, but were not intended to be read by the other.

[45] Now at UBC, NCC 2-13 ('Notebooks'); Dorothy edited his manuscripts severely at times, but this appears to be complete.

[46] UBC, NCC 2-13; dated by Hale as 24 October 1908 (p. 24) and pasted into the notebook at her request; this was long before their marriage, but White's ill-health would have precluded consummation.

One undeclared purpose was for Dorothy to justify their relationship, even while failing to hide the tensions caused by the knowledge that time for them was short. Hale was already 78 when they met, and soon in poor health. The reader could not guess the strength of opposition that came from both families. The report by Molly that 'old Horace Smith told father he must either marry Dorothy or her visits must cease' does not in any way signify approval.[47] The closeness of their friendship, and Dorothy's frequent visits to Groombridge, had caused disquieting gossip. Her parents surely intended the ultimatum to force separation, not precipitate marriage.

White's immediate family were completely against the union, his sister writing to him 'very sharply' about it.[48] Publication of the *Groombridge Diary* encouraged new expression of these feelings. For White's children in particular, the book showed that Dorothy was not to be trusted to give an accurate portrayal. She did not know their father well enough to provide one, and, most damningly, 'exploited her love (so called) for him for her own aggrandisement'.[49]

The Religion of the *Groombridge Diary*

It is difficult to overestimate the difference made to White's later years by the friendship with Dorothy. It was surrounded by a spiritual penumbra, and not all critics have been convinced that this was anything other than a reflection of Dorothy's own faith, which White was happy to mirror without really believing it. While the family regretted Dorothy's publication of the *Groombridge Diary* they did not suggest, as some modern critics tacitly do, that his recorded views on religious matters were untrue or misrepresented. The *Diary* appears to show that White valued the chance to share his deepest feelings on faith, with no indication that belief was something belonging in the past. He suggested that he had 'not altered much' since the 1850s, and even now 'did not change', though undoubtedly quickened.[50] Always his emphasis was upon 'those spiritual truths which the material forms embody', though this could also be a way of avoiding the issues of formal belief.[51] This primacy of individual judgement can be seen as the ultimate triumph of the protestant principle.

Under Dorothy's influence White was even persuaded occasionally to attend

---

[47] In a letter to her niece, Cecily White, 8 October 1924 (BPL, MR uncatalogued Stock deposit). Horace Smith, born in 1836, was surely horrified by his daughter's romantic attachment to one of his own generation.

[48] The letter of Annie White cited above, to her nephew Jack Hale White of 18 April 1913 (BPL, MR uncatalogued Stock deposit).

[49] Letter Molly to Cecily, 8 October 1924, as above.

[50] *Groombridge Diary*, p. 15, from a letter to Dorothy of 22 April 1908; secondly quoting from the 1910 MS (p. 2).

[51] *Groombridge Diary*, pp. 139-140.

church, going with her to a service at Westminster Abbey in July 1908. 'Was I false to my convictions?' he wondered - 'A thousand times No!'.[52] There may have been some unease about the credal affirmation required in Anglican worship, but he declared 'a strong *wish* to be able to belong to some Church'.[53] Dorothy was deeply involved in the teaching of a young people's Bible class in her home town of Beckenham, and White often discussed biblical passages for exposition with her. His heavily used Revised Version contained marginal notes from careful and sustained reading over many years; 'he tells me that he reads the Bible every morning and has done so for fifty years'.[54] In this unexpected way White indirectly returned to the Sunday school teaching which he had undertaken as a fourteen year old in Bedford.

He was eager to share his understanding of texts with Dorothy, and, through her, others, and his pleasure in doing so is palpable.[55] He often wrote detailed suggestions for the presentation of particular stories or ideas, full of practical advice, such as on withstanding temptation by prayer and calling to mind the example of Jesus.[56] (No trace of Spinozan sophistication here.) This was in accord with his belief in 'a teaching or preaching which consisted in perpetually holding up for love and admiration a noble image, to talk (for example) about the Master week after week, year after year, rather than about sin and punishment and reward and prayer and church and Bible reading, &c., &c. (except incidentally)'.[57] In addition to this indirect teaching, he and Dorothy began to share the Sunday readings together each Saturday (before she returned home to take her class). This was at Dorothy's suggestion, though by her account Hale was 'very glad' of this time together.[58] In their brief marriage they spent some time each morning in prayer.[59] It is impossible to know Hale's state of mind by this stage, when his health was deteriorating, but he seems to have been pleased to follow such routines. This essentially private record therefore confirms the other sources which demonstrate, as a minimum, a definite belief in God, an attachment to the person and example of Jesus, the practice of prayer, and a deep reverence for the Bible. His sense of the

---

[52] From his own 'Dorothy Book', cited in the *Groombridge Diary*, p. 62, note 1; 'convictions' here might include scruples about the content of Anglican worship, not simply belief generally.

[53] *Groombridge Diary*, p. 139, original italics; possibly regarding himself as barred by the undue restrictions of creeds or membership requirements – or speaking of his own mental reservations?

[54] *Groombridge Diary*, p. 5.

[55] Though he could sometimes be strangely jealous and alarmed by the boys' affection for their teacher; see pp. 352-353 below.

[56] *Groombridge Diary*, p. 342.

[57] *Groombridge Diary*, p. 375.

[58] *Groombridge Diary*, p. 407.

[59] *Groombridge Diary*, p. 449.

sacredness of the Christian tradition and mystical spiritual awareness are also clear signs of faith.

Reactions to the *Groombridge Diary*

The emotional controversy behind the text explains the strong reaction of family and friends.[60] One set of notes on the *Diary*, surviving without attribution but almost certainly by his granddaughter Cecily (and so endorsed by a later hand), questions some of Dorothy's claims, such as that Molly had encouraged her to visit Groombridge - rather Dorothy had assiduously sought an invitation.[61] Almost all the references from the *Diary* collected together by 'Cecily', whether or not challenges on accuracy, are to Dorothy's judgements on Hale. This text is undated, but probably arises from a correspondence which suggests Molly may have shared some of the information with her niece. A letter from Molly to Cecily of October 1924 contained impressions of the *Diary*, including the correction to Dorothy's 'wholly misleading' account of the first meeting with Hale.[62] Molly was outraged by publication of the *Diary*, but understandably did not wish to break openly with Dorothy. She believed Dorothy had manipulated her father, and forced a marriage which 'made him miserable'.[63] Cecily's document shows hostility to Dorothy's dominance and represents the common family view. Molly seems to have moved from acceptance of Dorothy's presence at Groombridge for her father's sake to a much greater, though often concealed, resentment.

Another source, again preserved anonymously, also questions Dorothy's representation of White. Apparently extant only as a partial typescript in the British Columbia archive, with a copy at Bedford which has the inscription added 'could be Lady Cecil', the 'Refutations of the Groombridge Diary' can be assigned to Frances Low.[64] Her complaints about intrusion and mis-description are not restricted to Dorothy, but include critics like Henry

---

[60] Since critics were not aware of the family tensions behind the *Diary* account the reaction of contemporary reviewers has been largely excluded from consideration.

[61] Manuscript (of just three densely written pages) now at UBC, NCC 6-22. Cecily was Jack's daughter; other evidence given here shows how concerned her father was about misrepresentation by Dorothy. Material omitted from the *Groombridge Diary* makes it plain that Dorothy shamelessly angled for an invitation.

[62] The impetus was largely from her side; letter of 8 October 1924 already cited. Cecily was then living with her parents in South America.

[63] Same letter, original emphasis.

[64] UBC, NCC 7-14 / BPL, MR archive JHW 10. Authorship based on internal evidence; p. 19a; the writer has a sister Florence, and brother Walter who died at 31, as did Walter Low. Biographical information from D. Chapman-Huston, *The Lost Historian: A Memoir of Sir Sidney Low* (London: John Murray, 1936). See p. 344 above for further information on the Lows.

Massingham and Robertson Nicoll, for 'these biographers knew him but slightly and … the Diarist did not know him at all till he had passed his seventy-fifth year, when his vigour, vitality and true personality no longer existed'.[65] The essence of Low's complaint is that Dorothy treated White like one of her Sunday school children, blind to his greater insight into matters they discussed, while alternately bullying and cajoling him. Her lack of respect, and tendency to blunder into the most sensitive of subjects, is shown in particular, Low contends, in the portrayal of White's religious views, exposed without any sense of the great reserve he showed in such matters.

Low herself was certain that White was a believer, but emphasized his reluctance to be tied to creeds or doctrines. She could not reconcile her knowledge of the man with the sentences Dorothy reported White writing in her pocket-book; 'don't let anyone think that, because I use the word [God] so rarely I don't believe in God. I do. It is the only thing in which I do believe'.[66] She refused to countenance that White would have so expressed himself, leaving unsaid the accusation that Dorothy manipulated him, or fabricated the statement. But White always controlled the level of his disclosure to those he met, and it is no surprise if some did not recognise the man they knew in the testimony of others. Dorothy undoubtedly occupied a unique position, and might be expected to reveal a most intimate knowledge. The subject of the *Autobiography* had written of his impatience with trivialities, such that 'it came to pass that only when tempted by unmistakeable sympathy could I be induced to express my real self on any topic of importance', and this was surely the case between Hale White and Dorothy in matters of religion.[67] Also in the *Autobiography* Rutherford had confessed a great need to feel loved, presumably reflecting the author's experience, possibly rooted in an unhappy childhood, and a desire to share deeply within a trusting relationship.[68]

It is difficult not to suspect some jealousy, Frances piqued as young women before had been when White's attention became focussed upon another admirer. There is no reason why White should not have shared his deepest feeling with Dorothy, even in matters he had kept from other close friends, who were perhaps not believers themselves. The signs are that he was glad of the chance to confide in her, as well as taking interest in her Bible class preparation, even while resenting the time she spent at Beckenham. And it was not just the time; something of the physicality of her relationship with boys (including playing cricket) was certainly disturbing to him. When it seemed possible that one of them was sexually fixated upon her this troubled the old

---

[65] UBC, NCC 7-14 / BPL, MR archive JHW 10, page 16, original underlining. Massingham wrote an introduction to the 1923 Fisher Unwin reissue of the novels.

[66] UBC, NCC 3-23, original underlining; vol. 2, p. 142 (p. 193 in the published *Diary*).

[67] *Autobiography*, pp. 23-24, Ch. II.

[68] *Autobiography*, pp. 109-110, Ch. VIII.

man greatly, probably because it also aroused frustrated desire within him.[69]

Fatally to her possible defence against critics, Dorothy acknowledged that at times she was confused in her reporting of conversations with Hale, an admission naturally seized on by Low to invalidate what she wrote.[70] Low may have been partly making points for family members like Molly who could not express them personally, and this would explain why the most obvious silence in the narrative - nothing about opposition to the marriage - was not mentioned, as being simply too private.[71] To some extent the criticism of Dorothy's reporting of White's religious beliefs stood proxy for a deeper revulsion about her behaviour which could not be voiced. It is hard to see on what grounds the portrayal of his religious beliefs could be challenged. No-one else was better placed than Dorothy to describe them, and she does not seem to have approached White with a preconception that the novels were tales of loss. It is not surprising that the *Groombridge Diary* is full of references to faith. Dorothy quizzed White about his beliefs, and he seemed very willing to talk. His published letters show that he had often in that way entered into discussion on questions of religion with those he trusted. It is unlikely that Dorothy's interest was felt by Hale to be too intrusive, though her eager persistence seems so to the modern reader.

The many reports of conversation on religious themes make it impossible to deny a serious faith commitment which found expression in private devotions and outward action, using the terminology of Christian tradition even while avoiding doctrinal statements. The refusal to entertain dogma must not be taken simply to imply doubts and difficulties, as a letter to Dorothy on the worth of the Bible cited in the text shows; 'I cannot endure negative criticism ... I find that I have enough to do in the extraction of one thousandth part of the positive value of the Bible ... I will add that the New Testament without the miracles would be ruined, and that no doctrinal statement could convey what they teach'.[72] The separation here between the event and any attempt to infer a dogmatic system from it crystallises White's objection to anything which confuses the sign with what it signifies; the story of the Temptation is a 'divine' one, to which nothing can be added by doctrinal extrapolation.[73] He had advised Dorothy, on the basis of his own experience, to avoid the 'dark wood

---

[69] See Simon Nowell Smith's report of 'The Case of Arthur Craven', *The Malahat Review*, 13 (1970), 47-54, showing the Victorian fascination with self-abuse. The young man was Arthur Coward, but Smith circumspectly disguised his true identity.

[70] Dorothy aimed at accuracy, but could not always be sure of her facts, *Groombridge Diary*, p. 32, note 2; see also p. 209.

[71] Unless this is in the lost portion of the typescript, the non-survival of which could then be attributed to its more controversial subject matter.

[72] *Groombridge Diary*, p. 3, from a letter of 10 February 1908.

[73] An example cited in his letter of February 1908 referred to above, *Groombridge Diary*, p. 3.

of metaphysics and theology [and] be satisfied with the Love of God' instead.[74]

That White as an adult did not attend any place of worship doubtless caused observers to infer that he had ceased to believe, or that his private views were incompatible with orthodox Christianity. The evidence of his disciplined Bible reading and private devotion goes some way to counter such views, but the retreat into the self was unhealthy. The importance of peer group support, and the inspiration of compelling preachers and leaders in the post-expulsion period has been documented, and Dorothy sensed the significance of this. She encouraged him to join in the prayers she recited, with some success, but could not make him enjoy hymns, concluding 'I don't think he was suited to a congregational form of religion'.[75] From an early letter of Caleb Morris, Dorothy noted that White had once appreciated the value of 'social' religion, for Morris had affirmed to his young friend that 'the importance which you attach to *Public Worship* is just and godly. The *Social* element of our nature must be frequently and formally drawn near to God, or instead of bearing wholesome fruit for Self and Society, it will get sour, sick, dead, offensive!'.[76] Morris and Dorothy here undoubtedly pinpoint a cause of many of White's difficulties, as in maturity he withdrew more and more from company, partly because of his first wife's illness, but later also by choice. This is not apparent only in relation to church, for the horror of the crowd or the mob kept him from active participation in matters of political and social reform too, though he often wrote in support of them.[77]

The profound religious interest, commitment and experience described and reported in the *Diary*, like that confessed in the *Early Life*, is incompatible with an interpretation of White based on reading the novels as his own story on a simplistic loss of faith model, or the equally misleading interpretation of the New College expulsion as resulting from corrosive doubt. These views prevent a sympathetic understanding of the vital sources on White's mature beliefs. An important whole-life standpoint for analysing faith development is then lost.

The Close of White's Life

The *Groombridge Diary* includes information about White's death and burial, though with insufficient detail to allow very clear conclusions to be drawn about the implied spiritual understanding surrounding these events.[78]

---

[74] *Groombridge Diary*, p. 147.

[75] *Groombridge Diary*, p. 450.

[76] *Groombridge Diary*, pp. 450-51, note 3, original emphasis.

[77] Drink could turn a crowd into a riotous mob, as in the description of polling day in Cowfold, *Revolution*, pp. 348-353, Ch. XXV; also *Deliverance*, p. 65, Ch. V, on 'our civilisation' as 'but a thin film or crust lying over a volcanic pit' which might one day erupt and 'destroy us all'.

[78] *Groombridge Diary*, pp. 452-454.

Unsurprisingly they show the important role played by Dorothy at the end, and it is not easy to separate her influence from Hale White's own wishes. Death had come on 14 March 1913 after several days of increasing debilitation. Sir William and Dorothy had his instructions for cremation and disposal of the ashes. Everything was to be kept as simple as possible. This is not unusual in the context of his personal modesty, and current reaction against the extravagant ceremonies of Victorian mourning, and may not have any larger significance. Sir William was to arrange the cremation, a wish registered with the Cremation Society and carried out at Golders Green, and Dorothy be entrusted with the ashes.

Cremation had been of uncertain legality in Britain until 1885, when the first crematory at Woking was brought into operation. In 1902 the Golders Green site was opened, where George MacDonald was cremated three years later. The reason then was a practical one. His wife Louisa had predeceased him, dying in Italy in 1902, and his ashes were taken to be interred in her grave at the British cemetery of Bordighera. This method was still the choice of the few however, and only in 1911 had the annual total of such disposals risen over one thousand.[79] It was favoured most often by those from scientific, medical and literary backgrounds, and hence drawn largely from the middle and upper classes. Sir William may have encouraged his father to choose this modern and hygienic end. Its association with health and sanitary reform is in accord with Hale's known interests. As one leading exponent advised, here was a method for those who preferred 'purification to putrefaction, cremation to corruption'.[80] While official medical opinion wavered, many senior doctors were enthusiasts.[81] The chairman of the Cremation Society (founded in 1874), the surgeon Sir Henry Thompson, was a Wimpole Street neighbour of Sir William, who would have known many of the other leading medical supporters. It would not be safe to infer from White's choice any particular belief about life after death. The churches were slow to endorse this new option, but it had always been believed that God could raise up on the last day those who had been burnt as martyrs. Fire was no obstacle to a bodily resurrection.[82]

Material omitted from the published version of the *Diary* reveals a little more. There was a special anxiety about interment, with a desire not to be

---

[79] Figures in Peter C. Jupp, *From Dust to Ashes: Cremation and the British Way of Death* (Basingstoke: Palgrave Macmillan, 2006), p. 94.

[80] Sir Spencer Wells, cited in Brian Parsons, *Committed to the Cleansing Flame: The Development of Cremation in Nineteenth-Century England* (Reading: Spire Books, 2005), p. 157.

[81] Some opposition arose from the fear that evidence of poisoning would be destroyed by cremation and murderers go unpunished.

[82] White might have relished the knowledge that both martyrs *and* heretics had been burned. The hostility of many churchmen gave cremation a radical tone, but it did not necessarily involve any repudiation of Christian beliefs.

finally parted by death. Burial of ashes, rather than scattering, was still the usual final act at this date. Dorothy chose for them to be interred in Groombridge churchyard, and White's instructions stipulated the wording for a gravestone (see Figure 7 below).[83] The inscription he drafted, 'Sacred to the memory of William Hale White, who was born at Bedford on the 22 December 1831, and died at _____ on the _____', apart from the significant 'sacred', can be seen as avoiding Christian language of any kind, but the true significance may lie in the delicate silence about any other person, especially his wives.[84] Dorothy wrote as if Hale had wished her name to be included, but 'I preferred that [it] should not appear', though she shared the hope that this would change in the future.[85] She intended to be buried alongside him when the time came, presumably then having her name added to the tombstone, despite anticipating that his children would be distressed. As she put it, 'at death, if I am living, he gives himself to me. I shall have the right to say where he is to be laid, to say how he is to be laid ... I will leave directions that at my death I am to be laid beside him'.[86] This suggests that the 'Funeral Directions' as reproduced in the *Diary* are the result of a joint effort to carry out these wishes in a way that could not be subverted by the family.

It would be a mistake to read too much into the simplicity of the memorial wording, which is entirely in keeping with White's preference for plain and economical language.[87] By being laid to rest at St John's White was exercising the ancient right of burial within the parish (assuming it not to have been Dorothy's choice alone). In a way it was a return to the family's earlier religious allegiance, and although surely arising from practical considerations implies at least a degree of assent to an act framed within the traditional Christian ritual and language of the Anglican funeral service.[88]

---

[83] Given in the *Groombridge Diary*, pp. 453-454.

[84] Later the names of Jack, Ernest and Molly were added. It seems that even in death Willie wanted to keep Groombridge at a distance.

[85] Typescript of omissions from the *Groombridge Diary* at BPL, MR (no reference number) p. 11; manuscript of whole diary at UBC, NCC 3-22 to 4-1.

[86] Omissions from the *Groombridge Diary*; BPL, MR (no reference number) p. 12. Church records from Groombridge show no sign that her wish was fulfilled, and initial enquiries have failed to locate a grave in either Sherborne, where she retired, or nearby Sturminster Newton where she spent her final months in a nursing home. Her will did not include any request about cremation or burial, and if the executor, Simon Nowell Smith, made the choice, then Oxford is the most likely site; near to his home and believed to be the burial place of her parents.

[87] For an equally plain, fictional, Dissenters memorial, note 'Sacred to the Memory of Hetty, the Beloved Wife of Frederick Rivers' in *Frederick Rivers: Independent Parson*, p. 400, and see William Leask's strictures on epitaphs in *Struggles for Life*, pp. 200-201.

[88] Others might read this as a final capitulation to Dorothy, given his earlier resistance to Anglicanism; it is impossible to be sure. The service had been conducted by the Revd

Note continues on following page

Figure 7 : White's tombstone, St John's Church, Groombridge

It is tempting to see the choice of cremation as expressing something of White's disquiet about bodily passions. It could also accord with the idea of personal survival only as part of the Divine mind, rather than an expectation of embodiment, though this is speculation. He does not seem to have had any very certain view, but to Gladys Easdale he wrote 'I cannot believe that the end is not to be peace. There is something within me which steadfastly resists any other conclusion'.[89] The discussions Hale and Dorothy had about funeral

C.H. Coe, Curate-in-Charge, and among the floral tributes was one from Thomas Fisher Unwin; details from a local newspaper report, *The Courier*, 21 March 1913, p. 17.

[89] Quoted in *Middle Age*, p. 217 (an undated reference, within 'a few years' of his death).

arrangements emphasized their increasing isolation from the rest of White's family, which reinforced the strength of their private bond. Before the burial Dorothy's sister Marion wrote to their nephew Simon Nowell Smith urging him to attend, revealing Dorothy's desolation at this time of need; 'I can't help feeling (quite quite private) that she can get no comfort from any of his relations - they are so odd, so afraid of each other, & the Doctor, (as you probably know) has always been detestable to Dorothy'.[90]

Unpublished Material from the 'Hale's Book' Manuscript

The survival of the manuscript 'Hale's Book', and the author's collation of sections excluded provides an opportunity to review how it was prepared for the press as the *Groombridge Diary*.[91] Her introductory notes are defensive, as if aware of the harsh judgement some would make of the *Diary*, but she insisted that her 'many erasures' hid 'no sad secrets or tragedies'.[92] Much of the material deals with Hale's expressions of love for Dorothy, presumably kept back because of their very personal nature. Extracts showing the old man's frequent sense of utter dependence may have been left out as too pathetic. Some references must have been judged too sensitive for publication, but were retained here to vindicate their relationship, and Dorothy's part in it.

For example, Molly's reaction to being told by Dorothy of the intimacy developing with her father is recorded as wholly positive; she was 'very much pleased'.[93] This may truly reflect Molly's initial (polite or shocked) response, perhaps in hoping that her own burden of caring would be relieved, but difficulties did soon arise. Hale is reported as telling Molly that he regarded Dorothy as 'indispensable', and Dorothy adds to this apparent admonition the rider, 'I said I was glad he had spoken so openly (he said many others things besides) as in the future it may be a comfort to me to have Molly to appeal to if I am attacked in any way. I am glad too for another reason, namely that expression is good for him, and happier both for him and Molly'.[94] Hale was learning, painfully, to choose between family and Dorothy. Some sections which reflect on faith support the *Diary* picture of a particular affinity between them in this area. The omissions as a whole do not materially affect the picture of the *Groombridge Diary* itself. Critical studies, often without explanation, have tended to play down or ignore Dorothy's portrayal of Hale White as a

---

[90] Letter of 1 March 1913, Stock deposit. Original underlining. 'The Doctor' of course is Sir William. What were they afraid of? Marion seems to be suggesting that the known coolness of Sir William about the second marriage held back others in the family from befriending Dorothy.

[91] UBC, NCC 3-22 to 4-1 (four volumes).

[92] Note to the reader, 'Hale's Book', vol. I (UBC, NCC 3-22).

[93] 'Hale's Book', vol. I, p. 60 (UBC, NCC 3-22).

[94] 'Hale's Book', vol. III, p. 11 (UBC, NCC 3-22).

thoroughly religious figure, even while accepting the love story which she weaves, which ironically there was evidence to question if only it had been sought. Failure to challenge this romantic ending may have been due to sensitivity towards the family, but the unwillingness to take faith seriously results from an over-emphasis on the novels as telling White's whole story, often accompanied by preconceptions about a secularising development.

Contributions by Jack and William Hale-White

If the sources above show that Molly for one did not care to speak out against Dorothy and the marriage at the time, later family records make plain the depth of opposition evoked. These must be mentioned, since once again the question of how to understand White (including his beliefs) arises in this context. Of all the children, Jack (John Harry, White's second son) was most concerned that a full and accurate record of their father's life should be made. All deferred to Sir William (always 'Willie' to his siblings) as the oldest son, but he was happy for Jack to collect and preserve what family material he could. Jack's journal contains his thoughts on this matter, as well as details of the information he gathered about his father's life.[95] On 1 August 1931, recording conversations with Willie and his sister, he noted that Dorothy 'had not acted with due consideration for us [the children] when publishing her "Diary"'.[96] Suffering alienation from their father in life due to this liaison, after his death the children became preoccupied with the fear that Dorothy would seek to control his legacy, and especially to impose her own view of his final years as a triumphant love story. This concern lay behind the refusal to countenance Dorothy's nephew Simon Nowell Smith as a biographer.[97] Agreeing with Willie that this request must be declined, Jack was mindful of the danger:

> I impressed upon him [Willie] the danger that Dorothy, who had had, so far, the field to herself, might continue to create an atmosphere favourable to her own defence and which it might become very difficult, eventually, to dissipate when the moment arrives to write a definite biography. For this reason I told him that I did think we should ourselves use our best endeavours to leave behind us materials for such a work which should restore the real course of events. I urged this also on Molly who is the only person who knew the inside of the history of those years after Miss Horace Smith made their acquaintance.[98]

---

[95] Manuscript now at British Columbia, NCC 6-24, covering the years 1931-1934.

[96] Reported in his Journal, as above.

[97] Sir William wrote to Nowell Smith saying all the children were against such a biography; letter of 20 July 1931, BPL, MR 22/4. Annotations on earlier correspondence make it clear that the connection with Dorothy made him unacceptable (see his notes on an undated pencil draft reply to Smith, BPL, MR 22/2).

[98] Journal, as above, the entry for 1 August 1931.

This explains the origins of 'Notes' made by Willie and Jack.[99] The sons were hampered by the fact that they were not close to their father as adults, and had incomplete memories of their childhoods. They had access to few independent sources, relying mainly on the family papers left to them. They did not consult those in Dorothy's custody. Sir William was naturally regarded as head of the family after his father's death, and along with Dorothy was the first point of contact for those seeking information about 'Mark Rutherford'. It had been a cause of concern to the children that Hans Klinke, the earliest researcher of White's life, had relied almost entirely on sources supplied by Dorothy. She had entertained him at her home in Sherborne and taken a great deal of trouble to supply copies of primary sources, the sort of cooperation also afforded to later scholars. It was clear to the children that maintaining the kind of discreet silence their father would have wished for could only result in increasing Dorothy's influence over his legacy and reputation. The immediate spur to their decision to create their own record seems to have been the 1932 centenary of Hale White's birth, marked by a commemorative event in Bedford (thankfully, Willie noted to Jack, 'Dorothy and the Milfords did not show up') and a measure of renewed critical interest.[100]

Willie wrote to Jack about the requests he was receiving; 'as you know several people have been to me during the last year or two for information about Mark Rutherford so to save the trouble of getting it out afresh for them every time, I have drawn up the enclosed and have added some few personal reminiscences to supplement yours'.[101] Willie had already seen the informal 'Notes' which Jack had prepared. From Jack's reply of 24 September the enclosures can be identified as a 'collection of data, letters and personal reminiscences which any one who admires father's work will find of great interest and value, and which will be indispensable to his future biographer'.[102] Compilation of the material had required a good deal of detective work, especially in compiling as full a list as possible of his often anonymously

---

[99] 'Notes on William Hale White (Mark Rutherford), by his eldest son, Sir W. Hale-White, May 1932' (typescript, BPL, MR 14/1) and 'William Hale White: "Mark Rutherford", 1831-1913. Notes by his Second Son,' Geneva 1931 (BPL, MR 15/1), typescript also in the Bodleian Library, Oxford (MSS. Eng. Misc. c. 443-447) and copy at UBC, NCC 6-23.

[100] Letter of 23 December 1931 (UBC, NCC 6-8); Jack had retired to Cannes and did not travel to Bedford for the day.

[101] Letter dated 6 September 1932 (UBC, NCC 6-8); notice the distancing effect of referring to 'Mark Rutherford'. Their father was in part a stranger even to them.

[102] As Jack described it, 24 September 1932 (UBC, NCC 6-8); Willie's notes now at Bedford (BPL, MR 14/1); all the material is gathered in a folder entitled 'Notes on Mark Rutherford by his eldest son 1932'. The 'Personal Reminiscences' are item 'm' within this file.

published articles.[103] The brothers did not have ready knowledge of these, though they were aware of his books. Jack recalled to his daughter Cecily how he and Willie had as children read reviews of the fiction including quotations which they felt sure indicated that their father was the writer, but recognising that 'absolute incognito was necessary to him', they did not mention it.[104] Jack acknowledged that together they could at best venture only a partial record of their father's life and achievement; the few letters from the 1850s which survived, referring to the expulsion, were 'of quite special importance seeing how little first-hand information we have of those early years'.[105]

Given this fact, combined with their father's reticence, it was likely that the record would be stronger on external facts, and impressions of character, than on his intellectual or spiritual development. Willie chose 'not to say anything about our father's attitude to life, belief and thought' merely 'filling up a few gaps and ... amplifying some of my brother's remarks on other matters'.[106] This supplementary matter was mainly intended to show that White in his prime was quite unlike the feeble old man portrayed by Dorothy. Also, in contrast with the negative depiction of his working life by Dorothy (and, it must be admitted, sometimes from Hale's own pen), the dedication and satisfactions of his Admiralty career are noted. Although a shy and serious man, he relaxed among friends, and enjoyed a sense of humour. Willie wanted to correct the impression (from the *Groombridge Diary*?) of 'a glum, unhappy man who got little or no enjoyment out of life and disliked his fellow creatures. I am certain that this is entirely wrong'.[107] Undoubtedly Dorothy, though nowhere mentioned, is a reason for some of these emphases.

Jack's notes, dated February 1931, include a review of White's religious opinions and experience.[108] His own journal reveals a spiritual quest which seems to have made him a sensitive interpreter of his father's beliefs. Lady Robert Cecil wrote to Molly, who had lent her a copy of these notes, that 'the analysis of your father's religious views seemed to me especially satisfactory'.[109] Jack's earliest memories begin in 1869, aged eight, and his father 38, living at Carshalton and well established at the Admiralty. They were times marked by his mother's failing health, which threw a shadow over family

---

[103] Which even so did not extend to the weekly newspaper columns.

[104] Recorded by Cecily in her unpublished typescript 'Jack and Agnes Hale-White: A Tribute by their Daughter', p. 5 (UBC, NCC 6-21). Agnes Hale-White was the daughter of Arthur Hughes, the painter.

[105] From the letter to William already cited (UBC, NCC 6-8), 24 September 1932.

[106] From his 'Personal Reminiscences', item 'm', p. 1, with the 'Notes on William Hale White' (BPL, MR 14-1).

[107] 'Personal Reminiscences', item 'm', p. 12.

[108] 'William Hale White "Mark Rutherford", 1831-1931, Notes by his second son' (UBC, NCC 6-23 and Bedford, BPL, MR 15/1).

[109] Letter of 10 March 1932 (UBC, NCC 6-15).

life and caused his father much anguish. Jack was careful to deny that the illness caused unhappiness in the marriage, reflected in White's fictional mismatched couples, though the vividness of his father's writing on this subject does suggest a personal origin.

Despite Lady Robert's appreciative remarks, there are considerable gaps in the account of Hale White's beliefs. His immersion in the Bible is noted - 'the book he knew almost word for word' - but Jack disputes the idea 'that he came, in time, to take a more orthodox view of the inspiration of the Bible' rather than accepting it for its 'intrinsic qualities'.[110] Its inspiration was not 'of a different order to that of other great books'. It is possible that Jack has Dorothy in mind as misleadingly suggesting a later orthodoxy, though there are problems with the evidence cited for his own assertion that Hale's 'vital convictions did not change' over time.[111] His claim is first that the *Early Life* account of the expulsion shows a non-supernatural view of scripture, and secondly that White quotes Wordsworth and Greek writers alongside the Bible without privileging the latter. Jack asserts that for his father the Bible was a text 'primus inter pares', without recognising that this itself is a view of inspiration which could effectively amount to a difference in kind. In this way the sacred writings were like the incarnation (possibly in a Schleiermacher-derived understanding), a unique and particular expression of the divine revelation. Claiming 'such was the teaching I received from him in my youth', he goes on to show how his father was keen to distinguish the various flawed English translations from the text recovered by critics like Kautsch, usually siding with the Revised Version's marginal corrections of the Hebrew.[112] From the *Early Life* section to which Jack refers it is clear that all White rejects is that inspiration can be defined or proved, very much his view about all doctrines; the 'doctrine of Biblical Inspiration ... has gone the way of many other theological dogmas. It has not been settled by a yea or nay, but by indifference, and *because yea or nay are both applicable*'.[113]

He recalls his father's recognition that the human mind can never explain or understand the divine, hence 'his was not a dogmatic faith and just in proportion as it was profound, it escaped definition'.[114] A warning note about

---

[110] 'Notes by his second son', p. 13 (UBC, NCC 6-23).

[111] 'Notes by his second son', p. 13 (UBC, NCC 6-23). A claim which could cut both ways; White achieved spiritual enlightenment in his early college years which never left him, or (as Jack suggests) he lost an inherited orthodox belief and hesitated to claim any definite faith afterwards.

[112] 'Notes by his second son', p. 14 (UBC, NCC 6-23).

[113] *Early Life*, p. 68, emphasis added; Jack does not cite any particular passage, and may have simply registered the claim that the three expelled denied the authority and inspiration of the Bible, without investigating other evidence. There may be an echo of Carlyle's 'everlasting yea' here.

[114] 'Notes by his second son', p. 19 (UBC, NCC 6-23).

the use of Jack as a source is sounded when he writes of his mother Harriet as 'before her marriage a Unitarian', for which there is not the slightest evidence elsewhere; possibly he means his father's mother - he may then have been confused by the later Unitarian attachment of White's cousin, William Chignell, and assumed that the Chignell family, including White's mother, had been of Unitarian descent.[115] Harriet read the Bible with the children, and was responsible for the 'simply prayers and hymns' they learned, in which his father was not involved, but it would be unjustified to infer too much from this for Hale was constantly busy with work or writing.[116] The children were not baptised as infants, but this was foreign to White's background at Bunyan, and again may not be significant.[117] In behaviour 'Christian conduct' was 'constantly' held before them as the ideal.[118] Jack never doubts the depth of his father's religious belief, quoting notes from his commonplace book published in *Last Pages* - 'there is one thought which never fails, a rock which amidst all doubt is never shaken, and it is our own weakness; our powerlessness to comprehend, although we may apprehend, the infinity of God. It swallows up death and every earth-begotten limit'.[119] In this awe before God is White's ultimate faith; he does not deny the truth of Christian doctrines but realises their provisional nature. It is at one with the Independent emphasis on the personal confession of faith alone as necessary and sufficient testimony, not subscription to any particular creed or set of doctrines. As Jack recognised, his 'father's writings are steeped in the sense of the omnipresent divine'; in part this lies behind the 'Thou in me and I in Thee' moment described in the short piece 'An Epoch' when the separation between self and the divinely-imbued creation is transcended, an experience which also suggested the overcoming of death itself.[120]

Jack's reconstruction of his father's belief is largely based on a reading of his published works. While it confirms the firmly theistic nature of that belief, and a rooted-ness in the Christian moral tradition, it also reflects Jack's ignorance about his father's early intellectual and spiritual development. His assessment is noticeably *not* based upon reports of intimate conversations or privileged knowledge. Significantly, he does not address the question of Dorothy's influence in this area, despite his very negative views about the relationship, nor does he criticise the apparent effect of this upon Molly. Her

---

[115] 'Notes by his second son', p. 20 (UBC, NCC 6-23).

[116] 'Notes by his second son', p. 20 (UBC, NCC 6-23).

[117] See above for Willie's letter from school asking why he had not been baptised, p. 168.

[118] 'Notes by his second son', p. 21 (UBC, NCC 6-23).

[119] 'Notes by his second son', p. 22 (UBC, NCC 6-23), from the material in *Last Pages*, p. 286.

[120] Notes by his second son', p. 24 (UBC, NCC 6-23). 'An Epoch' was published in *More Pages*, pp. 181-183.

decision to seek baptism and confirmation at Groombridge very probably owed something to Dorothy's example of Anglican devotion (for she then regularly accompanied Dorothy to services in the parish church), and Jack admits that his father made no objection; a reminder that Molly was at times close to Dorothy, whatever the tensions later revealed. This he took to be a sign of mature toleration; 'when my sister joined the Anglican Church he wrote to me saying that he approved of her action, and blamed himself for not having sooner discerned what she needed'.[121] (White may have been making a virtue out of necessity, for elsewhere he shows dismay about those of nonconformist ancestry who became Anglicans.[122]) Nonetheless in itself this material suggests that while later scholars (and some friends) thought that Dorothy re-shaped or misrepresented Hale White's beliefs, Jack did not. Though not uniquely revealing, Jack's record helpfully shows his father's consistent and deep, if hardly definable, religious belief.

Centenary Celebrations: White for a New Generation

Hale White was remembered in Bedford on the centenary of his birth. Sir William, along with other members of the family, attended the unveiling of a memorial tablet in the High Street to mark the birthplace. Comment by journalists and scholars gives the chance to assess White's reputation nearly twenty years after his death. Three areas are of particular interest; the literary appreciation which reveals White's critical standing, Bedford's reaction to its own son, and the Dissenting churches uncertainty about one who might be owned or disowned.

Among the articles celebrating White was one in the *Glasgow Herald* headed 'An Honest Doubter', an early application of this phrase to White.[123] The anonymous piece failed to shed light on his religious views, except to suppose some unspecified heterodoxy. Other centenary treatments made a better attempt to explain White's abiding worth (though Frances Low, in the *Birmingham Daily Post* was content to use the opportunity to settle a score over Dorothy's depiction of White in the *Groombridge Diary*).[124] It was naturally in Bedfordshire that White was most remembered, the local newspaper devoting a special issue to the anniversary weekend. The lengthy treatment of his life and times stopped short of fully endorsing the fictional portrayal of Bedford in the Mark Rutherford novels, commending Eastthorpe as 'the best description of

---

[121] 'Notes by his second son', p. 25 (UBC, NCC 6-23).

[122] See references in the unpublished Colenutt correspondence, p. 292 above.

[123] *Glasgow Herald*, 19 December 1931, p. 5.

[124] 'Mark Rutherford of the Books', 23 December 1931, p. 5; the writer is hardly disguised (if that had been intended) by signing simply as 'F.H.L', and on internal evidence is clearly Frances Low.

Bedford in the forties' offered by White, yet at the same time referring to the 'excellent description' of the early-Victorian town by Thomas Wright in his biography of Frederick Burnaby.[125] There is a sense of awkwardness about White's link with Bunyan Meeting, for while the chapel is remembered as the place where 'he received his early religious instruction' and the later expulsion is described, there is no mention of the estrangement this event caused between the White family and the Meeting.[126] This may reflect the common situation that those who knew the external facts of White's life, even in its religious aspect, struggled to understand what it meant for his spiritual life or beliefs.

This coverage was in advance of the tablet unveiling scheduled for the anniversary itself (22 December), and the same newspaper commented further after the event. Bunyan Meeting had been well represented at the gathering, and the minister, Bernard Cockett, was among the speakers. He had the delicate task of celebrating their famous member while defending Bunyan Meeting from his censures; in the end it had to be recognised that the Dissenting culture White criticised had been the chief former of his genius.[127] The *Observer's* 'special correspondent' dwelt at length on White's relations with Bunyan Meeting, fully admitting the rupture caused by a perceived lack of support during the New College crisis, while suggesting that the chapel's representation at the centenary event meant it was now 'reconciled to the broader, more humane views that White stood for'.[128] This emphasis arose from the idea that White might have been more at home in a less narrow or tightly defined church (or faith), a coming great church, ignoring the fact that his deepest sympathy and essential kinship was precisely with the historic Puritan tradition.

The centenary encouraged praise rather than significant analysis of Hale White, but it helped to keep his name alive until the first wave of critical studies appeared. The importance of the event lay in the incentive it provided to the preservation of sources, especially by White's sons. At the same time it also showed some typical features; local tributes remembered their famous son, but failed to notice how strangely inaccurate was his portrayal of Victorian Bedford; his pronounced religiosity confounded those who tried to claim him for the churches, as well as the rationalists; finally, the concentration of records in two opposing camps hampered efforts to more fully understand the man. It was fitting to honour White in the town of his birth, but this was still a sign of local significance. With time the wider and lasting value of his writings would

---

125 *The Bedfordshire Times and Independent*, 18 December 1931, pp. 13-15.

126 *The Bedfordshire Times and Independent*, 18 December 1931, p. 13.

127 *The Bedfordshire Times and Independent*, 25 December 1931; Cockett was an Australian, and so perhaps felt remote from White and nineteenth-century English Dissent.

128 *Observer*, 20 December 1931, 'The Centenary of Mark Rutherford' (page numbers missing from the clipping used here).

become clearer, even if uncertainty remained about the life from which they had emerged.

Summary

Consideration of the reception of the *Early Life*, and of its influence over the years, shows how contested the depiction of White has been. The memoir was only one aspect of the sometimes conflicting efforts to preserve and celebrate his artistic achievement. Individuals with access to only a limited range of sources inevitably found it difficult to sum up his private nature, including his religious beliefs. Their attempts could be controversial, disputed, or misleading. While the predominant feature of the posthumous comment, at least as far as the family were concerned, was the role of Dorothy (during his life, and in promoting or exploiting his reputation afterwards), the question of his beliefs was never far from the surface. This review suggests that she did not greatly distort the faith held and practised towards the end of his life. If others accused her of this, it showed only that they were not close enough to enjoy his confidence in such matters.

For those ready to understand it, the text of the *Early Life* itself clearly indicated a spirituality buffeted by the crisis of his youth but resilient and renewed in later life. There is nothing easy or triumphalistic about White's Christian faith, but it is nonetheless strong and essential to his being. Friends of his retirement years did not always understand this because he avoided facile statements of belief, but to Dorothy he did reveal a deep religious longing. She could be controlling and manipulative, but she does not essentially misrepresent the reality of his faith.

CHAPTER 12

Re-Reading William Hale White

Reading the life and writings of Hale White without the blinkers represented by Mark Rutherford and with a necessary degree of independence from the novels reveals a significant gap between the fiction and the life of its creator. This would be unexceptional if White's own story had not been too often conformed to that image, a practice which has been especially damaging in respect of his religious development, compounded by the distorting effects of the crisis of faith hypothesis. The potential of the *Early Life* to counteract these tendencies has been stifled by a readiness to align it with the novels, and a failure to attend to its meaning. There has also been too little engagement with the intellectual context, especially in respect of contemporary Dissent, where it quickly becomes apparent that White's beliefs were by no means unusual, or the expression of them sufficient in itself to justify or explain exclusion.

Though some of the portrayal of his childhood in this final memoir has been shown to be partial and even misleading, its significance for faith has been demonstrated. The historical findings will be briefly rehearsed before the cumulative effect of reconsidering the material about his religious progress is considered.

The History of William Hale White

There is reason to question received wisdom about White's early years at home and in church, based as it seems to be on slight evidence or selective readings. The lack of any positive reports about the pleasures of home or family life is striking, especially alongside comparable accounts. There is a neutral tone to the extensive references to his father in the *Early Life*. When Molly settled upon a picture of the young Hale with his father as a frontispiece she was probably unaware of the undercurrents which made this text a significant commentary on their relationship. It must be concluded that family life was not always happy, and that there were tensions between husband and wife. Whatever the reason for Hale's discretion it means that almost nothing can be gleaned of his early religious instruction in the home.

That he describes equally little of his learning in Sunday school is an additional handicap to reconstructing those years and influences. However what he does recall about his young life in Bedford needs to carefully weighed, and this research has shown how even apparently enlightening sources (from White and others) need to be used with a caution not always evident in earlier studies.

It is impossible to do justice to the vitality of early-Victorian Bedford by reading White. The representation of the town which readers of his novels have appreciated for its strong evocation of place, and which has attracted the notice of social historians, has been shown to be a construct and not a report. Although often cited as evidence for conditions in the early to mid-nineteenth century, White exhibits a strong backward-looking bias in the novels and the *Early Life* which if overlooked leads to a falsely archaic picture. Taken together, these historical findings on Hale White and Victorian Bedford challenge Mark Rutherford's depiction of a sleepy and backward birthplace.

White's record of Bunyan Meeting is also not to be taken at face value. Although he is championed above all as the insider telling the story of Dissent from a personal and sympathetic engagement (modified at times by estrangement), on this score too White can easily mislead the unwary. This is all the more dangerous when his word is taken on trust, and no attempt is made to check his picture against others. Contrary to his portrayal of the church, there was much to stimulate faith, including the regular example of those preparing for missionary service, an aspect of church life hardly mentioned. The Sunday school too was carefully organised for the benefit of its members. His treatment of John Jukes is prejudiced and unfair, and does not accurately reflect the man as either pastor or teacher, one whose 'solid and sound instruction' prepared so many of the missionary college students for their work overseas.[1] A rather more generous judgement on Dissent is applicable. Like so many other nonconformist causes, the faith community of White's birth 'was a society within a society. It was localized and it was atomized. It was a negation. Its accents were provincial', and yet it was also 'a society which transcended society', with 'horizons [which] easily encompassed the Empire and great tracts beyond, for their limits were bounded only by eternity'.[2]

The representation of Cheshunt and New College too is a serious distortion of both people and events. The training system has not been adequately treated, nor the nature of the teaching itself. John Harris has been unfairly described, and viewed in a wider perspective the expulsion takes on a different character. Everything has been presented to justify Hale White in his self-imposed (and strictly unnecessary) withdrawal from church life.

---

[1] The description of Joseph King, fellow Bedford student and biographer of *W.G. Lawes of Savage Island and New Guinea* (London: Religious Tract Society, 1909) p. 10.

[2] So Clyde Binfield on the nature of Dissenting communities (at their best); 'Hebrews Hellenized? English Evangelical Nonconformity and Culture, 1840-1940', in *A History of Religion in Britain: Practice and Belief from Pre-Roman Times to the Present*, ed. by Sheridan Gilley and W. J. Sheils (Oxford: Blackwell, 1994), pp. 322-345 (p. 322).

Self-Writing and Truth-Telling

This is not in itself unpredictable. All texts of an autobiographical nature, whether avowedly fictional or offered as simple memoirs, are based on an interpretation of the life described, and one which affects even the apparently historical detail included. They will often be innocently misleading; 'little white lies'. The work which appears to be most straightforwardly autobiographical, the *Early Life*, needs to be taken more seriously than hitherto, but read critically in the light of its genre. The nature of the text is not the only consideration in assessing the evidential value of White's writings. There are new possibilities from studies which have begun to throw light on the processing of memories, demonstrating the importance of the subject's self-understanding at the time of recall, and the significance of apparently trivial markers in the text.

White and Victorian Doubt

Although the inclusion of White in the list of Victorian doubters is not without some warrant, it is unhelpful. It obscures the complexity of his spiritual ancestry, and the persistence of faith. It might be better to think of him as one disturbed by faith rather than troubled by doubt, something perhaps closer to his self-understanding, without playing down the real difficulties which attended his earthly pilgrimage. Only by denying the strong statements of later works, including the *Early Life*, and the evidence from life (and private letters) can he be classed as one who somehow 'lost' faith. That this commonly happens reflects the power of the crisis of faith model, and is a warning of the dangers of this superficially attractive but distorting paradigm. His late attachment to Dorothy Smith stimulated faith, but the revival was in tune with what had gone before. As other examples have shown, White belongs to the class of those brought up within the faith who need to discover it for themselves, a process often involving painful dislocation.

White Domesticated - or Finally Understood?

This personal struggle for faith needs to be emphasized because of the assumption by some scholars that Dorothy misrepresented his beliefs, or that he, under her influence, suppressed his true, sceptical, views. This supposition cannot be substantiated, and again may have been derived from assumptions about a pattern of loss among Victorian thinkers imposed upon the sources. In fact too many critics, blinded by the romanticised version of Hale and Dorothy's relationship, have failed to identify the real tragedy of White's last years, the alienation from his family caused by the second marriage.

White as a Representative Figure

It is not surprising that the literary quality of White's novels has ensured continued reference to him as a witness to nineteenth-century Dissent. But this very feature, especially as expressed in the psychological portrait of Mark Rutherford, has its dangers. To take Rutherford or White as representative figures is inevitably misleading, with its strong temptation to fit an imagined pattern. This reappraisal suggests that White is not a 'typical' doubter, and the status of others so categorised also needs re-examining. Since faith is not so simply gained or lost, students of literature and historians who draw on fiction for evidence must engage with research about faith development, and the psychology of conversion in particular. If this is not done the complexity of Victorian religion, and its social and personal significance, will continue to be underestimated and misrepresented. This is not to deny that White experienced any crisis, for he suffered from a series, but they cannot be fitted into any pre-determined schema. Recognising that the spiritual breakdown described in the *Autobiography* might better be understood as a form of testing akin to the dark night of the soul may help to explain the stark contrast with other evidence of Hale White's faith. On this basis an outline of his development can be tentatively sketched.

The Crises and Continuities of White's Life

The reader of Mark Rutherford encounters one who undergoes a trial of faith, yet the novels are far from a complete picture of William Hale White's life and spiritual journey. It is misleading to simply interpret the experiences described as a loss of faith, or to transfer them directly to the writer.[3] Yet the evocation of loss, and the sense of spiritual disintegration, is so strong that White has been simplistically classed as a doubter, despite a lack of other evidence from life.

This can happen even then the careful reader is alert to differences from many other so-called doubters. In a study of similar texts of the period David Wee classed him as at best an agnostic or 'partial apostate' rather than an enemy of Christian faith; among those who 'criticize Christianity, but ... do not hate it'.[4] This judgement captures something of the sense of spiritual openness in White, but says too little about positive belief. Any loss is regretted, and though the breach with the church is painful, it is caused by following the truth.

---

[3] A comparable problem in reverse is the description of unhappy marriages, denied by his family as representing life, but surely finding a basis in some direct or indirect personal experiences.

[4] See 'The Forms of Apostasy: The Rejection of Orthodox Christianity in the British Novel, 1880-1900' (unpublished doctoral thesis, Stanford University, 1966) p. 212; a weaker view of his faith than argued for here however.

The old vessel cannot contain the new wine of a reinvigorated spirituality. In his fiction White struggles to describe a spiritual evolution which involves reconceptualising key elements of Christian faith. The direct and intuitive nature of his experience - awakened by Wordsworth's vision of the divine impress of the natural world, and in tune with Schleiermacher's feeling of absolute dependence - loosened the grip of organised religion, but this is not to be interpreted as a total rejection of the church. Participation in less formal networks of like-minded seekers after deeper truths continued to be important (until work and family pressures largely prevented it), recognition of the social and corporate dimensions of faith. There is also something of the prophet about White; the one who looks to the vital core of belief, denounces false religion (here 'Christendom'), and remains set apart. The conclusion of the *Early Life* that faith remained alive, and indeed revived, is not to be doubted. This testimony has been consistently down-played or ignored in previous studies because the novels have typically dominated reconstructions of the writer's life and thought. By contrast, here other sources have been given a greater place.

The elements of crisis in White's own experience can be relocated and reinterpreted in the convergence of several factors. On their own each might have produced quite different outcomes in his life. These successive disturbances are linked, though causation is hard to demonstrate.

They are (in order, though White was not always aware of their connection or importance until after the events); first, a crisis of conversion. Evidence has been gathered to show that understandings of the nature of conversion were in a state of flux from early in the century. Sudden conversions were not always to be expected, and the status of the children of believing parents was a special concern. While White does not record anything like his fellow-student Robert Theobald's unease as an 'anxious enquirer', in adulthood he reflects on the true meaning of conversion and the unsatisfactory nature (to him) of his testimony before Bunyan Meeting to such a change of heart. What he records about the frightening stories of sudden death and damnation thought suitable for evoking a response from children has some parallels with a fellow-sufferer whose early faith 'depended very much on the art of not thinking on the hateful mystery' by which the non-elect were eternally condemned.[5] The contrast with those like Theobald who in adulthood recalled youthful disquiet suggests that White did not at the time find difficulty in the content of belief and the nature of commitment at his Bunyan confession but had unreflectively 'accepted without

[5] A memory of the 1830s from Edward White, in a letter cited by F. A. Freer in *Edward White: His Life and Work* (London: Elliot Stock, 1902), p. 7. A student at Glasgow University at the same time as John D. Morell, Edward White became a proponent of conditional immortality. No relation of Hale White, but a significant Congregationalist of the period (1819-1898).

question' Calvinist teaching.[6] The experience generated through reading Wordsworth is nearer to a true conversion for White, but significantly not one which tied him to the church or any particular doctrinal formulation of faith.

Hale's was also a crisis of vocation. He had not chosen a ministerial career, but had acceded to his mother's desire that he should train for one. The tension between his own hopes of a different future, then the idealistic zeal of his emerging spirituality and the reality of the pettiness of chapel life, was intolerable to him. At the very least he became determined not to accommodate himself to the reduced expectations of his likely congregations, and may actively have welcomed the chance to leave New College early which the 1852 crisis presented. This outcome might have been proof to those concerned that the stress upon an educated ministry opened up too large a gulf between the thought world (and aspirations) of a minister and his congregation. The expulsion incident itself has been shown to be less easily explicable than normally suggested, and not an episode to be associated with the loss of faith.

It produced a crisis of commitment. Cheshunt and New College had not adequately provided the nourishment his soul sought (and already found in 'Nature'), and the engagement at Ditchling notwithstanding it was far from certain that chapel members would respond to his preaching or share his views.[7] George MacDonald and Henry Julius Martyn in their different ways show how easily pastor and flock could become alienated. Since the authorities at New College, like the family's minister in Bedford, had failed to show any commitment to him, so in the future he was unable to trust himself to the privileges or responsibilities of church membership. No doubt this was reinforced by his resistance to the sort of confession which an application for membership would require.

This highlights a crisis of conscience, the ethic which lies behind White's constant refusal to identify himself with particular statements of belief. Resistance towards credal subscription was an honourable tradition in Independency, where any tests except the testimony of Christian experience (which White declined to repeat after a troubled reinterpretation of his adolescent confession) could be viewed with suspicion. There is every reason to believe that he would have concurred with Thomas Binney's verdict that 'the act of subscription would either indicate the death within me of the moral man, or it would inflict such a wound that he would soon die'; a sin against God and

---

[6] *Early Life*, p. 60; only in retrospect was its teaching on predestination branded 'a terrible invention'.

[7] Assuming that his willingness to serve there meant it was not as bleak as the fictional parallels.

self.[8] Binney had Anglicanism in his sights but White, with his later embarrassment about the confession in applying for membership at Bunyan Meeting ('I had no experience to give') was unwilling to talk even of personal 'experience', let alone formal Christian beliefs.[9] In the circumstances this stance is not to be taken as a sign of disbelief, but of principled exception to such demands. He stands alongside many others instinctively opposed to doctrinal tests, of whom David Simon has been seen to be a prominent example.

It is not misleading in this context to talk of a crisis of church. The existence, and importance, of informal groupings, especially of students, around gifted preachers and teachers like Caleb Morris, F. D. Maurice, and others, points to a widespread need for greater stimulation than many churches could provide. If doubts and questions could not be expressed except in such gatherings there was a clear danger of disaffection among those most touched by the intellectual ferment of the age. Ministers who could read the signs of the times, in whose preaching the Bible became alive and mediated a sense of encountering the living God, were too rare. It is noticeable that those who tried to reclaim him for the church after death effectively blamed the church for failing to recognise the youthful White's true spirituality, the prophet in their midst.[10] Though the ministries of famous preachers were widely valued, especially by ministerial students and the young, it may be significant that as with Morris there was often a suspicion of their being not quite orthodox. Of their importance however there was no doubt. Thomas Binney's impact on the young was recalled in a tribute in the *Nonconformist*:

> [He] held awe-struck the masses of young men and serious burghers who listened to his ministrations ... which turned Scripture stories into living history, made the dry bones of antiquity move again, and vanquished incredulity by the mere realisation of the miracles.[11]

White's gradual removal from such spheres was undoubtedly detrimental to his spiritual life.

If the quality of ministers was an issue for White, so too the status of organised religion raised serious questions for him, a crisis of Christendom. Crucial here was the social and ethical teaching of the churches, and the

---

[8] Cited in E. Paxton Hood, *Thomas Binney*, p. 38. Compare White's attack on the 'clerical sophisms' of an Oxford education in a letter of 1897 published in *Letters to Three Friends*, p. 163.

[9] *Autobiography*, p. 11, Ch. I.

[10] This is reflected for example in Sperry's tribute, 'Mark Rutherford', *Harvard Theological Review*, 7 (1914), 166-192.

[11] Cited in Hood, *Thomas Binney*, p. 290. On the revival of preaching heralded by men like Binney see Watts, *The Dissenters, vol. II*, pp. 177-178.

attitudes prevalent in an avowedly Christian country. Faith cannot be divorced from political questions, for if Christianity 'has nothing to do with politics or daily life it is not a religion'.[12] The divided witness of the churches over the South African war was a particular cause of White's condemnation of what may be pejoratively termed 'Christendom'. He believed that the nonconformist churches had failed to provide a distinctive voice, and the Established Church was compromised by its status. While no defender of Anglican privileges, he was not a vociferous supporter of the campaigns for greater rights for Dissenters since the quest for power too easily corrupted the principles for which earlier generations had fought and suffered. Some of the issues which preoccupied nonconformists zealous to protect their position *vis-à-vis* Anglicanism, as over schooling, were less urgent than the social deprivation in the poorer parts of London and the divide between rich and poor.[13] The social and political failure of the churches was therefore a reason - if possibly also an excuse - for White to withhold his allegiance.

Lastly, White's case shows something of an intellectual crisis in Christianity. He explored new ways of understanding faith, including through the philosophy of Spinoza, and while not ultimately of great value, his study highlights a need for the intellectual reinvigoration of belief against the challenges of the century. White did not take advantage of theological routes to new understandings of faith, but there can be no doubt about the call for them. Had they been more accessible he might have found help and not been condemned to a largely self-imposed lonely search. If his scant references to major doctrines such as the incarnation make it difficult to be certain exactly what he believed, this can also be said of many nonconformist thinkers who eschewed dogmatic statements.[14]

As has become clear, believing has an important social dimension. The complex relationship between belief and belonging has a special poignancy in White's case. While rejecting in the spirit of a reformer much that the nonconformity of his day stood for he nonetheless bound up his whole identity with the Dissenting tradition, often evoking the solid values of Puritanism. This strong bond made it impossible in practice to find a spiritual home in any other church when distanced from his roots. Though this may have suited (and sprung from) his sense of not being a 'joiner' or 'belonger', it inevitably cut

---

[12] From a letter to Mabel Marsh, 16 July 1901, in *Letters to Three Friends*, pp. 211-212. It is partly a misreading of this letter which leads Peter Allen to suggest that White meant to disavow Christianity itself as a belief-system, rather than to critique its social role; 'Mark Rutherford: The Anatomy of a Failure', pp. 158-159 (note 24).

[13] Concerns expressed in a letter of February 1906, in *Letters to Three Friends*, pp. 132-133.

[14] And if profession of an experiential faith was all that mattered for church membership, why should doctrines be a suitable test of faith in later life?

him off from other sources of spiritual nourishment. There is a sense in which White seems always to have felt somewhat alone or apart, a trait arguably distinguishable even in his portrayal of early years.

Most of these issues were not unique to White or to his generation, and it is therefore possible to relate some of his problems to the lives of modern believers. His experiences as well as his writings can speak beyond their time.

White and Modern Spirituality

While this account has underlined White's sense of connection with a Dissenting past his emphasis upon personal belief also links him to the present age. With Wordsworth began the 'massive subjective turn' which Heelas and Woodhead identify as shaping the face of belief in modern times.[15] The importance of external factors upon the individual's faith journey has been shown here, along with the significance of groups in which issues of personal faith could be addressed for mutual encouragement. There is a degree of similarity with more recent forms of alienation from traditional religious expression. David Tacey has outlined the shift described as 'losing my religion, recovering the sacred' by charting a progress which is not so very far from that suggested for Hale White; a 'natal faith' is tested during adolescence, and renounced over time. The secular world then inhabited fails to satisfy (mainly because of its gross materialism), and the disillusioned seeker builds a new spirituality outside recognised religious traditions.[16] Research shows that the degree of congruence between the final faith position and the formally inherited beliefs is affected by the extent to which the past connection is valued.

It would be interesting to compare White's case further with these contemporary trends which (if the claims of the 'detached' believers reported by Tacey are taken seriously) are examples of loss *and* gain. The apparently growing attraction of a personal spirituality outside ecclesiastical structures means that research on church leaving and returning also has some overlap with the sort of issues which arose in White's life.

These are not the only possible links with contemporary debates about the place of religion. The understanding of sin has proved important in assessing the spiritual journeys of the three expelled, and some work might be done to relate this to modern debates about the causes and implications of secularisation. Dominic Erdozain has suggested that changing concepts of sin

---

[15] *The Spiritual Revolution: Why Religion is Giving Way to Spirituality* by Paul Heelas and Linda Woodhead (Oxford: Blackwell, 2005), p. 2.

[16] In *The Spirituality Revolution: The Emergence of Contemporary Spirituality* (London: Routledge, 2004), pp. 106-107. His subjects report weakening parental faith allegiances over the same period, an interesting parallel to William White perhaps, where evidence about his ties to Bunyan Meeting has been mixed.

in the nineteenth century are linked to later decline, as sin was gradually redefined in terms of external behaviour rather than as an ontological state.[17] Traditional soteriology was thereby damagingly undermined. The exploration of these changes within the churches could usefully be developed alongside the study of published and unpublished personal narratives giving insights to the life of faith.

Stories Still to be Told

This is clearly far from the last word on White - its aim has been more modest - and there remain many gaps in the available knowledge on his life. The standard accounts of a happy childhood have been challenged, but much is uncertain about his upbringing, while his siblings remain almost completely unknown. The newly discovered Colenutt letters show him reporting in 1898 that his sister Henrietta's husband had been bankrupted in a business failure, but there is scant evidence to show how these family relationships developed over the years.[18] There is reference also to some apparent scandal attached to his cousin Polly ('a dismal story'), again without any detail.[19] His own family life was certainly strained, though it is impossible to say to what extent this was due to his wife's illness, and sources on this are likely to be difficult to find. The emotional consequence seems to have been severe, affecting his relationship with the children. Writing to Erica Storr in 1910 he lamented that he could not 'remember any pleasure or instruction derived from my infants as infants. I suppose I never took to them really, although I was ashamed to confess it'.[20] Further research, especially among his extensive newspaper contributions which have not yet been fully collected or examined, may yield further biographical clues, and even some insights on belief. Now that the role of Dorothy Smith is better understood an attempt might also be made to seek more evidence about her years with White which may in the past have been discreetly overlooked, particularly on relations with his family, and her concern for his reputation. A full study of her life is itself desirable.

More might be said about the sometimes surprising instances where White's influence has been felt in the English literary tradition. It has been a commonplace to cite favourable references in writers such as D. H. Lawrence

[17] 'The Secularisation of Sin in the Nineteenth Century', *Journal of Ecclesiastical History*, 62 (2011), 59-88.

[18] A letter of August 1898 partly reproduced in *Letters to Three Friends* (pp. 87-88), but with this passage omitted (numbered 103 in the unpublished sequence).

[19] Letter of 23 October 1893 reproduced in *Letters to Three Friends* (pp. 63-64), with this section omitted (numbered 81 in the unpublished sequence).

[20] Letter of 9 November 1910, continued on 12 November, when he regretted his remark but did not cancel it. University of Sussex: Mark Rutherford Letters SxMs6, no. 27.

and Arnold Bennett, but other connections may be waiting to be discovered. Of the Auden generation, Edward Upward professed a debt to the first two Mark Rutherford novels in shaping his style, worked out in the *Spiral Ascent* trilogy. Surely it was more than a matter of form too, as Upward's fiction charted his own struggle with dogma in striving to keep the pure Marxist-Leninist faith while increasingly disenchanted with the British Communist Party. He was introduced to White's work through his Congregational family background, especially represented in holidays with grandparents of that allegiance living on the Isle of Wight.[21] Possible links with other writers nurtured to a greater or lesser extent in nonconformity would be worth investigating.

In the context of faith, the significance of changing ideas of conversion and the availability of more sensitive genre-specific literary readings suggest possibilities of parallel research in autobiographical records of all kinds. These may constitute a further challenge to the supremacy of the crisis of faith hypothesis, and could usefully give special attention to those at the borderlines of belief. The route by which some who stepped outside the bounds of orthodoxy retained a live spirituality while others succumbed to secular influences needs more research. In this area, as in the case of White, received opinions about Victorian 'doubt' have obscured the need for a closer look at the evidence. A clearer appreciation of the psychology of faith development would also help to banish the crude and misleading opposition of faith and doubt.

It will then be properly acknowledged that 'religious beliefs can coexist with scepticism and despair', and become easier to understand those like William Hale White who continue to search for faith among their perplexities - in his case doing justice to one who despite being unable to 'encompass God with a well-marked definition' could nevertheless truly declare 'I believe in Him'.[22]

---

[21] The acknowledgement was made by Upward in a private letter of 1992 to Katherine Bucknell, cited in her essay 'The Achievement of Edward Upward', in *W.H. Auden, 'The Language of Learning and the Language of Love': Uncollected Writing, New Interpretations*, ed. by K. Bucknell and N. Jenkins (Oxford: Clarendon Press, 1994), pp. 165-184 (p. 167).

[22] From jottings in the "White" Notebook of ca. 1907-1912, p. 7 of an unpaginated manuscript (UBC, NCC 3-1) and secondly as Mark Rutherford, *Autobiography*, p. 88, Ch. VI.

APPENDIX

Selected Lines of Hale White's Family Tree

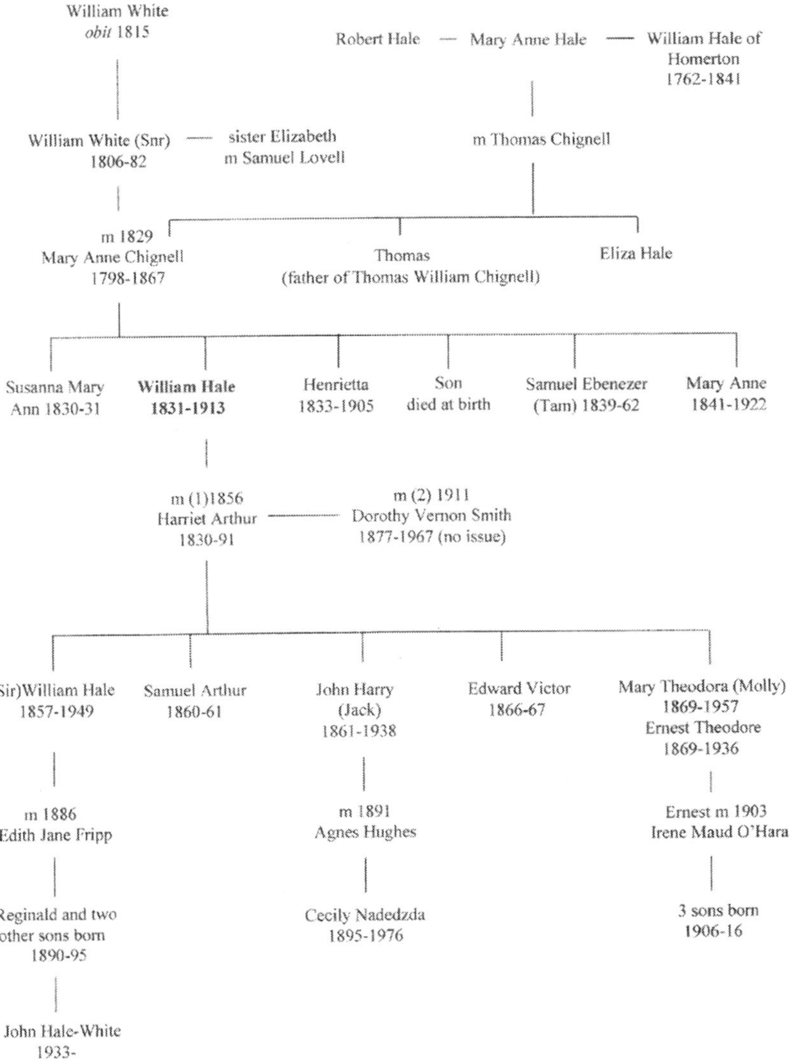

Information from genealogies at British Columbia drawn from family sources (UBC, NCC 6-19)

Bibliography

(a) Works by William Hale White (by date of first publication)

White, W.H. *An Argument for an Extension of the Franchise: A Letter Addressed to George Jacob Holyoake, Esq.* (London: F. Farrah, 1866).

— *Letter Written on the Death of Mrs Elizabeth Street* (London: W. P. Griffith & Son, Printers, 1877).

— 'Ixion', *The Secular Review*, 11 September 1880, pp. 164-165.

— *The Autobiography of Mark Rutherford*, The Works of Mark Rutherford, 1 (London: T. Fisher Unwin, n.d.). [First published 1881]

— *Mark Rutherford's Deliverance*, The Works of Mark Rutherford, 2 (London: T. Fisher Unwin, n.d.). [First published 1885]

[Printed by T. Fisher Unwin in 1924 as *The Deliverance of Mark Rutherford*; and under licence to Jonathan Cape for the Travellers' Library, 1927, same title.]

— *The Revolution in Tanner's Lane*, The Works of Mark Rutherford, 3 (London: T. Fisher Unwin, n.d.). [First published 1887]

— *The Autobiography of Mark Rutherford and Mark Rutherford's Deliverance*. [First published 1888]

— *Miriam's Schooling and Other Papers*, The Works of Mark Rutherford, 4 (London: T. Fisher Unwin, n.d.). [First published 1890]

— *Catharine Furze*, The Works of Mark Rutherford, 5 (London: T. Fisher Unwin, n.d.). [First published 1893]

— *Clara Hopgood*, The Works of Mark Rutherford, 6 (London: T. Fisher Unwin, n.d.). [First published 1896]

— *An Examination of the Charge of Apostasy Against Wordsworth* (London: Longmans, Green, 1898).

— *Coleridge's Poems: A Facsimile Reproduction of the Proofs and MSS. of Some of the Poems*, edited by the late James Dykes Campbell, with Preface and Notes by W. Hale White (Westminster: Archibald Constable, 1899).

— 'Caleb Morris', *The British Weekly*, 6 March 1902, p. 532 (Reprinted in *Last Pages from a Journal*).

— *John Bunyan* (London: Hodder and Stoughton, 1905).

— Letter, 'Mr W. S. Lilley and the Times', *The Speaker*, 10 February 1906, pp. 457-458.

— *Pages from a Journal With Other Papers*, 2nd edn (London: Oxford University Press, 1910). [First edition 1900]

— *More Pages from a Journal With Other Papers* (London: Oxford University Press, 1910).

— *The Early Life of Mark Rutherford* (W. Hale White) (London: Oxford University Press, 1913).
— *Last Pages from a Journal With Other Papers*, ed. by Dorothy White (London: Oxford University Press, 1915).
— *Letters to Three Friends* [ed. by Dorothy White] (London: Oxford University Press, 1924).
White, W.H. (ed.) *A Description of the Wordsworth and Coleridge Manuscripts in the Possession of Mr T. Norton Longman*. With three facsimile reproductions. Edited with Notes by W. Hale White (London: Longmans, Green, 1897).
— *Selections from Dr Johnson's 'Rambler'*. Edited, with Preface and Notes, by W. Hale White (Oxford: Clarendon Press, 1907).
White, W.H. (trans.) *Ethic: Demonstrated in Geometrical Order, and Divided into Five Parts, etc. by Benedict De Spinoza*, translated from the Latin by William Hale White (London: Trübner, 1883); second edition, T. Fisher Unwin, 1894; third edition, Duckworth & Co., 1899; fourth edition, Oxford University Press, 1910.
— *Tractatus de Intellectus Emendatione: Et de Via, Qua Optime Veram Rerum Congnitionem Dirigitur*, Translated from the Latin of Benedict De Spinoza by W. Hale White. Translation revised by Amelia Hutchison Stirling M.A. (Edin.) (London: T. Fisher Unwin, 1895) Reprinted by Duckworth & Co., 1899.
White, W.H. (journalism)
— 'Metropolitan Notes' Aberdeen Herald, 24 August 1861, p. 4; 28 September 1861, p. 4; 5 October 1861, p. 4; 18 January 1862, p. 4; 1 February 1862, p. 4; 8 March 1862, p. 4; 24 May 1862, p. 4; 4 November 1871, p. 5.
— 'How it Strikes a Stranger' Nonconformist, 3 April 1872, pp. 350-351; 28 August 1872, p. 890; 6 November 1872, pp. 1129-1130; 15 January 1873, p. 69.
— 'Our London Letter' Norfolk News, 26 October 1872, p. 5; 21 December 1872, p. 4; 8 February1873, p. 5; 14 March 1874, p. 5.

(b) Manuscripts and Unpublished Typescripts

Mark Rutherford Collection, Bedford Public Library

MR 1/6. Letter, John Harris to William White, 16 February 1852.
MR 1/10. Letter, John Harris to William White, 21 February 1852.
MR 1/33. Letter, John Jukes to William White, 8 April 1853.
MR 6/13. Letter, W. Hale White to George J. Holyoake, 20 January 1882.
MR JHW 26. William Hale White, Will, 17 April 1911.
MR 25/8. Letter, H. Furniss to (Sir) William Hale White, 14 May 1914.
[Stock deposit] Letter, Marion Milford to Simon Nowell Smith, 1 March 1913 (uncatalogued).

[Stock deposit] Letter, Annie White to Jack Hale-White, 18 April 1913 (uncatalogued).
[Stock deposit] Letter, Molly White to Cecily White, 8 October 1924 (uncatalogued).
MR 14/1. Willie Hale-White, 'Notes on William Hale White (Mark Rutherford) by his eldest son, May 1932'.
MR 15/1. 'Notes by his second son, Geneva, 1931' (Jack Hale-White).
MR 22/2. Pencil draft letters, Sir William Hale-White to Simon Nowell Smith, undated.
MR 22/4. Letter, Sir William Hale-White to Simon Nowell Smith, 20 July 1931.
MR JHW 10. 'Refutations of the Groombridge Diary'. [Frances Low]
[D. White] Omissions from the Groombridge Diary (uncatalogued typescript),

British Library, London

Add. Ms. 44891. William Hale White, 'Autobiographical Notes'.

Bodleian Library, Oxford

Mss Eng. Misc. c.443-447. Jack Hale-White, 'William Hale White : "Mark Rutherford", 1831-1913. Notes by his Second Son', Geneva 1931.

Brotherton Library, University of Leeds

Ms 11190-07. Letter, W. Hale White to Miss Edwards, 18 October 1907.

Bunyan Meeting, Bedford (at Bedfordshire County Record Office)

BY 9/2. Trustees of Bedford Old Meeting Minute Book.

Cheshunt College Archive, Westminster College, Cambridge

C1/7. Trustees' Minute Book 1837-50.
C8/1. Cheshunt College Preaching Book, April 1844- [to May 1851].

Houghton Library, Harvard University

Ms.Am.800.20. Letter, W. Hale White to William Howells, 25 February 1886.

New College Archives, Dr Williams's Library, London

154/1. Register of Student Declarations.
159. Senate Minute Book, vol. I.

218/18-25. Application to Homerton College, F. M. White (1848).
336/4/1. Letter, W. Hale White to New College, 6 May 1850.
336/4/2. Cheshunt College, permission for W. Hale White to transfer to New College.
366/13. Application to New College, Robert M. Theobald (15 June 1850).
366/14. Completed questions form, application to New College, Robert M. Theobald (15 June 1850).

Norman Colbeck Collection, University of British Columbia

This collection is gathered into fonds as numbered below. Neither the printed handlist nor the microfilms of the texts themselves include individual reference numbers (therefore some identifiers are repeated for different items).

1-7. Letter Frederick Pollock to W. Hale White, 15 December 1880.
1-19. Correspondence, W. Hale White / Kegan, Paul, Trench, Trübner & Co.
1-22 to 2-2. Letters, W. H. White to S. Partridge (used in Letters to Three Friends).
2-4. Correspondence, W. Hale White to (drafts)/from T. Fisher Unwin.
2-7. Letter, W. Hale White to Rose Paul, 18 February 1900.
2-10. W. Hale White, '1910 MS'.
2-11. Notebooks, W. Hale White.
2-13. Notebook (The 'Dorothy Notebook'), W. Hale White.
3-1. "White" Notebook, W. Hale White (c.1907-1912).
3-22 to 4-1. Dorothy White, 'Hale's Book' (manuscript of Groombridge Diary).
4-9 to 4-15. Letters and Publisher's Accounts; T. Fisher Unwin, Duckworth, and Oxford University Press (1895-1912).
4-9. Letter, T. Fisher Unwin to W. Hale White, 7 July 1910.
4-13. Letter, W. Hale White to Humphrey Milford, 11 February 1910.
6-7. Letter, Catherine Maclean to Reginald Hale-White, 10 November 1955.
6-8. Letter, Willie Hale-White to Jack Hale-White, 23 December 1931.
6-8. Letter, Willie Hale-White to Jack Hale-White, 6 September 1932.
6-8. Letter, Jack Hale-White to Willie Hale-White, 24 September 1932.
6-15. Letter, Lady Robert Cecil to Molly White, 10 March 1932.
6-16. Letter, Lady Robert Cecil to Molly White, 31 October 1934.
6-19. Genealogical tables (undated).
6-21. Cecily Hale-White, 'Jack and Agnes Hale-White: A Tribute by their Daughter'.
6-22. Anon ['Cecily'] Notes on the Groombridge Diary.
6-23. Notes by his second son, Geneva, 1931 (Jack Hale-White).
6-24. Jack Hale-White, Journal.
7-1 to 7-4. Mary White, Diaries, 1854-66 (lacking 1862 and 1864).
7-14. 'Refutations of the Groombridge Diary'. [Frances Low]

17-4. Letter, Director of British Museum to Sir William Hale-White, 10 October 1936.
17-4. Letter, Molly Hale-White to Humphrey Milford, 12 June 1913.
17-4. Letter, Molly White to Willie Hale-White, 15 July 1936.
17-5. Letter, Molly White to Humphrey Milford, 3 May 1913.
17-4. Letter, James Pinker & Son to Sir William Hale-White, 24 February 1936.
17-5. Oxford University Press Early Life Royalties Account, March 1914.

Chelwood Papers, Hatfield House (Lady Robert Cecil)

CHE 35/65-66. Letter, W. Hale White to Lady Robert Cecil, 24 July 1911.
CHE 35/81. Letter, W. Hale White to Lady Robert Cecil, 19 February 1912.
CHE 35/83-84. Letter, W. Hale White to Lady Robert Cecil, 6 March 1912.

Gladys Ellen Easdale, University of Reading

RUL MS 4991/4. Letters, W. Hale White to G. E. Easdale.
RUL MS 4991/29. Account of her life, written ca. 1904.

Thomas William Chignell Papers, Harris Manchester College

MS. Chignell 2. Scrapbook with newspaper cuttings and associated material from Chignell's time in Exeter.

Mark Rutherford Letters, University of Sussex

SxMs6. Letters of William Hale White to Erica Storr, 1905-1912.

Other

Milford, H. Unpublished letter to J. G. Wilson, 1943 (from catalogue of bookseller Richard Ford, London, 2007).

(c) Unpublished Theses

Brealey, M. A. '"What I now set down is fact": A Study of The Early Life of Mark Rutherford by William Hale White (1831-1913), with Special Reference to the Development of his Faith' (unpublished doctoral thesis, University of Bristol, 2008).
Crees, M. 'Before Mark Rutherford: The Translations, Journalism and Essays of William Hale White' (unpublished doctoral thesis, University of Liverpool, 1999).

Davies, L. J. 'An Awkward Rectitude: The Evolution of William Hale White's Fiction' (unpublished doctoral thesis, University of Liverpool, 1994).

Hubbard, T.F. 'Born in Exile: The Lower-Class Intellectual in the Fiction of William Hale White ("Mark Rutherford"), George Gissing and H. G. Wells, 1880-1911 (unpublished doctoral thesis, University of Aberdeen, 1982).

Ledger, S. 'History, Politics and Women: A Contextual Analysis of the Writings of William Hale White ("Mark Rutherford")' (unpublished doctoral thesis, University of Oxford, 1990).

Smith, H.A. 'The Life and Thought of William Hale White' (unpublished doctoral thesis, University of Birmingham, 1938).

Warner, A.J. 'Mark Rutherford, A Victorian Pilgrim: A Study of the Mind and Writings of William Hale White (1831-1913)' (unpublished thesis, University of Witwatersrand, 1949).

Wee, D. 'The Forms of Apostasy: The Rejection of Orthodox Christianity in the British Novel, 1880-1900' (unpublished doctoral thesis, Stanford University, 1966).

(d) Primary Sources

Anon. *The Church Awakened: Report of Special Meetings for the Revival of Religion, Held in Surrey Chapel, London, November 5th, 1838, and following days* (London: Thomas Ward, 1838).

Anon. 'Prospectus', *The Biblical Review, and Congregational Magazine*, 1 (1847), 1.

Anon. 'The Present State of the Greek Testament Text', *The Biblical Review, and Congregational Magazine*, 4 (1847), 38-49.

Anon. 'Consultations with Homeopaths', *British Journal of Homeopathy*, 21 (1863), 332-333.

Anon. Review of *Chapters from the Autobiography of an Independent Minister*, *The British Quarterly Review*, 150 (1882), 476.

Anon. 'Mark Rutherford and Democracy', *The Speaker*, 3 March 1906, pp. 518-519.

Anon. Review of *The Early Life*, *Spectator*, 9 August 1913.

Anon. Review of *The Early Life*, *Journal of Education*, October 1913.

Anon. Review of *The Early Life*; 'Shorter Notices', *Times Literary Supplement*, 8 August 1913, p. 330.

Anon. Obituary, W. Hale White, *The Times*, 17 March 1913.

Anon. Obituary, W. Hale White, *The Times* Weekly Edition, 21 March 1913.

Anon. Obituary, W. Hale White, *The Courier*, 21 March 1913, p. 17.

Anon. Obituary, W. Hale White, *The Nation*, 22 March 1913 ('Wayfarer' column).

Anon. Obituary, W. Hale White, *The Athenaeum*, 22 March 1913, p. 335.

Anon. 'An Honest Doubter', *Glasgow Herald*, 19 December 1931, p. 5.

Anon. 'Mark Rutherford: Centenary Tribute', *The Bedfordshire Times and Independent*, 18 December 1931, pp. 13-15.

Anon. 'The Centenary of Mark Rutherford', *The Observer*, 20 December 1931 (by a 'Special Correspondent').

Anon. 'Unveiling of a plaque to Mark Rutherford', *The Bedfordshire Times and Independent*, 25 December 1931.

Anon. Obituary, Dorothy Hale White, *The Times*, 28 July 1967. [by Simon Nowell Smith; personal information from his son Geoffrey Nowell-Smith]

Anon. Obituary, Reginald Hale-White, *The Times*, 2 November 1967, p. 12.

Adderley, J.G. *Stephen Remarx: The Story of a Venture in Ethics* (London: Edward Arnold, 1893).

Admiralty. *The Navy List, Corrected to the 20th June, 1859* (London: John Murray, 1859).

Admiralty. *The Navy List, Corrected to the 20th December, 1869* (London: John Murray, 1870).

Aged Minister, An. 'Unhealthy State of the Churches', Letter to the Editor, *The Congregational Magazine*, February 1844, pp. 124-128.

Alliott, R. *Psychology and Theology: or, Psychology Applied to the Investigation of Questions Relating to Religion, Natural Theology, and Revelation* (London: Jackson and Walford, 1855).

Arnold M. *Culture and Anarchy: An Essay in Political and Social Criticism* (London: Smith, Elder, 1869, repr. ed. by Stefan Collini, Cambridge: Cambridge University Press, 1993).

Ashton, J. *The Story of the Life of John Ashton ("Bishop of Stagsden")* (Bedford: H. Burt, 1904).

Bedford Medico- Ethical Society. 'Meeting of the Medical Practitioners of Bedford and its Neighbourhood' [Report], *The Lancet*, 11 July 1863, p. 51.

Betham-Edwards, M. *Reminiscences* (London: George Redway, 1898)

— *Mid-Victorian Memories* (London: John Murray, 1919).

Binney, T. (ed.) *Christians at the Grave: Paul at the Cross: and Christ on the Mount. The Funeral Services Occasioned by the Death of the Late Rev. John Harris, D.D., Principal of New College* (London: Ward & Co.; Jackson & Walford, 1857).

British Medical Association. 'The Week', *British Medical Journal*, 18 July 1863, p. 64.

Bushby, D. W. (ed.) *Bedfordshire Ecclesiastical Census, 1851*, Publications of the Bedfordshire Historical Record Society, 54 (Bedford: Bedford Historical Record Society, 1975), pp. 109-200.

Bushnell, H. *Christian Nurture*, 3rd edn (London: Alexander Strahan, 1866).

Campbell, J. 'Academic Reform', in *John Angell James: A Review of His History, Character, Eloquence, and Literary Labours, etc.* (London: John Snow, 1860), pp. xvii-xxxii.

Campbell, J. (ed.) *The British Banner*.

Carlyle. T. *The Life of John Sterling: With an Introduction by W. Hale White*, new edn (London: Oxford University Press, 1907).

— *The Collected Letters of Thomas and Jane Welsh Carlyle, vol. 27: 1852*, ed. by C. de L. Ryals, K.J. Fielding, and others (Durham, NC: Duke University Press, 1999).

Cecil, Lady Robert. 'Mark Rutherford', *The Nation and Athenaeum*, 27 October 1923, p. 151-152.

Cheshunt College. *Report of the Trustees of the late Countess of Huntingdon's College, Cheshunt ... 1849.*

— *Report of the Trustees of the late Countess of Huntingdon's College, Cheshunt ... 1850.*

— *Centenary Celebration of Cheshunt College: 25th June 1868* (London: Hodder and Stoughton, 1868).

Chignell, T.W. Welcome address at Exeter, report in *Devon Weekly Times*, 25 April 1862.

Child, H.H. Review of *The Groombridge Diary*, *Times Literary Supplement*, 15 May 1924, p. 299.

Coleridge, S.T. *Biographia Literaria*, ed. by J. Shawcross, 2 vols (Oxford: Clarendon Press, 1907).

Conference etc. *Minutes of the Proceedings of a Conference of Delegates from the Committees of Various Theological Colleges Connected with the Independent Churches of England and Wales, Held in the Congregational Library, Blomfield Street, London, on Tuesday the 7th, and Wednesday the 8th of January, 1845* (London: Blackburn & Pardon, Printers, 1845).

Coombs, J. Letter to the Editor, *The Lancet*, 14 February 1863, p. 192

— *Recollections, Personal and Political* (Bedford: Arthur Ransom, 1889).

Cornish, F.W. *Sunningwell* (London: Archibald Constable, 1899).

Cross, J.W. (ed.) *George Eliot's Life as Related in Her Letters and Journals*, new edn (Edinburgh: William Blackwood & Sons, 1885).

Dale, R.W. *The Old Evangelicalism and the New* (London: Hodder and Stoughton, 1889).

Dawson, W.J. *The Redemption of Edward Strahan: A Social Story* (London: Hodder and Stoughton, 1891).

Dickens, C. *Little Dorrit* (London: Bradbury and Evans, 1857).

Easdale, G. *Middle Age: 1885-1932* (London: Constable, 1935).

Evans, D.T. *The Life and Ministry of the Rev. Caleb Morris, who was Minister of the Tabernacle, Narberth; and of Fetter Lane Chapel, London* (London: Alexander and Shepheard, 1902).

Finney, C.G. *Memoirs of Rev. Charles G. Finney, the American Evangelist, Written by Himself* (London: Hodder and Stoughton, 1876).

— *The Memoirs of Charles G. Finney: The Complete Restored Text*, ed. by Garth M. Rosell and Richard A.G. Dupuis (Grand Rapids, MI: Academie Books/Zondervan, 1989).

Freer, F.A. *Edward White: His Life and Work* (London: Elliot Stock, 1902).

Froude, J.A. *The Nemesis of Faith* (London: J. Chapman, 1849).

— *Thomas Carlyle: A History of the First Forty Years of His Life, 1795-1835*, 2 vols (London: Longmans, Green, 1882).

General Medical Council. 'General Council of Medical Education and Registration. Winter Session, 1894' [Report] *British Medical Journal*, 8 December 1894, pp. 1329-1335.

Gosse, E. *Father and Son: A Study of Two Temperaments*, ed. by Peter Abbs (Harmondsworth: Penguin Books, 1983).

Grand, S. *The Beth Book: Being a Study of the Life of Elizabeth Caldwell Maclure, a Woman of Genius* (London: W. Heinemann, 1897; repr. London: Virago Press, 1980).

Grant, B. 'The Expelled Students, and their Doctrine of Inspiration', *The Bible and the People*, 2 (1852), 252-260.

— *The Dissenting World: An Autobiography*, 2nd edn (London: W. Macintosh, 1869).

Gregory, W. *Letters to a Candid Inquirer on Animal Magnetism* (London: Taylor, Walton, and Maberly, 1851).

Haight, G.S. (ed.) *The George Eliot Letters, vol. I: 1836-1851* (London: Oxford University Press, 1954).

Hamson, J. *Bedford Town and Townsmen: Record of the Local History of Bedford During the Last Half Century* (Bedford: Bedfordshire Times Office, 1896).

Harris, J. *The Great Teacher: Characteristics of Our Lord's Ministry* (London: Thomas Ward and Co., 1835).

— 'The Importance of an Educated Ministry: A Discourse Delivered on the Occasion of the Opening of the Lancashire Independent College, Manchester, at the Preparatory Service, on the 25th of April, 1843'; reprinted in *Sermons and Addresses Delivered on Special Occasions, by John Harris, D.D., Second Series*, ed. by Philip Smith (London: James Nisbet & Co., 1857), pp. 230-256.

— 'The Christian Ministry'; reprinted in *Sermons and Addresses Delivered on Special Occasions, by John Harris, D.D., Second Series*, ed. by Philip Smith (London: James Nisbet & Co., 1857), pp. 203-229.

— *The Pre-Adamite Earth: Contributions to Theological Science* (London: Ward and Co., 1846).

— *Man Primeval: Or, the Constitution and Primitive Condition of the Human Being. A Contribution to Theological Science* (London: Ward and Co., 1849).

— 'The Inspiration of the Scriptures', in *New College, London: The Introductory Lectures Delivered at the Opening of the College, October 1851* (London: Jackson and Walford, 1851), pp. 3-65.

Harris, R. (ed.) *The Reminiscences of Sir Henry Hawkins, Baron Brampton*, popular edn (London: Edward Arnold, 1905).

Hedderwick, J.B. *The Captain's Clerk* (London: Hutchinson, 1957).

Hewitson, A. *Our Churches and Chapels, Their Parsons, Priests, and Congregations; Being a Critical and Historical Account of Every Place of Worship in Preston* (Preston: Chronicle Office, 1869).

Hood, E.P. *Thomas Binney: His Mind Life and Opinions, Doctrinal, Denominational, Devotional, and Practical* (London: James Clarke, 1874).

Howells, W.D. 'Editor's Study', *Harper's New Monthly Magazine*, 72 (1886), 481-487.

International Congregational Congress. *The International Congregational Council: London, 1891. Authorised Record of Proceedings* (London: James Clarke, 1891).

Jefferson, R. 'Mark Rutherford', *Morning Post*, 17 March 1913.

Jenkyn, T.W. *On the Extent of the Atonement, in its Relation to God and the Universe* (London: Hamilton Adams, 1833).

Jones, D.A. *The Life and Letters of Henry Arthur Jones* (London: Victor Gollancz, 1930).

Jukes, J. *A Brief History of Bunyan's Church, Compiled, Chiefly from its Own Records; Accompanied With a Concise Statement of its Present Requirements, Obligations, and Intentions* (London, Bedford: Partridge & Oakey, Rowland Hill, 1849).

Kent, W. 'Mark Rutherford', *The Literary Guide*, March 1932, p. 58.

— *The Testament of a Victorian Youth: An Autobiography* (London: Heath Cranton, 1938).

King, J. *W.G. Lawes of Savage Island and New Guinea* (London: Religious Tract Society, 1909).

Linton, E.L. *The True History of Joshua Davidson* (London: Strahan, 1872).

— *The Autobiography of Christopher Kirkland*, 3 vols (London: Bentley & Son, 1885).

Layard, G.S. *Mrs Lynn Linton: Her Life, Letters and Opinions* (London: Methuen, 1901).

Leask, W. *Struggles for Life: Or, the Autobiography of a Dissenting Minister* (London: W. & F.G. Cash, 1854).

Lewis, S. *A Topographical Dictionary of England, vol. I* (London: S. Lewis & Co., 1831).

Littledale, R.F. Review of *The Autobiography of Mark Rutherford*, *The Academy*, 21 May 1881, p. 370.

— Review of *Mark Rutherford's Deliverance*, *The Academy*, 21 February 1885, p. 131.

— Review of *The Revolution in Tanner's Lane*, *The Academy*, 7 May 1887, p. 322.

London, University of. *The London University Calendar, 1849* (London: Richard and John Edward Taylor, 1848).

Low, Florence. 'Walks and Talks with Mark Rutherford', *The Contemporary Review*, 187 (1955), 405-409.

Low, Frances. 'Mark Rutherford of the Books: As I Knew Him', *Great Thoughts from Master Minds*, 96 (1931), 122-124.

— 'Mark Rutherford of the Books', *Birmingham Daily Post*, 23 December 1931, p. 5.

MacDonald, G. *Within and Without: A Dramatic Poem* (London: Longman, Brown, Green, 1855.

— *Annals of a Quiet Neighbourhood*, 3 vols (London: Hurst and Blackett, 1867).
— *The Miracles of Our Lord* (London: Strahan, 1870).
— *England's Antiphon* (London: Macmillan, 1874).
— *The Marquis of Lossie*, 3 vols (London: Hurst and Blackett, 1877).
— *Castle Warlock: A Homely Romance*, 3 vols (London: Sampson Low, 1882).
— *An Expression of Character: The Letters of George MacDonald*, ed. by G.E. Sadler (Grand Rapids, MI: William B. Eerdmans, 1994).
Mackenzie, W.D. *John Mackenzie: South African Missionary and Statesman* (London: Hodder and Stoughton, 1902).
Martineau, J. *A Study of Spinoza* (London: Macmillan, 1882).
Martyn, H. J. *Chapters from the Autobiography of an Independent Minister*. (London: Williams and Norgate, 1882) [Published anonymously]
— *The Autobiography of an Independent Minister, to Which is Now Added for the First Time a Second Part, Containing Six Chapters, as Also a New Preface to the First Part* (London: Williams and Norgate, 1887).
Massingham, H.W. 'Memorial Introduction', in *The Autobiography of Mark Rutherford* (London: T. Fisher Unwin, 1923), pp. v-xxv.
Mattei, C. *Electro-Homeopathic Medicine: A New Medical System, Being a Popular and Domestic Guide Founded on Experience*, 2nd edn, trans. by R. M. Theobald (London: David Stott, 1891).
Matthiason, J.H. *Bedford and Its Environs; or An Historical and Topographical Sketch of the Town of Bedford and Places Adjacent, Containing Accounts of Its Public Institutions, Schools, Charities, Societies, &c & Brief Notices of Every Thing Most Remarkable and Important Relating to the Town and Neighbourhood* (Bedford: W. White, Printer, 1831).
Moffat, R.U. *John Smith Moffat, C.M.G., Missionary: A Memoir* (London: John Murray, 1902).
Morell, J.D. *The Philosophy of Religion* (London: Longman, Brown, Green, and Longmans, 1849).
New College, London. *Report of New College, London, 1852.*
— New College: Rules (London: Printed for Private Circulation, n.d.).
Nicoll, W.R. 'Mark Rutherford', *The British Weekly*, 9 July 1896, p. 185 (as 'Claudius Clear').
— 'Memories of Mark Rutherford', in *A Bookman's Letters* (London: Hodder and Stoughton, 1913), pp. 364-412.
— Review of *The Early Life*, *The British Weekly*, 7 August 1913 (as 'Claudius Clear').
Pope, A.C. (ed.) *Homeopathic Medical Directory of Great Britain and Ireland, and Annual Abstract of British Homeopathic Serial Literature, 1869* (London: Henry Turner, 1869).
Ritchie, J. E. *Christopher Crayon's Recollections: The Life and Times of the Late James Ewing Ritchie, As Told by Himself* (London: James Clarke, 1898).

Robson, W. *Robson's Commercial Directory of the Six Counties Forming the Norfolk Circuit: viz. Beds, Bucks, Cambridgeshire, Hunts, Norfolk, and Suffolk* (London: William Robson & Co., 1839).

Rogers, J.G. *J. Guinness Rogers: An Autobiography* (London: James Clarke, 1903).

Scargill, W.P. *The Autobiography of a Dissenting Minister* (London: Smith, Elder, 1834). [A disputed attribution]

Schleiermacher, F. *Brief Outline of the Study of Theology, Drawn up to Serve as the Basis of Introductory Lectures*, trans. by William Farrer (Edinburgh: T. & T. Clark, 1850).

Selby, T.G. *The Theology of Modern Fiction* (London: Charles H. Kelly, 1896).

Shorter, C.K. *C.K.S., An Autobiography: A Fragment by Himself*, ed. by J. M. Bulloch (London: Privately Printed, 1927).

Smart, R. (ed.) *The Bousfield Diaries: A Middle-Class Family in Late Victorian Bedford*, Publications of the Bedfordshire Historical Record Society, 86 (Woodbridge: Boydell Press for The Bedfordshire Historical Record Society, 2007).

Spender, J.A. *Life, Journalism and Politics*, 2 vols (London: Cassell, 1927).

[Spender, J.A.] *The Story of the Liberator Crash: With Some Account of the Career and Character of Jabez Spencer Balfour* (London: Westminster Gazette, 1893).

Spinoza, B. *The Chief Works of Benedict de Spinoza*, trans. by R. H. M. Elwes, 2 vols (London: George Bell & Sons, 1883-84).

— *Ethics*, trans. by George Eliot, ed. by Thomas Deegan (Salzburg: Institut für Anglistik und Amerikanistik, Universität Salzburg, 1981).

Stead, W.T. 'Matteism, its Successes and its Failures', *Review of Reviews*, November 1894, p. 475.

Stoughton, J. 'The Nature and Value of the Miraculous Testimony to Christianity', in *Modern Scepticism: A Course of Lectures Delivered at the Request of the Christian Evidence Society* (London: Hodder and Stoughton, 1871), pp. 179-227.

Stowell, W. (ed.) *A Memoir of the Life and Labours of the Rev. William Hendry Stowell, D.D.* 2nd edn (London: Judd and Glass, 1860).

Syme, E. 'The Bible and the Truth: The New College Heresy', *The People: A Journal of Social, Educational, and Religious Progress*, 8 May 1852, pp. 149-151.

Theobald, M. *Spirit Workers in the Home Circle: An Autobiographic Narrative of Psychic Phenomena in Family Daily Life Extending Over a Period of Twenty Years* (London: T. Fisher Unwin, 1887).

Theobald, R.M. *Statement of Facts Connected With the Expulsion of Three Students from New College London* (London: Robert Theobald, 1852).

— *Memorials of John Daniel Morell, M.A., LL.D., Her Majesty's Inspector of Schools* (London: W. Stewart, 1891).

— *Shakespeare Studies in Baconian Light* (London: Sampson Low, Marston, 1901).

— '"Mark Rutherford": Some Reminiscences of Mr William Hale White', *Westminster Gazette*, 17 March 1913, p. 10.
— *Passages from the Autobiography of a Shakespeare Student* (London: Robert Banks & Son, 1912).
Tempest, E.V. 'Optimism in "Mark Rutherford"', *Westminster Review*, 180 (1913), 174-184.
Thomas, D. 'Caleb Morris'[Memoir], in *Pulpit Memorials: Photographs and Specimen Sermons of Twenty Congregational Ministers, With Brief Memoirs by Several Friends*, ed. by E.J. Evans and W.F. Hurndall (London: James Clarke, 1878) pp.381-398.
Thompson, E.J. *Introducing the Arnisons* (London: Macmillan, 1935).
— *John Arnison* (London: Macmillan, 1939).
Thompson, R.W. *Griffith John: The Story of Fifty Years in China*, Popular edition (London: Religious Tract Society 1908).
Todd, J. *Lectures to Children, Familiarly Illustrating Important Truths; First Series* (London: George Routledge and Sons, n.d.).
— *Truth Made Simple: Being a System of Theology for Children on the Attributes of God* (London: Ball, Arnold & Co., 1839).
Trollope, A. *The Three Clerks: A Novel*, 3 vols (London: Bentley, 1858).
Vickers, J.A. (ed.) *The Religious Census of Sussex, 1851* (Lewes: Sussex Record Society, 1989).
Walker, G.A. *Gatherings from Grave-yards: Particularly those of London. With a Concise History of the Modes of Interment Among Different Nations, etc* (London: Longman, 1839).
Ward, H. *Robert Elsmere*, 3 vols (London: Smith, Elder, 1888).
West, A. *Recollections: 1832 to 1886* (London: Thomas Nelson and Sons, 1899).
— *Contemporary Portraits: Men of My Day in Public Life* (London: Thomas Nelson and Sons, 1924).
White, D. V. *The Groombridge Diary* (London: Oxford University Press, 1924).
White, F.M. 'Life and Logic: or, The Life of Jesus in Relation to Modern Speculations', *Pitman's Popular Lecturer and Reader*, 5 (1863), 129-148.
White, W. *To Think or Not to Think?: Remarks Upon the Late Expulsions from New College* (London: Robert Theobald, 1852).
— *The Inner Life of the House of Commons*, ed. by Justin McCarthy, 2 vols (London: T. Fisher Unwin, 1897).
White, W.H., White, F.M., & Theobald, R.M., Letter to the Editor, *The Nonconformist*, 31 March 1852, p. 240.
Whitmee, S.J. *Personal Experience in the Use of Count Mattei's Remedies* (London: T. Cheverton, 1895).
— 'Mark Rutherford', *The British Weekly*, 3 April 1913, p. 3.
Williamson, F. *Frederick Rivers: Independent Parson* (London: Williams & Norgate, 1864). [pseudonym of William Kirkus]
Wordsworth, W. *The Poetical Works of William Wordsworth*, ed. by E. De Selincourt, 5 vols (Oxford: Clarendon Press, 1940-49).

Wordsworth, W. & Coleridge, S.T., *Lyrical Ballads, With a Few Other Poems* (Bristol: J. Cottle, 1798; repr. ed. by Michael Schmidt, London: Penguin Books, 1999).
Young Minister, A. 'Unhealthy State of the Churches', Letter to the Editor, *The Congregational Magazine*, March 1844, pp. 199-202.

(e) Secondary Sources

Anon. Obituary, 'Principal Sir James Donaldson', *The Athenaeum*, 13 March 1915, p. 238.
Anon. 'An Open Trust: Note on the Ditchling Trust Deed', *Transactions of the Unitarian Historical Society*, 1 (1916-18), 23-24.
Abrams, M.H. *Natural Supernaturalism: Tradition and Revolution in Romantic Literature* (New York: W.W. Norton, 1971).
Agar, N.E. *The Bedfordshire Farm Worker in the Nineteenth Century*, Publications of the Bedfordshire Historical Record Society, 60 (Bedford: Bedford Historical Record Society, 1981).
Allen, P. 'Mark Rutherford: The Anatomy of a Failure' in *The View from the Pulpit: Victorian Ministers and Society*, ed. by P.T. Phillips (Ontario: Macmillan of Canada, 1978), pp. 143-159.
Apfel, W. & P. Dunkley. 'English Rural Society and the New Poor Law: Bedfordshire 1834-47', *Social History*, 10 (1985), 37-68.
Ashton, R. *142 Strand: A Radical Address in Victorian London* (London: Chatto & Windus, 2006).
Atkins, D. *George Eliot and Spinoza* (Salzburg: Institut für Englische Sprache und Literatur, Universität Salzburg, 1978).
Balls, F.E. 'The Endowment of Education in the Nineteenth Century: The Case of the Bedford Harpur Trust', *History of Education*, 6 (1977), 103-113.
Barbour, J.D. *Versions of Deconversion: Autobiography and the Loss of Faith* (Charlottesville, VA: University Press of Virginia, 1994).
Barkway, S. 'An "Incredible Goose" and a "Country Flapper": Virginia Woolf and the Easdales', *Virginia Woolf Bulletin of the Virginia Woolf Society of Great Britain*, 28 (2008), 5-35.
Bartholomew, R.E. '19th Century Missiology of the LDS Bedfordshire Conference and its Interrelationship with Other Christian Denominations', *International Journal of Mormon Studies*, 2 (2009), pp. 108-127.
Bassett, T.J. 'T. Fisher Unwin's Pseudonym Library: Literary Marketing and Authorial Identity', *English Literature in Transition (1880-1920)*, 47 (2004), 143-160.
Bates, L.M. *Somerset House: Four Hundred Years of History* (London: Frederick Muller, 1967).
Baylen, J. 'The Mattei Cancer Cure: A Victorian Nostrum', *Proceedings of the American Philosophical Society*, 113 (1969), 149-176.
Bebbington, D. 'Evangelical Conversion, c.1740-1850', *Scottish Bulletin of Evangelical Theology*, 18 (2000), 102-127.

Bebbington, D., with K. Dix & A. Ruston (ed.) *Protestant Nonconformist Texts, vol. 3: The Nineteenth Century* (Aldershot: Ashgate, 2006).

Bell, P.L. *Belief in Bedfordshire* (Bedford: Belfry Press, 1986).

Bell, H.I. 'Autographs of Nathaniel Hawthorne and "Mark Rutherford"', *The British Museum Quarterly*, 11 (1936-37), 79-80.

Bendroth, M. 'Horace Bushnell's Christian Nurture', in *The Child in Christian Thought*, ed. by Marcia J. Bunge (Grand Rapids, MI: William B. Eerdmans, 2001), pp. 350-364.

Binfield, J.C.G. *George Williams and the Y.M.C.A.: A Study in Victorian Social Attitudes* (London: Heinemann, 1973).

— *So Down to Prayers: Studies in English Nonconformity, 1780-1920* (London: J.M. Dent & Sons, 1977).

— 'Hebrews Hellenized? English Evangelical Nonconformity and Culture, 1840-1940', in *A History of Religion in Britain: Practice and Belief from Pre-Roman Times to the Present*, ed. by Sheridan Gilley and W.J. Sheils (Oxford: Blackwell, 1994), pp. 322-345.

Blaxill, E.A. *History of Lion Walk Congregational Church, Colchester, 1662-1937* (Colchester: Benham & Company, Printers, 1938).

Boase, G.C. 'Harris, John, D.D. (1802-1856)' in *Dictionary of National Biography*, ed. by Leslie Stephen and Sidney Lee, vol. XXV (London: Smith, Elder, 1891), pp. 15-16.

Borsay, P. *The English Urban Renaissance: Culture and Society in the Provincial Town 1660-1770* (Oxford: Clarendon Press, 1989).

Boylan, A.M. *Sunday School: The Formation of an American Institution, 1790-1880* (New Haven, CT: Yale University Press, 1988).

Brewer, W.F. 'What is Recollective Memory?', in *Remembering Our Past: Studies in Autobiographical Memory* ed. by David C. Rubin (Cambridge: Cambridge University Press, 1999), pp. 19-66.

Briggs, J.H.Y. 'The Baptist Contribution to the Sunday School Movement in the Nineteenth Century', in *The Sunday School Movement: Studies in the Growth and Decline of Sunday Schools*, ed. by Stephen Orchard and John H.Y. Briggs (Milton Keynes: Paternoster, 2007), pp. 42-63.

— *Two Congregational Denominations: Baptist and Paedobaptist* (London: Congregational Memorial Hall Trust, 2010).

Brodribb, G. *Hastings and Men of Letters* (Hastings: Old Hastings Preservation Society, 1971).

Brookes, G.H. 'Fictional Forms in William Hale White's Autobiography of Mark Rutherford and Mark Rutherford's Deliverance', *Biography: An Interdisciplinary Quarterly*, 9 (1986), 247-268.

Broome, F.H. 'The Scientific Basis of George MacDonald's Dream-Frame', in *The Gold Thread: Essays on George MacDonald, ed. by William Raeper* (Edinburgh: Edinburgh University Press, 1990), pp. 87-108.

Brown, K.D. 'The Congregational Ministry in the First Half of the Nineteenth Century: A Preliminary Survey', *Journal of the United Reformed Church History Society*, 3 (1983) 2-15.

— *A Social History of the Nonconformist Ministry in England and Wales, 1800-1930* (Oxford: Clarendon Press, 1988).

Brown, N. *Dissenting Forbears: The Maternal Ancestors of J.M. Keynes* (Chichester: Phillimore, 1988).

Bruss, E. *Autobiographical Acts: The Changing Situation of a Literary Genre* (Baltimore, MD: Johns Hopkins University Press, 1976).

Buchmann, U. *William Hale White (Mark Rutherford) and the Problem of Self-Adjustment in a World of Changing Values* (Zurich: Juris-Verlag, 1950).

Bucknell, K. 'The Achievement of Edward Upward', in *W.H. Auden, 'The Language of Learning and the Language of Love': Uncollected Writing, New Interpretations*, ed. by K. Bucknell and N. Jenkins (Oxford: Clarendon Press, 1994), pp. 165-184.

Bull, F.W. 'The Newport Pagnell Academy', *Transactions of the Congregational Historical Society*, 4 (1910), 305-322.

Bunge, M.J. 'Introduction', in *The Child in Christian Thought*, ed. by Marcia J. Bunge (Grand Rapids, MI: William B. Eerdmans, 2001), pp. 1-28.

Burd, V.A. *Ruskin, Lady Mount-Temple and the Spiritualists* (London: Brentham Press, 1982).

Burnett, J. (ed.) *Destiny Obscure: Autobiographies of Childhood, Education and Family from the 1820s to the 1920s* (Harmondsworth: Penguin Books, 1984).

Butler, A. *Victorian Occultism and the Making of Modern Magic: Invoking Tradition* (Basingstoke: Palgrave Macmillan, 2011).

Carlile, J.C. *Alexander Maclaren, D.D.: The Man and His Message. A Character Sketch* (London: S.W. Partridge, 1901).

Carwardine, R. *Transatlantic Revivalism: Popular Evangelicalism in Britain and America, 1790-1865* (Westport, CT: Greenwood Press, 1978).

Cashdollar, C. *A Spiritual Home: Life in British and American Reformed Congregations, 1830-1915* (University Park, PA: Pennsylvania State University Press, 2000).

Cashman, B. *A Proper House: Bedford Lunatic Asylum (1812-1860)* (Bedford: North Bedfordshire Health Authority, 1992).

Chambers, B. *Printed Maps and Town Plans of Bedfordshire, 1576-1900*, Publications of the Bedfordshire Historical Record Society, 62 (Bedford: Bedfordshire Historical Record Society, 1983).

Chandler, R.A., J. R. Edwards, & M. Anderson. 'Disciplinary Action Against Members of the Founding Bodies of the ICAEW', *Accounting, Auditing and Accountability Journal*, 21 (2008), 827-849.

Chandler, R.A. & N. Fry. 'Audit Failure, Litigation, and Insurance in Early Twentieth Century Britain', *Accounting History*, 10 (2005), 13-38.

Chapman-Huston, D. *The Lost Historian: A Memoir of Sir Sidney Low* (London: John Murray, 1936).

Cirket, A.F. 'The 1830 Riots in Bedfordshire - Background and Events', in *Worthington George Smith and Other Studies: Presented to Joyce Godber*, Publications of the Bedfordshire Historical Record Society, 57 (Bedford: Bedfordshire Historical Record Society, 1978), pp. 75-112.

Cliff, P.B. *The Rise and Development of the Sunday School Movement in England, 1780-1980* (Redhill: National Christian Education Council, 1986).

Cockshut, A.O.J *The Unbelievers: English Agnostic Thought, 1840-1890* (London: Collins, 1964).

Coe, R.N. *When the Grass was Taller: Autobiography and the Experience of Childhood* (New Haven CT: Yale University Press, 1984).

Cooper, J.W. *Panentheism: The Other God of the Philosophers. From Plato to the Present* (Nottingham: Apollos, 2007).

Crippen, T. G. 'The Fakenham Theological Seminary', *Transactions of the Congregational Historical Society*, 8 (1920), 50-53.

Cunningham, V. *Everywhere Spoken Against: Dissent in the Victorian Novel* (Oxford: Oxford University Press, 1975).

— *In the Reading Gaol: Postmodernity, Texts, and History* (Oxford: Blackwell, 1994).

Cupitt, D. 'Introduction', *The Autobiography of Mark Rutherford and Mark Rutherford's Deliverance* (London: Libris, 1988), pp. vii-xxiii.

Daiches, D. *Some Late Victorian Attitudes* (London: André Deutsch, 1969).

Daniels, E.A. *Jessie White Mario: Risorgimento Revolutionary* (Athens, OH: Ohio State University Press, 1972).

Davie, D. *A Gathered Church: The Literature of the English Dissenting Interest, 1700-1930* (London: Routledge & Kegan Paul, 1978).

Davies, H. *Worship and Theology in Britain: From Newman to Martineau, 1850-1900* (London: Oxford University Press, 1962).

Davies, L 'Introduction', *Clara Hopgood* (London: J.M. Dent/Everyman, 1996), pp. xxv-xlvii.

Dawson, C. *Prophets of Past Time: Seven British Autobiographers, 1880-1914* (Baltimore, MD: Johns Hopkins University Press, 1988).

Dearborn, K. *Baptized Imagination: The Theology of George MacDonald* (Aldershot: Ashgate Publishing, 2006).

Delany, P. *British Autobiography in the Seventeenth Century* (London: Routledge & Kegan Paul, 1969).

de Man, P. 'Autobiography as De-Facement', in *The Rhetoric of Romanticism* (New York: Columbia University Press, 1984), pp. 67-81.

Donagan, A. 'Spinoza's Theology', in *The Cambridge Companion to Spinoza*, ed. by D. Garrett (Cambridge: Cambridge University Press, 1996), pp. 343-382.

Donajgrodzki, A.P. 'New Roles for Old: The Northcote-Trevelyan Report and the Clerks of the Home Office 1822-48', in *Studies in the Growth of Nineteenth-Century Government*, ed. by Gillian Sutherland (London: Routledge & Kegan Paul, 1972), pp. 82-109.

Eakin, P.J. *Touching the World: Reference in Autobiography* (Princeton, NJ: Princeton University Press, 1992).

Ebbatson, R. *Lawrence and the Nature Tradition: A Theme in English Fiction, 1859-1914* (Brighton: Harvester Press, 1980).

Egan, S. *Patterns of Experience in Autobiography* (Chapel Hill, NC: University of North Carolina Press, 1984).

Ellis, I. 'Schleiermacher in Britain', *Scottish Journal of Theology*, 33 (1980), 417-452.

English, M.P. *Victorian Values: The Life and Times of Dr Edwin Lankester, M.D., F.R.S.* (Bristol: Biopress, 1990).

Erdozain, D. 'The Secularisation of Sin in the Nineteenth Century', *Journal of Ecclesiastical History*, 62 (2011), 59-88.

Escott, H. *A History of Scottish Congregationalism* (Glasgow: Congregational Union of Scotland, 1960).

Evans, G.E. *Vestiges of Protestant Dissent, etc.* (Liverpool: F. & E. Gibbons, 1897).

Floyd, R. *Church, Chapel and Party: Religious Dissent and Political Modernization in Nineteenth Century England* (Basingstoke: Palgrave Macmillan, 2008).

Fowler, J.W. Stages of Faith: The Psychology of Human Development and the Quest for Meaning (New York: Harper & Row, 1981).

Fraenkel, C. 'Maimonides' God and Spinoza's Deus sive Natura', Journal of the History of Philosophy, 44 (2006), 169-215.

Gilbert, A.D. Religion and Society in Industrial England: Church, Chapel and Social Change, 1740-1914 (London: Longman, 1976).

Gill, S. *Wordsworth and the Victorians* (Oxford: Clarendon Press 1998).

Gilley, S. *Newman and His Age* (London: Darton, Longman and Todd, 1990).

Glover, W.B. *Evangelical Nonconformists and Higher Criticism in the Nineteenth Century* (London: Independent Press, 1954).

Godber, J. *The Harpur Trust, 1552-1973* (Bedford: Harpur Trust, 1973).

— *History of Bedfordshire: 1066-1888* (Bedford: Bedfordshire County Council, 1969; repr. 1984).

Goldsworthy, S. 'English Nonconformity and the Pioneering of the Modern Newspaper Campaign: Including the Strange Case of W. T. Stead and the Bulgarian Horrors', *Journalism Studies*, 7 (2006), 387-402.

Goode J. 'Mark Rutherford and Spinoza', *English Literature in Transition*, 34 (1991), 424-453.

Gregory, J. *Reformers, Patrons and Philanthropists: The Cowper-Temples and High Politics in Victorian Britain* (London: Tauris Academic Studies, 2010).

Grieve, A.J. 'A Hundred Years of Ministerial Training', *Transactions of the Congregational Historical Society*, 11 (1932), 258-264.

Hambrick-Stowe, C. *Charles G. Finney and the Spirit of America Evangelicalism* (Grand Rapids, MI: William B. Eerdmans, 1996).

Hamilton, C.I. *The Making of the Modern Admiralty: British Naval Policy-Making 1805-1927* (Cambridge: Cambridge University Press, 2011).

Hamilton, G. *Mr Norris and I: An Autobiographical Sketch* (London: Allan Wingate, 1956).

Harland, C.R. *Mark Rutherford: The Mind and Art of William Hale White* (Columbus, OH: Ohio State University Press, 1988).

Harley, J.B. 'Maps, Knowledge, and Power', in *The Iconography of Landscape: Essays on the Symbolic Representation, Design and Use of Past Environments*, ed. by D. Cosgrove and S. Daniels (Cambridge: Cambridge University Press, 1988), pp. 277-312.

Havighurst, A.F. *Radical Journalist: H. W. Massingham (1860-1924)* (Cambridge: Cambridge University Press, 1974).

Heelas, P., & L. Woodhead. *The Spiritual Revolution: Why Religion is Giving Way to Spirituality* (Oxford: Blackwell, 2005).

Hein, R. 'George MacDonald: A Portrait from His Letters', *Seven: An Anglo-American Literary Review*, 7 (1986), 5-19.

— *George MacDonald: Victorian Mythmaker* (Nashville, TN: Star Song Publishing, 1993).

Helmstadter, R. 'Condescending Harmony: John Pye Smith's Mosaic Geology', in *Science and Dissent in England, 1688-1945*, ed. by Paul Wood (Aldershot: Ashgate, 2004), pp. 167-195.

Hempton, D. *Evangelical Disenchantment: Nine Portraits of Faith and Doubt* (New Haven, CT: Yale University Press, 2008).

Henderson, H. *The Victorian Self: Autobiography and Biblical Narrative* (Ithaca, NY: Cornell University Press, 1989).

Higgs, E. *Life, Death and Statistics: Civil Registration, Censuses and the Work of the General Register Office, 1836-1952* (Hatfield: Local Population Studies, 2004).

Hinchliff, P. *Benjamin Jowett and the Christian Religion* (Oxford: Clarendon Press, 1987).

Hindmarsh, D.B. *The Evangelical Conversion Narrative: Spiritual Autobiography in Early Modern England* (Oxford: Oxford University Press, 2007).

Hobsbawm, E.J. & G. Rudé. *Captain Swing* (London: Lawrence and Wishart, 1969).

Hodgson, P.C. 'Editor's Introduction', *David Friedrich Strauss, The Life of Jesus Critically Examined* (London: SCM Press, 1973), pp. xv-l.

Hopkins, M.T.E. *Nonconformity's Romantic Generation: Evangelical and Liberal Theologies in Victorian England* (Carlisle: Paternoster Press, 2004).

Howe, E. *The Magicians of the Golden Dawn: A Documentary History of a Magical Order, 1887-1923* (London: Routledge & Kegan Paul, 1972).

Howsam, L. *Kegan Paul: A Victorian Imprint. Publishers, Books and Cultural History* (London; Toronto, ON: Kegan Paul International; University of Toronto Press, 1998).

Hughes, L. 'Madge and Clara Hopgood: William Hale White's Spinozan Sisters', *Victorian Studies*, 18 (1974), 57-75.

Humberstone, T.L. *University Reform in London* (London: George Allen & Unwin, 1926).

Hunter, G. 'Spinoza on Miracles', *International Journal for Philosophy of Religion*, 56 (2004), 41-51.

Jackson, G. 'Mark Rutherford's Scrap-Books', *London Quarterly Review*, 131 (1919), 191-204.

James, S. 'Freedom, Slavery, and the Passions' in *The Cambridge Companion to Spinoza's Ethics*, ed. by O. Koistinen (Cambridge: Cambridge University Press, 2009), pp. 223-241.

Jantzen, G. '"Where Two are to Become One": Mysticism and Monism', in *The Philosophy in Christianity*, ed. by Godfrey Vesey (Cambridge: Cambridge University Press, 1989), pp. 147-166.

Jefferson, G. *Edward Garnett: A Life in Literature* (London: Jonathan Cape, 1982).

Jeffs, E.H. 'Hale White: 1831-1913', in *Great Christians*, ed. by R.S. Forman (London: Ivor Nicholson and Watson, 1933), pp. 607-615.

Johnson, D. A. 'The End of the "Evidences": A Study in Nonconformist Theological Transition', *Journal of the United Reformed Church History Society*, 2 (1979), 62-72.

— 'Popular Apologetics in Late Victorian England: The Work of the Christian Evidence Society', *Journal of Religious History*, 11 (1981), 558-577.

— *The Changing Shape of English Nonconformity, 1825-1925* (New York: Oxford University Press, 1999).

Johnson, M.D. *The Dissolution of Dissent, 1850-1918* (New York: Garland Publishing, 1987).

Jones, R.T. *Congregationalism in England, 1662-1962* (London: Independent Press, 1962).

Jupp, P.C. *From Dust to Ashes: Cremation and the British Way of Death* (Basingstoke: Palgrave Macmillan, 2006).

Kersley, G. *Darling Madame: Sarah Grand and Devoted Friend* (London: Virago Press, 1983).

Kirk, S. *Philip Webb: Pioneer of Arts and Crafts Architecture* (Chichester: Wiley-Academy, 2005).

Klinke, H. *William Hale White (Mark Rutherford). Versuch einer Biographie* (Frankfurt: Wilhelm Bohn, 1930).

Lago, M. *"India's Prisoner": A Biography of Edward John Thompson, 1886-1946* (Columbia, MO: University of Missouri Press, 2001).

Lamm, J.A. *The Living God: Schleiermacher's Theological Appropriation of Spinoza* (University Park, PA: Pennsylvania State University Press, 1996).

— 'Romanticism and Pantheism', in *The Blackwell Companion to Nineteenth-Century Theology*, ed. by David Fergusson (Chichester: Wiley-Blackwell, 2010), pp. 165-186.

Lamont, P. 'Spiritualism and a Mid-Victorian Crisis of Evidence', *The Historical Journal*, 47 (2004), 897-920.

Larsen. T. 'Honorary Doctorates and the Nonconformist Ministry in Nineteenth-Century England', in *Modern Christianity and Cultural Aspirations*, ed. by David Bebbington and Timothy Larsen (London: Sheffield Academic Press, 2003), pp. 139-156.

— 'Biblical Criticism and the Crisis of Belief: D. F. Strauss's Leben Jesu in Britain', in *Contested Christianity: The Political and Social Contexts of Victorian Theology*, by Timothy Larsen (Waco, TX: Baylor University Press, 2004), pp. 43-58.

— 'Biblical Criticism and the Secularist Mentality: Charles Bradlaugh and the Case Against Miracles', in *Contested Christianity: The Political and Social Contexts of Victorian Theology*, by Timothy Larsen (Waco, TX: Baylor University Press, 2004), pp. 97-112.

— *Crisis of Doubt: Honest Faith in Nineteenth-Century England* (Oxford: Oxford University Press, 2006).

Ledger-Thomas, M. '"Glimpses of the Great Conflict": English Congregationalists and the European Crisis of Faith, circa 1840-1875', *Journal of British Studies*, 46 (2007), 826-860.

Lehman, D. *Signs of the Times: Deconstruction and the Fall of Paul de Man* (London: André Deutsch, 1991).

Lejeune, P. *On Autobiography*, ed. and with a foreword by Paul John Eakin, trans. by Katherine Leary (Minneapolis, MN: University of Minnesota Press, 1989).

Lewis, M. 'The Newport Pagnell Academy, 1728-1850', *Journal of the United Reformed Church History Society*, 5 (1994), 273-282.

Lightman, B. 'Robert Elsmere and the Agnostic Crises of Faith', in *Victorian Faith in Crisis: Essays on Continuity and Change in Nineteenth-Century Religious Belief*, ed. by Richard J. Helmstadter and Bernard Lightman (Stanford, CA: Stanford University Press, 1990), pp. 283-311.

Livingstone, D.N. *Adam's Ancestors: Race, Religion, and the Politics of Human Origins* (Baltimore, MD: Johns Hopkins University Press, 2008).

Lloyd, G. *Spinoza and the Ethics* (London: Routledge, 1996).

Lownsdale, S. 'Faith Development Across the Life Span: Fowler's Integrative Work', *Journal of Psychology and Theology*, 25 (1997), 49-63.

Lucas, J. *The Literature of Change: Studies in the Nineteenth-Century Provincial Novel*, 2nd edn (Brighton: Harvester Press, 1980).

MacDonald, G. *George MacDonald and His Wife* (London: George Allen & Unwin, 1924).

— *Reminiscences of a Specialist* (London: George Allen & Unwin, 1932).

Mackennal, A. *Sketches in the Evolution of English Congregationalism* (London: James Nisbet, 1901).
Maclean, C.M. *Mark Rutherford: A Biography of William Hale White* (London: Macdonald, 1955).
Macquarrie, J. *The Scope of Demythologizing: Bultmann and His Critics* (London: SCM Press, 1960).
Maison, M.M. *Search Your Soul, Eustace: A Survey of the Religious Novel in the Victorian Age* (London: Sheed and Ward, 1961).
Mandel, B.J. 'Full of Life Now', in *Autobiography: Essays Theoretical and Critical*, ed. by James Olney (Princeton, NJ: Princeton University Press, 1980), pp. 49-72.
Marcus, L. *Auto/biographical Discourses: Criticism, Theory, Practice* (Manchester: Manchester University Press, 1994).
Marshall, P. *Mystical Encounters with the Natural World: Experiences and Explanations* (Oxford: Oxford University Press, 2005).
Mason, R. *The God of Spinoza: A Philosophical Study* (Cambridge: Cambridge University Press, 1999).
Matthews, W. (com.) *British Autobiographies: An Annotated Bibliography of British Autobiographies Published or Written Before 1951* (Hamden, CT: Archon Books, repr. 1968).
McCraw, H.W. 'Two Novelists of Despair: James Anthony Froude and William Hale White', *The Southern Quarterly*, 13 (1974), 21-51.
McGillis, R. 'Fantasy as Miracle: George MacDonald's The Miracles of Our Lord', in *George MacDonald: Literary Heritage and Heirs*, ed. by Roderick McGillis (Wayne, PA: Zossima Press, 2008), pp. 201-215.
McGowen, R. 'Civilizing Punishment: The End of the Public Execution in England', *The Journal of British Studies*, 33 (1994), 257-282.
McGrath, A.E. *The Open Secret: A New Vision for Natural Theology* (Oxford: Blackwell Publishing, 2008).
McKie, D. *Jabez: The Rise and Fall of a Victorian Rogue* (London: Atlantic Books, 2004).
McNaughton, W.D. *The Scottish Congregational Ministry, 1794-1993* (Glasgow: Congregational Union of Scotland, 1993).
— *Early Congregational Independency in the Highlands and Islands and the North-East of Scotland* (Tiree: Trustees of Ruaig Congregational Church, 2003).
Mercer, M.J. 'New College, London: Its Origins and Opening', *Journal of the United Reformed Church History Society*, 6 (1999), 327-336.
Merton, S. *Mark Rutherford (William Hale White)* (New York: Twayne Publishers, 1967).
Moser, E. 'The Crescent, Bedford', in *Bedfordshire Historical Miscellany: Essays in Honour of Patricia Bell*, Publications of the Bedfordshire Historical Record Society, 72 (Bedford: Bedfordshire Historical Record Society, 1993), pp. 205-218.
Mullan, J. *Anonymity: A Secret History of English Literature* (London: Faber and Faber, 2007).

Munson, J. *The Nonconformists: In Search of a Lost Culture* (London: SPCK, 1991).

Murry, J.M. 'The Religion of Mark Rutherford', in *To the Unknown God: Essays Towards a Religion* (London: Jonathan Cape, 1924), pp. 260-275.

Nadler, S. *Spinoza's Ethics: An Introduction* (Cambridge: Cambridge University Press, 2006).

Nelson, J.G. *The Early Nineties: A View from the Bodley Head* (Cambridge, MA: Harvard University Press, 1971).

Nesta, F. 'The Series as Commodity: Marketing T. Fisher Unwin's Pseudonym and Autonym Libraries', in *The Culture of the Publisher's Series, vol. I: Authors, Publishers and the Shaping of Taste*, ed. by John Spiers (London: Palgrave Macmillan, 2011), pp. 171-187.

Newey, V. 'Mark Rutherford's Salvation and the Case of Catharine Furze', in *Mortal Pages, Literary Lives: Studies in Nineteenth-Century Autobiography*, ed. by Vincent Newey and Philip Shaw (Aldershot: Scolar Press, 1996), pp. 172-203.

Newman, J. *Somerset House: Splendour and Order* (London: Scala Publications, 1990).

Nicholls, P.A. *Homeopathy and the Medical Profession* (Beckenham: Croom Helm, 1988).

Oakes, R.A. 'Classical Theism and Pantheism: A Victory for Process Theism?', *Religious Studies*, 13 (1977), 167-173.

— 'Does Traditional Theism Entail Pantheism?', in *The Concept of God*, ed. by Thomas V. Morris (Oxford: Oxford University Press, 1987), pp. 57-71.

Olney, J. 'Autobiography and the Cultural Moment: A Thematic, Historical, and Bibliographical Introduction', in *Autobiography: Essays Theoretical and Critical*, ed. by J. Olney (Princeton, NJ: Princeton University Press, 1980) pp. 3-27.

Oppenheim, J. *The Other World: Spiritualism and Psychical Research in England, 1850-1914* (Cambridge: Cambridge University Press, 1985).

Orchard, S.C. 'Fakenham Academy in 1845', *Journal of the United Reformed Church History Society*, 2 (1978), 9-17.

— *Cheshunt College: A Record of the College Founded by Selina, Dowager Countess of Huntingdon, etc* (Cheshunt: Governors of Cheshunt College, ca. 1968).

— 'From Catechism Class to Sunday School', in *The Sunday School Movement: Studies in the Growth and Decline of Sunday Schools*, ed. by Stephen Orchard and John H.Y. Briggs (Milton Keynes: Paternoster, 2007), pp. 1-16.

Owen, A. *The Darkened Room: Women, Power and Spiritualism in Late Victorian England* (London: Virago Press, 1989; repr. Chicago. IL: University of Chicago Press, 2004).

— *The Place of Enchantment: British Occultism and the Culture of the Modern* (Chicago IL: University of Chicago Press, 2004).

Owen, W.T. *Edward Williams, D.D., 1750-1813: His Life, Thought and Influence* (Cardiff: University of Wales Press, 1963).

Paffard, M. *Inglorious Wordsworths: A Study of Some Transcendental Experiences in Childhood and Adolescence* (London: Hodder and Stoughton, 1973).

— *The Unattended Moment: Excerpts from Autobiographies with Hints and Guesses* (London: SCM Press, 1976).

Parsons, B. *Committed to the Cleansing Flame: The Development of Cremation in Nineteenth Century England* (Reading: Spire Books, 2005).

Pascal, R. *Design and Truth in Autobiography* (Cambridge, MA: Harvard University Press, 1960).

Payne, C. 'Rural Virtues for Urban Consumption: Cottage Scenes in Early Victorian Painting', *Journal of Victorian Culture*, 3 (1998), 45-68.

Perovich, A.N. 'Taking Nature Mysticism Seriously: Marshall and the Metaphysics of the Self', *Religious Studies*, 47 (2011), 165-183.

Pillemer, D.B., M.L. Picariello, A.B. Law and J. S. Reichman, 'Memories of College: The Importance of Specific Educational Episodes', in *Remembering Our Past: Studies in Autobiographical Memory*, ed. by David C. Rubin (Cambridge: Cambridge University Press, 1999), pp. 318-337.

Powicke, F.J. *David Worthington Simon* (London: Hodder and Stoughton, 1912).

Prickett, S. *Romanticism and Religion: The Tradition of Coleridge and Wordsworth in the Victorian Church* (Cambridge: Cambridge University Press, 1976).

Pye-Smith, A. *Memorials of Fetter Lane Congregational Church, London* (London: Warren Hall and Lovitt, 1900).

Qualls, B. *The Secular Pilgrims of Victorian Fiction: The Novel as Book of Life* (Cambridge: Cambridge University Press, 1982).

Raeper, W. *George MacDonald* (Tring: Lion Publishing, 1987).

Rambo, L.R. *Understanding Religious Conversion* (New Haven, CT: Yale University Press, 1993).

Renza, L.A. 'The Veto of the Imagination: A Theory of Autobiography', in *Autobiography: Essays Theoretical and Critical*, ed. by James Olney (Princeton, NJ: Princeton University Press, 1980), pp. 268-295.

Robb, D.S. 'George MacDonald at Blackfriars Chapel', *North Wind*, 5 (1986), 3-20.

— 'George MacDonald and Animal Magnetism', Seven: An Anglo-American Literary Review, 8 (1987), 9-24.

Robb, G. *White-Collar Crime in Modern England: Financial Fraud and Business Morality, 1845-1929* (Cambridge: Cambridge University Press, 2002).

Roberts, L. (comp.) *Arthur Hughes: His Life and Works. A Catalogue Raisonné, with a Biographical Introduction by Stephen Wildman* (Woodbridge: Antique Collectors' Club, 1997).

Robertson, C. *Who Was Sophie?: My Grandmother, Poet and Stranger* (London: Virago Press, 2008).

Rodger, N.A.M. *The Admiralty* (Lavenham: Terence Dalton, 1979).

Rogerson, J. *Old Testament Criticism in the Nineteenth Century: England and Germany* (London: SPCK, 1984).

Rose, K. *The Later Cecils* (New York: Harper & Row, 1975).

Rubin, D.C. 'Introduction', in *Remembering Our Past: Studies in Autobiographical Memory*, ed. by David C. Rubin (Cambridge: Cambridge University Press, 1999), pp. 1-15.

Salgado, G. 'The Rhetoric of Sincerity: The Autobiography of Mark Rutherford as Fiction', in *Renaissance and Modern Essays: Presented to Vivian de Sola Pinto in Celebration of his Seventieth Birthday*, ed. by G. R. Hibbard (London: Routledge & Kegan Paul, 1966), pp. 159-168.

Saunders, M. *Self Impression: Life-Writing, Autobiografiction, and the Forms of Modern Literature* (Oxford: Oxford University Press, 2010).

Savage, B. 'Jonathan Cape and the Travellers' Library ', *The Private Library*, n.s. 4 (1971), 165-183.

Schieder, R.M. 'Loss and Gain?: The Theme of Conversion in Late Victorian Fiction', *Victorian Studies*, 9 (1965), 29-44.

Schweitzer, F. 'Developmental Views of the Religion of the Child: Historical Antecedents', in *Stages of Faith and Religious Development: Implications for Church, Education and Society*, ed. by J.W. Fowler, K.E. Nipkow and F. Schweitzer (London: SCM Press, 1992), pp. 67-81.

Scotland, N. *Squires in the Slums: Settlements and Missions in Late-Victorian London* (London: I.B. Tauris, 2007).

Sell, A.P.F. *Dissenting Thought and the Life of the Churches: Studies in an English Tradition* (San Francisco, CA: Mellen Research University Press, 1990).

— *Commemorations: Studies in Christian Thought and History* (Calgary, AB; Cardiff: University of Calgary Press; University of Wales Press, 1993).

— *Philosophical Idealism and Christian Belief* (Cardiff: University of Wales Press, 1995).

— 'From Worms to Sunbeams: The Dilution of Calvinism in English Congregationalism', *Journal of the United Reformed Church History Society*, 7 (2004), 253-274.

— *Enlightenment, Ecumenism, Evangel: Theological Themes and Thinkers 1550-2000* (Milton Keynes: Paternoster, 2005).

— *Hinterland Theology: A Stimulus to Theological Construction* (Milton Keynes: Paternoster, 2008).

Sellers, I. *Nineteenth-Century Nonconformity* (London: Edward Arnold, 1977).

Shaw, G.B. 'In the Days of my Youth', in *Sixteen Self Sketches* (London: Constable, 1949), pp. 42-47.

Shaw, I.J. *High Calvinists in Action: Calvinism and the City; Manchester and London, c.1810-1860* (Oxford: Oxford University Press, 2002).

Smith, S.N. 'Mark Rutherford: A Short Bibliography of the First Editions', *Supplement to The Bookman's Journal*, 1930, 1-23.

— 'The Case of Arthur Craven', *The Malahat Review*, 13 (1970), 47-54

Snell, K.D.M. & P. S. Ell. *Rival Jerusalems: The Geography of Victorian Religion* (Cambridge: Cambridge University Press, 2000).

Sperry, W.L. 'Mark Rutherford', *Harvard Theological Review*, 7 (1914), 166-192.

Stace, W.T. *Mysticism and Philosophy* (London: Macmillan, 1961).

Stephens, W.B. *Education, Literacy and Society, 1830-70: The Geography of Diversity in Provincial England* (Manchester: Manchester University Press, 1987).

Stock, I. *William Hale White (Mark Rutherford): A Critical Study* (London: George Allen and Unwin, 1956).

Stockdale, E. *A Study of Bedford Prison, 1660-1877*, Publications of the Bedfordshire Historical Record Society, 56 (Bedford: Bedfordshire Historical Record Society, 1977).

Stone, W. *Religion and Art of William Hale White ("Mark Rutherford")* (Stanford, CA; London: Stanford University Press; Oxford University Press, 1954).

Sutherland, J. *Victorian Novelists and Publishers* (London: Athlone Press, 1976).

Sutton, C.W. 'Stowell, William Hendry', in *Dictionary of National Biography*, ed. by Sidney Lee (London: Smith, Elder, 1898), vol. 55, pp. 7-8.

Swann, C. 'William Hale White's (Mark Rutherford) Revisions to the Second Edition Preface of His Translation of Spinoza's Ethic', *ANQ: American Notes and Queries*, 13 (2000), 16-28.

— 'Autobiografiction: Problems with Autobiographical Fictions and Fictional Autobiographies. Mark Rutherford's Autobiography and Deliverance, and Others', *Modern Language Review*, 96 (2001), 21-37.

Symondson, A. (ed.) *The Victorian Crisis of Faith* (London: SPCK, 1970).

Tacey, D. *The Spirituality Revolution: The Emergence of Contemporary Spirituality* (London: Routledge, 2004).

Theobald, M.B. *Three Levels of Consciousness: An Autobiography* (London: John M. Watkins, 1960).

Thompson, D. (ed.) *Nonconformity in the Nineteenth Century* (London: Routledge & Kegan Paul, 1972).

Thompson, D. 'The Christian Socialist Revival in Britain: A Reappraisal', in *Revival and Religion since 1700: Essays for John Walsh*, ed. by J. Garnett and C. Matthew (London: Hambledon Press, 1993), pp. 273-295.

Thompson, E.P. *The Making of the English Working Class* (London: Victor Gollancz, 1965).

Thompson, J.H. *A History of the Coward Trust: The First Two Hundred Years, 1738-1988* (Cambridge: United Reformed Church History Society, 1998).

Thomson, P. 'The Novels of Mark Rutherford', *Essays in Criticism*, 14 (1964), 256-267.

Thorp, M.R 'Early Mormon Confrontations with Sectarianism, 1837-40', in *Mormons in Early Victorian Britain*, ed. by Richard L. Jensen and M. R. Thorp (Salt Lake City, UT: University of Utah Press, 1989), pp. 49-69.

Thwaite, A. *Glimpses of the Wonderful: The Life of Philip Henry Gosse, 1810-1888* (London: Faber & Faber, 2002).

Tibbutt, H.G. *Bunyan Meeting, Bedford: 1650-1950* (Bedford: Trustees of Bunyan Meeting [1950]).

— *A History of Howard Congregational Church Bedford* (Bedford: Howard Congregational Church, 1961).

— 'The Bedford Congregational Academy', *Transactions of the Congregational Historical Society*, 20 (1966), 114-118.

— 'From Stagsden to Samoa', *Bedfordshire Magazine*, 2 (1968), 192-196.

Tomalin, C. 'Afterword', *Clara Hopgood* (London: Hogarth Press, 1985). [unpaginated]

Tomes, R. '"We are hardly prepared for this style of teaching yet": Samuel Davidson and Lancashire Independent College', *Journal of the United Reformed Church History Society*, 5 (1995), 398-414.

— '"Learning a New Technique": The Reception of Biblical Criticism in the Nonconformist Colleges', *Journal of the United Reformed Church History Society*, 7 (2004), 288-314.

Towers, L.T. 'The Bedford Missionary Training College, and its Connection with the London Missionary Society', *Transactions of the Congregational Historical Society*, 15 (1945), 33-40.

Treuherz, J. *Hard Times: Social Realism in Victorian Art* (London: Lund Humphries in association with Manchester City Art Galleries, 1987).

Troup, R. *The Missionar Kirk of Huntly* (Huntly; Edinburgh: Joseph Dunbar; John Menzies, 1901).

Turner, F. 'The Victorian Crisis of Faith and the Faith that was Lost', in *Victorian Faith in Crisis: Essays on Continuity and Change in Nineteenth-Century Religious Belief*, ed. by Richard J. Helmstadter and Bernard Lightman (Stanford, CA: Stanford University Press, 1990), pp. 9-38.

Underhill, E. *Mysticism: A Study in the Nature and Development of Man's Spiritual Consciousness*, 14th edn (London: Methuen, 1942).

Unwin, P. *The Publishing Unwins* (London: Heinemann, 1972).

Unwin, S. *The Truth About a Publisher: An Autobiographical Record* (London: George Allen & Unwin, 1960).

Varley, J. 'A Bedfordshire Clergyman of the Reform Era and his Bishop', in *Worthington George Smith and Other Studies: Presented to Joyce Godber*, Publications of the Bedfordshire Historical Record Society, 57 (Bedford: Bedfordshire Historical Record Society, 1978), pp. 113-140.

Walther, L. 'The Invention of Childhood in Victorian Autobiography', in *Approaches to Victorian Autobiography*, ed. by George P. Landow (Athens, OH: Ohio State University Press, 1979), pp. 64-83.

Watts, M.R. *The Dissenters, vol. II: The Expansion of Evangelical Nonconformity* (Oxford: Clarendon Press, 1995).

Weatherall, M. 'Making Medicine Scientific: Empiricism, Rationality, and Quackery in mid-Victorian Britain', *Social History of Medicine*, 9 (1996), 175-194.

Welch, E. (ed.) *The Bedford Moravian Church in the Eighteenth Century*, Publications of the Bedfordshire Historical Record Society, 68 (Bedford: Bedfordshire Historical Records Society, 1989).

Wilde, O. *The Artist as Critic: Critical Writings of Oscar Wilde*, ed. by Richard Ellmann (London: W. H. Allen, 1970).

Willey, B. *More Nineteenth Century Studies: A Group of Honest Doubters* (London: Chatto and Windus, 1956).

— 'Introduction' in *Autobiography and Deliverance* [Mark Rutherford] (Leicester: Leicester University Press, 1969), pp. 7-20.

Williamson, D. *The Life of Alexander Maclaren: Preacher and Expositor* (London: James Clarke; Baptist Union Publication Department, 1910).

Wolff, R.L. *Gains and Losses: Novels of Faith and Doubt in Victorian England* (London: John Murray, 1977).

Woodhead, L. 'Introduction', in *Reinventing Christianity: Nineteenth-Century Contexts*, ed. by Linda Woodhead (Aldershot: Ashgate, 2001), pp. 1-21.

Wright T. *The Life of the Rev. Timothy Richard Matthews, Friend of Edward Fitzgerald* (London: C. J. Farncombe & Sons, 1934).

Yalden, P. 'Association, Community and the Origins of Secularisation: English and Welsh Nonconformity, c.1850-1930', *Journal of Ecclesiastical History*, 55 (2004), 293-324.

Young, D. *F. D. Maurice and Unitarianism* (Oxford: Clarendon Press, 1992).

Zaehner, R.C. *Mysticism Sacred and Profane: An Inquiry into Some Varieties of Preternatural Experience* (Oxford: Oxford University Press, 1957).

(f) Electronic Sources

Boase, G.C. 'Harris, John', in Oxford Dictionary of National Biography rev. A.B. Baker <http://www.oxforddnb.com/view/article/12402> [accessed 8 July 2008].

Brock, W.H. 'Gregory, William', in Oxford Dictionary of National Biography <http://www.oxforddnb.com/view/article/11475> [accessed 9 July 2010].

Buckland, A.R. 'Morell, John Daniel', in Oxford Dictionary of National rev. C. A. Creffield Biography <http://www.oxforddnb.com/view/article/19200> [accessed 19 March 2008].

Carlyle, T. The Carlyle Letters Online <:http://www.carlyleletters.dukejournals.org/> [accessed 20 September 2010].

Cunningham, V. 'White, William Hale', in Oxford Dictionary of National Biography <http://www.oxforddnb.com/view/article/36864> [accessed 19 March 2008].

Hamilton, C.I. 'The Difficulties of an Admiralty Reformer in the Later Nineteenth Century: The Case of E. N. Swainson', International Journal of Naval History, 7 (2008) <http://www.ijnhonline.org/volume7_number1_apr08/article_hamilton_apr08.htm> [accessed 8 March 2011].

Mark Rutherford Resource http://www.concentric.net/~djfrench/index.htm [accessed 10 March 2011].

Reynolds, K.D. 'Stowell, William Hendry', in Oxford Dictionary of National Biography <http://www.oxforddnb.com/view/article/26615> [accessed 20 August 2010].

Surman Index. <http://www.surman.english.qmul.ac.uk/start.php> [accessed 20 November 2010].

Yvard, J-M. 'Appartenance confessionnelle et allégeances politiques: William Hale White (<< Mark Rutherford >>) et l'évolution de la non conformité religieuse en Grande-Bretagne en XIXe siècle', La Revue LISA/Lisa e-journal, 9 (2011), 20-35 <http://www.lisa.revues.org/4094> [accessed 20 July 2011].

GENERAL INDEX

Page numbers with suffix n indicate one or more references in the footnotes.

PATERNOSTER

STUDIES IN CHRISTIAN HISTORY AND THOUGHT

New titles in the series, 2012

Raymond Brown, *Spirituality in Adversity. English Nonconformity in a period of Repression 1660-1689* – 9781842277850 - £34.99

Larry Siekawitch *Balancing Head and Heart in Seventeenth Century Puritanism. Stephen Charnock's Doctrine of the Knowledge of God* – 9781842276709 - £24.99

Michael Parsons (ed.), *Since we are Justified by Faith. Justification in the Theologies of the Protestant Reformations* – 9781842277775 - £24.99

Adam Hood (ed.), *John Oman: New Perspectives* – 9781842277317 - £24.99

Some future titles in the series

Van Vliet, *Marrow of the Theology and Piety of the Reformed Traditions* - 9781842273944

Clifford B. Boone, *Puritan Evangelism: Preaching for conversion in late-seventeenth century English Puritanism as seen in the works of John Flavel* - 9781842277843

Aaron T. O'Kelley, *Did the Reformers Misread Paul? A Historical-Theological Critique of the New Perspective* - 9781842277942

Brian Talbott, *In the Shadow of Geneva* - 9781842277959

Michael Pasquarello, *Hugh Latimer* - 9781842277973

Martin Wellings (ed.), *Protestant Nonconformity and Christian Missions* - 9781842277980

Edwin E. M. Tay, *The Priesthood of Christ in the Atonement Theology of John Owen (1616-1683)* - 9781842277997

Roger Standing, *The Forward Movement: evangelical pioneers of 'Social Christianity'* –9781842278031

Michael Parsons (ed.), *Aspects of Reformation. Reforming Theology and Practice* – 9781842278061

Other available titles

[volumes published *before* 2008 are half price while stocks last: contact paternoster@authenticmedia.co.uk]

David Thompson, *Baptism, Church and Society in Britain. From the Evangelical Revival to* Baptism, Eucharist and Ministry – 9781842273937 (2009) - £19.99

Tom Aitken, *Blood and Fire, Tsar and Commissar. The Salvation Army in Russia (1907-1923)* – 9781842275115 (2007) - £12.50

Byung-Ho Moon, *Christ the Mediator of the Law. Calvin's Christological Understanding of the Law as the Rule of Living and Life-giving* – 9781842273180 (2006) - £15.00

Andrew Partington, Church and State. *The Contribution of the Church of England Bishops to the House of Lords during the Thatcher Years* – 9781842273340 (2006) - £15.00

Linda Wilson, *Constrained by Zeal. Female Spirituality amongst Nonconformists, 1865-1875* – 9780853649724 (2006) - £12.50

Anthony Rich, *'Discernment' in the Desert Fathers* – 9781842274316 (2007) - £15.00

Anna Robbins, *Ecumenical and Eclectic. The Unity of the Church in the Contemporary World* – 9781842274323 (2007) - £12.50

Anthony Cross, *Ecumenism and History* – 9781842271353 (2005) - £15.00

Jack Whytock, *An Educated Clergy. Scottish Theological Education and Training in Kirk and Session, 1560-1850* – 9781842275122 (2007) - £12.50

Alan Sell, *Enlightenment, Ecumenism, Evangel. Theological Themes and Thinkers, 1550-2000* – 9781842273302 (2005) - £15.00

Kevin Hester, *Eschatology and pain in St Gregory the Great* – 9781842274378 (2007) - £10.00

Michael Thomas, *The Extent of the Atonement. A Dilemma for Reformed Theology from Calvin to the Consensus* – 9780853648284 (1997) - £12.50

Ruth Gouldbourne, *Flesh and the Feminine. Gender and Theology in the Writings of Casper Schwenckfeld* – 9781842270486 (2004) - £12.50

Tim Larsen, *Friends of Religious Equality. Nonconformist Politics in Mid-Victorian England* – 9781842274026 (2007) - £12.50

Stuart Clarke, *The Ground of Election. Jacob Arminius' Doctrine of the Work and Person of Christ* – 9781842273982 (2006) - £10.00

Andrew Daunton-Fear, *Healing in the Early Church. The Church's Ministry of Healing and Exorcism from the First to the Fifth Century* – 9781842276235 (2009) - £19.99

Alan Sell, *Hinterland Theology. A Stimulus to Theological Construction* – 9781842273319 (2008) - £39.99

Carole Spencer, *Holiness – the Soul of Quakerism* – 9781842274392 (2008) - £29.99

M. Knell, *The Immanent Person of the Holy Spirit from Anselm to Lombard: Divine Communion of the Spirit* – 9781842275610 (2009) - £24.99

William Evans, *Imputation and Impartation. Union with Christ in American Reformed Theology* – 9781842274361 (2008) - £24.99

Harold Hill, *Leadership in the Salvation Army. A Case-Study in Clericalism* – 97812842274293 (2006) - £15.00

Mark Garcia, *Life in Christ. Union with Christ and the Twofold Grace in Calvin's Theology* – 9781842275726 (2009) - £29.99

Tim Grass, *The Lord's Watchman. Edward Irving* – 9781842274262 (2011) - £24.99

Dennis Ngien, *Luther as a Spiritual Advisor* – 9781842274613 (2007) - £10.00

Brian Shelton, *Martyrdom from Exegesis to Hippolytus. The Early Church's Presbyter's Commentary on Daniel* – 9781842275689 (2008) - £24.99

John Darch, *Missionary Imperialists? Missionaries, Government and the Growth of the British Empire in the Tropics, 1860-1885* – 9781842275603 (2009) - £24.99

Stephen Orchard, *Nonconformity in Derbyshire. A Study in Dissent, 1600-1800* – 9781842276204 (2009) - £19.99

Shawn Wright, *Our Sovereign Refuge. The Pastoral Theology of Theodore Beza* – 9781842272527 (2004) - £12.50

Martin Sutherland, *Peace, Toleration and Decay. The Ecclesiology of Later Stuart Dissent* – 9781842271520 (2003) - £12.50

Donald Fortson, *Presbyterian Creed. A Confessional Tradition in America, 1729-1870* – 9781842274248 (2009) - £24.99

Colin Bulley, *The Priesthood of Some Believers. Developments from the General to the Special Priesthood in the Christian Literature of the First Three Centuries* – 9781842270349 (2000) - £15.00

Galen Johnson, *Prisoner of Conscience. John Bunyan on Self, Community and the Christian Faith* – 9781842272237 (2003) - £12.50

James Bruce, *Prophecy, Miracles, Angels and Heavenly Light. The Eschatology, Pneumatology and Missiology of Adomnan's* Life of Columbia – 9781842272275 (2004) - £12.50

Alan Sell & Anthony Cross, *Protestant Nonconformity in the Twentieth Century* – 9781842272213 (2005) - £15.00

Clark and Trueman, *Protestant Scholasticism. Essays in Reassessment* – 9780853648536 (1998) - £15.00

Crawford Gribben, *Puritan Millennium. Literature and Theology, 1550-1682* – 9781842273722 (2008) - £24.99

J.S. Yuille, *Puritan Spirituality. The Fear of God in the Affective Theology of George Swinnock* – 9781842275627 (2008) - £24.99

William Black, *Reformation Pastors. Richard Baxter and the Ideal of the Reformed Pastor* – 9781842271902 (2004) - £15.00

C. Clement, *Religious Radicalism in England, 1535-1565* – 9781842278449 (1997) - £15.00

Jeff McInnis, *Shadows and Chivalry. C.S. Lewis and George MacDonald on Suffering, Evil and Goodness* – 9781842274309 (2007) - £10.00

Susan Tara Brown, *Singing and the Imagination of Devotion. Vocal Aesthetics in Early English protestant Culture* – 9781842274071 (2008) - £19.99

Orchard & Briggs, *The Sunday School Movement. Studies in the Growth and Decline of the Sunday School* – 9781842273630 (2007) - £10.00

Mark Thompson, *A Sure Ground on Which to Stand. The Relation of Authority and Interpretive Method in Luther's Approach to Scripture* – 9781842271452 (2004) - £15.00

Guy Richard, *The Supremacy of God in the Theology of Samuel Rutherford* – 9781842275740 (2008) - £24.99

Roy Kearsley, *Tertullian's Theology of Divine Power* – 9780946068616 (1998) - £10.00

Brian Kay, *Trinitarian Spirituality. John Owen and the Doctrine of God in Western Devotion* – 9781842274088 (2008) - £19.99

Garnet Milne, *The Westminster Confession of Faith. The Majority Puritan Viewpoint on Whether Extra Biblical Prophecy is Still Possible* – 9781842275214 (2007) - £12.50

Lightning Source UK Ltd.
Milton Keynes UK
UKOW041305250712

196539UK00002B/1/P